W9-DBI-225

HISTORICAL ENCYCLOPEDIA OF
AMERICAN BUSINESS

HISTORICAL ENCYCLOPEDIA OF
AMERICAN
BUSINESS

Volume 1
Accounting industry—Google

Edited by

Richard L. Wilson
University of Tennessee, Chattanooga

SALEM PRESS
Pasadena, California   Hackensack, New Jersey

Editorial Director: Christina J. Moose   *Production Editor:* Joyce I. Buchea
Acquisitions Editor: Mark Rehn   *Layout:* Mary Overell
Development Editor: R. Kent Rasmussen   *Design and Graphics:* James Hutson
Project Editor: Rowena Wildin   *Photo Editor:* Cynthia Breslin Beres
Manuscript Editor: Andy Perry   *Editorial Assistant:* Dana Garey

Cover photo: Hulton Archive/Getty Images

Library of Congress Cataloging-in-Publication Data

Historical encyclopedia of American business / edited by Richard L. Wilson.
    p. cm.
Includes bibliographical references and index.
    ISBN 978-1-58765-518-0 (set : alk. paper) — ISBN 978-1-58765-519-7 (vol. 1 : alk. paper) —
ISBN 978-1-58765-520-3 (vol. 2 : alk. paper) — ISBN 978-1-58765-521-0 (vol. 3 : alk. paper) 1. United
States—Commerce—History—Encyclopedias. 2. Industries—United States—History—Encyclopedias.
3. Industrial management—United States—History—Encyclopedias. 4. Business enterprises—United
States—History—Encyclopedias. I. Wilson, Richard L., 1944-
    HF3021.H67 2009
    338.097303—dc22

                                                                                         2009002942

PRINTED IN CANADA

Table of Contents

Publisher's Note

Historical Encyclopedia of American Business is a three-volume encyclopedic reference set with 477 alphabetically arranged articles, ranging in length from 300 to 3,000 words, that cover the breadth of American business history—from the earliest trade between Native Americans and Europeans on the North American continent to modern online commerce and the financial crisis of 2008. The set provides broad, basic coverage of the business world, addressing the forces that shaped business, the regulations and organizations that kept it in balance, and the major issues and ideas that emerged over the course of history. The essays, taken as a whole, reveal how the modern American business world has developed.

SCOPE

Most of the essays are overviews at least 1,000 words in length discussing sectors of the economy such as agriculture, banking, and services; individual industries such as advertising, automobile manufacturing, chemicals, and electronics; and more general topics and concepts such as bank failures, business cycles, consumer boycotts, inventions, labor strikes, and outsourcing. There are also overviews on broad legal topics such as antitrust legislation, bankruptcy law, incorporation laws, and patent laws. These essays describe historical developments and relate them to the business environment of the twenty-first century.

This is a reference work on American business history, but it devotes considerable space to American business relations with the rest of the world. It examines U.S. trade policies, from the tariffs and duties that marked its initial relations with Great Britain to the movement toward free trade through articles on international economic issues, tariffs, the North American Free Trade Agreement, and the World Trade Organization. The set has substantial essays on American trade with Canada, Mexico, Japan, China, and other regions of the world.

Because this is primarily a history set, it pays special attention to historical events and eras. It contains long essays on such topics as colonial economic systems, the American Industrial Revolution, slavery, and the impact on business of both individual wars—from the Revolutionary War to the Iraq wars—and war in general. Virtually every significant economic depression and "panic" has its own article, including the financial crisis of 2008, and additional essays cover such events as the Boston Tea Party, Coxey's Army, the Crédit Mobilier scandal, the Dust Bowl of the 1930's, and the energy crisis of 1979. The set also contains many, mostly brief, essays on individual laws such as the Clayton Antitrust Act of 1914 and overviews on areas of law such as contract and land law. The set's appendix section contains annotated lists of 123 laws and 140 court rulings.

Although the main thrust of this set is on broad topics and historical trends, it also offers brief biographies of 37 individuals who have played exceptional roles in American business or are outstanding representative types. These figures range from some of the nation's towering Founders, Benjamin Franklin, Alexander Hamilton, and George Washington, to some of the giants of twenty-first century business, such as Bill Gates, Warren Buffett, Indra K. Nooyi, and Martha Stewart. All the biographical essays focus on the business contributions of their subjects. Some readers will be surprised to learn that George Washington was one of the most important American businessmen of his time. Readers will also find briefer sketches of more than 150 other business leaders in an appendix directory.

Another group of essay topics covers individual companies, corporations, labor unions, and government agencies. Among individual business that are subjects of essays are Apple, Bell Labs, Coca-Cola, eBay, General Motors, and Wal-Mart. An appendix directory has brief sketches of more than 85 additional American businesses and corporations. Labor unions rating essays include the AFL-CIO, the Brotherhood of Sleeping Car Porters, the International Brotherhood of Teamsters, and the United Mine Workers of America. Labor is also covered in two overview essays on history and strikes, and in individual essays on strikes and issues in labor such as child labor, wages, and women in business.

Articles on agencies and cabinet-level departments of the federal government examine the role that each agency or department has played in business. Some entities are now gone, such as the First Bank of the United States; some have been with the country since its early days, such as the U.S. Department of the Treasury; and some are relatively new, such as the U.S. Department of Homeland Security. Brief sketches of more than 50 federal government agencies and commissions are collected in an appendix. The set also includes long overview essays on Congress and the presidency and has separate essays on the impact of the U.S. Supreme Court on banking law, commerce, contract law, labor law, and land law.

A final subject category in *Historical Encyclopedia of American Business* is the media. In addition to broad overviews on the roles of journalism, literature, radio, television, and films in business history and how each medium has depicted business, the set offers articles on individual business publications such as *Fortune* and *Forbes* and television networks.

ORGANIZATION AND FORMAT

Like Salem's other encyclopedic works, *Historical Encyclopedia of American Business* is organized and formatted to be student friendly. Essays are arranged alphabetically under the headwords students are most likely to check, and additional help is offered in the form of textual cross-references (e.g., "Cycles. *See* Business cycles"), "see also" cross-references at the end of each essay, and a complete list of contents in every volume.

The categorized list of essays in volume 3 allows readers to find all entries in a subject area. As befits a historical set, the largest number of essays, 88, is in the category of Events and Eras. The nineteenth century is represented in 69 essays and the Colonial Era and New Republic in 29 essays. Government Regulation has 70 entries, followed by Labor, 50; Transportation and Travel, 47; Corporations, 43; Government Agencies, 42; Financial Industry, 42; Retail Trade, 40; People, 38; Manufacturing Industries, 36; Agriculture, 34; Banking, 31; Foreign Trade, 31; Media and Publishing, 29; Technology, 28; Communications, 27; Food Industries, 25; Natural Resources, 23; Military and Warfare, 22; Energy, 21; Crime, 17; Depressions, Recessions, and Panics, 17; Infrastructure, 17; Service Industries, 16; Land Policy, 16; Entertainment, 15; Stock Markets, 15; Taxation, 14; High-tech Industries, 11; Animal Husbandry and Fishing, 10; Medical and Health Care Industries, 9; Education, 8; Real Estate Industry, 8; Internet, 7; Marketing, 5; Demographics, 5; Advertising, 4; Household Products Industries, 3; Native Americans, 2; Sports, 3; and Housing and Construction, 2.

Individual essays use the same types of ready-reference top matter for which Salem reference works are noted, and every essay begins with a brief summary of its topic's significance in American business history. Dates and places are highlighted in the top matter when relevant, such as for events and biographies. All essays at least 500 words in length have "Further Reading" lists, and bibliographical citations in longer essays are annotated.

In addition to the appendixes mentioned earlier, volume 3 also has an annotated general bibliography, a glossary of business terms, and a lengthy time line. Besides the categorized list of entries mentioned already, there is an index of personages and a general subject index.

ACKNOWLEDGMENTS

Salem Press would like to thank the more than 140 scholars who contributed original articles to *Historical Encyclopedia of American Business*. Their names and affiliations are listed in the pages that follow here. This publication is especially indebted to its editor, Richard L. Wilson of the University of Tennessee, Chattanooga, whose contributions have been many and substantial.

Contributors

Terry A. Anderson
American Medical Writers Association

Philip Bader
Pnom Penh, Cambodia

Amanda J. Bahr-Evola
Southern Illinois University,
Edwardsville

Jane L. Ball
Yellow Springs, Ohio

Rikard Bandebo
Washington, D.C.

Maryanne Barsotti
Warren, Michigan

Eric Bellone
Suffolk University

Alvin K. Benson
Utah Valley University

Milton Berman
University of Rochester

R. Matthew Beverlin
University of Kansas

Pegge Bochynski
Salem State College

Kevin L. Brennan
Ouachita Baptist University

Howard Bromberg
University of Michigan Law School

Brandy M. Brooks
Northeastern University

Michael A. Buratovich
Spring Arbor University

Michael H. Burchett
Limestone College

William E. Burns
George Washington University

Gary A. Campbell
Michigan Technological University

Richard K. Caputo
Yeshiva University

Sharon Carson
University of North Dakota

Jack Carter
University of New Orleans

Frederick B. Chary
Indiana University Northwest

Dennis W. Cheek
Ewing Marion Kauffman Foundation

Douglas Clouatre
MidPlains Community College

Sarah J. Damberger
Northeastern University

Frank Day
Clemson University

Paul Dellinger
Wytheville, Virginia

Richard A. Dello Buono
New College of Florida

Mark DeStephano
Saint Peter's College

James I. Deutsch
Smithsonian Institution

Joseph Dewey
University of Pittsburgh, Johnstown

M. Casey Diana
University of Illinois,
Urbana-Champaign

Marcia B. Dinneen
Bridgewater State College

Thomas Du Bose
Louisiana State University, Shreveport

Julie Elliott
Indiana University, South Bend

Howard C. Ellis
Millersville University of Pennsylvania

Robert P. Ellis
Worcester State College

Victoria Erhart
Strayer University

Thomas R. Feller
Nashville, Tennessee

Dale L. Flesher
University of Mississippi

Janet E. Gardner
University of Massachusetts,
Dartmouth

Gilbert Geis
University of California, Irvine

Richard A. Glenn
Millersville University

Christian V. Glotfelty
Lock Haven University of
Pennsylvania

Nancy M. Gordon
Amherst, Massachusetts

Michael Haas
College of the Canyons

Jan Hall
Columbus, Ohio

Maurice Hamington
University of Southern Indiana

Randall Hannum
New York City College of Technology

A. W. R. Hawkins
Texas Tech University

Bernadette Zbicki Heiney
*Lock Haven University of
Pennsylvania*

James J. Heiney
*Lock Haven University of
Pennsylvania*

Peter B. Heller
Manhattan College

Mark C. Herman
Edison College

Russell Hively
Neosho, Missouri

Paul W. Hodge
University of Washington

Marsha M. Huber
Otterbein College

Mary Hurd
East Tennessee State University

W. Turrentine Jackson
University of California, Davis

Edward Johnson
University of New Orleans

Lee Ann Jolley
Tennessee Technological University

Mark S. Joy
Jamestown College

David Kasserman
Rowan University

Linda M. Kelley
*University of Illinois, Urbana-
Champaign*

Leigh Husband Kimmel
Indianapolis, Indiana

Paul M. Klenowski
Thiel College

Gayla Koerting
Nebraska State Historical Society

Grove Koger
Boise State University

Eugene Larson
Los Angeles Pierce College

J. Wesley Leckrone
Widener University

Denyse Lemaire
Rowan University

Thomas Tandy Lewis
St. Cloud State University

Roy Liebman
Los Angeles Public Library

Peter D. Lindquist
University of Denver College of Law

Victor Lindsey
East Central University

Alar Lipping
Northern Kentucky University

M. Philip Lucas
Cornell College

R. C. Lutz
Madison Advisors

Edward W. Maine
California State University, Fullerton

Nancy Farm Mannikko
*Centers for Disease Control and
Prevention*

Martin J. Manning
U.S. Department of State

Carl Henry Marcoux
University of California, Riverside

Laurence W. Mazzeno
Alvernia College

Scott A. Merriman
Troy University

Beth A. Messner
Ball State University

Randall L. Milstein
Oregon State University

William V. Moore
College of Charleston

Andrew P. Morriss
University of Illinois College of Law

Alice Myers
Bard College at Simon's Rock

Michael V. Namorato
University of Mississippi

Leslie Neilan
Virginia Tech University

Caryn E. Neumann
Miami University of Ohio, Middletown

William A. Paquette
Tidewater Community College

Robert J. Paradowski
Rochester Institute of Technology

James Pauff
Tarleton State University

Roger Pauly
University of Central Arkansas

David Peck
*California State University,
Long Beach*

Allene Phy-Olsen
Austin Peay State University

Erika E. Pilver
Westfield State College

Michael Polley
Columbia College

David L. Porter
William Penn University

Jessie Bishop Powell
Montgomery, Alabama

Steven Pressman
Monmouth University

Victoria Price
Lamar University

Aaron D. Purcell
Virginia Tech University

Steven J. Ramold
Eastern Michigan University

R. Kent Rasmussen
Thousand Oaks, California

H. William Rice
Kennesaw State University

Betty Richardson
*Southern Illinois University,
Edwardsville*

Alice C. Richer
Spaulding Rehabilitation Center

Robert B. Ridinger
Northern Illinois University

Edward A. Riedinger
Ohio State University

Joseph R. Rudolph, Jr.
Towson University

Sajay Samuel
Pennsylvania State University

Kurt M. Saunders
California State University, Northridge

Sean J. Savage
Saint Mary's College, Indiana

Brion Sever
Monmouth University

Houman B. Shadab
George Mason University

Taylor Shaw
*ADVANCE Education and
Development Center*

Martha Sherwood
Kent Anderson Law Associates

R. Baird Shuman
*University of Illinois, Urbana-
Champaign*

Alan L. Sorkin
*University of Maryland,
Baltimore County*

Karel S. Sovak
University of Mary

Theresa L. Stowell
Adrian College

Cynthia J. W. Svoboda
Bridgewater State College

Melinda Swafford
Tennessee Technological University

Peter Swirski
University of Hong Kong

Glenn L. Swygart
Tennessee Temple University

John M. Theilmann
Converse College

Jennifer L. Titanski
*Lock Haven University of
Pennsylvania*

Anh Tran
Wichita State University

Paul B. Trescott
Southern Illinois University

Richard Tuerk
Texas A&M University, Commerce

William T. Walker
Chestnut Hill College

Donald A. Watt
Dakota Wesleyan University

Shawncey Webb
Taylor University

Marcia J. Weiss
Point Park University

Twyla R. Wells
University of Northwestern Ohio

Christine A. Wernet
University of South Carolina, Aiken

Richard L. Wilson
University of Tennessee, Chattanooga

Scott Wright
University of St. Thomas

Complete List of Contents

Volume 1

Volume 2

Volume 3

HISTORICAL ENCYCLOPEDIA OF
AMERICAN BUSINESS

A

AAA. *See* **American Automobile Association**

A&P. *See* **Great Atlantic and Pacific Tea Company**

Accounting industry

DEFINITION: Enterprises concerned with designing financial information systems, recording economic transactions, auditing financial statements, and offering business services such as tax planning, payroll processing, and valuation of assets

SIGNIFICANCE: The accounting industry serves all sectors of the economy, including for-profit enterprises, nonprofit organizations, and local, state, and national governments. It compiles and interprets data to enable informed business decisions and coordinate business relationships. The industry has been crucial to the efficient management of American business, and accounting is sometimes called "the language of business."

The demand for audited financial records in American business emerged as early as 1628, when the Massachusetts Bay Company was chartered as a joint-stock company to finance the Pilgrims bound for New England. Modern accounting can be traced back to around 1817 in the classrooms of the United States Military Academy at West Point, New York. The academy established the technique of measuring human perfor-

mance in the context of grading students. This effort to measure human productivity then spread to the burgeoning railroad industry.

The railroads were a commercial enterprise of unprecedented scale. They required enormous sums of capital and large numbers of workers and managers, and they posed numerous challenges of organization and operation. Accounting data began to be used not only to run the railroads efficiently but also to manage their business profitably and to control the behavior of employees. These uses of accounting information within organizations soon spread to the rest of the large corporations that made up the American economy. Such innovations as the well-known Du Pont model of financial ratios would cement the use of accounting information as an indispensable tool of management.

As part of the Progressive movement for government and business reform toward the end of the

---

THE DU PONT MODEL OF FINANCIAL RATIOS

The Du Pont model of financial ratios became a common equation in the accounting industry for examining a corporation's return on equity (ROE). Its purpose is to break down the corporation's ROE into separate components to understand each component's contribution to the bottom line. The basic formula is as follows:

ROE = Net Profit Margin × Asset Turnover × Equity Multiplier

Thus, the Du Pont formula models a company's ability to turn equity into profit as a function of three factors:

- the ability to sell goods for more than they cost to make or obtain (net profit margin)
- the ability to sell and restock inventory efficiently (asset turnover)
- the ability to leverage assets effectively (equity multiplier)

Different businesses may rely more heavily on different components of the ROE, but they all must take all three into account when evaluating financial performance.

nineteenth century, accountants began to organize themselves as a public profession. Beginning with New York in 1897, state societies of public accountants formed to institute educational standards, licensing requirements, and codes of conduct to raise and regulate the quality of accountants auditing corporate financial statements. In addition, by the early twentieth century, university-based research contributed to the development of accounting theory as a framework for accounting practice.

The public accounting industry was put on a firm footing with the passage of the Federal Securities Acts of 1933 and 1934. These laws and others like them, including the Sarbanes-Oxley Act of 2002, are aimed at protecting investors by regulating the content and form of financial information about publicly traded corporations. By the early twenty-first century, the accounting industry had become an integral part of American business in general and American capital markets in particular. It assisted investors and enabled managers in running businesses more efficiently and profitably.

Sajay Samuel

FURTHER READING

Edwards, John Richards, ed. *The History of Accounting: Critical Perspectives on Business and Management.* 4 vols. New York: Routledge, 2000.

Eichenwald, Kurt. *Conspiracy of Fools.* New York: Broadway, 2005.

Fleischman, Richard, ed. *Accounting History.* 3 vols. London: Sage, 2006.

SEE ALSO: Banking; Business crimes; Enron bankruptcy; Income tax, corporate; Internal Revenue Code; Service industries; Taxation.

Advertising industry

DEFINITION: Enterprises that use various media to announce, offer, or promote goods, services, or ideas to create a demand for them

SIGNIFICANCE: The advertising industry persuades people to buy products and services that, without advertising, might go unnoticed by the consumer. Consequently, advertising has been vital in promoting all kinds of businesses and products, often creating a demand for things neither necessary nor of any real value. On the other hand, it has created competition among businesses and organizations that causes them to continually improve their products and services to the advantage of the consumers.

Making other people aware of something for sale is mostly beneficial and profitable. Advertising goes back to ancient times. For centuries, vendors of foods, items of clothing, and other necessities used painted signboards and symbols to show potential customers what could be obtained at a particular location. This method's drawback, however, was that customers had no way of knowing where a vendor was located except by passing by and seeing the sign or by word of mouth.

By the sixteenth century, the printing press allowed posters and handouts containing information about goods and services for sale to be printed on easily distributed sheets. The first newspaper advertisement in the American colonies appeared in the eighteenth century: A person owning property in New York advertised it in *The Boston News-Letter.* In 1729, Benjamin Franklin placed advertisements in his *Pennsylvania Gazette,* and by 1742, his *General Magazine* carried the first magazine advertisements in the colonies. Franklin cleverly used illustrations and headlines to catch the reader's eye and call attention to what was for sale. Also, rather than bunch all the advertisements together on a separate page, as had been the practice, he placed some advertisements near editorial material to ensure that readers would see them.

Some early American outdoor signs using drawings or statuettes—such as the wooden Indian and the little black boy—were used by tobacco shops. Such devices, along with product illustrations, were useful and necessary to communicate to a population with limited literacy. People who could not read well, or at all, could still recognize what was being offered. Advertising of this type was widespread because many painters and art students were available to create the signboards and carve the statuettes, and they were more reliable than printing presses, which were prone to frequent breakdowns.

When the printing press ushered in weekly, then daily, newspapers in the American colonies, it did not take long for advertising to become an integral feature of newspapers. The one-cent dailies that came out after 1830 were so affordable that they increased newspaper readership, making advertising in the newspaper a good way to reach the public. Advertisements were placed not only by legitimate businesses but also by some makers of quack remedies, as well as brothels and prostitutes. Everyone who had something to sell recognized the value of advertising it.

THE ADVENT OF AGENCIES

Though illustrations usually were what attracted readers to advertisements, copy also was important. Well-written, interesting, and informative copy was vital to selling a product. Early on, copy was written by professional writers, known as literary men, who either freelanced, providing their writing services for a fee to anyone who hired them, or were employed by a business to write copy solely for that company.

In 1841 in Philadelphia, Volney Palmer set up what is considered the first advertising agency. His agency and those that quickly followed concerned themselves with soliciting advertisements for newspapers. Then George P. Rowell found it more profitable for an advertising agency to buy newspaper space cheaply and sell it at retail price to businesses wanting to advertise. To bolster his contention that newspaper advertising was profitable, he published the first volume listing all the newspapers in the United States, along with fairly accurate estimates of their circulation numbers. In this way, he showed customers that by using his services, they could guarantee their advertisements would be seen by a certain number of potential customers. These early agencies were mainly brokers for newspaper space.

With the mission of advertising agencies firmly established—they were to ensure that advertisements were bought and paid for—agencies expanded their services to include writing the ad copy. Depending on the product or the newspaper in which the advertisement would run, the copywriters concerned themselves with aiming at "Everyman" and "Everywoman," without worrying too much about the diversity of the readers. However, as more media became available and specialization of content became the rule and not the exception, copywriters adjusted by adapting their copy to the specialized interests of the consumers. They also recognized that copy for newspapers, for magazines, and for direct mail had to be different: Newspaper readers were usually more apt to scan and toss; magazines readers, on the other hand, often kept the magazine around for days if not weeks and, therefore, would have occasion to retrace their reading and have numerous opportunities to see an advertisement. Direct mail, because of its resemblance to a personal communication, had to immediately convince readers that the message was meant for them in particular.

During the late 1860's, copywriter John Powers developed a writing style called "honest copy," in which he wrote the literal truth about a product. Telling the sometimes "awful truth" about a product was risky, but Powers thought that if the consumer believed the company was telling the complete truth about the product, the company, and therefore the product, could be trusted. Some clients did not like the style; possibly they felt the bad might overshadow the good and cost them sales. However, many other clients experienced excellent sales with this style of copywriting, which became known as the Powers style and was considered to be years before its time.

During the mid-nineteenth century, new technologies allowed businesses to produce new products quickly. However, the existence of these new products and even some older ones went unnoticed in many areas of the United States. Manufacturers wanted to make potential consumers not only aware of the products but also eager to buy them. They wanted to create new markets for the goods being produced. To help them do this, advertising agencies became full-service agencies, meeting all their clients' needs, not only producing the ad copy and artwork but also doing market research and ultimately placing the advertisements in the various media.

The oldest full-service agency was N. W. Ayer & Son, which started in 1869 and for a while mainly served the patent medicine business. It went on to work for Montgomery Ward, Ferry Seeds, and Singer Sewing Machines, and later Procter & Gamble, Burpee Seeds, and Gold Dust Cleanser. Though at first it used only newspaper advertising, it gradually was pressured by the competition to add magazine and outdoor advertising by 1898.

The 1880's saw the beginning of national advertising of branded products. Companies such as Montgomery Ward and Sears, Roebuck and Company started using mail-order catalogs to inform and entice rural customers, who made up the majority of the American population until the 1920's. Advertising volume rose from about $200 million in 1880 to almost $3 billion in 1920.

MEDIA

During the early 1920's, advertising got a new medium when radio stations began broadcasting. Most early radio programs were used to promote the sale of radios, but before long, other entities—nonprofit organizations such as schools, civic groups, and clubs—set up radio stations of their own, sponsored by businesses in exchange for acknowledgment by name on the air. Soon station owners realized they could generate more money if they got more sponsors, so they began the practice of selling small segments of air time on each program to as many businesses as could be fitted into the air space. The radio advertisements not only entertained the listeners, as they were often creative, dramatic, or humorous, but also, and most important, informed them. The new products or services offered were presented in such a way as to persuade the listeners that they should be one of the first to own them or that the product was something they needed. Sometimes the commercials, as the radio advertisements were called, explained new uses for products that were already familiar to the consumer.

Radio programs were written to appeal to particular audiences. There were shows meant mainly for children, teenagers, women, men, the family, and for adults in general. Advertisers could place commercials for specific products on programs with the appropriate audience. This practice of target marketing proved a valuable technique when television came along.

Television programs have identifiable demographics, as do cable channels, which are sometimes devoted to a particular audience, such as sports enthusiasts, women, or ethnic minorities. Early television advertisers had editorial control of programming, allowing them to control a program's content. They could veto certain aspects of a proposed program or insist on additions or deletions to favor their product, with little concern for the effect such changes might have on the program's creative aspects. Selling small blocks of broadcast time to several advertisers was seen as the way to limit the power of any one business to control the programming. This strategy, credited to National Broadcasting Company (NBC) executive Sylvester Weaver,

was known as the magazine concept and participation advertising. It ushered in "the commercial break" that most television programs use approximately every fifteen minutes.

In addition to commercials, television shows allow for product placement, which allows advertisers to circumvent the tendency of some viewers to fast forward past commercials on shows that they have recorded. The clearly labeled product is highly visible in a scene and even sometimes is called to the reader's attention by dialogue. This technique is also used to include advertising in films.

In the twentieth century, print media became increasingly diversified, as newspapers and magazines targeted to a specific age group, gender, or interest became more prevalent than ever. Knowing the demographics of the readers was a boon to advertisers, who could target the people most likely to be interested in specific products.

Other advertising media include direct mail, outdoor billboards, transit advertising, and the Internet. Direct mail is advertising that sends its message to individual consumers, first using the United States postal service and later adding the telephone (telemarketing) and e-mail. Although letters or flyers, using words and pictures alone to persuade the reader to take a particular action, are a relatively inexpensive direct-mail medium, direct mail has also taken the form of coupons, samples, and specialty items such as magnets, key chains, pencils, or ballpoint pens inscribed with a business logo or message. Specialty items tend to be kept and used by consumers and therefore remind them of products or services for a longer period.

Outdoor advertising, which harks back to the earliest advertising strategies, uses billboards of various kinds and sizes as well as wallscapes (advertisements displayed on already standing surfaces, such as the sides of buildings). Traditional billboards were set up along well-traveled highways to catch drivers' eyes. Some were huge, impossible-to-ignore displays, 14 feet high and 48 feet wide, but others were smaller. Few were as small as the famous sequential Burma Shave shaving cream signs so popular between 1925 and 1963. They were a sequence of five or six 18-by-40-inch boards, painted red with white lettering, placed alongside the road about 100 feet apart. They always spelled out, a few words at a time, a jingle-style message about almost anything as long as the punch line clearly referred to Burma Shave, the only words on the last board. One jingle on six signs read, "I proposed/ To Ida/ Ida refused/ Ida won my Ida/ If Ida used/ Burma Shave." Outdoor advertising is also common at sporting venues such as baseball and football stadiums, racetracks, and soccer fields.

Transit advertising is advertising placed on or in major forms of transit and at points where passengers board or exit transit. Advertisements range from small posters in and on buses, trolleys, and trains to wraps that cover entire cars and buses.

Advertisements on bus shelters and benches, walls, and pillars in subway or train stops are daily reminders of the product or service advertised. Airplanes and blimps have also been used to advertise products in areas where many people are gathered, such as outdoor sporting events.

The advent of the Internet brought another advertising medium to the mix. The Internet allows numerous outlets for advertisements, including banners, pop-ups, links to advertisements that appear during searches, and mass e-mails. Many sites also send targeted advertisements to those who visit them.

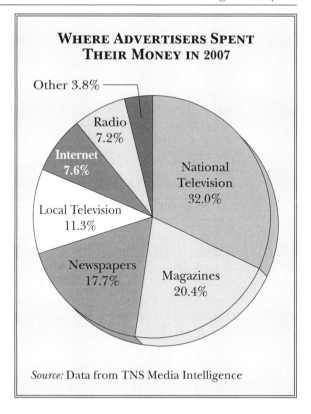

WHERE ADVERTISERS SPENT THEIR MONEY IN 2007

Other 3.8%
Radio 7.2%
Internet 7.6%
Local Television 11.3%
Newspapers 17.7%
National Television 32.0%
Magazines 20.4%

Source: Data from TNS Media Intelligence

STRATEGIES

As media for distributing advertising messages increased, the strategies for competing for consumer dollars changed. Advertising agencies have become more specialized in all aspects of their services. To learn the needs, desires, aspirations, and incomes of potential customers for their products, they do extensive and even intensive research. They analyze age, gender, ethnicity, and educational demographics of the targeted consumer. They ascertain consumer behavior. For example, they might consider advertising a particular toiletry in a particular magazine. They will then research the magazine's readership to decide if their proposed advertisement would appeal to the consumer likely to use the product. When they are satisfied that the magazine is a good choice, they must then decide what would be the best approach, visually and verbally, to grab that consumer's attention amid all the other editorial and pictorial distractions as the consumer reads through the magazine.

The same kind of strategizing is necessary for advertising successfully on radio or television. With so many programs aired on the media, advertisers need to know who actually listens to or watches par-

ticular programs. The kind of advertisement is vital: Placing a frivolous commercial on a serious program or an earnest one on a comedic program would more likely repel than attract the consumer. With the high cost of both making commercials and airing them on popular programs, advertisers must also consider whether the size of the audience is worthwhile. Some advertisers apparently feel that quantity is more important than quality and are apt to spend their advertising dollars to run short, ten- to fifteen-second commercials several times during an hour or two of television programming. Others believe an engrossing thirty-second commercial strategically placed in a popular prime-time program will reap more impressive benefits.

IMPACT

Advertising is so much a part of the twenty-first century world that its impact is constantly debated. It invades public spaces such as schools and is considered by some to be a kind of child exploitation. Those who favor its positive effects are often those who profit the most from it. There is little doubt that advertisements and commercials have a strong influence on the buying practices of the American public. In the years since pharmaceutical companies, law firms, and other such entities began advertising, these businesses have grown. Brand names are so well known that many of them have become part of the national vocabulary. People are as likely to say "Kleenex" as to say "tissue." Many toys and food items are purchased at the insistence of children who have watched television commercials promoting the products.

The idea that advertising helps to sell a profusion of products goes hand in hand with the idea that more and more goods are manufactured because advertising creates a demand for them. Advertisements increasingly equate consumers' personal happiness with their consumption of goods. Because people often feel owning things is a sign of success, advertisers are quick to encourage conspicuous consumption. Excessive consumption of some products, however, has the potential to cause social harm, and therefore many people are critical of advertising for alcoholic beverages, tobacco products, gambling venues, junk food, and fast-food restaurants, especially when the advertisements are directed toward minority populations or children.

The original mission of advertising was to apprise potential consumers of the availability of things they needed and could use. Over time it came to affect the media it uses. Television programs, ostensibly presented for the entertainment and edification of the viewer, are often modified, at the insistence of the advertiser, so that viewers will pay at least as much attention to the commercials as to the program. Researchers have found that programs that require little concentration and barely stimulate the viewer's mental abilities make the viewer sit longer and thus sit through the commercials. When the commercials are more entertaining than the actual program, the viewer pays them more attention, thereby achieving the aim of the advertiser.

Advertisements are almost everywhere consumers go—on the walls of airports, on public address systems in stores, on the telephone when consumers are put on hold, and even on grocery carts. Advertising pays off for the agencies as well as for the businesses that use it. According to TNS Media Intelligence, advertisers in the United States in 2006 spent more than $150 billion. Worldwide expenditure was $385 billion. The industry sees only progressive growth, with a projected advertising expenditure by 2010 of $500 billion.

Jane L. Ball

FURTHER READING

Fox, Stephen. *The Mirror Makers: A History of American Advertising and Its Creators.* Rev. ed. Urbana: University of Illinois Press, 1997. Contains the stories of some of the earliest advertisers, from the nineteenth century to the 1970's, and of the ten biggest advertising agencies from 1945 to 1995. Considered by some to be one of the best histories of advertising ever written.

Marchand, Roland. *Advertising the American Dream: Making Way for Modernity, 1920-1940.* Berkeley: University of California Press, 1985. Discusses advertising agency employees of the 1920's and 1930's, how advertising graphically records American culture in the popular media, and how advertisements promote the consumption of goods.

Margolin, Victor, Ira Brichta, and Vivian Brichta. *The Promise and the Product: Two Hundred Years of American Advertising Posters.* New York: Macmillan, 1979. Explores advertising through posters from colonial days to the 1970's. More than three hundred illustrations, some in full color. Features some advertising campaigns and graphic depictions that influenced Americans' daily lives.

Michelet, John. *Advertising: Industry in Peril.* Tigard, Oreg.: Olympian, 2006. Discusses the flaws of advertising and provides suggestions on how to correct them. Identifies major issues needing change, arguing that billions of dollars are wasted each year with unimpressive advertisements that consumers ignore.

Silvulka, Juliann. *Soap, Sex, and Cigarettes: A Cultural History of American Advertising.* Belmont, Calif.: Wadsworth, 1997. Describes advertising history from the days of the colonial newspapers to modern-day Web sites, also details the influence of advertising agencies that reflect trends and introduce new ones to capture consumers' interest and money. Illustrated.

SEE ALSO: Christmas marketing; Franklin, Benjamin; Internet; Magazine industry; Newspaper industry; Retail trade industry; Tobacco industry; Truth-in-advertising codes.

Advice books. *See* How-to-succeed books

Affirmative action programs

DEFINITION: Publicly mandated and private programs designed to increase employment and education opportunities for traditionally underserved or underrepresented groups, usually racial minorities and women

SIGNIFICANCE: Affirmative action programs were designed to equalize opportunities for disenfranchised groups. They have been controversial since their inception, from the standpoints of both public policy and constitutional law. Critics and supporters alike would agree, however, that they significantly changed hiring and recruitment practices throughout the country, altering the composition of the workforce within several major industries.

On March 6, 1961, newly inaugurated president John F. Kennedy issued Executive Order 10925, which required businesses receiving contracts with the federal government not only to refrain from discriminating in employment but also to "take affirmative action to ensure that employees are treated during employment without regard to their race, creed, color, or national origin." The requirement was then understood to mean that employers should desegregate, ending all-black and all-white work units, departments, and divisions. On June 22, 1963, Kennedy's Executive Order 11114 empowered federal agencies to terminate contracts with businesses disobeying Executive Order 10925. Nevertheless, southern firms continued to resist compliance, as enforcement was weak.

CIVIL RIGHTS ACT OF 1964

The term "affirmative action" next appeared in Title VII of the Civil Rights Act of 1964, which empowered courts to require employers guilty of discrimination to engage in "such affirmative action as may be appropriate." The statute went into effect on July 1, 1965, and suggested such remedies as hiring or reinstatement of employees with back pay.

So long as complainants were required to file lengthy and costly lawsuits in order to gain relief for illegal discrimination, discriminatory employers were at a definite advantage. Therefore, advocacy groups urged President Lyndon B. Johnson to require federal contractors to take "affirmative action" in advance of complaints by empowering an administrative agency to enforce requirements and monitor compliance. On September 24, 1965, Johnson issued Executive Order 11246, which extended affirmative action to the recruitment, screening, and selection of new employees. Enforcement was assigned to the U.S. Department of Labor. The Equal Employment Opportunity Commission (EEOC), empowered to enforce Title VII, then asked errant employers to draw up "affirmative action plans," that is, blueprints for changes in policies, practices, and procedures identified as responsible for discrimination.

On October 13, 1967, Johnson issued Executive Order 11375, extending affirmative action to cover sex discrimination. On May 28, 1968, the Labor Department for the first time required contractors to prepare written "affirmative action programs."

THE PHILADELPHIA PLAN AND BACKLASH

Although affirmative action was understood to mean including ethnic groups and women in occupations from which they were formerly excluded, many employers provided only token responses to the new orders and regulations, such as hiring just one African American or woman in a particular job. In 1968, to deal with this tokenism, the Labor Department's Philadelphia office began to require contractors to demonstrate compliance quantitatively.

What became known as the Philadelphia plan involved comparing employees and applicants for employment with statistical norms. For example, if Labor Department statistics showed that 30 percent of all forklift operators working in the Philadelphia area were African American, each contractor was required to ensure that close to 30 percent of its forklift operators were African American. Similarly, employers had to demonstrate that rates of promotion, salaries, and other aspects of employment treated both sexes and all ethnic and racial groups equally. If they could not do so, they were required to state specific reasons why disparities existed and correct the deficiencies.

The Philadelphia plan insisted that, where disparities were found, employers must draw up time-

Allan Bakke arrives at the Medical School of the University of California at Davis in 1978. He successfully sued the university for reverse discrimination after it rejected him in 1973 and 1974. (AP/Wide World Photos)

tables for removing those disparities. It became a nationwide standard on February 5, 1970, when the Labor Department issued new guidelines for affirmative action known as Revised Order 4. The order required employers to assess whether they perpetuated patterns of exclusion or underemployment of minorities or women. If so, changes were to be made in any personnel policies, practices, or procedures that were deemed responsible for the anomalous patterns; goals and timetables for such changes were required. Failure to make an analysis or to correct deficiencies was deemed to constitute bad faith, placing a contract in jeopardy.

Although the Philadelphia plan was acceptable to civil rights groups, some white men saw the hiring of an increasing number of minorities and women as "reverse discrimination." Employers also began to complain of the cost of collecting, organizing, and analyzing detailed statistics about their employees.

Affirmative action has not always been implemented in a manner consistent with federal guidelines, leading to court challenges on some occasions. Judges, in turn, have supported affirmative action only when remedies have been narrowly tailored to remedy specific deficiencies in reasonable periods of time. In 1995, President Bill Clinton announced four standards for "mending" affirmative action: Affirmative action should not establish quotas, give preference to unqualified applicants, involve reverse discrimination, or continue beyond the existence of a demonstrable need. That policy continued through the beginning of the twenty-first century.

Michael Haas

FURTHER READING

Anderson, Terry H. *The Pursuit of Fairness: A History of Affirmative Action.* New York: Oxford University Press, 2005. Traces affirmative action from the presidential executive orders of the 1960's through the early twenty-first century, evaluating critiques and court challenges.

Bergman, Barbara. *In Defense of Affirmative Action.*

New York: Basic Books, 1996. An advocacy book that points out that affirmative action is an antidote to preferences for whites who rely on social connections with those in authority for advancement.

Carter, Stephen L. *Reflections of an Affirmative Action Baby.* New York: Basic Books, 1991. Many African Americans hired during the era of affirmative action programs were accused of being unqualified, even though affirmative action is designed to benefit only qualified minorities and women. Carter describes how affirmative action served to exacerbate racial tensions for African Americans.

Curry, George E., ed. *The Affirmative Action Debate.* New York: Perseus, 1996. Eight essays detail the pros and cons of affirmative action.

Ezorsky, Gertrude. *Racism and Justice: The Case for Affirmative Action.* Ithaca, N.Y.: Cornell University Press, 1991. Coherent legal rebuttal to objections to the concept of affirmative action.

Glazer, Nathan. *Affirmative Discrimination: Ethnic Inequality and Public Policy.* Cambridge, Mass.: Harvard University Press, 1987. Vigorous critique of the concept of affirmative action as a form of discrimination.

SEE ALSO: Equal Employment Opportunity Commission; Labor, U.S. Department of; Presidency, U.S.; Supreme Court and commerce; Supreme Court and labor law; Women in business.

AFL-CIO

IDENTIFICATION: Federation encompassing more than fifty national and international labor unions
DATES: Founded in 1955; AFL founded in 1886; CIO founded in 1932
SIGNIFICANCE: The unions represented by the AFL-CIO (American Federation of Labor and Congress of Industrial Organizations) fought for and won American workers' rights to collective bargaining, employer-sponsored health care plans, the eight-hour workday, workplace safety provisions, pensions and other retirement plans, and the procedures for dealing with grievances arising from workplace issues. The AFL-CIO influences local and national political elections by endorsing candidates sympathetic to worker-friendly policies and laws.

Founded by Samuel Gompers in 1886, the American Federation of Labor (AFL) was a union limited to skilled craftsmen. This policy distinguished the early AFL from other trade unions such as the Knights of Labor, which admitted semiskilled laborers, employers, and even strikebreakers. Although the early AFL stated that it was open to anyone who wished to join, it was openly hostile to African Americans, women, recent immigrants with limited ability to speak English, Chinese railroad workers, and all workers employed in factories manufacturing mass-produced goods. In the few instances when the AFL did support nonwhite or female workers, it did so in whatever way would help these workers while protecting the jobs and wages of white men.

AVERTING VIOLENCE

Gompers and other high-ranking members of the AFL saw the damage that violent labor strikes organized by the Knights of Labor inflicted on company profits and reputations as well as on those participating in the strikes. He vowed that the AFL would not engage in any tactics that might lead to the deaths of striking workers. He believed that physical confrontations during strikes led to legislation designed to criminalize labor organizing activities. Gompers preferred the AFL to pursue less antagonistic policies. For decades, the AFL concentrated on basic workplace issues such as job safety and security, as well as wage stabilization. One of the AFL's most significant early achievements was the passage of the Clayton Antitrust Act in 1914, formally granting workers the right to strike. The U.S. Supreme Court, however, ruled that the act did not permit secondary boycotts by sympathetic unions.

Gompers was not particularly interested in political issues. The AFL did not make attempts to form a third political party at any point in its history, although the AFL-CIO became strongly aligned with the Democratic Party in the latter part of the twentieth century and has endorsed candidates in national political races. Before his death in 1924, Gompers organized the AFL to be largely a national-level administrative body that would provide visibility as well as organizational and fund-raising skills for unions under its umbrella. At one time, more than fifty separate unions, with member rolls numbering in the tens of millions, belonged to the AFL. The AFL is supported by a portion of the dues

UNIONS IN THE AFL-CIO, 2008

Air Line Pilots Association (ALPA)
Amalgamated Transit Union (ATU)
American Federation of Government
  Employees (AFGE)
American Federation of Musicians of the
  United States and Canada (AFM)
American Federation of School Administrators
  (AFSA)
American Federation of State, County and
  Municipal Employees (AFSCME)
American Federation of Teachers (AFT)
American Federation of Television and Radio
  Artists (AFTRA)
American Postal Workers Union
  (APWU)
American Radio Association (ARA)
American Train Dispatchers Association
  (ATDA)
Associated Actors and Artistes of America
  (4As)
Bakery, Confectionery, Tobacco Workers and
  Grain Millers International Union
  (BCTGM)
Brotherhood of Railroad Signalmen (BRS)
California Nurses Association/National Nurses
  Organizing Committee (CNA/NNOC)
California School Employees Association
  (CSEA)

Communications Workers of America
  (CWA)
Farm Labor Organizing Committee (FLOC)
Federation of Professional Athletes
  (Professional Athletes)
Glass, Molders, Pottery, Plastics and Allied
  Workers International Union (GMP)
International Alliance of Theatrical Stage
  Employes, Moving Picture Technicians,
  Artists and Allied Crafts of the United States,
  Its Territories and Canada (IATSE)
International Association of Bridge, Structural,
  Ornamental and Reinforcing Iron Workers
  (Iron Workers)
International Association of Fire Fighters
  (IAFF)
International Association of Heat and Frost
  Insulators and Allied Workers (AWIU)
International Association of Machinists and
  Aerospace Workers (IAM)
International Brotherhood of Boilermakers,
  Iron Ship Builders, Blacksmiths, Forgers and
  Helpers (IBB)
International Brotherhood of Electrical
  Workers (IBEW)
International Federation of Professional and
  Technical Engineers (IFPTE)

that union members pay. The unions in the AFL pursue their own policies to benefit each union's members.

Beginning early in the twentieth century, the AFL began to accept unions representing industrial (semiskilled) workers, although the AFL continued to prefer craft unions representing skilled workers. The AFL's reluctance to fully support the concerns of industrial unions created room for much more militant unions affiliated with the AFL, such as the United Mine Workers of America led by John L. Lewis, to pursue their own agendas. This eventually forced a showdown between these unions and the AFL, leading to the expulsion of many of these unions. The AFL remained nonpolitical, even as it continued to stand up for workers' rights.

During the Great Depression, Congress passed the National Industrial Recovery Act of 1933 and the National Labor Relations Act of 1935. Union membership grew in both unions represented by the AFL and those outside it. Unemployment benefits became a much more common employee benefit.

POSTWAR DEVELOPMENTS

After the start of World War II, most unions cooperated with government policies to limit strikes and demands for higher wages. Many union workers were exempt from military conscription because their labor was considered essential for the war effort. After the war, however, union workers struck for increased wages and removal of restrictions on

UNIONS IN THE AFL-CIO, 2008 *(continued)*

International Longshore and Warehouse Union (ILWU)

International Longshoremen's Association (ILA)

International Plate Printers, Die Stampers and Engravers Union of North America

International Union of Allied Novelty and Production Workers (Novelty and Production Workers)

International Union of Bricklayers and Allied Craftworkers (BAC)

International Union of Elevator Constructors (IUEC)

International Union of Operating Engineers (IUOE)

International Union of Painters and Allied Trades of the United States and Canada (Painters and Allied Trades)

International Union of Police Associations (IUPA)

Marine Engineers' Beneficial Association (MEBA)

National Air Traffic Controllers Association (NATCA)

National Association of Letter Carriers (NALC)

National Postal Mail Handlers Union (NPMHU)

Office and Professional Employees International Union (OPEIU)

Operative Plasterers' and Cement Masons' International Association of the United States and Canada (OP&CMIA)

Seafarers International Union of North America (SIU)

Sheet Metal Workers International Association (SMWIA)

Transport Workers Union of America (TWU)

Transportation Communications International Union/IAM (TCU/IAM)

United American Nurses (UAN)

United Association of Journeymen and Apprentices of the Plumbing and Pipe Fitting Industry of the United States and Canada (UA)

United Automobile, Aerospace & Agricultural Implement Workers of America International Union (UAW)

United Mine Workers of America (UMWA)

United Steel, Paper and Forestry, Rubber, Manufacturing, Energy, Allied Industrial & Service Workers International Union (USW)

United Transportation Union (UTU)

United Union of Roofers, Waterproofers and Allied Workers (Roofers and Waterproofers)

Utility Workers Union of America (UWUA)

Writers Guild of America, East Inc. (WGAE)

---

union activities. Congress, however, was in no mood to negotiate. In 1947, Congress passed the Taft-Hartley Act, which restricted labor union power. President Harry S. Truman vetoed the bill. Congress overrode the presidential veto, and Truman, despite his initial opposition to the bill, invoked the act a dozen times during his eight years in office.

The AFL has always been the largest union administrative body and generally the most conservative. Its rival union administrative body, and sometime partner, is the Congress of Industrial Organizations (CIO). Always smaller and much more aggressive in advocating workers' rights, the CIO was founded in 1932 as the Committee for Industrial Organization by John L. Lewis. The CIO ac-

cepted unions whose members were organized along industrial or geographical lines regardless of whether the workers were classified as skilled or semiskilled. The CIO actively pursued involvement in national as well as state and local politics. Lewis and his CIO union members battled AFL procedures and preferences for craft unions during the brief period, 1935-1938, when the AFL and CIO tried to operate as a unified body.

Being expelled from the AFL freed the CIO to focus on organizing efforts in the rubber, automotive, and steel industries, as well as among electrical and radio workers. By the end of 1936, the United Electrical Workers claimed more than 600,000 dues-paying members. In 1936-1937, General Motors employees occupied manufacturing buildings in Flint,

Michigan, for forty-four days, despite attempts by the police and National Guard troops to forcibly remove them. As a result of this sit-down strike, the CIO helped workers form the United Auto Workers (UAW). The CIO-affiliated UAW gained the right to represent General Motors workers. The strike at General Motors caused a national sensation. Chrysler and Ford executives agreed to allow employees to form unions under UAW control. U.S. Steel, a major supplier to the automotive industry, agreed to a collective bargaining agreement with the CIO-affiliated Steel Workers Organizing Committee (SWOC) and avoided a strike. The CIO sponsored a West Coast longshoremen's union in 1937. The formation of unions at other steel companies was unsuccessful, probably because of the violence and deaths of union members that occurred in several strikes during the decade. CIO-sponsored attempts to organize southern textile mill workers during the 1940's also failed because of systematic legal discrimination against African Americans.

The presence of communists or communist sympathizers in CIO senior administrative positions was far more damaging to the CIO than unsuccessful attempts to organize workers. In 1940, Congress passed the Alien Registration Act, commonly referred to as the Smith Act. This act allowed for the prosecution of any person threatening violence against the U.S. government. Regardless of whether socialistic or communistic statements made by union leaders were actually threats of violence against the government, these statements made it easy for conservatives to target CIO union leaders and force them out of their jobs. Trying to save its own reputation, the CIO expelled several member unions accused of being communist led or inspired.

MERGER

In 1952 and 1953, both the AFL and the CIO lost their longtime presidents. Walter Reuther of the CIO and George Meany of the AFL realized that both groups could be more effective in organizing and increasing union membership if the two groups reunited, which they did in 1955. From 1955 until 2005, the AFL-CIO represented the vast majority of craft and industrial workers in the United States. During the 1970's, the AFL-CIO claimed more than 23 million dues-paying members. However, beginning during the 1980's, manufacturing jobs traditionally held by union members began to be out-

sourced, as manufacturing facilities and jobs were transferred to countries with lower labor costs and less restrictive environmental controls. The AFL-CIO lost members. Union organizers began to target workers in service industries, particularly teachers; government employees at the city, county, and state levels; and employees in the hotel and tourism industry. Industrial workers and service industry workers sometimes had opposing concerns. By 2005, several of the largest service industry unions had left the AFL-CIO to form the Change to Win Federation, an organization more focused on service worker concerns. In 2008, the AFL-CIO claimed a worldwide membership of 10.5 million members among fifty-six national and international labor unions.

Victoria Erhart

FURTHER READING

Dubofsky, Melvyn, and Joseph McCartin, eds. *American Labor: A Documentary Collection.* New York: Palgrave Macmillan, 2004. This collection of essays focuses on gender and ethnic issues within American labor history.

Forbath, William. *Law and the Shaping of the American Labor Movement.* Cambridge, Mass.: Harvard University Press, 1991. The author discusses American legal history as it relates to the history of labor in the United States.

Leab, Daniel. *The Labor History Reader.* 2d ed. Urbana: University of Illinois Press, 1985. Covers the development of labor movements in the United States since colonial times.

Lichtenstein, Nelson. *State of the Union: A Century of American Labor.* Princeton, N.J.: Princeton University Press, 2003. The author's thesis is that labor movements are essential to ensure a functioning democracy.

Sinyai, Clayton. *Schools of Democracy: A Political History of the American Labor Movement.* Ithaca, N.Y.: ILR Press, 2006. Examines the intermingled history of labor activism and American politics.

SEE ALSO: Gompers, Samuel; International Longshoremen's Association; Knights of Labor; Labor, U.S. Department of; Labor history; Labor strikes; Lewis, John L.; National Labor Relations Board; Sitdown strike of 1936-1937; Taft-Hartley Act; United Mine Workers of America; United States Steel Corporation.

Agency for International Development, U.S.

IDENTIFICATION: Independent agency of the U.S. government that provides financial assistance to foreign countries

DATE: Founded on November 3, 1961

SIGNIFICANCE: The primary purpose of USAID is to implement long-term overseas economic and development assistance. The agency also provides humanitarian relief following disasters and seeks to support the democratization of other nations.

The United States Agency for International Development (USAID) is an independent federal agency, although the secretary of state broadly oversees its work. USAID is responsible for supporting long-term economic growth in developing countries through projects in agriculture, democracy and governance, economic growth, natural-resources management, education and training, and health. In 2008, USAID awarded about $4 billion in federal contracts and grants to American businesses. This money allowed the businesses to administer technical assistance projects and to purchase and distribute commodities and equipment. USAID works through nearly four thousand American companies and nongovernmental organizations (NGOs).

HISTORY OF U.S. FOREIGN AID AND USAID

USAID traces its roots to various attempts by the U.S. Congress to address the needs of other nations for military, economic, political, and social stability. The first attempt was the 1948 Marshall Plan, which aided in the reconstruction of Europe after World War II. Successive attempts to create a U.S. international development organization included the Mutual Security Agency in 1951, the Foreign Operations Administration in 1953, the International Cooperation Administration and the Food for Peace program in 1954, and the Development Loan Fund in 1957.

Support by the American public for foreign aid had lagged dramatically by the late 1950's, owing in part to the 1958 publication of *The Ugly American* by Eugene Burdick and William Lederer. This novel described arrogant American aid workers in Southeast Asia, and it negatively influenced public perception of aid workers and diplomats generally. This and other issues prompted Congress and the ad-

ministration of President Dwight D. Eisenhower to refocus U.S. aid toward developing nations, and the subject became important in the 1960 U.S. presidential campaign.

John F. Kennedy became president in 1961 with the promise to repair America's image in the world, and he made foreign assistance a high priority. Kennedy said that the U.S. response to the world's poorest nations was inadequate and that it was vitally important that the United States and other industrialized nations help less developed nations become economically self-sufficient.

Spurred by the presidential campaign, on September 4, 1961, Congress passed the Foreign Assistance Act, which called for a separation of military and nonmilitary foreign aid programs and the creation of an agency to administer economic assistance programs. One result of the act was the establishment of USAID on November 3, 1961. Congress folded into USAID various operations of the International Cooperation Agency, the Development

Rwandan Agnes Mukanshijo is participating in a USAID income-generation project. She is growing geraniums in the hope of selling their oil to the perfume industry. (USAID)

Loan Fund, the Export-Import Bank of the United States, and the Food for Peace program.

FOREIGN AID PHILOSOPHY

The American economist and political theorist Walt Whitman Rostow had an influential role in determining how USAID would carry out its work. Rostow was a strong proponent of capitalism and free enterprise and a steadfast opponent of communism. One of the first USAID programs was the 1961 Alliance for Progress, which sought better economic cooperation between the nations of North America and South America. The charter that established the alliance called for, among other things, an annual increase in per capita income of 2.5 percent, the elimination of adult illiteracy by 1970, price stability, land reforms, and equitable income distribution.

Early USAID projects in Africa were designed to provide stability to nations that had newly declared their independence from European colonizers. In Asia, projects were primarily designed to counteract the spread of communism and the influence of the People's Republic of China.

REORGANIZING FOREIGN AID PROGRAMS

By the early 1970's, Americans had again become skeptical of foreign aid, in part as a result of disdain for the Vietnam War. Up until then, USAID had managed many large projects that involved building roads, bridges, and schools in developing nations, and it had made direct donations of money and goods to foreign countries. In 1973, the House of Representatives amended the Foreign Assistance Act to stipulate that foreign aid should focus on promoting basic human needs, such as education, basic health maintenance, and agriculture.

An attempt was made to reorganize American foreign assistance projects in 1979, when the International Development Cooperation Agency was established and some programs under the Economic Support Fund program were delegated to the USAID director. Another attempt was made in 1988, when the House Committee on Foreign Affairs sought completely to overhaul the 1961 Foreign Assistance Act. The bill died in committee, however.

The role of USAID in administering U.S. foreign aid was reexamined in 1991, when the administration of President George H. W. Bush sought to rewrite the Foreign Assistance Act. That attempt also failed, when some members of Congress complained that the administration was seeking too much discretionary authority in directing foreign aid. Another attempt to rewrite the Foreign Assistance Act occurred in 1994, during the administration of President Bill Clinton, but the bill was not introduced in the Senate, nor did it pass through the appropriate committees in the House of Representatives.

U.S. foreign aid was again the subject of reform in 2003, when President George W. Bush established the Millennium Challenge Corporation to provide aid to the world's poorest countries. The mission of the corporation was to reduce global poverty by promoting sustainable economic growth in countries committed to adopting significant economic and political reforms. In 2008, USAID provided economic and other developmental assistance to 120 countries, with a budget of approximately $17.6 billion.

Terry A. Anderson

FURTHER READING

Berrios, Rubén. *Contracting for Development: The Role of For-Profit Contractors in U.S. Foreign Development Assistance.* Westport, Conn.: Praeger, 2000. Contains an overview of the complexities of the consulting market in international development and explains how for-profit firms can do business with USAID.

Graham, Carol, et al. *The Other War: Global Poverty and the Millennium Challenge Account.* Washington, D.C.: Brookings Institution Press, 2003. Explains the Millennium Challenge Account and cautions against the dangers of creating another foreign aid agency.

Lancaster, Carol, and Ann Van Dusen. *Organizing U.S. Foreign Aid: Confronting the Challenges of the Twenty-first Century.* Washington, D.C.: Brookings Institution Press, 2005. Argues that the U.S. foreign aid program is in disarray and offers advice for making it more effective.

United States Agency for International Development. *USAID Primer: What We Do and How We Do It.* Washington, D.C.: Author, 2006. A publication by the agency itself that offers a practical overview of how USAID operates and where it works.

SEE ALSO: Export-Import Bank of the United States; Government spending; International economics and trade; Marshall Plan.

Agribusiness

DEFINITION: Mass commercial production and distribution of agricultural commodities

SIGNIFICANCE: The growth of U.S. agribusiness has corresponded with a decrease in the number of small, family farms in the country. Moreover, American multinational corporations have helped drive an international trend toward the replacement of subsistence farming with commercial farming.

First coined in 1955, the term "agribusiness" denoted an increasing consolidation of American agricultural resources that was driven by considerations of efficiency. This process began during the Industrial Revolution, when large farms with access to technological resources developed a competitive advantage over smaller, poorer farms. Wealthy farmers could purchase tractors and other machinery that made agriculture more efficient. They could cultivate more land and harvest crops more easily, benefiting from economies of scale unavailable to those working on smaller farms. Also as a result of the Industrial Revolution, people no longer had to produce their own food to survive. Instead, they could work in factories and earn enough money to purchase food. These factories provided poor farmers with a strong incentive to leave the land.

During the late 1960's, the third agricultural revolution, also known as the Green Revolution, made farming an even more expensive activity. Scientists succeeded in altering the genetics of seeds so they could produce more food. To maximize the benefits of these genetically altered seeds, however, one needed to use irrigation and pesticides, increasing the cost of the capital outlay needed for competitive agricultural production. As had been the case during the Industrial Revolution, those most likely to benefit from these new techniques were the wealthier producers. Smaller, poorer producers were forced out of business. Thus, advances in agricultural technology inadvertently contributed to reducing the number of producers in this sector of the economy.

Agribusiness has been controversial in a variety of contexts. Opponents of agribusiness point to the sharp reduction in the number of producers of agricultural products. They fear that this situation could lead to an increase in the price of food as competition dwindles. Moreover, some environmentally conscious consumers have become concerned over the large carbon footprint of national and international agribusiness. They advocate eating food produced locally, rather than centrally produced food that is shipped long distances.

Furthermore, in developing nations, there are not enough urban jobs to accommodate all of the people leaving farms and moving to cities. In addition, the wages earned by industrial workers in developing nations are relatively low. Thus, opponents of agribusiness argue that the concentration of food production in the hands of a small number of large, multinational corporations exacerbates poverty and world hunger.

Advocates of agribusiness argue that global food production has increased as corporate farming has become more common, reducing rather than increasing world hunger. Corporations such as Cargill and Monsanto are able to use the most advanced agricultural technology, as well as management and organizational techniques, to produce food as efficiently as possible, thus bringing down the cost of food over time.

Kevin L. Brennan

FURTHER READING

Elliot, Jack. *Agribusiness: Decisions and Dollars.* Clifton Park, N.Y.: Delmar, 1999.

Jansen, Kees, and Sietze Vellema. *Agribusiness and Society: Corporate Responses to Environmentalism, Market Opportunities, and Public Regulation.* London: Zed Books, 2004.

Ricketts, Cliff. *Introduction to Agribusiness.* Clifton Park, N.Y.: Thomson Delmar Learning, 1999.

SEE ALSO: Agriculture; Agriculture, U.S. Department of; Beef industry; Farm labor; Farm protests; Food-processing industries; Pork industry; Poultry industry; Rice industry; United Farm Workers of America.

Agriculture

DEFINITION: Deliberate management of crops and livestock to produce foods and other agricultural products

SIGNIFICANCE: Farming advances and efficiencies have made the United States one of the world's largest exporters of agricultural products. However, U.S. agriculture has come under censure internationally because of its farm subsidies and tariffs and domestically because of environmental concerns, its inhumane treatment of animals, and its employment and treatment of immigrant workers.

Farming practices were first brought to America during the colonial years, when England granted large tracts of land to private companies or individuals for farming and development. After America won its independence in 1783, all unsettled lands came under the supervision of the federal government. Poor settlers, known as squatters, would often farm these tracts of land and claim ownership. Wheat, barley, rice, indigo, tobacco, maize, potatoes, and cotton were some of the first crops cultivated in the United States. In 1839, Congress set aside $1,000 to fund the distribution of seeds for crops and to collect agriculture statistics. The Homestead Act of 1862 offered vast amounts of land in the West for settlement, and by the mid-nineteenth century, American agriculture was a vital part of the economy, becoming a business operation that advanced the United States as a nation.

THE INDUSTRIAL REVOLUTION

The American Industrial Revolution, occurring between 1820 and 1870, was significant to the U.S. economic evolution. Mills and factories expanded, waterways and railroads were built to ship goods long distances, and new inventions made production more efficient and quicker. Farm equipment, such as plowshares, reapers, the cotton gin, steam tractors, and the combine, made farming easier and faster. By 1860, there were approximately 2 million farms with an average size of 199 acres, which produced a variety of goods. Some of the agricultural products were consumed by farmers, some were sold domestically, and some were exported.

As the number of farms increased to supply the growing population, farmers began to organize to have more of a say in the governmental policies that affected them. The U.S. Agricultural Society was organized by farmers in 1852 to protect their interests and was active in all areas of farming. Although it disbanded in 1860, its influence still can be seen in U.S. agricultural policy. The U.S. Agricultural Society demanded a national bureau of agriculture to regulate farming issues, and the U.S. Department of

Agriculture (USDA) was established in 1862 to meet its demands. The early mission of the USDA was to disseminate information about agricultural methods and distribute new and valuable seeds and plants.

In 1867, a group of farmers known as the National Grange of the Patrons of Husbandry was organized to plan educational events and social gatherings for farming families. Other groups, such as the Greenback Party during the 1870's, the Farmers' Alliance during the 1880's, and the Populist Party during the 1890's, soon evolved into political groups that advocated for and protected farmers. Because middlemen, bankers, and shippers often took unfair advantage of farmers economically, farming advocacy efforts resulted in government regulations and the formation of bank cooperatives that strengthened the economic viability of the farming community.

FEDERAL INTERVENTION

President Abraham Lincoln appointed Isaac Newton, a successful farmer, the first commissioner of the USDA (1862-1867). Under his progressive leadership, the USDA set up the Bureau of Animal Industry along with botany, chemistry, entomology, statistics, forestry, and other departments that advanced agricultural practices. In 1862, the Homestead Act gave public land to anyone willing to farm it, and the Morrill Land-Grant Act established colleges with agricultural education programs. Commissioner and Secretary of Agriculture Norman J. Colman (1885-1889) was instrumental in passing the Hatch Act in 1887. The Hatch Act established Office of Experiment stations and funded agricultural experiments to advance better and efficient farming practices.

In 1897, James Wilson became secretary of agriculture, and he served for sixteen years. Under his astute management, the USDA became well known for quality research, regulations, and education programs. He established extension services; initiated soil conservation, reforestation, and farm credits; expanded research into plant disease and insect control; and began experimental farms and labs. These experimental farms and extension services were valuable for teaching farmers how to implement new farming techniques that improved crop yields. Many of these programs helped prevent or cure plant and animal diseases, improved nutrition and fattened animals in less time, used selective breeding for healthier animals, developed new disease-resistant hybrid seeds, and increased crop production through use of new fertilizers.

The first two decades of the twentieth century saw cities and the U.S. population continue to grow. Prices for farm products were high, as demand for goods increased and land values soared. During World War I, the United States became the primary supplier of food and agricultural goods to other countries involved in the war. Soon after the war ended, so did the higher demand for agricultural products, and prices fell. Despite economic prosperity in the rest of the country, farmers fell on hard times as their incomes plummeted. They pleaded with the U.S. government for assistance, but to no avail. The stock market crash of 1929 and the resulting Great Depression soon brought the rest of the nation into the same economic plight. Farming conditions in parts of the midwestern and southern plains soon became worse, as weather cycles took a downturn and turned once-productive farmlands into dust bowls. The burgeoning American economy was in tatters.

DEPRESSION AND RECOVERY

The federal government regarded the agriculture industry as an integral component of the U.S. economy. In 1929, President Herbert Hoover created the Federal Farm Board, which raised prices without limiting production and provided economic stability for farmers by regulating farm markets. Target prices for the commodity crops of wheat, corn, and rice were legislated. Deficiency payments were made to farmers based on the difference between the crop target price and the average market price, regardless of market demand in the state in which they farmed.

New farming techniques, gasoline- and electric-powered equipment, and widespread use of pesticides and chemical fertilizers also created work efficiencies that continued to increase food production. Although this was good for the overall economy, it was bad for farmers, because high yields meant increased supply, which meant lower prices. The new farming techniques also required the purchase of large, expensive equipment and chemicals, raising the farmers' cost of production. These combined to decrease their profits and ability to make an adequate living from farming. President Franklin D. Roosevelt and the Congress passed the Agri-

cultural Adjustment Act of 1933, which provided economic incentives to farmers for decreasing their production of hog and dairy products and soil-depleting crops. The act was in part designed to remedy the farming practices that had resulted in the soil erosion that added to the Dust Bowl problem. Many later farm bills would similarly contain conservation measures. Farmers who willingly decreased production received parity payments that balanced prices between farm and nonfarm products and set up a system of price supports that guaranteed farmers a price equal to prices they would have received during favorable times. Some excess crops were purchased by the government and stored for sale during lean years.

The Farm Credit Act of 1933 also kept farmers solvent by allowing them to refinance one-fifth of their farm mortgages over an eighteen-month period. Infrastructure supports, such as extending power lines into rural areas (through the Rural Electrification Administration) and building a network of farm-to-market roads, helped farmers market their goods in distant cities and towns. All-risk insurance programs were begun in 1939 to protect farmers against crop failures due to natural disasters. Improvements in storage and transport, such as cold-storage warehouses, refrigerated railroad cars and trucks, air freight, and eventually development of quick-freeze processes, also allowed perishable foods to be shipped to all areas of the United States. By 1935, there were more than 6 million farms with an average size of 155 acres.

Before World War II, low farm prices were largely the result of business cycles, bad weather, lack of adequate transportation methods, and credit difficulties. World War II and the Korean War temporarily boosted farm prices, as U.S. farmers supplied agricultural products to foreign countries hard hit by the war. After World War II, overproduction of crops became the main reason for decreased farm product prices and decreased profits for farmers. During the 1950's and 1960's, programs were started to use excess agricultural products. In 1954, Congress created the Food for Peace program, exporting U.S. agricultural goods to poor countries. President Lyndon B. Johnson established the Food Stamp Program in 1961, which gave eligible Americans coupons for commodity foods. Surplus foods were also used in school meal programs available to schools in poorer areas.

The Agricultural Act of 1956, also called the Soil Bank Act, continued the effort to decrease production of specific crops and convert cropland to soil-conserving reserve lands through incentive payments to farmers. Although advanced agricultural techniques—use of hybrid plants and better feeding and breeding methods for livestock—had increased food production dramatically, they had created overproduction, which was wasting land and water resources and depressing farm product prices.

GOOD TIMES AND BAD TIMES

The Agriculture and Consumer Protection Act of 1973, an omnibus farm bill, dealt with soil conservation, lowered the limit on farm program payments, provided direct disaster payments, and shifted to a market-oriented farm policy. The Food and Agriculture Act of 1977 continued the market-oriented loan and target price policies of the 1973 legislation and further limited farm program payments. It created an extended storage program for grains, known as the farmer-reserve program, in an attempt to deal with surpluses. The Agricultural Credit Act of 1978 increased the amount of credit available to farmers. For much of the 1970's, the worldwide demand for agricultural products was growing, creating higher land prices and incomes and reducing surpluses. However, as farmers borrowed money at low interest rates to expand their businesses by purchasing equipment and land, many became overextended. As market prices for agricultural crops fell, land prices dropped and credit became tighter. Farms began going into foreclosure, and manufacturers and sellers of farm equipment, seed, and fertilizer, along with rural banks, also experienced economic difficulties. The embargo in 1980 on U.S. food exports to the Soviet Union, through which President Jimmy Carter canceled sales of 17 million metric tons of corn, soybeans, and wheat, also reduced demand for agricultural products. The Soviet grain embargo ended in 1981.

In 1983, the Payment-in-Kind program was implemented in an attempt to reduce government surplus holdings of grains, rice, and cotton by removing 25 percent of farming land from production. A crop insurance program was also implemented to provide relief to farmers from natural disasters. However, the government had amassed large stockpiles of farm products and could not sell them. Gradually, market prices began to strengthen, but the cost of farming support programs exceeded $4 billion annually.

FARMS AND FARMLAND, 1850-2006

Year	Farms (1,000's)	Total Acreage (1,000's)	Average Acreage Per Farm
1850	1,449	293,561	203
1860	2,044	407,213	199
1870	2,660	407,735	153
1880	4,009	536,082	134
1890	4,565	623,219	137
1900	5,740	841,202	147
1910	6,366	881,431	139
1920	6,454	958,677	149
1930	6,295	990,112	157
1940	6,102	1,065,114	175
1950	5,388	1,161,420	216
1960	3,962	1,176,946	297
1970	2,954	1,102,769	373
1980	2,428	1,042,000	429
1990	2,146	987,000	460
2000	2,167	945,000	436
2006	2,090	932,000	446

Sources: Data from *Historical Statistics of the United States: Colonial Times to 1970* (Washington, D.C.: U.S. Department of Commerce, Bureau of the Census, 1975); *Statistical Abstract of the United States, 1981* (Washington, D.C.: U.S. Department of Commerce, Bureau of the Census, 1981); *Statistical Abstract of the United States, 2008* (Washington, D.C.: Department of Commerce, Economics and Statistics Administration, Bureau of the Census, Data User Services Division, 2008)

In 1985, President Ronald Reagan and the Congress enacted the Food Security Act, also known as the 1985 Farm Bill. This legislation lowered commodity prices and subsidies and established a dairy-herd buyout program. Loan deficiency payments, compensation for crops when market prices fell below a government-set minimum, were implemented to protect farmers when market prices were low. The result did reduce crop surpluses and made U.S. agricultural products more attractive to other countries.

Legislation in 1990 encouraged farmers to raise crops for which they had not received subsidy payments and reduced the amount of payments for which they could qualify. In 1996, Congress worked to stop farming reliance on government assistance altogether. The Federal Agriculture Improvement and Reform Act (FAIR Act), also called the Freedom-to-Farm Act or 1996 Farm Bill, dismantled price and income supports, allowed farmers to plant crops for global markets without restriction, and phased out dairy price supports.

Congress eased the transition for farmers with the Agricultural Market Transition Act (AMTA) of 1996. The AMTA provided deficiency payments over a seven-year period for corn, wheat, grain sorghum, barley, oats, cotton, and rice crops, and government stockpiles for these crops were eliminated. By 1999, an estimated 30 million acres that would have been idle were in production, with crops that allowed farmers to respond to changing market and climate conditions. Overseas exports slumped, however, and livestock and crop prices plunged in 1998. The government responded with a number of emergency appropriation bills, again boosting farm subsidies to keep the agricultural business stable.

Besides crop deficiency payments, the loan program for farmers started during the 1930's also acts as a subsidy for farmers. Under this loan program, farmers originally would repay loans plus interest after their crops were sold in the marketplace. These loans had no penalty for nonpayment, except that the low-value crop was defaulted to the government. When the FAIR Act was implemented, the requirement to default low-value crops was removed, and the loan became a direct subsidy for the farmer. Loan deficiency payments (LDP) were also implemented and allowed farmers to bypass the loan process and receive a subsidy payment instead. This created a system in which farmers could take loan subsidies when market prices were low and sell their crops when market prices improved.

In 1985, the Conservation Reserve Program (CRP) was implemented and set aside millions of acres of farmland in highly erodable or environmentally sensitive areas. Farmers were paid per acre for a ten- to fifteen-year period to not grow crops but instead plant native grasses on the land or create riparian areas. The FAIR Act lessened the total number of acres that could be enrolled under the conservation program from 45 million acres to 39.2 million acres.

TWENTY-FIRST CENTURY POLICY

In the twenty-first century, improvements in soil conservation, farm machinery, fertilizers and seeds, irrigation methods, and pest control have continued to increase crop yields. At the same time, these new methods have increased the costs of producing crops. Agriculture remains a capital-intensive industry with large fixed costs and uncertain outcomes, influenced by weather (drought, flooding) and the ups and downs of the commodity markets, both domestically and globally.

There were 2.1 million farms in the United States in 2002, with an average size of 441 acres, compared with nearly 5.4 million farms with an average size of 215 acres during the 1950's. Many small American farms have been replaced by agribusinesses ranging from small hog-confinement operations to huge multinational firms. Although agribusinesses often result in cost-effective production of agricultural products, they have been criticized for producing pollution and environmental problems (often caused by disposal of animal wastes or large-scale use of pesticides), creating inhumane environments for animals (such as confinement sheds), and being the main beneficiaries of farm subsidies, rather than small family farms. Agribusinesses have also been criticized because they employ migrant workers, some of whom may be in the country illegally, and expose them to harsh working conditions.

Many small farmers must work part-time in addition to farming because of high land and equipment costs and the difficulty of earning enough to support their families. Continued federal subsidies for wheat, corn, rice, cotton, and soybeans as well as loan and set-aside program have shielded farmers from the ravages of market supply and demand but have cost the American government an estimated

$20 billion per year in 2001, up from about $9 billion per year during the early 1990's.

Farm subsidies have also caused problems at the global level. For example, the World Trade Organization has repeatedly called for fewer government subsidies for American cotton growers. The organization claims that the U.S. government is illegally subsidizing American cotton farmers, which drives down cotton prices on the world market, creating poverty in other cotton-producing countries. Brazil won a ruling at the World Trade Organization against the United States for providing subsidies to cotton farmers; this may result in the creation of a tariff against American cotton in Brazil.

Proponents of farm subsidies argue that price supports, which are paid when market prices fall below a certain point, are caused by falling prices and certainly do not trigger them. Also, because farmers have fixed costs of production, falling prices—not subsidies—will trigger overproduction as farmers strain to recoup their investments. Proponents argue that because farmers cannot control commodity prices, the government should use a combination of price supports and supply controls to avoid the negative effects of rapidly falling prices, which include farmer bankruptcies, land loss, accelerated consolidation of farms, and pressure to switch to input-intensive farming methods (such as factory farming).

Toward the end of the first decade of the twenty-first century, fuel concerns in the United States increased the demand for biofuels. This in turn drove up the demand and price for corn, a source of biofuel that supporters praise as a renewable source of energy and critics say is an inefficient source of energy and lucrative for farmers largely because of subsidies. Increased demand for grains by China and India, coupled with a weak American dollar, drove up market prices for corn and other grains. Higher grain prices translated into increased costs for beef, dairy, and poultry producers. The result has been higher consumer food costs worldwide. Domestically, higher prices and increased demand have reduced the amount of surplus commodities held by the Department of Agriculture, which means food banks are receiving less food from the government. The increase in demand means that farmers will increase production to increase supply and drive down costs, but if the market for agricultural products decreases, that will again result in overproduction. The fluctuations in farm prices due to market forces and uncontrollable weather conditions may require occasion federal interventions to maintain an adequate food supply and ensure that the economy thrives. However, the costs of these interventions must be carefully examined.

Alice C. Richer

Further Reading

Cochrane, Willard W. *The Curse of American Agricultural Abundance.* Lincoln: University of Nebraska Press, 2003. Ironic account of the negative consequences of the vast productive capacity of American farms and farmlands.

Etter, Lauren, and Greg Hitt. "Bountiful Harvest: Farm Lobby Beats Back Assault on Subsidies." *The Wall Street Journal,* March 27, 2008. Details the battle over farm subsidies on Capitol Hill.

Fitzgerald, Deborah. *Every Farm a Factory: The Industrial Ideal in American Agriculture.* New Haven, Conn.: Yale University Press, 2003. Analysis of the costs and benefits of the industrialization of American agriculture.

Gardner, Bruce L. *American Agriculture in the Twentieth Century: How It Flourished and What It Cost.* Cambridge, Mass.: Harvard University Press, 2002. Comprehensive economic history of twentieth century U.S. agriculture.

Hurt, R. Douglas. *American Agriculture: A Brief History.* West Lafayette, Ind.: Purdue University Press, 2002. Historical overview of agriculture in the United States.

See also: Agribusiness; Agriculture, U.S. Department of; Beef industry; Cereal crops; Cotton industry; Dairy industry; Farm Credit Administration; Farm labor; Farm protests; Farm subsidies; Pork industry; Poultry industry.

Agriculture, U.S. Department of

Identification: Cabinet-level department of the federal government responsible for aiding and regulating food production

Date: Established in 1862

Significance: The Department of Agriculture was created to boost national agricultural production, but it later acquired responsibility for ensuring the safety of the nation's food supply as well.

Established in 1862, the United States Department of Agriculture (USDA) was created to improve productivity in American farming. The department helped farmers acquire and use technology and fertilizers and rotate crops effectively. It became a cabinet-level department in 1889. At the beginning of the twentieth century, its mission expanded, as two significant divisions were added to the department: The Forest Service was formed in 1905, and the Food and Drug Administration (FDA) was established in 1906, shaping the USDA into a major regulatory agency. The FDA was later removed from the department, but some of its original regulatory duties remained with the USDA after the separation.

The modern USDA regulates much of the food production and distribution process in the United States, setting guidelines for food safety and offering aid to farmers to increase production and lower prices. The department works closely with business, including small and corporate farms, wholesale food distributors, and retailers such as grocery stores. The USDA's central duties are divided into three broad spheres of influence: farming and rural communities, food safety, and conservation.

FARMING AND RURAL COMMUNITIES

The isolation and distances associated with rural communities have been a particular focus of the USDA since its creation. Early in its existence, the department began providing agricultural research and funding to educate farmers about new technologies and planting techniques. As technology became more important to successful farming, agricultural communities began to require conveniences more commonly found in urban areas.

During the Great Depression, the USDA began providing grants to expand and maintain the nation's rural infrastructure. The 1935 Rural Electrification Act provided electricity to many rural communities for the first time. The expansion of electric power lines to isolated farms was prohibitively expensive for local communities, so federal funding was necessary. The rural electrification program was a success, but technology continued to advance over time, and rural, agricultural communities continued to need assistance to adopt new technologies, including communications technologies such as telecommunications and, later, the Internet.

The Depression also highlighted the economic uncertainties of the farming community. The USDA is primarily responsible for administering the federal subsidy programs that provide a guaranteed income for farmers. The Farm Service Agency (FSA) is the government's safety net for American farmers. It provides loans for land, equipment, and crop purchases—mainly to new farmers, who lack the credit to receive bank loans. The FSA is also responsible for providing farmers with bridge loans, that is, interim funds they can use until they have harvested their crops. Bridge loans help prevent farmers from being forced to sell their commodities at a time when the market price is low. The USDA also makes loans to farmers when weather or other natural disasters destroy crops. Price supports are a larger program for agribusiness, as the federal government sets minimum prices for farm commodities.

In addition to helping increase food production and providing income supports to farmers, the USDA has helped increase domestic and foreign consumption of American-grown food. The USDA's Agriculture Marketing Service (AMS) division advertises American agricultural products. The AMS has engaged in high-profile, national campaigns, including the popular "Got Milk?" promotion since 1993. It is financed by mandatory fees charged to producers.

The USDA also works to increase food consumption by administering programs designed to provide food to the poor. The National School Lunch Program is responsible for feeding tens of millions of school children daily. The program provides free or subsidized lunches while setting nutritional standards for each meal. The USDA was granted control of the program as part of its mission to dispense food surpluses. The department also runs the food stamp program, providing subsidized food for adults and families. The food stamp program also aids businesses, increasing their sales and revenue by making it possible for impoverished Americans to purchase more food than they otherwise could.

The USDA has also sought to increase overseas demand for American agricultural commodities. It has conducted studies on alternative uses for food crops, including using them as fuel. The department educates farmers on how to increase their exports under international trade agreements and the regulations of the World Trade Organization (WTO).

Complementing the efforts of the USDA, the Office of the United States Trade Representative

An Iowa farmer uses a tractor bought with a loan from the Farm Security Administration (later the Farmers Home Administration) in 1939. (Library of Congress)

(USTR) negotiates and implements trade agreements. The USTR, through its effort with the WTO, can have a positive impact on agribusiness, opening new markets for American farmers by lowering foreign trade barriers. Trade agreements can also have a negative impact, however, as they may eliminate subsidies to American farmers, decreasing their income and increasing the cost of food.

The USDA analyzes markets and the demand for certain agricultural products. The department makes short-term and long-term forecasts of the expected global and domestic production of farm commodities, helping farmers make plans for the next decade. The department also projects possible alternative uses for existing commodities, such as the conversion of corn into the biofuel ethanol.

FOOD SAFETY

The USDA has worked to protect American consumers from food-borne illnesses. During the 1990's, the crisis of bovine spongiform encephalopathy (BSE, commonly known as mad cow disease) and its spread from animals to humans heightened public awareness of food-borne illnesses and the role of the USDA's Food Safety and Inspection Services (FSIS) on the front lines of food safety. The FSIS guarantees that animals slaughtered for sale do not have diseases that might spread to people eating their meat. With a considerable amount of American meat being shipped overseas, the FSIS must prove to foreign governments that the slaughtering of animals by U.S. producers follows safety guidelines. If meat is considered unsafe, foreign countries may halt imports, much as Japan did after mad cow disease was discovered in some American beef.

The USDA has become more active in its inspections of foreign food producers as well. Although the department imposes strict regulations on American beef and poultry producers, it is often forced to depend on other governments to regulate their own industries. USDA inspectors, however, do examine foreign countries' regulations and inspect food production plants and farms to ensure that food safety is maintained among exporters to the United States. They coordinate these efforts with foreign governments. The department thus works to ensure that the feeding and treatment of animals destined to become part of the U.S. food chain are properly regulated. In the absence of such regulations, the USDA can impose import bans on potentially unsafe food.

The Animal and Plant Health Inspection Service was created to protect American agriculture from infestation from insects and other pests. The service has the authority to impose a quarantine on foreign or domestic food products that are found to contain pests. It also works with the U.S. Customs and Border Protection Bureau to ensure that pests do not enter the country on the clothes or belongings of foreign visitors or Americans returning from abroad. The service also researches the best methods for fighting and defeating these pests and provides information to domestic producers on how to prevent infestations.

CONSERVATION

Conserving the resources of public and private lands is another duty of the USDA. The best-known conservation agency within the USDA is the United States Forest Service, which produced the popular Smokey the Bear advertising campaign to prevent forest fires. The Forest Service also has a close relationship with business: As a protector of national forests, the service works with private companies that harvest trees in national forests. It regulates where and how trees will be cut to preserve the national forests while also allowing harvesting of lumber needed to build houses and to thin the forests.

Finally, the Natural Resources Conservation Service researches and dispenses information on the conservation of topsoil and water and the proper use of irrigation systems. It educates farmers and gardeners alike, teaching them to prevent fires, to use natural and artificial fertilizers effectively, and to rotate crops to maintain soil integrity.

Douglas Clouatre

FURTHER READING

Hurt, R. Douglas. *Problems of Plenty: The American Farmer in the Twentieth Century.* Chicago: Ivan R. Dee, 2003. Historical look at American farming, including the various government programs used to improve agriculture and the financial condition of farmers.

Morgan, Kevin, Terry Marsden, and Jonathan Murdoch. *Worlds of Food.* New York: Oxford University Press, 2006. Discusses the growing competition among world food producers and the difficulties in regulating worldwide food production.

Murphy, Denis. *People, Plants, and Genes.* New York: Oxford University Press, 2007. Describes the technological movement toward genetically enhanced foods and the regulatory environment for those foods.

Pasour, E. J., and Randall Rucker. *Plowshares and Pork Barrels.* Washington, D.C.: Independent Institute, 2005. Critical analysis of the American government's farm programs, ranging from agricultural subsidies to the food stamp program.

Southgate, D. Douglas, Douglas Graham, and Luther Tweeten. *The World Food Economy.* Hoboken, N.J.: Wiley-Blackwell, 2006. Introduction to the international food economy; explains how overseas producers have complicated the American food market and how American farmers have sought to compete with international producers.

SEE ALSO: Agribusiness; Agriculture; Bracero program; Dairy industry; Environmental movement; Farm Credit Administration; Farm subsidies; Food Stamp Plan; Meatpacking industry; World Trade Organization.

Air traffic controllers' strike

THE EVENT: Strike by government employees seeking better working conditions and compensation
DATE: August 3, 1981
PLACE: United States
SIGNIFICANCE: The air traffic controllers' strike of 1981 violated federal law and the terms of the controllers' contract. The president responded to the strike by terminating striking workers, significantly weakening both PATCO and the American organized labor movement generally.

By the 1980's, American unions had become less powerful. In 1981, one of those unions, the Professional Air Traffic Controllers Organization (PATCO), sought to improve its members' pay while reducing the stress its workers faced on the job. The controllers' principal employer, the Federal Aviation Administration (FAA), refused the union's demands, and PATCO decided to call a strike during the peak of the travel season. The union believed that the government would have no choice but to concede to prevent the airline, shipping, and tourist industries from being crippled. President Ronald Reagan instead responded with an ultimatum: The air traffic controllers were to return to work within forty-eight hours or face termination.

Although federal employees had a mandated no-strike clause, PATCO felt that it had the right to call a strike because negotiations had failed to achieve the desired results and other federal workers in the past had used similar tactics. By the end of July, union president Robert E. Poli had been working on a deal with the government for six months to no avail: The government's offer was rejected by 95 percent of the union's membership. On August 3, 1981, a strong majority of that membership took to the picket lines.

PATCO sought higher wages, a shorter workweek to alleviate the stress of the job, and better retirement benefits. At the time, the airline industry enjoyed revenues of $30 billion per year, and the union assumed that drastic government action would jeopardize that revenue. However, after the president fired the striking controllers, the FAA implemented a contingency plan that successfully restored air traffic standards to normal operating levels within a few weeks.

More than eleven thousand air traffic controllers lost their jobs as a result of the strike. Moreover, on October 22, 1981, the Federal Labor Relations Authority decertified PATCO, removing its ability to engage in collective bargaining on behalf of its members. In 1987, collective bargaining power would be reassigned to the National Air Traffic Controllers Association. The illegal strike was never supported by the public, which instead tended to agree with the president.

The air traffic controllers' strike had significant effects on American business. In addition to breaking the union's hold on the airline industry, it sent a message to other unions and their members, as well as to management in other industries: Organized labor was weakening, and the administration of President Reagan was willing to exert its influence on the side of management.

This power shift in labor-management relations corresponded with advancements in technology that increased productivity, allowing managers to accomplish more with fewer workers. Many other industries sought to use technology to increase the power of management and weaken that of labor. For many years after the air traffic controllers' strike, unions were not respected as a valuable tool by employers. Many companies cut jobs, pensions, and other employee benefits. It would take almost fifteen years for the unions to regain their strength and worth in the workplace.

Karel S. Sovak

FURTHER READING

Nordlund, W. *Silent Skies: The Air Traffic Controllers Strike.* Westport, Conn.: Praeger, 1998.

Round, Michael A. *Grounded: Reagan and the PATCO Crash.* Rev. ed. New York: Routledge, 1999.

SEE ALSO: Air transportation industry; Aircraft industry; Labor history; Labor strikes; Presidency, U.S.; Transportation, U.S. Department of.

Air transportation industry

DEFINITION: Business sector that uses aircraft to transport passengers, cargo, and mail

SIGNIFICANCE: One of the leading business sectors in the American economy, the air transportation industry employed nearly half a million people during the early twenty-first century, not including travel agencies, hotels, and car rental companies. In 2004, the average American flew 2.2 times a year.

The Wright brothers flew the first powered airplane in 1903, and World War I demonstrated the airplane's military potential. In 1919, Deutsche Luft-Reederei (later Lufthansa) began flying passengers between Berlin and Weimar, Germany. The air transportation industry began in the United States in 1925, when Juan T. Trippe and others persuaded Congress to privatize the airmail system. The U.S. Post Office initially granted twelve contracts. Trippe's company, Colonial Aviation, won the New York-Boston route, but Trippe later lost control of the company. Airplane manufacturer William Boeing received the contract for Chicago-San Francisco and founded the airline that later became United Airlines. Pitcairn Aviation obtained the New York-Atlanta and Atlanta-Miami contracts and later became Eastern Air Lines. A company called Robertson Aviation flew the St. Louis-Chicago route and employed a then-unknown pilot named Charles A. Lindbergh.

THE FIRST AIRLINES

In 1927, Trippe's new company, Pan American World Airways (Pan Am), received the contract to fly the mail from Key West, Florida, to Havana, Cuba. Trippe felt that he could increase profits by transporting a few passengers along with the mail. One of his first customers was the gangster Al Capone.

In 1930, the U.S. Post Office awarded the following contracts: New York-California via Chicago to United, New York-California via St. Louis to Trans World Airlines (TWA), New York-California via Dallas to American, and several routes along the east coast to Eastern. Two regional airlines that later became international also received routes: Braniff International Airways got the Chicago-Dallas route and Delta Air Lines got Atlanta-Chicago.

The controversial millionaire (later billionaire) Howard Hughes made three important technical innovations during the 1930's. They were retractable landing gear, flushed rivets, and an oxygen feeder system. The first two streamlined airplane designs and increased their speed. The third allowed planes to fly at higher altitudes and also increased their speed.

Two aircraft, the Douglas DC-3 and the Boeing 315, boosted the air transportation industry during the 1930's. The Douglas DC-3 had two engines, flew at 180 miles per hour, was easier to fly than previous passenger planes, and was more comfortable for passengers. The Boeing 315, also known as the China Clipper, was a four-engine plane with pontoons as big as fishing boats. It landed and took off from water, so it could land anywhere in the ocean in an emergency, carried seventy-four passengers, had a 175-mile-per-hour cruising speed, and offered a range of 3,500 miles without refueling. As the nickname indicates, it was designed to fly from the United States to China, so Pan Am built refueling stations on islands such as Oahu, Wake, and Guam for its Hong Kong-San Francisco and New Zealand-San Francisco routes. It was the largest passenger plane ever regularly flown until the Boeing 747 came along.

THE CIVIL AERONAUTICS BOARD PERIOD

By 1938, there were 250 passenger flights each day in the United States. However, the system was perceived as too chaotic by the administration of Franklin D. Roosevelt, which considered airlines to be a kind of utility. In line with the prevailing pro-regulation ideology, Congress passed the Civil Aeronautics Act of 1938. Not only did it create the Civil Aeronautics Board (CAB) to regulate routes and rates, but it also froze all existing airmail contracts in perpetuity.

Prices for flights were determined by the CAB based on the costs provided by the airlines themselves so that the airlines

were guaranteed to make a profit. Eventually airlines made a distinction between first class and coach, but even flying coach was so expensive that Pan Am partnered with the Household Finance Corporation to help middle-class travelers pay for tickets through installments.

Hughes bought a majority of TWA stock in 1939 and worked with the Lockheed Corporation to develop the L-049 Constellation. It had a pressurized cabin that allowed it to fly at high altitudes, four engines that made it twice as fast as the DC-3, and the same range as the China Clipper. In 1955, Pan Am began flying the first passenger jet, the Boeing 707, and flight times were reduced even further. Pan Am started flying the Boeing 747, the first jumbo jet, in 1970.

American Airlines developed the first computerized reservation system, Sabre, during the early 1960's. It enabled American to manage its inventory of planes and seats more efficiently and eventually accumulated reams of data. United build the second system, called Apollo, and other airlines such as Eastern, Delta, and TWA built their own systems as well. In 1976, United offered to place its terminals in the offices of travel agents, although American actually placed more Sabre terminals in those offices

Passengers board a Trans World Airline Constellation aircraft during the mid-1940's. (Library of Congress)

than any other airline. By the mid-1980's, American's terminals were in 34 percent of the 30,000 travel agencies in the United States, and United's were in about 25 percent.

In 1969, the CAB allowed the airlines to offer discount fares such as youth and family fares. Two airlines, however, began offering low-price tickets as the norm, not the exception. Pacific Southwest Airlines (PSA) and Southwest Airlines both flew within the borders of just one state, PSA in California and Southwest in Texas. Consequently, they were not subject to CAB regulations and could set their own prices. The volume on PSA's route between San Francisco and Los Angeles was so high that the airline could sell a one-way ticket for $10. In 1971, Southwest began flying between Houston, San Antonio, and Dallas Love Field Airport and charged $26 for a one-way ticket, except for the last flight of the day, for which it charged $10.

Braniff, also based in Texas, cut ticket prices within Texas even further, to $13 for a one-way ticket. Texas International Airlines received permission from CAB to offer "peanuts fares," which were 50 percent off their regular rates. Continental Airlines countered with "chickenfeed fares," and American introduced "super saver" fares that required advance purchase and one-week layovers.

A service company, founded in 1971, revolutionized the air cargo business. Originally based in Little Rock, Arkansas, Federal Express (better known as FedEx) moved to Memphis in 1973. Its concept was to guarantee next-day delivery of packages via a central hub. The company started with fourteen airplanes connecting twenty-five cities.

DEREGULATION

Deregulation began as a post-Watergate affair reform. American and Braniff were caught giving illegal campaign contributions to Richard M. Nixon's 1972 re-election campaign in return for favorable treatment by the CAB. Also, the 1970's were the years of the highest inflation in American history, and pro-free-market economists proposed deregulation as a means of lowering airline ticket prices. Deregulation laws were enacted in 1978.

Southwest was the airline best prepared for deregulation because of its low costs. Before deregulation, Southwest had added more cities in Texas to its schedule. However, before it could expand outside the state, it had to deal with one last remnant of reg-

ulation. Democrat Jim Wright represented the congressional district that included the Dallas-Fort Worth International Airport and the headquarters of Braniff and American. In 1979, he introduced a bill to prevent any airline from flying from Dallas Love Field Airport to any airport outside Texas. Fortunately for Southwest, it had enough support in Congress to force a compromise. It was allowed to fly from Love Field to airports in the adjacent states of Louisiana, Arkansas, Oklahoma, and New Mexico. (Wright's law was repealed in 2006.) Southwest's first interstate flight went from Dallas to New Orleans. Southwest added Chicago's Midway Airport in 1985 and Baltimore-Washington International Airport in 1993. With flights to cities in California, it became a national airline, not just a regional one.

Acquisitions were the first result of deregulation. For instance, Pan Am acquired National Airlines, American purchased AirCal, United obtained Air Wisconsin, PSA was taken over by US Airways, FedEx took over the Flying Tiger Line, and even Southwest bought a small airline called Morris Air, based in Salt Lake City.

Texas International Airlines formed a holding company called Texas Air, which acquired Continental, People Express Airlines, and Eastern. It also created a new airline called New York Air. Texas International, People Express, and New York Air were eventually merged into Continental. Eastern continued to operate as a separate company but was forced to sell its computerized reservation system, its gates in Newark, New Jersey, and several widebody jets to Texas Air at bargain prices. Eastern also had to pay Texas Air a management fee and buy its fuel from an affiliated company. Finally, Eastern's sales department was transferred to Continental. Texas Air allowed Eastern to file bankruptcy in 1989, and it stopped flying.

For the first time since 1938, the airlines had to compete on price, and some never adapted to the new situation. In 1982, Braniff became the first of the old airmail carriers to stop flying. Just before going under, it leased its Latin American routes to Eastern. During liquidation, American bought Braniff's Dallas to London-Gatwick route. Pan Am survived longer, generating cash by selling its Pacific routes to United in 1985. It kept flying until 1991, when Delta purchased its East Coast and transatlantic routes. United acquired Pan Am's Latin American routes during liquidation. TWA operated in bankruptcy in 1992 and 1995 before it was finally taken over by American in 2001.

American created the first loyalty program, using its Sabre system, by assigning different numbers to individual passengers. The airline also used Sabre to develop the concept of yield management, by which programmers could develop algorithms to automatically discount and, even more important, to refrain from discounting fares. This enabled American to increase profits even when involved in price wars.

FedEx took advantage of deregulation to expand its fleet of planes and the number of cities it connected. In 1979, the company started using computers to track packages and expanded to Canada in 1981 and Asia in 1984.

AFTER SEPTEMBER 11, 2001

Because of the terrorist attacks of September 11, 2001, the entire U.S. air transportation system was shut down for two full days and took months to recover. About 16 percent of flights were eliminated in the process. US Airways took the lead when it cut 24 percent of its flights and laid off roughly the same percentage of employees.

NUMBER OF AIRLINE PASSENGERS BY ROUTE, 2007, IN THOUSANDS

Route Area	Fare Class	
	First and Business	Economy
Domestic (total)	73,440.6	1,175,698.9
International (total)	69,838.5	760,701.6
Within Europe	15,609.1	298,030.2
North Atlantic	12,596.6	69,103.7
Within Asia	9,455.0	114,975.9
Europe-Asia	5,659.1	38,306.4
North and Mid Pacific	3,736.9	25,435.1
Within North America	3,176.5	16,364.5
North America-Central America	2,557.0	38,084.5
Europe-Middle East	2,460.8	14,052.4
Within Middle East	1,896.1	11,932.3
Middle East-Asia	1,621.2	23,276.6
Europe-Southern Africa	1,575.3	12,437.7
Asia-Southwest Pacific	1,507.2	14,168.9
Europe-Northern Africa	1,243.2	17,501.1
North America-South America	1,226.5	8,751.6
Within Africa	1,077.5	10,407.8
Africa-Middle East	1,020.5	9,272.3
Within South America	698.6	8,617.2
Europe-Southwest Pacific	590.5	3,915.1
South Pacific	487.1	3,024.1
Central America-South America	450.5	3,784.6
Mid Atlantic	380.5	2,561.8
Within Central Europe	318.5	6,785.5
Within Southwest Pacific	314.7	6,250.0
Africa-Asia	310.3	2,794.7
Middle East-Southwest Pacific	80.9	409.8
Africa-Southwest Pacific	60.5	457.7

Source: Data from International Air Transport Association

United entered Chapter 11 bankruptcy in 2002 and emerged from it in 2006. Both Northwest and Delta filed for bankruptcy, kept flying, and were in the process of merging in early 2009. Of the old airmail carriers, only American has operated without having to merge or file bankruptcy. In 2008, four smaller airlines—Aloha, Skybus, ATA, and Frontier—filed for bankruptcy, and many others cut costs and capacity in the face of rising fuel prices. However, Southwest and other low-cost carriers have increased their market share. In 2007, South-

west became the number one airline in the world in terms of the number of passengers flown. In 2008, as other airlines experienced trouble, Southwest reported a profit in its second quarter, the sixty-ninth profitable quarter in a row.

Thomas R. Feller

FURTHER READING

Brown, Peter Harry, and Pat H. Broeske. *Howard Hughes: The Untold Story.* Cambridge, Mass.: Perseus Books, 1996. The story of Hughes, who was an aviation pioneer and controlled TWA from 1940 to 1959.

Gittell, Jody Hoffer. *The Southwest Airlines Way: Using the Power of Relationships to Achieve High Performance.* New York: McGraw-Hill, 2003. Analysis of Southwest's management techniques in comparison with those of American, United, and Continental.

Hengi, B. I. *Airlines Remembered: Over Two Hundred Airlines of the Past.* Leicester, United Kingdom: Midland, 2000. Brief, illustrated histories of two hundred defunct airlines.

_____. *Airlines Worldwide.* Leicester, United Kingdom: Midland, 2004. Brief, illustrated histories of 360 airlines still flying as of 2004.

Lovegrove, Keith. *Airline: Identity, Design, and Culture.* New York: teNeues, 2000. Illustrated history of airline uniforms, food, interior design, and logos.

Newhouse, John. *Boeing Versus Airbus: The Inside Story of the Greatest International Competition in Business.* New York: Vintage Books, 2007. A history of the air transportation business from the point of view of the two largest aircraft manufacturers of the early twenty-first century.

Petzinger, Thomas, Jr. *Hard Landing: The Epic Contest for Power and Profits That Plunged the Airlines into Chaos.* New York: Random House, 1995. A history of the airline industry with emphasis on the period after deregulation.

SEE ALSO: Air traffic controllers' strike; Aircraft industry; Airships; DC-3 aircraft; Hotel and motel industry; Postal Service, U.S.; September 11 terrorist attacks; Shipping industry; Supersonic jetliners; Tourism industry; Transportation, U.S. Department of.

Aircraft industry

DEFINITION: Enterprises designing, developing, manufacturing, and deploying commercial, private, and military aircraft

SIGNIFICANCE: Among the many products developed and sold by American industries, aircraft have been one of the most successful and most conspicuous. Throughout most of the world, American aircraft have dominated the field for many years.

The beginning of America's aircraft industry can be traced back to the Wright brothers, Orville and Wilbur, whose successful first flight of a piloted airplane in 1903 was followed by their application for a patent. This was followed in 1909 by the formation of the Wright Company and the first sales of airplanes to the public. A rival company was started by Glenn Curtiss, an adventurous flyer whose designs soon proved to be more attractive than those of the Wrights, and the Curtiss Aeroplane Company soon dominated the market. By the time of the U.S. entry into World War I in 1917, there were three airplane manufacturers in the United States: the Wrights' company (which primarily built airplane engines), Curtiss's company, and the Glenn A. Martin Company, newly formed in California. All three were involved in supplying aircraft to the military during the war.

POST-WORLD WAR I EXPANSION

During the 1920's, three more major aircraft companies came into being: Douglas Aircraft Company, the Boeing Company, and the Lockheed Corporation. The primary customers of the time were the newly created airlines such as United, Trans World Airlines, and American Airlines, as well as the armed forces. The military foresaw the potential importance of airplanes in the event of another global war and encouraged aircraft builders to develop planes that would have long ranges and a capacities for heavy cargo. Curtiss built a popular trainer called the "Jenny," and Martin built some of the first bombers.

Passenger planes did not at first command a very big market. Well-publicized plane crashes made potential passengers wary, and costs were high. Airlines survived primarily because of airmail subsidies. The first successful airliners were the Lockheed Vega, the Douglas DC-2, and the Boeing 247, all of which were capable of crossing the country in three or four hops. Overhead was high, and they carried few passengers (the Vega carried only six, the Boeing 247 carried ten, and the DC-2 carried fourteen).

Urged to create a better plane with longer range by the head of American Airlines, Douglas brought out a revolutionary new plane, the DC-3. Introduced in 1936, the DC-3 quickly cornered the market. It carried twenty-one passengers, could fly nonstop from New York to Chicago, had a kitchen for serving hot meals, and developed a safety record unparalleled in the industry.

Boeing turned its efforts to the military market. Its first large bomber was the B-17, which was first flown in 1935 but fully realized its potential after the start of World War II. Boeing also developed the B-29 bomber, which played a very important role in the war, as did the various military airplanes built by Lockheed, Curtiss, Douglas, Convair, and other smaller companies. More than 300,000 airplanes were built by the American aircraft industry during the war years.

Post-World War II Developments

Postwar conditions were similar to those that followed the end of World War I: Few new orders for planes were received by the aircraft companies, because used planes from the war were abundant and inexpensive. The DC-3, which had been called the C-47 in its military version, could be bought, converted to airline specifications, and flown very inexpensively.

In due time, largely because of the improved speed, comfort, and safety records of the airlines, more people chose to fly. Gradually, the demand for new and better aircraft led to renewed activity in the airplane companies. Douglas brought out the DC-4 and DC-5, but not until the introduction of the DC-6 did the airlines buy large numbers. The DC-6 was a much bigger craft, with four engines, retractable landing gear, and a pressurized cabin to allow flying above the weather. Furthermore, the long-range version of the DC-6 could fly across the Atlantic. Boeing also introduced a larger airliner, called the Stratocruiser. It was especially designed for long-distance flights and was unique for the era in having two decks, with the lower deck serving as a lounge or first-class cabin. Lockheed came out with an elegant design for a long-range liner, called the Constellation. Rather than a long, straight cylinder, the fuselage of the Constellation was tapered and curved in a streamlined shape, and the tail had triple fins. At the end of the era of propeller planes, Lockheed was building a larger version of the Constellation called the Super Constellation, and Douglas was building the DC-7.

Jet planes first became practical during the late 1940's. Military jets were developed first, and they saw their first extensive use during the Korean War. Jet fighters were manufactured by Lockheed, North American Aviation, and Republic. Long-range bombers were developed by Boeing, which introduced the sleek B-47 in 1947 and the eight-engine B-52 a few years later.

The first commercial jet was the British De Haviland Comet, which first saw service in 1952. After several tragic crashes, the Comets were withdrawn from service in 1954, and commercial jets were not reintroduced until 1958, when the Boeing 707 went into service. This was truly a turning point for the industry. With the rapid speed of the new jets and their improved safety record, people abandoned trains and ocean liners, and the transportation industry was taken over by the airlines. Even some freight was switched from ships and trains to airplanes.

Boeing's 707 was followed by others in the 700 series, some for shorter legs (the 727 and 737), some for intercontinental flights (the 747 and 777),

Number of Airports and Pilots, 1930-2005

Year	Airports[a]	Certified Pilots
1930	1,782	15,280
1940	2,331	69,829
1950	6,403	580,574[b]
1960	6,881	783,232
1970	11,261	732,739
1980	15,161	827,071
1990	17,490	709,659
2000	19,281	625,581
2005	19,854	609,737

Sources: Data from *Historical Statistics of the United States: Colonial Times to 1970* (Washington, D.C.: U.S. Department of Commerce, Bureau of the Census, 1975); *Statistical Abstract of the United States, 2008* (Washington, D.C.: Department of Commerce, Economics and Statistics Administration, Bureau of the Census, Data User Services Division, 2008)

[a] Airports are existing airports, heliports, seaplane bases, and the like recorded with the Federal Aviation Administration. Military airports with joint civil and military use are included.

[b] Data for 1950 were not available; data for 1951 are shown here.

and some for increased efficiency (the 757 and 767). Douglas developed the DC-8 as its first jet and later the tri-motor jumbo jet DC-10. Lockheed, after putting out a jet-prop hybrid called the Electra, which had wing-failure problems, introduced the L1011, and Convair came out with the short-lived 880 and 990. However, by the end of the twentieth century, only the Boeing planes were still in production in the United States. The Boeing Company's revenue in 2007 totaled $66 billion. During the early decades of the twenty-first century, serious competition from Europe's Airbus Industrie had begun to erode the near monopoly that the American aircraft industry had enjoyed for so long.

Paul W. Hodge

FURTHER READING

Bilstein, Roger. *The American Aerospace Industry: From Workshop to Global Enterprise.* New York: Twayne, 1996. A solid historical examination of corporate development in American aviation. The book also examines the role of general aviation manufacturers such as Cessna and Piper.

_____. *Flight in America: From the Wrights to the Astronauts.* Rev. ed. Baltimore: Johns Hopkins University Press, 1994. A good overview of aviation and space travel that also examines technological trends in aviation.

Boyne, Walter J. *Beyond the Horizons: The Lockheed Story.* New York: Thomas Dunne Books, 1998. Examination of Lockheed from one of America's foremost aviation historians.

Francillon, Rene. *McDonnell Douglas Aircraft Since 1920.* Annapolis Md.: Naval Institute Press, 1990. Discusses the civilian and military aircraft developed by both companies prior to their merger and after their combination.

Heppenheimer, T. A. *Flight: A History of Aviation in Photographs.* Richmond Hill, Ont.: Firefly Books, 2004. Thoroughly illustrated history of the aircraft industry.

_____. *Turbulent Skies: The History of Commercial Aviation.* New York: John Wiley & Sons, 1998. A comprehensive history of commercial aviation from the biplane era to the end of the twentieth century.

Millbrooke, Anne. *Aviation History.* Englewood, Colo.: Jeppeson Sanderson, 2000. International history of aircraft engineering and aviation.

SEE ALSO: Air traffic controllers' strike; Air transportation industry; Airships; Arms industry; DC-3 aircraft; Hughes, Howard; Supersonic jetliners; Transatlantic steamer service; Transcontinental railroad.

Airships

DEFINITION: Lighter-than-air craft that can be propelled in desired directions and that can take off, maintain a given altitude, and land
SIGNIFICANCE: Giant German airships were used on commercial trans-Atlantic flights during the early twentieth century. Although these airships were replaced by airplanes, smaller, nonrigid airships called blimps are still used for special purposes, such as advertising and photography.

Airship history began as early as 1785, when the French inventor Jean-Pierre Blanchard flew across the England Channel from France to England in a hot-air balloon. The craft was hand powered by winglike flaps and looked much like a hot-air balloon with a double tail. It took nearly one hundred years for the concept of lighter-than-air flight to advance beyond that level. What was needed were better aeronautical engineering and lightweight engines.

By 1900, many blimps had been built and flown by inventive adventurers in Europe and America, but it was not until Count Ferdinand von Zeppelin in Germany built his first rigid airship, the Luftschiff Zeppelin LZ1, that the full possibilities for commerce were realized. Convinced that airships were the transport of the future, Zeppelin created the world's first airline, the Deutsche Luftschiffahrts-AG (the German airship travel company). By the time of World War I, the dirigibles built by this company had traveled some 120,000 miles, carrying a total of forty thousand passengers. The war, however, brought this commerce to an end.

Following the war, airships were reintroduced as commercial vehicles. Both tourist jaunts and long-range transport were promoted, primarily in Europe. The Zeppelin company was building large airships for peaceful use. The Graf Zeppelin, launched in 1928, was the first commercially successful dirigible of a period sometimes dubbed the "golden age of the dirigible." Almost eight hundred feet long,

The Hindenburg *just after bursting into flames on May 6, 1937.* (Library of Congress)

the Graf Zeppelin attracted great interest, especially when it circumnavigated the world with passengers in twenty-one days, traveling a total of thirty-two thousand miles. The passenger facilities included sleeping rooms, a dining hall, bathrooms, a library, and many of the amenities associated with ocean liners. The golden age lasted a decade but ended spectacularly in 1937, when the company's largest airship, the *Hindenburg,* caught fire while landing in New Jersey, killing thirty-five of its ninety-seven passengers and crew.

In the years since the *Hindenburg* disaster, commercial use of airships has been limited to smaller, nonrigid or semirigid craft used for special purposes. The famous Goodyear blimp is the most familiar example of an airship used for advertising. Airships have also been used as stable platforms for aerial photography, for mapping, and for mineral resource exploration.

Paul W. Hodge

FURTHER READING

Botting, Douglas. *Dr. Eckener's Dream Machine.* New York: Henry Holt and Company, 2001.

Brooks, Peter. *Zeppelin: Rigid Airships, 1893-1940.* London: Putnam Aeronautical Books, 2004.

Shock, James R., and David R. Smith. *The Goodyear Airships.* Bloomington, Ill.: Airship International Press, 2002.

SEE ALSO: Air transportation industry; Aircraft industry.

Alaska gold rush. *See* Klondike gold rush

Alaska Pipeline

THE EVENT: Construction of a controversial pipeline to move crude oil across Alaska
DATE: March 24, 1977-May 31, 1977
PLACE: Alaska
SIGNIFICANCE: The pipeline across Alaska was one of the most ambitious and debated construction efforts mounted by private industry in American history. It presented construction problems, such as how to avoid damaging the permafrost, and aroused intense political controversy at both the state and national levels.

In 1967, Governor Walter Hickel, formerly a wealthy real estate developer, issued oil leases to a section of Alaska's North Slope that led to the 1968 discovery and verification of substantial oil reserves in Prudhoe Bay on the Arctic Ocean. Previously, all active exploration for major exploitable oil and gas fields had taken place in southeastern Alaska, beginning with the Richfield strike on the Kenai Peninsula in 1957, although small-scale fields had been known and operated since the 1920's and Arctic prospecting had been under way since the 1950's.

ORIGINS OF THE PROJECT

The possibility of transporting Arctic oil south by tanker was tested in the exploratory voyage of the *Exxon Manhattan* in 1969, which successfully transited from the Atlantic to the Beaufort Sea via the Northwest Passage but was forced to alter course because of sea ice. The *Exxon Manhattan*'s experience meant that transport by land was the only viable option. On February 10, 1969, plans to construct the Trans-Alaska Pipeline System were announced. This forty-eight-inch pipeline across interior Alaska would move heated crude oil south from Prudhoe Bay to the ice-free port

of Valdez. By September, 1969, all major surveys of the proposed overland route had been completed, and a seven-company consortium led by British Petroleum, Atlantic Richfield, and Humble Oil was formed under the name Alyeska, with lease rights to portions of the new field opened for bid by the state of Alaska.

The announcement of the existence of this new oil field touched off a complex national and local debate, which was in full swing by the autumn of 1969. On one side was an array of conservationists, environmentalists, and Native Alaskans, whose chief concerns were the project's immediate and long-term damages to the Alaskan wilderness ecosystem, on which much of the state's tourist economy depended, and potential threats to the fisheries of Prince William Sound from tanker pollution. On the other side, defending the pipeline, were oil company executives and others in the Alaskan business community, who recognized the necessity of developing the North Slope field to expand Ameri-

The last portion of the Alaska Pipeline is installed. (Library of Congress)

can oil reserves and stimulate the Alaskan economy in both the public and private sectors by increasing its resource base. A nine-volume environmental impact statement, prepared by a task force from the U.S. Geological Survey and including pipeline project data provided by the oil companies, was presented to the President's Council on Environmental Quality and the public on March 20, 1972, emphasizing the numerous unknowns of the project. These ranged from how migratory moose and caribou populations would interact with the pipeline and the effects of Alaska's frequent seismic activity, to fears of heat from the pipeline melting the supporting permafrost (creating the potential for warping and possible ruptures) and construction as a source of erosion in an already fragile environment. The design of the pipeline incorporated crossing areas to allow unimpeded passage of animals along known migration routes and used an elevated frame where necessary to remove the threat to the permafrost base. A further complication was the legally valid claim by the Alaskan Native populations to hundreds of acres of land in the absence of treaties or other historical agreements between them and the federal government that could be used as precedent for corporate acquisition or assignment of use rights.

On November 16, 1973, President Richard Nixon signed the Trans-Alaska Pipeline Authorization Act into law. Construction of the pipeline lasted from March 24, 1974, to May 31, 1977. It was built in six sections; spanned three mountain ranges and more than eight hundred bodies of water, including several rivers; and had an overall zigzag plan to allow for expansion. The Arctic oil supply was seen as addressing the problem of American vulnerability to interruptions in access to foreign petroleum sources (as demonstrated by the 1973 energy crisis) by significantly expanding exploitable reserves and as providing a new source of income to redress an unfavorable national balance of payments.

AFTER THREE DECADES

The impact of the project on the financial structure and institutions of Alaska was diverse, placing new burdens on every aspect of the economy from housing to banking, construction, and transportation (in particular the airlines), and resulting in a major cash influx that stimulated price inflation in many sectors. The primary contribution of the pipe-

line was to generate revenue to provide nearly 90 percent of the income of the state of Alaska, which had no sales tax or personal income tax. By the end of the first decade of operation, concerns arose over problems of internal and external corrosion. However, despite these concerns, the success of the pipeline project served as a model for further construction in the Alaskan arctic, centered on deposits of natural gas rather than petroleum, which continued into the early twenty-first century.

Although the problem of potential spills was emphasized by an accident in 1978 and an act of sabotage in 2001 that involved someone shooting at the pipeline while intoxicated, the overall record of management and maintenance supports the pipeline proponents' claims that the project has been of significant financial benefit to both Alaska and the United States. The Trans-Alaska Pipeline System monitors its environmental impact on fish populations, derivative erosion, bird nesting patterns (over 170 species have been identified along the pipeline route), and permafrost dynamics, the latter of major concern, with 75 percent of the total pipeline course lying within permafrost terrain of some type. By 2007, the pipeline was moving more than 15 million barrels of oil per year, although declining overall production stimulated reexploration of the North Slope and interest in potential new fields beneath the Arctic Ocean.

Robert B. Ridinger

FURTHER READING

"Alaska, North Slope Producers Strike Deal on Pipeline." *American Gas* 88, no. 4 (May, 2006): 11. Useful summary of early planning efforts for the proposed natural gas pipeline.

Berry, Mary Clay. *The Alaska Pipeline: The Politics of Oil and Native Land Claims.* Bloomington: Indiana University Press, 1975. Discussion of the political issues (especially internal Alaskan matters) surrounding the project and the financial settlements that were required to build the pipeline system.

Coates, Peter A. *The Trans-Alaska Pipeline Controversy: Technology, Conservation, and the Frontier.* Bethlehem, Pa.: Lehigh University, 1991. The Alaska Pipeline and the consequences of its construction are considered within the history of conflict between supporters of development and environmentalists.

Cooper, Bryan. *Alaska: The Last Frontier.* London: Hutchinson, 1972. An account of Alaska as it was during the early 1970's, with the effect of the proposed construction of the pipeline discussed in detail.

Gimbel, Barney. "The Hunt for Oil at the Top of the World." *Fortune* 157, no. 9 (May 5, 2008): 96-102. Discusses the proposals for accessing the oil deposits beneath the Arctic Ocean.

Lasley, John. "Steps to a North Slope Gas Pipeline." *Oil and Gas Investor* (October, 2005): 64. Brief summary of the four envisioned stages of the gas pipeline development.

Nelson, Daniel. *Northern Landscapes: The Struggle for Wilderness Alaska.* Washington, D.C.: Resources for the Future, 2004. A status report on technology and wilderness in Alaska at the beginning of the twenty-first century, with a chapter on the legacy of the Alaska Pipeline project.

SEE ALSO: Equal Employment Opportunity Commission; Labor, U.S. Department of; Presidency, U.S.; Supreme Court and commerce; Supreme Court and labor law; Women in business.

Alaska purchase

THE EVENT: U.S. acquisition of the Alaska territory from the Russian Empire

DATE: Treaty completed on July 27, 1868

PLACE: United States, Alaska

SIGNIFICANCE: The United States purchased Alaska to boost American fishing and whaling industries, increase the nation's control of commerce in the Pacific, and create a bridge to Asian markets.

The American entrepreneur Perry McDonough Collins had a vision as early as 1857 of expanding U.S. trade into Siberia, Manchuria, and northern China, foreseeing a million-dollar market for cotton manufactures alone. To this end, Collins promoted a telegraph line running from San Francisco up the Pacific coast and across the Bering Strait to the Amur River. In 1862, the United States agreed to pay for the line through Russian territory and receive in return a right of way in Russian America (the future Alaska). This grand scheme collapsed when the Russian Empire objected to paying rebates on messages transmitted to and from the United States.

U.S.-RUSSIAN NEGOTIATIONS

In 1866, the territorial legislature of Washington petitioned President Andrew Johnson to seek Russian permission for American fishermen to visit Alaskan harbors. The petition was also sent to Secretary of State William H. Seward, who used it as an excuse to bring up the future of Alaska with Edouard de Stoeckl, Russia's ambassador to the United States. Later that year, a San Francisco fur dealer named Louis Goldstone sought a commercial lease in Alaska, and although nothing came of his request, Stoeckl became aware of American economic interest in Alaska. Fortuitously, the Treaty of Peking (1860) had recently enlarged Russia's Asian territory, and its acquisition of Vladivostok lessened St. Petersburg's interest in Alaska.

Upon Stoeckl's return to St. Petersburg in late 1866, he was queried about selling Alaska to the United States by the Russian finance minister, Michael Reutern, who through Grand Duke Constantine and Prince Aleksandr Mikhailovich Gorchakov secured the emperor's approval to begin negotiations. Acquiring Alaska suited Seward's vision of the United States becoming a world power by increasing its economic strength. When Stoeckl arrived back in the United States in 1867 with instructions to tempt the United States into making an offer for Alaska, Seward was happy to offer $7.2 million, and the details of the sale were worked out that same night, March 29, 1867.

With the treaty completed, Seward was faced with the challenge of guiding it through the Senate. He began by arranging news stories in the New York *Commercial Advertiser* and the *New York Tribune.* Henry Raymond, the editor of *The New York Times,* published a story emphasizing the need for harbors to accommodate the United States' "fast-growing commerce with northeast Asia." Only Horace Greeley, in his *New York Tribune,* opposed the treaty, and even he soon relented and described Alaska as an "American Norway," rich in fish and fur. Resistance soon surfaced in the Senate, however. The Committee on Foreign Relations, composed mainly of easterners with little interest in the West Coast, scoffed at the project. Help for Seward came from Professor Spenser Baird of the Smithsonian Institution, who wrote to Senator Charles Sumner, the committee's chair, that "the shores of the North Pacific are swimming with animals of economical importance, cod, salmon, fur seals, etc."

The United States issued this check on August 1, 1868, to purchase Alaska from Russia. (NARA)

By early April, the treaty's prospects looked better, and Seward hosted a round of dinner parties, hoping that food and wine would soften his critics' hearts. On April 8, Sumner argued for approval in a three-hour speech that stressed potential commercial profits, observing that Hong Kong was closer to San Francisco by way of the Aleutians than by way of Honolulu. Sumner had studied his subject well, noting Alaska's coal deposits, its gold, and its timberlands. Sumner admitted, however, the role of politics in his thinking, citing Russia's friendliness during the Civil War and the need that many Americans felt to reward Russia's support. Sumner's speech was decisive, and the next day the Senate ratified Seward's treaty.

FUNDING THE PURCHASE

Seward's next challenge was persuading the House to appropriate the $7.2 million to complete the purchase. He cleverly arranged for 250 American troops to sail into Sitka harbor on October 18, 1867, and claim possession of Alaska in a ceremony attended by the Russian governor. With the American flag flying over the new territory, the House could hardly reject approving payment for it. The biggest obstacle still left was a claim for $373,613 by the widow of Benjamin Perkins, who had agreed to sell arms to Russia during the Crimean War. The rifles were never shipped, but Anne Perkins nonetheless sued for the money to be held back from the Alaska appropriation. The claim was thin and was warded off by Seward's maneuvering.

After some heated debate over whether the House was bound to appropriate money for a treaty signed by the Senate, the House endorsed the appropriations bill on July 27, 1868. One key factor in this decision was the representatives' anticipation of a large increase in trade with China. Representative Green Berry Raum of Illinois exulted that "the whole of the rich trade of the East . . . will . . . necessarily fall into our hands."

The Alaska purchase helped facilitate trade, but it attained greater significance as the natural resources of the region were discovered and exploited. When gold was discovered in Canada's Yukon Territory, many Americans traveled to and through Alaska, as the nearest launching point for gold expeditions. Oil was also discovered in the territory during the mid-twentieth century, and the combination of Alaskan oil fields and the territory's strategic importance during World War II led to Alaska becoming a state in 1959.

Frank Day

FURTHER READING

Farrar, Victor J. *The Annexation of Russian-America.* 1937. Reprint. Washington, D.C.: W. F. Roberts,

1966. Account of the purchase of Alaska based on State Department records and Russian sources in the National Archives.

_____. "Background to the Purchase of Alaska." *Washington Historical Quarterly* 13 (1922): 93-104. Reviews Alaska's role in the United States' early relations with Russia.

Jensen, Ronald J. *The Alaska Purchase and Russian-American Relations.* Seattle: University of Washington Press, 1975. Comprehensive, well-written survey of the treaty, beginning with the early Russian-American discussions in 1854 and concluding with a chapter on questions surrounding the disposition of some of the money meant for transfer to Moscow.

Reynolds, Robert L. "Seward's Wise Folly." In *America and Russia.* New York: Simon & Schuster, 1962. Strong defense of the Alaska Purchase.

Taylor, John M. *William Henry Seward: Lincoln's Right Hand.* Washington, D.C.: Brassey's, 1991. Chapter 24, "The Empire Builder," provides a concise account of the negotiations between Seward and Stoeckl concerning Alaska.

Woldman, Albert A. *Lincoln and the Russians.* New York: World, 1952. Broad account of U.S.-Russian relations during Abraham Lincoln's presidency, with good commentary on the financial issues involved.

SEE ALSO: Alaska Pipeline; Exploration; Fur trapping and trading; International economics and trade; Klondike gold rush; Land laws; Louisiana Purchase; Petroleum industry.

Alcoholic beverage industry

DEFINITION: Enterprises involved in the production and distribution of wine, beer, and distilled spirits such as bourbon and vodka

SIGNIFICANCE: As the United States became increasingly urbanized and industrialized, alcohol similarly became a mass-produced commodity distributed both in stores and in bars and restaurants. After the enactment and repeal of Prohibition, the federal government created a three-tier distribution system, from suppliers to wholesalers to retailers, to ensure the existence of a layer of distribution between suppliers and retailers.

The alcoholic beverage industry in the United States has evolved over time, both in terms of methods of production and in terms of the typical locations and circumstances of consumption. Alcohol was initially brewed primarily at home. Taverns and small breweries and distilleries began to produce beverages in somewhat greater quantities to serve their own clienteles, and eventually a small number of corporate producers began selling larger quantities.

At first, Americans tended to drink alcohol at home and on the job. Later, bars and taverns became popular, until the home again became the primary locale of consumption. This choice of locale had an effect not only on alcohol production but also on distribution and marketing, as during the height of bars' popularity (1870 to 1920), corporate brewers and distillers could enjoy direct links to consumers through their ownership of or exclusive contracts with bars. Changes in working conditions wrought by industrialization led some workers to engage in binge drinking. Violence against women and workers' absenteeism increased, leading to an increasing backlash against the alcoholic beverage industry.

The regulation and taxation of alcoholic beverages have also evolved since colonial days. With the practice of corporate bar ownership and exclusive contracts ending after Prohibition, a three-tier distribution system was instituted by the federal government, to be regulated by the states. Wholesalers were introduced into the distribution chain to mediate between suppliers and retailers.

BEFORE PROHIBITION

Beer came to North America from England with the early seventeenth century Pilgrim settlers, who packed it with them on the *Mayflower,* and alcohol played an important part in the settlers' social and political lives. Home brewing was very common. Puritans disliked distilled liquor but felt that beer was acceptable. The first commercial breweries began in the United States in the eighteenth century. New York and Philadelphia had the most, but the Adams family brewery—based in Boston—was a growing business. Taverns were a popular place for people to congregate and discuss the major events of the day, and tavern owners were considered among the most respected businessmen in town. For example, in seventeenth century Massachusetts, Eric Burns writes, "only voters and church members . . . 'the colony's elite' were allowed to purchase and operate taverns." As beer was mainly being manufactured in urban areas, distilled liquor was a rural venture. Early attempts at making wine were unsuccessful, so it was mostly imported (the first successful commercial winery in the United States was established in Pennsylvania in 1818). Drinking was an accepted part of everyday life; workers were encouraged to drink on the job, and shopkeepers offered free drinks to customers.

By the mid-nineteenth century, a number of German immigrants were operating successful breweries throughout the United States, such as Anheuser-Busch, Schlitz, Hamm, and Schmidt. As was true of most businesses during the industrial era, alcohol manufacturing became more centralized, moving from a number of smaller brewers and distillers to fewer, larger manufacturers. In addition to brewing the product, many brewers and liquor distillers owned bars, where they could sell their product directly to their customers. Others offered saloon owners exclusive contracts. The owners agreed to sell only one company's products. In return, the company provided the bar's food, equipment, and decorations.

Both bar ownership and exclusive contracts proved to be lucrative for large beer and liquor companies. By 1909, 70 percent of the saloons in the United States had such arrangements. These corporate saloons can be seen as an early example of the chain restaurant: Customers could go to one anywhere and know what kind of food and alcohol they would get.

By this time, the saloon culture of the working class was in full swing, with bars serving as places for workers to organize as well as to indulge. Many unions used bars as meeting places as well as for socializing. In the wake of industrialization, workers found themselves having to drink on an "industrial timetable" instead of drinking small amounts of alcohol all day, as they had done during preindustrial times. As a result, some began to engage in binge drinking.

This binge drinking brought on more noticeable effects of alcohol abuse, such as missed work and violent behavior. The temperance movement, upset over the violence—particularly against women—brought on by drinking, and the anti-immigration movement, which felt that it was immigrants who were doing the drinking, teamed together to put pressure on the government to enact prohibition. This was not the first time that prohibition was advocated by temperance groups. Short-lived state prohibition laws had been passed in Maine and a handful of other northern states during the 1840's, with short-lived success, as they were either vetoed or eventually stricken down by the state governments. With the creation of the Anti-Saloon League in 1895, the temperance movement finally had a strong lobbying presence, and it stepped up its push for national prohibition.

The federal government tried to avoid making any laws that would regulate alcohol distribution and sales, and many politicians avoided the question as being politically dangerous. The prohibition movement earned financial support from industrialists such as Henry Ford and John Rockefeller, who felt that workers who drank were bad for their businesses. The beer industry tried to separate itself from distilled liquor and wine to be seen as a more moderate choice, but it was unsuccessful. The movement gained steam during the early twentieth century, with states such as Mississippi and Alabama voting to become dry. Once World War I started, the prohibition movement had its best political argument yet—that the alcoholic beverage industry used resources needed for food. Prohibition advocates also took advantage of anti-German sentiment (most major brewers being of German descent), and the movement gained the pull with government that it needed to push Prohibition through. It lasted fourteen years.

Prohibition was not a success. Bootleggers, who manufactured liquor or smuggled it into the country from Canada or from the Caribbean, were in high demand, and organized crime soon got involved in the smuggling. Distilled liquor during this time was often made from dubious sources and could be lethal. Distilled spirits rose in popularity over beer, simply because it was easier to move. Many people began home brewing beer again, as this activity was not outlawed. (The home distilling of hard liquor or "moonshine" was prohibited, however.) Since the federal government did not provide sufficient funds for Prohibition enforcement, illegal manufacturing and consumption of alcohol continued throughout the era, and Prohibition was finally repealed in 1933.

AFTER PROHIBITION

In 1933, the Federal Alcohol Administration (FAA) was established to enforce the newly mandated three-tier system of distribution to avoid the problems encountered when suppliers had direct contact with retailers. Although the Bureau of Alcohol, Tobacco, Firearms, and Explosives (ATF) oversees the FAA, specific regulations vary from state to state. For example, the majority of states are "open" states, allowing licensed retailers and wholesalers to sell all kinds of alcoholic beverages. Other states, by contrast, are "control" states, which buy and sell alcohol through their own stores. This too can vary, as some states sell only distilled liquor from their stores, allowing wine to be sold at other retail outlets.

Every state allows beer to be sold in stores. In addition, thirty-two states allow counties and municipalities to decide whether alcohol may be sold in their jurisdictions. Local and state governments also determine sales taxes on alcoholic beverages.

Another outcome of Prohibition was a decrease in the number of breweries and distillers in business, as the major companies in both categories took over larger shares of the market. The wine industry had the hardest time bouncing back from Prohibition, but it has grown steadily since World War II, especially after the release of information about the possible health benefits of drinking wine in moderation.

Julie Elliott

FURTHER READING

Burns, Eric. *The Spirits of America: A Social History of Alcohol.* Philadelphia: Temple University Press, 2004. Covers the history of alcohol consumption in the United States and how it was affected by politics and culture.

Holleran, Joan. "Drinking Up." *Beverage Industry* 90, no. 5 (May, 1999): 17-21. Provides a summary of "The Maxwell Report: The Liquor Industry in

SPENDING ON ALCOHOLIC BEVERAGES, 1940-2007, IN MILLIONS OF DOLLARS

Year	At Home	Away from Home	Total
1940	977	1,602	2,579
1950	3,445	4,413	7,858
1960	5,793	5,734	11,527
1970	10,845	9,069	19,914
1980	24,788	20,656	45,444
1990	38,044	34,539	72,583
2000	52,674	58,935	111,609
2007	73,256	89,283	162,539

Source: Data from Economic Research Service, U.S. Department of Agriculture

1998." Gives a good overview of the state of the alcohol industry during the 1990's.

Holt, Mack P., ed. *Alcohol: A Social and Cultural History.* New York: Berg, 2006. Collection of essays related to international alcohol consumption; includes two important essays on the history of drinking in America: Madelon Powers's "The Lore of the Brotherhood," which covers the "saloon culture" era of pre-Prohibition, and Jack S. Blocker, Jr.'s "Kaleidoscope in Motion," a history of drinking in the United States from the colonial period to the early twenty-first century.

McGowan, Richard. *Government Regulation of the Alcohol Industry: The Search for Revenue and the Common Good.* Westport, Conn.: Quorum Books, 1997. Explores the three-tier distribution system and government regulation of alcohol. Provides an excellent historical overview of the beer and distilled liquor industries in the United States.

Whitman, Douglas Glen. *Strange Brew: Alcohol and Government Monopoly.* Oakland, Calif.: Independent Institute, 2003. Brief work that looks at problems with the three-tier distribution system and notes the attempts by small wineries to sell directly to consumers.

SEE ALSO: Cereal crops; Cola industry; Drug trafficking; Native American trade; Prohibition; Treasury, U.S. Department of the; Whiskey Trust.

American Automobile Association

IDENTIFICATION: Tax-paying, not-for-profit corporation made up of regional affiliates, which has the aim of improving roads and providing services for its members

DATE: Founded on March 4, 1902

SIGNIFICANCE: Reflecting the importance of automobiles in the United States, the American Automobile Association has promoted good roads and traffic safety, offered its members help in roadside mechanical emergencies, noted fuel prices, published maps, and performed other services to enhance the motoring experience.

The American Automobile Association (AAA; pronounced "triple A") was created at a meeting of nine automobile clubs in Chicago in 1902, with about fifteen hundred members—at a time when Americans relied much more on horses than on automobiles for transportation and when there were no roads for motorized vehicles.

The AAA campaigned initially for suitable roads, with a major accomplishment coming in the Federal Aid Road Act of 1916. The AAA also worked toward the Federal-Aid Highway Act of 1956, which began the system of interstate highways. In the latter part of the twentieth century, the AAA urged Congress not to divert the money collected from taxes and fees paid by drivers and airline passengers but to use it only for the maintenance and improvement of the infrastructure needed for ground and air transportation, respectively.

In addition to campaigning for good roads, the AAA has worked for the safety and convenience of drivers, their passengers, and pedestrians. The AAA sponsors the School Safety Patrol Program and educational programs for drivers. It advocates graduated driver licensing laws for adolescents and the use of seat belts and child-restraint systems. It offers insurance, travel planning, discounts at various businesses, hotel and restaurant ratings, and even cellular telephones.

The AAA, however, is best known for helping its members when they have car trouble, for reporting gasoline prices, and for publishing maps. Emergency Road Service is a program that began in St. Louis in 1915 and spread throughout the nation. Members of the AAA carry cards with toll-free numbers that they can call from almost anywhere if they need help. As for the price of gasoline, news agencies rely on the AAA's record keeping for stories about financial stress at pumps. Furthermore, the AAA produces both standard road maps and detailed strip maps designed for specific trips.

Despite designating some routes on maps as Scenic Byways and promoting the recycling of batteries and the efficient use of gasoline, the AAA has drawn criticism for being environmentally unfriendly because of its lobbying for better roads and bridges. According to its critics, it has allied itself with highway contractors, automobile manufacturers, and oil companies to promote suburban sprawl and the excessive use of road-clogging, air-polluting private automobiles at the expense of public transportation. The AAA, which has more than 50 million members, has replied that air pollution from automobiles has declined and that the organization tries to balance environmental concerns with its concern for the convenience and safety that Americans expect in their transportation.

Victor Lindsey

President Calvin Coolidge (holding emblem) receives a membership in AAA from club representatives in 1923. (Library of Congress)

FURTHER READING

Jackle, John A., and Keith A. Sculle. *Motoring: The Highway Experience in America.* Athens: University of Georgia Press, 2008.

Lubove, Seth. "Drive-By Shooting." *Forbes*, April 14, 2003, 66.

Silverstein, Ken. "Smitten with a Club." *Harper's Magazine*, May, 2002, 52-53.

SEE ALSO: Arab oil embargo of 1973; Automotive industry; Ford Model T; Ford Motor Company; General Motors; Highways; Rubber industry.

American Bimetallic League national convention

THE EVENT: Convention of supporters of adding a silver standard to the gold standard to increase the American money supply

DATE: August, 1893

PLACE: Chicago, Illinois

SIGNIFICANCE: The American Bimetallic League sought to pressure the federal government to mint silver dollar coins to be reintroduced into general circulation as legal tender. These free silver advocates wanted the government to set a standard valuation of silver against gold as a 16:1 ratio and allow payments of government debts in silver.

In 1893, the United States was facing serious financial problems. Advocates of a silver and gold standard thought that adoption of a bimetallic standard would increase the country's monetary supply, control inflation, and raise commodity prices to benefit farmers—an important consideration for an economy that was still primarily agricultural rather than industrial. Free silver advocates argued that the Panic of 1873 had been caused by the removal of the silver dollar coin from general circulation. They met in early August of 1893 to discuss strategy.

The Panic of 1893 followed very shortly after the American Bimetallic League national convention. U.S. gold stocks had dropped to dangerously low levels, in part as a result of gold exports and in part because of a decline in gold mining production in Nevada and California.

The free silver movement reached its apex three years later, when presidential candidate William Jennings Bryan gave his famous "Cross of Gold" speech at the Democratic National Convention. The speech, and the issue, earned him the nomination of his party. However, it lost him the backing of many Democratic newspapers, and William McKinley defeated him in the 1896 general election. Bimetallism continued as an issue, but it was associated with the fringes rather than the mainstream of economic and political theory.

Victoria Erhart

FURTHER READING

Bayoumi, Tamim, et al. *Modern Perspectives on the Gold Standard.* New York: Cambridge University Press, 2008.

Lewis, Nathan. *Gold: The Once and Future Money.* New York: John Wiley & Sons, 2007.

Timberlake, Richard H. *Monetary Policy in the United States: An Intellectual and Institutional History.* Chicago: University of Chicago Press, 1993.

SEE ALSO: Black Friday; *Coin's Financial School;* "Cross of Gold" speech; Currency; Fort Knox; Gold standard; Klondike gold rush; Mint, U.S.; Monetary policy, federal; Panic of 1893.

American Federation of Labor-Congress of Industrial Organizations. *See* AFL-CIO

American Revolution. *See* Revolutionary War

American Society of Composers, Authors, and Publishers

IDENTIFICATION: Professional performance rights organization

DATE: Founded on February 13, 1914

SIGNIFICANCE: ASCAP was the first American performance rights organization, tracking the performance of its members' compositions and collecting licensing fees on their behalf. The organization made it feasible for individual composers to receive the fees they were due by eliminating the need for them to dedicate their own time and resources to administrative overhead. With the advent of radio during the 1920's, followed later by other mass broadcast and computer technologies, ASCAP and other performance rights organizations assumed greater importance.

During the early and mid-nineteenth century, music publishers would often issue their own sheet music, with their own versions of popular tunes, generating huge profits for themselves without paying the original composers. Stricter copyright laws in the latter part of the century led to the creation of musical houses. Each house was responsible for enforcing the copyrights of its member composers, songwriters, and publishers.

A group of Tin Pan Alley musicians determined to disentangle this convoluted system gathered in 1914 and, on February 13, formed the American Society of Composers, Authors, and Publishers (ASCAP). The only way to join the society was through sponsorship by a member, and numerous copyright holders did join, so that the group represented most music creators in the United States by the end of the decade. Eventually, ASCAP membership was made open to all music composers, publishers, and songwriters.

The 1920's brought a new challenge, as radio grew in popularity. Initially, artists performed their music for free on the airwaves, but this novelty soon wore off, leaving a large group of creators in need of support from ASCAP. Radio stations were forced to pay copyright licensing fees for both live performances and prerecorded broadcasts.

In 1930, a much smaller performance rights organization, the Society of European Stage Authors and Composers (SESAC), was formed. Originally, SESAC promoted only European and gospel music. Although it later expanded to include a more diverse membership, SESAC screens its applicants and remains deliberately small in size.

Many radio stations considered ASCAP's fees too high. In 1939, Broadcast Music Incorporated (BMI) was founded to compete with ASCAP by offering lower fees. In 1941, radio stations nationwide organized a boycott of ASCAP musicians, attempting to demonstrate that ASCAP did its artists more harm than good by charging high copyright fees. However, the boycott failed utterly, and public demand for the ASCAP artists quickly brought a compromise in the dispute.

The three major performance rights organizations, ASCAP, SESAC, and BMI, serve the same function for their members, collecting copyright fees from broadcasting groups to distribute to the appropriate copyright holders. ASCAP and BMI both operate on a not-for-profit basis, keeping only administrative fees, while SESAC retains an undisclosed profit from the royalties it collects.

Jessie Bishop Powell

FURTHER READING

Choate, Pat. *Hot Property: The Stealing of Ideas in the Age of Globalization.* New York: Knopf, 2005.

Passman, Donald S. *All You Need to Know About the Music Business.* Rev. ed. New York: Simon & Schuster, 2000.

Ryan, John. *The Production of Culture in the Music Industry: The ASCAP-BMI Controversy.* Lanham, Md.: University Press of America, 1985.

SEE ALSO: Apple; Copyright law; Digital recording technology; Music industry; Radio broadcasting industry.

American Stock Exchange

IDENTIFICATION: Smallest of the three major stock exchanges in the United States

DATE: Founded in 1842 as the New York Curb Market

SIGNIFICANCE: Although listing mostly smaller and riskier stocks than the larger American stock exchanges, the AMEX has instituted innovative techniques and technologies, such as hand signals and ticker tape machines, that have gone on to influence the other markets.

Originally known as the New York Curb Market, the American Stock Exchange (AMEX) first met outdoors on Broad Street, near Exchange Place, in New York City. The exchange moved indoors to a building at 86 Trinity Place in New York City on June 27, 1921. When the exchange was located outdoors, the noise from traffic, as well as the increasing volume of

A curbside trader holding a megaphone signals a trade in New York in about 1920. (Hulton Archive/Getty Images)

trading, necessitated the creation of a system of hand signals to allow brokers to communicate with traders despite the noise. These hand signals have remained in use on trading floors around the world.

The AMEX has never been big enough to rival the New York Stock Exchange (NYSE), known as the "Big Board." From its beginning, the AMEX specialized in smaller, relatively unknown stocks for which there was no established market. The brokers at the AMEX were often called "two-dollar brokers," because that was how much money they made on a trade. They were essentially freelance brokers who advertised for companies that needed to raise capital by issuing stocks and for buyers who were willing to invest in highly speculative stocks.

Purchasing stocks that traded on the AMEX was much closer to gambling than investing. Many of the securities were unauthorized and were from un-

listed companies. They were not always worth the paper on which they were printed. Many AMEX brokers were part-time or temporary workers. They made money however they could and then moved on, leaving shareholders to fend for themselves. Neither the brokers nor their trading practices were closely regulated. The AMEX had no central clearinghouse to register transactions and deliver stock certificates to purchasers.

The free-for-all atmosphere at the AMEX and the negative publicity it generated embarrassed the much more respectable NYSE. Directors of the NYSE planned to move the AMEX inside the NYSE building, where its operations could be controlled and eventually dismantled. This threat of extinction forced AMEX brokers to find their own building and to institute regulations against the most disreputable brokers and practices. After a series of scandals in 1922-1923, the AMEX helped create a bull market in low-priced securities.

The AMEX created a central clearinghouse for transactions and deposits and invented a network of ticker machines throughout the country to provide prices of securities. By 1930, almost every large city in the United States had at least one ticker machine at a broker and banker's office. The Great Depression during the 1930's nearly wiped out the AMEX and its securities, as many undercapitalized companies listed on the exchange went bankrupt. The exchange managed to survive, however.

To remain competitive after World War II, the AMEX continued to employ more lenient listing requirements than did the NYSE. The AMEX also created new financial products for investors, including options, derivatives, and exchange-traded funds (ETFs). The NASDAQ bought the AMEX in 1998, but both exchanges continued to operate separately. The AMEX building was heavily damaged in the World Trade Center attacks on September 11, 2001, and the exchange's operations were temporarily moved to Philadelphia. In 2003, AMEX Membership Corporation bought the exchange back from NASDAQ. In January, 2008, NYSE Euronext acquired the AMEX for $260 million in stock.

Victoria Erhart

FURTHER READING

Sobel, Robert. *AMEX: A History of the American Stock Exchange, 1921-1971.* Reprint. Frederick, Md.: Beard Books, 2000.

_____. *The Curbstone Brokers: The Origins of the American Stock Exchange.* Reprint. Frederick, Md.: Beard Books, 2000.

SEE ALSO: NASDAQ; New York Stock Exchange; Stock markets.

AMEX. *See* American Stock Exchange

Amtrak

IDENTIFICATION: Quasi-public corporation created by the federal government to operate passenger train service in the United States
DATE: Began operations on May 1, 1971
SIGNIFICANCE: The federal government's creation of Amtrak allowed private railroad companies to abandon their passenger services, which had become highly unprofitable. Amtrak and the sizable federal subsidies supporting it make it possible to maintain a national rail passenger service that would otherwise be financially unsustainable.

After World War II ended in 1945, the automobile and airline industries began to make major inroads into the customer base of commercial passenger trains, threatening the major U.S. railroad companies. By the late 1960's, passenger rail service faced a serious crisis. Many railroads wanted to end passenger service, but government regulations made it difficult to suspend unprofitable trains. In 1970, Congress passed the Rail Passenger Service Act, which President Richard Nixon signed into law on October 30 of that year. The law created Amtrak (National Railroad Passenger Corporation) to maintain railroad passenger service while allowing the private railroads to stop carrying passengers.

Advocates of the Amtrak system believed that with improve- ments in service and the rationalization of routes, passenger trains could operate profitably, so the legislation creating Amtrak mandated that it should make a profit. Amtrak was free from Interstate Commerce Commission regulations that had often kept the private railroads from cutting money-losing trains. However, Amtrak did not prove to be free from the political pressures that might be brought to keep operating underutilized lines.

Relatively modest federal subsidies in Amtrak's early years proved to be wholly inadequate. For several years, annual subsidies of more than $1 billion were required. Later, deficits were decreased, and subsidies were cut to between $600 million and $700 million per year. Significant gains in performance were achieved by the mid-1980's, and by the 1990's, Amtrak had largely replaced the outdated equipment it inherited from the private railroads. The system remained unable to realize a profit, however.

The Northeast Corridor, from Washington, D.C., to Boston, Massachusetts, is the most heavily used part of the system. Amtrak owns the track in the Northeast Corridor. In other parts of the country, Amtrak pays fees to use the tracks owned by the freight railroads. In the Northeast Corridor, many trains operate on frequent service schedules. In the rest of the country, long-distance trains operate much less frequently (often one train runs per day

The Amtrak Vermonter, *pictured here in 1996, heads south on its run from St. Albans, Vermont, to Washington, D.C.* (AP/Wide World Photos)

in each direction). In parts of the Midwest and along the West Coast, there are regional corridors that provide more frequent service.

In addition to its own intercity trains, Amtrak operates commuter trains on a contract basis in several large metropolitan areas. Amtrak operates twenty-one thousand miles of routes, serving over five hundred communities, and employs about nineteen thousand people. In fiscal 2007, Amtrak carried more than twenty-five million passengers, and its revenues covered about 67 percent of its operating expenses.

Mark S. Joy

FURTHER READING

Edmondson, Harold A., ed. *Journey to Amtrak: The Year History Rode the Passenger Train.* Milwaukee: Kalmbach, 1972.
Martin, Albro. *Railroads Triumphant: The Growth, Rejection, and Rebirth of a Vital American Force.* New York: Oxford University Press, 1992.
Solomon, Brian. *Amtrak.* St. Paul, Minn.: MBI, 2002.

SEE ALSO: Air transportation industry; Automotive industry; Postal Service, U.S.; Public transportation, local; Pullman Strike; Railroad strike of 1877; Railroads; Transportation, U.S. Department of.

Annapolis Convention

THE EVENT: Meeting of representatives from five states to discuss shortcomings of the nation's first constitution, the Articles of Confederation
DATE: September 11-14, 1786
PLACE: Annapolis, Maryland
SIGNIFICANCE: The representatives at the Annapolis Convention decided that the Articles of Confederation needed to be replaced and that a constitutional convention should be held to reinvent the federal government. Many of the perceived shortcomings to be remedied involved the extremely limited financial power of the federal government.

The Articles of Confederation were written in 1777 and ratified in 1781. This first attempt at creating a collective American union was famously ill executed. The power of the central government under the Articles of Confederation was extremely weak.

There was no central judiciary or executive, only a legislature. This first legislature was funded by the individual states and composed of people appointed by state governments. Each state, no matter how large, had a single vote.

Although a noble starting point, this first attempt at colonial self-government resulted in a conundrum. The country, then called a confederation, lacked a national military or bureaucracy. The body of the nation existed without a head. In this primitive configuration, the states were more like independent member nations of a body resembling the modern-day European Union. The confederation was quite unlike the integrated body of fifty subnational governments it would become.

Business interests in the confederation were at the mercy of independently acting state governments with divergent economic profiles. Rhode Island, for example, was no longer ruled by prerevolutionary British royalists. This meant that power had shifted from wealthy landowners under the Articles of Confederation to small shop owners and farmers. Economic traditions such as sound inflation policy were cast aside in favor of legislation preferred by a less economically oriented group of citizens.

Domestic currency issues got out of control, as each state printed its own money without any necessary support by gold or silver. International trade represented an even greater problem for eighteenth century American business owners. John Adams was selected by Congress to negotiate a treaty of commerce with Great Britain. Britain declared, however, that it would not negotiate with one American government but with each state government individually. Adams had little recourse in the face of this pronouncement. Under the Articles of Confederation, then, foreign countries pitted each state against the others in tariff and trade policies.

In response to the manifest failure of the Confederation, George Washington and the Virginia legislators invited delegations from each state to meet at Mount Vernon, Washington's home, to discuss the situation. Ultimately, only five states attended, and the group met in Maryland. The principal concern of the group—as expressed by Alexander Hamilton, who served as its secretary—was the "power of regulating trade." No early economy could be built without more cohesive policy making and concentrated negotiating powers. Hamilton recorded the recommendation of the group "to meet at Philadelphia on the second Monday in May next, to take into consideration the situation of the United States." The die had been cast, and the idea of the constitutional convention was conceived. Under the new Constitution, business would no longer be so subject to the disparate policies of each state.

R. Matthew Beverlin

FURTHER READING
Beard, Charles A. *An Economic Interpretation of the Constitution of the United States.* New York: Free Press, 1913.
Kammen, Michael. *The Origins of the American Constitution: A Documentary History.* New York: Penguin Books, 1986.
Morris, Richard B. *Alexander Hamilton and the Founding of the Nation.* New York: The Dial Press, 1957.

SEE ALSO: Articles of Confederation; Constitution, U.S.; Currency.

Anthracite coal strike. *See* Coal strike of 1902

Antique and art markets

DEFINITION: Markets in which furniture and housewares older than one hundred years and items of artistic value, such as paintings, sculpture, prints, and drawings, are sold

SIGNIFICANCE: The markets for art and antiques have satisfied both consumers' quest for elaborate furnishings and decorative objects to add beauty and status to their lives and people's desire to invest in objects that are likely to appreciate, largely independent of fluctuations in the stock market.

Antiques and art are sometimes grouped into the same market not only because they are often sold together but also because these objects depend on subjective appeal and social acceptance to determine their value in the marketplace. Antiques, which include many objects such as domestic items and furniture, derive their value primarily from

their age and condition, rarity, and the items' beauty or craftsmanship. Art, in the context of antique and art markets, most often refers to the visual arts, including painting, sculpture, and printmaking. The appreciation and collection of both antiques and art are considered to be an indicator of status in many societies, including that of the United States.

RISE OF THE MARKETS

Although many artists and artisans produced works even during the colonial days and many antiques and artworks had been imported into the United States, the relative youth of the country, its small number of museums, and a seeming lack of tradition caused the country to be a lesser player in the antique and art markets for many years. However, the American antique and art markets gained international prominence during the 1950's, when Sotheby's, one of the leading auction houses, opened a branch in New York City. The city's reputation as a leader in the antique and art markets became solidified in 1964, when Sotheby's purchased Parke-Bernet, which was the leading fine-art auctioneer in the area at that time.

Although ownership of antiques and art is typically transferred through ordinary marketplace transactions (through inheritance, retail shops, auctions, and online purchases), one of the most important relationships in the antique and art markets is between the art dealer or collector and museums and galleries. Through the acquisition and exhibition of antiques and works of art, museums and galleries provide exposure and add legitimacy to these objects and the artists or craftspeople who produced them. Such acquisitions and exhibitions increase the value of the items involved as well as the value of any similar items in private collections. Similarly, media coverage of artists, antiques, and artworks can enhance the value of antiques and art. Articles in reputable art magazines and books from art publishers can increase the perceived value of an item.

ANTIQUES AND ART AS INVESTMENTS

Most individuals who actively participate in the antique and art markets view the purchase of both antiques and art as not only an aesthetic pursuit but also as an investment. Investment in both markets requires specialized knowledge: For the antique market, the investor must know what items were

SELECTED PRICES FROM A 2008 CHRISTIE'S SALE OF IMPRESSIONIST AND MODERN ART

Work Title	Artist	Form of Art	Price ($ millions)
The Railroad Bridge at Argenteuil	Monet	painting	41.4
Standing Woman II	Giacometti	bronze	27.4
Portrait with a Blue Coat	Matisse	painting	22.4
Eve, the Large Version	Rodin	bronze	18.9
Caress of the Stars	Miró	painting	17.0
City Square II	Giacometti	sculpture	14.6
Family Group	Henry Moore	bronze	4.0
Working Model for Reclining Figure: Angles	Henry Moore	sculpture	3.2

Source: Data from Carol Vogel, "Monet and Rodin Set Price Records at Christie's," *The New York Times*, May 7, 2008

Note: The Monet painting was purchased in 1988 for $12.6 million, and the Miró painting had sold for $11.7 million in 2004.

produced in a particular historical period and must be able to identify the items' notable characteristics, whereas for artworks, the investor must gain specialized knowledge of individual artists.

The general perception is that investment in the antique and art markets is purely speculative; however, this is not borne out by evidence. Although there is a risk with any investment, the antique and art markets have proven to be considerably less volatile than the stock market. The idea that the antique and art markets are volatile may have been created when the bullish stock market of the 1980's seemed to have encouraged unusually high levels of investment in artwork and antiques, followed by a significant correction, or downturn, in the markets during the 1990's. For the most part, market analysts believe that the correction was only to be expected in view of the runaway prices of the 1980's. Nonetheless, the antique market later proved to be surprisingly stable during a period of economic unrest; from 1997 to 2004, the quarterly fluctuation, as reported by the Artprice Global index, proved to be half or two-thirds that of the Dow Jones Industrial Average over the same period. The same type of stability had previously held true for the antique and art markets during and after the Vietnam War and continued to do so in the wake of both September 11, 2001, and the start of the Iraq War in 2003.

Market analysts believe that there are several reasons that the antique and art markets are able to maintain, and even increase, their numbers of participants even during times of social and economic unrest. The most important reason cited for the stability of the antique and art markets is that of precedence; throughout the history of these markets, prices have, overall, increased at a fairly predictable rate. The antique and art markets seem, according to analysts, to be somewhat unusual in that investors can reasonably expect that the value of a given good will increase over time, notwithstanding the fluctuations of the stock market.

Sarah J. Damberger

FURTHER READING

Luecke, Marjorie Ann. *The International Antiques Market: A Guide for Collectors and Investors.* South Brunswick, N.J.: A. S. Barnes, 1979. Provides an overview of the various categories of antiques, including price guides with projected price trends.

McAndrew, Clare. *The Art Economy: An Investor's Guide to the Art Market.* Dublin: Liffey Press, 2007. An interesting overview of the global art market from the point of view of an investor; discusses the value of art as a financial investment with comparisons of the returns on art investment in comparison with those on stocks and other assets.

McNulty, Tom. *Art Market Research: A Guide to Methods and Sources.* Jefferson, N.C.: McFarland, 2006. Provides an introduction to the art market, including information about artwork analysis and valuation. Also includes a list of pertinent periodicals and auction houses.

Parker, Philip M. *The 2007 Import and Export Market for Antiques Over One Hundred Years Old in the United States.* San Diego, Calif.: ICON Group International, 2006. An overview of the global antique market with a focus on the United States market, providing estimated figures for the volume of imports and exports per country and by region, providing a comparison of the United States market with other major country markets.

Robertson, Iain. *Understanding International Art Markets and Management.* New York: Routledge, 2005. An overview of the international art market, including a discussion of the reasons that the market is dominated by the United States and Western Europe.

SEE ALSO: Advertising industry; Business cycles; Counterfeiting; Jewelry industry; Retail trade industry.

Antitrust legislation

DEFINITION: Federal legislation restricting monopolistic actions by business firms

SIGNFICANCE: Antitrust regulation had a dampening effect on the growth of big business by dismantling monopolistic companies, reducing predatory behaviors such as price fixing, and restricting mergers.

The federal government's Sherman Antitrust Act of 1890 initiated federal antitrust policy and remained a legislative centerpiece for the following century. The law was a response to widespread public distress over the rise of big business and the alleged predatory conduct of railroad corporations and John D. Rockefeller's Standard Oil Company. In 1889-1891, eighteen individual states also adopted antitrust laws.

SHERMAN ANTITRUST ACT

The Sherman Antitrust Act was relatively simple. It prohibited any contract, combination, or conspiracy in restraint of trade, as well as monopolization or attempts to monopolize. The law authorized the United States attorney general to prosecute violations or to bring civil suits against violators, seeking relief. In addition, private persons claiming injury could sue alleged violators and recover triple the amount of proven damages.

The provisions were vague and were gradually given detail by court cases. Loose combinations of several firms were frequently convicted for agreeing to fix prices, allocate markets, or agree on other elements of competitive behavior. Early cases involved railroads (Trans-Missouri Freight Association, 1897) as well as industrial firms (Addyston Pipe and Steel Company, 1899). The form of anticompetitive agreement was sufficient to constitute illegal behavior, regardless of whether the results significantly harmed others. This contract component remained consistent throughout antitrust history.

The provision against monopolization was not very effective. One of the greatest waves of corporate mergers occurred after 1890, culminating in the formation of the United States Steel Corporation in 1901. The presidency of Theodore Roosevelt saw a few actions against giant monopolies. In 1904, the first trust-busting episode involved the dissolution of Northern Securities Company, a giant railroad holding company. In 1911, successful prosecutions were brought against Standard Oil and American Tobacco. Both had been formed by extensive mergers. Each was broken up into several separate companies.

During the presidency of Woodrow Wilson, antitrust legislation was significantly extended by two related measures. The Clayton Antitrust Act of 1914 forbade a number of specific business practices, including price discrimination, tying contracts and exclusive-deal agreements, purchases of corporation stock by other corporations, and interlocking directorships. Price discrimination involved large corporations charging lower prices in areas where they faced significant competitors and charging higher prices in areas where competition was lacking. The practice of tying required a customer to buy a second product to get the one they wanted (often a patented product). However, these actions were judged to be illegal only if they tended to lessen competition or to create a monopoly, and these conditions were difficult to establish.

The Federal Trade Commission (FTC) Act of

1914 established a specialized agency to enforce the Clayton Act and also outlawed "unfair methods of competition" in general. The authorities maintained effective restraint on collusive behavior, as evidenced by *United States v. Trenton Potteries* (1927). However, antitrust prosecutions against such giant firms as United States Steel (1920) and International Harvester (1927) were not upheld in court.

THE GREAT DEPRESSION

Policy changed dramatically with the onset of the Great Depression in 1929. The National Industrial Recovery Act (NRA) of 1933 was predicated on the false theory that the depression resulted from overproduction and excessive competition. Businesses were encouraged to join together to create and enforce "codes of fair competition," which frequently were collusive agreements to reduce competition. When approved by the government, such codes were exempt from antitrust.

The NRA was declared unconstitutional in 1935; however, elements of it were reenacted to protect such sectors as coal mining, airlines, petroleum extraction, and truck transport against "destructive" competition. Antipathy toward competition also helped motivate the Robinson-Patman Act of 1936, which enlarged the scope of prohibited price discrimination. The new law aimed to protect small retailers against the ability of large chain-store retailers to extract price concessions from suppliers. Antimonopoly and procompetition attitudes were strengthened by the prosperity and inflation of the 1940's. Successful cases were brought against the giant Aluminum Company of America (1945) and against the major cigarette manufacturers in 1946.

The relatively ineffective restrictions on corporate mergers in the Clayton Act were greatly strengthened by the Celler-Kefauver Act of 1950. This act was extended by the Hart-Scott-Rodino Act of 1976, which required firms contemplating mergers to file prior notification, giving the government authorities the capacity to negotiate as well as forbid.

Two noteworthy big-business prosecutions ended in 1982. The government's case against International Business Machines (IBM) was withdrawn after being in the works from 1969. American Telephone and Telegraph Company (AT&T) accepted a consent decree to separate into a number of component companies. Both industries were sub-

---

POETICAL OBSERVATIONS ON ANTITRUST LEGISLATION

Business is a useful beast,
We should not hate it in the least;
Its profits should not be sequestered,
And yet it should be mildly pestered.
To pester, rather than to bust,
Should be the aim of antitrust.

Source: Kenneth Ewart Boulding, *Principles of Economic Policy* (Englewood Cliffs, N.J.: Prentice-Hall, 1958)

---

ject to rapid technological change. IBM soon lost its dominant position in computers to firms such as Microsoft and Hewlett-Packard. The AT&T settlement, along with deregulation of rates, significantly opened the way for the rise of new telecommunications firms such as Sprint and the ill-fated WorldCom.

Other countries began to imitate U.S. antitrust measures, beginning with the forced breakup of cartels in Japan and Germany after World War II. Globalization greatly reduced the capacity for industrial firms to maintain monopoly positions, and the World Trade Organization and the European Union restrained the capacity of governments to aid their favored local monopolies.

American antitrust policy has always generated controversy among economists. Its biggest benefits have come from reducing collusion and preventing large firms from unfairly using their power to prevent the rise of competitors.

Paul B. Trescott

FURTHER READING

Armentano, Dominick T. *Antitrust Policy: The Case for Repeal.* 2d ed. Auburn, Ala.: Mises Institute, 1998. Argues that antitrust policies often restrict competition and interfere with business efficiency.

Hovenkamp, Herbert. *Federal Antitrust Policy: The Law of Competition and Its Practice.* 3d ed. St. Paul, Minn.: Thomas/West, 2005. An examination of antitrust law and the cases involved.

Kovacic, William E., and Carl Shapiro. "Antitrust Policy: A Century of Economic and Legal

Thinking." *Journal of Economic Perspectives* 14, no. 1 (Winter, 2000): 43-60. Analyzes the importance of judicial rulings and economic analysis in the evolution of antitrust.

Kovaleff, Theodore P., ed. *The Antitrust Impulse.* Armonk, N.Y.: M. E. Sharpe, 1994. Numerous essays express divergent views: Part 3 showcases both critics and defenders of antitrust law.

Peritz, Rudolph J., Jr. *Competition Policy in America, 1888-1992: History, Rhetoric, Law.* New York: Oxford University Press, 1996. History of federal government policies relating to antitrust issues. Includes a substantial bibliography and an index.

Reed, O. Lee. *The Legal and Regulatory Environment of Business.* 14th ed. New York: McGraw-Hill/Irwin, 2008. Lengthy work covers antitrust legislation in detail, examining the statutes and cases. Contains much other material on business ethics.

Wilcox, Clair, and William G. Shepherd. *Public Policies Toward Business.* Homewood, Ill.: Richard D. Irwin, 1975. Chapters 5 through 10 deal comprehensively with antitrust policies and their effects.

See also: Clayton Antitrust Act; Congress, U.S.; Federal Trade Commission; International Business Machines; Justice, U.S. Department of; Northern Securities Company; Price fixing; Robber barons; Sherman Antitrust Act; Standard Oil Company; United States Steel Corporation.

Apple

Identification: Computer and consumer electronics company

Date: Founded on April 1, 1976

Significance: Apple has been one of the driving forces in innovation in the personal computer and consumer electronics industries. Even at times when the company was considered a niche player in personal computing, features that it pioneered often made their way into products marketed by its more successful competitors. In the twenty-first century, with its iPod MP3 player, the company expanded from computing to marketing "digital lifestyle" devices, and it grew to become the world's largest online purveyor of digital music files.

Apple (originally Apple Computer) was founded by Steve Wozniak and Steve Jobs, who had close ties to the 1960's counterculture, and the corporate culture of Apple reflected that mind-set. The Apple motto, Think Different, was not only a counterpoint to Think, the decades-old motto of International Business Machines (IBM), but also a paean to counterculture nonconformity. When Jobs first sought outside investors, he had no idea how to compose a business plan. He had to learn how to relate to corporate executives and produce formal business documents to acquire capital.

Apple quickly established its reputation for innovation. The Apple II personal computer had floppy disk drives at a time when other personal computers still depended on magnetic tape drives for data and software storage. As a result, Apple II users were able to load and operate complex programs such as VisiCalc, the original spreadsheet application and the original "killer app" (that is, a software application that by itself justifies the purchase of the hardware on which it runs). In 1984, Apple introduced the Macintosh, which boasted the first graphical user interface (GUI) on a consumer computer. Users were no longer required to memorize arcane codes for data paths and commands. Instead, a visual representation of a desktop containing folders and files allowed for more intuitive manipulation of applications and data.

By the middle of the 1990's, Apple was in serious trouble. Its product line had become confused, and its market share was shrinking. There were even speculations that the company could fail. In a bold stroke, the board of directors brought back ousted cofounder Jobs to become interim chief executive officer (CEO) in 1997. Jobs immediately cleaned house, simplifying Apple's product line and concentrating on creating innovative, elegant products. His first offering was the iMac, an all-in-one computer that harked back to the original Macintosh while replacing several key interfaces with the new universal serial bus (USB). USB soon became a standard across the industry. Jobs followed that coup with the iBook, a colorful laptop also aimed at the consumer market.

Once Apple was back on a solid financial footing, Jobs began investigating the possibility of marketing a digital music player. The result was the iPod, which was introduced in October of 2001. To go with it, Apple also introduced the iTunes Music Store, an online store that allowed people to purchase and

Steve Jobs, chair of the board of Apple Computers, holds up an Apple II computer in 1984. (AP/Wide World Photos)

download music files to play on their iPods over the Internet. The iPod and iTunes Music Store were runaway successes that quickly positioned Apple as a major player in the digital music business and redefined the core mission of the company. In January of 2007, acknowledging the importance of "digital lifestyle" devices such as the iPod, iPhone, and AppleTV to its business model, Apple Computer renamed itself Apple, Inc.

Leigh Husband Kimmel

FURTHER READING

Levy, Steven. *The Perfect Thing: How the iPod Shuffles Commerce, Culture, and Coolness.* New York: Simon & Schuster, 2006.

Malone, Michael S. *Infinite Loop: How Apple, the World's Most Insanely Great Computer Company, Went Insane.* New York: Doubleday, 1999.

Young, Jeffrey S., and William L. Simon. *iCon Steve Jobs: The Greatest Second Act in the History of Business.* Hoboken, N.J.: John Wiley & Sons, 2005.

SEE ALSO: Computer industry; Digital recording technology; Gates, Bill; International Business Machines; Music industry; Online marketing; Video rental industry.

Arab oil embargo of 1973

THE EVENT: The cessation of oil exports from Arab states to the United States and some Western European countries that supplied the Israeli military as a result of American support of Israel during the 1973 Yom Kippur War

DATE: October 17, 1973-March 17, 1974

PLACE: United States, Arab states, Western Europe

SIGNIFICANCE: The immediate effect of the 1973 oil embargo was a decrease in the amount of crude oil and petroleum products available to American businesses. The long-term effects were large increases in the price of oil that motivated the United States and other nations to begin developing large-scale conservation efforts to reduce their dependence on oil, as well as increased domestic exploration to reduce the dependence on foreign oil.

Following World War II, two series of events shaped the Middle East. Politically, the creation of the state of Israel sent shock waves through the region. Three wars were fought within twenty years between the new Jewish state and its hostile neighbors. Economically, the development of the oil fields in and around the Persian Gulf brought great wealth to the region. However, until the early 1970's, American and Western European oil companies were able to keep the price of crude oil relatively low and relatively stable. In 1973, these political and economic forces came together, resulting in the Arab oil embargo.

In the fall of 1973, the Organization of Petroleum Exporting Countries (OPEC) sought to increase the price of oil, because the dollar was losing value. On October 6, Egypt and Syria attacked Israel, starting the Yom Kippur War. The Persian Gulf oil producers sought to weaken the ties between the United States and Israel, which relied on U.S. support. Thus, on October 17, OPEC decided to end exports to the United States and any other countries supporting Israel. Within two days, all the Arab oil exporters joined in this action. In just over two weeks, OPEC cut its production by one-fourth. Although the war lasted only twenty days, the embargo lasted five months.

The cut in oil production by the Arab states represented only about 7 percent of the petroleum available to the United States. The psychological impact of the embargo, however, was strong. American oil consumption dropped in response to the embargo, but there were still extensive areas of the country that experienced gasoline shortages. By the time gas prices stabilized, they had increased by about 45 percent. The entire country was affected, and businesses either passed on their increased costs to their customers or went out of business. Prices increased across the economy. The threat of another oil embargo gave the government an incentive to encourage more domestic oil production and exploration. The OPEC embargo was thus the first step toward the creation of the global free market in crude oil.

One long-term effect of the embargo was to encourage the government, businesses, and individuals to seek ways to conserve energy. The government would eventually pass a law mandating fuel efficiency standards in automobiles and provide incentives to companies seeking alternative sources of energy. The U.S. industry most affected by the crisis and its aftermath was the automotive industry. With the advent of substantially higher gas prices, the demand for smaller, more fuel-efficient cars increased. The crisis marked the beginning of the decline of the American auto industry, as Japanese firms associated with smaller cars grew rapidly.

Donald A. Watt

FURTHER READING

Pelletiere, Stephen. *America's Oil Wars*. Westport, Conn.: Praeger, 2004.

Zalloum, Abdulhay Yahya. *Oil Crusades: America Through Arab Eyes*. London: Pluto Press, 2007.

SEE ALSO: Automotive industry; Chrysler bailout of 1979; Energy crisis of 1979; "Gas wars"; General Motors; International economics and trade; Organization of Petroleum Exporting Countries; Petroleum industry.

Arms industry

DEFINITION: Private enterprises researching, developing, manufacturing, marketing, and distributing weaponry for military clients

SIGNIFICANCE: Starting with small, government-owned facilities as some of the first industrial facilities in the United States, the arms industry has expanded into large corporate entities. The arms industry has been one of the leading drivers of American technology in pursuit of superior weaponry for the defense of the United States. During the country's wars, the arms industry provided the tools to defend U.S. interests, but it often struggled to survive in times of peace.

The American arms industry began with government facilities that produced weapons solely for the U.S. military. Determined to be independent of foreign sources of weaponry, President George Washington created the first arms facilities to provide small arms for the Army and ships for the Navy. In 1794, Washington signed legislation that created the first two armories for the U.S. Army. One was located in Springfield, Massachusetts, and the other was placed in Harpers Ferry, Virginia (later West Virginia). Both locations were strategically located to support armies in both the northern and the southern portions of the country. Both were also close to sources of waterpower to operate the machinery, and both also sat astride major transportation routes. Whereas the Harpers Ferry armory existed entirely as a manufacturing and storage facility, the Springfield armory had the additional function of weapons design. The Springfield Armory designed and manufactured every major small arm of the U.S. Army until the 1960's. Other arsenals supplemented the work at Springfield and Harpers Ferry.

The Frankford Arsenal, established in 1816 near Philadelphia, was the major producer of ammunition for the Army until it closed in 1977. The Watervliet Arsenal, founded in 1813 near Troy, New York, was the main producer of artillery for the United States, a function it continues to serve. Ships for the U.S. Navy came from a series of government-run naval yards. The first naval yard, established at League Island near Philadelphia in 1801, was a major production facility, building and maintaining a large number of ships until the base closed in 1995.

Most major coastal cities boasted a ship facility by the 1830's, with the most important yards at Boston, Brooklyn, Philadelphia, and Norfolk, Virginia.

THE LATE NINETEENTH CENTURY

The structure of the American arms industry remained primarily in government hands throughout the nineteenth century. The United States fought few major wars, and the wars that did occur did not require much additional production outside the government-owned facilities. Even the demands of the U.S. Civil War could be met by these limited facilities. When new weapons technology emerged in the nineteenth century, the government-run facilities absorbed the new technology instead of placing orders with nongovernment firms. When new technology emerged, government arsenals simply adapted the existing weapons to accept the new technology. Likewise, Navy shipyards adapted new marine technologies into older accepted production methods, preserving the government's control over its supply of arms. The only major exception to this tradition was the Colt Manufacturing Company. The company's founder, Samuel Colt, set up a factory in Hartford, Connecticut, to produce his greatest invention, the world's first practical revolving chamber pistol. Because the new invention was so superior to earlier pistols, the Army wished to adopt it, but Colt held the patent to his invention and would not give up control of his pistol to the government. Instead, Colt sold pistols to the Army for more than a century, and it was the largest private arms producer in America until the late nineteenth century.

SHIFT TO THE PRIVATE SECTOR

By the close of the nineteenth century, circumstances had changed the American arms industry. The rapid expansion of technology was changing existing weapons at such a rate that the existing armories and yards could not keep up. More important, private research and innovation were generating new technology outside the control of government-owned facilities, and if the Army and Navy wanted the new technology, they would have to pay for it. In 1892, for instance, the Army needed a new rifle to replace its obsolete models. Unable to produce a suitable rifle at the Springfield Armory, the War Department eventually purchased the rights to the Krag rifle from its designers, although the Army would manufacture the rifle at the Springfield Armory.

Springfield also wound up producing other outside designs at the armory, most notably the designs of John Moses Browning, the greatest American firearms designer. Springfield Armory eventually manufactured pistols, rifles, and machine guns designed by Browning. The Navy was also forced to use outside companies and designs when its own yards could not keep pace with technology. The USS *Indiana*, America's first modern battleship, was constructed in 1893 at the William Cramp & Sons Shipbuilding Company in Philadelphia, because no Navy yard was capable of launching a ship of its size. Eventually, the Navy began to produce large ships in its own yards, but most of the early American battleships were constructed in private yards. After John Philip Holland introduced his first practical submarine in 1897, the Navy had to purchase submarines from the private Electric Boat Company in Groton, Connecticut, a company started by Holland and Isaac Rice to market the new device.

In World War II, the American arms industry played a huge part in the United States' military success. Private firms, especially the aerospace industry, provided key technological breakthroughs that the U.S. government could not produce itself. While existing government armories produced small arms and artillery for the Army, new military technology came from the arms industry. Companies such as Boeing, North American, Martin, and Consolidated produced aircraft far more advanced than anything the government could produce.

The arms industry also provided the ability to produce in quantities that the war demanded. Private yards produced most of the thousands of vessels procured by the U.S. Navy. A good example was the landing craft, vehicle/personnel (LCVP), an innovative amphibious landing craft designed by Andrew Jackson Higgins used in dozens of beach landings throughout the war. Private arms production also churned out mass-produced merchant vessels, the Liberty ships, in numbers the government could not hope to produce. World War II also marked the beginning of commercial businesses' entry into the defense industry as companies created arms industry wings. A good example of this was the Ford Motor Company. Instead of producing cars during World War II, Ford built automotive vehicles (like trucks and tanks) for the Army, but also diversified

World War II workers assemble Garand rifles in an armory as part of the war effort. (Library of Congress)

into aircraft production. Private arms manufacturers, however, still had to accommodate government demands. Boeing Aircraft, for instance, developed the B-29 Superfortress, the most advanced bomber in the world at the time, but the government forced Boeing to share its production secrets with the Martin Company, which built the B-29 under license at its plant near Omaha, Nebraska. Boeing did not like the situation, but it had to accede, because Boeing lacked the production capacity to build the aircraft in the numbers the government needed on such short notice.

THE COLD WAR ERA

After World War II, the intensification of the Cold War and the advent of new wartime technology led to a decline in government arms production and almost total reliance on the arms industry. As the pace of technological advancement increased, the portion of the U.S. military's equipment produced by government armories and shipyards declined. Private technological research had so outpaced government research that the government could no longer compete. Also, as technological breakthroughs occurred, the patents for the new technology remained in private or corporate hands, and if the U.S. military wanted access to those break-

throughs, it would have to buy from the private producers.

The Cold War also played a large part in the shift to private producers. Unlike earlier wars, when technology plateaued and defense budgets fell, the threat of the Soviet Union forced the United States to spend large amounts on defense and procure the best weaponry available. That meant it had to rely on the private arms industry to maintain a technological and qualitative edge over Soviet weaponry, which government facilities could not provide. As a consequence, government armories and shipyards lost most of their traditional roles and began to close. Even the venerable Springfield Armory lost its traditional tasks when the Army adopted the civilian-designed M16 rifle in 1961, the first non-Springfield-produced rifle in the U.S. Army's history.

Most of the weaponry produced during the Cold War came from a new manifestation of the arms industry: the defense contractor. Whereas companies like Ford switched to weapons production during World War II before going back to their prewar civilian products, the defense contractors of the Cold War made military hardware as their only line of work. A few major defense contractors (such as Boeing, which produced both civilian airliners and military aircraft) still had a civilian side, but most of the new companies built only military equipment or had only a small presence in nonmilitary industries. Aviation companies such as Northrop, Grumman, McDonnell, Douglas, and Lockheed relied almost entirely on military orders to survive, and each tried to carve out a niche market for itself. Grumman and McDonnell, for example, specialized in carrier aircraft for the U.S. Navy, while Lockheed was a major producer of transport aircraft.

Civilian shipyards, such as Newport News Shipbuilding in Virginia, specialized in the construction of aircraft carriers and other large vessels, replacing construction in Navy yards. Other defense contractors emerged as the result of mergers of smaller armament industries. The best example of this type of company was General Dynamics, founded in 1952. The company started out as the Electric Boat Company, the submarine company started by Holland. After government orders for submarines ended after World War II, Electric Boat began to acquire other companies to diversify its offerings in the armaments industry. General Dynamics acquired the Canadian aircraft producer Canadair and the American aircraft and missile company Convair, making General Dynamics a strong contender in several major defense fields. By the 1990's, General Dynamics was producing F-16 fighters for the Air Force, M-1 battle tanks for the Army, and ships for the Navy all at the same time. The intense competition for business, however, drove some companies to illegal action. During the 1960's and 1970's, several defense contractors, including Lockheed and Northrop, were found guilty of bribery and other criminal activity aimed at obtaining contacts for their companies.

AFTER THE COLD WAR

With the end of the Cold War during the 1980's, the arms industry changed yet again. The decrease in general defense spending caused a huge contraction in the arms industry. Companies without a civilian market and with no means of sustaining themselves either merged or went out of business. In 1967, for instance, McDonnell had merged with Douglas to survive, only to be purchased by Boeing in 1997. Lockheed merged with Martin in 1985 to survive, while Northrop and Grumman merged in 1994. General Dynamics also changed to stay solvent. The company sold off its aviation and missile branches during the 1990's to concentrate on land vehicle and ship production. Its original company, Electric Boat, still exists as the only submarine producer in the United States. Competition has also become very fierce for the limited defense dollars, as companies stake their future on obtaining the few major defense procurement projects still available. To make matters worse, the globalization of the world economy opened the door for foreign defense contractors, creating still more competition for government contracts.

Steven J. Ramold

FURTHER READING

Ball, Robert W. D. *Springfield Armory Shoulder Weapons, 1795-1968.* Norfolk, Va.: Antique Trader, 1997. A survey of the small arms produced by the Springfield Armory throughout its long contribution to the American arms industry.

Boorman, Dean K. *A History of Colt Firearms.* New York: Lyons, 2001. An examination of the significant contributions of Samuel Colt to the American arms industry. Colt firearms equipped the U.S. Army for most of its history, and Colt has a close relationship with the Springfield Armory.

Davis, Kenneth S. *Arms, Industry, and America.* New York: Wilson, 1971. Somewhat outdated, but still the best general history of the American arms industry, especially in the twentieth century.

Goodwin, Jacob. *Brotherhood of Arms: General Dynamics and the Business of Defending America.* New York: Times Books, 1985. A lengthy history of General Dynamics' rise to the top of the defense contractor industry, and the diverse products it has produced.

Morris, Charles R. *Iron Destinies, Lost Opportunities: The Arms Race Between the USA and the USSR, 1945-1987.* New York: Harper & Row, 1988. A critical analysis of the role of the arms industry in exacerbating the Cold War and the economic impact of defense spending.

Singer, Peter W. *Corporate Warriors: The Rise of the Privatized Military Industry.* Ithaca, N.Y.: Cornell University Press, 2003. A study of the newest manifestation of the defense contractor. Privatized defense companies not only produce weapons but also provide hired troops to be used outside the scope of established national armies.

SEE ALSO: Aircraft industry; Industrial research; Industrial Revolution, American; Iraq wars; Military-industrial complex; War surplus; Wars; World War I; World War II.

Army Corps of Engineers, U.S.

IDENTIFICATION: Agency of the Department of Defense responsible for military and public works projects domestically and abroad

DATE: Established on March 16, 1802

SIGNIFICANCE: The U.S. Army Corps of Engineers has provided vital indirect support to business enterprises through its work supporting the nation's infrastructure, most notably waterways and harbors, and has been a major employer in the construction industry.

Since its establishment by Congress in 1802, the U.S. Army Corps of Engineers (USACE) has played an important role in the growth and sustainability of American business. Early in the nineteenth century, USACE officers were instrumental in mapping areas between the Mississippi River and the Pacific coast, facilitating the settlement of the West. In 1824, the USACE was assigned to improve navigation on America's rivers. That mission was expanded after the U.S. Civil War to include construction of levees and again in 1936, when the USACE was made responsible for nationwide flood control. During the early nineteenth century, the USACE built defenses at many of the nation's harbors, and over time, the agency took on the task of ensuring the safety and navigability of the country's key ports. The USACE's work has made it possible for American businesses to transport goods by water and operate safely on land near major waterways without undue concern for flooding.

In 1925, Congress authorized the USACE to develop hydroelectric power stations. By the end of the century, the agency was operating seventy-five plants, providing one-fifth of the nation's hydroelectric power. During World War II, the USACE constructed facilities for the Manhattan Project, the government's program to develop the first nuclear weapon. Techniques developed on this project became useful to civilian firms building nuclear power facilities after the war.

In 1970, the USACE was assigned responsibility for environmental management of hundreds of areas adjacent to waterways and for cleanup of numerous sites contaminated by toxic waste. For these projects, USACE officials contracted with civilian firms specializing in work of this nature. During the twentieth century, the USACE developed partnerships with the National Park Service and various states to provide recreational activities on hundreds of lakes and rivers. In 2007, the USACE was employing approximately 600,000 workers to operate these sites, which were visited by millions of Americans each year.

By 2000, the USACE had become the largest public-engineering and construction-management agency in the world. Its responsibilities included levee construction and repair, flood control, shore protection, disaster response, construction and maintenance of facilities at Army and Air Force installations, environmental protection, and toxic-

A worker from the U.S. Army Corps of Engineers surveys the scene four days after the terrorist attacks on the New York City World Trade Center. (U.S. Army Corps of Engineers)

waste cleanup. The USACE also sponsored research and development activities in areas such as engineering design for building construction, infrastructure, and management of coastal and riverine operations. Most of its annual civil-works budget, approximately \$5 billion during the early twenty-first century, was allocated to pay private firms to carry out this work, generating a significant source of revenue for those businesses.

Laurence W. Mazzeno

FURTHER READING

The History of the U.S. Army Corps of Engineers. Arlington, Va.: U.S. Army Corps of Engineers, 1998.

Mazmanian, Daniel A., and Jeanne Nienaber. *Can Organizations Change? Environmental Protection, Citizen Participation, and the Corps of Engineers.* Washington, D.C.: Brookings Institution, 1979.

Morgan, Arthur E. *Dams and Other Disasters: A Century of the Army Corps of Engineers in Civil Works.* Boston: Porter Sargent, 1971.

SEE ALSO: Canals; Dams and aqueducts; Highways; Military-industrial complex; Mississippi and Missouri Rivers; Public utilities.

Articles of Confederation

IDENTIFICATION: First constitution of the United States
DATE: Ratified on March 1, 1781
SIGNIFICANCE: The Articles of Confederation created an extremely weak central government, leaving each state in control of its own trade, taxation, and currency. The failure of this system led the states to produce a new constitution that centralized economic and trade powers in the new federal government.

The Articles of Confederation and Perpetual Union—a "league of friendship" among the former colonies—were adopted by the Second Continental Congress on November 15, 1777, and went into effect on March 1, 1781, following state ratification. The Articles, which reflected the former colonists' distrust of a strong central government, created a confederation in which each state retained its "sovereignty, freedom, and independence." The national government consisted of a one-house Congress with no independent executive or judiciary. Congress had few powers: It could make peace and war, coin money, and negotiate treaties, but little else. Most important, coining money and negotiating treaties were not its exclusive province, as the states were free to do so as well. This proved to be the chief weakness of the government.

The Articles contributed to political and economic near disaster. Because all important proposals required support from two-thirds of the states, any five states could prevent action. While the national government could coin money, it had no resources to back up the value of its currency. Congress could ask, but not compel, the states to pay taxes, leading to perpetual bankruptcy. The national government lacked the authority to regulate commerce, resulting in limited foreign trade and many commercial disputes among the states. Finally, because the Articles did not prohibit states from printing their own money, which was often unsupported by gold or silver, the new nation's economy produced rampant inflation, angry creditors, and public rebellions.

The economic problems created by the Confederation contributed to the impetus for constitutional reform. The Articles were replaced by the U.S. Constitution on June 21, 1788.

Richard A. Glenn

SEE ALSO: Annapolis Convention; Bank of the United States, First; Banking; Constitution, U.S.; Land laws; Mint, U.S.; Revolutionary War; Shays's Rebellion; Washington, George.

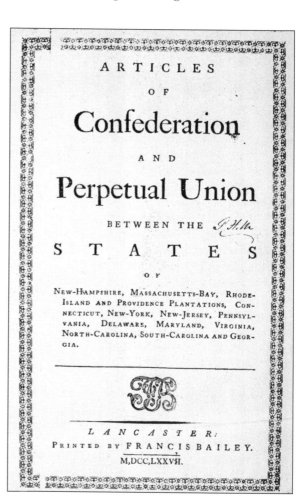

Published copy of the Articles of Confederation. (Hulton Archive/Getty Images)

ASCAP. *See* **American Society of Composers, Authors, and Publishers**

Asian financial crisis of 1997

THE EVENT: Drastic decline in the value of the currencies of several Asian nations, leading to significant economic contraction in those nations

DATE: Summer, 1997-summer, 1998

PLACE: Primarily Thailand, Indonesia, and South Korea

SIGNIFICANCE: The Asian financial crisis demonstrated the risks of speculating in foreign currencies. As a result of the crisis, American businesses and private citizens became hesitant to invest in developing countries. Growth in such countries slowed, and U.S. investors were forced to reevaluate their options and priorities.

The Asian financial crisis emerged when traders in foreign currencies became convinced that several Asian currencies were overvalued. As a result, the value of Thailand's currency, the baht, fell by 50 percent against the U.S. dollar in the summer of 1997. Not long after this, the Malaysian ringgit, the Indonesian rupiah, and the Philippine peso also sharply depreciated. By autumn, the South Korean won dramatically decreased in value as well.

The significant decline in the value of these currencies led to a major economic downturn in much of the region. Although the ability of Asian nations to export products increased because of their weak currencies, the cost of their imports skyrocketed. Thus, these nations received less money despite the increase in their foreign sales, while their ability to purchase foreign goods drastically diminished. Multiple Asian countries had zero or negative economic growth during the crisis, thus falling into recession. Thailand was perhaps in the worst condition, as its economy contracted by 12 percent in 1998. Furthermore, unemployment rates increased, and some countries in the region experienced record levels of business failures.

The impact of the Asian financial crisis was not limited to Asian economies. As a result of the crisis, these economies, which had experienced significant economic growth since the late 1960's, re-duced their demand for expensive imports, including petroleum. This led to a decline in the price of oil, which in turn threatened the economies of oil-producing nations. Russia was especially vulnerable, as it was attempting to make the transition to capitalism after stagnating under a government-owned, centrally planned economy for decades.

Individuals and businesses from the wealthy, Western countries suddenly became reluctant to invest in developing nations, even in those nations that had experienced major economic growth for a few decades. Political leaders and economists feared that what started as a currency issue in Asia could lead to a severe, global economic downturn. American investors lost a significant growth market and had to look elsewhere for investments that would balance potentially high returns with an acceptable level of risk.

The International Monetary Fund responded to the situation with an economic assistance package that provided approximately $120 billion in loans to the countries most affected by the crisis. The package was controversial, as it placed conditions on the loans that would be painful in the short term to their recipients. These conditions included privatization, deregulation, and reductions in government spending. Although the affected economies eventually came out of their recession, some experienced long-term decreases in their standards of living. Also, the tough conditions associated with the loans caused tensions between some recipient nations and the United States.

Kevin L. Brennan

FURTHER READING

Goldstein, Morris. *The Asian Financial Crisis: Causes, Cures, and Systemic Implications.* Washington, D.C.: Institute for International Economics, 1998.

Haggard, Stephan. *The Political Economy of the Asian Financial Crisis.* Washington, D.C.: Institute for International Economics, 2000.

Sharma, Shalendra D. *The Asian Financial Crisis: Crisis, Reform, and Recovery.* New York: Palgrave Macmillan, 2003.

SEE ALSO: Asian trade with the United States; Bretton Woods Agreement; Currency; Financial crisis of 2008; International economics and trade; Organization of Petroleum Exporting Countries; Petroleum industry.

Asian trade with the United States

SIGNIFICANCE: U.S. trade with Asia grew rapidly in volume, significance, and complexity in the last quarter of the twentieth century, affecting what the United States produced and what it imported. U.S. companies have been major players in exploration, production, and trade of Middle Eastern and Southwest Asian oil.

Free trade with foreign nations was one of the key principles of the Declaration of Independence in 1776. Merchants of the newly formed United States looked to Asia for business. China constituted a major opportunity, as many other Asian countries had become European colonies. Of the colonial powers, only the Netherlands agreed to sign a most-favored-nation treaty with the United States in 1782. This treaty also covered Dutch Southeast Asian possessions.

U.S. trade with China was especially lucrative. In 1789, Congress passed the first Tariff Act, levying a duty of 10 percent on imported chinaware, as porcelain was called. Average duties were only 8.5 percent, indicating that the young nation sought to maximize public revenue from the Asia trade.

After the War of 1812 ended, U.S. trade policy became more protectionist. High tariffs protected U.S. manufacturers. However, since key imports from Asia such as tea, silk, spices, and coffee were not produced domestically, trade in these items continued regardless of higher duties. Because of the United States' comparatively small manufacturing base, the value of U.S. goods sold in Asia remained low.

To protect the interests of American traders in Asia, the United States appointed consuls to Manila in the Philippines in 1817 and Batavia (later Jakarta, Indonesia) in 1818. In 1830, U.S. president Andrew Jackson concluded a treaty between the United States and the Ottoman Empire. In 1832, Congress ratified a commercial treaty with Muscat (later Sultanate of Oman) in Arabia.

More trade treaties with Asian nations followed. However, although the 1833 treaty with Siam (later Thailand) and the 1850 treaty with Brunei were fair, the 1844 treaty with China was unfair. Like the treaty imposed on Japan in 1854, the unfair treaties set low duties for U.S. exports to China and Japan and imposed high duties on goods exported from these countries to the United States. The United States made duty exemptions only for desired Asian materials such as silk and agricultural products such as tea.

AFTER THE U.S. CIVIL WAR

The American Civil War severely limited Asian trade, but it recovered quickly. China remained the United States' main trading partner. Trade with China reflected the typical pattern of nineteenth century U.S.-Asian trade. Asian countries tended to export more to the United States than they imported from American manufacturers.

Despite India's status as a British colony, limiting American access to its markets, India was an important trading partner for U.S. merchants. India's tea was an especially desired commodity. In 1868, imports from India to the United States were worth $6.4 million. This was ten times the value of U.S. exports to India. However, in spite of the importance of Asian materials such as silk and cotton for the United States' manufacturing industry, U.S. trade with Asia remained a niche market. It accounted for less than 3 percent of all U.S. trade in the post-Civil War period.

U.S. business was deeply aware that European colonialism hampered American access to Asian markets. In 1899, the $6.5 million of U.S. exports to India and the $32.7 million of Indian imports to the United States were worth just 8 percent of India's trade with Great Britain. In that year, to avoid the creation of a colonial stranglehold over China, the United States proclaimed the start of the Open Door Policy in China, demanding equal trade access for all foreign nations. Free trade in China served U.S. business interests well. Unlike the situation in India, in 1899, the $60 million in trade between the United States and China was rather close to the $74 million in trade between Great Britain and China.

Until 1913, the United States protected its developing industries through high tariff barriers on manufactured goods and commodities. Thus, U.S. companies sold locomotives in Siberia and to the Ottoman Empire, while raw materials and noncompetitive goods from Asia enjoyed lower import duties. To gain the favor of the Philippines, which the United States had taken from Spain in 1898, Philippine sugar entered the United States duty-free, beginning in 1909. This did no harm to businesses in continental America as no sugar was produced there.

BETWEEN THE WORLD WARS

American businesses vigorously expanded trade with Asia in the period between the world wars from 1918 to 1941. Trade was aided by lower U.S. tariffs. Discovery of oil in the Middle East and Southwest Asia aroused the interest of American oil companies. They obtained stakes in the consortiums that were given concessions by local governments. In 1925, American oil companies participated in oil discovery in Iraq.

U.S.-Asian trade flourished. American companies gained from growing Asian markets, especially China, Japan, and India. By 1929, U.S. exports to Asia were worth $643 million and accounted for 12.3 percent of U.S. exports. By March, 1930, the United States had granted most-favored-nation status to China, Persia (later Iran), and Turkey.

The Great Depression severely shrank trade, and many countries erected trade barriers. American exports to Asia shrank by 40 percent, to $386 million in 1931. This decline was not as sharp as elsewhere, so Asia's share of American exports increased to 16 percent. By 1932, the $292 million of U.S. exports to Asia made up 18 percent of U.S. exports. Asian trade helped U.S. manufacturers in the deepest troughs of the Great Depression.

In 1933, the United States shifted its policy to free trade. That same year, American oil companies founded the California-Arabian Standard Oil Company in Saudi Arabia, which struck oil in 1938. The 1939 trade agreement with Turkey was the first one with a Middle Eastern country concluded under the new American Reciprocal Trade Agreements Program, which sought to revive world trade.

The United States responded to Japanese aggression in China and other Asian countries with an oil embargo to Japan after July, 1941. It was only a few months before the Japanese attack on Pearl Harbor effectively ended peacetime U.S. trade with Asia. Trade did not resume until the Japanese surrender, announced on August 15, 1945.

POSTWAR U.S. MARKETS

At the end of World War II, the United States decided to promote the integration of the economies of the free world, including those of Asian nations, through free trade. The United States opened its domestic market on an unprecedented scale. Asian nations quickly availed themselves of this opportunity for their exports, primarily of commodities.

A major blow to U.S. business in Asia occurred when Chinese communists won control of the country in 1949. U.S. trade with mainland China ceased to exist from 1951 to 1972. On the other hand, because of U.S. support, Japan gained admission to the free world's trade zone in 1955.

With its economy booming, the United States could afford generosity toward Asian companies accessing the huge American market. The first pressures appeared when the American textile industry suffered from cheap Asian competition. However, during the Cold War, foreign policy concerns overrode domestic business concerns regarding cheap imports from Singapore, the Republic of China (Taiwan), Japan, and South Korea. During the Kennedy Round of the General Agreement on Tariffs and Trade (GATT) from 1964 to 1967, the United States was decidedly in support of free trade.

American oil companies enjoyed huge earnings from trade with the Middle East. In 1951, when Prime Minister Mohammad Mossadegh of Iran nationalized the British oil company that was exploiting Iran's oil fields, the United States supported the British. The boycott of national Iranian oil was very effective, and Mossadegh was toppled from power with covert U.S. help in 1953. Because of favorable royalty agreements with Southwest Asian and Arabian nations, U.S. oil companies earned massive profits until the Arab oil embargo of October, 1973.

When the Tokyo Round of the GATT opened in 1973, the American economy had lost some of its postwar vigor. Increased competition from East Asia as well as Japanese protectionism severely strained the U.S. steel, textile, and apparel industries. Taiwan, South Korea, and Japan enjoyed rapid economic growth because of free access to the U.S. market. The United States also absorbed goods from developing Asian countries such as Malaysia, Indonesia, Sri Lanka, India, and Pakistan. For political reasons during the Cold War, American business had to bear the burden of an open market while encountering trade barriers in Asia.

By the 1980's, the U.S. trade balance had become decisively negative. Oil prices jumped in 1973 and 1979, and while American companies trading in Middle Eastern and Southwest Asian oil made profits, higher energy costs led to a global recession. To achieve a favorable balance of payments, East and Southeast Asian nations such as Japan, South Korea, Taiwan, Malaysia, and Indonesia flooded the American market with goods. U.S. businesses complained about dumping. Under the administrations of U.S. presidents Ronald Reagan and George H. W. Bush from 1981 to 1993, the antidumping clauses of the 1979 Trade Agreement Act were more strictly enforced. American businesses won 58 percent of the seventy-eight cases they brought against Japanese manufacturers, 66 percent of the thirty-eight cases against Chinese companies, and 54 percent and 44 percent, respectively, of the forty-one cases filed against South Korean and Taiwanese producers.

During the 1990's, American businesses' fears of being overtaken by Japanese companies faded with the burst of the Japanese bubble economy. The Asian financial crisis of 1997 underscored the vulnerability of the East and Southeast Asian economies. A long, acrimonious human rights and business dispute between the United States and the People's Republic of China was solved with the signing of the Agreement on Market Access of November 15, 1999. This enabled the People's Republic of China to join the World Trade Organization in 2001.

EARLY TWENTY-FIRST CENTURY

In 2006, the People's Republic of China surpassed Mexico as the United States' number two trading partner. By mid-2008, China accounted for 11.2 percent of all U.S. trade, behind Canada's 17.9 percent share but ahead of Mexico's 10.7 percent share. U.S. trade with Japan decreased to 6.2 percent in mid-2008, assuaging American fears of Japanese economic domination. Three more Asian nations were among the top fifteen U.S. trading partners. South Korea held a share of 2.5 percent and was ranked seventh, followed by Saudi Arabia with 2 percent and a rank of ninth, and Taiwan with 1.9 percent and a rank of eleventh.

From its modest beginnings during the nineteenth century as a niche market, Asia grew enormously in importance as a trading partner for the United States. Indicative of the shift from Asian countries as providers of raw materials and commodities to exporters of the latest in consumer electronics was Malaysia. Although Malaysia had formerly been known for its exports of rubber and palm oil, the greater part of its $32 billion exports to the United States in 2007 consisted of consumer electronics and electrical appliances. This was also true for other Asian nations. Japan and South Korea were major car exporters to the United States.

The United States had a negative trade balance with most countries in the world by 2008, and Asia was no exception. Indeed, beginning in the eighteenth century, the United States tended to import more goods from Asia than it exported to Asia. However, as Asian countries began to employ protectionism for their developing industries, much as the United States had done in the nineteenth century, critics worried that the United States might not be able to pay for its Asian imports without drastically devaluing its currency. At the same time, America's oil trade with the Middle East became

TOP TRADING PARTNERS OF THE UNITED STATES, TOTAL TRADE IN GOODS, 2007

Rank	Country	Exports ($ billions)	Imports ($ billions)	Total Trade (%)
1	Canada	248.9	313.1	18.0
2	China	65.2	321.5	12.4
3	Mexico	136.5	210.8	11.1
4	Japan	62.7	145.5	6.7
5	Germany	49.7	94.4	4.6
6	United Kingdom	50.3	56.9	3.4
7	South Korea	34.7	47.6	2.6
8	France	27.4	41.6	2.2
9	Taiwan	26.4	38.3	2.1
10	Netherlands	33.0	18.4	1.6
11	Brazil	24.6	25.6	1.6
12	Venezuela	10.2	39.9	1.6
13	Italy	14.1	35.0	1.6
14	Saudi Arabia	10.4	35.6	1.5
15	Singapore	26.3	18.4	1.4

Source: Data from Foreign Trade Statistics, U.S. Census Bureau
Note: Trade figures are from the U.S. perspective.

characterized by extreme volatility and political risks.

R. C. Lutz

FURTHER READING

Bailey, Jonathan. *Great Power Strategy in Asia: Empire, Culture, and Trade, 1905-2005.* New York: Routledge, 2007. In the context of American-Japanese rivalry, this work covers U.S. trade with East Asia, especially Japan and China. It also analyzes trade's importance for the postwar U.S.-Japanese relationship and the outlook for U.S. trade with China.

Dudden, Arthur Power, ed. *American Empire in the Pacific: From Trade to Strategic Balance, 1700-1922.* Burlington, Vt.: Ashgate Variorum, 2004. Individual essays focus on early U.S.-China trade, the reasons for U.S. trade interests in Asia, and the connection between trade and U.S. foreign policy in Asia. U.S. colonial trade in the Philippines and U.S. trade with Japan are covered in detail.

Eckes, Alfred E., Jr. *Opening America's Market: U.S. Foreign Trade Policy Since 1776.* Chapel Hill: University of North Carolina Press, 1995. Excellent overview of U.S. trade policy that makes reference to U.S.-Asian trade and puts it into perspective. The author was a member of the U.S. International Trade Commission from 1981 to 1990. The work shows how postwar Japan successfully copied nineteenth century U.S. protectionism.

Kalicki, Jan H., and Eugene K. Lawson, eds. *Russian-Eurasian Renaissance? U.S. Trade and Investment in Russia and Eurasia.* Washington, D.C.: Woodrow Wilson Center Press, 2003. This useful overview of U.S. trade with the Central Asian republics that were part of the Soviet Union until 1991 focuses on the investment climate, the economic drivers, specific industries and their potential in the new republics, and the problems affecting U.S. trade there.

Oren, Michael. *Power, Faith, and Fantasy: America in the Middle East, 1776 to the Present.* New York: W. W. Norton, 2007. Comprehensive look at American interests in Southwest Asia, with good coverage of trade issues, particularly regarding oil. Chronology includes milestones in U.S.-Middle East trade history.

Strobridge, William, and Anita Hibler. *Elephants for Mr. Lincoln.* Lanham, Md.: Scarecrow Press, 2006.

A close look at U.S. trade with Southeast Asia from its beginning to the post-Civil War era. The title refers to the Thai king's proposal to aid the Union war effort with a gift of war elephants. The work focuses on the actual experiences of early American traders in Southeast Asia and the damage wrought by Confederate raiders in local waters targeting Union shipping. Readable and informative.

SEE ALSO: Asian financial crisis of 1997; Automotive industry; Chinese trade with the United States; General Agreement on Tariffs and Trade; Immigration; Korean War; Nixon's China visit; Rice industry; Spanish-American War; Taiwanese trade with the United States; Tariffs.

Astor, John Jacob

IDENTIFICATION: First American multimillionaire

BORN: July 17, 1763; Waldorf, near Heidelberg, Baden (now in Germany)

DIED: March 29, 1848; New York, New York

SIGNIFICANCE: Astor's commercial success anticipated the rags-to-riches stories popularized by nineteenth century novelists. His first American job was selling baked goods in the streets. By 1820, he was considered the wealthiest man in America.

One of eleven children of a butcher, Johann Jakob Astor was educated until age fourteen. He later joined an older brother in London, where he sold musical instruments, learned English, and changed his name to John Jacob. In 1783, the twenty-year-old Astor set sail for New York. After selling baked goods, he worked for a fur merchant before branching out on his own. In 1785, he married Sarah Todd, the daughter of his poor but well-connected New York landlady.

Astor's success was influenced by his character and his marriage. He was frugal, hardworking, eager and quick to learn, fearless, and single-mindedly determined to gain financial success. His wife brought a dowry and, through her family, important contacts. In 1786, he advertised musical instruments and supplies at his lodging, later buying fur there. Until he could afford to hire agents to act for him, Astor went on buying trips into the wilderness.

John Jacob Astor. (Hulton Archive/Getty Images)

His wife ran his store during these absences, despite her pregnancies.

In 1808, Astor founded the American Fur Company, which was probably the first holding company, forming its first subsidiary, the Pacific Fur Company, in 1810. By 1836, he controlled the American fur trade east of the Mississippi. To achieve greater profits, he also traded with China, sending ships to purchase furs on the Pacific coast, shipping the furs to China, buying Chinese goods—especially tea, which was popular in America—and, in New York, loading the ships with goods to purchase more Pacific furs. Astor created many trading posts, envisioning an overland trading route between the two coasts. His long-range plan demanded a permanent post at Fort Astor, later Astoria, on the Columbia River. He sent two expeditions to found this post, one by land and one by sea. Both ended disastrously. Noted writer Washington Irving described these catastrophes in *Astoria* (1836).

By the 1830's, American demand for furs and Chinese tea was decreasing, and the development of railways and paddlewheel steamers pointed to major changes in commercial distribution. Astor began dismantling his trade empire in 1834. As early as 1789, he had begun investing in real estate, primarily in Manhattan. By 1830, real estate investment was his most profitable business activity, although, by that time, his affairs were largely in the hands of his son, William Backhouse Astor. In 1834, however, he built Astor House, New York's first luxury hotel. At the time of his death in 1848, the worth of Astor's estate was estimated at between $20 million and $30 million.

Betty Richardson

FURTHER READING
Madsen, Axel. *John Jacob Astor: America's First Multimillionaire.* New York: John Wiley & Sons, 2001.
Smith, Arthur D. Howden. *John Jacob Astor: Landlord of New York.* 1929. Reprint. New York: Cosimo, 2005.
Wilson, Derek. *The Astors, 1763-1992: Landscape with Millionaires.* New York: St. Martin's Press, 1993.

SEE ALSO: Carnegie, Andrew; Chinese trade with the United States; Fur trapping and trading; Gates, Bill; Rockefeller, John D.

Automation in factories

DEFINITION: The substitution of machine power for human effort and attention

SIGNIFICANCE: Factory automation has allowed companies to leverage their workers' labor to increase productivity many thousandfold and to produce goods that could not be produced by traditional craft methods.

The automation of factories began with the application of mechanical power to replace human and animal muscular effort, particularly in heavy industry. Such devices as windmills and watermills can be traced back to classical antiquity, but they truly began to come of age during the late eighteenth century with the development of the steam engine.

The mercantilist policies of the British crown prevented the American colonies from developing their own industry, but after the Revolutionary War, northern business leaders began to develop their own textile and other industries, helped by protectionist tariffs that made it difficult for the cheap goods of industrialized Britain to compete. Soon cities such as Lowell, Massachusetts, and Pittsburgh, Pennsylvania, were dark with the smoke generated by the thousands of power-driven textile and steel mills.

The development of machine tools for the forming and shaping of various components in large numbers led to various mechanical controls that permitted manufacturers to reach far finer tolerances in their parts than had been possible by depending on human senses. Throughout the nineteenth century and the first part of the twentieth, industry continually improved on these control systems, at first with mechanical controllers and later with electromechanical ones.

ENTER THE DIGITAL AGE

The development of the computer meant that even more sophisticated automated controls could be applied to industrial processes, particularly in fields such as aeronautics and astronautics in which high-value parts had to be made to extremely close tolerances. Human eyes and hands simply did not have the precision to guide the machines that closely, and many companies were routinely failing ninety-nine out of a hundred parts. By using computers to control the milling machines, companies were able to reverse those ratios, failing only 1 percent of the parts they produced.

The next major development was the construction of the robotic arm, which could move in three dimensions to perform complex tasks. By the 1960's, computer control had reached the point at which such robotic arms could be produced not just as experimental devices but as productive equipment.

The first tasks to be automated by industrial robots were both dangerous and repetitive. The danger involved in these tasks meant that costly safety precautions had to be taken to protect workers. For instance, the task of spray painting automobiles in-

Assembly line robots weld the cab of Chrysler's 2009 Dodge Ram pickup at the Warren Truck Plant in Warren, Michigan. (AP/Wide World Photos)

volved enormous amounts of electricity to run the ventilation fans that brought fresh air to the workers and the purchase and maintenance of breathing apparatuses for workers who had to operate in spaces that could not be ventilated. If a company could replace the human spray-gun operators with robots, supervised by a single human operator in a ventilated booth overlooking the factory floor, the cost of the robots could quickly be recouped from what the company would save in reduced electricity bills, safety equipment costs, and workers' wages.

Auto-body welding was another area of heavy industry that was automated with robot arms at a very early stage. Welding exposes a human welder to heat, high-current electricity, ultraviolet radiation, and fragments of hot metal showering off the electrode. Furthermore, it is very difficult to make all the welds in every auto body correctly, which can make the vehicle less sturdy and therefore not as safe in a crash. By contrast, an industrial robot can be programmed to make hundreds of welds one after another, all perfectly positioned, and never tire or become bored.

ROBOTS

The earliest industrial robots tended to work in isolation. Each was designed for its specific task, with little thought of how it could fit into a larger system. In 1978, General Motors introduced the Programmable Universal Machine for Assembly (PUMA), an integrated system of conveyor belts, parts feeders, and small robots that could work in the same space as human employees. The PUMA could perform repetitive tasks, and human employees could do the tasks that required more complex judgment.

The development of the microprocessor had major implications for industrial robotics. Putting the entire circuitry of a computer's central processing unit on a single piece of silicon meant that robots no longer depended on a giant mainframe in a distant computer room but could be controlled locally. In addition, microprocessors could be produced in large numbers very cheaply. As a result of Moore's Law (microprocessor circuitry doubles in complexity every eighteen months, and the price of an existing microprocessor drops by half during that same period), it became inexpensive to get older versions of popular microprocessors in large numbers to run basic industrial robots.

As a result, it became economically feasible to automate a range of repetitive assembling jobs that had not been sufficiently dangerous to make the savings in safety measures and equipment pay for the robots. Many of these tasks were generally boring enough that human workers had a tendency to let their attention wander while working, resulting in incorrectly assembled parts and lost money in the long term. Because robots were not subject to boredom, it was often easier to automate the process than to implement measures to keep human workers' minds focused on the task.

Leigh Husband Kimmel

FURTHER READING

Colestock, Harry. *Industrial Robotics: Selection, Design, and Maintenance.* New York: McGraw-Hill, 2005. Practical information on robot designs commonly used in industry.

Espejo, Roman, ed. *What Is the Impact of Automation?* Detroit: Greenhaven, 2008. A collection of essays on automation that examine its effects on labor, particularly manufacturing jobs, and its application in farming, health care, and smart homes for the elderly.

Hodges, Bernard. *Industrial Robots.* Oxford, England: Newnes, 1992. Focuses on the development of the industrial robot, although it does note earlier automation efforts.

Ichiban, Daniel. *Robots: From Scence Fiction to Technological Revolution.* New York: Henry Abrams, 2005. General history of robotics from its literary roots to the factory floor.

Reid, T. R. *The Chip: How Two Americans Invented the Microchip and Launched a Revolution.* New York: Random House, 2001. A basic history of the development of the microchip, critical to the development of modern robotics.

SEE ALSO: Automotive industry; Computer industry; Ford, Henry; Ford Model T; Ford Motor Company; Gompers, Samuel; Industrial Revolution, American.

Automotive industry

DEFINITION: Enterprises that design, manufacture, distribute, and market motor vehicles

SIGNIFICANCE: Since the early twentieth century, thousands of businesses, large and small, have participated in the manufacture, marketing, and sale of motor vehicles, providing employment for millions of Americans and requiring huge capital investments.

Gasoline-powered vehicles were invented primarily by Europeans during the late nineteenth century, but they were improved and made into the center of a large-scale industry in the United States. Over the years, many domestic companies have tried to manufacture automobiles, but the vast majority failed to earn a profit. In 1900, there was only one car for every ninety-five hundred Americans; ten years later, the ratio was one car per two hundred; by 1930, the ratio had shrunk to one for every five Americans. The history of the industry has always involved numerous interrelated components, including innovations in technology, marketing strategies, and adaptations to changing needs and cultural values. American manufacturers—particularly General Motors (GM), the Ford Motor Company, and Chrysler Motors—maintained global dominance from the early twentieth century until the last two decades of the century, but thereafter Japanese and Korean products grew more successful, at Detroit's expense.

THE BEGINNING OF THE INDUSTRY

Many people in many different places were responsible for the invention of the automobile. Étienne Lenoir, a Belgian, made the first successful internal combustion engine in 1860, and twenty-five years later Carl Benz, a German engineer, was the first to build a usable vehicle powered by such an engine. In 1893, Charles E. and J. Frank Duryea built America's first successful automobile in Springfield, Connecticut, and two years later their vehicle prevailed in a car race against German-built competitors. The Duryea car averaged seven miles per hour in the fifty-five-mile race from Chicago to Evanston, Illinois. At this time, accidents and breakdowns were extremely common, and many people looked on motor vehicles as a passing fad.

During the 1890's, numerous entrepreneurs were competing in an attempt to develop a commercially profitable vehicle. In 1897, Colonel Albert A. Pope of Hartford, Connecticut, established the Pope Manufacturing Company, which is considered the true beginning of the U.S. automobile industry. That same year, Francis and Freeman Stanley began making steam automobiles in Newton, Massachusetts, and they built a few hundred Stanley Steamers before the advantages of the internal combustion engine become clear. The first truly successful company, the Olds Motor Works, founded by Random E. Olds in 1899, sold five thousand cars during its first five years of operations. The "Merry Oldsmobile" was dependable, affordable, and simple to operate. Olds was the first to apply the assembly-line principle to the automobile and the first to build a factory specifically designed to manufacture automobiles.

In 1902, Henry M. Leland founded the Cadillac Automobile Company, which was named after the founder of Detroit. In 1903, David Dunbar Buick founded the Buick Motor Company. That same year Henry Ford, an engineer who had failed in two earlier business ventures, established the Ford Motor Company, which for its first three years simply assembled parts supplied by other companies. Although Thomas Alva Edison encouraged Ford to persevere, Edison disdained the noise and pollution of gasoline engines, investing his time and money in an unsuccessful attempt to build an electric car.

The majority of the earliest automobile manufacturers paid a royalty of about 1 percent to the Association of Licensed Motor Vehicles (ALAM), which existed only because George Selden had obtained a patent for making automobiles in 1895. Although Selden did not actually build an automobile until 1904, he obtained a patent based on a crude model that he had first submitted in 1877, after observing a two-cycle engine built by George Brayton. Henry Ford refused to pay royalties to ALAM, and after a long legal battle, a federal appellate court in 1911 ruled in Ford's favor, holding that Selden's patent applied only to automobiles using the obsolete Brayton engine. Publicity from the litigation helped enhance Ford's reputation as an opponent of unmerited gain at the public's expense.

AUTOMOBILES BECOME MAINSTREAM

During the first two decades of the twentieth century, Ford's company emerged as the leading American manufacturer of automobiles. In 1906, Ford successfully produced a popular vehicle, the Model N, which he priced at $500, significantly undercutting his competition. By 1908, Ford had sold twelve thousand Model Ns. His basic strategy was to design a car for a mass market and then search for the means to produce it as cheaply as possible. Based on his intuition and a long heritage of American manufacturing, he emphasized five principles of production: standardization of product, interchangeability of parts, efficient mechanization, continuous flow production, and the minimal use of skilled labor.

In 1908, Ford introduced his famous Model T, also known as the Tin Lizzie, and he sold ten thousand of the model in the first year. After opening a large Highland Park plant in 1911, Ford controlled 20 percent of the business within a year. In 1913, he introduced the moving assembly line, in which individual workers stayed in one place and performed only one or two simple operations, as the automobiles rolled by them. The resulting efficiency allowed Ford to further reduce prices, quickly propelling the Model T to represent 40 percent of the U.S. market. In 1914, Ford decided to reward workers by paying them $5 per day, which was more than twice the average industrial wage. Continuing to improve his product, Ford was the first manufacturer to use vanadium steel and regional assembly plants.

With the need for military vehicles and trucks during World War I, annual investments in new plants grew from $600 million in 1914 to $2.5 billion in 1918. Detroit was the fastest growing city in the country, going from a population of 465,000 in 1910 to 994,000 in 1920. The prosperity of the 1920's was a boon to the industry, as was the Federal Highway Act of 1921, which provided states with matching funds for highway construction. During the decade, production soared from 1.1 million units in 1920 to 5.3 million in 1929. President Warren G. Harding observed that "the motorcar has become an indispensable instrument of our political, social, and industrial life."

For many years, Ford's River Rouge Complex, which was constructed between 1917 and 1928, was the largest integrated factory in the world. By 1921, the Model T controlled over 55 percent of the U.S. market. Ford continually improved mechanization to employ fewer skilled workers, and by 1914, three-fourths of the company's workforce was unskilled. Many were immigrants, and it was said that they needed only to understand one command, "hurry

up." Most of the savings from mechanization were passed on to the consumer. The price of the Model T, which was $690 in 1911, dropped to only $265 in 1927, the last year of its production. By then, more than 15 million Model T's had been sold.

During the 1920's, General Motors (GM) began to challenge Ford's dominance of the automobile industry. In 1908, William Crapo Durant, a flamboyant businessman, had founded GM as a holding company for Buick, and he then added Oldsmobile, Cadillac, and Pontiac. After Durant lost control of GM to a banking trust in 1910, he and race car driver Louis Chevrolet founded the Chevrolet Company. By 1916, Durant had earned enough money to purchase a controlling interest of GM, and he retook control of the company through a dramatic proxy war. In 1919, Durant successfully established the innovative finance division, General Motors Acceptance Corporation (GMAC), but he made the bad mistake of overexpanding during an economic downturn. Pierre Du Pont and other investors forced Durant to leave GM in 1920, and they replaced him with the more practical Alfred Sloan, who served as president from 1923 to 1946 and as chairman of the board from 1937 to 1956.

Credited with coining the term "professional manager," Sloan emphasized order, careful research, and joint decisions based on the bottom line. In organizing GM's autonomous divisions, his goal was "decentralized operations with coordinated control." In contrast to Henry Ford's pragmatic view of the automobile as simply a means of transportation, Sloan recognized that an automobile was a personal statement of aspiration and status. Appreciating the differences in consumers, he used the motto "a car for every purse and purpose." Under Sloan's leadership, GM's sales grew from $304 million in 1921 to $1.5 billion in 1929.

During the Great Depression of the 1930's, the production of automobiles plummeted from 5.5 million units in 1929 to only 1.5 million in 1932. Automobile ownership had already become so firmly entrenched in U.S. culture, though, that gasoline sales declined by only 4 percent. One of the consequences of the Depression was that it forced dozens of small manufacturers out of business. In 1929, the independents held about one-quarter of the market; by 1941, their share was only 10 percent. Passage of the National Labor Relations Act (also called the Wagner Act) in 1935, which established workers' right to collective bargaining, also had a great impact on the automobile industry. GM was persuaded to negotiate with the United Auto Workers (UAW) as a result of the Flint sit-down strike of 1936-1937. Despite Henry Ford's disdain for labor unions, a strike combined with government pressure finally coerced him to recognize the UAW in 1941.

AFTER WORLD WAR II

Although the U.S. government prohibited production of passenger automobiles during World War II, the industry earned large profits by producing 8.6 million military vehicles, 3.8 million tanks, 2.5 million trucks, and 660,000 jeeps. When production of passenger automobiles was resumed in 1945, there was a tremendous pent-up demand. In 1945, about 25 million vehicles were registered in the country, with more than half older than ten years. In the next five years, some 21 million vehicles were produced, thereby replacing most of the prewar fleet. The UAW effectively took advantage of its bargaining position by negotiating with a single company at a time. With limited competition from foreign imports, U.S. companies avoided costly strikes by agreeing to generous benefits—health care insurance, retirement pensions, and cost-of-living wage adjustments. Few people at the time recognized the extent to which fringe benefits would create onerous "legacy costs" when the number of workers would later plummet.

By the 1960's, a growing consumer movement was calling for governmental controls to force manufacturers to produce automobiles that were safer, consumed less energy, and emitted less pollution. Ralph Nader's influential book *Unsafe at Any Speed: The Designed-In Dangers of the American Automobile* (1965) helped promote this movement. In 1965, Congress first mandated emissions standards in the Vehicle Air Pollution and Control Act, which would be modified frequently in subsequent years. The National Traffic and Motor Vehicle Safety Act of 1966 mandated a number of improvements for passenger safety. In 1975, moreover, Congress passed the Energy Policy and Conservation Act, which attempted to double the fuel efficiency of new cars by 1985 by mandating the Corporate Average Fuel Economy standards (CAFE) for passenger cars.

Until the 1970's, American manufacturers increasingly built vehicles that were larger and more powerful. During the 1960's, a small number of Americans were purchasing small and relatively inexpensive Volkswagens, and during the 1970's, manufacturers became alarmed about the growing popularity of Japanese imports. Detroit was unprepared for the explosion of oil prices in 1973 and 1979, which increased demand for small, energy-efficient cars. Factories closed, and some 300,000 workers were laid off. After the downturn almost forced Chrysler Corporation into bankruptcy, Congress in 1979 reluctantly passed legislation guaranteeing Chrysler with a loan of $1.5 billion. By trimming costs, closing old plants, and adding a number of popular models, Chrysler managed to make profits and begin paying off the loan by the mid-1980's.

With growing automation and the continuing challenge of foreign competition, the number of U.S. autoworkers continued to decline. In 1978, 2.4 million Americans were employed in the industry; four years later, the number dropped to 1.8 million; by 2002, the number had dropped to 1.16 million; and by 2007, there were only 860,000. The share of the market held by the Big Three companies declined from 70 percent in 1998 to 49.4 percent in

NEW MOTOR VEHICLE SALES AND LEASES, 1970-2005, IN THOUSANDS

	Cars		Trucks	
Year	Domestic	Imported	Domestic	Imported
1970	7,119	1,280	1,746	65
1975	7,053	1,571	2,249	229
1980	6,209	2,327	1,809	451
1985	8,205	2,838	3,902	780
1990	6,897	2,403	3,957	603
1995	7,128	1,506	5,691	391
2000	6,833	2,019	7,651	841
2005	5,480	2,187	8,065	1,216

Sources: Data from the *Statistical Abstract of the United States, 2000* and the *Statistical Abstract of the United States, 2008* (Washington, D.C.: Department of Commerce, Economics and Statistics Administration, Bureau of the Census, Data User Services Division, 2000, 2008)

2007. With their huge losses, financial analysts warned that one or more of the companies could be forced into bankruptcy. The crisis of the Big Three was due to a combination of factors, including a general decline in demand, legacy costs not faced by competitors, the public's view that foreign automobiles were of better quality, and rising gasoline prices that caused consumers to prefer smaller vehicles. Toyota had become the largest producer of automobiles in the world. The number of Japanese imports, however, had actually declined since the 1990's, for by 2007 almost two out of every three Japanese nameplates sold in the United States was domestically made. Another trend was the movement of factories to the South, where labor costs were lower. Whereas the South was home to only 7 percent of automobile workers in 1972, it was home to 17 percent thirty years later.

In 2008, with rising gasoline prices that made sport-utility vehicles (SUVs) and trucks less popular and a credit crisis in the fall, the Big Three (and the Japanese automakers as well, although to a lesser extent) saw their sales and profits drop. In October, the Big Three automakers appealed to the federal government for financial aid, as Chrysler and General Motors faced possible bankruptcies. On December 19, President George W. Bush announced that $13.4 billion in emergency loans would be made available to keep Chrysler and General Motors afloat, with an additional $4 billion to be available in February. However, the automakers were given the loans on condition that they make major concessions and organizational changes by March 31, 2009, to demonstrate that they could return to profitability. Ford, which was in a better financial state, was not expected to make use of the federal loans. On February 18, 2009, General Motors and Chrysler asked for an additional $14 billion in aid, while presenting restructuring plans designed to return their companies to profitability.

Thomas Tandy Lewis

FURTHER READING

Halberstam, David. *The Reckoning.* New York: Morrow, 1986. A well-written account of how and why the automobile industry experienced relative decline as it struggled to meet the challenge of Japanese competition.

Maynard, Micheline. *The End of Detroit: How the Big Three Lost Their Grip on the American Car Market.* New York: Doubleday, 2004. Argues that the Big Three's decline since the 1990's was primarily due to the failure to provide quality and fuel efficiency at reasonable cost.

Pelfrey, William. *Billy, Alfred, and General Motors: The Story of Two Unique Men, a Legendary Company, and a Remarkable Time in American History.* New York: AMACOM, 2006. Compelling and scholarly account of how William Crapo Durant founded the company and how Alfred P. Sloan developed it into one of the most successful enterprises in U.S. history.

Rae, John R. *The American Automobile Industry.* Boston: Twayne, 1984. A succinct general history with many fascinating anecdotes, providing an excellent introduction to the topic.

Shimokawa, Koichi. *The Japanese Automobile Industry: A Business History.* London: Athlone Press, 1994. A relatively brief account of the dramatic growth of the Japanese industry after World War II.

Watts, Steven. *People's Tycoon: Henry Ford and the American Century.* New York: Knopf, 2006. Puts forward the thesis that Ford's great success was shaped by the emergence of consumer capitalism, bureaucracy, mass culture, and the corporate state.

SEE ALSO: American Automobile Association; Arab oil embargo of 1973; Chrysler bailout of 1979; Drive-through businesses; Ford, Henry; Ford Model T; Ford Motor Company; General Motors; Iacocca, Lee; Rubber industry.

B

Bank failures

DEFINITION: Closure of financial institutions resulting from their inability to pay their depositors and other creditors

SIGNIFICANCE: Before the 1940's, bank failures were a major contributor to business depressions, depriving depositors of their money and reducing the availability of loans. Since then, insurance provided by the FDIC has helped minimize the effects of failures on the overall U.S. economy.

The U.S. banking system has long been characterized by a large number of relatively small banks, mostly operating on a local basis only. Such small institutions are often unable to diversify their assets, and they are thus at risk for insolvency. Further, banks have often faced liquidity problems—that is, they have found it difficult to maintain enough cash on hand to meet depositors' demands. After 1933, the operations of the Federal Reserve and the Federal Deposit Insurance Corporation (FDIC) greatly reduced both the solvency and the liquidity problems of American banks.

THE EIGHTEENTH AND NINETEENTH CENTURIES

After the United States achieved independence, banks were organized in major cities, mostly chartered by state governments. They received little government supervision. The banks financed their loans by issuing banknotes, which circulated as money. Fraudulent operators could print such notes, "lend" them to themselves, spend them a long way from home, and then disappear before the notes were presented for payment. The Farmers Exchange Bank of Gloucester, Rhode Island, for example, failed in 1809 with $800,000 in note liabilities and $86 in cash assets.

The first (1792-1812) and second (1816-1841) federally chartered Banks of the United States held the nation's other banks accountable, constantly returning their notes for payment. The Second Bank aroused the ire of President Andrew Jackson and lost its federal charter. It became heavily involved in loans intended to raise the export price of cotton during the 1830's, and it failed in 1841—the largest

bank failure to that date. The economy experienced a violent boom-and-bust after 1837, and about one-fourth of American banks failed between 1839 and 1842, reducing the money supply from $250 million during the mid-1830's to about $170 million in 1841-1842. Banks that were not insolvent often temporarily suspended the conversion of their liabilities into cash and continued to operate.

Although a number of states established effective bank supervision, thinly settled frontier areas remained vulnerable to "wildcat banking." Another boom-and-bust sequence occurred during the 1850's, but by 1860, there were more than 1,500 banks. During the Civil War, the National Banking Acts of 1863 and 1864 authorized federal chartering of "national" banks. A punitive tax on state institutions' banknotes persuaded most existing banks to join the national system. National banks could issue banknote currency, but only by pledging collateral of U.S. Treasury securities. Banknote holders were thus protected against loss.

Cash reserves were required for deposits, but banks outside the major cities could hold part of their reserves on deposit with a big-city bank, thus "pyramiding" reserves. The system was still vulnerable to panics involving deposits. One such panic in 1873 resulted from the failure of Philadelphia financier Jay Cooke's banking firm, which was heavily invested in new issues of railroad bonds that it could not sell.

THE EARLY TWENTIETH CENTURY

After another banking panic in 1907-1908, Congress in 1913 created the Federal Reserve system to furnish an "elastic currency"—Federal Reserve notes, which could expand in supply when members of the public insisted on cashing their bank deposits. National banks were required, and other banks were permitted, to become "member banks," holding reserves with the Federal Reserve and privileged to borrow from it. The expectation was that banks would borrow newly issued currency to meet panic demands from their depositors.

In 1900, the United States had about 12,000 banks, and that number was rising rapidly, reaching 30,000 in 1921—the all-time peak. Most of these were small banks in small communities. Federal Reserve estimates of bank suspensions averaged 130 per year between 1892 and 1900, despite 491 banks failing in the panic year of 1893. The estimate fell to 81 failures per year between 1901 and 1910 and 94 per year from 1911 to 1920. Then things changed. In 1921-1922, the economy experienced a sharp recession, which was followed by a sustained deflation of farm prices. The failure rate among small rural banks escalated as farm loans went into default. Between 1921 and 1929, a staggering 5,700 banks failed. These failing institutions held about $1.6 billion in deposits, but their depositors ultimately lost only about one-third of this total.

In mid-1929, the U.S. economy entered the worst economic downswing in its history, and bank failures were an important contributing factor. A major New York City bank, the Bank of the United States, failed in December, 1930, unleashing a nationwide run on the banking system. The bank had been heavily involved in stock and real estate speculation. By the time the panic ended in 1933, 9,000 banks holding deposits of $6.8 billion had suspended operations, and their depositors had lost $1.3 billion.

Most of the banks that failed in 1930-1931 had already been in shaky condition when the downswing began, but others were dragged down by deteriorating business conditions. The mass failures depleted the national money supply, which declined from $27 billion in 1929 to $20 billion in 1933. Bank lending declined to the same degree. These factors help explain why the Great Depression was so long and so severe.

AFTER 1933

On his inauguration in March, 1933, President Franklin D. Roosevelt declared a national bank holi-

Worried customers gather outside a New York City bank after it was closed in April, 1932. (National Archives)

day, closing all the banks and administering another deflationary shock. As the banks reopened, however, depositor confidence returned. The Banking Acts of 1933 and 1935 created a federal program of insurance of bank deposits, and virtually all banks joined. The newly created FDIC was given the power to regulate insured banks. From 1934, the number and impact of bank failures decreased to such an extent that their effects on the U.S. economy became inconsequential. In the recession of 1937-1938, 59 banks failed, and that was the highest number of failures in any year between 1934 and 1941.

Bank failures were not eliminated, for individual banks continued to take risks. One major failure, for example, involved the Franklin National Bank in 1974—then the nation's twentieth-largest bank. Other major episodes involved the Penn Square Bank (1982) and Continental Illinois (1984). After a flurry of failures during the early 1990's, the annual failure rate dropped into single digits from 1995 through 2007, except during 2002, when 12 banks failed.

THE 2008 FINANCIAL CRISIS

Involvement of banks in subprime mortgage lending led to a rise in bank failures in the 2007-2008 financial crisis, reaching a level not experienced since 1994. IndyMac, which failed in July, 2008, had roughly $1 billion in uninsured deposits held by 10,000 depositors. Washington Mutual (WaMu) failed in late September, 2008. With more than $300 million in reported assets, it was the largest bank failure in American history. JPMorgan Chase took over the bulk of WaMu's deposits and branches. However, the transaction wiped out WaMu's stockholders and most of its nondeposit creditors. In early October, Wachovia was rescued by absorption into Wells Fargo on terms that preserved value for all depositors.

The financial rescue legislation of October 3, 2008, the Emergency Economic Stabilization Act, reduced the likelihood of further bank failures by in-

---

TEN BIGGEST BANK FAILURES, 1937-2008

1. Washington Mutual, Seattle, 2008, $307.0 billion
2. Continental Illinois National Bank and Trust, Chicago, 1984, $40.0 billion
3. First Republic Bank, Dallas, 1988, $32.5 billion
4. IndyMac, Pasadena, California, 2008, $32.0 billion
5. American S&L Association, Stockton, California, 1988, $30.2 billion
6. Bank of New England, Boston, 1991, $21.7 billion
7. MCorp, Dallas, 1989, $18.5 billion
8. Gibraltar Savings, Simi Valley, California, 1989, $15.1 billion
9. First City Bancorporation, Houston, 1988, $13.0 billion
10. Homefed Bank, San Diego, 1992, $12.2 billion

Source: Data from Federal Deposit Insurance Corporation, October, 2008

---

creasing deposit insurance coverage from $100,000 to $250,000.

Paul B. Trescott

FURTHER READING

Hammond, Bray. *Banks and Politics in America from the Revolution to the Civil War.* Princeton, N.J.: Princeton University Press, 1957. Extensive coverage of scandals and controversies; good exposition of the rise and fall of the Second Bank of the United States.

Mishkin, Frederic S. *The Economics of Money, Banking, and Financial Markets.* 8th ed. New York: Pearson/Addison Wesley, 2006. This excellent undergraduate text deals with modern bank failures in chapter 11.

Wicker, Elmus. *Banking Panics of the Gilded Age.* New York: Cambridge University Press, 2000. A distinguished economic historian looks at the interaction between bank panics and economic fluctuations during the late nineteenth century.

_____. *The Banking Panics of the Great Depression.* New York: Cambridge University Press, 1996. Wicker's earlier work details the causes and effects of the Great Depression within the banking industry.

SEE ALSO: Bank of the United States, First; Bank of the United States, Second; Banking; Bankruptcy law; Currency; Federal Deposit Insurance Corporation; Federal Reserve; Financial crisis of 2008; Great Depression; Panic of 1857; Panic of 1873; Panic of 1907.

Bank of the United States, First

IDENTIFICATION: Federally chartered, quasi-private central bank

DATE: 1791-1811

SIGNIFICANCE: The First Bank of the United States helped stabilize the finances of, pay the debts of, and establish international credit for the fledgling nation's federal government. The debate over its existence shaped the course of constitutional law and led to the founding of the United States' first two political parties.

Independence from Great Britain brought the United States and its constituent states considerable debt. The amount of state and national debt increased under the Articles of Confederation. The lack of a stable national currency further undermined the new nation's international credibility. After the adoption of the Constitution, Congress in October, 1789, asked Secretary of the Treasury Alexander Hamilton to study the problem and create a report on the nation's credit. Hamilton's *Report on the Public Credit, January, 1790* advocated establishing the credit of the United States by assuming responsibility for the debts of the Articles of Confederation government, the debts incurred during the Revolutionary War, the foreign debt principally owed to France, and the debts of the states. The report recommended chartering a national bank that would be responsible for issuing a national currency and levying protective tariffs to raise revenue.

SECTIONAL AND POLITICAL CONTROVERSY

James Madison was opposed to Hamilton's plan because a large portion of the war debt was held by speculators in New York, Pennsylvania, and Maryland who stood to gain from the plan. Madison was opposed to wealth obtained by speculation but not to wealth acquired from slave labor. Hamilton reminded Madison that he had supported the April 26, 1783, resolution of the Continental Congress

pledging not to discriminate against those who obtained the government debt.

The southern slave-owning states of Maryland and Virginia had paid their war debts and were against helping South Carolina and the northern states that had not. The largest share of the state debt was owed by the northern states. Hamilton persuaded the southern states to accept the payment of state debts in exchange for the construction of the national capital along the Potomac River. Pennsylvania approved Hamilton's plan when it was offered the chance to house the temporary national capital in Philadelphia for a ten-year period.

The First Bank of the United States was chartered as a private institution in 1791, with a capital stock of $10 million. Some 20 percent of the stock was owned by the federal government, with the remainder sold to private citizens. The charter, modeled on that of the Bank of England, authorized the bank to serve as a source of deposit, to act as the fiscal agent of the government, to loan money to the government, and to establish a credible national currency. Before signing the Bank Act, President George Washington requested that both Hamilton and Secretary of State Thomas Jefferson submit opinions about the bank.

Jefferson wrote *On the Constitutionality of the Bank, February 5, 1791*, in which he argued that the bank was unconstitutional under the Tenth Amendment, because creating a national bank was not an enumerated power or a granted power of Congress. Jefferson became the national advocate of strict construction of the Constitution. Hamilton's response in *On the Constitutionality of the Bank, February 23, 1791* centered on the critical and urgent financial needs of the new nation. He argued that the government must have the power to undertake its duties. Using the doctrine of implied powers, Hamilton stated that powers not explicitly denied to the government under the Constitution permitted the bank's creation, establishing the broad constructionist position toward the Constitution. Hamilton's argument eventually persuaded President Washington to sign the bill that had passed in the Senate on January 20, 1791 and—with more heated debate—in the House of Representatives on February 8, 1791. The bill passed in the House by a vote of 39 to 20. In the House, there was only one northern vote against the bank's creation, while there were only three southern votes in favor.

POLITICAL PARTIES EMERGE

The difference of opinion between Hamilton and Jefferson on the bank led to the creation of the United States' first political parties. Hamilton's Federalist Party advocated acceptance of the First Bank of the United States along with a broad, less literal, interpretation of the Constitution. The Federalists supported the right of the national government to expand its authority, even at the expense of the states. Secretary Hamilton's position was further argued before Congress in his December, 1791, *Report on Manufactures*, which blamed the dire financial situation on the nation's dependence on agriculture. Hamilton urged the United States to expand its manufacturing and commerce sectors to generate revenue from national tariffs, subsidies, bounties, and premiums. Jefferson countered with the creation of the Democratic-Republican Party, supporting state's rights and a strict interpretation of the Constitution. Under this view, any power not specifically enumerated in the Constitution belonged to the states alone, and the federal government could not exercise it.

The first board of the First Bank of the United States had twenty-five members. Three were U.S. senators, four were members of the House of Representatives, one was a doctor, and the rest were lawyers, merchants, and brokers. The Federalist Party held the majority of seats, with 80 percent of the board's members hailing from the cities of New York, Boston, and Philadelphia. Thomas Willing, a Philadelphia merchant, was elected as the bank's first president on October 25, 1791. Branches were opened in Boston, New York City, Baltimore, and Charleston, South Carolina.

During Washington's second administration, the government sold its stock in the bank to pay debts without raising taxes. Later, President Jefferson was forced to modify his views about the Constitution and the bank. Jefferson's purchase of Louisiana would have been complicated without the existence of the First Bank of the United States to finance it. The bank stabilized the nation's credit at home and abroad, established the U.S. dollar as a convertible currency in specie, and led to the creation of the United States Mint. The First Bank of the United States' twenty-year charter expired in 1811. It was not renewed, because the Democratic-Republican majority in Congress remained opposed to it.

The First Bank of the United States was housed in Carpenter's Hall, Philadelphia, from 1791 to 1795. From 1795 until 1811, it occupied a classical revival-style structure at 120 Third Street, designed by architects Samuel Blodgett and James Windrim. The new building's architectural plan was inspired by Greek designs and was meant to connect the U.S. government with the democracy of ancient Greece. Atop the portico was an eagle, the first symbol of the United States. The cost of the building's construction was $110,168.

William A. Paquette

FURTHER READING

Chernow, Ron. *Alexander Hamilton.* New York: Penguin Press, 2004. Thorough and meticulously documented biography of the first major figure in American financial history. Offers new information about Hamilton's ancestry, his personality, and his relationships with other Founders.

Cowen, David Jack. *The Origins and Economic Impact of the First Bank of the United States, 1791-1797.* New York: Garland, 2000. Drawing on previously untapped evidence, this close study of the First Bank of the United States explores the bank's origins, its shifting policies, and its strong impact on the nascent national economy.

Ferguson, E. James. *The Power of the Purse: A History of American Public Finance, 1776-1790.* Durham: University of North Carolina Press, 1961. Study of American financial history that reveals how important Hamilton's measures were in saving the country from "currency finance" and creating an environment favoring economic growth and stability.

Gordon, John Steele. *Hamilton's Blessing: The Extraordinary Life and Times of Our National Debt.* New York: Walker, 1997. Study revealing the long history of American national debt and showing how it originated with Hamilton's ideas that a national debt could create a vital economy.

Moulton, R. K., comp. *Legislative and Documentary History of the Banks of the United States from the Time of Establishing the Bank of North America, 1781, to October, 1834.* 1834. Reprint. Clark, N.J.: Lawbook Exchange, 2008. Reprint of a valuable early nineteenth century collection of contemporary documents on the creation and operation of the two early national banks. Especially useful for its documentation of contemporary opinions about the banks.

Wright, Robert E., and David J. Cowen. *Financial Founding Fathers: The Men Who Made America Rich.* Chicago: University of Chicago Press, 2006. Illuminating study of the contributions to American financial history made by Hamilton and his successors, including Albert Gallatin, Stephen Girard, and Nicholas Biddle. A valuable study of early banking institutions that is suitable for both beginning and advanced students.

SEE ALSO: Articles of Confederation; Bank of the United States, Second; Banking; Constitution, U.S.; Currency; Federal Reserve; Monetary policy, federal; Supreme Court and banking law.

Bank of the United States, Second

IDENTIFICATION: Federally chartered, quasi-private national bank

DATE: January 1, 1817-1841

SIGNIFICANCE: The financial stability of the United States and its currency was compromised by the expiration of the charter of the First Bank of the United States in 1811 and by the expenses incurred by the War of 1812. The Second Bank of the United States was chartered to promote a common U.S. currency, repay loans, and reestablish the nation's international credit.

In 1811, Congress failed to recharter the First Bank of the United States, because the majority Democratic-Republican Party believed that its existence was unconstitutional. This decision left the nation without a unified currency. Local and state banks used paper currency that lost value during the financial strains of the War of 1812, because it was not backed by specie (gold or silver). American bankers and businessmen, as well as foreign shippers, refused to accept local currencies. Congress thus had little choice but to establish a new national bank to create a new national currency.

The bill authorizing the Second Bank of the United States was introduced by Senator John C. Calhoun of South Carolina and was approved with little opposition. The Second Bank was similar to Alexander Hamilton's First Bank: It was chartered for twenty years and authorized to serve as a source of deposit, act as the fiscal agent of the government, loan money to the government, and establish a credible national currency. Congress agreed to provide $7 million of the $35 million required as operating capital, and five of the twenty-five members of the bank's board would be appointed by the federal government. The bank's first president was William Jones, who was more a Democratic-Republican political loyalist than an economic talent. The new bank helped facilitate Henry Clay's expansionist scheme to develop the interior of the United States with a transportation network connecting the Great Lakes and the Ohio and Mississippi Rivers and a tariff system to encourage domestic manufacturing.

PANIC OF 1819

Jones established a policy of easy credit and allowed branches to open without sufficiently scrutinizing their banking practices. As a result, the bank extended too many loans to farmers to purchase equipment, seed, and other materials. The European continent was plagued at the time by wars and revolution, so American agricultural products were in demand. A return to political stability in Europe decreased the demand for American farm goods, however.

With reduced markets for their products, American farmers could no longer pay their debts. The Second Bank was authorized to regulate currency values and credit rates and to regulate state banks by accepting state currency only if it was sufficiently backed by specie. As a result, state and local bank loans could be recalled at the discretion of the Second Bank. Further credit to loan money was curtailed. Farms were repossessed, and factories closed. The Second Bank's regulatory actions contributed to the Panic of 1819, making the bank nationally unpopular.

MCCULLOCH V. MARYLAND

Jones resigned the bank's presidency in 1819 and was quickly replaced by Langdon Cheves. Cheves's leadership resolved the bank's liquidity problems and restored financial confidence within a year. The new president reduced the number of loan notes in circulation, regulated interest rates, and stabilized the nation's currency. However, reducing the dividend rate being paid to stockholders won Cheves opponents, who joined forces with state banks opposed to the Second Bank's requirement that loans be repaid in specie.

The states of Maryland, Tennessee, Georgia,

North Carolina, Kentucky, and Ohio passed legislation taxing branches of the Second Bank. Indiana and Illinois refused to permit branches to operate in their states. The conflict between state banks and the Second Bank of the United States culminated in the case of *McCulloch v. Maryland* (1819), which was appealed to the U.S. Supreme Court. At issue was whether Congress had the right to charter a bank and whether a state could tax a federal institution.

The Court, led by Chief Justice John Marshall, ruled in favor of the bank, arguing that the state's powers were outweighed by the sovereignty of the people of the United States acting through Congress to carry out the federal government's responsibilities. The Maryland law permitting the taxing of a federal institution was declared unconstitutional. In 1823, when Cheves stepped down as president, the Second Bank emerged as a strong financial institution, saving the national government over $1 million by transferring funds directly from the Treasury to the bank, securing funds for the federal government to borrow, maintaining specie payments at both the state and federal levels, and permitting easier credit and currency for the West and South.

BIDDLE VERSUS JACKSON

The appointment of Nicholas Biddle as bank president in 1823 continued to strengthen the nation's fiscal confidence. However, a controversy developed over the amount of specie backing the nation's paper currency. The controversy generated criticism of the bank from those who did not understand the institution's function; they were joined by state bankers who felt increasingly constrained by the bank's regulatory practices.

President Andrew Jackson made the bank an issue during his first term as president. For Jackson, the bank violated his interpretation of the proper spheres of action of the states and the federal government. He urged that the private business of the bank be taxed by the states. Jackson challenged the Supreme Court's verdict in *McCulloch v. Maryland*, believing the Second Bank to be unconstitutional. He sought to expand the scope of the Tenth Amendment, which reserves to the states or the people all powers not delegated to the central government. He believed it was wrong for a private banking institution to act as a central bank for the federal government and as a potential rival in financial policy to the president and the Congress.

President Jackson, in championing himself as the voice of the people, placed himself against the perceived moneyed interests of the East, represented by Biddle. Jackson warned Biddle not to renew the bank's charter early. Biddle listened instead to Jackson's political rival, Henry Clay, who persuaded Biddle to renew the charter in 1832 instead of 1836.

ANDREW JACKSON QUESTIONS THE BANK OF THE UNITED STATES' CONSTITUTIONALITY

In his first state of the union address, on December 8, 1829, President Andrew Jackson argued against the renewal of the Bank of the United States' charter on constitutional grounds. He asked Congress to pass laws establishing a more acceptable financial institution to function in place of that bank.

The charter of the Bank of the United States expires in 1836, and its stock holders will most probably apply for a renewal of their privileges. In order to avoid the evils resulting from precipitancy in a measure involving such important principles and such deep pecuniary interests, I feel that I can not, in justice to the parties interested, too soon present it to the deliberate consideration of the Legislature and the people. Both the constitutionality and the expediency of the law creating this bank are well questioned by a large portion of our fellow citizens, and it must be admitted by all that it has failed in the great end of establishing an uniform and sound currency.

Under these circumstances, if such an institution is deemed essential to the fiscal operations of the Government, I submit to the wisdom of the Legislature whether a national one, founded upon the credit of the Government and its revenues, might not be devised which would avoid all constitutional difficulties and at the same time secure all the advantages to the Government and country that were expected to result from the present bank. . . .

The charter renewal passed both houses of Congress by the summer of 1832, but Jackson vetoed it on July 10, 1832. Jackson's stubbornness and Biddle's arrogance led them to butt heads during the 1832 election campaign, making the constitutionality of the bank part of the national election debate.

Jackson won the election, bringing about the demise of the bank. Federal funds were not immediately withdrawn, but no new funds were deposited. Biddle raised interest rates excessively in 1834, undermining any chances of Congress revisiting the bank's charter. When the Second Bank's charter expired in 1836, the federal government's funds were withdrawn. The state of Pennsylvania granted the bank a charter, however, and it continued to do business until 1839, when it was forced to close because it had extended too many loans. The remaining resources of the Second Bank of the United States were liquidated in 1841. The government's failure to renew the charter of the Second Bank of the United States contributed to the Panic of 1837 and a six-year economic downturn in the U.S. economy.

William A. Paquette

FURTHER READING

Bodenhorn, Howard. *A History of Banking in Antebellum America: Financial Markets and Economic Development in an Era of Nation-Building.* New York: Cambridge University Press, 2000. Examination of American banking policies in the years leading up to the U.S. Civil War, with attention to the Bank of the United States.

Brown, Marion A. *The Second Bank of the United States and Ohio, 1803-1860: A Collision of Interests.* Lewiston, N.Y.: Edwin Mellen Press, 1998. Study of conflicts between the Second Bank of the United States and the state of Ohio.

Ellis, Richard E. *Andrew Jackson.* Washington, D.C.: CQ Press, 2003. Excellent biography of President Jackson that explores his life, career, policies, and legacy.

Govan, Thomas P. *Nicholas Biddle: Nationalist and Public Banker, 1786-1844.* Chicago: University of Chicago Press, 1959. Well-written biography that provides rich background information on the development of the Second Bank of the United States.

Kaplan, Edward S. *The Bank of the United States and the American Economy.* Westport, Conn.: Greenwood Press, 1999. Wide-ranging economic study of the role of the Bank of the United States in American economic history.

Sharp, James R. *The Jacksonians Versus the Banks: Politics in the States After the Panic of 1837.* New York: Columbia University Press, 1970. Examines the ruinous aftereffects of the demise of the national bank and the rise of untrustworthy state banks.

Timberlake, Richard H. *Monetary Policy in the United States: An Intellectual and Institutional History.* Chicago: University of Chicago Press, 1993. Broad history of American monetary policy. The third chapter, focusing on the Second Bank of the United States, regards the institution as a comparatively primitive central bank that was constrained by its commitment to the gold standard.

Watson, Harry L. *Liberty and Power: The Politics of Jacksonian America.* New York: Noonday Press, 1990. Analyzes the political forces that elevated the bank battle to become the primary issue in the 1832 presidential campaign.

SEE ALSO: Articles of Confederation; Bank of the United States, First; Banking; Constitution, U.S.; Currency; Federal Reserve; Monetary policy, federal; Panic of 1819; Panic of 1837; Presidency, U.S.; Supreme Court and banking law.

Banking

DEFINITION: Business of storing, transmitting, loaning, and exchanging funds

SIGNIFICANCE: The establishment and subsequent expansion of banking services in America contributed to the westward development of the country. It also led to the creation of major businesses. Availability of credit and savings products for individual consumers also gave rise to increased consumption of goods and services provided by American businesses.

Banks provide three services. They give their clients a way to store value for later use (in savings, checking, and other deposit accounts). They make future value available for present use (by offering loans), and they provide a way for individuals to exchange value with other people without being in direct contact with them.

EARLY BANKING

Few banks existed in the colonies. England exerted significant control over the colonists' financial affairs, and there was limited commerce within the colonies themselves. The general lack of banks and banking services meant that the exchange of goods and services was largely governed by bartering or the use of commodity money, including such goods as beaver pelts, tobacco, rice, and other commodities.

As America gained its independence and enjoyed increased manufacturing and business activity, particularly in the northern colonies, a more efficient method of exchange became necessary. More businesses and individuals, as well as trading partners in other countries, required cash rather than warehouse bills for payment. As a result, the nation's first three commercial banks were founded.

The first of these was the Bank of North America, chartered by the Congress of the Confederation in 1781. This bank was granted near monopoly power for banking services in the Confederation, although the wide distances between major population centers limited its effective reach to Philadelphia and the surrounding area. The bank issued paper currency that, according to its face, was convertible to gold or silver. The bank, however, was allowed to maintain a fractional reserve system, meaning that it was not required to back the issued notes on a one-to-one basis with gold or silver.

The Bank of North America was relatively short-lived. In a recurring situation, businesses and individuals in more outlying areas of the country found it difficult to convert paper money issued by the bank to spendable funds in their communities. (Consider the challenge of traveling from Charleston, South Carolina, to Philadelphia to convert these notes to gold.) They therefore demanded a premium price for goods when paid with banknotes. The resulting inflation increased the demand for conversion of these notes back to gold or silver. The fate of the bank was sealed when demand for conversion exceeded the bank's gold reserves, leading to its closure in 1784.

New York and Massachusetts chartered their own state banks in 1784—the Bank of Massachusetts, in Boston, and the Bank of New York (founded by Alexander Hamilton, future secretary of the Treasury). These banks had higher reserve requirements than the Bank of North America and, at least initially, confined their operations to New York and Boston. Both banks flourished for centuries. Bank of Boston was acquired by Bank of America in 2005, and Bank of New York merged with Mellon Financial in 2007.

In 1791, the First Bank of the United States became the first central bank to be chartered by Congress. The bank was to issue a paper currency that would be used to pay government obligations and would be accepted in payment of taxes, effectively giving paper money legal tender status for the first time. These notes were also convertible to gold or silver on presentment to the bank. The unanticipated consequence of this new currency was a flood of money into the economy, which in turn created substantial wholesale price inflation. Private bank charters also began to increase in response to the rising demand for banking services: Eighteen new private banks were chartered by 1796.

FROM 1800 TO THE CIVIL WAR

The charter of the First Bank of the United States was not renewed by Congress in 1811 as a result of changing political influences, especially between advocates of a central bank with fractional reserves and advocates of one on a pure gold standard with no fractional reserves. Banks once again began issuing their own notes. The continued expansion of the country and its economy encouraged the formation of even more new banks, so by the time the Second Bank of the United States was chartered in 1816, well over two hundred banks were in existence.

The Second Bank of the United States was also designed to establish a national currency that would be more stable than the multitude of notes issued by state banks. As had been true of the First Bank of the United States' currency, these notes would be accepted in payment of federal taxes and would be redeemable for gold or silver. The confidence in the new currency inspired by federal support resulted in another significant increase in the money supply, spurring higher demand for products and pushing prices higher.

In response to this situation in 1817, the bank systematically reduced credit availability, insisted that its branch banks redeem notes in gold, and refused to pay more than par for notes issued by the weaker of these branch banks. The net effect of this tightening was a large number of loan defaults, business bankruptcies, and bank failures. Real estate sales activity fell by more than 80 percent over a two-year period, and the country found itself the victim of the first real boom-bust cycle in American history. This experience also set the stage for the refusal of Congress to renew the charter of the Second Bank of the United States in 1832.

The operations of the Second Bank of the United States raised an important constitutional issue, which was adjudicated by the U.S. Supreme Court in the landmark case *McCulloch v. Maryland* (1819). Many states at the time did not support the idea of a national bank. Maryland levied a tax on all banks operating within its borders and not chartered by the state, including the local branch of the Second Bank of the United States. The federal bank refused to pay the state tax, and Maryland sued to compel payment. The Supreme Court determined that the chartering of a bank was a power implied by Article I, section 8, of the Constitution. Under the Constitution, states cannot impede federal laws, so Court ruled that the tax was unconstitutional. This ruling firmly established the doctrine of implied powers, broadening the scope of the federal government's constitutional authority and creating support for the expansion of federal power that followed.

During the 1820's and 1830's, the number of banks in the United States continued to grow, and they issued more private banknotes. At the same time, the silver reserves of these banks grew at a rapid pace as a result of increased importation of Mexican silver. The increased silver reserves encouraged ever more generous lending terms and increased speculation in land and other commodities. This situation came to a temporary halt in 1836, when President Andrew Jackson decreed that payments on government land contracts would no longer be accepted in paper currency but would have to be made in gold or silver. Together with fiscal tightening in Great Britain, this decree reduced inflation, but it also reduced business activity, pushing the country into another recession.

The nation's boom-bust cycles encouraged congressional leaders to consider a ban on fractional reserve banking as a way to bring stability to the economy. Instead, the government allowed banks to lend against their holdings of treasury notes and then began to accept these bank-issued notes (currency) in payment of federal taxes. These two actions helped legitimize the independent banknotes that Jackson had tried to limit, so by 1860 more than ten thousand different issues were in circulation.

The enormous variety of banknotes in circulation also made it difficult for banks and merchants to determine the value of any given note. The resulting uncertainty eventually led to a slowdown in U.S. business activity, as companies became increasingly reluctant to accept payment in notes issued by far-off banks whose soundness, reserve levels, and even existence could not be readily determined. These issues would slowly begin to fade during the U.S. Civil War, as that conflict brought about drastic changes in the country.

FROM THE CIVIL WAR TO WORLD WAR II

In 1861, Secretary of the Treasury Salmon P. Chase proposed national banking legislation that was enacted in 1863 as the National Currency Act. For the first time, legislation defined the requirements for national bank charters and established examination and performance standards. These regulations provided stability to the institutions and thus allowed chartered banks to issue currency that would itself have a more stable value. The law also established the Office of the Comptroller of the Currency, a government agency responsible for examining national banks and enforcing the regulations.

The National Currency Act created the first truly national currency. Although notes were issued by individual banks, they were entered on the books of the comptroller and stamped by the Treasury prior to issuance. Banks could issue notes only after they purchased sufficient U.S. Treasury securities from the government to stand behind those notes. Thus, the notes were effectively backed by the federal government. The added security of this backing reduced previous concerns about banknotes' negotiability and value, resulting in a stable currency. These notes functioned as the national currency until the issuance of Federal Reserve notes in 1914.

In an effort to reduce private banknote issues by state banks, the government began taxing those banks' notes. This tax had the immediate effect of reducing the number of state banks. However, it also encouraged the development of demand deposits, or checking accounts. Such accounts allowed the transfer of money between bank accounts without the use of paper notes or currency, thus avoiding the tax. The tax also created the dual banking system of state and federally chartered banks.

The new requirement that deposits be backed with Treasury securities created other problems. The value of these securities varied depending on prevailing market interest rates. When the value of Treasury notes fell as a result of rising interest rates, banks reduced loan availability to maintain proper reserve levels. Seasonal changes in liquidity resulting from shifts in farmers' demand for cash also plagued the banking system. These two issues combined in 1907 to create a serious panic within the banking industry.

A commission was appointed to find a solution to these problems; it recommended reestablishing a central bank. Six years later, the Federal Reserve Act, or Glass-Owen Act, of 1913 established the Federal Reserve and its twelve branches as the nation's central bank. The new institution would issue Federal Reserve notes, direct obligations of the federal government, to replace the old bank-issued notes that had existed since the founding of the country. Thus the familiar national currency came into existence.

The Federal Reserve Act ushered in a period of relative calm in U.S. financial markets despite the disruptions brought on by World War I. Banks lent more money, providing a relatively easy and stable source of funds to support increased wartime production. After the war, production continued to expand to meet demand for goods. Credit remained readily available, allowing the U.S. economy to grow and consumer consumption to increase. Economic growth and the availability of money also encouraged speculation in the stock market.

New stocks were issued to help finance the expansion of American business, and they were easily marketed to investors. At the time, the banks in New York not only held deposits and provided loans but also acted as the chief underwriters, buyers, and sellers of stocks. As a result, the same banks that created newly public companies' stocks also provided loans to investors to finance their purchase of those stocks. During the mid- to late 1920's, then, a person could borrow money from a bank's loan department, then use that money to purchase stocks from the same bank's securities department. This situation drove a wave of speculation and increased bank profits, until the speculation ended in October, 1929, when the stock market crashed.

The crash brought about massive financial losses for individual investors. They sought to sell their shares before they could fall any farther, pulling what little cash they could from the market. Investors who had bought stocks with borrowed money were caught in margin calls: The value of the stock securing their loans fell below a predetermined level and was no longer sufficient to support the loans. Investors withdrew so much money from deposit accounts to cover these margin calls that many banks ran out of cash and were unable to pay their depositors. This downward cycle fed on itself, as bank runs caused several thousand banks to fail over the following three years.

Shortly after President Franklin D. Roosevelt's inauguration in 1933, two pieces of bank legislation

The interior of the Dime Savings Bank in Detroit, Michigan, in the early 1900's. (Library of Congress)

were passed. The Emergency Banking Act closed every bank in the country for a four-day "holiday." This closure provided time for bank examiners to review every bank in the country; they permanently closed those that seemed unable to survive and reopened those that had sufficient resources to weather the crisis. This process helped restore some of the public's faith in the banking system.

Later in the year, the Glass-Steagall Act was passed, arguably the most important banking legislation passed until its repeal by the Gramm-Leach-Bliley Act of 1999. This act prohibited commercial banks from acting as investment banks. It also established the Federal Deposit Insurance Corporation (FDIC), which provides insurance coverage of bank deposits (up to $100,000; increased in October, 2008, to $250,000). The FDIC further improved public confidence in the banking industry, and the financial markets once again began to stabilize. This was not a rapid process given the depth and breadth of the Great Depression. However, the slowly improving financial condition of the banking industry allowed banks to begin issuing loans again, and individuals had fewer concerns about the safety of their savings. World War II broke out in Europe just as the nation was recovering from the ravages of the Depression. This had the immediate effect of significantly increasing demand for industrial production, especially of war materials needed by the British. This sudden and substantial demand was happily assisted through increased lending by banks. As the war went on, production (and the demand for funds) continued to increase. Another effect of this growth was the rapid expansion of earnings by American workers and service members, leading to an increase in savings deposits. As more deposits were available to banks, more bank loans became available to borrowers, and the country found itself with a growing economy.

AFTER WORLD WAR II

In the latter half of the 1940's and the 1950's, returning U.S. service personnel used their wartime earnings and increased wages from new jobs to purchase homes and consumer goods. A major benefit was provided to returning soldiers by the G.I. Bill of 1944, formally known as the Servicemen's Readjustment Act. This act provided for mortgage insurance from the Veterans Administration for home loans taken out by service members. This had the effect of

reducing the risk to banks, giving them the incentive to lend to more people.

Minimal changes occurred in general banking laws or practices over the following four decades. Few banks undertook anything but the most basic forms of lending or other services, with some notable exceptions: Car loans were developed during the 1950's, with terms increasing from twenty-four months during the early 1950's to forty-eight and sixty months during the 1980's. The credit card was also fully developed during this period. The first credit cards were issued during the 1930's as charge cards designed to increase sales of gasoline. The cards evolved into general-purpose credit instruments, as the first such card was issued in 1958 by Bank of America as the BankAmericard (later known as Visa).

By the 1980's, banks and other financial institutions were looking for ways to increase their revenues, and they were beginning to chafe at the restrictions still in place from the Glass-Steagall Act. Some relief was provided by the Depository Institutions Deregulation and Monetary Control Act of 1980 and the Depository Institutions Act of 1982. These laws increased competition and innovation in the financial services industry by allowing the development of new types of deposit accounts, such as interest-bearing checking accounts and money market deposit accounts. The acts also allowed savings and loans (S&Ls) to begin lending to businesses. The sudden expansion of lending by inadequately trained lenders resulted in huge loan losses for these institutions. The subsequent failures of many savings and loans resulted in such large losses that the obligations of the Federal Savings and Loan Insurance Corporation (FSLIC) had to be transferred to the FDIC in 1989.

In 1985, national branch banking was declared constitutional after more than two hundred years of banks being limited to maintaining branches in only one state. This change prompted the bank merger mania of the 1980's and 1990's, as it suddenly made sense for banks in multiple markets to merge operations. The mergers allowed better utilization of overhead and gave banks access to a more diverse customer base spread across a much larger geographical area. Both of these effects reduced risk and generally resulted in banks issuing more loans. The individual states remained in control of whether banks within their borders would be al-

TOP TWENTY BANKS IN THE WORLD, 2008, BY ASSETS, IN MILLIONS OF U.S. DOLLARS

Rank	Bank	Assets	Capital
1	Royal Bank of Scotland Group PLC, Edinburgh, UK	3,782,880	5,036
2	Deutsche Bank AG, Frankfurt am Main, Germany	2,953,727	1,985
3	BNP Paribas SA, Paris	2,477,272	19,696
4	Barclays PLC, London	2,442,996	3,286
5	Crédit Agricole SA, Paris	2,067,577	31,481
6	UBS AG, Zurich, Switzerland	2,007,224	183
7	Société Générale, Paris La Défense, France	1,566,904	852
8	ABN AMRO Holding NV, Amsterdam	1,498,849	1,586
9	UniCredit SpA, Milan	1,493,799	9,770
10	ING Bank NV, Amsterdam	1,453,382	768
11	The Bank of Tokyo-Mitsubishi UFJ, Tokyo	1,362,598	8,450
12	Banco Santander SA, Boadilla del Monte, Spain	1,334,671	4,572
13	JPMorgan Chase Bank National Association, New York	1,318,888	1,785
14	Bank of America NA, Charlotte, N.C.	1,312,794	2,879
15	Citibank NA, New York	1,251,715	751
16	Credit Suisse Group, Zurich, Switzerland	1,201,802	41
17	Fortis Bank SA/NV, Brussels, Belgium	1,121,656	—
18	Industrial and Commercial Bank of China, Ltd., Beijing	962,031	42,795
19	China Construction Bank Corporation, Beijing	903,353	31,994
20	Bank of Scotland PLC, Edinburgh, United Kingdom	890,936	853

Source: Data from BankersAlmanac

Note: Standings are as of July 31, 2008. The other U.S. banks making the top fifty were number 33, Wachovia Bank NA, Charlotte, NC, $653,269 million in assets and $455 million in capital; and number 47, Wells Fargo Bank NA, San Francisco, $467,861 million in assets and $520 million in capital.

lowed to branch; Colorado became the last state to authorize full branch banking with the passage of legislation in 1993.

Automated teller machines (ATMs) came into widespread distribution, increasing consumer access to funds while providing banks with both a source of fee income and a way to reduce overhead, as fewer tellers and other staff members were required to service customers. Banks continued to expand on automated services, offering Internet banking and other electronic services, further enabling them to reduce staff levels and potentially to generate fee income.

In 1999, the Gramm-Leach-Bliley Act repealed many of the restrictions enacted by the Glass-Steagall Act, once again allowing banks to maintain ownership in insurance companies, investment banks, and other financial service providers. The law led to another round of acquisitions and consolidations. Despite the continued consolidation of major banking companies, local banks have retained a healthy presence in their communities. These smaller institutions follow the same regulations and are afforded the same insurance coverage as their larger brethren, but they compete based on community attention, knowledge, and service. They remain major providers of credit to small and medium-sized businesses, as well as primary lenders to builders and developers within their communities.

Peter D. Lindquist

FURTHER READING

Brands, H. W. *The Money Men: Capitalism, Democracy, and the Hundred Years' War over the American Dollar.*

New York: W. W. Norton, 2006. Biographic study of five figures who shaped the history of U.S. monetary policy and paper currency.

Chernow, Ron. *The House of Morgan.* New York: Atlantic Monthly Press, 1990. Study of J. P. Morgan, who helped stabilize the markets after the Panic of 1907.

Deane, Marjorie, and Robert Pringle. *The Central Banks.* New York: Viking Penguin, 1995. Examination of the United States' central banks and their role in the national economy.

Grant, James. *Money of the Mind.* New York: Farrar Straus Giroux, 1992. Discusses the role of psychological factors in the history of credit.

Green, Edwin. *Banking: An Illustrated History.* New York: Rizzoli International, 1989. Provides useful illustrations of key institutions, financial instruments, and bankers.

Klein, Maury. *Rainbow's End: The Crash of 1929.* New York: Oxford University Press, 2001. Details the changes wrought by the stock market crash that began the Great Depression.

Mihm, Stephen. *A Nation of Counterfeiters: Capitalists, Con Men, and the Making of the United States.* Cambridge, Mass.: Harvard University Press, 2007. History of the pre-Federal Reserve United States and the often fraudulent printing and circulation of paper currency and banknotes before the advent of greenbacks.

Rothbard, Murray N. *A History of Money and Banking in the United States: The Colonial Era to World War II.* Auburn, Ala.: Ludwig von Mises Institute, 2002. Detailed examination of the personal and political motives of persons in power that led to bank failures and economic disasters over three hundred years of American history.

Warsh, David. *Knowledge and the Wealth of Nations: A Story of Economic Discovery.* New York: W. W. Norton, 2006. Extended treatment of the history of economics, focusing on the seminal works of Adam Smith in the eighteenth century and of Paul Romer in the twentieth century.

SEE ALSO: Bank failures; Bank of the United States, First; Bank of the United States, Second; Credit unions; Currency; Deregulation of financial institutions; Federal Deposit Insurance Corporation; Federal Reserve; Monetary policy, federal; Morris Plan banks; Postal savings banks; Savings and loan associations; Supreme Court and banking law.

Banking law, Supreme Court and. *See* Supreme Court and banking law

Bankruptcy law

DEFINITION: Statutes and common law providing a legal framework within which courts examine debtors' assets and creditors' claims, oversee distribution of those assets among creditors, and cancel remaining debts

SIGNIFICANCE: Uniform bankruptcy laws are pivotal in a rapidly growing, credit-based economy. Their purpose is to grant equitable treatment to creditors and give debtors fresh starts. Without them, lenders have no assurance that their claims will receive just treatment in the event of borrower default. Borrowers, conversely, are reluctant to commit to a risky enterprise if the consequences of failure are too dire.

Historically, American legislators have upheld national goals of economic growth and social mobility by passing bankruptcy laws more generous to debtors than those in most European countries. America has been a nation of debtors from the outset, as its settlers borrowed to pay for their passage from Europe, to buy and clear land, to build and operate mills, to purchase slaves, and to gamble and drink. Inevitably, some investments went sour, and some individuals failed to prosper, leaving them to face the eighteenth century English legal system, which valued commerce and capital over human life.

Legal bankruptcy was possible in colonial America, but it was not an attractive option. The law allowed seizure and sale of all a debtor's assets, including furniture, his wife's clothes, and the tools of his trade. In theory, debtors could be executed if they concealed anything of value from bankruptcy adjudicators. In practice, however, the handful of executions for debt in eighteenth century England involved massive corporate fraud. Although the total liquidation of debtors' assets bought release from debtor's prison, it did not result in cancellation of their debts. Creditors could renew collection efforts if a debtor's circumstances improved.

BANKRUPTCY IN THE NEW NATION

After the American Revolution, most states continued to follow English bankruptcy law well into the nineteenth century. Because entrepreneurs in the infant republic relied heavily on English capital to expand their business ventures, they were poorly situated to press for more debtor-friendly laws, which could have discouraged English lenders. The terms granting the United States independence at the close of the revolution specifically provided for repayment of prerevolutionary debts to English merchants. State bankruptcy laws that gave preferential treatment to more recent American creditors, in violation of the treaty, were a nontrivial factor in the deteriorating Anglo-American relations that culminated in the War of 1812.

Most bankruptcies in America before the mid-nineteenth century were involuntary, brought by creditors. In contrast, most business bankruptcies since 1898 and virtually all personal bankruptcies have been voluntary, initiated by debtors.

The U.S. Constitution empowers Congress to enact uniform bankruptcy laws. Congress passed such laws sporadically during the nineteenth century, always in response to economic downturns that highlighted the problem of business failures involving creditors in different states. Advocates for industrial and commercial interests favored federal bankruptcy laws, while farming and states' rights advocates in general opposed them. A key issue was whether a state law could discriminate against out-of-state creditors. The U.S. Supreme Court, in *Ogden v. Saunders* (1827), struck down a debtor-friendly New York state statute on the grounds that it impaired the obligation of interstate contracts. This decision left many individual provisions of state bankruptcy laws open to challenge.

The temporary federal bankruptcy laws passed in 1800, 1841, and 1867 were in effect for a total of sixteen years. Impetus for a permanent law grew during the 1880's and coalesced during the Panic of 1893. The Bankruptcy Act of 1898, sponsored by Jay Torrey, established the shape of bankruptcy in the United States for the next century. It provided for uniform, equitable distribution of assets to creditors, leaving the states to decide which assets were exempt, and it contained limited provisions for restructuring debts in bankruptcy. This act made individual bankruptcy more attractive to consumers. Since 1898, the proportion of bankruptcy filings brought by individuals, as opposed to businesses, has increased steadily. This increase reflects the more consumer-friendly laws passed beginning in 1898, but it also reflects an enormous rise in individual debt and a decline in the number of self-employed people operating family businesses.

The Great Depression produced a new round of bankruptcy reform legislation. There had long existed a special provision for railroads, the railroad receivership, which provided for a federal trustee to manage a bankrupt railroad with the aim of eventually selling it intact, often to the original bondholders, rather than liquidating its assets piecemeal. Bankruptcy reform legislation of 1933-1934 eliminated separate treatment of railroads and made reorganization and restructuring of debts, under the supervision of a United States trustee, an option for any corporation. The 1938 Chandler Act extended the restructuring option to the increasing numbers of bankrupt individuals who had no assets to liquidate but could pay some of their debt from future income.

Rates of bankruptcy filing, both individual and corporate, declined after 1938 and remained low during the 1940's and 1950's. Thereafter, individual bankruptcy rates rose steeply, peaking in 2004-2005. They dropped sharply following the 2005 bankruptcy reform act but have since risen in response to an economic downturn. The absolute number of business bankruptcies has not risen, but the dollar amounts in some recent business failures have been staggering.

In 1978, Congress enacted a uniform, comprehensive bankruptcy code incorporating the 1898 act, the Chandler Act, and other legislation. The new code's provisions, outlined in more than two hundred pages of regulations, recognize four types of bankruptcy. Chapter 7, total liquidation, can apply to individuals or businesses. With some notable exceptions (including child support, criminal restitution, and student loans), a person emerges from Chapter 7 free of debt.

Chapter 11 governs corporate reorganization in bankruptcy. In some cases, a United States trustee assumes control of the corporation during Chapter 11 reorganization; in others, the trustee merely supervises the operations. Chapter 13, often called "wage-earner bankruptcy," applies to individuals and small businesses. In Chapter 13, an individual can retain assets but is required to submit a bare-bones budget and turn over all disposable income to the trustee, for a period of three or five years. At the end of that period, most remaining debts are discharged. Chapter 12 contains special provisions for farmers and commercial fishermen, and Chapter 15, added later, covers international bankruptcies.

Two trends during the 1980's and 1990's contributed to a public perception that there was widespread abuse of the generous provisions of the 1978 act. Those decades saw an explosion of consumer debt, fueled by the credit card industry and by inflated housing costs. A small number of highly publicized cases of students filing for bankruptcy to shed student loan debt before embarking on lucrative careers led first to a five-year waiting period before such loans could be discharged (1982) and later (1998) to complete exemption of federal student loans from bankruptcy discharge in the absence of undue hardship. The courts have always had the option, under the substantial abuse provisions of the 1978 act, of refusing bankruptcy protection to people who use credit cards profligately.

CORPORATE BANKRUPTCY AFTER 1978

Although individual abuse of the 1978 bankruptcy law has been exaggerated, substantial corporate abuses slipped under the congressional radar. The intervening decades have seen the growth of a phenomenon known as strategic bankruptcy, in which a company's management makes decisions enhancing short-term profits while incurring future obligations it intends to avoid through a Chapter 11 bankruptcy. Corporate executives and others with privileged inside information are able to sell their stock before the company files for bankruptcy, and they often retain their munificent salaries during reorganization. By contrast, labor contracts and pension plans, future benefits negotiated by employees as part of their compensation, are often destroyed by bankruptcy proceedings, and most stockholders, who have no advance warning, suffer when stock prices decrease dramatically in response to the company's bankruptcy filing.

Deliberate strategic planning has been suspected in the 1982 bankruptcy of Johns-Manville, which liquidated most of its assets and then folded in anticipation of massive asbestos-exposure claims, as well as in the 1983 bankruptcy of Continental Airlines, in

BUSINESS AND CONSUMER BANKRUPTCY FILINGS, 1980-2007			
Year	Business	Consumer	Total
1980	43,694	287,570	331,264
1985	71,277	341,233	412,510
1990	64,853	718,107	782,960
1995	51,959	874,642	926,601
2000	35,472	1,217,972	1,253,444
2005	39,201	2,039,214	2,078,415
2007	28,322	822,590	850,912

Source: Data from American Bankruptcy Institute

which generous provisions of a union contract were at stake. Reorganization during Chapter 11 proceedings allows a business to fire older employees and then rehire them under much less favorable terms.

Enron's strategy before 2001 involved plans to take advantage of Chapter 11 bankruptcy to shed obligations to employees and stockholders while shielding top executives from the consequences of fiscal irresponsibility. The fraud went much further than that, however, because the company had very few capital assets. Its value to investors lay almost entirely in income being generated by the month-to-month operation of the company. Enron's deceptive accounting practices created the illusion of income where none in fact existed. When the company filed for bankruptcy, there were no assets to liquidate for the benefit of creditors and no future income to pay them either. Employees and stockholders were ruined financially, and at least a few of those responsible would be imprisoned.

THE 2005 BANKRUPTCY ACT

The first comprehensive overhaul of American bankruptcy laws since 1978, the Bankruptcy Abuse Prevention and Consumer Protection Act of 2005 (BAPCPA) is, as the name suggests, mainly aimed at individual bankruptcies. A handful of provisions under Title XIV increase protections for employee wages and pensions in corporate bankruptcies. BAPCPA created a requirement for individuals to obtain credit counseling within ninety days before filing for bankruptcy and to complete a financial management course before receiving discharge. Attorneys and others who work with debtors find that the requirement, while not difficult to meet, accomplishes little.

The BAPCPA further constrains consumers by creating a means test to determine whether a person can file for Chapter 7 liquidation or must file under Chapter 13 and make payments into a plan for five years. If family income is above the median income for the state, a person is presumed to be able to make payments under a Chapter 13 plan.

These two provisions, as well as others, made filing consumer bankruptcy more complicated and expensive than it had been formerly and temporarily depressed the U.S. bankruptcy rate. Contrary to a popular perception that was reinforced by creditors and so-called debt-reduction companies, the 2005 law did not remove bankruptcy as an option for consumers overwhelmed by debt.

REAL ESTATE IN BANKRUPTCY

When it enacted BAPCPA, Congress did not envision that the ensuing three years would produce an explosion in consumer bankruptcies tied to the real estate market. Deregulation of financial markets coupled with soaring real estate values led many homeowners to enter into purchase or refinancing agreements secured by their homes. Lenders ignored the future ability of borrowers to repay the loans from their income, counting on appreciation of home values to recoup their investments in the event of sales or foreclosures. Further, most of these loans were bundled and sold to investors far from the homes' locations. These lenders had neither the incentive nor the ability to work with individuals on the brink of default to prevent foreclosures that would hurt borrowers and lenders alike.

Declining home values and a generally stagnant economy after 2006 produced a chain reaction. Individual homeowners, unable to meet payments or to sell their homes for as much money as they owed on them, declared bankruptcy. The companies making the loans were also unable to sell them, and a number of such companies were themselves forced to declare bankruptcy.

Martha Sherwood

FURTHER READING

Coleman, Peter J. *Debtors and Creditors in America: Insolvency, Imprisonment for Debt, and Bankruptcy, 1607-1900.* Frederick, Md.: Beard Books, 1999. Contains a wealth of information on sociological factors behind bankruptcy legislation.

Delaney, Kevin J. *Strategic Bankruptcy: How Corporations and Creditors Use Chapter 11 to Their Advantage.* Berkeley: University of California Press, 1992. Case studies of large corporations that use bankruptcy as part of a business plan.

Skeel, David A. *Debt's Dominion: A History of Bankruptcy Law in America.* Princeton, N.J.: Princeton University Press, 2001. Thorough and scholarly, with coverage from the colonial period through the end of the twentieth century.

Sommer, Henry J. *Consumer Bankruptcy Law and Practice.* Boston: National Consumer Law Center, 2004. Aimed at attorneys, with a focus on individual bankruptcies under the 1978 bankruptcy reform legislation and its revisions.

Sullivan, Theresa, Elizabeth Warren, and Jay Westbrook. *As We Forgive Our Debtors: Bankruptcy and Consumer Credit in America.* Oxford, England: Oxford University Press, 1989. Based on a large study of consumer bankruptcies; focuses on economic trends and provides good treatment of women's issues.

SEE ALSO: Chrysler bailout of 1979; Credit card buying; Enron bankruptcy; Great Depression; Incorporation laws; Supreme Court and contract law; WorldCom bankruptcy.

Barron's

IDENTIFICATION: Weekly financial magazine for investors

DATE: Founded in 1921

SIGNIFICANCE: *Barron's* provides advice and information to individuals seeking to manage their own money effectively. This advice empowers individuals and, as a result of *Barron's* large readership, it can itself influence financial markets.

The entirety of U.S. and world markets is a complex topic but one of great importance to private investors. *Barron's* is a weekly publication that attempts to make these markets comprehensible and financial information manageable so that readers can make better decisions about trading and finance. The magazine's columns and stories can examine individual companies, whole industries, or entire economic sectors.

Barron's caters to a wide range of readers, from individual investors to senior corporation executives, whom it helps understand and anticipate market events. This anticipation and the confidence it generates can translate into action, as investors, having read an article in *Barron's*, may trade stock as a result. The magazine may thus influence the stock values of those companies and sectors it discusses, causing them to fluctuate. This influence can be either positive or negative, depending on the tenor of the coverage.

Articles in the magazine usually focus on what happened in the prior week and what is projected for the future. The prior week's coverage focuses on commodities, stocks, and bond options, especially the statistics relevant to those securities. Future projections are based on coverage of certain firms or economic sectors, including relevant demographic or investment trends, political developments, and general market conditions. Readers can also become aware of such issues as stock fraud by reading *Barron's* investigative features.

Jan Hall

SEE ALSO: Bloomberg's Business News Services; Bond industry; *The Economist*; *Forbes*; *Fortune*; Magazine industry; Stock markets; *The Wall Street Journal*.

Baseball strike of 1972

THE EVENT: First players' strike in Major League Baseball, motivated by the players' desire for better pension benefits and salary arbitration rights

DATE: April 1-13, 1972

PLACE: United States and Canada

SIGNIFICANCE: The 1972 baseball strike was the first organized player strike against Major League Baseball's team owners. The event provided the precedent for future players' strikes.

Confrontations between players and management have occurred throughout the history of baseball. Players were always at a disadvantage because of the reserve clause. The reserve clause of players' contracts stipulated that, on a contract's expiration, a player's team retained the exclusive rights to that player. Thus, unless a team formally released or traded one of its players, that player could not play for any other team, even after he was no longer being paid to play for the first team. The reserve clause allowed owners to dictate the fates of players.

In 1966, Marvin Miller was hired as the executive director of the Major League Baseball Players Association (MLBPA). Miller transformed the MLBPA into a bona fide union. In 1968, Miller was able to negotiate the first collective bargaining agreement in baseball. In 1972, Miller represented players in negotiations with owners. The major negotiation items included player pension funds, a minimum salary, player arbitration, and whether a player could veto a trade. Owners were reluctant to meet the demands of players. As a result, players on every team went on strike for the first time in baseball. The strike lasted thirteen days, and the owners and players agreed on several benefits to players. The players received a $500,000 increase in their pension fund. A system of arbitration was put into place in which players who had disagreements with a team's salary offer could submit a proposal to an impartial arbitrator. A "ten-and-five" rule was also agreed on. This agreement would allow a player to veto a trade if he had played for ten years in the major leagues and had been with the same team for the last five years. In addition, the minimum salary for players was increased to $16,000. The arbitration gains made by players during the 1972 strike led the way to free agency (the ability of an athlete to negotiate a contract with any team), as players commenced signing lucrative contracts beginning during the mid-1970's.

Alar Lipping

FURTHER READING
Dworkin, James B. *Owners Versus Players: Baseball and Collective Bargaining*. Boston: Auburn House, 1981.

Korr, Charles P. *The End of Baseball as We Knew It: The Players Union, 1960-1981*. Champaign: University of Illinois Press, 2002.

Miller, Marvin. *A Whole Different Ball Game: The Sport and Business of Baseball*. Secaucus, N.J.: Carol Publishing Group, 1991.

SEE ALSO: Labor history; Labor strikes; Sports, intercollegiate; Sports franchises; Supreme Court and labor law.

Beef industry

DEFINITION: Enterprises breeding, raising, and slaughtering cows and processing, distributing, marketing, and selling their meat

SIGNIFICANCE: From its beginnings during the early stages of colonial settlement, the raising of cattle has grown steadily in the United States. Following its greatest period of expansion—the era known as the Cattle Kingdom on the Great Plains in the second half of the nineteenth century—the beef industry has continued to be a major American food production industry.

Cattle were introduced to the Western Hemisphere by the Spanish during the early period of exploration and settlement. They were also brought into the British colonies to the north quite early in the settlement process. By the end of the seventeenth century, cattle were being raised in the backcountry for sale in eastern cities such as Philadelphia; Charleston, South Carolina; and Baltimore. They were generally left to forage on the land and then captured and driven in herds to their final destination. This pattern continued through the first half of the nineteenth century, as settlement pushed west.

WESTWARD EXPANSION

During the late 1860's, however, the production of beef for commercial purposes took on a new meaning, primarily as a result of railroad construction and continued western expansion. The advent of the railroad made the transportation of livestock much easier. When the railroad reached Chicago in 1852, several different railway companies established stockyards there to facilitate the shipment of cattle eastward, and Chicago quickly became a major rail center for the industry. At this time also, a major new mode of beef production began to develop with the rise of what would come to be known as the "beef bonanza" or Cattle Kingdom in the Great Plains region.

As the railroads pushed west and the market for beef in the eastern cities grew, the Cattle Kingdom took shape.

Utilizing a style of raising cattle introduced by the Spanish in Mexico several centuries earlier, the process involved the open grazing of cattle on the plains. Large herds of a particularly hardy breed known as longhorns, which had also been introduced by the Spanish, were allowed to graze freely, watched over by individuals called by such names (depending on the region) as "cowboys," "cowpunchers," or "buckaroos."

When cattle were mature enough for market, they were driven along cattle trails, some of them hundreds of miles in length, to towns along the newly constructed railroads. The individual credited with originating this system was Joseph McCoy of Illinois, who began putting it into effect during the late 1860's, using the town of Abilene, Kansas, located on the Kansas Pacific Railroad, as his principal shipping point. For the next twenty years, this system expanded, helping create the rich cultural traditions of the Wild West that have been celebrated in Western films and novels. Terms like "roundup," "cattle drives," "broncobuster" (reflecting the importance of the horse as a tool of the cowboy), and "rodeo" permanently entered the American vocabulary at this time. As the economic importance of the cattle industry grew, Chicago continued to serve as a major rail terminus and processing center. The Union Stockyards built there in

BEEF SUPPLY AND USE, 1990-2006, IN MILLIONS OF POUNDS

Year	Production	Imports	Supply	Exports	Consumption
1990	22,742	2,356	25,434	1,006	24,031
2000	26,888	3,032	30,332	2,468	27,338
2003	26,339	3,006	30,036	2,518	27,000
2004	24,650	3,679	28,847	460	27,750
2005	24,784	3,599	29,020	698	27,751
2006	26,172	3,073	29,816	1,150	28,035

Source: Data from the *Statistical Abstract of the United States, 2008* (Washington, D.C.: Department of Commerce, Economics and Statistics Administration, Bureau of the Census, Data User Services Division, 2008)

Note: Weight is the weight of the animal minus entrails, head, hide, and internal organs but with fat and bone. Total supply equals production plus imports plus remaining stocks of previous year.

1865 and the large meatpacking plants such as Swift's and Armour's that grew up around the stockyards brought rapid economic growth to that city.

RISE OF THE MODERN INDUSTRY

The age of the Cattle Kingdom lasted only through the 1880's. Permanent agricultural settlement spread onto the Great Plains as a result of the Homestead Act of 1862 and the beginning of the wheat boom during the later years of the century. The amount of land available for open grazing declined. The continued development of a rail system in the region eliminated the need for the long cattle drives of the earlier period, and the introduction of barbed wire (developed by Joseph Glidden during the 1870's) enabled wheat farmers and eventually cattle ranchers to fence in their land. Several years of bad weather, including the drought of 1883 and the severe winter of 1886-1887, further undercut the system. By the 1890's, the raising of cattle on fenced-in ranches had largely replaced open grazing, although the old system was still practiced in some areas into fairly modern times.

Over time, other dimensions of the industry also changed. Although Chicago remained a major meat-processing center and destination point for cattle into the second half of the twentieth century, a process of decentralization within the industry gradually took place. Refrigerated railroad cars, initially a boon to centralization, in the end also made it possible (and cheaper) to slaughter animals where they were raised rather than transport them to large urban centers. During the 1950's, both Armour's and Swift's closed their Chicago plants, and in 1971, the Union Stockyards also closed, bringing another key part of the old system to an end.

Beef production remains a major food industry in the United States. Beginning with the National Cattle Growers Association in 1884, various organizations have been formed to encourage unity among cattle producers as well as to promote consumer interest in beef products. Scientific practices, including understanding and treatment of animal diseases and animal feed requirements, have been introduced. The beef industry, in both its historical development and its present practices, stands as one of the leaders in the shift from independent producers to what is known as modern agribusiness.

Scott Wright

FURTHER READING

Carlson, Paul H., ed. *The Cowboy Way: An Exploration of History and Culture.* Lubbock: Texas Tech University Press, 2000. A collection of essays on cowboy life and culture including several on non-whites—Mexican Americans, African Americans, and Native Americans—who made up approximately one-third of the cowboy workforce.

Dale, Edward Everett. *The Range Cattle Industry: Ranching on the Great Plains from 1865 to 1925.* Rev. ed. Norman: University of Oklahoma Press, 1960. Originally published in 1930, this work remains a classic study of the Great Plains cattle industry of the late nineteenth and early twentieth centuries.

Dykstra, Robert R. *The Cattle Towns.* New York: Alfred A. Knopf, 1968. Examines the effects of the cattle industry on the development of five famous Kansas cattle towns—Abilene, Dodge City, Ellsworth, Wichita, and Caldwell.

Gressley, Gene M. *Bankers and Cattlemen.* New York: Alfred A. Knopf, 1966. A study of the role of eastern capital in the rise and fall of the Cattle Kingdom.

Skaggs, Jimmy. *Prime Cut: Livestock Raising and Meatpacking in the United States, 1607-1983.* College Station: Texas A&M University Press, 1986. Covers the history of beef production in America from colonial to modern times, integrating the topic with other forms of livestock raising (primarily sheep and hogs), as well as with the associated growth of the meatpacking industry.

SEE ALSO: Agribusiness; Agriculture; Agriculture, U.S. Department of; European trade with the United States; Fast-food restaurants; Food-processing industries; Meatpacking industry; Poultry industry; Restaurant industry.

Bell, Alexander Graham

IDENTIFICATION: Scottish American inventor
BORN: March 3, 1847; Edinburgh, Scotland
DIED: August 2, 1922; Baddeck, Nova Scotia
SIGNIFICANCE: Bell, a prolific inventor and philanthropist, is best known as the inventor of the telephone. He founded Bell Telephone, which would eventually become the communications giant American Telephone and Telegraph.

Alexander Graham Bell was a distinguished Boston University professor and instructor of the deaf with a long history of interest in acoustics when he began experimenting during the mid-1870's with the telegraph, a system of communication then nearly thirty years old. Bell, whose mother and wife were both deaf, had pioneered in the controversial field of teaching deaf children to speak rather than signing. The telegraph had significant limitations as a communication device. Telegraph messages, sent in Morse code, could go only one way at a time. Moreover, employees of telegraph companies had to act as intermediaries to relay those messages to their intended recipients.

Bell envisioned a telegraph system capable of conveying multiple messages (he used the model of a chord in music) and capable of being directed into individual homes. He sought to redesign and improve telegraphic communication equipment, assisted by another scientist interested in new electrical theories, Thomas A. Watson.

After months of frustrating experimentation on his so-called harmonic telegraph, on June 2, 1875, Bell, working near a receiver in a separate room from Watson, happened to hear by chance the sound of Watson working on a clock device. Hearing that sound across nearly sixty feet of wire inspired Bell radically to alter his concept of telegraph improvement. He turned rather to the idea of transmitting speech across wires, sending the actual voice rather than just a message. Over the next several months, Bell and Watson worked furiously to perfect a working transmitter and receiver in order to secure the first patent, competing against a number of other scientific groups that were also closing in on the technology necessary to transmit speech. Bell was first: On March 7, 1876, he secured patent number 174,465, among the most lucrative single patents ever issued by the U.S. government.

Even as Bell undertook a whirlwind promotional tour for his new machine (including historic demonstrations at the 1876 Philadelphia Centennial Exhibition), he had to withstand an assault of nearly seven hundred separate lawsuits from inventors claiming they had perfected the technology first. Given the fierce competition in Gilded Age America among inventors and given the exorbitant sums of money that stood to be earned from a successful patent, Bell defended himself with integrity. His greatest challenge came from the Western Union tele-

Alexander Graham Bell. (Library of Congress)

graph company, whose communication monopoly was suddenly challenged by the telephone. Bell had offered Western Union the opportunity to buy his telephone patent outright for $100,000. The company declined the offer, instead pursuing alternative telephone patents using some of the most familiar scientists of the day, most notably Thomas Alva Edison.

Bell's patent survived all lawsuits, largely because Bell had kept copious laboratory notes that clearly established the time line of his invention, as well as his methodology. Bell's invention made him famous and wealthy when he was only in his forties. He did not personally direct the day-to-day workings of Bell Telephone. Rather, he spent the better part of the next five decades working on a variety of other scientific interests, among them perfecting early models of air-conditioning, metal detectors, hydroplanes, fiber optics, and the iron lung. In addition, Bell used his resources to found the National Geographic Society and to introduce the groundbreaking mass-market magazine *Science*.

Joseph Dewey

FURTHER READING

Bruce, Robert V. *Alexander Graham Bell and the Conquest of Solitude.* Ithaca, N.Y.: Cornell University Press, 1990.

Gray, Charlotte. *Reluctant Genius: Alexander Graham Bell and the Passion for Invention.* New York: Arcade, 2006.

Shulman, Seth. *The Telephone Gambit.* New York: Norton, 2008.

SEE ALSO: Bell Labs; Edison, Thomas Alva; Electronics industry; Gilded Age; Industrial Revolution, American; Inventions; Patent law; Telecommunications industry; Western Union.

Bell Labs

IDENTIFICATION: Telecommunications research and development company

DATE: Founded in 1925

SIGNIFICANCE: One of the most productive research and development concerns in the United States during the twentieth century, Bell Telephone Laboratories, commonly known as Bell Labs, produced numerous inventions that shaped communication, commerce, and everyday life during the twentieth century.

The venture that became known as Bell Labs grew out of Western Electric, the manufacturing division of the American Telephone and Telegraph Company (AT&T). In 1925, AT&T president Walter Gifford established the Bell Telephone Laboratories division to assume the duties of the electrical engineering department of Western Electric, which had been responsible for a number of early advances in telephone technology. From its inception, Bell Labs employed some of the world's most prominent scientists, producing some of the most dramatic technological advancements of the twentieth century. Among its early inventions were the facsimile (fax) machine, long-distance television transmission, the solar energy cell, and stereo radio broadcasts.

With the outbreak of World War II, Bell Labs refocused its research on the war effort, but it produced a number of inventions during the postwar era that revolutionized modern communications and commerce. Among the most dramatic of these inventions were the transistor, invented in 1947, and the laser, first described in a paper by Charles Townes and William Schawlow in 1957. The transistor made possible the use of smaller, higher-quality, and more durable audio equipment and communications devices, while the laser led to the development of numerous technologies, including laser surgery, highly accurate measuring and timekeeping devices, compact discs (CDs), and digital versatile discs (DVDs).

One of the most significant and controversial technological achievements of Bell Labs was the development of cellular telephone technology during the 1970's. Several companies worked simultaneously on developing cellular communications during the late twentieth century—including the Motorola Corporation, which produced the first practical handheld cellular telephone—yet the federally sanctioned domination of the telephone industry that the Bell System enjoyed during this period led to the granting of federal approval to Bell Labs to implement its Advanced Mobile Phone System (AMPS) during the late 1970's, giving it a significant advantage over its competitors. Despite this controversy, Bell Labs continued to dominate the evolution of cellular telephone technology during the 1980's.

The establishment of Bell Labs symbolized the decreasing role of the individual inventor and the rise of the corporate research laboratory in the development of new technology. Although individual scientists continued to receive credit—and often fame and fortune—for their inventions, technological advances increasingly came to fruition under the financing and supervision of corporations.

Bell Labs' parent company, AT&T Technologies, was renamed Lucent Technologies in 1996 and was downsized following a financial downturn in the telecommunications industry during the early twenty-first century. Lucent merged with the French telecommunications company Alcatel in 2006 to form Alcatel-Lucent. The Bell Laboratories division subsequently remained operational but drastically scaled down, as many of its locations across the United States were closed.

Michael H. Burchett

FURTHER READING

Endlich, Lisa. *Optical Illusions: Lucent and the Crash of Telecom.* New York: Simon & Schuster, 2004.

Gehani, Narain. *Bell Labs: Life in the Crown Jewel.* Summit, N.J.: Silicon Press, 2003.

SEE ALSO: Antitrust legislation; Bell, Alexander Graham; Electronics industry; Telecommunications industry.

Black Friday

THE EVENT: Economic panic caused by the failed attempt of two financiers to corner the gold market on the New York Gold Exchange

DATE: September 24, 1869

PLACE: United States

SIGNIFICANCE: The financiers' attempt to control the gold market failed when the U.S. government released $4 million in gold on Friday, September 24, 1869, known as Black Friday. The resulting panic severely disrupted the U.S. national economy.

In 1869, the first year of Ulysses S. Grant's presidency, speculators attempted to make a fortune by cornering the gold market on the New York Gold Exchange. After befriending banker Abel Rathbone Corbin, who was Grant's brother-in-law, financiers James Fisk and Jay Gould sought to ingratiate themselves with the president and convince Grant not to sell U.S. Treasury gold. Fisk and Gould planned to buy up enormous quantities of gold at low prices and then sell the gold for massive profits once the price of gold went back up. Also involved in the scheme was General Daniel Butterfield, assistant treasurer of the United States, who promised to provide inside knowledge about the government's time frame to sell gold. In addition, Fisk and Gould reasoned that the increase in the price of gold would ensure a rise in the price of wheat and cause farmers in the West to ship east—and thus increase rail freight for the Erie Railroad, which the financiers owned.

During the summer of 1869, the market fell, and Gould and Fisk began to buy up large quantities of gold, which led to other financiers similarly buying up gold. This in turn caused the price of gold to rise. In September, the price of gold soared even higher—indeed by then the price of gold had risen 30 percent—in part because Gould and Fisk refused to sell the gold they had accumulated. However, Secretary of the Treasury George S. Boutwell and President Grant found out about the scheme and issued orders to sell $4 million worth of U.S. Treasury gold to stabilize the market. After the gold reached the market, the value of gold plummeted, falling from $160 to $130 in minutes. This sudden downward shift caused a panic and an immediate sell-off.

Consequently, Black Friday, as it came in time to be known, led to a two-week slide in the gold market, which severely disrupted the entire U.S. economy and lasted until the following year. Foreign trade was brought to a complete standstill, stock prices fell 20 percent, and the price of grain fell 50 percent. Butterfield was forced to resign from the U.S. Treasury, and President Grant was harshly criticized for apparently tolerating or condoning the conspiracy in its early stages.

M. Casey Diana

FURTHER READING

Ackerman, Kenneth D. *The Gold Ring: Jim Fisk, Jay Gould, and Black Friday, 1869.* New York: Dodd, Mead, 1988.

McAlpine, R. W. *The Life and Times of Colonel James Fisk, Jr.* New York: Arno Press, 1981.

Renehan, Edward. *Dark Genius of Wall Street: The Misunderstood Life of Jay Gould, King of the Robber Barons.* New York: Basic Books, 2005.

SEE ALSO: American Bimetallic League national convention; Banking; Commodity markets; Currency; Gold standard; Gould, Jay; Monetary policy, federal; Panic of 1857; Panic of 1873.

Black Hills gold rush

THE EVENT: Discovery of gold in the Dakota Territory and subsequent influx of prospectors and development

DATE: 1874-1876

PLACE: Dakota Territory (now in South Dakota)

SIGNIFICANCE: The gold rush led to the development of the Homestake mine, which operated for 125 years and produced 10 percent of the world's supply of gold.

In the summer of 1874, the U.S. Army directed Lieutenant Colonel George Armstrong Custer to lead an expedition to explore the Black Hills in what was then the southwestern corner of the Dakota Territory. The official purpose of the expedition was to map a route to connect with the road to Fort Laramie and to find a location for a planned new military post. Unofficially, the Army hoped to settle questions about the presence of gold in the region. Under the terms of the Fort Laramie Treaty of 1868, the Black Hills had been promised to the Native American Sioux tribes; persistent rumors of gold in the hills threatened to undermine that agreement.

Custer's force left Fort Lincoln, located near the site of present-day Bismarck, North Dakota, in early July and traveled south along the western side of the Black Hills. The one-thousand-man expedition turned east into the hills on July 22, 1874. It proceeded as far east as the site of present-day Custer, South Dakota, where it stayed for one week. While Custer and other military officers explored and mapped the area, the two civilian miners attached to the expedition checked local streams for traces of gold. They found some in French Creek.

Custer returned to Fort Lincoln and reported the gold find. Almost immediately, thousands of miners rushed for the Black Hills. The sheer volume of miners made it impossible for the military to keep them out of the region. The influx exacerbated the Indian wars that led to Custer's death at the Battle of the Little Bighorn two years later.

The first prospectors began searching for gold in the southern Black Hills, near the site of the initial discovery in French Creek. Results were poor, with only thin traces of gold being found. It was not until the search moved north that a true bonanza was discovered. The area around Deadwood Creek was rich with placer gold, large nuggets that had broken loose from a larger vein. On April 9, 1876, four miners—Alex Engh, Hank Harney, Frank Manuel, and Moses Manuel—filed a claim on a gold-bearing outcropping near the present-day Lead. They named their mine the Homestake.

Three men pan for gold in the Dakotas in the late 1800's. (Library of Congress)

Shortly afterward, a consortium of San Francisco investors led by George Hearst bought the Homestake for $70,000. Although the Black Hills gold rush lacked the drama of the two other major American gold rushes—in California in 1848 and in the Klondike in 1896—the Homestake vein proved to be the richest gold vein in American history. The impact of the 1848 gold rush was diffused, with multiple claims being filed and developed over a wide geographic area in northern California. Some 12 million ounces of gold were extracted from California claims during the first five years of the gold rush, but most claims were quickly exhausted. Similarly, the Klondike, with its harsh winter weather and arduous conditions, provided much human drama, but the gold rush there had less of an economic impact than did either the California or South Dakota rushes. Since the initial discovery of gold, the Klondike region in Canada's Yukon Territory has yielded approximately 12.5 million ounces of gold, a respectable amount but not even a third of the Homestake's production over the same period of time.

Profits from the Homestake were concentrated in the hands of a small group of investors, so they helped build some of America's best-known fortunes, such as that of the Hearst family. They also aided the growth of corporations such as Anaconda Mining. With company headquarters in San Francisco, Homestake Mining Company eventually expanded globally into other areas of mining, such as uranium and copper, in locations as far-flung as Australia and Chile. Thus, the economic impact of the Homestake continues to be felt into the twenty-first century.

Miners continued to prospect in the Black Hills, each hoping to strike a claim as rich as the Homestake, but no comparable veins of easily processed ore were found. The Homestake mine itself eventually became the deepest mine in the United States, with a depth of eight thousand feet. More than 40 million ounces of gold were removed from the mine before it closed in 2001.

Nancy Farm Mannikko

FURTHER READING

McDermott, John D., comp. *Gold Rush: The Black Hills Story*. Pierre: South Dakota State Historical Society Press, 2001.

Meldahl, Keith Heyer. *Hard Road West: History and Geology Along the Gold Rush Trail*. Chicago: University of Chicago Press, 2007.

Parker, Watson. *Gold in the Black Hills*. Pierre: South Dakota State Historical Society Press, 2003.

SEE ALSO: California gold rush; Currency; Exploration; Fort Knox; Gold standard; Klondike gold rush.

Black Monday

THE EVENT: Severe U.S. stock market crash that was preceded and followed by stock market crashes in other countries

DATE: October 19, 1987

PLACE: New York, New York

SIGNIFICANCE: The Black Monday crash, one of the worst in U.S. history, had an enormous impact on American and world business. Following numerous studies of the crash, reforms were implemented to forestall such an event happening again.

On October 19, 1987, Black Monday, Wall Street witnessed the loss of nearly $1 trillion in stock values. The Dow Jones Industrial Average fell 508 points—22.6 percent of its total value—to $1,738.74. The Standard and Poor's 500 index fell 20 percent to $224.84, and the NASDAQ composite index ended at $360.21. A significant number of stocks on the New York Stock Exchange (NYSE) experienced losses that day. The NYSE rebounded quickly, however, and the U.S. economy did not experience a subsequent depression. Unlike the aftermath of the stock market crash of 1929, the American economy revived, and the stock markets attempted to learn from the Black Monday phenomenon.

The rest of the world was not as fortunate as the United States. By the end of October, Hong Kong, Australia, Spain, the United Kingdom, Canada, and New Zealand all experienced significant losses on their stock exchanges, and their economies underwent serious economic dislocations.

CAUSES

Shortly after Black Monday, President Ronald Reagan ordered a study to be conducted on what caused the crash. The resulting exhaustive study of U.S. stock exchanges, the Brady report, offered potential explanations for the disaster. However, the

New York Stock Exchange traders join in the panic selling on Black Monday. (AP/Wide World Photos)

world's industrialized countries over monetary policy. In many ways, what all these explanations boil down to is that the U.S. stock exchanges had serious internal problems that were not addressed until it was too late. The end result was almost a complete collapse of the market structure. Fortunately, the U.S. market rebounded fairly quickly and recovered. More important, studies of Black Monday led to significant reforms of the stock exchanges.

REFORMS

The reforms implemented after Black Monday were designed to sustain the stock market's structure during a crisis. Circuit breakers or trading halts were instituted to forestall a complete collapse of the stock exchange: If the market's value were to fall by a certain number of points, trading would be automatically suspended for a specified period of time to allow brokers and investors to calm down. Other improvements included improved coordination among federal agencies and among the various markets, more authority being given to the SEC to act on an emergency basis, and restrictions being placed on computer trading. Over-the-counter (OTC) market specialists and market makers were held more accountable and were required to publicize their quotes more openly, clearance and settlement systems were improved, and cross-margining programs were implemented. These reforms collectively reduced but did not eliminate the possibility of another severe stock market crash.

Michael V. Namorato

Brady report was not the only study written. Literally scores of individuals, think-tank groups, business agencies, and government agencies such as the Securities and Exchange Commission (SEC) analyzed the crash. Given the nature of the problem and the number of different studies, it is not surprising that no one single cause or report was accepted by all involved.

Among the more widely accepted explanations of Black Monday advanced by scholars are the following. Program or computer trading, allowing computers to be involved in trades once certain guidelines were met, may have exacerbated the crash by causing mass sell-offs more quickly than humans could react. The market may have been widely overvalued, meaning that stocks were valued much higher than their worth. Portfolios may have been underinsured or uninsured. There may have been insufficient coordination within the exchanges.

Other widely accepted scholarly theories of causes contributing to the crash include illiquidity, or the problem of individuals and corporations being unable to convert their holdings to cash; failure of technology (too much stock activity occurred on Black Monday, and the technology controlling trading could not handle it all); investments in derivative securities (options and futures); U.S. trade and budget deficits; market psychology or overconfidence; and international disputes among the

FURTHER READING

Arbel, A., and Albert Kaff. *Crash: Ten Days in October . . . Will It Happen Again?* Chicago: Longman Financial Services, 1989. Analysis of the factors contributing to Black Monday and the likelihood of similar factors causing a similar event in the future.

Bernstein, Peter. *Capital Ideas: The Improbable Origins of Modern Wall Street.* New York: Free Press, 1992.

Historical study of the evolution of the U.S. stock markets, from their beginnings through the late twentieth century.

Kamphuis, Robert W., et al., eds. *Black Monday and the Future of Financial Markets.* Chicago: Mid-America Institute for Public Policy Research, 1989. Public policy-focused study of the lessons to be learned from Black Monday.

Lindsey, Richard, and Anthony Pecora. "Ten Years After: Regulatory Developments in the Securities Market Since the 1987 Market Break." *Journal of Financial Services Research* 13, no. 3 (1998): 283-314. Overview of the reforms instituted during the decade following the 1987 stock market crash.

Malliaris, A. G., and Jorge Urrutia. "The International Crash of October, 1987: Causality Tests." *Journal of Financial and Quantitative Analysis* 27, no. 3 (1992): 353-364. Another causal analysis of the crash, but focused globally rather than just on the American experience.

Schwert, G. William. "Stock Volatility and the Crash of '87." *Review of Financial Studies* 3, no. 1 (1990): 77-102. Looks at the role of volatility as a causal trigger in the stock market crash of 1987.

SEE ALSO: Derivatives and hedge fund industry; Financial crisis of 2008; Great Depression; NASDAQ; New York Stock Exchange; Securities and Exchange Commission; Stock market crash of 1929; Stock markets.

Bloomberg's Business News Services

IDENTIFICATION: Financial news, data, and software company

DATE: Company founded in 1981; news service founded in 1990

SIGNIFICANCE: Bloomberg's offered its clients up-to-the-minute and breaking news about financial markets, allowing them to respond immediately to events that could influence the value of investments. It was an early player in a trend toward using computer and communications technology that changed the nature of securities trading.

From its beginnings in 1981 (when it was known as Innovative Market Systems), Michael Bloomberg's business news company strove to cover news instantly by providing expensive wire-service terminals to its clients, mostly stock traders. Conventional business journalists had not been taking advantage of computer technology to move data as quickly as possible to readers. The Bloomberg system offered clients unprecedented speed of access, as well as a way to analyze the data.

Since the 1980's, the service has greatly expanded from its beginnings as a specialized computer data-delivery system. It maintains a presence across a variety of media, including books, magazines, online products, radio, handheld messaging devices, and television. In 1990, it was renamed as Bloomberg's Business News Services. Many other news providers base some of their stories on information they receive from Bloomberg's, treating the company as a source rather than as a competitor. These outlets enhance the Bloomberg's brand, motivating more customers to purchase the company's terminals.

The financial statistical information provided almost in real time by Bloomberg's terminals is not always significant to all investors, especially long-term investors. Short-term investors, however, are greatly aided by the company's ability to report even slight fluctuations in the markets. The success of Bloomberg's lies in this ability to disseminate up-to-the-second financial reports. The reports cover data from all over the world, and they are disseminated worldwide as well. Subscribers can log on to the service from anywhere with the use of biometric authentication.

Jan Hall

SEE ALSO: Barron's; CNBC; *The Economist*; *Fortune*; NASDAQ; New York Stock Exchange; Newspaper industry; Standard & Poor's; Stock markets; *The Wall Street Journal.*

Bond industry

DEFINITION: Enterprises—including government entities—that issue and trade in interest-bearing promissory notes, initially issues to raise money for a particular entity or project

SIGNIFICANCE: The bond industry enables governments to fund major infrastructure improvements and corporations to finance various stages of development.

Bonds are financial instruments by which buyers lend money to sellers under the terms outlined for each particular bond. They are thus debt instruments and are issued for a certain value (par value), for a set period of time (ending at their maturity date), at a given interest rate, and generally with some other provisions, such as whether the bonds can be "called early" (paid off prior to their maturity date). The interest paid on bonds represents their cost to the borrower/seller. This cost is affected by the bond purchaser's confidence that the interest payments and principal can be covered by the issuer. The less confidence the market has in a particular issuer, the more interest the issuer will need to offer to convince investors to bear the risk of purchasing its bonds.

Since 1909, rating systems have been used to indicate the general perception regarding an issuer's ability to make payments on its bonds. The less certainty there is that the issuing entity can make the needed bond payments, the lower the rating (AAA is the highest) will be—and the higher the interest demanded by those seeking to purchase its bonds. Once a bond has been issued, generally the purchaser of that bond can sell it to others before its maturity date. However, the value of the bond might not be the par value if interest rates have changed since the bond was issued or if the creditworthiness of the issuer has changed.

Bonds issued by state or local governments are generally issued for a specific purpose, such as building a school or constructing a bridge. The U.S. federal government uses bonds to cover budgetary deficits. Traditionally the maximum length of time for a bond to reach maturity is thirty years. U.S. government bonds are usually understood to be the safest in the world. Corporate bonds are issued by corporations for almost any imaginable purpose. Because the default risk is greater for corporations than for governmental entities, the interest rate on their bonds is generally higher than on government bonds.

Although there are substantial government regulations on the bond market, in the United States, most of the sales are done in private trades. This is because most bonds are not interchangeable, as are shares of stock. Although bonds such as those from the U.S. Treasury can be seen as comparable and are issued in large quantities, a bond for county bridge construction is not interchangeable with a bond for a private corporation to expand a manu-facturing plant. Internationally, there are large markets that account for about one-third of the world's debt trades. The Bond Market Association is an organization that represents these centers for debt securities trading.

Donald A. Watt

FURTHER READING

Goodman, Jordan E. *Everyone's Money Book on Stocks, Bonds, and Mutual Funds.* New York: Dearborn Trade, 2002.

Mishkin, Fredric S., and Stanley G. Eakins. *Financial Markets and Institutions.* 6th ed. Boston: Pearson Prentice Hall, 2009.

Wild, Russell. *Bond Investing for Dummies.* Indianapolis: Wiley, 2007.

SEE ALSO: Civil War, U.S.; Commodity markets; Government spending; Interest rates; Junk bonds; Mutual fund industry; Pension and retirement plans; Stock markets.

Book publishing

DEFINITION: Creation, marketing, and distribution of fiction and nonfiction books

SIGNIFICANCE: Book publishing has been a significant presence in America since colonial times, with almanacs, primers, and law books originally forming the foundation of the industry. Since 1640, when the first printed book was published in America, the book publishing industry grown into a multibillion-dollar industry.

Publishing came to America in 1639, when the Day (also spelled Daye) family imported a printing press from England. After the family printed its first book, *The Whole Booke of Psalmes*, in Cambridge, Massachusetts, in 1640, theology became the leading genre of American publishing for more than a century. Printing was restricted to Cambridge until 1674, when Marmaduke Johnson, a publisher who came to America to print an Indian Bible (1663), moved his press to Boston. The Boston-Cambridge area was to remain a center of publishing in the United States.

SEVENTEENTH AND EIGHTEENTH CENTURIES

Toward the end of the seventeenth century, other significant centers of publishing developed;

Philadelphia acquired a printing press in 1685, and New York City's first press arrived in 1693. The eighteenth century brought wider readership among the middle classes. Theology remained the leading genre, but almanacs, primers, and law books also formed foundations of the industry.

Commercial lending libraries appeared in America during the eighteenth century, and they were followed by free, public lending libraries in the nineteenth century. Public libraries generated concern among publishers, who believed that such free access to books would decrease sales. Instead, the increased circulation of books through libraries expanded audience size and stimulated sales.

NINETEENTH CENTURY

The nineteenth century marked a new era in publishing, as the industry's development was stimulated by advances in technology and transportation. Around the same time, New York City emerged as the leading center of the publishing industry in the United States, largely as a result of the founding of three large New York-based publishing houses: Harper Bros. in 1817, George Palmer Putnam and John Wiley's house in 1840, and Charles Scribner's house in 1846. New York's publishing houses were able to use the Erie Canal to expand their market base into the West. They took advantage of their larger market base, printing and shipping books in larger quantities to cut costs. Many small publishing houses could not compete effectively and were eventually driven out of business.

TWENTIETH CENTURY

At the beginning of the twentieth century, literary agents appeared. Literary agents represented authors in contract negotiations and were consistently able to obtain high rates of royalties and large advance payments for their clients. These higher sums for authors decreased the publishing houses' profit margins, making it more difficult and less common for houses to speculate on new authors. Literary agents may also have been indirectly responsible for the increased marketing efforts that appeared around the same time: As higher payments to the author became common, publishing houses placed additional emphasis on generating sales to maintain reasonable profits.

In spite of resource shortages, Word War I had a relatively small impact on the American publishing industry. One significant effect of the war was a decrease in purchasing power among the middle class, and publishers began to look to other markets to maintain their profits. During this time period, universities grew significantly in both number and size, causing the demand for college textbooks to grow rapidly. Eventually, many publishing houses depended on their educational departments to generate income and support less profitable undertakings. Textbooks were also in demand in primary and secondary schools; these textbooks became another significant income generator, as the adoption of a textbook or series guaranteed large-scale sales, with the likelihood of a long-term relationship.

The Great Depression had an immediate effect on America's publishing industry, bringing drastically decreased sales, minimal profits, and numerous bankruptcies. Publishers began to experiment with new marketing techniques to attract readers, including holding the first book fair in America, which was held by *The New York Times* during the 1930's. To mitigate the effects of the Depression on

---

BOOKS SOLD IN UNITED STATES, 2006

Type of Book	Books Shipped (millions)
Juvenile trade	873
Adult trade	824
Mass market paperback	575
Professional	281
Religious	263
Elementary/high school textbook	177
College textbook	77
University press	25

Source: Data from the *Statistical Abstract of the United States, 2008* (Washington, D.C.: Department of Commerce, Economics and Statistics Administration, Bureau of the Census, Data User Services Division, 2008)

Note: Books sold equals net publishers' shipments after returns.

booksellers, Simon & Schuster developed the policy of accepting returns on unsold books for credit against future purchases. Other publishers quickly followed, and the practice became standard in the industry.

As did World War I, World War II had minimal negative impact on the publishing industry, and postwar boom conditions stimulated significant economic growth. The middle class grew quickly, causing the book market to expand, and the number of publishing houses grew in response. In addition, the paperback was reintroduced to the market after the war, allowing publishers to sell cheaper books to a wider audience. By the early 1950's, the paperback had become the most widely distributed type of book; this remained true into the twenty-first century.

Toward the end of the twentieth century, the publishing industry became increasingly centered in a few large conglomerates. As had been the case in the nineteenth century, small publishers were unable to compete and were forced out of business. Around the same time, a new category of publishers was created: the nonprofit press. Nonprofit presses are typically focused on putting forth the work of a particular genre or set of genres, but they all share the mission of producing work that otherwise might be passed over by the larger publishers as lacking in commercial appeal.

A new medium, e-books, or electronic books, appeared in 1971, when Michael Hart created the first electronic book: a copy of the Declaration of Independence. In spite of initial concerns about e-books infringing on the traditional book market, major publishing companies began to work at the end of the twentieth century to understand and establish themselves in the e-book market. During the early twenty-first century, e-books began to gain mainstream acceptance and expanded into new formats, such as installment books compatible with cell phone displays.

Sarah J. Damberger

FURTHER READING

Epstein, Jason. *Book Business: Publishing Past, Present, and Future.* New York City: W. W. Norton, 2002. Based on a series of lectures given by Jason Epstein, the former editorial director of Random House, this book provides a unique perspective on the publishing industry.

Greco, Albert N. *The Book Publishing Industry.* 2d ed. Philadelphia: Lawrence Erlbaum, 2004. Detailed summary of the book publishing business and a bibliography of related literature.

Kirsch, Jonathan. *Kirsch's Handbook of Publishing Law: For Authors, Publishers, Editors, and Agents.* Marina del Rey, Calif.: Acrobat Books, 1994. Comprehensive overview of publishing law.

Rosenthal, Morris. *Print-on-Demand Book Publishing: A New Approach to Printing and Marketing Books for Publishers and Self-Publishing Authors.* Springfield, Mass.: Foner Books, 2004. Self-published book exploring print-on-demand publishing.

Tebbel, John. *A History of Publishing in the United States.* 4 vols. Harwich Port, Mass.: Clock & Rose Press, 2003. Historical overview of book publishing in the United States.

SEE ALSO: Catalog shopping; *Coin's Financial School*; Copyright law; Great Depression; How-to-succeed books; *The Jungle*; Literary works with business themes; Magazine industry; Newspaper industry; Printing industry; *Reader's Digest*.

Boston Tea Party

THE EVENT: The boarding of British ships and dumping of tea in Boston Harbor by Boston merchants disguised as Mohawk warriors

DATE: December 16, 1773

PLACE: Boston, Massachusetts

SIGNIFICANCE: This dramatic act of rebellion became an important symbol of American dissatisfaction with Great Britain's colonial economic policies, particularly the imposition of taxes without granting colonists representation in Parliament, and helped lead to the American Revolution.

Before 1767, most residents of the British American colonies drank smuggled Dutch tea rather than pay the high British tax on tea. The Townshend Acts of that year, named for Charles Townshend, Chancellor of the Exchequer, lowered the tax but made more efficient the collecting of it. Townshend's power to collect taxes was enhanced by the illness of the prime minister, which allowed Townshend to become the functional leader of the government.

Many Americans continued to boycott British tea, demanding the removal of all import taxes.

By 1773, the British East India Company had a surplus of seventeen million pounds of tea. The company faced bankruptcy as the value of its stock dropped by almost one-half. On May 10, 1773, Parliament passed the Tea Act as a means of saving the British East India Company. This act lowered the tea tax but granted the company a virtual monopoly on the tea trade to America, allowing it to sell directly to select American consignees. The consignees in Boston included two sons and a nephew of Thomas Hutchinson, the royal governor of Massachusetts.

Three tea ships arrived in Boston Harbor in late November. Other merchants demanded the resignation of the consignees who were to handle the tea for the British East India Company. The consignees in Philadelphia and New York eventually complied, but those in Boston refused. By November 30, people had gathered in mass meetings in Boston, demanding that the tea be returned to England, but Governor Hutchinson refused to comply.

On the evening of December 16, another mass meeting, chaired by Sam Adams, was held at Boston's Old South Church. After being informed of the governor's final refusal, Adams gave the signal for three companies of fifty men each, dressed as Mohawks, to board the three ships and dump their tea into the harbor. Working throughout the night, the men dumped 342 chests of tea. No other property on the ships was damaged. British warships anchored nearby made no attempts to intervene.

Similar events took place in Charleston, South Carolina. On December 2, another tea ship, the *London*, had arrived in Charleston Harbor. A mass meeting led to the resignation of the Charleston consignees. The *London*'s tea was seized on December 22 and stored in government warehouses until July, 1776, when it was sold to raise funds for the revolution.

To punish Boston for leading the colonial defiance of British policy, Parliament passed the Coercive Acts of 1774-1776, which closed the Port of Boston and reduced the level of autonomy of Massachusetts. However, these actions only increased the colonists' resolve to take control of their own destiny.

Glenn L. Swygart

This 1864 lithograph shows people cheering as tea is dumped overboard in Boston Harbor in 1773. (Library of Congress)

FURTHER READING
Burgan, Michael. *The Boston Tea Party.* Minneapolis: Compass Point Books, 2000.
Zinn, Howard, and Anthony Arnove. *Voices of a People's History of the United States.* New York: Seven Stories Press, 2004.

SEE ALSO: Chinese trade with the United States; Colonial economic systems; Great Atlantic and Pacific Tea Company; Parliamentary Charter of 1763; Revolutionary War; Taxation; Tea Act of 1773; Townshend Act.

Boycotts, consumer

DEFINITION: Socially or politically motivated refusal to patronize particular businesses or industries

SIGNIFICANCE: Consumer boycotts are used by various political and social-awareness groups and individual consumers in an effort to effect change or simply to punish a company for a perceived injustice. The length and severity of the boycott can affect the health of the boycotted firms or industries and therefore the jobs of the people employed by them.

Boycotts of consumer products are generally triggered by a corporate policy or action and are designed to effect change, accomplish punishment, or both. Boycotts can severely affect a company's profit margin and result in the loss of jobs. The word "boycott" entered the English language in 1880, after Irish landlord Captain Charles Boycott demanded unreasonable rent from his tenants and evicted them from his land when they were unable to pay. In retaliation, his workers fled, neighbors shunned him, businesspeople ostracized him, his harvest was ruined, and he was forced to leave Ireland.

REASONS FOR BOYCOTTS

When consumer product companies adopt harmful policies or engage in unfair business practices, consumers often band together and refuse to buy the companies' products until they change their offensive practices. Avon, Anheuser-Busch, American Airlines, Bristol-Myers, Bumble Bee Seafoods, Burger King, Campbell's Soup, Chrysler, Clorox, Domino's Pizza, Exxon, General Motors, General Electric, KFC, Johnson's Wax, Nestlé, Nike, Marathon Oil, Marlboro, Mary Kay Cosmetics, Philip Morris Company, Procter & Gamble, Purina, and Target are just a few of the major companies that have at one time been boycotted.

As part of the social justice movement, American consumers have been encouraged by various political, protest, and social-awareness groups representing such movements as environmental protection and animal rights to resist buying various products. Such boycotts are meant to help the groups achieve either political or social goals and to right perceived wrongs. However, the refusal of consumers to purchase products as a means of protest to bring about social change is not a recent phenomenon. In an effort to bring attention to the plight of Jews under the German Nazi regime, in 1933 the United States boycotted German goods. As an act of passive resistance in India, Mahatma Gandhi instigated a boycott of British products—which he called "baubles of Britain"—that helped bring about Indian independence. During the 1980's, corporations banded together and refused to purchase South African products to oppose that country's apartheid regime.

Historically, consumer boycotts have been viewed as authentically American. Indeed, boycotts have played a significant role in American history. For instance, before the American Revolution, colonists opposed the Stamp Act of 1765, which required them to purchase tax stamps from Britain. They boycotted British-made goods for a year, leading to the repeal of the Stamp Act and, ultimately, the establishment of the United States of America. Similarly, in 1830, northern Americans protested slavery by refusing to purchase slave-produced products such as tobacco and sugar.

Other examples of boycotts that received a great deal of publicity are the boycott of the anti-Semitic Henry Ford's manufactured automobiles and the grape and lettuce boycott led by César Chávez and his United Farm Workers union between the 1960's and the 1990's. The French opposition to the Iraq War also led to boycotts in the United States against French wines.

TWENTY-FIRST CENTURY BOYCOTTS

Advances in technology have made boycotts easier to set into motion by means of Internet Web sites, blogs, USENET newsgroups, and e-mail mailing lists. Indeed, within a matter of hours, consumer watchdog groups can arrange for thousands of consumers to boycott a product with a simple e-mail message. In addition, consumer boycotts often focus on advertisers of television shows. For instance, gays and lesbians boycotted the advertisers of the *Dr. Laura* talk show in response to Laura Schlessinger's statements about their community. Other twenty-first century boycotts have involved Wal-Mart for unfair labor practices and Philip Morris for continuing to manufacture cigarettes.

In the political arena, concerned consumers may band together and boycott the companies that make contributions to a candidate who fails to support their issues. For instance, after George W. Bush failed to ratify the Kyoto Protocol, consumers were urged to boycott products made by Bush's corporate funders. However, boycotts have begun diminishing in favor to some degree because of the recognition that these actions may miss their mark, failing to harm a company's bottom line but causing its employees and their families to suffer. Writing large numbers of letters to corporate executives stating that their company's products will continue to be purchased, but only if changes are brought about, seems to be an effective alternative.

M. Casey Diana

FURTHER READING

Ettenson, Richard, N. Craig Smith, and Jill Klein. "Rethinking Consumer Boycotts." *Marketing* 47, no. 4 (2006): 6-7. Brings to light the idea that boycotts might not be effective because of the loss of workers' jobs.

Friedman, Monroe. *Consumer Boycotts: Effecting Change Through the Marketplace and Media.* New York: Routledge, 1999. Social history of the boycott and an exploration of its dynamics. Academic book suitable for students seeking to understand boycotts, social activists engaged in boycotts, corporate executives affected by boycotts, and researchers.

Glickman, Lawrence B. "Boycott Mania: As Business Ethics Fall, Consumer Activism Rises." *The Boston Globe*, July 31, 2005. American historian argues that a new wave of consumer boycotts is facilitated by a diverse group of protesters, including labor and civil rights activists, through the use of the Internet.

_____. *Consumer Society in American History: A Reader.* Ithaca, N.Y.: Cornell University Press, 1999. Comprehensive exploration of American consumer history traces consumerism more than three centuries, from the colonial era to the 1990's, and demonstrates how such forces as politics, immigration, race, gender, and class affect consumers. Includes a section on consumer boycotts.

Innes, Robert. "A Theory of Consumer Boycotts Under Symmetric Information and Imperfect Competition." *Economic Journal* 116, no. 4 (2006): 355-381. Scholarly article describing how oftentimes targeted companies accede to boycott demands quickly.

SEE ALSO: Chávez, César; Civil Rights movement; Farm protests; Labor history; Labor strikes; Supreme Court and labor law; United Farm Workers of America.

Bracero program

IDENTIFICATION: Government-sponsored program to bring temporary agricultural laborers to the United States from Mexico
DATE: January, 1942-December, 1964
PLACE: Western United States
SIGNIFICANCE: Instituted during World War II, the bracero program brought a much-needed influx of Mexican laborers to the fields of the American West, making California the breadbasket of the United States and of much of the world. The program brought such economic rewards that it was extended until 1964.

By 1942, the United States was fully involved in World War II and experienced a severe shortage of domestic labor, especially in the agricultural sector in the West. Previous experience offered a solution. Mexican workers (called *braceros*, "those who use their arms to work," in Spanish) had been exempted from the immigration quotas that had been established by Congress in 1921, so they were able to work in the greatly expanded agricultural industry in the South and West. With the coming of the Great Depression in 1929, many Mexicans were deported back to their homeland, as there was no longer any need for their labor. By 1942, however, the United States was once again in need of foreign agricultural workers. The U.S. and Mexican governments therefore signed the International Agreement of Migratory Workers, which legalized the introduction of Mexican agricultural workers into the farms of the southern and western United States.

The war curtailed production in warring nations and virtually eliminated agricultural competition in world markets, and the U.S. agricultural industry expanded dramatically. There was a shortage of men to work the fields, however, because most able-bodied rural men either were serving in the armed forces or had moved to the cities to secure better-paying factory jobs. Under the program administered by the U.S. Department of Agriculture, the braceros were guaranteed housing, meals, proper sanitary conditions, transportation, and a minimum wage of 30 cents an hour. However, Mexico refused to send workers to Texas, where threats had been made against the lives of Mexican workers.

By 1945, 68,000 Mexican workers labored to construct railroads. At the end of the first phase of the program, in 1947, some 250,000 braceros, all male, had moved to the United States to take up work. The initiative had been so successful that the legislature authorized a series of informal agreements with Mexico to extend the program, allowing Mexicans to continue to come to the United States even after soldiers returned from Europe. With the advent of the Korean War, even Texas allowed braceros to work in its agricultural sector.

Despite government oversight, enforcement of the bracero program's regulations was difficult, and some abuse of workers did occur. Nonetheless, legislation extended the life of the program every two years until 1964, when it was mutually decided to bring the initiative to a close. In all, approximately five million Mexican workers came to work in the United States under the bracero program. The pre-

Mexican farmworkers top sugar beets in a field near Stockton, California, in 1943. (Library of Congress)

cedent for migration from Mexico to the north had been set. While most Mexican agricultural workers came to the United States legally during the years of the program, it is believed that several million others came illegally. This practice, too, set a precedent for the future.

Mark DeStephano

FURTHER READING

Boye, De Mente. *NTC's Dictionary of Mexican Cultural Code Words.* Lincolnwood, Ill.: NTC, 1996.

Gonzales, Manuel G. *Mexicanos: A History of Mexicans in the United States.* Bloomington: Indiana University Press, 1999.

Gutiérrez, David G., ed. *The Columbia History of Latinos in the United States Since 1960.* New York: Columbia University Press, 2004.

SEE ALSO: Agriculture; Agriculture, U.S. Department of; Farm labor; Immigration; Labor history; Latin American trade with the United States; Mexican trade with the United States; North American Free Trade Agreement; United Farm Workers of America; World War II.

Bretton Woods Agreement

THE EVENT: International convention that reached an agreement establishing the International Monetary Fund and the International Bank for Reconstruction and Development

DATE: July 1-July 22, 1944

PLACE: Bretton Woods, New Hampshire

SIGNIFICANCE: The International Monetary Fund maintains a system of fixed exchange rates centered on gold and the U.S. dollar, and the International Bank for Reconstruction and Development provides economic assistance to developing countries. By creating them both, the Bretton Woods Agreement began a new era of international finance and monetary policy.

The Bretton Woods Agreement is the common name for the agreement arising out of the United Nations Monetary and Financial Conference, which was held in Bretton Woods, New Hampshire, from July 1 to July 22, 1944. Many nations had responded to the Great Depression during the 1930's by adopting nationalist measures focused within each nation's borders: They devalued their currencies, adopted high tariff barriers, and established unfair trading blocs. Rather than solving the global economic problems, these tactics led to further instability and brought many global leaders to conclude that economic cooperation was the only way the world could achieve peace and prosperity.

On August 9, 1941, U.S. president Franklin D. Roosevelt and British prime minister Winston Churchill crafted the Atlantic Charter, which called for global economic cooperation and lower trade barriers. The charter was announced on August 14 and was quickly adopted by the Allied nations.

By 1942, John Maynard Keynes, an adviser to the British treasury, and Harry Dexter White, an assistant to the U.S. secretary of the Treasury, had drafted plans for an organization to provide financial assistance to nations undergoing economic difficulties. Their plans called for fixed exchange rates, which, in theory, were expected to lead to expanded world trade. Between 1942 and 1944, representatives of the United States and Great Britain met several times to work out the details of this mechanism, and on April 21, 1944, the nations issued the Joint Statement by Experts on the Establishment of an International Monetary Fund, which formed the basis of the Bretton Woods negotiations.

As World War II neared its end, the United States invited more than seven hundred delegates from forty-four Allied nations to agree on a new series of rules to govern and manage the international monetary system. The resulting agreements brought order to the international financial and monetary system and established the International Monetary Fund (IMF) and the International Bank for Reconstruction and Development (IBRD).

The IMF serves as a forum in which nations consult on macroeconomic issues. It is entrusted with maintaining a system of fixed exchange rates centered on gold and the U.S. dollar. Its task is to expand world trade by providing financial assistance to countries facing short-term deficits in their balance of payments.

The IBRD provided financial assistance at first for reconstruction in countries that had been damaged during World War II. It later provided economic assistance to developing nations.

The United States became a member of the IMF and IBRD in July, 1945, when Congress passed the Bretton Woods Agreements Act. The two organizations were officially established on December 27, 1945.

Terry A. Anderson

FURTHER READING

McClure, Paul S., ed. *A Guide to the World Bank.* Washington, D.C.: World Bank, 2003.

Peet, Richard. *Unholy Trinity: The IMF, World Bank, and WTO.* London: Zed Books, 2003.

Woods, Ngaire. *The Globalizers: The IMF, the World Bank, and Their Borrowers.* Ithaca, N.Y.: Cornell University Press, 2007.

SEE ALSO: Gold standard; International economics and trade; Marshall Plan; World Trade Organization; World War II.

Bridges

DEFINITION: Structures, typically of metal, wood, or stone, that span a river or other waterway

SIGNIFICANCE: Bridges are important to commerce in that they permit travel by roadway over otherwise impassable bodies of water, thus making trading easier and faster. Some of the earliest American corporations formed to create bridges.

Since ancient times, human societies have built bridges across waterways, particularly narrow bodies of water such as streams. As local economies increasingly became regional and national economies, the need for bridges increased. At first, ferryboats were used to transport individuals across streams. As the level of trade increased, however, the loads became too large for the boats to handle efficiently, and the cost of making multiple trips by ferryboat resulted in high prices for the goods being ferried. Bridges began to present an economical alternative. In some cases, owners of ferryboats built toll bridges to replace their own ferry services. Early bridges were built of wood, but iron and steel became the materials of choice during the late nineteenth century, particularly for larger bridges.

When the young American states began chartering corporations shortly after the end of the Revolutionary War, private enterprises constructing and running toll bridges were among the first to be incorporated in each state. Bridges were not yet considered to be a public good that would be provided by the government, so their construction had to be financed privately. As the country spread westward, additional states joined the union, and their legislatures also saw fit to permit entrepreneurs to construct toll bridges. As a result, toll bridges were among the first corporations to be chartered in the eastern and midwestern states. The only corporations to predate toll bridges were canal builders and financial institutions. Even toll roads were not chartered as corporations until after toll bridges were incorporated. In fact, some experts speculate that entrepreneurs were inspired to build toll roads only after it became evident that toll bridges were so successful.

SUCCESSFUL TOLL BRIDGES

The toll bridges built by the early corporations were indeed among the most successful of early American businesses. The bridges over smaller rivers required only a small amount of capital for construction and virtually no working capital. The smallest bridges were often individually owned, but larger bridges required a degree of capital that only incorporating can provide. The first toll bridge corporation, formed in Boston in 1785, was the Charles River Bridge company. The bridge was completed one year later. It was so successful that two more Boston bridge corporations were chartered in 1787. No additional bridge corporations were formed until one in Maryland in 1791. The following year, ten bridge corporations were chartered in four states—Massachusetts, New Hampshire, Rhode Island, and

		Number
Age	*Year Built*	*of Bridges*
0-4	2003-2007	25,405
5-9	1998-2002	37,476
10-14	1993-1997	39,594
15-19	1988-1992	43,154
20-24	1983-1987	41,106
25-29	1978-1982	36,383
30-34	1973-1977	40,974
35-39	1968-1972	50,188
40-44	1963-1967	55,058
45-49	1958-1962	52,375
50-54	1953-1957	35,084
55-59	1948-1952	27,713
60-64	1943-1947	8,152
65-69	1938-1942	24,642
70-74	1933-1937	22,994
75-79	1928-1932	23,954
80-84	1923-1927	9,889
85-89	1918-1922	7,602
90-94	1913-1917	3,727
95-100	1908-1912	3,812
100+	1907 and before	9,993

AGE IN YEARS OF U.S. BRIDGES AS OF 2007

Source: Data from Federal Highway Administration, U.S. Department of Transportation

New Jersey. The first bridge corporation in New Jersey was called the President, Managers, and Company of Rancocus Toll-Bridge. The company sold one hundred shares of stock at $80 each, providing total capital of $8,000.

By the end of 1800, a total of seventy-two bridge companies had been incorporated in ten of the original colonies (none in Virginia, Delaware, or North Carolina), plus one in Kentucky. The Kentucky firm was the Frankfort Bridge Company, founded in 1799 to build a bridge in that city (the state capital). This was the only corporation of any kind chartered in Kentucky before 1800. The number of bridge companies increased greatly during the early nineteenth century. Some of these enterprises had rather long lives. For example, the Piermont Bridge Corporation, chartered in New Hampshire in 1827, was still operating during the 1860's.

RAILROAD BRIDGES

Bridges had to precede the growth of railroads. Railroads covered long distances and permitted trade among buyers and sellers located hundreds of miles apart, but transporting freight over great distances meant that many rivers had to be crossed. The most costly components of a railroad, and the most time-consuming to complete, were the bridges. Railroad bridges had to be of superior construction to support the weight of steel tracks and fully loaded trains. In many cases, because of the cost of building the bridges, some railroads had to initially use ferryboats to get trains across wide rivers until the bridges could be built. For example, the Illinois Central Railroad used large steamboats to ferry entire trains across the Ohio River for several years until the bridge was completed at Cairo, Illinois, in 1869. The importance of railroad bridges is demonstrated by the fact that the railroad bridges in the Confederate states were among the favorite targets of Northern troops during the U.S. Civil War.

Bridges provided the link that allowed for countrywide transportation services—whether roads or railways. Although railroads still own their own bridges, the era of privately owned toll bridges connecting roads ended during the early twentieth century, when these bridges were taken over by state highway departments. In some cases, the tolls continued but were assessed by a quasi-governmental bridge authority.

Bridges are still as valuable as ever, and their impor-

tance has made them a public good, built and maintained by state funds. The collapse of a bridge on Interstate 35W over the Mississippi River in Minneapolis in August, 2007, raised questions about the conditions of the country's aging bridges. The Federal Highway Administration subsequently issued a report stating that, as of 2007, more than 150,000 of the nearly 600,000 bridges in the United States were in need of repairs or upgrading, estimated to cost $140 billion.

Dale L. Flesher

FURTHER READING

Ambrose, Stephen E. *Nothing Like It in the World.* New York: Simon & Schuster, 2000. Discusses the role of bridge building for the Transcontinental Railroad and includes several photos of the building process.

Davis, Joseph Stancliffe. *Essays in the Earlier History of American Corporations.* Cambridge, Mass.: Harvard University, 1917. A collection of essays on various types of early corporations, including toll bridges.

Dilts, James D. *The Great Road.* Stanford, Calif.: Stanford University Press, 1993. An excellent history of the Baltimore and Ohio Railroad, including extensive discussion of railroad bridges.

Jackson, Robert W. *Rails Across the Mississippi: A History of the St. Louis Bridge.* Urbana: University of Illinois Press, 2001. An excellent history of the Eads Bridge over the Mississippi River that was started in 1867.

Schuyler, Hamilton. *The Roeblings: A Century of Engineers, Bridge-Builders and Industrialists.* Princeton, N.J.: Princeton University Press, 1931. History of three generations of a family of bridge builders.

Toll Facilities in the United States: Bridges, Roads, Tunnels, Ferries. Washington, D.C.: U.S. Department of Transportation, 1995. An overview of all modern toll facilities in the United States, including bridges.

SEE ALSO: Army Corps of Engineers, U.S.; Canals; Construction industry; Highways; Railroads; Transcontinental railroad; Transportation, U.S. Department of; Turnpikes.

Broadcasting industry. *See* Radio broadcasting industry; Television broadcasting industry

Brotherhood of Sleeping Car Porters

IDENTIFICATION: Labor union representing African American railroad porters

DATE: Founded on August 25, 1925

SIGNIFICANCE: The Brotherhood of Sleeping Car Porters was the first national union of any profession to be organized by African Americans. For over five decades, the brotherhood worked to oppose racism and class prejudice in hiring practices, both within and outside the transportation industry, and many of its members became leaders of the 1960's Civil Rights movement.

The Brotherhood of Sleeping Car Porters was secretly organized on August 25, 1925, under the leadership of journalist and activist A. Philip Randolph. It would eventually represent some 250,000 members during its corporate existence. The four major railway-related labor unions of the time (serving engineers, firemen, trainmen, and conductors) refused to admit African Americans as members. Thus, in 1925, the predominantly African American porters lacked the rights and bargaining leverage gained by other members of the American labor force through national union representation.

A. Philip Randolph. (Library of Congress)

The union's creation challenged the severely restrictive labor policies of the privately held Pullman Company, the chief manufacturer and operator of railroad sleeping cars in the American market. The company did not recognize the legitimacy of independent labor organizations and refused to deal with them, preferring instead to maintain a company union under its complete control. The first nine years of the brotherhood's existence were marked by struggles not only against the company but also against white organized labor organizations such as the American Federation of Labor, which were indifferent to racially discriminatory hiring and workplace practices. The union also confronted a federal government that repeatedly failed to investigate allegations of racism in the labor force.

The economic impact of the Great Depression provided the brotherhood with opportunities more effectively to challenge unfair practices, and the Amended Railway Labor Act of 1934 specifically outlawed company unions, requiring a company to negotiate with the union that represented a majority of its employees. Porters enjoyed a high social status within the group of service professionals such as waiters and cooks considered to perform "negro work." This status was matched by the union's emphasis on working to achieve racial integration and job parity in other fields outside the railway companies by forging political alliances with the federal government.

The interstate mobility of the brotherhood's members also allowed them to use the rails as a network over which information and strategies could be widely shared. The union helped create local chapters of the National Association for the Advancement of Colored People (NAACP) and distributed copies of the *Chicago Defender* across the South to educate prospective migrants seeking jobs in the North and Midwest about the job markets they would find in those regions.

On February 28, 1978, the brotherhood merged with the Brotherhood of Railway and Airline Clerks. This merger reflected the diminished importance of railway travel in the United States, the 1970 collapse of the Penn Central Railroad (which had merged with the Pullman Company), and a decline in the union's membership that was due to the aging and changing employment patterns of African Americans in the national workforce.

Robert B. Ridinger

FURTHER READING

Chateuvert, Melinda. *Marching Together: Women of the Brotherhood of Sleeping Car Porters.* Urbana: University of Illinois Press, 1998.

Harris, William H. *Keeping the Faith: A. Philip Randolph, Milton P. Webster, and the Brotherhood of Sleeping Car Porters.* Urbana: University of Illinois Press, 1977.

Wilson, Joseph W. *Tearing Down the Color Bar: A Documentary History and Analysis of the Brotherhood of Sleeping Car Porters.* New York: Columbia University Press, 1989.

SEE ALSO: Labor strikes; Pullman Strike; Railroads; Randolph, A. Philip; Transcontinental railroad; World War II.

Buffett, Warren

IDENTIFICATION: Successful and well-known American investor who became one of the richest people in the world

BORN: August 30, 1930; Omaha, Nebraska

SIGNIFICANCE: Buffett turned a talent for business and a head for numbers into a very successful investment career. His investment strategies and business plans have been both copied and criticized.

Warren Buffett bought his first stock at the age of eleven, later selling it for a profit of $5 per share. He enrolled in Columbia University in 1950 to study under Benjamin Graham, author of *The Intelligent Investor* (1949). Buffett worked at Graham's investment management company from 1954 to 1956 before returning to Omaha. There, he persuaded seven friends and relatives, including his sister Doris and his aunt Alice, to give him $105,000 to invest. In 1965, he took control of Berkshire Hathaway, a textile manufacturer, and in 1967, he bought National Indemnity, an insurance company, to generate more cash for investing. Buffett developed his own variation of Graham's method of identifying and buying undervalued companies, which is known as value investing. He invested so successfully that he made the *Forbes* 400 (an annual list of the richest people in the world) in 1979 and was named the richest person in the world in 2008 by the magazine.

Nicknamed the Oracle of Omaha, Buffett is famous for living modestly despite his enormous wealth. His salary is about $100,000, the lowest of all the chief executive officers in the *Fortune* 500 list of companies. The headquarters staff for Berkshire Hathaway consists of about fifteen people, also the lowest in the *Fortune* 500. He lives in the same house in Omaha that he bought in 1958 for $31,500. Buffett also is a noted philanthropist. In 2006, he gave away stock worth more than $30 billion to the Bill and Melinda Gates Foundation.

In 2008, during the financial crisis, Buffett invested $5 billion in the Goldman Sachs Group and his Berkshire Hathaway (a holding company) agreed to buy $3 billion in preferred stock of ailing General Electric. These investments were viewed as being in line with Buffett's strategy, which is to invest in good companies when they are experiencing weakness. His moves were regarded as providing the companies with a boost not only to the companies' bottom lines but also to their reputations.

Thomas R. Feller

Warren Buffett. (AP/Wide World Photos)

FURTHER READING

Buffett, Warren. *The Essays of Warren Buffett: Lessons for Corporate America*. Edited by Lawrence A. Cunningham. New York: Cunningham Group, 2001.

Lowenstein, Roger. *Buffett: The Making of an American Capitalist*. New York: Random House, 1995.

O'Loughlin, James. *The Real Warren Buffett: Managing Capital, Leading People*. London: Nicholas Brealey, 2004.

SEE ALSO: Financial crisis of 2008; *Forbes*; Gates, Bill; Gould, Jay; NASDAQ; Rockefeller, John D.; Stock markets.

Bush tax cuts of 2001

THE EVENT: President George W. Bush's signing of the Economic Growth and Tax Relief Reconciliation Act

DATE: Signed on June 7, 2001

PLACE: Washington, D.C.

SIGNIFICANCE: The Economic Growth and Tax Relief Reconciliation Act was designed to give tax breaks to business owners and the upper class in an effort to stimulate the market. Although some experts argue that the act initially helped the economy, many note that it had negative effects by reducing government revenues.

The Economic Growth and Tax Relief Reconciliation Act (EGTRRA), signed into law on June 7, 2001, by George W. Bush, affected many areas of the tax code. The two major changes were the elimination of the estate tax and a decrease in income tax rates. The law also altered other aspects of the tax code, including the basis of inherited property, the marriage penalty, child tax credits, pension plans, education savings accounts, and the alternative minimum tax.

The estate tax is to be phased out under the provisions of the tax cuts. Before the passage of the act, an estate worth less than $675,000 was exempt from estate taxes, while significantly larger estates could pay taxes at rates of over 50 percent. The act slowly increased the exemption amount for estates and decreased the tax rate over a number of years. By 2009, all estates worth less than $3.5 million were to be exempt from paying estate taxes, and the maximum amount of tax that larger estates will have to pay is not to exceed 45 percent.

EGTRRA was also designed to reduce income taxes over the course of several years. By 2006, individuals who were paying 28 percent of their income in taxes saw their tax rate reduced to 25 percent. Those in slightly higher tax brackets (31 percent and 36 percent) also had their taxes reduced by 3 percent. The biggest tax cut went to those who had higher incomes and were paying 39.6 percent of their income in taxes. These individuals saw their taxes decrease by 4.6 percent.

The two major components of EGTRRA, the elimination of the estate tax and a reduction in income tax rates, strongly favored those in the highest income brackets. The 2001 tax cuts were a short-term fix that was designed to generate economic growth, but as of 2008, this plan had not safeguarded the economy from decline. Additionally, in 2010, the tax cuts are due to expire, and in the absence of further action by Congress, the tax rates are to return to pre-2001 levels.

Christine A. Wernet

SEE ALSO: Income tax, corporate; Income tax, personal; Presidency, U.S.; September 11 terrorist attacks; Supply-side economics; Taxation; Trickle-down theory.

Business crimes

DEFINITION: Crimes committed by individuals or corporations during the course of business, usually for economic reasons

SIGNIFICANCE: White-collar crimes such as embezzlement, fraud, tax evasion, false advertising, and unfair labor practices have occurred with regularity throughout the history of businesses and corporations. Whether committed at the individual or corporate level, these crimes can destroy companies and the lives of employees and investors as well as hurt customers and everyday Americans.

Although business crimes can be perpetrated by business owners, most white-collar crimes are committed by individuals who work for or manage businesses. Therefore, business crime in the United States has developed hand in hand with the growth of large businesses. As businesses grow too large for every aspect of their operation to be overseen by their owners, the opportunities for fraud and embezzlement multiply. Corporations, in which ownership and management are separated, are especially vulnerable to white-collar crime. One of the earliest forms of corporations, the railroads, were subject to fraud for a number of reasons: They had lots of cash, assets were spread out over miles of countryside, and the business was too large for a single manager to oversee operations. Therefore, the early railroad companies experienced numerous instances of fraud. By the 1870's, half of the railroads in America were in receivership, many because of the illegal acts of corporate managers.

HISTORICAL FRAUDS

The largest railroad fraud of the nineteenth century involved Crédit Mobilier of America, the construction company that built the transcontinental railroad. An 1872 article in the powerful *New York Sun* accused noted politicians of accepting stock in Crédit Mobilier in exchange for their influence in Congress. The company's objective was to ensure that Congress would not delay federal money being funneled into railroad construction. To make the matter worse, it was determined that Crédit Mobilier intended to defraud the government by overcharging for construction of the tracks. Insiders at the Union Pacific Railroad had created the construction company so that they could pay themselves millions of dollars.

The most widely held securities in the United States during the 1920's were the stocks and bonds of Kreuger & Toll, a Swedish match conglomerate. In 1932, the bankruptcy of Ivar Kreuger's empire of shell companies following his suicide led to a national outcry that resulted in congressional passage of the 1933 Securities Act. Before 1933, companies that depended on stockholder financing were not required to have audits. That changed largely because of Kreuger.

In 1938, the McKesson & Robbins drug company was the victim of insider fraud perpetrated by Philip Musica. As president of the drug company, Musica had used a facade of false documents to conceal the fact that $19 million in inventory and receivables were nonexistent. During the 1960's, the news centered on the salad oil swindle at the Allied Crude Vegetable Oil Refining Corporation and the mis-

deeds of Texan Billie Sol Estes, an associate of Lyndon B. Johnson.

The salad oil swindle was perpetrated by Anthony "Tino" DeAngelis, who moved a small amount of soybean oil around in hundreds of large tanks. He then got the American Express Field Warehousing Company to certify that all the tanks were full of oil, when in reality the tanks were full of water with a small amount of oil on the top. Based on the phony warehouse receipts, DeAngelis was able to get bankers to lend him hundreds of millions of dollars.

Texas businessman Estes fraudulently collected federal subsidies on cotton that he claimed to have grown and stored by purchasing allotments from other farmers. He also had used nonexistent fertilizer tanks as collateral in the allotment scheme. An investigator in Estes's case died, and although the death was originally believed to be a suicide, it was later determined to be a murder. Some of Estes's business associates also died. Estes later claimed that Johnson was involved in the scandal, and perhaps even involved in the deaths. The salad oil swindle tended to give big business a bad name, as many people believed that all business deals were at least somewhat shady, and the Estes case led some people to believe that government was involved in business crime.

MODERN HIGH-TECH FRAUDS

The 1970's witnessed the dawn of computer fraud, with extensive news coverage of the use of computers to defraud shareholders at Equity Funding Corporation of America, a Los Angeles-based financial firm that sold life insurance and mutual funds to individuals. At Equity Funding, top management created nonexistent insurance policies on the computer, deceiving investors and regulators. At that time, auditors were not familiar with computers and failed to uncover the fraud. Two former employees revealed the company's misdeeds.

During the 1980's, hundreds of financial institutions, primarily savings and loan associations, failed because of insider fraud, leading to a congressional investigation headed by Michigan congressman John Dingell. The oddest part about the cases of the 1980's was that so many companies were involved, and most of them were in the same industry.

In the twenty-first century, HealthSouth, Global Crossing, Tyco International, Enron, and World-Com were all involved in scandals that were reminis-

Former head of Qwest Communications, Joe Nacchio, arrives at the federal courthouse in Denver for sentencing on insider trading charges in July, 2007. He was one of many top-level executives targeted by a government task force established in 2002. (AP/Wide World Photos)

cent of the nineteenth century railroad cases and the Kreuger debacle. In every case, the corporate governance system broke down or did not exist, and greedy individuals either took corporate assets for their personal use or manipulated stock prices to defraud stockholders. The seemingly endless string of financial frauds in public corporations has cast doubt on the credibility of even untarnished corporations. Such trust, once lost, is slow to return. The result of these highly publicized white-collar crimes was doldrums in the financial markets during the 1870's, 1930's, the 1960's, the 1980's, and the early years of the twenty-first century.

Dale L. Flesher

FURTHER READING

Cooper, Cynthia. *Extraordinary Circumstances: The Journey of a Corporate Whistleblower.* New York: Wiley, 2008. The full story of the downfall of WorldCom by the internal auditor who uncovered the fraud.

Fox, Loren. *Enron: The Rise and Fall.* Hoboken, N.J.: Wiley, 2003. Examines Enron's culture and what led to the fraud there. Also discussed are the impacts on the financial markets and the U.S. economy.

Miller, Norman C. *The Great Salad Oil Swindle.* New York: Coward McCann, 1965. Tells the story of how one man manipulated millions of gallons of nonexistent salad oil, resulting in the bankruptcy of two Wall Street brokerage houses; caused the demise of a subsidiary of American Express Company; and destroyed the stability of the stock market.

Minkow, Barry. *Clean Sweep.* Nashville, Tenn.: Thomas Nelson, 1995. Autobiographical work describing the author's leadership at ZZZBest, involcing one of the largest frauds of the 1980's.

Pilzer, Paul Zane, and Robert Deitz. *Other People's Money: The Inside Story of the S&L Mess.* New York: Simon & Schuster, 1989. The story behind the frauds at savings and loan associations during the 1980's.

Shaplen, Robert. *Kreuger: Genius and Swindler.* New York: Alfred A. Knopf, 1960. Explains the role of Ivar Kreuger in what at the time was the largest corporate bankruptcy in history. Kreuger's securities were the most widely held in the world.

SEE ALSO: Computer industry; Enron bankruptcy; Gambling industry; Identity theft; Justice, U.S. Department of; Organized crime; Ponzi schemes; Private security industry; Racketeer Influenced and Corrupt Organizations Act; Secret Service, U.S.; Treasury, U.S. Department of the.

Business cycles

DEFINITION: Fluctuations in overall economic activity—expansions in overall output, followed by declines and subsequent revivals—that occur in countries where most of the goods are produced in private, for-profit firms

SIGNIFICANCE: Business cycles have been an important part of American business history. For example, severe depressions occurred in 1818-1819, 1837-1843, 1873-1879, and 1929-1933, causing major declines in the standard of living of the average worker. Since the end of World War II, the strength of expansions has greatly exceeded contractions, resulting in significant business prosperity.

The term "business cycle" is slightly misleading, because fluctuations in overall output and related economic indicators do not occur at precisely regular intervals. These economic aggregates, however, do move with a degree of regularity that has been observed in the United States for nearly two hundred years. Business cycles vary greatly in magnitude as well as duration, yet they have certain features in common. First, they are national or international in scope. Second, they have direct impacts on production, employment, wages, prices, retail sales, construction, and international trade. Third, they are persistent, meaning that they last for several years. In general, the expansion in business activity lasts for a longer period of time than the decline. This result has been observed not only in the United States but also in Great Britain, France, and Germany.

PRINCIPAL FEATURES

Most industries and other economic sectors exhibit a fluctuating pattern of economic activity that generally conforms to the overall cyclical movement of the economy. An important exception is the agricultural sector. Agricultural production depends more on the weather and improvements in technology than on overall business conditions. The production of producer and consumer durable goods moves with a high degree of association with overall business conditions, and producer durable goods demonstrate wide cyclical movements in production, employment, and inventories. Fluctuations in production and employment are smaller for nondurable goods and services. One reason is that purchases of nondurable goods and services (items such as food, clothing, and medical care) are less readily postponed in difficult economic times than those of durable goods (such as automobiles).

Private investment expenditures are much smaller in the aggregate than overall consumer spending. However, the level of investment is much more volatile than the level of consumption. Aggregate investment depends critically on business expectations, which can be highly variable over time; consumer expenditures are considerably more stable. The level of business profits varies closely with the overall business cycle and indicates a much greater amplitude of cyclical movements than the level of wages and salaries, dividends, net interest, or rental income.

The level of wholesale prices tends to have wider fluctuations over the course of the business cycle than the levels of retail prices and wages. This is primarily because business-to-business sales (wholesale) are much more variable than sales from business to the consumer (retail). Virtually all recessions or depressions before 1950 were associated with declines in wholesale prices. Since 1950, wholesale prices have never fallen during an economic decline; however, in each of the nine U.S. recessions from 1953 through 2001, there was a temporary reduction in the rate of price increase. In contrast to prices for consumer and producer goods, however, prices of industrial commodities continued to show a high degree of sensitivity to business cycles, often declining even in periods of slow economic growth as well as during absolute declines in overall economic activity.

An increase in unemployment is a universal occurrence in recessions. As new business orders and

REAL GROSS DOMESTIC PRODUCT PER CAPITA IN THE UNITED STATES

Period	Avg. Annual Change (%)
1979-1990	2.0
1990-1995	1.2
1995-2000	2.9
2001-2002	0.6
2002-2003	1.5
2003-2004	2.7
2005-2006	1.9
2006-2007	1.2
1979-2007	1.8

Source: Data from U.S. Department of Labor, Bureau of Labor Statistics, Office of Productivity and Technology, "Comparative Real Gross Domestic Product per Capita and per Employed Person" (Washington, D.C.: Author, 2008)

Note: Real gross domestic product (GDP) is expressed in 2005 U.S. dollars. Real GDP is the value of all market and some nonmarket goods and services produced within a country, stated using the base-year price level. Per capita GDP is used to measure a country's prosperity.

output decline, workers are laid off. Wage stability prevents workers from easily finding new jobs at lower wage rates. Thus, during the declining phase of the business cycle, unemployment increases. When business revives, unemployment often declines slowly. This is because businesses want to be sure that the cyclical expansion will be sustained before they rehire workers or train new employees. Therefore, in 2002 and 2003, unemployment remained relatively high, even as the economy rebounded from the recession of 2001 and production surpassed prerecession levels.

During severe recessions, such as those in 1973-1975 and 1981-1982, a significant portion of unemployment is characterized as long term. This refers to workers who have been unemployed for fourteen weeks or longer. Long-term unemployment poses a particular problem because the economic resources that families have available, primarily their personal savings and unemployment insurance, often are exhausted after several months.

A DIFFERENT CYCLE

Growth cycles need to be distinguished from business cycles. Most economic fluctuations begin with much-reduced but still positive growth rates, which then develop into actual declines. However, some slowdowns do not result in absolute declines in economic growth and subsequently move into a phase of increased expansion, not recession. This phenomena is known as a growth cycle.

Since 1950, declines in growth in the United States that have not led to actual declines in economic activity occurred in 1951-1952, 1962-1964, 1966-1967, 1979, and 2007. Their adverse effects were felt primarily in areas of particular cyclical sensitivity, notably in housing starts and stock prices. Unemployment ceased declining but did not rise significantly, and profits declined slightly rather than falling dramatically. Thus, the overall impact of any of these slowdowns in economic activity was definitely less than even the mildest of recessions.

Alan L. Sorkin

FURTHER READING

Glasner, David, ed. *Business Cycles and Depressions: An Encyclopedia.* New York: Garland, 1997. Comprehensive volume that includes theories of business cycles and descriptions of individual panics or depressions.

Gordon, Robert J., ed. *The American Business Cycle: Continuity and Change.* Chicago: University of Chicago Press, 1986. Outstanding advanced treatise on the courses of business cycles and the economic policies that are formulated to deal with them.

McEachern, William A. *Macroeconomics: A Contemporary Introduction.* Mason, Ohio: Southwestern, 2006. Chapter 5 contains a good basic overview of the economic indicators of business cycles.

U.S. Department of Commerce. *Economic Report of the President, 2008.* Washington, D.C.: U.S. Government Printing Office, 2008. This report gives a detailed treatment of overall business conditions and provides large numbers of tables of relevant economic statistics.

Valentine, Lloyd, and Dennis Ellis. *Business Cycles and Forecasting.* Cincinnati: Southwestern, 1991. Well-written textbook for a basic course on business cycles. Readers should be familiar with the essentials of macroeconomics.

SEE ALSO: Banking; Depression of 1808-1809; Great Depression; Interest rates; Recession of 1937-1938; Securities and Exchange Commission; Stock market crash of 1929.

Business schools

DEFINITION: Schools that are designed to teach people the skills and knowledge to be successful in business

SIGNIFICANCE: The establishment of business schools changed the way many businesspeople were educated. Instead of entering apprenticeships, people attended schools where they followed a course of study designed to teach them business.

Before the mid-nineteenth century, an apprenticeship was required to learn to be a businessperson. The apprentice would begin as an office boy and work his way up in an organization. These apprenticeships were usually poorly paid and occasionally unpaid positions. During the 1830's, private proprietary business schools began operating in major cities to provide, in a few months, the training that it might take an apprentice several years to learn. B. F. Foster, who had written books on accounting, started a commercial school in Boston in 1834 and then in 1837 moved to New York, where he started Foster's Commercial Academy. Other authors of business books soon followed, starting schools in other eastern cities. Such schools were common by the start of the U.S. Civil War. Traditional colleges were reluctant to offer business courses, so the proprietary schools had a monopoly on the subject. The most successful of the proprietary schools were those owned by H. B. Bryant, H. G. Stratton, and Silas Packard. By the 1870's, these names were almost synonymous with business education. In fact, companies competed to hire "Packard boys" and eventually "Packard girls," because graduates of these schools, branches of which existed in many cities, were known to be well trained.

EARLY BUSINESS SCANDALS

During the late nineteenth century, a few universities began considering business schools. The first such school was established at the University of Pennsylvania in 1881, when Joseph Wharton made a contribution to support it. The University of Chicago followed in 1898, Dartmouth in 1899, and New York University in 1900. Business education had become a legitimate subject taught at major universities.

The quality of collegiate business education was enhanced in 1916, when the first accreditation agency for business schools was established. The agency, the Association to Advance Collegiate Schools of Business (AACSB) International (formerly known as the American Association of Collegiate Schools of Business), traces its roots to a meeting at the University of Chicago in 1916. Representatives from seventeen business schools met to form an Association of Collegiate Schools of Business. This represented just over half of the thirty schools of business then housed in American universities. During the 1920's, the number of business schools grew, and the number of AACSB members increased as well. In 1925, the AACSB approved new membership standards, including that a school must offer courses in five areas: finance, accounting, business law, marketing, and statistics.

By the beginning of World War II, the AACSB had fifty-five members. By 1951, it had seventy members, one-fifth of which had been admitted in the two preceding years. Member schools employed 2,790 business faculty, nearly double the number employed five years earlier.

REPORTING ON EDUCATION

The 1950's ended with the publication of two major studies: the report by Robert Aaron Gordon and James Edwin Howell, *Higher Education for Business* (1959), and the report by Frank C. Pierson and others, *The Education of American Businessmen: A Study of University-College Programs in Business Administration* (1959). These major studies, which had been funded by the Carnegie and Ford Foundations, would do much to professionalize business schools during the 1960's.

The 1960's was a busy time in business education, partly because the impact of the independent 1959 reports was immediate and substantial. The two foundation reports gave business schools a focus and a mission for at least the next decade and perhaps longer. Because schools began to implement the recommendations of the two reports, business education began to achieve a degree of legitimacy in the larger higher education community. Major universities had been dominated by the arts and sciences, and business schools had ranked somewhere below colleges of education and agriculture. What had previously been viewed as vocational programs achieved high levels of respect on university campuses, and faculty shared in the respect by becoming among the most highly paid employees at most universities. This rise in status can be attributed to the two 1959 foundation reports.

In 1984, on the twenty-fifth anniversary of

TOP TEN BUSINESS SCHOOLS, AS RANKED BY *U.S. News & World Report* IN 2008

1. Harvard University
2. Stanford University
3. University of Pennsylvania (Wharton)
4. Massachusetts Institute of Technology (Sloan)
5. Northwestern University (Kellogg)
   University of Chicago (tied)
7. Dartmouth College (Tuck)
8. University of California, Berkeley (Haas)
9. Columbia University
10. New York University (Stern)

the Pierson and the Gordon and Howell reports, the AACSB commissioned Lyman W. Porter and Lawrence E. McKibbin to reexamine the state of business education. Their report, *Management Education and Development: Drift or Thrust into the Twenty-first Century?* (1988), was the most significant publication in the history of the AACSB. Unlike the 1959 studies, Porter and McKibbin found that business schools were more esteemed than they had been in the earlier period, but many faculty had used that sense of appreciation to justify complacency and self-satisfaction—attributes that threatened the continued existence of effective business education. As with the 1959 reports, the Porter and McKibbin study was to be the foundation for much of what business schools would do in the future.

The period from the late 1960's through the first decade of the twenty-first century has been a time of spectacular growth for business schools. In 1966, the AACSB had 106 member schools, all of which were accredited. By 2006, the organization had more than 1,000 member schools, of which 506 were accredited. By 1966, member schools typically granted 23,000 bachelor's degrees and 6,600 master's degrees in business each year. By 2008, AACSB members were granting more than 210,000 bachelor's degrees in business and more than 104,000 master's degrees per year.

Dale L. Flesher

FURTHER READING

The American Association of Collegiate Schools of Business, 1916-1966. Homewood, Ill.: Richard D. Irwin, 1966. This history covers most changes in business education during the early twentieth century.

Flesher, Dale L. *The History of AACSB International.* Tampa, Fla.: AACSB International, 2007. This volume covers the history of business schools and their relationship to the accreditation agency during the period from 1916 to 2006.

Pierson, Frank C. *The Education of American Businessmen: A Study of University-College Programs in Business Administration.* New York: McGraw-Hill, 1959. This book of more than seven hundred pages summarizes the findings of a survey, sponsored by the Carnegie Foundation, of business education during the late 1950's.

Porter, Lyman W., and Lawrence E. McKibbin. *Management Education and Development: Drift or Thrust into the Twenty-first Century?* New York: McGraw-Hill Book Company, 1988. Excellent overview of business education during the late 1980's.

Previts, Gary J., and Barbara Dubis Merino. *A History of Accountancy in the United States.* Columbus: Ohio State University Press, 1998. Includes a history of nineteenth century accounting education.

SEE ALSO: *Coin's Financial School*; Education; Junior Achievement; Management theory; Washington, Booker T.

Professor Brian Bushee lectures in 2006 at Wharton, the first business school in the United States. (AP/Wide World Photos)

C

Cable News Network

IDENTIFICATION: Cable television channel dedicated to twenty-four-hour news coverage
DATE: Launched on June 1, 1980
SIGNIFICANCE: The original all-news station, CNN proved the commercial viability of broadcasting to a niche market.

The Cable News Network (CNN) was the brainchild of Atlanta, Georgia, media mogul Ted Turner. Turner had already created one of the first cable television superstations, transmitting the signal of local independent television station WTCG to a communications satellite and selling the resulting feed to cable companies across the nation. He saw in the growth of cable the possibility of a market for more specialized stations.

At the time, the model of the generalist station, broadcasting a mix of different types of programming, remained so strong that few expected CNN to succeed when it was launched on June 1, 1980. However, it was successful enough that two years later Turner launched CNN Headline News, which specialized in thirty-minute news summaries rather than the more in-depth coverage that was found on CNN.

Another innovation pioneered by CNN was the open newsroom, in which there was no backdrop set behind the anchor desk. Instead, viewers could look beyond the news anchors to see reporters at their desks, preparing news stories. This innovation was copied in 1982 by the Weather Channel, and as MSNBC, CNBC, and FOX News Channel each entered the twenty-four-hour news niche, they too arranged their sets to allow viewers to see the newsroom at work.

Although CNN was somewhat successful throughout the 1980's, it was the 1991 Gulf War that brought it to prominence. As a result of a combination of factors, CNN was the first channel to be able to provide live reports of the air war directly from Baghdad. Correspondents such as Bernard Shaw and Peter Arnett soon became household names, and CNN became the go-to channel for people seeking world news reports. Because CNN provided twenty-four-hour newscasts without other programming, the news was always available whenever someone wanted to tune in.

The September 11, 2001, terrorist attacks proved another scoop for CNN, which aired a report, complete with an image of the north tower of the World Trade Center on fire, minutes after it was struck. For the next two days, CNN ran continual news coverage, sacrificing millions of dollars of advertising revenue to bring the latest developments as they happened. To present repetitious bits of information while covering ongoing developments, CNN pioneered the news ticker, a constant crawl of textual information across the bottom of the screen similar to stock-ticker crawls on business channels.

Since 1995, CNN has maintained a presence on the World Wide Web. During particularly important breaking news events, traffic to the site can become so heavy that it exceeds the servers' capabilities.

Leigh Husband Kimmel

FURTHER READING

Pike, Sidney. *We Changed the World: Memoirs of a CNN Satellite Pioneer.* St. Paul, Minn.: Paragon House, 2005.
Schonfeld, Reese. *Me and Ted Against the World: The Unauthorized Story of the Founding of CNN.* New York: Cliff Street, 2001.
Whittemore, Hank. *CNN: The Inside Story.* Boston: Little, Brown, 1990.

SEE ALSO: CNBC; *Fortune*; National Broadcasting Company; Newspaper industry; Radio broadcasting industry; Telecommunications industry; Television broadcasting industry; *USA Today*.

California gold rush

THE EVENT: The migration of tens of thousands of individuals from around the world to California after the discovery of gold
DATE: 1848 to mid-1850's
PLACE: California
SIGNIFICANCE: The gold rush era led to the creation of the institutions that still govern American mining, sparked the development of the American West, brought rapid population growth to Sacra-

mento and San Francisco, and created demand for transcontinental railroads and telegraphs and for international shipping between California and all parts of the world.

On January 24, 1848, a carpenter working on a millrace found a piece of gold about half the size of a pea, exclaimed "Boys, I believe I have found a gold mine," and launched the California gold rush. Nine days later, before news of the discovery reached the outside world, Mexico ceded California and much of the American West to the United States to end the Mexican War.

THE RUSH

As the news spread around the world, California's population grew from a few thousand to twenty thousand by the end of 1848; ninety thousand people arrived during 1849 alone. Hundreds of thousands more came over the next decade, transforming a sleepy backwater into a major population center with thriving businesses. Most important, the gold rush occurred in an institutional vacuum, because miners started mining long before California's government was established. Indeed, the population boom outpaced Congress's ability to decide how to organize the newly acquired territories, and California ultimately entered the union as a state without first acquiring territorial status.

CREATING MINING LAW

The gold rush produced institutions that would continue to govern hard rock mineral mining in the United States. Because gold was discovered before the United States had organized its new acquisition or even established the basic functions of its government, miners were able to create their own institutions. Through camp meetings, miners established simple rules: a system of private ownership of mineral rights based on discovery, a sparse set of prohibitions on violence enforced through group action, a property registry, and respect for contracts. By simply moving onto the

land and engaging in mining, they established de facto the principle of free access to public land for those seeking minerals.

Because California became a state almost immediately after gold's discovery and because miners dominated early California politics, mining interests enjoyed vigorous representation in Congress. This representation enabled them to stall efforts to assert federal ownership of the mineral resources of the newly acquired West. Furthermore, as gold prospectors spread to other locations, following other mineral booms, they carried the institutions created in California with them. As a result, by the time the federal government finally legislated on mining in

PRESIDENT POLK ACKNOWLEDGES CALIFORNIA'S GOLD

On December 5, 1848, President James K. Polk announced to Congress in his state of the union address the discovery of phenomenal amounts of gold in California, thereby giving credibility not only to the gold rush but also to the state itself. His words opened the floodgates to miners from around the world.

It was known that mines of the precious metals existed to a considerable extent in California at the time of its acquisition. Recent discoveries render it probable that these mines are more extensive and valuable than was anticipated. . . .

The effects produced by the discovery of these rich mineral deposits and the success which has attended the labors of those who have resorted to them have produced a surprising change in the state of affairs in California. Labor commands a most exorbitant price, and all other pursuits but that of searching for the precious metals are abandoned. Nearly the whole of the male population of the country have gone to the gold districts. Ships arriving on the coast are deserted by their crews and their voyages suspended for want of sailors. Our commanding officer there entertains apprehensions that soldiers can not be kept in the public service without a large increase of pay. Desertions in his command have become frequent, and he recommends that those who shall withstand the strong temptation and remain faithful should be rewarded.

This abundance of gold and the all-engrossing pursuit of it have already caused in California an unprecedented rise in the price of all the necessaries of life.

1866, it had little choice but to accept the existing mining practices. (Congress consolidated federal mining law in the General Mining Law of 1872.) Thus, the gold rush decisively shaped the laws governing the mineral industry in the United States. Both critics and supporters of the 1872 General Mining Law agree that it originated in the gold rush, even as they disagree about whether maintaining that statute in the twenty-first century is appropriate.

CREATING THE CALIFORNIA MARKET

The creation of the state of California itself was a major contribution of the gold rush. The state's vibrant economy (if the state were an independent country, its economy now would be the seventh largest in the world) and its sprawling cities make it hard to imagine the time during the mid-nineteenth century when the Mexican territory of California was a backwater populated at most by a few thousand ranchers and missionaries, as well as roughly 150,000 Native Americans. Because the region was too far from Mexico's centers of population to play a major role in supplying agricultural goods to urban centers, its major economic activity consisted of raising cattle for the production of hides and tallow.

The gold rush brought not only miners but also businesspeople and farmers to supply the miners. For example, San Francisco grew from a collection of ramshackle buildings to a thriving city of over fifty-six thousand in 1860, one of the fastest rates of growth of any city in history. Modern California's lucrative agricultural sector has its origins in the production of food for miners.

Although most miners went to California intending to stay only a year or two before returning to their homes in the eastern United States, Australia, Britain, Chile, China, Mexico, and elsewhere, many found the mild climate, fertile soil, and growing business opportunities to be reasons to stay in the state even after they left the mines. With the mining population providing a large market with money to spend, California's business community grew almost as rapidly as did the mines. The lure of California's riches led to the construction of transcontinental railroads and telegraph lines, as well as luring ever more migrants to the new state. In many respects, the gold rush created America as a transcontinental nation.

Andrew P. Morriss

FURTHER READING

Clappe, Louise Amelia Knapp Smith. *The Shirley Letters: From the California Mines, 1851-1852*. Berkeley, Calif.: Heyday, 1998. Insightful and entertaining collection of first-person reports from the gold fields by Dame Shirley, one of the first women visitors to the goldfields during the early 1850's.

Holliday, J. S. *The World Rushed In*. New York: Touchstone, 1981. Thorough synthesis of thousands of letters, diaries, and other primary source documents; brings the gold rush alive and offers a perceptive account of the miners' experiences.

Leshy, John D. *The Mining Law: A Study in Perpetual Motion*. Washington, D.C.: Resources for the Future, 1987. Leshy, later general counsel for the U.S. Department of the Interior, takes a critical view of the history of the gold rush and the resulting statutes.

Morriss, Andrew P. "Miners, Vigilantes, and Cattlemen: Overcoming Free Riders in the Private Provision of Law." *Land and Water Law Review* 33, no. 2 (1998): 581-696. Focuses on the economics of the institutions the miners created and provides a guide to the secondary literature through footnotes.

Umbeck, John. *A Theory of Property Rights with Applications to the California Gold Rush*. Ames: Iowa State University Press, 1981. Umbeck examines hundreds of mining camp records and explores the spontaneous order that arose in the chaos of the gold rush.

SEE ALSO: Black Hills gold rush; "Coolie" labor; Exploration; Gold standard; Klondike gold rush; Mexican War; Mineral resources; Mint, U.S.; Panic of 1857; Pony Express; Vanderbilt, Cornelius.

Canadian trade with the United States

SIGNIFICANCE: Canada is the most important trading partner of the United States and the major export market for thirty-five U.S. states. It is the United States' largest market for food and also is a major market for manufactured goods. The United States imports more agricultural products from Canada than from any other nation and depends on it for forest products and energy.

Major trading between Canada and the United States began with the Canadian-American Reciprocity Treaty in 1854. Before this time, Great Britain had functioned as a ready market for Canadian grain and timber products. Britain's Corn Laws, import tariffs that were created by the Importation Act of 1815, supported the import of grain (primarily wheat) grown in the British colonies rather than foreign-grown, often cheaper, grain. However, when Great Britain repealed its Corn Laws with the Importation Act of 1846, Canada needed to find new markets for its raw materials.

Aware that this act placed a serious hardship on Canada, Britain negotiated the Canadian-American Reciprocity Treaty (Elgin-Marcy Treaty) of 1854 with the United States to provide a market for Canadian raw materials, especially wheat and timber. In accepting the treaty, the United States agreed to eliminate its tariff of 21 percent on the import of raw materials. In exchange, the United States was granted fishing rights off Canada's east coast. In addition, each country received some navigation rights on the other's lakes and rivers.

The treaty resulted in rapid growth in Canada's economy, as exports to the United States grew rapidly, eventually increasing by 33 percent. Exports from the United States to Canada, however, increased by only 7 percent. Trade between the two countries doubled by 1864. Then in 1866, the United States decided to end the treaty, citing three reasons. First, it seemed that only Canada was benefiting from the treaty. Second, the implementation of the Cayley-Galt Tariff, enacted in 1858, imposed a tariff of 20 percent on manufactured goods and of 10 percent on partially manufactured goods imported into Canada. Third, the United States, angered by British aid to the Confederacy, saw the canceling of the treaty as a means of retaliation against Great Britain.

OPPOSITION TO FREE TRADE

In 1871, negotiations for the Treaty of Washington began. Although the treaty for the most part addressed issues other than free trade, its acceptance in 1873 did allow free entry into U.S. markets for Canadian fish in return for the admission of U.S. fishermen into Canada's inshore fisheries for a period of twelve years.

From about 1875 to 1900, neither Canada nor the United States was in favor of free trade. In 1891,

Canadian Liberals ran on a platform of unrestricted free trade and lost the election. Many Canadians feared political takeover by the United States because free trade would increase Canada's economic dependence on the United States. Free trade was also opposed by the United States, which maintained a protectionist attitude and a policy of high tariffs on all imports.

In spite of the distrust between the two countries, U.S. companies invested large amounts of money in the Canadian commercial sector, and Canada's developing unions affiliated with their American rather than British counterparts. This increase in economic ties paved the way for an attempt at negotiating a new free trade agreement between the two countries.

In 1911, President William Howard Taft and Prime Minister Wilfrid Laurier concluded an agreement to provide limited free trade on a significant number of manufactured items. In a surprising reversal of its protectionist attitude, the U.S. Congress passed the agreement. However, the Conservative opposition defeated the agreement in Parliament. Laurier himself was defeated in the following general election. Too many Canadians still believed that free trade with the United States would lead to political annexation of Canada.

The early 1930's witnessed continuing opposition to free trade from both Canada and the United States. In 1930, Congress passed the Smoot-Hawley Tariff Act, pushing duties on imports to the United States higher than they had ever been. Canada responded by raising its tariffs in 1932.

TOWARD FREE TRADE

In 1934, the situation began to change, as the United States passed the Reciprocal Trade Agreements Act. The two countries started negotiations to further lower tariffs the following year and signed a new treaty in 1938. During World War II, trade relations continued to improve, as Canada and the United States collaborated economically for the war effort. In 1941, President Franklin D. Roosevelt and Prime Minister William Lyon Mackenzie King met at Hyde Park, New York, to implement an agreement for cooperative war production. The Hyde Park Declaration was signed on April 20, 1941.

After the war, Canada was once again wary of economic dependence on the United States, and having seen its imports from the United States rise to twice as much as it was exporting, Canada preferred multilateral trade agreements and relied on the General Agreement on Trade and Tariffs (GATT) and the agreements reached under the North Atlantic Treaty Alliance (NATO). However, economic involvement between the two countries continued to increase. Canada possessed enormous stores of raw materials but needed the industrial supplies and technology of the United States.

In January, 1965, the Automotive Products Trade Agreement, or Auto Pact (APTA), was signed by Prime Minister Lester B. Pearson and President Lyndon B. Johnson. The agreement eliminated tariffs on cars, buses, trucks, tires, and automobile parts. To protect Canadian workers, the agreement stated that the three major U.S. automobile manufacturers, General Motors, Ford, and Chrysler, would make three of every five cars sold in Canada in Canadian plants. It also ensured that Canadian auto production would not fall below the 1964 level. Although the Auto Pact provided many blue-collar jobs in Canada and thus stimulated the economy, it was detrimental to Canada from the standpoint of creating a large trade deficit, as more cars produced in the United States were sold in Canada. The agreement also prohibited Canada from free trading in automobiles with other nations. In 2001, the Auto Pact was declared illegal by the World Trade Organization; however, other treaties between the United States and Canada had already reduced it to an agreement of relatively little importance.

FREE TRADE

From the 1960's to the 1980's, United States-Canadian trade relations vacillated between a move toward free trade and the imposition of tariffs or surcharges in various areas of trade. In 1983, Prime Minister Pierre Trudeau's government entered into negotiations for free trade in certain economic sectors. Then, in 1985, Prime Minister Brian Mulroney began negotiating a free trade agreement with the United States. In October, 1987, the treaty was drawn up and subsequently ratified by the U.S. Congress and the Canadian Parliament. Within a ten-year period, starting in January, 1989, all tariffs between the two countries were to be eliminated by the treaty.

However, the subject of free trade soon became a

United States Trade with Canada, 1985-2005, in Millions of Dollars			
Year	Exports	Imports	Balance
1985	47,251	69,006	–21,755
1990	83,674	91,380	–7,706
1995	127,226	144,370	–17,144
2000	178,941	280,838	–91,897
2005	211,899	280,384	–68,485

Source: Data from U.S. Census Bureau, Foreign Trade Division, Data Dissemination Branch, Washington, D.C.
Note: Trade figures are from the U.S. perspective.

topic of interest to politicians not only in Canada and the United States but also in Mexico. In December, 1992, President George H. W. Bush, Prime Minister Mulroney, and Mexican president Carlos Salinas de Gortari signed the North American Free Trade Agreement (NAFTA). Agriculture remained an area of contention between Canada and the United States, and this made a single trilateral signing of the treaty impossible. Therefore, three separate agreements were signed by each pair of countries. The agricultural agreement between Canada and the United States still contained tariffs and restrictions on certain agricultural products, including poultry, dairy, and sugar.

The treaty had to be ratified by the legislative body in each of the countries. In all three, it met with strong opposition as fears of job losses, economic dependence, and political annexation arose. However, the treaty was ratified by all three legislative bodies and went into effect on January 1, 1994. In general terms, NAFTA brought about free trade among the three countries.

The treaty has not solved all the problems and controversies surrounding trading between Canada and the United States. The imposition of a 27 percent tariff on the import of Canadian softwood lumber by the United States has caused considerable argument. Canada has been concerned about the provision in NAFTA that states that once anything is sold as a commodity, governments are prohibited from stopping its continued sale as such. The "commodity" causing the problem is water from Canadian lakes and rivers. Another issue involves the importation of banned substances. There has also been dissension over certain changes that Canada has made to its taxation laws.

Public opinion about the benefits of or harm done by NAFTA remain varied, as free trade has been an ongoing issue between Canada and the United States since their first exchange of goods. Whether free trade eliminates or increases jobs, whether it creates a dangerous economic dependence between countries, or whether it has the potential to destroy a country's autonomy all remain unresolved topics of debate associated with trade between the United States and Canada.

Shawncey Webb

FURTHER READING

Anastakis, Dimitry. *Auto Pact: Creating a Borderless North American Auto Industry, 1960-1971.* Toronto: University of Toronto Press, 2005. Views the Auto Pact as good for the Canadian economy, although it eliminated a Canadian automotive industry. Illustrations, bibliography, and appendixes.

Corsi, Jerome R. *The Late Great U.S.A.: The Coming Merger with Mexico and Canada.* Los Angeles: World Ahead Media, 2007. Sees NAFTA as leading to a North American community like the European Union and predicts dangers for the United States. Illustrations, foreword, and appendixes.

Hakim, Peter, and Robert E. Litan, eds. *The Future of North American Integration: Beyond NAFTA.* Washington, D.C.: Brookings Institution Press, 2002. Discusses the issue of how fully NAFTA addresses the relationship among the United States, Canada, and Mexico, and contains essays by experts from the countries.

Orchard, David. *The Fight for Canada: Four Centuries of Resistance to American Expansion.* Westmount, Que.: Robert Davies Multimedia, 1998. Discusses the history of opposition to free trade, U.S. investment in Canada, and the dangers of Canadian economic dependence on the United States.

Thomas, David M., and Barbara Boyle Torrey, eds. *Canada and the United States: Differences That Count.* Peterborough, Ont.: Broadview Press, 2007. Gives insights into Canadian and American attitudes, and can be useful to understand the un-

derlying cultural differences that cause problems in trading, especially free trade.

Thompson, John Herd, and Stephen J. Randall. *Canada and the United States: Ambivalent Allies.* Athens: University of Georgia Press, 2008. Covers Canadian-United States relations from the American Revolution to the present.

Weintraub, Sidney, ed. *NAFTA's Impact on North America: The First Decade.* Washington, D.C.: Center for Strategic and International Studies, 2004. In-depth, unbiased analysis of NAFTA and its effects.

SEE ALSO: Agriculture; Automotive industry; Fishing industry; Forestry industry; Fur trapping and trading; General Agreement on Tariffs and Trade; International economics and trade; Mexican trade with the United States; Multinational corporations; North American Free Trade Agreement; War of 1812.

Canals

DEFINITION: Combinations of natural waterways and engineered improvements that provide water transportation

SIGNIFICANCE: Canals opened the American frontier, creating new markets for eastern factories and providing access to the raw materials in the Midwest. They enabled businesses to become more efficient; however, several states suffered bankruptcies during the 1830's because of investments in canals.

Small canals were first created in the United States during the late eighteenth century. One canal project, the Powtomack Company, was led by George Washington, who thought that canals offered the nation the best hope of linking its regions into a united country. However, the first major canal to influence American business was the Erie Canal, completed in 1825. Governor DeWitt Clinton persuaded the New York legislature to invest $7 million in the construction of a 363-mile waterway to link Lake Erie in western New York to the Hudson River at Albany. The Hudson's path through New York City would make that municipality the greatest port in the world. Lake Erie's connection to the other Great Lakes opened up the frontier (including western Pennsylvania and what would become the states

The locks at the Panama Canal in 1912, before the gates were placed. (Library of Congress)

of Ohio, Indiana, Illinois, Michigan, Wisconsin, and Minnesota) to settlers. The completed canal was considered the engineering marvel of the nineteenth century. The benefits of the Erie Canal were immediate; settlers quickly moved west. Freight rates from Buffalo to New York, which had been $100 per ton by road, dropped to $10 per ton for shipments by canal. Whereas freight rates had previously often exceeded the value of the goods being shipped, the canal rates made it economical to ship more kinds of products. In only nine years, the tolls collected on the Erie Canal were sufficient to recoup the entire cost of construction.

The lower freight rates that resulted from the opening of the Erie Canal made New York City the port of choice for both domestic and foreign shippers. Other New York cities benefited as well; almost every major city in the state falls along the trade route established by the Erie Canal. As a result of the economies demonstrated by the Erie Canal, there was a boom in canal construction in other locales, and a search for alternative forms of transportation that might offer similar economies.

ALTERNATIVE FORMS OF TRANSPORTATION

Some experts argue that even the invention of railroads can be attributed to the opening of the Erie Canal. For example, the Baltimore and Ohio (B&O) Railroad was formed in 1827, when merchants of Baltimore sought to preserve their city's commercial advantage as a seaport link with the American interior. Baltimore had risen to the third largest city in the United States because of the construction of the Cumberland Road that bridged the Allegheny Mountains from Cumberland, Maryland, to the Ohio River Valley and on to the Mississippi

Valley of the Midwest. However, even with the Cumberland Road, travel by wagon was arduous, slow, and costly. The opening of the Erie Canal in 1825 threatened to ruin Baltimore's commercial role, as transport to the Ohio and Mississippi River Valleys shifted to waterborne shipment via canal, lake, and river through New York City.

Because Baltimore did not have direct river access to the west, merchants were willing to consider any ideas. Banker Philip E. Thomas had been corresponding with his brother, Evan, who was in England and was excited about "railed roads" there. The two believed that the cost of construction of a railroad, even over the mountains, would be less than the cost of building the Chesapeake and Ohio Canal (the nearest competitive alternative). The brothers also felt that the railed road offered a mechanical advantage in that horse-drawn wagons in a train could be pulled efficiently on the smooth rails. The merchants of Baltimore quickly warmed to the railed road idea.

Negative Aspects

Although the eastern canals were mostly successful, such was not the case in the Midwest. Canals offered a definite advantage in frontier areas. Compared with railroads, canals could be built using more local materials, allowing money to be expended locally instead of flowing to outside interests. In the case of railroads, the steam engines and the rails had to be imported. Several midwestern states approved laws, often called internal improvements acts, during the 1830's to fund the building of canals. The bonds were to be paid off from revenues generated from canal tolls. Such revenues never materialized, and the bonds, many of which were held by British investors, were never paid off. As a result, these states either had to declare bankruptcy or, at minimum, found they could no longer issue bonds for any purpose. Due to financial mismanagement and the Panic of 1837, the internal improvements in the Midwest came to an end. The longest canal in the Midwest was the Wabash and Erie Canal, which was started in Fort Wayne, Indiana, in 1832. When completed twenty-one years later, the canal stretched from Toledo, Ohio, on Lake Erie to Evansville, Indiana, on the Ohio River. At 468 miles, it was the longest canal ever built in the United States. Its completion created a series of connective waterways from New York City to New Orleans.

Canals were the interstate transportation system of the first half of the nineteenth century, but following the U.S. Civil War, the railroad industry had grown to such an extent that canals became less profitable. In the twenty-first century, many of the old canals had become little more than tourist attractions.

Dale L. Flesher

Further Reading

Bernstein, Peter L. *Wedding of the Waters: The Erie Canal and the Making of a Great Nation.* New York: W. W. Norton, 2005. Engagingly written history of the Erie Canal that considers it in the broad context of nineteenth century American history and demonstrates its impact on national development.

Bourne, Russell. *Floating West: The Erie and Other American Canals.* New York: W. W. Norton, 1992. Series of histories about various American canals; includes bibliographic references.

Hecht, Roger W. *The Erie Canal Reader, 1790-1950.* Syracuse, N.Y.: Syracuse University Press, 2003. Collection of fiction, poetry, essays, and other works about the Erie Canal written over the course of its history.

Rubin, Julius. *Canal or Railroad? Imitation and Innovation in the Response to the Erie Canal in Philadelphia, Baltimore, and Boston.* Philadelphia: American Philosophical Society, 1961. Discusses community responses to the completion of the Erie Canal.

Scheiber, Harry N. *Ohio Canal Era: A Case Study of Government and the Economy, 1820-1861.* Athens: Ohio University Press, 1969. Although this book deals with the problems of the Ohio canals, the situations were similar in the other midwestern states.

Shaw, Ronald E. *Canals for a Nation: The Canal Era in the United States, 1790-1860.* Lexington: University Press of Kentucky, 1990. An excellent history of the canal era; includes bibliography and index.

Sheriff, Carol. *The Artificial River: The Erie Canal and the Paradox of Progress, 1817-1862.* New York: Hill & Wang, 1996. Uses archival research to document the varied responses of ordinary people who lived along the waterway.

See also: Bridges; Clay's American System; Cumberland Road; Erie Canal; Highways; Mississippi and Missouri Rivers; Panama Canal; Railroads; Stagecoach line, first; Turnpikes; Water resources.

Carnegie, Andrew

IDENTIFICATION: Industrialist who launched the steel industry in Pittsburgh with Carnegie Steel Company and who later was devoted to philanthropy

BORN: November 25, 1835; Dunfermline, Scotland

DIED: August 11, 1919; Lenox, Massachusetts

SIGNIFICANCE: Andrew Carnegie began the steel industry in Pittsburgh and innovated in both the organization of steel companies and the uses of steel in engineering and manufacturing. He became one of the wealthiest men in history and pioneered the idea that American business could be philanthropic.

Andrew Carnegie immigrated to the United States with his humble Scottish family in 1848; they settled in Allegheny, Pennsylvania. As an adult, he realized success in many business ventures, including those in oil, Great Lakes trade, and railways. He invested well, with good timing and insight about the needs and direction of the country. Many of his projects revolutionized businesses. For example, he promoted the first viable sleeping cars for the railroads. Carnegie and his associates also became the first bridge-building firm to use iron rather than wood. In 1875, he started a Pennsylvania steel plant and began supplying track for the railroads. He merged with Henry Clay Frick, a coke dealer, in 1881. By the end of the decade, Carnegie's operations had made the United States the world's leading exporter of steel.

Carnegie's association with Frick would prove to have dire consequences for Carnegie's reputation as a supporter of American workers. While Carnegie was in Europe on vacation, he asked Frick to manage a labor problem at his company. Although Frick knew that Carnegie was a defender of unions, Frick ordered a lockout, and a strike ensued. Frick enlisted the Pinkerton National Detective Agency, a notorious union-busting security company. Pinkerton agents engaged in a twelve-hour shootout against the striking workers, who finally retaliated. The state militia was required to intervene to reopen the mill.

Eventually, Carnegie organized Carnegie Steel Company. This company became the most influential firm in the world. As owner of the world's biggest steel company, he became extremely wealthy. Adjusted for inflation, he is commonly listed as the second wealthiest person in the history of the world.

Not only did Carnegie originate numerous projects beneficial to the public, but he also urged American business to do more to promote the welfare of others. In a time of robber barons who plundered the country, his good works underscored the message to industrialists of his famous 1889 essay, "The Gospel of Wealth": Those who are successful in business should do as much as they can to contribute to humanity. (It is important to note that Carnegie dreamed of becoming a philanthropist in 1868, long before his great financial success.)

Carnegie's legacy includes museums, schools, research facilities, funds for education, and institutions devoted to the study of peace and ethics. In 1901, he sold his steel company to J. P. Morgan, who turned it into the United States Steel Corporation (U.S. Steel). Considering Carnegie's contributions to the U.S. economy and philanthropy, it seems fitting that a dinosaur is named after him: *Diplodocus carnegiei* can be seen at the Carnegie museum in Pittsburgh. It was discovered on a trip sponsored by the philanthropist.

Jan Hall

Andrew Carnegie. (Library of Congress)

FURTHER READING

Carnegie, Andrew. *"The Autobiography of Andrew Carnegie" and "The Gospel of Wealth."* New York: Signet, 2006.

Nasaw, David. *Andrew Carnegie.* New York: Penguin Press, 2006.

Standiford, Les. *Meet You in Hell: Andrew Carnegie, Henry Clay Frick, and the Bitter Partnership That Transformed America.* New York: Crown, 2005.

SEE ALSO: Education; Gilded Age; Homestead strike; Morgan, J. P.; Panic of 1907; Robber barons; Rockefeller, John D.; Steel industry; United States Steel Corporation.

Carver, George Washington

IDENTIFICATION: African American agricultural scientist

BORN: July 12, 1861(?); near Diamond Grove, Missouri

DIED: January 5, 1943; Tuskegee, Alabama

SIGNIFICANCE: Carver conducted scientific research on such crops as peanuts, soybeans, sweet potatoes, and pecans. Products derived from this research reached the market during the early twentieth century, revitalizing the economy and business activity of the South by liberating the region from an excessive dependence on cotton.

While participating in farmwork during his youth in Missouri, George Washington Carver developed a great interest in and love for plants. After graduating from Iowa Agricultural College in 1894, he was hired there as a faculty member and spent many hours working on agricultural and botanical projects in the school's greenhouses. In 1897, he was hired as the director of agriculture at Tuskegee Institute in Alabama.

At Tuskegee, Carver discovered that crop rotation could be used to maintain soil nutrients. In particular, peanuts, peas, sweet potatoes, soybeans, and pecans would enrich soils that had been depleted by growing cotton. Carver developed more than 300 different uses for peanuts, from cooking oil to printer's ink; over 150 uses for sweet potatoes; over 50 uses for pecans; and many practical uses for soybeans, including making paints and stains. The implementation of proper crop rotation, along with the

George Washington Carver. (National Archives)

exploitation of the vast number of new applications of peanuts, sweet potatoes, soybeans, and pecans, created new markets for farmers in the South. By 1938, peanuts had become a $200 million business.

As Carver's fame grew, business leaders and American presidents sought his help to stimulate business and boost the economy. Henry Ford worked with Carver to solve the problems caused by the rubber shortage during World War II by making synthetic rubber using sweet potatoes and goldenrod, a weed. Through the use of science and technology, Carver helped Americans meet societal, business, and financial needs at a critical time in the history of the United States.

Alvin K. Benson

FURTHER READING

Hersey, Mark. "Hints and Suggestions to Farmers: George Washington Carver and Rural Conservation in the South." *Environmental History* 11, no. 2 (April, 2006).

Holt, Rackham. *George Washington Carver: An American Biography.* Rev. ed. Garden City, N.Y.: Doubleday, 1963.

McMurry, Linda O. *George Washington Carver: Scientist and Symbol.* New York: Oxford University Press, 1981.

SEE ALSO: Agribusiness; Agriculture; Cotton gin; Cotton industry; Ford, Henry; Garvey, Marcus; Inventions; Washington, Booker T.; World War II.

Catalog shopping

DEFINITION: Purchase of consumer and business products by mail, based on their descriptions in print or online catalogs

SIGNIFICANCE: The advent of catalog shopping created a new source of revenue and a new business model for marketers and manufacturers, who emphasized to consumers the increased convenience and selection available when ordering products by mail. Catalog outlets contributed to the growth and diversity of American retail businesses.

Benjamin Franklin is credited with starting the first mail-order business in America. In 1744, he published a catalog featuring scientific and academic materials. Franklin understood that customer satisfaction was the key to repeat business and offered a guarantee: "Those persons who live remote, by sending their orders and money to B. Franklin may depend on the same justice as if present."

The early nineteenth century brought changes to the American landscape that encouraged the growth of the mail-order business. The steam engine, steamboat, and railway provided a distribution system that enabled merchandisers to transport goods quickly and efficiently. Newspapers, books, and magazines became cheaper to produce; literacy was on the rise; and the U.S. Post Office (later U.S. Postal Service) expanded into agrarian areas.

By the 1850's, specialized catalogs were a fixture in provincial households, offering goods that were difficult to find in local stores. Early catalogers included Orvis, which sold fishing tackle; E. Remington & Son, which sold guns and ammunition; and D. M. Ferry, which offered seeds. After the U.S. Civil War, direct mail came into its own. Several factors contributed to this growth: Increased immigration and a higher birthrate swelled the rural population. Catalogs kept farmers up to date on the latest inventions and offered the convenience of purchasing machinery, animals, and seeds through the mail. Finally, postage, manufacturing, and shipping costs declined after the war.

MONTGOMERY WARD AND SEARS, ROEBUCK

E. C. Allen of Augusta, Maine, was the first American entrepreneur to offer a general catalog that featured more than a single product line. He mailed more than 500,000 copies in 1871. Allen's success paved the way for Montgomery Ward to enter the market. During the late 1860's, farmers formed the National Grange of the Patrons of Husbandry. Ward induced the National Grange to name his company, Montgomery Ward, the official supply house for the organization. In 1872, he founded what would become the longest continually operating catalog business in the United States by using the network of National Grange halls as a conduit for sales. By 1876, Ward was selling a wide selection of items, including red flannel, jeans, hoop skirts, paper collars, lace curtains, and oilcloth tablecloths.

Ten years later, in 1886, R. W. Sears published a specialty catalog that featured watches. His superb salesmanship and persuasive advertising copy captured the attention of consumers. In 1893, Sears, Roebuck and Company issued a general catalog that included a diverse product line, much like Montgomery Ward's, but Sears's items were often cheaper. Although the country was suffering a depression, Sears, Roebuck and Company pulled in $400,000 in sales that year. Eventually, Sears became Montgomery Ward's chief competition. The "catalog war" between the two giant mail-order retailers lasted several decades.

POSTAL INNOVATIONS AND GROWTH SPURTS

During the late nineteenth and early twentieth centuries, two postal improvements further spurred the growth of the catalog industry: rural free delivery (RFD) and parcel post. In 1891, Postmaster General John Wanamaker first proposed a rural free delivery system, which was designed to eliminate the need for residents to pick up their mail at the local post office. Instead, carriers delivered letters to roadside boxes. Parcel post, instituted on January 1, 1913, also offered residents the convenience of having packages delivered directly to their doors.

New catalog businesses proliferated throughout the twentieth century. In 1912, Leon L. Bean founded a mail-order business in Freeport, Maine, and L. L. Bean grew to become one of the most recognized brands in the catalog industry. Eddie Bauer found similar success on the West Coast with the establishment of his retail store in Seattle, Washington, in 1920, and his catalog business in 1945. Chicago-based clothing retailer Spiegel mailed out its first catalog in 1905.

Although catalog sales slowed during the Great Depression, the mail-order industry experienced renewed growth during the post-World War II boom of the 1950's and 1960's. No longer a staple of farm life, catalogs became popular with the urban and suburban population, as the American economy grew more industrialized and affluent. In this fertile environment, niche catalogs such as Lillian Vernon, a household and fashion accessory retailer established in 1951, thrived.

TECHNOLOGY AND THE INTERNET

During the 1980's, the catalog industry experienced record growth. The use of sophisticated computers and software aided companies in better targeting their customer mailing lists and managing inventory. A greater number of working families and the elderly enjoyed the flexibility of shopping from home. Acceptance of credit cards streamlined

the payment process, and the prevalence of toll-free "800" numbers made ordering easy and economical for consumers.

By the early 1990's, the catalog business had matured and revenues were flat. The arrival of the World Wide Web, however, transformed the industry during the mid-1990's. Online mail-order companies such as Amazon.com, Cyberian Outpost, and eToys proliferated. Many such companies failed when the dot-com bubble burst, but those left standing proved both lucrative and influential.

The success of online catalogs such as Amazon.com prompted traditional catalog houses to develop their own Web sites. Many companies not only mailed their catalogs but also published them online. At first, paper catalogs produced more sales than did Web sites, as the established customer base of paper catalogs did not immediately transition to online sales. Eventually, however, the situation changed. Web browsers became ubiquitous, encryption technology (necessary to safeguard credit card numbers from computer hackers) improved and was more widely trusted, and companies began offering "Web only" specials—specific products or discounted prices that were available only online. As a result, Internet sales caught up with, and in most instances outpaced, those of print catalogs.

The success of the Web catalog in conjunction with search engines such as Google began to transform the retailing landscape, since—unlike print catalogs—Web catalogs are universally and instantly available to anyone with a computer and Internet access. Consumers need not subscribe to or receive a catalog to have access to an online company's products. They are also able easily to compare a brick-and-mortar retailer's prices with those of online companies. Thus, the advent of Web catalogs greatly broadened the field within which an individual business must compete to sell its products, making every bookstore, for example, a rival of Amazon.com.

Two women in Pie Town, New Mexico, order from the Sears Roebuck catalog. People in rural areas especially benefited from catalog shopping. (Library of Congress)

Pegge Bochynski

FURTHER READING

Gorman, Leon. *L. L. Bean: The Making of an American Icon.* Boston: Harvard Business School Press, 2006. Written by a former president of L. L. Bean and the grandson of the founder, this authoritative account offers an insider look at the challenges of building and maintaining an iconic brand.

Hoge, Cecil C., Sr. *The First Hundred Years Are the Toughest: What We Can Learn from the Century of Competition Between Sears and Wards.* Berkeley, Calif.: Ten Speed Press, 1988. Detailed study of the fierce rivalry between the two largest mail-order houses in the United States.

Marcus, James. *Amazonia: Five Years at the Epicenter of the Dot.com Juggernaut.* New York: New Press, 2004. Recounts the shaky initial rise of Amazon.com from the point of view of a literary expert who produced and edited reviews for the site.

Montgomery, M. R. *In Search of L. L. Bean.* Boston: Little, Brown, 1984. Folksy look at the founder of L. L. Bean, family rivalry, and the societal trends that shaped the company.

Weil, Gordon L. *Sears, Roebuck, U.S.A.* New York: Stein and Day, 1977. History of the company that focuses on the contributions of Richard W. Sears, Julius Rosenwald, and Robert Wood.

SEE ALSO: Credit card buying; Fuller Brush Company; Home Shopping Network; Montgomery Ward; Online marketing; Postal Service, U.S.; Retail trade industry; Sears, Roebuck and Company; Tupperware; Warehouse and discount stores.

Cereal crops

DEFINITION: Grains or seeds from plants of the grass family that are suitable for consumption

SIGNIFICANCE: The United States has long been a world leader in the production and exportation of cereal crops, especially corn. The ability of corn to withstand variations in climate and soils, combined with advances in hybridization, almost ensure the continued superiority of U.S. cereal production. Production of corn has risen from an average of 27 bushels per acre in 1900 to an expected average of 155 bushels per acre in 2008.

The United States is the top corn producer in the world and a major exporter of the crop. Of the corn crop for 2007, about 54 percent went for livestock feed; 27 percent was used to produce a huge assortment of food and industrial products, including sweeteners, corn oil, alcohol, and fuel ethanol; and about 19 percent was exported. The primary importer of U.S. corn is Japan, followed by Mexico, South Korea, Taiwan, Egypt, and others.

MAJOR GRAIN CROPS

The United States, the world's largest exporter of wheat, was estimated in 2008 to produce 2.462 billion bushels. Although wheat is grown in virtually every state in the United States, its prime locus is the southern Great Plains area, including Kansas, Texas, Oklahoma, Nebraska, and Colorado, where hard red winter wheat—which accounts for about 40 percent of the entire wheat crop—is grown. The United States grows more wheat than it uses, exporting about half of its yield, while using some for livestock feed and most of the remainder for flour. The domestic demand for wheat increased after 1970, leading to overproduction in 1990-1995, causing a drop in prices and a long period in which supply exceeded demand. In 2002, bad weather in other countries, and the opening of new export markets for the United States resulted in a slow increase of wheat production. The year 2006 was a record year for wheat production in the United States.

Barley represents barely 3 to 4 percent of total crop acreage in the United States, which ranks as one of the five major barley producers in the world. The northern plains states and the Pacific Northwest are primary production areas of barley, which is exported primarily to Saudi Arabia, Japan, and republics of the former Soviet Union. Of the remaining barley, most is used for livestock feed and malt.

The U.S. share of the world trade market for grain sorghum stands at 70 percent—a figure bolstered by U.S. exports to Mexico, Japan, Israel, and South Africa, among other nations. Traditionally used for food products, grain sorghum blends with other flours, ending up frequently in snack foods. It is a also a nutritious livestock feed, and as much as 12 percent of it proceeds to the manufacturing of ethanol. Rice production in the United States is a smaller, more expensive industry that exports about

U.S. DEPARTMENT OF ENERGY ON BIOFUELS

Findings of the Department of Energy (DOE) regarding biofuels presented in 2008:

- Without ethanol, the DOE estimates that gasoline prices would be between 20 and 35 cents higher per gallon.
- Ethanol saves the typical household $150 to $300 per year.
- Without biofuels, the DOE estimates that the United States would use 7.2 billion additional gallons of gasoline in 2008 to maintain existing levels of travel.
- U.S. corn ethanol reduced greenhouse gas emissions 19 percent compared with gasoline over the "life" of ethanol—from growing corn to producing ethanol and burning it.
- In 2007, 13 million tons of greenhouse gases were not emitted because of biofuel production and use.
- Cellulosic biofuels—made from switchgrass, corn stover, wood chips, and various nonfood sources—are estimated to reduce greenhouse gas emissions by 86 percent compared with gasoline.
- Cellulosic biofuel sources can be produced on land not suitable for food crops.
- Biofuels represent only a small part of the increase in global food prices, the other causes being higher oil and gas prices that increase the costs of fertilizer and of harvesting and transporting crops, increased demand as developing nations become more affluent, two years of bad weather and drought in various parts of the world, and export restrictions imposed by some nations.

Source: U.S. Department of Energy, "Fact Sheet: Gas Prices and Oil Consumption Would Increase Without Biofuels," June 11, 2008

half of its yield. The international rice market, however, is highly competitive, threatening the U.S. interest in it. The remaining half of the U.S. rice yield finds its way into the domestic market, where it is used in the production of food—mostly processed foods, beer, and pet food.

CONTROVERSIES

Genetic engineering, or methods of modifying crops to breed desirable traits, has drawn much criticism. The process of altering the genetic composition of a crop by the introduction of a gene from any species into a plant to achieve a desired plant characteristic has raised fears of human contamination upon consumption of the plant food. However, with much of the world's population starving and increased crop production vital to the nation's economy, the U.S. government approved the first use of Bt corn, a genetically modified organism, in 1995. Found in soil bacterium and possessing a lethal effect on certain insects, the *Bacillus thuringiensis* (Bt) delta endotoxin was introduced to corn to combat the European corn borer caterpillars and, later, the Western corn rootworm. Cereal crop yields, enhanced by the development of Bt corn, are also increased by drought-resistant wheat and flooding-resistant rice.

Mapping of the barley genome, scheduled to be completed by 2012, will lead to genetically modified barley seeds that not only are pest and disease resistant but also will improve malt quality. Despite the use of genetic modification in the United States for more than ten years and unceasing research to further it, the process continues to attract controversy. The controversy is not abated by the fact that crops are often grown to be more resilient and produce higher yields at the expense of their taste and nutritional value. That is, they are bred to be better commodities rather than to taste better.

As oil prices climbed during the early twenty-first century, researchers looked for the best means to make fuel from plants. Plants high in starch content, primarily corn and sorghum, can be turned into biofuels and are treated with enzymes to convert starch into alcohol and ethanol. Corn, however, is not an efficient biofuel, and its preferential use for ethanol is more a result of the fact that the crop is readily available and that domestically produced, corn-based ethanol is subsidized by the government than of any scientific reason for choosing corn over other, more promising sources of ethanol.

As the ethanol production process is quicker and cheaper for plants high in sugar content—such as the sugarcane of Brazil—the United States has begun to integrate tropical maize into the corn grown in the Midwest. The maize stalks grow about 15 feet tall, compared to the 7.5-foot hybrid corn stalk; with fewer ears, maize contains more concentrated sugar in the stalk. The growth of corn for fuel raises concerns about the possibility of a decrease in the acreage devoted to production of corn and other grains for food; also, ethanol plants have been viewed as the impetus for the rising price of corn. Nevertheless, ethanol has been in production in the United States since 2001, and most automobile manufacturers equip new automobiles with the ability to use a 10 percent ethanol additive to gasoline. Some cities and states have passed laws requiring ethanol additives in an attempt to improve air quality.

Mary Hurd

FURTHER READING

Abdel-Aal, Elsayed, and Peter Wood, eds. *Specialty Grains for Food and Feed*. St. Paul, Minn.: American Association of Cereal Chemists, 2005. This collection of essays examines specialty cereal grains, including emmer wheat, waxy wheat, spelt, rye, sorghum, amaranth, and buckwheat, as foodstuffs and livestock feed.

Blume, David. *Alcohol Can Be a Gas: Fueling an Ethanol Revolution for the Twenty-first Century*. Santa Cruz, Calif.: International Institute for Ecological Agriculture, 2007. Aimed at the nonscientific reader, this reference book is a massive tome of information about alcohol—its production and viability for powering vehicles.

Dongarra, Jack, ed. *Cereals and Pseudocereals*. New York: Springer, 2007. Looks at six international cereal crops and their possible use to prevent overemphasis on the reliable major cereal crops.

Murphy, Denis J. *People, Plants, and Genes: The Story of Crops and Humanity*. New York: Oxford University Press, 2007. A thorough history of cereal crops and their effects on humanity, from earliest times to the present.

Nicholl, Desmond S. T. *An Introduction to Genetic Engineering*. London: Cambridge University Press, 2008. Basic information for students concerning molecular biology and the manipulation of genes. Contains diagrams and maps.

SEE ALSO: Agribusiness; Agriculture; Alcoholic beverage industry; Colonial economic systems; Farm labor; Farm subsidies; Food-processing industries; Rice industry.

Chávez, César

IDENTIFICATION: Mexican American labor and civil rights activist
BORN: March 31, 1927; near Yuma, Arizona
DIED: April 23, 1993; San Luis, Arizona
SIGNIFICANCE: Chávez advanced the standing of minority workers and strengthened labor institutions in the United States. He founded several significant labor organizations, and at the time of his death, he was the president of the AFL-CIO.

The family of César Chávez ran a small farm and a local store in Yuma, Arizona, but with the onset of the Great Depression, his family lost everything. His father packed up the family and moved to California, so that he could pursue employment as a migrant worker—an insecure way of life that hundreds of thousands of Americans, especially Latinos, were forced to adopt to survive harsh economic conditions. Young César quickly began to realize that the economic misfortunes his family faced were part of a greater injustice in the U.S. labor system, and his childhood experiences would contribute greatly to his later life as an activist.

When Chávez reached adulthood, he followed in his father's footsteps, becoming a farmworker picking beets, lettuce, and apricots on California farms. He grew frustrated with the poor wages and long hours that Latinos like himself were forced to withstand, and he began to take action to make working conditions better for farmworkers. Chávez studied leaders such as Mahatma Gandhi and believed that true change could be brought about through peaceful protest and strikes that were designed to end injustice without violence.

Chávez's quest to improve the working conditions of migrant laborers led him to participate in worker strikes and in 1952 led him to join the Community Service Organization (CSO), where he organized strikes and promoted voter registration among farmworkers. In 1962, he founded the National Farm Workers Association (NFWA), which later became the United Farm Workers of America

(UFW). The union grew, and in 1965, a five-year strike by grape pickers began at Chavez's request. The strike led farmers to negotiate with their workers, who achieved higher wages, better hours, health care, and some pension benefits as a result.

Chávez's aim was to secure better working environments for Latino farmworkers, but he achieved much more. His peaceful methods of fasts, strikes, and boycotts led to legislation, such as the 1975 Agricultural Labor Relations Act, that gave farmworkers' unions negotiating powers that had been reserved for industrial laborers. Chávez is thought of as one of the most influential people in the labor movement, and he rose to become the president of the AFL-CIO. Chávez continued his battle for better conditions and working processes for farmers until his death in 1993, and he is remembered among the Latino and farmworker communities as a hero.

Jennifer L. Titanski

FURTHER READING

Ferriss, Susan, Diana Hembree, and Ricardo Sandoval. *The Fight in the Fields: César Chávez and the Farmworkers Movement.* Bel Air, Calif.: Harvest/HBJ Book, 1998.

Levy, Jacques E., and Barbara Moulton. *César Chávez: Autobiography of La Causa.* Minneapolis: University of Minnesota Press, 2007.

SEE ALSO: AFL-CIO; Agriculture; Boycotts, consumer; Bracero program; Farm labor; Labor history; Labor strikes; United Farm Workers of America.

Chemical industries

DEFINITION: Enterprises that create, manipulate, or exploit substances through the use of chemistry

SIGNIFICANCE: Chemicals have played an important role in the development and modern prosperity of the United States and of various businesses. Manufacturers of such bulk chemicals as sulfuric acid and fertilizers, as well as such light chemicals as pharmaceuticals and synthetic fibers, helped transform chemical industries from the small, unoriginal, and inefficient enterprises of the eighteenth century into the world's largest, most innovative, and most highly efficient oligopolies in the twenty-first century.

Great Britain's mercantilist policies in the eighteenth century encouraged the export from its American colonies of such raw materials as pig iron and potash but discouraged the production of high-quality steel and gunpowder. As a result, American chemical industries during and after the Revolutionary War were much inferior to those in England and other European countries. Were it not for the importation of high-quality gunpowder from France, the American war for independence might well have failed. Eleuthère Irénée du Pont, who had learned to make excellent gunpowder under Antoine Lavoisier in Paris, came to the United States and, in 1802, began manufacturing high-quality powder. The DuPont company, which became the chief manufacturer of explosives for the American government, grew, diversified, and prospered along with the nation.

NINETEENTH CENTURY INDUSTRIES

Throughout the nineteenth century, the United States was a predominantly agricultural society, and chemical businesses, which manufactured the most-needed acids and alkalis, were largely family-type establishments. Some firms began to manufacture chemical fertilizers to supplement materials derived from such nitrogenous wastes as manures, compost, fish meal, and guano. During the American Industrial Revolution of the first half of the nineteenth century, some industries, such as iron and steel, became large and prosperous, but many scholars have restricted the scope of chemical industries by separating them from the steel and petroleum industries.

Scholars, engineers, and businessmen have distinguished two chief categories of chemical industries. In heavy chemical industries, such inorganic chemicals as sodium carbonate and sulfuric acid are produced in great amounts in large factories, whereas in light chemical industries, such organic chemicals as dyes and pharmaceuticals are produced in modest factories with specialized equipment. The origin and development of both types of chemical industries were mainly European. For example, the Leblanc process for manufacturing sodium carbonate was developed in France, and the production of such sophisticated chemicals as dyes and drugs took place mostly in Germany.

Despite reliance on Europeans for standard as well as new processes and chemicals, some Ameri-

This Copperhill, Tennessee, copper mining and sulfuric acid plant, pictured in 1939, produced sulfuric acid, a chemical that played a significant role in the U.S. chemical industry. (Library of Congress)

cans attempted to found new chemical businesses, with mixed results. For example, after Charles Goodyear patented vulcanization in 1844, he tried to establish rubber industries in the United States and Europe, but his failures left his widow with gigantic debts. On the other hand, Charles Pfizer founded a Brooklyn company in 1849 that pioneered fermentation techniques in the manufacture of organic acids, which led to successes in the production of pharmaceuticals and varnish resins.

The U.S. Civil War stimulated the expansion of certain chemical industries in the North, and this growth continued after the war. For example, in 1867 Graselli Chemical constructed a sulfuric acid plant in Cleveland, near a Rockefeller refinery whose patronage led to success great enough to foster expansion to several states in the Midwest, East, and South. During the 1890's, General Chemical Company, which later became part of the Allied Chemical Corporation, also had success in the manufacture of sulfuric acid, a bulk chemical that has often been characterized as a significant indicator of a country's technological progress.

THE PATH TO MARKET DOMINANCE

During the latter decades of the nineteenth century and throughout the twentieth century, chem-

ists working in industrial research laboratories, first in Europe and then in the United States, helped make chemicals a significant part of Western economies. For example, aluminum, which had been a prohibitively expensive metal, became an important element in the world economy after the American chemist Charles Martin Hall in 1886 discovered an efficient and inexpensive electrolytic process for making this light and useful metal. The Pittsburgh company that first capitalized on the Hall process later became the Aluminum Company of America.

Similarly, Herbert H. Dow adopted an electrolytic process for making caustic soda (sodium hydroxide) that contributed to the early success of the Dow Chemical Company. Research chemists also helped make the Schoelkopf Aniline and Chemical Company the largest American producer of coal-tar dyes, and chemicals and chemical engineers—by developing an improved method for making sulfuric acid—also helped make the Allied Chemical Corporation a success. DuPont's chemists, working in the company's General Experimental Laboratory, created a smokeless gunpowder that was a phenomenal success throughout the world.

The event that, more than any other, fostered the rapid development of American chemical industries was World War I. The war deprived the United States of access to the drugs, dyes, and other organic chemicals produced in Germany. American firms thus had to expeditiously expand productivity and create new chemical industries to meet military and domestic needs. They were aided by government actions such as the confiscation of German patents and the implementation of large tariffs. A good example of a new company that benefited from these policies was Union Carbide, formed in 1917 to manufacture various chemicals from petroleum. Other companies such as Kodak, Monsanto, Hercules, and American Cyanamid also became prosperous and powerful by expansion and diversification.

During the decades following World War I, American firms established over one thousand industrial research laboratories, and chemical businesses profited from discoveries made in their laboratories. For example, during the late 1920's Thomas Midgley, Jr., discovered odorless and nontoxic organic fluorine compounds (freons) that replaced ammonia as a refrigerant. During the years before World War II, Wallace Carothers, a DuPont chemist, headed a research group that created the first wholly synthetic rubber (later known as neoprene) and a synthetic fiber, nylon, that was put on the market in 1939. Nylon would go on to earn the company more than $25 million. During World War II, well-established companies, such as DuPont, and many new firms produced the large amounts of explosives, synthetic rubber, pharmaceuticals, and other chemicals needed by the U.S. military.

Because of pent-up consumer demand and the success of new chemical products, American chemical businesses continued to prosper in the postwar years. Although such petroleum companies as Exxon, Texaco, and Mobil were the largest corporations in the second half of the twentieth century (and some would categorize these as chemical companies), such strictly chemical corporations as Dow, DuPont, Union Carbide, and Allied Chemical took the place, in total assets and productivity, of automobile and iron-and-steel firms, which suffered because of poor management and increased domestic and foreign competition. U.S. chemical industries grew, through mergers and acquisitions, into oligopolies, and they increased their investments in the research and development of new products, driving their success.

Concrete evidence for this success is the increasing number of chemical corporations in lists of the nation's top one hundred companies and the increasing proportion of U.S. patents generated by these companies' researchers, compared with those in other industries. By the early years of the twenty-first century, the American chemical industry was by far the world's largest and most productive. Despite growth in assets, workforce, products, and markets, however, American chemical businesses encountered environmental and safety problems, as their products were blamed for polluting the land, water, and air; for precipitating accidents that killed people and damaged property; for overcharging consumers for drugs; and for retrenching on investment in research and development during a period of intense global competition. Nevertheless, some companies continue to exhibit healthy growth, and many new and successful chemicals continue to find their way to eager customers in an increasingly diverse and demanding marketplace.

Robert J. Paradowski

FURTHER READING

Chandler, Alfred D., Jr. *Shaping the Industrial Century: The Remarkable Story of the Evolution of the Modern Chemical and Pharmaceutical Industries.* Cambridge, Mass.: Harvard University Press, 2005. This book, part of the Harvard Studies in Business History series, insightfully analyzes the evolution of influential chemical industries in the twentieth century, while showing why some companies prospered and others failed. Index.

Haynes, William. *American Chemical Industry: A History.* 6 vols. New York: Van Nostrand, 1945-1954. This comprehensive history of the American chemical industry, written by a business historian, traces developments from the colonial period to the start of World War II. This indispensable work emphasizes the organizational and economic aspects of numerous chemical companies. Illustrations, chronologies, and appendixes.

Hounshell, David, and John Kenly Smith, Jr. *Science and Corporate Strategy: Du Pont R&D, 1902-1980.* New York: Cambridge University Press, 1988. Hounshell, an expert on the development of industrial research in the United States, focuses on a company that has been important in the evolution of the American chemical industry. Index.

Spitz, Peter H., ed. *The Chemical Industry at the Millennium: Maturity, Restructuring, and Globalization.* Philadelphia: Chemical Heritage Foundation, 2003. Spitz heads a team of scholars who analyze the scientific, technological, economic, political, and environmental factors that have influenced the development of various chemical companies in the recent past.

Thackray, Arnold, et al. *Chemistry in America, 1876-1976.* Dordrecht, Holland: D. Reidel, 1985. Collects much useful and relevant information on the history of American chemistry and the chemical industry. Charts, graphs, tables, extensive bibliographies, and index.

SEE ALSO: Arms industry; Colonial economic systems; DDT banning; Environmental Protection Agency; Food-processing industries; Occupational Safety and Health Act; Petroleum industry; Pharmaceutical industry; World War I.

Child labor

DEFINITION: Employment of girls and boys, often under the legal age to work

SIGNIFICANCE: Children were a cheap, submissive source of labor for textile, mining, glass, and other industries in the United States until the early twentieth century, when social reform began to produce legislation that protected children from unfair or unsafe working conditions and from other forms of exploitation by employers.

Child labor, in one or another form, has been part of the American economy since the founding of the United States, when labor shortages encouraged the use of children in agriculture, domestic service, home-based businesses, and industries. During the earliest years, children primarily worked on their families' farms or served as indentured servants and apprentices. Children's rights issues usually did not extend to agricultural labor, because children usually worked without wages for their parents on family farms, where activists thought of them as safe from harm.

EARLY EMPLOYERS

Outside the home, the textile industry was one of the largest employers of children, preferring girls over boys because they were often more submissive. Textile work began at home in the form of carding and spinning wool and moved to factories as the industry became mechanized. Industrialization increased the number of working children. In 1820, half of the textile workers in one Massachusetts city were children. As late as 1832, more than 40 percent of mill workers were boys younger than twelve. Other early industries that regularly used child labor included glass, tobacco, and coal. Regardless of the industry, child labor was a problem, because children were overworked (often putting in ten- to fourteen-hour days), underpaid or unpaid, and regularly exposed to corporal punishment.

Child labor was generally accepted in the United States during the country's formative years. It was not seen as a problem, in part because it was more widespread than people realized. The government did not keep records of the use of children as workers. In addition, because American children were not as egregiously abused as were English children, U.S. employers of children benefited from comparisons with their counterparts in England.

Economic factors also contributed to the acceptance of child labor. Child workers helped support their families. Their income increased their families' economic success, helped keep their families off public charity, and aided in providing savings for their parents' old age. Some industries even paid one wage to a parent for an entire family's labor. Because men with spouses and larger families were paid better than were single men or men with small families, parents often had more children. Some people also believed that work kept children morally on track. A busy child would learn positive lessons, including responsibility. In an effort to limit

During the nineteenth century, children could often be found working at menial tasks, such as oyster shucking. (Library of Congress)

idleness among children, one state law even encouraged county commissioners to choose young children from poor families for work in public flax houses. Meanwhile, businesses reduced their costs by employing children or families more cheaply than they could employ an entirely adult workforce.

Child labor abuses started to be more widely recognized during the mid- to late nineteenth century. States began to pass laws mandating minimum levels of education and minimum ages of employment. Those laws often went unenforced, however. By the early twentieth century, many children between ten and fifteen years old were working full-time factory jobs.

During the 1890's, Illinois governor and children's rights advocate John Peter Altgeld appointed reformer Florence Kelley to oversee factories that used child labor and to monitor legislation concerning child labor. Kelley was later appointed director of the National Consumers League in New York, where she made additional advances toward reforming the use of child workers. Kelley also associated with Jane Addams, whose work included child labor reform. Another activist, Lewis Hine, was connected with the National Child Labor Committee. Hine became known for his photographic documentation of working children. His photos clearly displayed the conditions under which American children worked.

Despite reform movements, the Great Depression found many children working in substandard conditions. The newspaper industry hired large numbers of boys either to deliver newspapers to subscribers or to hawk them on the streets. Other young boys were trained as salesmen, going door to door to sell newspaper subscriptions. In addition to the health dangers these children faced, undue stress was placed on the boys as they attempted to take on challenges beyond the capabilities of people so young.

LEGISLATION

Concern over the lack of education among the nation's youth was one of the driving forces behind child labor legislation. Early laws either required the teaching of math, writing, and reading or specified minimum school attendance for children, usually requiring three months per year of formal education. Though laws were passed as early as 1813 in the eastern states, a lack of enforcement too often rendered them useless.

During the middle of the nineteenth century, only seven states had passed laws limiting hours for child workers, and Pennsylvania alone limited the type of work children could perform. By 1909, only six states did not have such laws.

There were three main problems with the legislative attempts to reform and regulate child labor. First, many manufacturers argued that businesses in states without regulations had an unfair advantage over those in states that had strong laws. Second, the laws were often difficult to implement, and businesses breaking the laws were seldom prosecuted. Finally, during the early twentieth century, a number of federal attempts to legislate child labor were overturned, partly because they infringed on states' rights.

Despite some laws being overturned, the twentieth century brought more effective reform movements, starting with Alabama's establishment of the first State Child Labor Committee (1901). The National Child Labor Committee was created in 1904. The oldest federal agency regulating child labor, the Children's Bureau, was founded in 1912. Although it directed early reform on child labor issues, by the middle of the twentieth century the Children's Bureau came to focus on children's health rather than labor issues. Now a part of the Department of Health and Human Services, the bureau concentrates on child development, protection, welfare, and adoption. The labor committees, the Children's Bureau, and other groups successfully promoted a number of new laws that regulated child labor.

On September 1, 1916, the Child Labor Act (also known as the Keating-Owen Act) was passed. This act regulated the transportation across state lines of products made by children under the age of sixteen. The Supreme Court overturned the act on June 3, 1918, primarily as a result of the language in the act. The original language regulated only the products themselves and the transportation of the products, rather than the age of those who made the products. The Court was also concerned that transportation of goods from a state with lenient child labor laws might negatively affect the level of regulation in states receiving those goods.

In 1933, Congress passed the National Industrial Recovery Act (NRA), which (among many other provisions) outlawed child labor in industry, but it was struck down by the Supreme Court in 1935.

Newsboys were the only exception to the law, which was ironic given that publishers were among the first to condemn other industries for relying on child labor. Among the groups that opposed the NRA were the American Newspaper Publishers' Association, the International Circulation Managers' Association, the American Bar Association (which offered an alternative amendment), and a group called the National Committee for the Protection of Child, Family, School, and Church. In 1938, the Fair Labor Standards Act successfully reintroduced the labor regulation provisions of the NRA, enacting minimum wages, maximum hours and days, and a minimum age for workers. This law survived judicial scrutiny, although it would subsequently be revised and amended many times over the years.

During the early part of the twenty-first century, child labor issues have continued to pose quandaries. Hours and times that children sixteen and over can work are often poorly regulated. Furthermore, enforcement of guidelines is limited. Some activists argue that the laws have become too lenient.

ONGOING ISSUES

By the 1950's, most unfair and unsafe U.S. child labor practices had been eliminated or lessened dramatically. The businesses that employed children changed after that decade as well. Whereas children during the early part of the twentieth century and before worked in factories, late twentieth and early twenty-first century working teens were employed by department stores, grocery stores, restaurants, and other retail companies.

Dangers vary for children in the twenty-first century. One problematic area is an increased level of decision-making responsibility given to teens who may not be developmentally capable of choosing the best options. This responsibility may result in the children taking unwise risks that can cause injury. Sexual harassment of young female workers is another danger.

Education remains a concern as well. Studies show that academic performance is negatively affected by long hours and stressful work situations. In addition, research suggests that children working at least twenty hours per week during their high school years are regularly involved in illegal or borderline activities, increasing their chances of school suspension. School attendance is also affected by teen employment.

As in the past, moreover, child agricultural workers are regularly ignored or excluded from legislative and regulatory measures. A significant percentage of laborers aged sixteen and younger are injured or killed in work-related accidents on farms owned by their parents. Changes in legislation and regulatory practices could theoretically prevent many of these accidents. Further, the many migrant children, primarily Latino, working on farms are still treated poorly in many areas of the country. Employers reportedly make these children work more than ten hours per day and expose them to dangerous chemicals, among other violations.

Theresa L. Stowell

FURTHER READING

Greene, Laura Offenhartz. *Child Labor: Then and Now.* New York: Franklin Watts, 1992. This simple overview of American child labor from the beginnings of the country until the early 1990's provides information on the history, reformation, and legislation of child labor.

Hindman, Hugh D. *Child Labor: An American History.* Armonk, N.Y.: M. E. Sharpe, 2002. Provides excellent historical and theoretical commentary through both primary and secondary sources on the subject. Though the focus of the book is on child labor history, the author connects the history to twenty-first century problems in America and beyond.

Levine, Marvin J. *Children for Hire: The Perils of Child Labor in the United States.* Westport, Conn.: Praeger, 2003. Levine challenges the idea that there are no longer major problems with child labor. He argues that child labor laws have become too lenient and that not enough has been done to keep American children safe in the workforce.

Manheimer, Ann, ed. *Child Labor and Sweatshops.* Detroit, Mich.: Greenhaven Press, 2006. Addresses political, economic, and social aspects of child labor through a series of articles that are reprinted from a variety of sources. The simple format is easy to follow and provides a strong overview.

Trattner, Walter I. *Crusade for Children: A History of the National Child Labor Committee and Child Labor Reform in America.* Chicago: Quadrangle Books, 1970. Overview of the relationship between the National Child Labor Committee and the child labor reform movement beginning during the early twentieth century. Focuses on child labor legislation and its progress in making changes in the lives of working children in the United States.

Zelizer, Viviana A. *Pricing the Priceless Child: The Changing Social Value of Children.* New York: Basic Books, 1985. Provides a synopsis of the way adults have valued children over the last few centuries, including how children's labor has varied between a moral and an economic issue.

SEE ALSO: Agriculture; Child product safety laws; Farm labor; Indentured labor; Industrial Revolution, American; Supreme Court and labor law; United Farm Workers of America; Women in business.

Child product safety laws

DEFINITION: Laws regulating the design, marketing, and packaging of products geared toward children to protect them from harm

SIGNIFICANCE: Child product safety laws, by requiring warning labels and prohibiting harmful components or design elements, protect young people from potentially dangerous toys and other products, while adding expenses to manufacturers creating and marketing those products.

Two important laws affecting child product safety are the Federal Trade Commission Act of 1914 and the Consumer Product Safety Act of 1972. The Federal Trade Commission Act established the Federal Trade Commission (FTC). As one of the first agencies to oversee consumer protection, the FTC's primary responsibilities are to enforce consumer protection laws and to assist in resolving consumer issues. The Consumer Product Safety Act created the Consumer Product Safety Commission (CPSC). The CPSC's primary responsibility is to protect the public from risks from more than fifteen thousand different products. The CPSC oversees the evaluation of product safety, assists businesses in developing standards, helps minimize conflicting state and local regulations, maintains a database of product-related injuries and deaths, and conducts research into the causes and prevention of product-related deaths, illness, and injuries.

Children have been the innocent victims of ill-ness, injuries, and even deaths resulting from the use of consumer products. Children's products and toys are often manufactured in countries that do not comply with U.S. child product safety laws. More than 70 percent of the toys sold in the United States are manufactured overseas, with the majority imported from China. In addition, selective classification of products may also exclude products that are not intended for children's use but that often fall into their hands. To ensure child product safety, the CPSC defines children's products as items designed or intended for use by children twelve years of age or younger. Children's toys are defined as products designed or intended for use in play by a child twelve years of age or younger. Child-care articles are defined as products designed or intended to facilitate sleep, the feeding of children, or young children's suckling or teething.

In 2008, Congress passed a comprehensive consumer safety law, the Consumer Product Safety Improvement Act. This act significantly affected U.S. child product safety requirements. The law banned phthalate, phthalate alternatives, and lead in children's products; mandated third-party testing and certification of children's products; and ordered the creation of a public product safety database containing information on use of consumer products. It increased civil penalties for violations of product safety laws and introduced provisions for enforcement of product safety laws by state attorneys general. It also mandated warnings in advertising and Web sites for toys and games, established whistleblower protection for employees reporting safety violations, and increased the authority of the CPSC to dictate the terms of product recalls. Finally, it instituted greater enforcement efforts involving other federal agencies, foreign product safety regulators, and state health agencies.

Lee Ann Jolley

FURTHER READING:

Felcher, E. M. "Product Recalls: Gaping Holes in the Nation's Product Safety Net." *Journal of Consumer Affairs* 37, no. 1 (2003): 170-180.

Peterson, K. F. "A Clear and Present Danger: Consumer Product Safety and Recall." *Trial* 44, no. 1 (2008): 9.

Swartz, J. A. "Danger at Play: Inquisitive Children Invariably Handle the Products They Encounter in Their Homes." *Trial* 39, no. 12 (2003): 40-44.

SEE ALSO: Child labor; Chinese trade with the United States; Christmas marketing; Federal Trade Commission; Occupational Safety and Health Act; Promotional holidays.

Chinese trade with the United States

SIGNIFICANCE: Trade between communist China and the United States went from nearly nonexistent to hundreds of billions of dollars of imports in the twenty-first century, making China a major U.S. trading partner and a key supplier of many goods.

Largely closed to foreign business interests until the nineteenth century, China limited most of its trade with foreign powers to Macao and, on the mainland, to one port city: Guangdong. It was there that the British first made inroads into Chinese markets and where they could obtain goods that were highly prized in Europe, such as tea, porcelain, and silk. Although relations between Great Britain and China were strained, the two powers signed a number of agreements that slowly opened China to Western merchants. The Treaty of Nanking (1842) allowed for open trade between China and the West, and it was followed by the Treaty of Tianjin (1858) and the Treaty of Beijing (1860). The latter agreement also led to China signing commercial treaties with other Western powers such as France, Germany, Russia, and the United States. Western traders enjoyed greater openness in Chinese markets, and Western companies increased their investments in Chinese industries. This is not to say that financial cooperation had not existed before 1860. For example, Americans had established several plants in China for the production of ships. In 1856, a forty-ton steamer was built under the supervision of the American Captain Baylies, which marked the beginning of a long period of American production of ships on the mainland. In 1863, Americans introduced the boiler and machinery parts to shipbuilding in China, which revolutionized the industry.

After the negotiation of the Treaty of Beijing, other business interests came to China in search of vast, new markets. Several United States-based banks greatly increased their activities on the mainland after 1860. These included various California banks that had been linked to China through India, such as the Exchange Bank Corporation, the English & American Bank, the British & California Banking Company, and the American-China Development Company. In 1867, the Ezra R. Goodridge Company opened several plants for the manufacture of silk and ribbon.

Throughout the 1880's, several American companies built flour-milling plants in China and engaged in fierce competition for control of the Chinese markets. The Sperry Milling Company, Golden Gate Flouring Mills, Centennial Mills, and the Portland Flour Company, all of which began their operations in Hong Kong, struggled to gain the upper hand in the lucrative trade in flour with the mainland. The American concern Mustard & Company began to import cigarettes into China in 1890. Following its defeat in the First Sino-Japanese War, China signed the Treaty of Shimonoseki (1895), which allowed for the further expansion of foreign business concerns in the interior as well as for the establishment of permanent foreign settlements in China, especially in coastal cities.

THE TWENTIETH CENTURY

The dawn of the twentieth century found American trade with China to be stronger than at any other time since its inception during the 1850's. In 1902, the British-American Tobacco Company established itself in China, building its first factory in Shanghai, and later expanded its operations into numerous Chinese cities such as Shanghai, Tianjin, Mukden (later Shenyang), Hankou, Qingdao, and Harbin. American shipping groups such as the Pacific Mail Steamship Company and the Shanghai Steam Navigation Company continued to do business in China, although the American presence in the industry was minimal in that the American firm Russell & Company had sold its Chinese operations to local businesspeople during the 1870's. Textiles were of great importance, and the American Trading Company soon established operations in China through its subsidiary, the International Cotton-Manufacturing Company, which enjoyed great profits garnered through its mainland operations. With the new electrical age, American business interests also scored great financial successes in China. The General Edison Company opened its first plant for the production of lamps in Shanghai in 1918 and, with the growth of the business itself, realized the construction of a larger plant in the same city in 1926 by its new International General Electric Company. This was complemented by the American-owned Shanghai Power Company.

China imported agricultural products such as tobacco and raw cotton, timber, automobiles, kerosene, gasoline, and machinery and other heavy equipment throughout the first decades of the century. For its part, the United States also imported a range of Chinese goods: textiles, electronic products, leather goods, footwear, skins, bristles, soybeans, silk, tea, and glass. The founding of the Republic of China (1911) marked a new interest by reform-minded leaders in modernizing both the Chinese political system and the economy, and by 1936, the United States had become China's largest trading partner. Yet all this was to change quickly. With the Japanese invasion in 1937 and the simultaneous military revolt of the Communists under Mao Zedong, business production declined precipitously, and China quickly slid into economic disaster. Only vast amounts of American aid to the Nationalist government propped up the economy and the military sufficiently for Chiang Kai-shek and his government to limp their way to the island of Formosa (Taiwan) in late 1949, there to establish the new seat of the Republic of China in exile.

COMMUNIST CHINA

From the founding of the People's Republic of China in 1949 under the communist rule of Mao Zedong until 1978, China isolated itself from contact with much of the outside world, especially the United States. Trade between the United States and China was virtually nonexistent, and it was not until the summit of 1972 between Mao and U.S. president Richard M. Nixon that diplomatic and trade channels were once again opened. Deng Xiaoping's embracing of the outside world in his 1978 Open-Door Policy saw China's full engagement in diplomatic and economic relations with other nations, which culminated in formal reestablishment of diplomatic relations between the United States and China in January, 1979.

Following on the heels of the political rapprochement, in July of 1979, the two countries signed the Bilateral Trade Agreement. Between 1981 and 1990, China's economy grew at an average rate of 10.3 percent, and its trade grew at an annual rate of 16 percent. Trade between the United States and China has grown from $2.3 billion in 1979 to more than $386.6 billion in 2007, making China the fourth-largest trading partner of the United States. In 1980, the United States granted China most-favored-nation status, and China also gained access to both the International Monetary Fund (IMF) and the World Bank. In 1992, China agreed to lower trade barriers, and in 1995, it entered into an agreement with the United States to protect intellectual property.

By 2007, U.S. exports to China were valued at $65.2 billion, while its imports from China reached an all-time high of $321.4 billion—a negative trade balance of some $256.2 billion. China is a major supplier of numerous products, including toys, sporting goods, apparel, foodstuffs, metals and metal products, textiles, apparel, automotive parts, plastic materials, games, footwear, chemicals, raw materials, machine tools, handicrafts, telecommunications equipment, computers and other electronic machinery, agricultural chemicals, fertilizers, cereals, leather and travel goods, vehicles (not railway), and furniture. For its part, the United States also supplies China with many essential products: electrical machinery, air- and spacecraft, power-generation equipment, plastics and plastic products, iron, steel, optical and medical equipment, copper and copper articles, organic chemicals, pulp and paperboard, oil seeds, and oleaginous fruits. In 2007, the United States became China's top trading partner, while China was the fourth-largest trading partner with the United States. Combined with Hong Kong, however, China was the third-largest trading partner with the United Sates. As of 2008, the United States was China's major export location, and China was the fourth-largest import market of the United States.

EXPANDING TRADE

A review of trade statistics from 1985 to 2007 shows that American exports to China grew steadily and reached almost ten times their levels in 1985. Imports from China grew to alarmingly high levels. In 1985, the United States imported approximately $3.8 billion in goods, as compared with almost $321.4 billion in products in 2007. The huge trade deficit, which increased from $6 million in 1985 to $256.2 billion in 2007, became the center of an enormous economic and political controversy and the cause of increasingly strained relations between the United States and China. For its part, the United States claims that Chinese markets still remain closed to American products, while Chinese officials note that the value of U.S. products sold to China has also grown enormously, if not as dramatically as U.S. imports from China have increased. Many in Congress have clamored for the revaluation of the official Chinese currency, the *renminbi* (RMB, or, colloquially, the *yuan*), as it was pegged directly to the U.S. dollar as of 2008. Some contend that raising the exchange rate of the RMB will place American and Chinese companies on a more equal footing, thus encouraging Chinese purchase of American goods and discouraging U.S. purchase of Chinese products. Many economists warn, however, that the problem is far more complex. Some note that foreign direct investment in China became the largest in the world in 2007. Revaluing the RMB, and thus slowing Chinese exports, may cause these foreign investors to receive lower returns on their investments, thus harming the wider global economy. What is more, decreases in Chinese profits will adversely harm world asset market valuations. The resulting deflation of the Chinese economy might very well affect all retailers who sell Chinese products. Again, the negative effects of revaluation and a slowing of Chinese sales might not yield the result desired by American legislators. Chinese officials contend that the American trade deficit has little to do with a lack of reciprocal trade between the two nations but rather is a function of the American desire for material goods. They point out that, by the end of the 1990's, the U.S. trade deficit had not only grown dramatically with China, but also had reached its highest levels ever with other Asian trading partners, including Singapore, Hong Kong, Korea, and Taiwan.

Trade tensions between the United States and China have risen and declined, especially since the 1990's. Although American businesses recognize that China has become a large market for their products, many still fear that China's enormous economy will overtake that of the United States. This fear is not unfounded: The Chinese economy is projected to surpass that of the United States as the largest economy in the world by 2020. However, even this negative prediction has a bright side for

UNITED STATES TRADE WITH CHINA, 1985-2005, IN MILLIONS OF DOLLARS			
Year	Exports	Imports	Balance
1985	3,856	3,862	–6
1990	4,806	15,237	–10,431
1995	11,753	45,543	–33,789
2000	16,185	100,018	–83,833
2005	41,925	243,479	–201,554

Source: Data from U.S. Census Bureau, Foreign Trade Division, Data Dissemination Branch, Washington, D.C.
Note: Trade figures are from the U.S. perspective.

American businesses, which recognize that prospects for trade with a vast Chinese market may be still greater in the future. Some markets offer particular hope of growth for American interests: computers, cell phones, aircraft, and automobiles.

The Chinese have been accused of unfair trade practices, but China's entrance into the World Trade Organization (WTO) in December, 2001, offered hope that the vast "dragon economy" could gradually be brought into conformity with the regulations and procedures of the global business community. In 2006, China gained full membership in the WTO, although the United States has since complained that the Chinese response to international regulations has been tepid, at best, especially in the areas of product dumping and intellectual property rights. Also, tensions regarding the pegging of the RMB have remained. In December of 2003, Congress threatened to apply heavier tariffs to Chinese products unless Chinese markets were further opened. Tensions rose to such a point that some feared a U.S.-China trade war. If Chinese markets were not made more accessible to American businesses and if the RMB were not revalued, Congress threatened to levy an additional tariff of 27 percent on all Chinese imports. Although the tariff was not enacted, the issue has remained critical. In 2005, the Chinese government reiterated its commitment to full enforcement of intellectual property rights, but American regulators have continued to complain of random enforcement that is very public but only symbolic.

CONTINUING PROBLEMS

A host of other problems plague the trade relationship between the United States and China. A great reduction in manufacturing jobs in the United States has engendered a spirit of protectionism in some political and economic circles. Increasingly, pressure has been brought to bear on Congress to force the Chinese to come into parity with the rest of the international business community. The enormous trade imbalance between the two countries has exacerbated the problem, as has the question of Chinese investment in the United States. As of March, 2008, China was the second-largest holder of United States Treasury securities ($491 billion, or 19.5 percent of total foreign ownership of U.S. Treasury securities), and fears arose—irrationally—that the Chinese might, at any time, demand immediate payment, thus destroying the U.S. economy in one fell swoop. However, as economists were quick to note, such an action would eliminate the U.S. market for Chinese business and bring about a complete collapse of the world economy.

The thought of communist China "controlling" the U.S. economy raised the specter of disaster for many Americans, especially in the light of several other business developments involving China. During the early part of the twenty-first century, Chinese attempts to take control of some American businesses, especially those related to national security, raised controversy. Evidence of Chinese cyber espionage and cyber jamming made many in the business and political communities wary of Chinese intentions. China's launch of new communication and navigation satellites made some nations nervous, as these developments indicate that China is capable of launching nuclear weapons. Many in Congress have discussed greater controls on American exports of technological information and equipment as a response to growing nationalism and militarism in China. For the last decade, China has registered double-digit increases in military spending, apparently in an attempt to compete with the United States. Such expenditures have cast a pall over U.S.-China trade relations and have made some Americans wary of Chinese attempts to make peaceful overtures to the world community. Some American scholars and members of the business community have noted that the Chinese, known for their attempts to sinicize their potential adversaries, have shown signs of trying to do the same in the realm of economics. They have cautioned that, until China fully conforms to the regulations and procedures of the entire global community, the United States should deal very cautiously with Beijing.

An issue that continues to plague U.S.-China trade relations is the question of human rights. Global human rights groups have listed China as the nation that least respects human rights. Highly publicized imprisonments of Chinese journalists, activists, and even prominent business figures had led to stormy debates in Congress as to whether the United States should be dealing with the Chinese at all. Many legislators has stated that they believe that China must be forced into conformity with the human rights conventions of the United Nations and that, barring full compliance, it should be isolated from the American trading community. However, unilateral action by the United States in this matter would be difficult. More moderate legislators have urged American administrations to work more closely with world bodies such as the World Bank, the WTO, the United Nations, Association of SouthEast Asian Nations (ASEAN), and the Group of Seven to pressure China to respect human rights, especially in the area of religious tolerance. All agree that the situation has improved since 1979; however, much is still lacking in the Chinese human rights record. American companies have tried to institute fair labor practices in their factories in China and have also sought to instill a respect for human rights in Chinese managers and workers at every level.

Mark DeStephano

FURTHER READING

Henderson, Callum. *China on the Brink: The Myths and Realities of the World's Largest Market.* New York: McGraw-Hill, 1999. A study of the many difficult challenges that China faces on the road to economic development, especially as it deals with the suspicions of the global community. This work combines political analysis with economic realities.

Hinkelman, Edward G., ed. *China Business: The Portable Encyclopedia for Doing Business with China.* San Rafael, Calif.: World Trade Press, 1995. An excellent sourcebook for almost any aspect of doing business with China, this work provides a wealth of data and analysis of critical issues.

Hudson, Christopher, ed. *The China Handbook.* Chicago: Fitzroy Dearborn, 1997. This collection of essays, although topical, provides a fine overview of China's economic transition from the founding of the People's Republic of China to the late 1990's.

Hufbauer, Gary Clyde, et al. *U.S.-China Trade Disputes: Rising Tide, Rising Stakes.* Washington, D.C.: Institute for International Economics, 2006. This study of the economic tensions between the United States and China is balanced and scholarly.

Lardy, Nicholas R. *China in the World Economy.* Washington, D.C.: Institute for International Economics, 1994. An excellent analysis of the Chinese economy and its relation to the international economy. Chapter 4 is a particularly helpful overview of U.S.-China trade difficulties.

Studwell, Joseph. *The China Dream: The Quest for the Last Great Untapped Market on Earth.* New York: Atlantic Monthly Press, 2002. An interesting study of China's historical record in the realm of business and economic cooperation with the rest of the world. Provides important historical perspective.

Tong, Sarah Yueting. *U.S.-China Trade Balance: Why Such a Huge Discrepancy?* Singapore: East Asian Institute of the National University of Singapore, 2004. A scholarly analysis of the complex problems involved in the U.S.-China trade imbalance. Tong, an authority in this area, offers a clear presentation of the challenges facing both nations at the level of trade.

See also: Asian trade with the United States; Child product safety laws; "Coolie" labor; Counterfeiting; International economics and trade; Japanese trade with the United States; Nixon's China visit; Promotional holidays; Taiwanese trade with the United States.

Christmas marketing

Definition: Advertising and promotion of gifts and seasonal merchandise during the winter holiday season

Significance: Christmas is the most celebrated holiday in the United States and accounts for a large percentage of retailers' annual sales. As retailers have focused their efforts on capitalizing on the holiday season, some conservative Christian organizations have voiced objections that Christmas is losing its spiritual meaning and becoming secularized.

The Christmas season has become inextricably linked to the mass marketing and consumerism that helped forge a distinct American national identity throughout the nineteenth and twentieth centuries. Christmas has become a holiday in which spirituality, customs, and commerce collide. The figures for sales during the holiday season are staggering. In 1991, an average family spent $750 on gifts. A decade later, $6.1 billion was spent on home decorations, lights, and trees for the holidays, whereas sales for the entire season were approximately $200 billion. For individuals who are considered "dedicated collectors" and purchase Christmas-themed merchandise year-round, Christmas décor is now sold throughout the year at fifteen hundred stores nationwide, such as the G&L Christmas Barn in Windham, Connecticut.

Mass Marketing and Consumerism

The consumerism associated with the Christmas season emerged during the late nineteenth and early twentieth centuries. For the first time, technological and infrastructure advancements enabled goods produced by local retailers to be transported, distributed, and advertised on a national scale. The proliferation of advertising for Christmas began after 1820, when stores began to run advertisements for presents to give to loved ones and family.

The first Christmas tree with electric lights was displayed in New York in 1882 at the home of Edward Johnson, a colleague of Thomas Alva Edison. The General Electric Company saw this innovation as an opportunity and began to mass market bulbs during the 1880's. By 1903, the Ever-Ready Company manufactured the first Christmas lights, called festoons, which came with twenty-eight sockets. However, the bulbs were not affordable to the general public until the 1920's, and outdoor lighting did not begin to be promoted by General Electric until 1925.

In 1897, Marshall Field's became the first department store to design a special holiday window display. The early decorated windows were geared toward religious themes, but over the years, the windows began to display more secular images. They often took their themes not from spiritual sources but rather from such Christmas books as Dr. Seuss's *How the Grinch Stole Christmas!* (1957) or poems such as Clement Clarke Moore's "A Visit from Saint Nicholas" (1823; also known as "The Night Before Christmas").

The Great Depression was the impetus for President Franklin D. Roosevelt to move Thanksgiving festivities one week earlier in November, so stores could have an extra week to count toward raising Christmas revenue. In 1939, Montgomery Ward distributed to children copies of the song "Rudolph the Red-Nosed Reindeer," which was written by employee Robert L. May; in 1949, Gene Autry recorded Johnny Marks's popular song adaptation. The Rudolph story represented the company's decision to market Christmas to children and, through children, to their parents.

Christmas displays became popular with the middle class after World War II, as postwar economic prosperity shaped middle-class aesthetic values and favored the development of competitions among neighbors in creating such displays. Lights became cheaper, and popular magazines and stores heavily promoted decorating as part of the joy of the season. Before World War II, homemade decorations cut from paper were common. However, during the 1950's, mass-produced decorations became available because of the development of styrene, a plastic that could withstand the heat produced by illuminated figurines.

Santa Claus emerged as the embodiment of an American Christmas, beginning during the mid-nineteenth century after the publication of Moore's poem. Cartoonist Thomas Nast popularized the jolly and rotund image of Santa Claus during the early 1860's. Coca-Cola began to use Santa Claus as a pitchman in 1931, when the company commissioned illustrator Haddon Sundblom to develop an advertising campaign. Santa's image could be widely distributed, since no company or individual could lay claim to its copyright. Santa Claus also became part of a growing industry known as "event photography." By the mid-twentieth century, Santa Claus was present in malls and department stores throughout the United States as part the burgeoning event photography business. Having youngsters sit on Santa's lap did not correlate to increased sales at the stores, but it was profitable for companies that contracted out for photographers. The malls or stores received a share of profits from photos sold to customers.

TWENTIETH CENTURY DEVELOPMENTS

One-quarter of all annual retail business is conducted during the Christmas season. Toward the middle of the twentieth century, the consumerism

This talking Christmas tree, on sale at a Connecticut mall in 1997, is typical of the Christmas-themed merchandise offered in the holiday season. (AP/Wide World Photos)

and materialism surrounding Christmas began to draw sharp criticism from conservative Christian groups. These groups argued that modern, secular marketing and advertising obscured the true intent, customs, and religious traditions behind the holiday. Beginning in 1949, the Milwaukee Arch Confraternity of Christian Mothers developed the slogan "Keep Christ in Christmas" to remind Americans of what they saw as the true spirit of the season. During the early twenty-first century, retail chains such as Target; Sears, Roebuck; and Wal-Mart underwent attacks by conservative groups for using the more inclusive "Happy Holidays" rather than "Merry Christmas" in store advertisements. Because the holiday is such as significant part of the retail industry, Christmas sales are often analyzed closely for clues as to the state of the economy, especially during periods of slow growth or recession.

Gayla Koerting

FURTHER READING

Lavin, Mau, ed. *The Business of Holidays.* New York: Monacelli Press, 2004. Explores the American obsession with holidays and retail revenue in thirty-three essays on topics ranging from Groundhog Day to Christmas.

Nissenbaum, Stephen. *The Battle for Christmas.* New York: Alfred A. Knopf, 1997. Traces the political, economic, and social history of Christmas celebrations in America from the seventeenth through the twentieth centuries.

Restad, Penne. *Christmas in America: A History.* New York: Oxford University Press, 1995. Charts the evolution of the Christmas season from the colonial period to the late twentieth century. Also examines the emergence of Santa Claus as a quasi-religious figure representing hope, charity, and goodwill from 1820 to 1880.

Schmidt, Leigh E. *Consumer Rites: The Buying and Selling of American Holidays.* Princeton, N.J.: Princeton University Press, 1995. Examines the connection between American religious and commercial culture, focusing on St. Valentine's Day, Easter, Mother's Day, and Christmas.

Thompson, Sue Ellen. *Holiday Symbols and Customs.* Detroit, Mich.: Omnigraphics, 2003. Provides a general overview of the traditions, customs, and symbols associated with holidays celebrated throughout the world.

SEE ALSO: Child product safety laws; Greeting card industry; Promotional holidays; Retail trade industry.

Chrysler bailout of 1979

THE EVENT: Federal financial assistance provided to an ailing major manufacturer in the automotive industry

DATE: 1979

PLACE: Detroit, Michigan

SIGNIFICANCE: Although Congress had declined to provide economic assistance to other companies in the past, the consequences of those decisions convinced the legislature that aiding Chrysler was necessary. Taxpayers and advocacy groups, however, warned that the bailout would set a bad precedent for American businesses.

After losing more than $200 million in 1978 and nearly the same amount in just the first quarter of 1979, the Chrysler Corporation was on the verge of bankruptcy. Many factors had contributed to Chrysler's decline: the costs of complying with federal regulations, an influx of foreign imports, and the gas crisis caused by the Arab oil embargo, which diminished market demand for Chrysler's large, gas-guzzling vehicles. Chrysler hired Lee Iacocca, a former Ford executive to turn the company around. Iacocca began restructuring Chrysler and also sought loan guarantees from the federal government. Advocates of government aid argued that a bankruptcy would result in a tremendous loss of jobs and disruption of the stock market, but opponents countered that government help would set a precedent of rewarding failure and involving the government in private business.

Congress provided aid in the form of the Chrysler Corporation Loan Guarantee Act of 1979, which provided Chrysler with $1.5 billion in federal loan guarantees. After the act's passage, the United Auto Workers made concessions worth many millions of

---

CHRYSLER'S ORIGINS

In 1925, Walter Percy Chrysler reorganized the financially troubled Maxwell Motor Company to create the Chrysler Corporation. The new company immediately began producing and selling the first automobile named the Chrysler. Boasting numerous design innovations, such as a high-compression engine, the car sold 19,960 units during its first year. In 1926, that number increased to 129,572. In 1928, Chrysler expanded, adding low-priced Plymouths, medium-priced De Sotos, and higher-priced Dodges to its line of cars with the Chrysler name. By the end of that year, Chrysler was the second-largest automobile producer in the world, behind General Motors. During the Depression years, Chrysler survived by reducing its debt and improving its product line. Chrysler maintained its second-place position into the early 1950's, when it was overtaken by Ford.

Bernadette Zbicki Heiney

dollars in their contract negotiations with the company. These concessions also helped the company recover from bankruptcy and regain a competitive position in the industry. In 1998, Daimler-Benz bought Chrysler and formed DaimlerChrysler. In August, 2007, the Chrysler group was sold to Cerberus Capital Management, and it was renamed Chrysler LLC.

In October, 2008, the Big Three automakers were suffering huge losses because of falling sales, legacy costs, and a drop in the popularity of sports-utility vehicles and trucks that were the mainstays of their product lines. They appealed to the federal government for financial aid, with Chrysler and General Motors facing possible bankruptcies. On December 19, President George W. Bush announced that $13.4 billion in emergency loans would be made available to prevent the automakers' collapse. However, the loans were given on condition that automakers make major concessions and organizational changes by March 31, 2009, to demonstrate that they could return to profitability. Ford, which was in a better financial state, was not expected to make use of the federal loans. On February 18, 2009, General Motors and Chrysler asked for $14 billion more in aid.

Karel S. Sovak

FURTHER READING

Breer, Carl, and Anthony J. Yanik. *The Birth of Chrysler Corporation and Its Engineering Legacy.* Warrendale, Pa.: Society of Automotive Engineers, 1995.

Dammann, George H. *Seventy Years of Chrysler.* Glen Ellyn, Ill.: Crestline Publishing, 1974.

Gup, Benton E. *Too Big to Fail: Policies and Practices in Government Bailouts.* Westport, Conn.: Praeger, 2004.

SEE ALSO: Automotive industry; Bankruptcy law; Congress, U.S.; Enron bankruptcy; Ford Motor Company; General Motors; Iacocca, Lee; WorldCom bankruptcy.

CIO. *See* AFL-CIO

Civil Rights Act of 1964

THE LAW: First federal civil rights legislation since the Reconstruction era

DATE: Signed into law on July 2, 1964

SIGNIFICANCE: Using its constitutional power to regulate interstate commerce, the U.S. Congress passed the Civil Rights Act of 1964 to outlaw segregation in public accommodations involved in interstate commerce, to declare discrimination in employment illegal, and to establish the Equal Employment Opportunity Commission.

On June 19, 1963, in response to sit-ins, marches, boycotts, and demonstrations by civil rights organizations, President John F. Kennedy proposed the strongest civil rights bill of the twentieth century. This bill included proposals dealing with voting rights, public school desegregation, discrimination in public accommodations, establishment of the federal Community Relations Service, continuation of the Civil Rights Commission, discrimination in federally assisted programs, and the creation of the Equal Employment Opportunity Commission. A year later, Congress passed the bill by a vote of 289 to 126 in the House of Representatives and 73 to 27 in the Senate. President Lyndon B. Johnson signed the bill into law on July 2, 1964.

The final bill was organized by broad provisions, or titles. Title I made illegal the unequal application of voter registration requirements. Title III prohibited state and local governments from denying access to public facilities based on race, religion, or ethnicity, while Title IV granted the attorney general the power to file suit to enforce school desegregation. Title X created the Community Relations Service to assist in community disputes involving claims of communications.

Other parts of the act specifically addressed issues related to discrimination in the private sector. Title II outlawed discrimination in hotels, motels, restaurants, theaters, and all other public accommodations engaged in interstate commerce, although it exempted private clubs. It also allowed individuals to file lawsuits to obtain relief. Title VI prohibited discrimination in any program or activity receiving federal funds. If an agency violated that provision, it could lose its federal funding. Title VII prohibited discrimination in employment on the basis of color, religion, sex, or national origin in any business that employed twenty-five people or more.

Title VII also created the five-member Equal Employment Opportunity Commission (EEOC) to implement the law. Later legislation would expand the role of the EEOC, which would be empowered to enforce laws that prohibited discrimination based on race, color, religion, sex, national origin, disability, or age in hiring, promoting, firing, setting wages, testing, training, or apprenticeship, as well as all other terms and conditions of employment. The commission was also given the power to investigate, create conciliation programs, file lawsuits, and conduct voluntary assistance programs.

The Civil Rights Act had a significant impact on both the public and the private sectors. Overnight, it virtually eliminated the legal segregation of public accommodations. The threat to government programs and businesses that discriminated in employment of losing federal funds, and the creation of the EEOC resulted in equal opportunity becoming a part of American life for minorities and women.

William V. Moore

FURTHER READING

Graham, Hugh Davis. *The Civil Rights Era: Origin and Development of National Policy, 1960-1972.* New York: Oxford University Press, 1990.

Hasday, Judy L. *The Civil Rights Act of 1964: An End to Racial Segregation.* New York: Chelsea House, 2007.

Loevy, Robert D., ed. *The Civil Rights Act of 1964: The Passage of the Law That Ended Racial Segregation.* Albany: State University of New York Press, 1997.

SEE ALSO: Affirmative action programs; Civil Rights movement; Equal Employment Opportunity Commission; Supreme Court and commerce; Supreme Court and labor law; Women in business.

Civil Rights movement

THE EVENT: A national struggle for legal, racial, and social equality led by African Americans

DATE: c. 1954-1968

PLACE: United States, particularly the South

SIGNIFICANCE: Long after the U.S. Civil War, many African Americans were still working in low-paying jobs that required few skills and had no

opportunities for advancement. They faced discrimination in education and the workplace that limited their progress. The Civil Rights movement helped transform the place of African Americans in the economy.

The South has historically been the most economically deprived region of the United States. During the early 1950's, the South maintained segregated services and institutions at considerable cost. Labor unions organized only fitfully, and although national leaders were sympathetic to African American problems, local officers were not, sometimes even being members of the Ku Klux Klan. Though labor was cheap in the South, businesses and industries frequently avoided this region because of its inferior schools, backward social conditions, and potential for racial unrest.

After World War II, the South rapidly began changing from a rural society to an urbanized, industrial one. The mechanization of farming and the decline of the cotton industry meant that fewer unskilled workers were needed in rural areas. Both white and black southerners migrated in large numbers to cities in the North, finding industrial jobs there. Although enlightened thinkers acknowledged problems, social patterns were slow to change. Whites generally believed they benefited from the system as it was, and in cities such as Atlanta, there was a black bourgeoisie that was relatively comfortable with its own privileges. In Birmingham, Alabama, men such as white banker Charles Zukoski met regularly with insurance executive A. G. Gaston, the wealthiest black citizen of Alabama. Though modest reforms were suggested, the major abuses of segregation continued.

PIONEERS OF THE MOVEMENT

Students, like those enrolled in the African American universities and seminaries of Nashville, Tennessee, were important during the early Civil Rights movement. Students Diane Nash, James Bevel, James Lawson, Marion Barry, and John Lewis quickly perceived the vulnerability of businesses to their organized sit-ins and boycotts. Within only a few weeks, these students were able to integrate six lunch counters in Nashville. The city's largest department store at that time, Harvey's, unlike its rival, Cain-Sloan's, had a forward-looking management that perceived the economic advantage in accommodating African American customers.

Despite economic disadvantages, African American family income in the South was growing. Even during the early 1960's, sales to African Americans constituted 15 percent of retail sales in Houston, 17 percent in Atlanta, and 24 percent in Memphis. These proportions would increase in the years that followed, as white people bought automobiles, moved out of the inner cities, and began to patronize suburban shopping centers, leaving behind African Americans who were largely dependent on public transportation. Inner-city variety stores started providing ethnic cosmetics, portraits of a black Jesus, and other products specifically designed for their increasingly African American clientele. These stores then began to employ African American clerks and managers.

In Montgomery, Alabama, E. D. Nixon, locally revered as "the father of the Civil Rights movement," convinced downtown merchants that it was to their advantage to address African American customers respectfully and allow them to use drinking fountains. Nixon recruited Martin Luther King, Jr., then minister of the Dexter Avenue Baptist Church, to lead the bus boycott initiated by Rosa Parks. In 1955, the boycott brought the system of public transportation to a halt in Montgomery. King well understood the importance of businesspeople in the racial struggle. He realized that in cities such as Birmingham, it would be easier to apply pressure to businessmen than to elected officials. By this time, the Civil Rights movement had learned to use the medium of television effectively. Many southern businesspeople were embarrassed when television sets throughout the United States showed footage of police officers using police dogs and fire hoses against demonstrating African Americans, including women and children.

THE MOVEMENT SHIFTS NORTH

The struggle in the South won African Americans legal access to better schools and public places, including theaters, restaurants, and hotels. When the focus shifted North, where African Americans had legal rights but often lived in impoverished areas separated from whites, these gains seemed irrelevant and middle class to many African Americans. Access to a luxury hotel was useless to someone paid minimum wage. In the North, the Civil Rights move-

The Civil Rights movement brought an end to businesses that, like this one, discriminated against nonwhites. (Library of Congress)

ment's goals became more pointedly economic. Businesses and professions were targeted, with activists promoting proposals for compensatory treatment for disadvantaged minorities. Although nonviolence had worked well as both theory and tactic in the South, where the movement was led by students and clergymen, less idealistic activists in the North leaned toward militancy. Organizations such as the Congress for Racial Equality (CORE) and the Student Nonviolent Coordinating Committee (SNCC) became more strident in their protests, as new leaders such as Stokely Carmichael preached of "black power." Some militants even advocated a separate economy, with black businesses to be patronized exclusively by African Americans.

OUTCOMES

Though not all economic goals were met, American society changed radically as a result of the Civil Rights movement. The impoverished, feudalistic South gradually faded away as the region came into a fuller partnership with the rest of the states economically, politically, and socially. African American politician Jesse Jackson observed that only an integrated Atlanta could have acquired the headquarters of Cable News Network (CNN) and been chosen to host the Olympic Games. African Americans started returning to southern states, bringing with them business and professional skills. After the movement, more and more African Americans enjoyed business success, becoming doctors, lawyers, and other professionals, and working in and rising to executive positions in businesses that had once been dominated by white Americans. For example, during the early twenty-first century, the chief executive officer position at several prominent companies was held by an African American: Kenneth I. Chenault at American Express (2001), John W. Thompson at Symantec (1999), and Richard D. Parsons at Time Warner (2002-2007). Oprah Winfrey, a talk show host, became owner of her own media company and one of the richest people in the United States.

Allene Phy-Olsen

FURTHER READING

Bloom, Jack M. *Class, Race and the Civil Rights Movement*. Bloomington: Indiana University Press, 1987. The best analysis of economics and the movement, demonstrating how idealism and economic reality brought racial advancement, as the South moved from an agrarian to an industrial society.

Branch, Taylor. *Parting the Waters: America in the King Years, 1954-1963*. New York: Simon & Schuster, 1988. Often regarded as the definitive history of the Civil Rights movement, this work concentrates on the life and career of Martin Luther King, Jr.

Draper, Alan. *Conflict of Interest: Organized Labor and the Civil Rights Movement in the South, 1954-1968*. Ithaca, N.Y.: ILR Press, 1994. An analysis of organized labor's inroads into the South and the ambivalent actions of white workers, who were anxious to improve working conditions while committed to the racial status quo.

Halberstam, David. *The Children*. New York: Random House, 1998. A highly readable account of the Nashville Civil Rights movement detailing the student sit-ins, economic boycotts, and the clever use of national publicity.

Marable, Manning, Immanuel Ness, and Joseph Wilson, eds. *Race and Labor Matters in the New U.S. Economy*. New York: Rowman & Littlefield, 2006. A collection of essays by sociologists and political scientists that examine the relationship between economics and ethnicity.

SEE ALSO: Affirmative action programs; Civil Rights Act of 1964; Equal Employment Opportunity Commission; Garvey, Marcus; Justice, U.S. Department of; Labor history; Poor People's Campaign of 1968; Randolph, A. Philip; Supreme Court and commerce; Women in business.

Civil War, U.S.

THE EVENT: Conflict between the Northern states (the Union) and the Southern states (the Confederacy)

DATE: April 12, 1861-April 9, 1865

PLACE: United States

SIGNIFICANCE: During the U.S. Civil War, the Union government demonstrated its capacity to raise large sums of money, and it established a national currency, a national banking system, and the nation's first income tax. The war promoted the economic growth of the Northern states, while it retarded development in the states of the Confederacy.

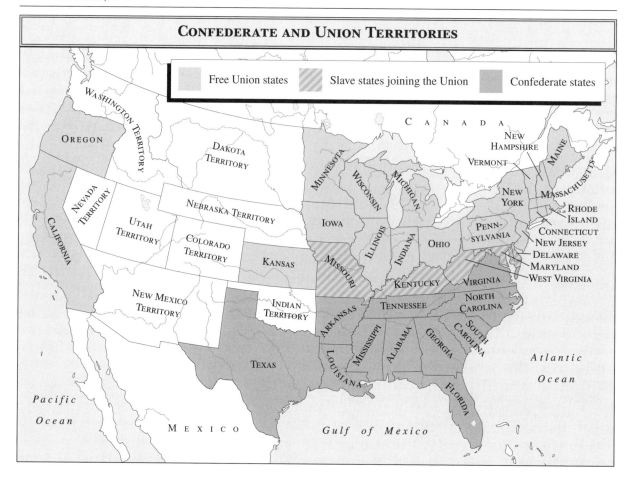

CONFEDERATE AND UNION TERRITORIES

Free Union states   Slave states joining the Union   Confederate states

With the outbreak of the Civil War, the Northern states experienced a severe recession (then called a "panic"). There were several causes for the downturn, including the disruption of trade with the South, inadequate banking reserves, and uncertainties about how the war would affect business. More than six thousand banks and commercial firms were forced to close their doors in 1861. Southerners owed Northern creditors more than $300 million, most of which was a complete loss. The prices paid for agricultural commodities dropped precipitously. In Illinois, for example, corn fell from almost $1 to as little as 10 cents per bushel. The recession continued into early 1862, but by the fall of that year, the Northern states were beginning to experience a wartime boom.

STRATEGIC OBJECTIVES

Like other wars, the ultimate success or failure of the armies in the Civil War was largely determined by their supplies of armaments, equipment, food, clothing, and other war materials. In turn, the availability of such materials depended on the underlying economic conditions of the sponsoring societies. From this perspective, the North had numerous advantages. According to the 1860 census, the twenty-five states of the Union had a population of 22.3 million, whereas the eleven states of the Confederacy contained 9.1 million people, including 5.47 million whites, 3.5 million slaves, and 130,000 free blacks. Ninety percent of the nation's manufacturing was located in the North. In addition, the Northern states had about five times the amount of personal wealth, two and a half times the number of railway miles, and more than four times the amount of personal wealth.

The Confederate states, nevertheless, had the advantage of fighting a defensive war. To obtain its goal of independence, the Confederacy did not have to win a military victory; rather, it only had to do well enough to convince a majority of Northerners that the goal of preserving the Union was not worth a great sacrifice in lives and money. Many Southerners, moreover, hoped to obtain help from abroad. Because cotton, the nation's major export commodity, was so essential to the textile mills of Great Britain and Western Europe, some Southern leaders proclaimed that "cotton is king." They expected that the Europeans' great appetite for cotton would force them to oppose the blockade, recognize Confederate independence, and eventually help the Southern cause with loans.

The strategy of King Cotton was a failure for several reasons. Although it was true that European manufacturers suffered from diminished supplies of cotton, other places in the world, including Egypt and the Caribbean islands, were able to expand production. European political and business leaders, moreover, were careful not to support a losing cause, and after the Northern victories of 1863, most informed observers expected that the Union forces would almost certainly prevail. In addition, after President Abraham Lincoln issued the Emancipation Proclamation in 1863, any support for the South would appear to endorse the institution of slavery, which was very unpopular in Europe.

CONFEDERATE FINANCES

One of the main reasons that the South failed to achieve independence was inadequate financial resources. Even if the Confederate government had pursued more effective policies, it is doubtful that victory would have been possible. The cost of the war to the Confederacy was an estimated $2 billion, and its total expenditures for the period were approximately $2.3 billion. More than 80 percent of this amount was obtained by printing paper money, which rapidly declined in value. When the war began in 1861, the Confederate government had assets worth about $27 million in money backed by gold or silver. The government also levied a small tariff on imports and a tax on cotton exports, but this brought in only $3.5 million during the entire war.

In large part because of its emphasis on state sovereignty, the Confederate Congress was hesitant to impose direct taxes. In August, 1861, the first tax law required most citizens to pay 0.5 percent of their assessed property values, with an exemption for heads of families having less than $500 in property. A pro-

vision of the law allowed the states to pay the tax on behalf of their citizens, and several states paid the tax with borrowed money. An 1862 law required Southern citizens to pay into the treasury the amount owed to their Northern creditors, but this measure proved almost impossible to enforce. In April, 1863, the Confederate Congress finally enacted a comprehensive tax law on almost everything taxable, including incomes, personal property, and agricultural products, but the deteriorating military situation increasingly prevented collection. Overall, the combination of taxes raised only about $200 million, which was less than 10 percent of Confederate expenditures.

Confederate officials initially expected to rely heavily on the sale of government bonds, even though most planters had debts and not many Southerners possessed large amounts of liquid capital. In early 1861, the first bond issue of $15 million was quickly sold out. Within a few months, however, Confederate bonds at 8 percent interest were selling slowly, not surprisingly in view of the inflation rate, which had reached 12 percent a month by the end of the year. By that time, moreover, the naval blockade was making it difficult for even the wealthiest of Southerners to obtain hard currency. Secretary Christopher Gustavus Memminger devised the idea of a "produce loan," which allowed farmers to obtain bonds in exchange for pledges for the proceeds of their cotton, tobacco, and other crops. This approach eventually resulted in bond sales of about $34 million. The government also tried to borrow money abroad. In early 1863, the French banker, Emile Erlanger, authorized the sale of $15 million dollars in cotton-backed bonds. The Northern victories in Vicksburg and Gettysburg, however, soon persuaded many Europeans that the Southern cause was probably doomed to failure, and they purchased only some $2.5 million in bonds. The total bond sales of the Confederacy totaled about $150 million, with at least two-thirds of this amount purchased with inflated Confederate paper money.

On March 9, 1861, the Confederate Congress, encouraged by Secretary of the Treasury Memminger, authorized the printing of $1 million in paper currency, which grew to $311 million by the end of 1861, representing three-quarters of the government's revenues for the year. The currency (called "treasury notes") was not backed by gold or silver, and each bill promised that the government "will pay the bearer with interest of two cents per day . . . six months after the ratification of a treaty of peace between the Confederate States and the United States." As the cost of the war mounted, the printing presses produced more and more notes. Memminger in 1862 warned that the excessive dependence on paper money could eventually result in "depreciation and final disaster," but the government appeared to have no other options for raising the necessary funds. By the war's end in 1865, more than $1.5 billion in Confederate currency was in circulation. By this time, moreover, many states, counties, and even cities were issuing their own notes, often crudely printed, making them easy to counterfeit.

Awash in a sea of paper money, the Southern states inevitably experienced runaway inflation, resulting in severe hardships for the civilian population. In December, 1861, the Confederate dollar was worth only 80 cents in gold; by 1863, it was valued at about 20 cents; and by early 1865, it had declined to less than 2 cents. In the relatively good year of 1862, the wages of urban workers increased about 55 percent, while prices grew by about 300 percent. The conditions on the farms, where most Southern whites lived, were even worse. With so many adult men away from home, the crop yields declined significantly. On March 26, 1863, Congress enacted an impressment law that required farmers and merchants to turn over surplus commodities to the government in exchange for Confederate currency. The law also applied to slaves, who were impressed to work for the army. By March, 1865, more than $500 million in currency of little value had been exchanged for goods and slaves.

Union Finances

One of the main reasons for the Union victory was the government's ability to obtain the funding required to fight the war, which amounted to $700 million in 1864 and over $1 billion in 1865. During the four years, the Union government raised some $3.2 billion, with about 25 percent coming from taxes and two-thirds from the sale of bonds and other securities. When Abraham Lincoln took office, the nation's public debt, having increased from the Panic of 1857, stood at $64 million. By the end of the conflict, the public debt had grown to $2.68 billion.

Despite the wealth and fundamental soundness of the economy, the government faced significant monetary and inflationary challenges. The financial panic that occurred after secession significantly reduced the specie (or gold holdings) of the U.S. Treasury and weakened the government's credit rating. Early in the conflict, moreover, the federal government did not have the machinery necessary to raise large sums of money. Before this time, governmental expenditures had been modest in comparison with the unprecedented expenditures of the war, and adequate revenue had been raised by a combination of the tariff and the sale of public lands.

Secretary of the Treasury Salmon P. Chase initially expected to finance the war primarily by the tariff and the sale of government bonds. In early 1861, Congress attempted to increase the government's revenue with the Morrill Act, which raised the tariff on dutiable goods to 36 percent, and three years later the tariff was further increased to 47 percent. At Chase's urging, in the summer of 1861, Congress authorized the sale of $50 million in twenty-year bonds paying a high rate of interest (7 percent). The relatively high interest rate was necessary because of the temporary weakness of the government's credit rating. In February, 1862, Congress authorized the issuance of another $514 million in bonds. When the bonds did not sell well, the administration contracted with a private firm, Jay Cooke and Company, to market them. Cooke, called the "financier of the Civil War," skillfully secured the help of the press and employed 2,500 salesmen.

As revenue demands increased, Chase decided it was necessary for the government to issue non-interest-bearing Treasury notes, which were commonly called greenbacks because of their color. The Legal Tender Act of 1862 authorized the printing of $150 million in greenbacks not exchangeable in specie (metal coin), and additional legislation resulted in a total printing of almost $450 million by the war's end. The notes announced: "Legal tender in payment of all debts, public and private, within the United States, except duties on imports and interest." Although backed by the federal government, the value of the greenbacks declined significantly in relation to gold. Their decline in value was one of the major causes for the inflationary conditions that heightened the government's growing need for funds. A greenback dollar purchased only 67 cents in gold by the spring of 1863, and it continued to decline until it was worth only 35 cents in gold at its lowest point, July 11, 1864, when troops under Confederate General Jubal Early were "at the doors of Washington." Although detested by most bankers and wealthy investors, the greenbacks were quite popular with the general public, particularly debtors.

On August 5, 1861, Congress enacted the nation's first income tax, which was expanded in 1862, 1863, and 1865. In its final form, incomes between $600 and $5,000 were taxed at the rate of 5 percent, and incomes above $10,000 were taxed at 10 percent. By the end of the war, the income tax brought in more than $20 million. On July 1, 1862, Congress passed the Internal Revenue Act of 1862, which levied a comprehensive system of taxes on all kinds of goods and services, including natural resources, manufactured items, transportation, farm products, bank deposits, newspapers, and insurance policies. An annual tax was levied on interest payments and other income in excess of $600, and stamp duties were also attached to all business and legal documents. To assess and collect the various taxes, the statute created the Office of Commissioner of Internal Revenue within the Department of the Treasury. The president was authorized, by executive order, to divide the country into collection districts and to appoint an assessor and collector for each district. Because of the complexities in developing new institutions, some of the taxes were not levied until May, 1863.

Early in the war, Secretary Chase advocated the creation of a national banking system to exercise control over the approximately 1,600 state banks that issued their own banknotes, resulting in more than 7,000 different forms of currency used in business transactions. However, many Americans, especially the Jacksonian Democrats, feared the power of a "monster bank." After President Lincoln effectively lobbied on behalf of the measure, Congress, by a narrow margin, passed the National Bank Act of 1863, which organized a network of National Banks chartered by the government. To qualify for a charter, a bank had to possess minimum capital of $20,000 to $200,000, depending on the size of the city in which it was located.

Each chartered bank was required to invest a minimum of either $30,000 or one-third of its capital in government bonds, and the bank then received a new type of hard currency, national banknotes, in an amount equal to 90 percent of its bond holdings. The banknotes could be used as legal tender for almost all purposes. From the government's perspective, the new institution had two major benefits: First, it helped sell government bonds, and second, it provided a uniform currency throughout the country. The system was also profitable to banks, because with the same capital, they could collect interest from the bonds and at the same time use the bank notes to make loans to customers. Initially, nevertheless, most banks, especially those in New York, were slow to apply for a national charter. In March, 1865, Congress drove the state banknotes out of circulation by imposing a 10 percent tax on them. Within a year, the vast majority of state banks had converted to federal charters.

ECONOMIC DEVELOPMENT

During the four years of war, the economies of the Union states generally grew in all major sectors,

---

WHOLESALE PRICE INDEXES, 1860-1866, BY PRODUCT GROUP (1910-1914 = 100)

Product Group	1860	1861	1862	1863	1864	1865	1866
Building materials	65	63	69	88	114	118	128
Foods	96	89	107	123	189	180	173
Fuel and lighting	98	80	87	125	197	214	160
Textile products	119	120	147	206	264	266	245
Metals and metal products	149	152	180	236	354	306	278

Source: Data from *Historical Statistics of the United States: Colonial Times to 1970* (Washington, D.C.: U.S. Department of Commerce, Bureau of the Census, 1975)

including manufacturing, agriculture, mining, financial institutions, and railroad construction. Government spending, which was only $60 million in 1860, rose to $1.2 billion in 1865. The availability of government contracts helped many businesses. The credit-rating service, R. G. Dunn, reported that the number of business failures in the Northern states declined from 2,733 in 1860 to only 510 in 1864. The war created particularly strong demand for iron products, which especially helped manufacturers in Pittsburgh and Cleveland. The shipment of iron ore from the Lake Superior region more than doubled during the Civil War. The woolen textile industry also experienced phenomenal growth because of the need for military uniforms combined with the inability of the cotton textile industry to obtain needed supplies. The amount of wool used by manufacturers grew from about 85 million pounds in 1860 to 200 million pounds in 1865.

Investors and speculators in the stock market made huge profits. The war stimulated a frenzy of trading that allowed many people to acquire great wealth, as least on paper. Between 1862 and 1864, people buying and selling stocks realized capital gains estimated at $250 million. This accumulation of capital helped prepare for the modernization and expansion of big business that occurred from the end of the Civil War until World War I.

The war years also promoted the expansion of Northern agriculture. The number of hogs butchered in Chicago, for example, grew from 270,000 in 1861 to 900,000 in 1865. Farmers found unusually good markets for their products. Civilian demand was greater than in peacetime, and the federal government purchased huge quantities of food. Also, poor European harvests from 1860 to 1862 helped drive up prices. The wheat production in the midwestern states grew from 80 million bushels in 1859 to 100 million bushels in 1865. Before the war, wheat sold for $1 or less per bushel, but the price for a bushel increased in many places to $2.25 in 1864. Because of the labor shortage, more farm machinery was manufactured than ever before. In 1864 alone, about 90,000 mowers and reapers were manufactured. Much of the farm labor was performed by women and children. The need for labor was partially met by the continuing stream of immigrants, many of whom were farmers. Although the number of immigrants declined to about 91,000 in 1862, it grew to 176,000 in 1863 and then to 248,000 in 1865.

The secession of the Southern states allowed the Republican-dominated Congress to enact a number of historical reforms that Northern political and business leaders had advocated for many years. The Pacific Railway Act of 1862 launched the construction of a transcontinental railroad. The Morrill Land-Grant Act of 1862 helped expand the public financing of higher education. The Homestead Act of 1862 allowed settlers to acquire 160 acres of free public land, provided that they agreed to reside on the land for five years. Other reforms included the establishment of a national currency, a national banking system, and an income tax (which was ruled unconstitutional in 1895). Several of these reforms helped lay the foundation for the industrial economy that emerged after the Civil War.

The war, unfortunately, devastated the economies of the eleven Confederate states. In addition to killing about one-quarter of the white men of military age, the war destroyed half the farm machinery, a third of the railroad mileage, and thousands of farms and businesses. It also increased the disparity in wealth between the North and the South. According to the census, Northern capital increased by 50 percent, compared with a 74 percent decline in the total capital of the Confederate states. In 1860, these states possessed about 30 percent of the national wealth, but the ratio declined to approximately 12 percent by the war's end in 1865. Inadequate capital and infrastructure would continue to retard the economic development of the South well into the middle of the twentieth century.

Thomas Tandy Lewis

FURTHER READING

Gallman, J. Matthew. *The North Fights the Civil War: The Home Front.* Chicago: Ivan R. Dee, 1994. A study of how the North mobilized and how it was changed by events and economic forces.

Goodwin, Doris Kearns. *Team of Rivals: The Political Genius of Abraham Lincoln.* New York: Simon & Schuster, 2005. A lively written account of Lincoln's cabinet members, their policies, and their disagreements.

McPherson, James C. *Battle Cry of Freedom: The Civil War Era.* New York: Oxford University Press, 1988. Although this outstanding text emphasizes military conflict, it provides excellent introductions to economic and political aspects of the war.

Massey, Mary Elizabeth. *Ersatz in the Confederacy: Shortages and Substitutes on the Southern Homefront.* Charleston: University of South Carolina Press, 1993. A study of the South's attempt to deal with desperate shortages of manufactured items and essential commodities.

Pauldan, Phillip Shaw. *A People's Contest: The Union and Civil War, 1861-1865.* New York: Harper & Row, 1988. An excellent source of detailed information about domestic affairs in the North.

Richardson, Heather Cox. *The Greatest Nation on Earth: Republican Economic Policies During the Civil War.* Cambridge, Mass.: Harvard University Press, 1997. Argues that the Republicans' probusiness policies established preconditions responsible for the growth and modernization of the postwar years.

Wagner, Margaret, Gary Gallagher, and Paul Finkelman, eds. *Civil War Desk Reference.* New York: Simon & Schuster, 2002. A concise and useful guide to almost all topics relating to the war, including business and finances.

SEE ALSO: Confederate currency; Cotton industry; Counterfeiting; Currency; Homestead Act of 1862; Immigration; Military-industrial complex; Panic of 1857; Slave era; Tariffs; Taxation; Transcontinental railroad; Wars.

Clay's American System

IDENTIFICATION: Economic plan to allow for the internal development of the United States by levying a protective tariff, establishing a national bank, and providing subsidies for the building of infrastructure

DATE: Instituted in 1824

SIGNIFICANCE: Clay's system helped define the nature and drive the development of U.S. business from the nineteenth through the twenty-first centuries.

Henry Clay, a nineteenth century U.S. representative and later senator from Kentucky, devised the American System to fashion a compromise to unite the United States into a single political unit by providing a way for all sections to benefit economically from national policies. After the War of 1812, Britain flooded the United States with cheap goods and undermined U.S. business growth. In 1816, Clay proposed a tariff to protect American industries, but this was opposed by western and southern agricultural interests who feared British retaliation against U.S. exports.

To make this tariff more attractive to agricultural interests, Clay proposed that the national government undertake major internal improvements, such as federally financed roads and canals paid for by the tariff revenue and public land sales. This compromise also depended on the Second Bank of the United States for economic stability. Although Clay saw this compromise as helping everyone, President Andrew Jackson vehemently opposed it. Jackson favored the antibusiness views of President Thomas Jefferson and saw Clay as continuing the probusiness ideas of Alexander Hamilton, the first secretary of the Treasury. Eventually the Clay-Jackson disagreements led to the founding of the Whig Party and later the Republican Party.

In a sense, the Clay-Jackson dispute is a precursor to the business philosophies in both Republican and Democratic Parties as late as the twenty-first century. Clay also lost virtually every battle he fought with Jackson, but his ideas won out in the long run. Clay had a vision of the federal government using its national revenue-raising power to fund a wide variety of internal improvements. In a single-member legislative district system (such as that used for both the U.S. House of Representatives and Senate), internal improvements based on pork barrel politics is a very likely outcome. Clay recognized this and provided the underlying rationale for the system widely used by both U.S. political parties from the nineteenth to the twenty-first centuries. Clay's American System can be seen in national internal improvement polices from the development of canals to railroads to the development of the interstate highway system. During the early twenty-first century, only comparatively minor differences over the degree of probusiness emphasis separate the Republican and Democratic Parties.

Richard L. Wilson

FURTHER READING

Baxter, Maurice G. *Henry Clay and the American System.* Lexington: University Press of Kentucky, 1995.

_____. *Henry Clay the Lawyer.* Lexington: University Press of Kentucky, 2000.

Watson, Harry L., ed. *Andrew Jackson vs. Henry Clay: Democracy and Development in Antebellum America.* Boston: Bedford/St. Martin's, 1998.

SEE ALSO: Bank of the United States, Second; Banking; Congress, U.S.; Constitution, U.S.; Government spending; Tariffs; Taxation.

Clayton Antitrust Act

THE LAW: Federal legislation that extended and modified antitrust regulation of businesses

DATE: Became effective on October 15, 1914

SIGNIFICANCE: Along with the Sherman Antitrust Act of 1890, the Clayton Antitrust Act protected competition in the marketplace by proscribing various anticompetitive business practices. It also exempted certain union activities from antitrust prosecution, preserving the ability of unions to exert reasonable pressure on employers during negotiations.

During the initial period following the enactment of the first federal antitrust law, the Sherman Antitrust Act of 1890, the law proved to be a disappointment to those who were anticipating its expansive and vigorous enforcement. The American economy was beset by a wave of corporate mergers between 1895 and 1905, leading to renewed concerns about greater concentration of power among fewer firms in various industries. Another disquieting development occurred with the emergence of the "rule of reason" standard of proof in antitrust cases. In the 1911 case *Standard Oil Co. v. United States,* the U.S. Supreme Court announced that only unreasonable contracts and combinations in direct restraint of trade were illegal. In the aftermath of this decision, many feared that the rule of reason would greatly impair future antitrust enforcement by allowing firms to assert any legitimate business reason in defense of their anticompetitive conduct.

As a consequence of these concerns, antitrust policy emerged as a major issue in the presidential election of 1912. All three principal candidates—Democrat Woodrow Wilson, Republican incumbent William Howard Taft, and independent for-

mer president Theodore Roosevelt—called for amendments to the Sherman Antitrust Act to strengthen federal antitrust enforcement. Following his election that year, President Wilson began work on a proposal to reform antitrust law. In January of 1914, Wilson addressed a joint session of Congress to urge the passage of new legislation that would explicitly delineate the anticompetitive practices outlawed by the Sherman Antitrust Act. The former law had simply but vaguely outlawed every "contract, combination in the form of trust or otherwise, or conspiracy in restraint of trade or commerce." Subsequently, Representative Henry D. Clayton, who was chair of the House Committee on the Judiciary, introduced a bill that was eventually enacted into law and became known as the Clayton Antitrust Act.

The Clayton Antitrust Act explicitly prohibited price discrimination, exclusive dealing, and tying—or the anticompetitive linking of a sale price to the purchase of other commodities. The act also outlawed mergers between firms that threatened substantially to lessen competition or to create a monopoly within an industry. If these practices reduced competition, they were rendered illegal by the act whether or not they were "reasonable" from a business perspective. In addition, the new statute exempted labor unions from antitrust regulation and expanded the availability of treble damages and injunctive relief to private plaintiffs who brought civil antitrust lawsuits.

Kurt M. Saunders

FURTHER READING

Hovenkamp, Herbert. *Federal Antitrust Policy: The Laws of Competition and Its Practice.* 3d ed. St. Paul: West, 1994.

Kinter, Earl W. *The Legislative History of the Federal Antitrust Laws and Related Statutes.* New York: MacMillan, 1978.

SEE ALSO: Antitrust legislation; Federal Trade Commission; Incorporation laws; Labor history; National Labor Relations Board; Northern Securities Company; Price fixing; Sherman Antitrust Act; Supreme Court and commerce; Supreme Court and labor law.

CNBC

IDENTIFICATION: Cable television channel that focuses on business and financial news
DATE: Launched in 1980
SIGNIFICANCE: Since its inception, CNBC has developed into a principal U.S. business and financial cable television network and one of the world's most important financial news sources.

The number of U.S. citizens owning stocks and bonds—often through various retirement plans—grew substantially in the second half of the twentieth century. It was thus probably inevitable that a major new financial information source would emerge on the most advanced communication network available. From a very modest beginning in 1980, CBNC grew until it was worth billions of dollars, becoming the nineteenth-most-valuable cable network.

CNBC started in 1980 as the Satellite Program Network (SPN), broadcasting low-cost programming such as old movies and instructional programs. The National Broadcasting Company (NBC) leased the channel in 1988 and changed the name to Consumer News and Business Network in 1989. At first, CNBC struggled in competition with the Financial News Network (FNN), but it prospered when FNN floundered and NBC bought out FNN and its other partners. By 1991, NBC began marketing the channel solely by its initials CNBC.

During the 1990's, CNBC grew dramatically, adding an Asian version in 1995 and a European version in 1996. By partnering with Dow Jones Newswire and *The Wall Street Journal*, CNBC gained access to the world's most respected business and financial news sources, and its prestige rose accordingly. In 2005, NBC Universal acquired full control of the network, although it continued to use its former partners as news sources.

CNBC has become a major international source of business and financial news, and it employs the most advanced "scroll" lines to provide a wide variety of financial data instantaneously. Operating from 4 A.M. to 8 P.M. daily, CNBC employs an extensive, high-quality on-air staff that has become prominent on other major news channels. The staff routinely interviews Federal Reserve chairs, cabinet officers, presidential candidates, and even sitting presidents.

Richard L. Wilson

SEE ALSO: Bloomberg's Business News Services; Cable News Network; National Broadcasting Company; Stock markets; Television broadcasting industry; *USA Today; The Wall Street Journal.*

CNN. *See* Cable News Network

Coal industry

DEFINITION: Enterprises that mine and process coal
SIGNIFICANCE: An important component of American industrial development since the early nineteenth century, coal has provided energy to industry and remained a major source of electrical power into the early twenty-first century. Coal mining has provided numerous jobs, and it served to spur railroad construction during the late nineteenth century, while persistent health and safety concerns for mine workers have placed the industry at the heart of the labor and regulation movements.

Coal has been mined in the United States since the colonial era. Early coal mines, primarily in Pennsylvania, were usually surface mines or shallow underground mines. Beginning during the 1840's, underground mines became more common in Pennsylvania and later in West Virginia and eastern

COAL PRODUCTION, 1980-2005, IN MILLIONS OF SHORT TONS

Year	Coal Produced
1980	830
1990	1,029
1995	1,033
2000	1,074
2005	1,133

Source: Data from the *Statistical Abstract of the United States, 2008* (Washington, D.C.: Department of Commerce, Economics and Statistics Administration, Bureau of the Census, Data User Services Division, 2008)

Kentucky. Underground mining continues to be a major form of mining in the eastern United States. During the mid-twentieth century, surface mining developed as a major extraction technique in all parts of the country. In Western states such as Wyoming, massive equipment is used to remove both the surface and the coal. Particularly in West Virginia and eastern Kentucky, a surface mining technique known as mountaintop removal has been deployed. In this technique, explosive charges blow the tops off hills into nearby valleys to make coal accessible to mining.

By the late twentieth century, the electric power industry consumed most of the coal mined in the United States. Because the United States has large coal reserves, coal could continue to provide energy well into the future. Coal mining and burning produce several forms of environmental pollution, however. One potential innovation has been seen in efforts to liquefy coal or turn it into a gas. Gasified coal would serve as a supplement to petroleum, as well as burning more cleanly than does solid coal. These projects are very high-cost, however, and synthesized coal liquids remain uneconomic, although increases in the price of crude oil may motivate additional research.

COAL AND THE ENVIRONMENT

The four basic types of coal, classified by their carbon content, are lignite (about 60 percent carbon), sub-bituminous (60-85 percent carbon), bituminous (about 85 percent carbon), and anthracite (almost pure carbon). Much of the early coal that was mined was anthracite, but by the late twentieth century most of the coal mined in the United States was lignite or bituminous coal. Coal contains various sorts of impurities, such as sulfur, nitrogen compounds, and some heavy metals. Lignite and sub-bituminous coal from the Powder River Basin in Wyoming have a lower heat content than does bituminous coal from Eastern states, but they also have a lower sulfur content, creating fewer environmental problems when burned. Many power plants turned to Western coal during the late twentieth century because of its low cost and low sulfur content.

Burning coal produces several forms of environmental pollution, such as acid rain from the sulfur and nitrogen in the coal. It also produces carbon dioxide, a greenhouse gas. Environmental regulations have led coal-fired power plants to adopt several technological innovations in an attempt to reduce emissions, as well as causing many plants to turn to low-sulfur coal. Although the coal industry has been critical of environmental regulation, claiming that regulations increase its costs, environmental regulators have tried to take into account the true cost of burning coal. Pollution that results from burning coal in an electric power plant, such as acid rain, is often imposed on people other than the consumers

Coal miners prepare for descent into a mine at Hazelton, Pennsylvania, in 1905. (Library of Congress)

of the plant's electricity, making simple market self-regulation unlikely. Environmental standards attempt to capture the true societal cost of burning coal, as well as to decrease environmental hazards.

Coal mining itself produces several costs that the mining industry often ignores. Underground mining has always been dangerous work, although innovations such as water-jet mining have somewhat reduced the danger to miners. When they are abandoned after their coal is extracted, underground mines may collapse, causing the surface to subside. Surface mining requires the disposal of the overburden to get at the coal. This material is usually dumped in nearby valleys, damaging water courses and creating pollution from the runoff of surface water. Mountaintop removal often creates hazards for nearby residents, as well as causing water pollution.

EMPLOYMENT IN THE COAL INDUSTRY

Employment in the coal industry peaked during the 1940's and has been in decline ever since. Increased use of technology has increased productivity in underground mines, requiring fewer workers, and surface mining also requires few workers. From 1973 to 2003, coal production nearly doubled. Underground production increased only slightly, with most of the increase coming from surface mines, particularly in the West. In 1950, underground mining accounted for 75 percent of the 560.4 tons of coal mined in the United States, but in 2003 underground mining accounted for only 33 percent of the 1,072 tons of coal production. In 1973, the coal industry employed 152,000 workers nationwide, with 73 percent in underground mines. In 2003, the coal industry employed 71,000 workers, with 56 percent in underground mines. Over that period, employment in Western mines more than doubled, as more mining was done in surface mines in the West. Nonetheless, in some communities in West Virginia and eastern Kentucky, coal mining continues to be the major source of employment.

Coal continues to be a major energy source in the United States despite its numerous environmental risks. The continuing push for clean energy will probably lead to a decline in the coal industry in the United States, but this decline is likely to be gradual, as coal continues to be a cheap alternative to oil as an energy source.

John M. Theilmann

FURTHER READING

Arnold, Barbara J., Mark S. Kilima, and Peter J. Bethell. *Designing the Coal Preparation Plant of the Future.* New York: Society for Mining Metallurgy and Exploration, 2007. Examines advances in producing "clean coal."

Goodell, Jeff. *Big Coal.* Boston: Houghton Mifflin, 2006. Excellent analysis of the role of coal in American industry and its environmental impact.

Lockard, Duane. *Coal.* Charlottesville: University Press of Virginia, 1998. Good analysis of the human impact of the coal industry.

Logan, Michale, ed. *Coal.* New York: Greenhaven, 2007. Compilation of various short pieces presenting opposing viewpoints regarding the coal industry.

Shnayerson, Michael. *Coal River.* New York: Farrar, Strauss and Giroux, 2008. Deals with the coal industry's use of mountaintop removal and the environmental problems generated by the process.

Smil, Vaclav. *Energy at the Crossroads.* Cambridge, Mass.: MIT Press, 2003. Places coal use in the larger context of global energy policies.

SEE ALSO: Coal strike of 1902; Energy, U.S. Department of; Energy crisis of 1979; Mineral resources; Nuclear power industry; Petroleum industry; Public utilities; United Mine Workers of America.

Coal strike of 1902

THE EVENT: Strike by Pennsylvanian anthracite coal miners seeking safer conditions, better pay, and recognition of the mine workers' union

DATE: May 12, 1902-October 23, 1902

PLACE: Eastern Pennsylvania

SIGNIFICANCE: The strike negotiations marked the first time a sitting president intervened in a strike, citing national safety as the reason.

Following 1897's successful bituminous coal strike, John Mitchell, president of the United Mine Workers of America (UMWA), led a strike in 1900 to benefit Pennsylvania's anthracite coal miners. Hoping to avoid an election-year disaster, the Republican Party negotiated a settlement, raising workers' salaries. However, some issues were left unresolved, including the fact that the UMWA was not recognized as a legal union. The Anthracite Coal Strike of 1902 resulted from these unresolved issues.

Mitchell tried to negotiate concessions for the anthracite coal miners similar to those granted to the bituminous coal miners. He wanted a 20 percent wage increase, an eight-hour workday, and recognition of the UMWA's legitimacy. When the mine owners refused to deal with Mitchell or to recognize the UMWA, a nonviolent strike was called. On May 12, the coal miners struck. They were joined by firefighters, pumpmen, and engineers on June 2. Of the 147,000 miners who struck, 30,000 permanently left the region; about 8,000 to 10,000 emigrated to Europe.

Fearing a heating-fuel shortage, President Theodore Roosevelt decided to intervene personally in the strike. Convinced by Attorney General Philander C. Knox that he needed to remain on the sidelines, Roosevelt appointed a panel to research the situation and make recommendations. Research showed that, although the mine workers' situation was not as bad as they claimed, there was room for reform. On October 3, Roosevelt called a meeting between Mitchell and the owners. The union appeared ready to negotiate in good faith; it accepted the creation of a commission to recommend reasonable reforms, but the owners did not. The owners' spokesperson, George Baer, claimed that the workers were not worthy of consideration and that God was on the side of the owners. This attitude caused public opinion to swing to the union's side. The meeting ended with the creation of a seven-member commission that represented the owners, businessmen, workers, politicians, and clergy. With the creation of the commission, the strike ended on October 23, 1902.

The commission's findings resulted in a series of compromises. The union's demands were all partially met; miners received a 10 percent wage increase, a nine-hour workday, and the establishment of a permanent arbitration board. The strike set a precedent for presidential involvement in settling labor disputes. It helped legitimize union representation and supported the development of progressive business practices.

Leslie Neilan

FURTHER READING

Janosov, Robert A. *Great Strike: Perspectives on the 1902 Anthracite Coal Strike.* Easton, Pa.: Center for Canal History and Technology, 2002.

Zane, J. Robert. *1902! The Great Coal Strike in Shenandoah, Pa.: A True Story of Martial Law in an Anthracite Mining Community.* Frackville, Pa.: Broad Mountain, 2004.

SEE ALSO: Coal industry; Labor history; Labor strikes; United Mine Workers of America.

Coca-Cola Company

IDENTIFICATION: Soft drink manufacturer and distributor
DATE: Founded on January 29, 1892
SIGNIFICANCE: The Coca-Cola Company is one of the largest American corporations, and its iconic, eponymous beverage is the best-selling soft drink in the world. Through the years, the company has deployed memorable advertising in all media, the latest technology, and a model production and distribution system to increase and maintain its success.

On May 8, 1886, an Atlanta pharmacist, John Stith Pemberton, invented Coca-Cola syrup and mixed it with carbonated water to create a soda fountain drink. Pemberton's bookkeeper, Frank Robinson, named the drink and designed the trademark, which would be registered in 1893. They sold the syrup to local soda fountains.

Before he died in 1888, Pemberton sold his business to several partners. By 1891, Atlanta pharmacist Asa G. Candler had acquired sole ownership for $2,300. On January 29, 1892, he formed the corporation, the Coca-Cola Company. Candler opened manufacturing plants in other states, and by 1895 Coca-Cola was sold throughout the United States. He also developed new marketing ideas, such as distributing coupons for free drinks, as well as selling calendars, clocks, and other souvenirs bearing the product's trademark. In 1899, Candler gave Benjamin Thomas and Joseph Whitehead exclusive rights to bottle and distribute Coca-Cola. They developed high-speed bottling and a distribution system that became a model for the American soft drink industry.

In 1919, investors led by Ernest Woodruff and W. C. Bradley purchased the company for $25 million. In 1923, Ernest Woodruff's son Robert Woodruff became president. During the 1920's, Woodruff introduced revolutionary merchandising tools

A boy sells Coca-Cola from a roadside stand in Georgia in 1936. (Hulton Archive/Getty Images)

such as a six-bottle carton and a metal, open-top cooler that enabled Coca-Cola to be sold ice-cold. He envisioned Coca-Cola as an international product. The Summer Olympics of 1928 saw the first sale of Coca-Cola at an Olympiad. The automatic fountain dispenser was introduced at the 1933 Chicago World's Fair. During World War II, Woodruff built more plants overseas to supply the armed forces, and many non-Americans tasted Coca-Cola for the first time.

In the following decades, global recognition and sales grew, as the company developed successful packaging, marketing, and new products. In 1955, new ten-, twelve- and twenty-six-ounce "king-size" and "family-size" bottles became popular, and plastic two-liter bottles arrived in 1977. The company's advertising slogans have been among the most recognized in American culture. They have included It's the Real Thing (1942, 1969), Coke Is It! (1982), and The Coke Side of Life (2006). While Coca-Cola

(sometimes sold as Coke) remained the company's flagship product, by 2008, the company produced and distributed more than 2,800 beverage products and 450 brands, accounting for 1.5 billion consumer servings per day and operations in more than two hundred countries.

Alice Myers

FURTHER READING

Hays, Constance. *The Real Thing: Truth and Power at the Coca-Cola Company.* New York: Random House, 2004.

Pendergrast, Mark. *For God, Country, and Coca-Cola.* New York: Basic Books, 2000.

Watters, Pat. *Coca-Cola: An Illustrated History.* Garden City, N.Y.: Doubleday, 1978.

SEE ALSO: Advertising industry; Alcoholic beverage industry; Cola industry; Food-processing industries; Multinational corporations.

Coin's Financial School

IDENTIFICATION: Book by William Hope Harvey
DATE: Published in 1894
SIGNIFICANCE: *Coin's Financial School* popularized the ideas of the Populist Party and the free silver movement. It formed the basis for presidential candidate William Jennings Bryan's "Cross of Gold" speech in 1896.

The 175-page *Coin's Financial School*, originally published by the Coin Publishing Company of Chicago, explains a technical financial issue in a manner that can be understood by average citizens. An organ of Populism, the economic text is interspersed with dozens of political cartoons. It begins with the premise that silver was secretly demonetized in the Coinage Act of 1873. (President Ulysses S. Grant later claimed that he did not know such a provision was in the bill.)

The motive for abolishing the free coinage of silver was to force the U.S. Civil War debt to Great Britain to be paid in gold rather than silver. British bankers had cornered the gold market, so it was to their advantage to ensure that gold was the only legal tender. The law—which eliminated half of the U.S. money supply—was damaging both to American debtors and to the nation's agricultural concerns.

Although the effects of the Coinage Act had been discussed during the period between 1873 and 1894, the depression brought on by the Panic of 1893 had increased tensions in the economy. Author William Hope Harvey's proposed solution was bimetallism: He argued that silver should be remonitized and valued at one-sixteenth the value of gold. He argued that reliance on gold as the only measure of value would result in a tight money supply. Unlimited coinage of silver, on the other hand, would result in higher farm prices and more jobs for miners.

Coin's Financial School was one of the most successful books on economics ever published, selling one million copies in its first three years. It was said that the book was sold by newsboys on every train. Harvard University Press published a reprint of Harvey's book in 1963 along with an eighty-page analysis by Richard Hofstadter.

Dale L. Flesher

SEE ALSO: American Bimetallic League national convention; Black Friday; "Cross of Gold" speech; Currency; Fort Knox; Gold standard; Klondike gold rush; Panic of 1893.

Cola industry

DEFINITION: Enterprises engaged in the creation, mass production, packaging, and distribution of cola drinks

SIGNIFICANCE: The cola industry produced one of the earliest nationwide, mass-produced consumer products that appealed to popular tastes. Driven in part by consistently innovative advertising campaigns, the giants of the industry, Coca-Cola and Pepsi-Cola, grew to become international brands, selling their products throughout the world.

The soft drink industry is one of the most competitive in the world, with companies employing global advertising campaigns to reach every available market. As a result, these companies have both produced and co-opted several American icons in their attempts to develop and maintain brand identity and loyalty. Although the industry has been dominated by the Coca-Cola Company and PepsiCo, the maker of Pepsi-Cola, other companies have sought

entry into the market and have affected the business practices of these two giants.

The formula for Coca-Cola (also known as Coke) was created by John Stith Pemberton, who mixed a coca extract syrup and carbonated water. His invention was first sold in Atlanta as a patent medicine, before it was served at soda fountains and mixed by hand in drug stores. During the early twentieth century, the Coca-Cola Company expanded through the United States. Then, during the 1920's, it began to expand overseas, as the company created a foreign bureau to sell the drink. During World War II, Coca-Cola became the favorite drink of American soldiers, with bottling plants being built near the front lines in Europe and North Africa. As the war ended, Coca-Cola became an American icon.

COCA-COLA VS. PEPSI COLA

The Pepsi-Cola company (which became PepsiCo in 1965 when it merged with Frito-Lay) also had ordinary beginnings, as Caleb Bradham, a North Carolina druggist, developed a formula for what would become a sweeter soft drink in 1898. Pepsi-Cola (also known as Pepsi) became a perennial also-ran to Coca-Cola, until Depression-era cost-cutting led to the development of the twelve-ounce bottle, which gave consumers of Pepsi more product for the same price as the much smaller Coca-Cola. Suddenly, impoverished consumers had a cheaper version of their favorite beverage, and Pepsi-Cola challenged Coca-Cola's supremacy during the postwar era.

PepsiCo used several tactics to seize market share from Coca-Cola. Its most famous and effective was the Pepsi Challenge of the 1980's: Consumers were asked to take blind taste tests, comparing Pepsi-Cola and Coca-Cola. The results touted in Pepsi-Cola's advertising campaign favored Pepsi-Cola. The ads worked, and Coca-Cola lost market share to Pepsi-Cola, setting the stage for the disastrous gamble of New Coke.

Preparing to celebrate a century of Coca-Cola, the company embarked on one of the worst public relations disasters in corporate history, reformulating Coca-Cola from the original recipe. Intended to recharge the Coca-Cola brand and defeat the challenge from Pepsi-Cola, New Coke instead energized a consumer revolt against the new formula. For months, fans of the original formula collected the old Coca-Cola under the assumption that it would run out, then they began a media campaign to convince the company to return to the original formula. With its new formula under attack, the company relented, selling New Coke alongside the original formula drink, which it renamed Coca-Cola Classic. Eventually New Coke would disappear from the shelves, ending the brief and disastrous attempt to change an icon.

The rivalry between Coca-Cola and PepsiCo moved from the companies' main products to their subsidiary ones; both corporations purchased or developed competing brands of bottled water, teas, and sports drinks such as Gatorade and Powerade. Old products, such as vanilla-flavored or cherry colas, were reintroduced and repackaged for a generation that had not known them. PepsiCo went a step further by expanding into the fast-food business, purchasing Pizza Hut (1977), Taco Bell (1978), and Kentucky Fried Chicken (1986; later KFC), and using these chains' thousands of outlets to sell PepsiCo products, thus creating a permanent market for Pepsi-Cola and its other soft drinks. In 1997, PepsiCo spun off these fast-food restaurants, creating Tricon Global Restaurants, which in 2002 acquired Long John Silver's and A&W Restaurants and became Yum! Brands.

Getting the product to customers is important for increasing market share. This Pepsi-Cola truck delivered the company's beverages to restaurants in 1943. (Library of Congress)

OTHER COMPETITORS

A third major competitor in the cola wars entered the market in 1905. Royal Crown cola was also invented by a curious chemist and quickly became the third leading cola in the United States. It was best known for its innovations, including being the first to use the taste-test format to compare itself with its rivals during the 1940's. In 1962, Royal Crown introduced the first diet cola, sending its popularity soaring, as healthy eating became the newest trend. Although Royal Crown enjoyed a third-place position in the competition during the 1960's and 1970's, it suffered from its image as a cheap imitation of Coca-Cola and Pepsi-Cola, ap-

pealing to consumer purse strings rather than their taste. Even its introduction of a caffeine-free cola in 1980 could not stop the brand's slide, and in 2000, it was purchased by the Canadian firm Schweppes. Since then Royal Crown cola has been one of several soft drinks sold by conglomerates.

In 1994, British billionaire Richard Branson challenged Pepsi-Cola and Coca-Cola, introducing his Virgin Cola into the English market, and at the turn of the century he sought to invade the American market. Unfortunately for Branson, his plans fizzled: Virgin Cola was unable to grasp a foothold in the United States, even with Branson's billions backing it. Because of this, few new colas are offered nationally, although supermarkets routinely carry regional products, such as Jones Soda, or discount colas under the stores' own logos.

Douglas Clouatre

FURTHER READING

Allen, Frederick. *Secret Formula.* New York: HarperBusiness, 1995. Highlights the development and growth of the Coca-Cola Company.

Hays, Constance. *The Real Thing.* New York: Random House, 2004. Recounting of the rise of Coca-Cola and its battle with PepsiCo and other soft drink companies.

Pendergrast, Mark. *For God, Country, and Coca-Cola.* New York: Basic Books, 2000. Explains how Coca-Cola and PepsiCo have battled for loyalty of consumers.

Rothacher, Albrecht. *Corporate Cultures and Global Brands.* Hackensack, N.J.: World Scientific, 2004. Examines how international brands of products have spread across the world and includes discussion of the Coca-Cola and PepsiCo companies.

SEE ALSO: Coca-Cola Company; Food-processing industries; Sugar industry.

Colonial economic systems

DEFINITION: European-rule systems under which North American settlers lived before the United States became independent

SIGNIFICANCE: During the years from 1607 to 1775, farmers and merchants in colonies on mainland North America developed a market economy and commercial practices that provided the basis for material success comparable to the most advanced nations of Europe and made possible nineteenth century expansion.

The earliest British settlements on the North American continent were business enterprises organized by British corporations expecting to profit from trade. The joint-stock Virginia Company—modeled after the East India Company, which had prospered by importing goods previously unobtainable in England—hoped to achieve similar success in the New World. The Pilgrims arrived in the Massachusetts Bay area in 1620, desiring to practice their religion freely, but the London merchants who organized a joint-stock company to finance their move anticipated earning significant profits from trading with Native Americans.

MERCANTILISM

Although the London merchants sought profit, it was not capitalism that ruled the English economy in 1600. The economic theory that justified chartering corporations and founding colonies was based on mercantilist ideas that required state intervention in economic affairs, precisely what Adam Smith excoriated in his 1776 *An Inquiry into the Nature and Causes of the Wealth of Nations.* Mercantilism stressed the importance of a strong central government and urged subordination of the economy to that goal. It assumed that the strength of a nation was measured by the gold it held, because the monarch could use that gold to raise armies to defeat his enemies and defend his country. Ensuring the flow of gold into the country required a favorable balance of trade in which exports exceeded imports. Government had an obligation to encourage and regulate overseas activities that could provide England with goods it would otherwise import, thereby limiting the movement of gold out of England. Even better than imported goods were commodities that England could resell to other countries for gold.

All European countries that founded American colonies—Spain, France, the Netherlands, and Sweden—were like the English in that they hoped to exploit the new lands according to mercantilist theory. The reality varied, depending on the natural features of the area settled, the composition of the indigenous population, the characteristics of the European settlers, and the degree of control by the home government. Only Spain succeeded in actually finding gold and silver in its colonies to bolster its position in Europe.

English kings did not have money available to support overseas expansion, but English merchants did. To encourage merchants to undertake risky enterprises, the English government granted charters creating limited liability joint-stock companies, guaranteeing each company a monopoly on trading rights to specific areas, and delegating governmental powers to exercise military and political control over distant trading posts.

The model worked well in the East Indies and Africa but less so in North America. Virginia Company stockholders never recovered their investments. The Pilgrims took decades to repay investors, who never realized significant profits. The Puritans took control of the Massachusetts Bay Company, whose charter—by accident or design—did not specify that its controlling board had to remain in London under the eyes of the government. They simply took their charter with them, establishing an autonomous government in the New World, something never contemplated in mercantilist theory.

The major economic factors governing development of the colonies were scarcity of labor and abundance of land. The effects of these factors varied from colony to colony depending on the climate, crops grown, and composition of each colony's population. Agricultural crops from the southern colonies, where specialized commercial agriculture developed, came closest to fitting original English mercantilist expectations from overseas expansion. The northern and middle colonies, although political successes, were economic anomalies. Only colonial merchants actually thought of themselves or acted like businessmen. Even when involved in international commerce, neither plantation owners nor farmers conceived their activities in strictly economic terms.

SPANISH TERRITORIES

Spain had an advantage over other European colonial powers because its empire controlled areas where a settled indigenous population could be plundered of its accumulated treasures and then heavily exploited for its labor, and where gold and silver could be mined. Organizing strict bureaucratic control of its empire, Spain achieved results consistent with mercantilist theory to a greater degree than any other colonial power.

Spain began constructing a centralized, bureaucratic structure in 1503 with the creation of the Casa de Contratación, or House of Trade, located in Seville, with authority over commerce, shipping, and finance related to America. The Casa granted a monopoly on trade with America to the merchant guild of Seville, which was expected to provide capital for the trade in return for protection from the Crown. The Casa organized traffic to the New World by a "flota" system, limiting shipping to fleets or convoys sailing at regular intervals to a limited number of harbors.

The flota system had obvious advantages in protecting shipments of gold and silver from the New World, but it failed to satisfy the trade needs of the colonies. Both merchants and the Crown held mercantilist ideas that claimed that the business practice of limiting production and charging high prices was the most profitable. This opened the way for interlopers from other European powers, often welcomed in cities far removed from the main trade routes. Because all ships were armed, it was not easy to tell if a non-Spanish vessel was a trader or a raider hoping to loot ill-defended Spanish cities.

The Spanish colonial economic system was more profitable to the home country than those of other European nations. However, it did little for Spain in the long run, since Spanish kings spent much of their revenue sending armies to fight endless European wars.

SOUTHERN AGRICULTURE

The Chesapeake region built a flourishing economy based on tobacco. Although the Virginia Company proved an economic failure, it established the system that led to a successful colony. When neither trade with Native Americans nor search for mineral resources proved profitable, the company realized it needed to turn Virginia into a settlement colony. Because land was plentiful and labor scarce, the company offered head rights of fifty acres per person to anyone bringing people to the colony. Those unable to pay their own way could receive the same grants if willing to indenture themselves as laborers for four or five years to repay the costs of their passage. However, the men who had procured large land grants on which they planned to create large plantations found indentured laborers to be an inefficient workforce because these laborers were eager to leave the plantations once they had served out their indentures.

Slavery provided the solution, but the institution developed slowly. Slavery did not exist as a legal status in English law in August, 1619, when a Dutch ship sold 20 Africans to eager planters. It is thought that they may have been treated in the same manner as European indentured servants, perhaps with longer terms of service. As late as 1651, some Africans who had completed their indentures received grants of land comparable to those offered to Europeans; there were only about 300 Africans then, in a total population of some 15,000. Because Africans were involuntary migrants, improving their treatment would not encourage more to come. Although conditions for European indentured servants improved, the status of Africans deteriorated, and by century's end, black slavery had been legally defined as servitude for life with the status inherited by children.

This development encouraged imports of Africans and fueled a massive growth in tobacco production as plantations were created along the sides of navigable rivers where oceangoing ships could conveniently pick up cargo. Despite uneasiness over the health effects of smoking and fulminations against tobacco by King James I, shipments were welcomed in England. Tobacco not only replaced previous imports from Spanish colonies but also could be processed and exported to continental Europe as snuff and pipe tobacco, helping the mercantilist drive for a positive balance of trade. To encourage production, the English government granted American colonies a monopoly on tobacco, forbade growing the plant in the British Isles, and placed heavy duties on imports from outside the empire.

Rice and indigo were profitable crops in the southern coastal region running from Cape Fear, North Carolina, to the Altamaha River in Georgia, centered on the port of Charleston. Large plantations staffed by slaves devoted to rice cultivation appeared during the 1690's. Africans were particularly valuable because a considerable number of them had cultivated rice in Africa and brought with them technical knowledge of when and how to control the water level in the fields. Rice production clearly fulfilled mercantilist expectations. The grain was not only consumed in Great Britain but also exported to northern Europe in significant amounts. The Navigation Acts permitted direct shipment of rice from Charleston to major markets in southern Europe and the Mediterranean.

Indigo, a deep-blue dye stuff much in demand by textile manufacturers, was more strictly channeled to England. Seventeenth century attempts to grow the plant in mainland colonies had failed when faced with competition from more efficient producers in the French West Indies. In the eighteenth century, British subsidies made indigo a profitable plant for growers in the rice districts; mercantilist theory approved of the subsidy on the grounds that keeping production within the empire was more useful to the British economy than getting less expensive supplies of the dye for England's textile industry. When the subsidy ended after independence, production of indigo declined drastically.

Tobacco, rice, and indigo planters preferred to think of themselves as

NEW FRANCE

The French colonial economic system in North America resembled that of the British in that it was theoretically based on mercantilist principles. However, Canada's far northern location limited possible exports to the fur trade. When the home country increased control, political and military goals became predominant.

Like the British, the French used a private joint-stock company, the Company of New France, also called the "Hundred Associates" for the number of its shareholders. Chartered in 1627 and given a monopoly on trade in return for promising to build the colony and convert natives to Catholicism, the company was a failure. Its only export was furs, and returns did not match expenses. In 1645, the company tried leasing the trade to a group of settlers who called themselves the Community of Habitants. Most entrepreneurs in the colony were involved with the fur trade, whether directly trading with the Native Americans, or handling processing and shipment of furs to France.

In 1663, Louis XIV made his Canadian territories a province of France on a par with other French provinces, placing control of the area in the hands of royal appointees. Both economic and political considerations encouraged rapid expansion westward over the Great Lakes and down the Mississippi to New Orleans. As fur-bearing animals became scarce in the immediate vicinity of the St. Lawrence River, traders pushed ever further out. Encircling the British colonies on the East Coast became the major objective of French policy, requiring military expenditures greatly exceeding any possible profit. As an economic enterprise, New France was an expensive failure. Demographically, it was a resounding success; the ten thousand French inhabitants of 1681 were the progenitors of over six million French-Canadians in the twenty-first century.

landed gentlemen rather than businessmen. However, unlike their English models, they could not depend on rents from tenants to sustain a lavish lifestyle. Because financial success depended on rational management of production of an export commodity, ignoring business considerations often meant running up large debts, endangering the future of the plantation and the planter's family.

NORTHERN AGRICULTURE

The distinguishing characteristics of farming in the north were family settlement and economic diversification. The Puritans who populated New England, the Presbyterians in New Jersey, and the Quakers and German Protestants in Pennsylvania came in families. Whether settling in cohesive townships in New England or in isolated farmsteads elsewhere, access to land ownership was the great magnet.

Farmers could not be simple businessmen in an age without social safety nets—survival of the family depended on how their farms functioned. Few could equal the boast of the legendary farmer who claimed that, save for salt and bar iron, he produced on his own acreage everything his family needed. However, achieving minimal self-sufficiency was feasible and a vital defensive strategy. Cash crops were a secondary, though highly desirable, consideration. Once established, most families wanted more than minimum subsistence, necessarily involving the farm in commerce. This might mean simply bartering with neighbors for items the farm did not produce, or with a local artisan—a blacksmith or a shoemaker—for needed services. However, the desire for a better quality of life led to a demand for textiles from Britain and for tea, coffee, sugar, and other goods, involving the mostly self-sustaining farmers in international trade and requiring that they raise crops that could be exported to pay for imports.

In Pennsylvania, the predominant cash crop was wheat, which, milled into flour, was in high demand in the West Indies sugar colonies. New England, where farms were less productive than in the middle colonies, found in the fisheries another commodity valued in international trade—dried salt cod was prized all over Catholic Europe. Local merchants became wealthy businessmen, managing commerce among the colonies and with the West Indies. The port cities, Boston, New York, Philadelphia, and Charleston, flourished. These operations violated mercantilist theory because they were in direct competition with the homeland. Wheat could have been grown in Britain rather than the colonies, and the fishing fleets and the colonial merchant marine duplicated British enterprises, yet the imperial government tolerated the competition.

Easy access to land encouraged a diversity of nationalities to come to British North America, except for New England. The close pattern of settlement by townships discouraged outsiders; when the Revolutionary War broke out, the overwhelming majority of New Englanders were descendants of English people who had come during the early seventeenth century. Every other colony attracted significant numbers of Welsh, Scots, and Protestant Irish; each considered themselves distinct nationalities. Protestant refugees driven out of Germany's Rhineland late in the seventeenth century by the scorched-earth tactics of Louis XIV arrived in New York, where large-scale landowners treated them as easily exploitable laborers on their estates. Word of their mistreatment filtered back to German lands and reinforced the efforts of the Penn family to recruit settlers for their colony. Pennsylvania became the most diverse of all the colonies. Its eighteenth century population was estimated as one-third German, one-third English, and one-third Scots and Irish. Each nationality brought its own skills and distinctive life patterns.

THE BACKCOUNTRY

Settlers in the backcountry, areas that lay beyond the core settlements of the mainland colonies and whose geographic position made marketing their products difficult, developed unique economic systems and living patterns. During the late nineteenth century, these regions would be praised as the great American frontier, where the true American character developed. In the eighteenth century, such areas were despised, reputed to be populated by uncouth, uncivilized people whose lifestyle and farming practices were equally slovenly.

The backcountry economy appeared in Virginia when settlement moved past the river systems that eased marketing of tobacco. It characterized parts of North Carolina between tobacco and rice areas, and appeared in every colony as settlement spread inland. The reactions of English and colonial travelers to this lifestyle were almost universally negative. They viewed the people as crude and uncultured, unable to recognize the superiority of their visitors, and the farming practices as ugly and wasteful, demonstrating willful ignorance of proper agriculture.

Farming methods in the hinterland were indeed untidy and wasteful, but also rational in an area where land was abundant and cheap, labor was scarce, and family survival depended on the work of husband and wife. The labor-saving method of turning forest into cropland was to girdle trees and plant corn (which unlike wheat did not require plowed fields) between the trees to feed the family. After the trees died, they were cut down and burned. Grain and tobacco were useless crops when the cost of carriage exceeded market value. However, cows and pigs could forage for themselves in the forest and be driven to distant markets on their own legs, where they often arrived weak and emaciated, further evidence of incompetent farming practices in the backcountry.

Forest products were an important part of colonial economic systems both north and south, especially, but not only, in backcountry areas. England had been largely deforested before 1600 and depended on importing timber and naval stores from Baltic countries for its navy and shipbuilders. America provided an alternate source of supplies, and England offered bounties when the colonists developed the techniques needed to produce satisfactory pitch, tar, and turpentine, vital in protecting wood and rope from corrosion by salt water. Tall New England white pines made ideal masts for Britain's Royal Navy, and the sap of southern long-leaf pines proved the best source of pitch and turpentine. Artisans learned to make barrel staves and heads needed to transport tobacco from the Chesapeake region and sugar from the West Indies, also a major market for construction timber. Trial and error led to the discovery that wood ash from the hardwood forests of New York and New England was best for making potash, the most important industrial chemical of the eighteenth century, used in producing glass, soap, drugs, and dyes.

COMMERCE

By the mid-seventeenth century, commerce originating in the North American colonies was of sufficient importance for England to begin regulating it in accordance with mercantilist theory. The 1651 and 1660 Navigation Acts, as well as eighteenth century additions, had three major provisions: Certain enumerated products of the colonies could be ex-ported only to England; most goods from Europe and Asia could not be imported directly by the colonies, but had to come through England; and ships engaged in trade with the colonies had to be owned and constructed in England or the colonies, have an English captain, and a crew three-quarters English. The original enumerated commodities were sugar, cotton, indigo, dyewoods, ginger, and tobacco; in 1660, all except tobacco were products of the West Indies. Later additions included naval stores, copper, rice (with an exception for shipments directly to southern Europe, which bought about one-third of the crop), potash, beaver and other furs, and tanned hides. Customs duties were collected on most of these commodities on their arrival in England, providing welcome funds for the royal exchequer. In some years, the import tax on tobacco exceeded the price paid to planters.

Acts to protect specific English economic interests by preventing American manufacturers from selling hats or woolen cloth outside the colony where they were produced were irritants in relations between the colonies and England. Attempts to collect significant duties on sugar and molasses, used to distill rum, the favorite colonial alcoholic beverage, caused major problems when England attempted to actually enforce such laws during the mid-eighteenth century.

Despite these problems, the Acts of Trade created relatively little dissension, primarily because American colonials and American-built ships counted as English under the acts. American merchants demonstrated considerable business acumen in competing on an equal basis with English merchants, although they lacked equal financial resources. Northern merchants dominated intercolonial trade, including shipments to and from the sugar islands, and participated in transatlantic trade. English merchants controlled the lucrative tobacco market, using their monetary power to finance both planters and European customers. Colonial shipping benefited from the services of the Royal Navy; without its protection against Mediterranean pirates, trade with southern Europe would have been much too risky.

Ships and rum were the primary manufactured products that entered international trade. Making barrel staves used to ship tobacco and sugar to England was a useful winter occupation for farm families, but most household production, whether of linen and woolen cloth or iron products from blacksmith's workshops, was consumed locally.

Shipbuilding flourished in New England, where skilled workmen and cheaper availability of masts, lumber, and naval supplies gave the colonists an economic advantage. American shipyards produced ships of all sizes besides the large warships and specialized great ships intended for the East Indies trade. One-quarter to one-half of the ships were purchased by English merchants. By 1770, about one-third of the ships used in the British coastal, as well as European trade, were made in America.

After 1763, Great Britain, in effect, abandoned the mercantilist system of economic regulations and began using taxes and customs duties to pay salaries of royal officials and costs of armies on the frontier. What had previously been irritations for colonists became major grievances, ultimately leading to demands for independence. By this time, the colonies had developed an economy and society comparable to the most advanced countries of western Europe. Boston, New York, Philadelphia, and Charleston were provincial capitals comparable in size and prosperity to other provincial centers in the British Empire, including Dublin, Edinburgh, and Belfast. American agriculture was productive enough to support nine years of warfare. The rich might not be as wealthy as aristocratic Europeans, but middling citizens shared a comfortable standard of material life, and the poor were infinitely better off. Although the country was overwhelmingly rural (perhaps as much as 90 percent of the population was engaged in farming), the colonial economic systems provided the basis for favorable entry into the Industrial Revolution and creation of the most prosperous nation in the world in the nineteenth century.

Milton Berman

NEW NETHERLAND AND NEW SWEDEN

Dutch and Swedish colonies in North America were short-lived. After seventeen years, New Sweden was conquered by the Dutch in 1655; New Netherland was in turn seized by Great Britain in 1664. Both failed to live up to mercantilist expectations because of a narrow focus on fur trading.

Henry Hudson's 1609 explorations revealed the Hudson River and the large harbor at its mouth to his Dutch sponsors. In 1621, the Dutch West India Company received a monopoly on trade from the New World and took control of the colony, centered on the small city of New Amsterdam on the tip of Manhattan Island, and claimed all land between the Delaware and Connecticut Rivers. Trading posts at Fort Orange (later Albany) and on the Delaware River produced New Netherland's only export—furs. The company tried to keep a tight rein on the trade, fending off individual entrepreneurs who attempted to take part in the business.

In 1638, Peter Minuit, who had been governor of New Netherland, offered his services to the New Sweden Company and led a group of settlers to the west bank of the Delaware. As in New Netherland, fur was the only profitable export. The Dutch objected to the competition, and a small military expedition in 1655 easily took over the Swedish settlement.

Seventeenth century Netherlands was at the peak of its power and prosperity; few Dutch were interested in leaving home. Almost half of New Netherland's inhabitants came from other countries; in 1643, eighteen different languages were spoken in New Amsterdam. The population remained small and defenses were negligible; when a British fleet appeared in 1664, resistance was impossible.

FURTHER READING

Eccles, W. J. *The French in North America, 1500-1783.* Rev. ed. East Lansing: Michigan State University Press, 1998. The classic narrative of the French experience in America brought up-to-date in a new edition.

Engerman, Stanley L. "Government in Colonial America." In *Government and the American Economy: A New History.* Chicago: University of Chicago Press, 2007. Examines the ways in which governments aided the development of the American colonial economy.

Engerman, Stanley L., and Robert E. Gallman, eds. *The Colonial Era.* Vol. 1 in *The Cambridge Economic History of the United States.* New York: Cambridge University Press, 1996. Nine articles by major scholars analyze significant aspects of colonial economic systems.

Hinderacker, Eric, and Peter C. Mancall. *At the Edge of Empire: The Backcountry in British North America.* Baltimore: Johns Hopkins University Press, 2003. A concise, readable narrative appraises the role of the backcountry in the expansion of colonial America.

Seavoy, Ronald E. *An Economic History of the United States: From 1607 to the Present.* New York: Routledge, 2006. Four chapters deal with the colonial period. Seavoy argues that farmers, the majority of the population, did not act or think like businessmen.

Shorto, Russell. *The Island at the Center of the World: The Epic Story of Dutch Manhattan and the Forgotten Colony That Shaped America.* New York: Doubleday, 2004. A superb account of New Netherland that includes the history of New Sweden.

Wright, Gavin. *Slavery and American Economic Development.* Baton Rouge: Louisiana State University Press, 2006. Challenges accepted views on the role of slavery in the American economy.

SEE ALSO: Boston Tea Party; Embargo Acts; French and Indian War; Navigation Acts; Plantation agriculture; Revolutionary War; Royal Charters of North American colonies; Slave era; Slave trading; Stamp Act of 1765; Tea Act of 1773; Townshend Act.

Colorado River water

DEFINITION: Waters of the primary river system draining the Southwest

SIGNIFICANCE: Diversion of the Colorado River has helped make possible the economic growth of the American West, particularly Southern California and the city of Los Angeles. The river's water is used for irrigation and the generation of electric power, and the lakes created by damming the river are recreation centers. Without the Colorado's water, it would be difficult to imagine the American Southwest as it exists in the twenty-first century.

Unlike other rivers that have been important to American economic development, the Colorado River is not a large river, and it has never played an important role in the transportation of goods and people. Because it is essentially an untamed river, the Colorado's flow varies dramatically from a few thousand cubic feet per second to more than two hundred thousand cubic feet per second. Not explored until 1869, the Colorado has become the source of water and electric power for much of the American West.

HOOVER DAM

In the arid West, politicians long had their eyes on the Colorado River as a source of water for their states. In 1922, California, Arizona, and Nevada (the lower basin states), together with Colorado, Utah, Wyoming, and New Mexico (the upper basin states), negotiated the Colorado River Compact at the direction of Secretary of Commerce Herbert Hoover. This agreement allocated the estimated flow of 17.5 million acre-feet per year. Some 7.5 million acre-feet were allocated to each basin, with a bonus of 1 million acre-feet given to the lower basin and 1.5 million acre-feet reserved to Mexico. Two problems remained: calculating the flow estimate and determining how to draw on the Colorado's water.

Rainfall had been plentiful in the Rockies during the early twentieth century, so the estimate of 17.5 million acre-feet seemed accurate. It was not. The rainfall during the early twentieth century was abnormally high, and the Colorado River has rarely produced 17.5 million acre-feet in flow since the compact was signed. Since the 1930's, the flow has averaged 11.3 million acre-feet per year. That problem would crop up in the future—the more immediate issue after the compact was agreed to was how to tap the river's water.

In 1930, Congress authorized Boulder Dam (renamed Hoover Dam), and construction began in 1931. It was jointly carried out by eight engineering firms, some of which (such as the Bechtel Corporation) would become massive construction firms in the future. Construction of Boulder Dam provided a stimulus to the Western economy, as large numbers of men worked on the project. The dam became a model for later projects throughout the world. It was completed and the first electric power generated in fall of 1936. Hoover Dam generated such a large amount of electric power that it paid for itself. Lake Mead extended upstream for a hundred miles, providing the water that could be used to irrigate and provide drinking water for California and the Southwest.

The population of California was growing during the 1930's, and the Colorado River was seen as a short-term solution to its water needs. Initially, much of California's water allocation went to agriculture, with nearly 3 million acre-feet irrigating the truck farms of the Imperial Valley. By the 1950's, California was already using its 4.4 million acre-foot allotment under the Colorado River Compact and was searching for additional sources of water both within its borders and elsewhere. It soon began to pump 700,000 additional acre-feet from the river. Initially, this was not a problem, but as the population of the intermountain states began to grow, they too wanted to ensure their allocations from the river. The small gambling town of Las Vegas, Nevada, started to grow during the 1950's, creating a significant new demand for electric power and water in the desert. Not only did the citizens of Las Vegas need a large amount of water for drinking and irrigation of their lawns, but the hotels of the city often had large decorative fountains and lakes. The Mirage Hotel, for example, uses more than 1 million gallons of water a day. Abundant water was part of the ambience of the Las Vegas hotels, an ambience that was enormously profitable to the city.

DAMS ALONG THE RIVER

The Bureau of Reclamation turned again to the Colorado in 1956 with the construction of Glen Canyon Dam, which formed Lake Powell. Between them, Lake Mead and Lake Powell have four times the capacity of the yearly flow of the Colorado, evening out the flow and providing a continual source of irrigation water and electric power. In 1964, the bureau wanted to construct another dam across the Colorado that would have drowned the Grand Canyon National Monument. Conservationists defeated the project, pointing out the scenic value of the canyon that would be flooded, as well as the waste through evaporation of the new lake.

The demand for water and electric power in the West appears insatiable. Other sources of water, including underground aquifers, have been tapped, as the Colorado is incapable of supplying all the water that is needed. The Colorado seemed capable of supplying at least a sizeable part of the water for the West, at least in 1999 when both Lakes Powell and Mead were full. Since 1999, the Rockies have experienced much less snowfall than usual. By 2007, Lake Mead was half empty, and Lake Powell was also

Boulder Dam, in 1938, viewed from the high mountain downstream. (Library of Congress)

in decline. The Colorado fed the dream of making the West bloom, and for a time it helped to make the dream a reality. By the early twenty-first century, the dream was coming into question.

John M. Theilmann

FURTHER READING

Gertner, Jon. "The Future Is Drying Up." *New York Times Magazine*, October 21, 2007, pp. 68-77, 104, 154-155. Examines the future role of the Colorado River as the climate of the Southwest becomes drier.

Pearce, Fred. *When the Rivers Run Dry*. Boston: Beacon Press, 2006. Places the Colorado in the wider question of water shortage.

Reisner, Marc. *Cadillac Desert*. Rev. ed. New York: Penguin Books, 1993. The classic book dealing with water in the American West, with two chapters devoted to the Colorado.

Reisner, Marc, and Sarah Bates. *Overtapped Oasis: Reform or Revolution for Western Water*. Washington, D.C.: Island Press, 1990. Account predicting a water crisis in the West, with extensive attention to the Colorado.

Ward, Diane Raines. *Water Wars*. New York: Riverhead Books, 2002. Deals with the political and engineering questions surrounding water, with attention to the Colorado.

SEE ALSO: Dams and aqueducts; Erie Canal; Mississippi and Missouri Rivers; Pike's western explorations; Tennessee Valley Authority; Water resources.

Commerce, Supreme Court and. *See* Supreme Court and commerce

Commerce, U.S. Department of

IDENTIFICATION: Cabinet department charged with promoting domestic and international trade, technological growth, and economic expansion

DATE: Established in 1903 as the Department of Commerce and Labor; became a separate department in 1913

SIGNIFICANCE: Probably no office of the United States government relates more directly to the American business community than does the Department of Commerce, which arranges for loans to businesses, monitors business opportunities both domestic and international, takes positive steps to control unemployment, and offers guidance to the nation's workforce and to the businesses that employ that workforce, as well as to Congress.

The United States experienced unprecedented growth in industry during the last quarter of the nineteenth century. Many influential industrialists felt that they needed a stronger tie to the federal government than they had at that time, and they especially favored the creation of a department that would represent them and their interests formally in the president's cabinet.

On February 14, 1903, during the presidential administration of Theodore Roosevelt, the United States Congress voted to establish the Department of Commerce and Labor, a designation that survived for just over a decade. On March 14, 1913, Commerce and Labor were divided into two separate, cabinet-level entities, each headed by a secre-

tary. By this time, with industrialism continuing to grow rapidly in the United States, it was clear that the regulation of this growth was too great for one department to handle efficiently. In 1913, President Woodrow Wilson appointed William C. Redfield the first secretary of commerce under the department's new configuration.

Congress placed on the new secretary of commerce the task of monitoring trade between the United States and other nations with special attention to the sale and transportation of commercial goods to and from the United States. The responsibility of maintaining an American merchant marine also fell to the secretary of commerce.

AGENCIES

The Department of Commerce, which employs approximately thirty-six thousand people, is a remarkably complex organization with operations both domestic and international. Many of its subdivisions have a profound influence on the overall business community of the United States. Its Minority Business Development Agency has done a great deal, for example, to encourage the growth of enterprises run by members of racial and ethnic minorities, thereby creating employment opportunities for many who had found it difficult to flourish in the workplace.

Every decade, the Bureau of the Census, also a branch of the Department of Commerce, undertakes the enormous task of counting the population of the United States and of classifying it in ways that are extremely useful to the business community in planning such initiatives as the establishment of new manufacturing and marketing facilities.

Through the census, determinations can be made about where certain groups are clustered and which areas of the country are increasing or decreasing in size. The demographic information provided by the census is indispensable to industry as it makes the long-term plans that such industries must necessarily consider if they are to succeed economically.

The protection of intellectual properties through copyrights and trademarks and of inventions through the issuance of patents is a function of the Department of Commerce. The protection that copyrights and patents guarantee is of the utmost importance in businesses ranging from entertainment to a broad range of manufacturing industries.

INTERNATIONAL OUTREACH

One of the most important mandates of the Department of Commerce is that of promoting American business and trade with foreign countries. It promotes this goal directly through its Economic Development Administration and its Import Administration. When the department was first established, United States industry was extremely dependent on foreign trade for its existence, so the early secretaries of commerce worked closely with their foreign counterparts to establish valuable trade relations. It also worked collaboratively with the Department of State to foster the trade relations with foreign countries that were so vital to its existence.

As part of its charge to promote technological advancement, the department engages in comprehensive research enterprises that monitor the advancement of technology within the United States but that also track technological advances throughout the world. A great many of the patents and trademarks issued by the Department of Commerce domestically relate directly to protecting America's daunting proliferation of technological advances and of the intellectual properties that relate to them.

A CHANGE IN EMPHASIS

Following World War I, the business communities of the United States tended to view foreign involvement with some suspicion. A new isolationism swept much of the country. It was in such an atmosphere that Herbert Hoover became President Warren G. Harding's secretary of commerce in 1921, a position in which he continued in 1923 when Calvin Coolidge assumed the presidency following Harding's death. Hoover sought to make the Department of Commerce preeminent among the administration's cabinets.

The economic surges that characterized the 1920's created an atmosphere that was advantageous to big business. Although the department continued to promote international trade, its major emphasis was gradually shifting to the promotion of domestic business. The economic excesses of this period, labeled "The Roaring Twenties," led eventually to the Harding administration's being widely discredited, but Hoover retained his position, and by 1928, his last year in his position as secretary, he had gained sufficient popularity and support—much derived directly from the business commu-

nity—that he ran for the presidency of the United States and was elected.

Shortly into Hoover's term as president, however, the economic bubble of the 1920's burst and the Great Depression ensued. In the next election, held in 1932, Hoover was overwhelmingly defeated, and Franklin D. Roosevelt replaced him as president of the United States. Under Roosevelt and his New Deal, the Department of Commerce had little choice but to turn its major attention to domestic matters as it struggled to return the nation to greater prosperity.

WORLD WAR II

The domestic emphasis of the Department of Commerce continued through the 1930's, at the end of which, in 1939, World War II erupted in Europe. With the onset of this war, the Department of Commerce again pressed for a more international emphasis as American industry began to recover from the economic downturn of the Great Depression and devote itself to providing the goods and equipment that a wartime economy demanded. With the entry of the United States into World War II in December, 1941, American industry was operating at optimal levels to meet the increased demand.

The Department of Commerce helped to expand the workforce as many in it entered military service and were, therefore, forced to leave their civilian jobs. As a result, women and members of racial minorities, who began to constitute a major portion of the American workforce, were assisted by the department as they prepared to enter manufacturing industries. With the need to rebuild much of Europe following World War II, the international emphasis of the Department of Commerce continued.

In 1977, President Jimmy Carter appointed Juanita Kreps, a Duke University economics professor, as the first female secretary of commerce. As secretary, Kreps worked assiduously to ensure women fair treatment in the workplace. She struggled to remove the so-called glass ceiling that prevented many talented women from advancing to the heights for which their abilities clearly qualified them.

ORGANIZATION

During the administration of Ronald Reagan, substantial changes were made in the organization of the Department of Commerce. Under this new organization, seven discrete offices were created below those of the secretary of commerce and the deputy secretary. Among these are the crucial offices of the agency's general counsel and of the assistant secretaries for congressional affairs and for administration.

Those who report directly to the secretary of commerce are the associate deputy secretary, the inspector general, the special assistant for regional development, and the director for public affairs. Seven assistant secretaries oversee such areas as tourism, economic affairs, trade development, productivity, technology, innovation, and communications and information. The broad range of activities assigned to these assistant secretaries gives one some notion of the scope of enterprises and interests that occupy those working in the United States Department of Commerce.

Of great importance to American business is the department's National Bureau of Standards, which is charged with monitoring such matters as weights and measures. The department's National Oceanic and Atmospheric Administration has grown in significance as interest in ecology and in such matters as global warming have increased in importance not only nationally but also throughout the world. The Bureau of Economic Analysis and the Bureau of Industrial Economics have helped American industries plot their course with much more confidence than they would have were it not for what the research of these two entities has revealed about the nation's business climate.

TRADE AND RESEARCH

The Department of Commerce continues to be much concerned with stimulating foreign trade. It works with the Department of State to formulate government policies regarding foreign trade and international commerce. It also distributes information about foreign trade opportunities throughout the world.

To achieve these ends, the department maintains a group of trade representatives based in foreign countries and, with their input, produces a staggering variety of publications that alert the business community to opportunities that the department has uncovered through its research and interactions with foreign governments and industries.

The Department of Commerce supports a broad and productive assortment of research activities re-

lated to American business interests, both domestic and international. Research is carried out on a regular basis by three major branches of the department, the National Bureau of Standards, the National Oceanic and Atmospheric Administration, and the National Weather Service.

The research produced by these three major entities continually informs the American business community of developments directly related to those communities. The department has extremely well-organized conduits for the dissemination of the information produced by the research arms of the department.

R. Baird Shuman

FURTHER READING

Borrelli, MaryAnne. *The President's Cabinet: Gender, Power, and Representation.* Boulder, Colo.: L. Rienner, 2002. A feminist account of the functions of the presidential cabinet and of how it helps to shape attitudes about race and gender.

Brinkley, Alan, and Davis Dyer, eds. *The Reader's Companion to the American Presidency.* Boston: Houghton Mifflin, 2000. Brinkley and Dyer devote twelve pages to Herbert Hoover, mostly to his term as president, although they comment briefly but cogently on his service as secretary of commerce.

Cicarelli, James, and Julianne Cicarelli. *Distinguished Women Economists.* Westport, Conn.: Greenwood Press, 2003. The authors devote four pages to a discussion of economist Juanita Kreps, who served as secretary of commerce in Jimmy Carter's administration.

Gould, Lewis L. *The Modern American Presidency.* Lawrence: University of Kansas Press, 2003. Gould devotes the first twenty-eight pages of his book to the relationship of the first secretary of commerce, George B. Cortelyou, to Presidents William McKinley and Theodore Roosevelt.

Holford, David M. *Herbert Hoover.* Berkeley Heights, N.J.: Enslow, 1999. In this comprehensive biography, Holford provides insights on how Hoover helped to transform the United States Department of Commerce during his tenure as secretary of commerce.

Kreps, Juanita Morris. *Sex, Age, and Work: The Changing Composition of the American Work Force.* Baltimore: Johns Hopkins University Press, 1975. An interesting account of how Kreps viewed the

American workforce in this book published two years before she became secretary of commerce.

Miller, Walter L. *The Life and Accomplishments of Herbert Hoover.* Durham, N.C.: Moore, 1970. An appreciative assessment of President Herbert Hoover's contributions to American business.

SEE ALSO: Federal Trade Commission; Homeland Security, U.S. Department of; Interior, U.S. Department of the; Labor, U.S. Department of; Presidency, U.S.; Small Business Administration; Supreme Court and commerce; Transportation, U.S. Department of.

Commodity markets

DEFINITION: Markets in which the products of primary economic activities, such as agriculture or mining, are traded

SIGNIFICANCE: The establishment of commodity markets allowed for efficient trading. As the United States grew, commodity trade and pricing drove the creation of standards for agricultural products, as well as transportation systems that could ensure their delivery. The development of futures contracts by the Chicago Board of Trade greatly facilitated agricultural development throughout the Midwest.

The purpose of modern commodity markets is to decrease the risk for the producers and consumers of commodities. Selling crops once they have been harvested often meant that the farmer had little choice but to accept the price offered the day the crops were brought to the market. Similarly, those needing the crops could not make good plans, as they were uncertain of the quality and quantity of crops being grown. There were also uncertainties regarding the price that would need to be offered to obtain the crop. The same was true for other commodities. By creating exchanges where futures con-

tracts, or their predecessors, were bought and sold, some of the risk was decreased. Farmers knew that they would get a predetermined price for their crops. Businesses needing those crops knew what their costs would be and the amounts of those crops that would be delivered at a set time. The one risk factor that could not be overcome was whether a particular crop would fail. However, with the development of an effective market mechanism, it became possible to replace a crop from one source with the same commodity from another source.

HISTORY

There is evidence that agricultural commodity markets, with possible futures contracts, existed in the ancient Middle East. However, during much of the more recent history of Europe, agricultural and mineral commodities were sold as they were produced. This was generally at the site of production or where the commodities were needed. It was only with the urbanization of the population and the ability of farmers to produce large crop surpluses that regional centers of trade became the focus of commodity economic activity.

In the United States, during the nineteenth century, midwestern agricultural production increased to such an extent that regional trading centers in cit-

The Chicago Board of Trade in session around 1900. (Library of Congress)

ies such as Chicago and Kansas City were needed. On the East Coast, large amounts of agricultural and mineral commodities were needed in the New York City area, so that commodity exchanges developed there as well. Although the majority of transactions in the nineteenth century involved commodities already produced, forward contracts started becoming more common. These guaranteed the delivery of a set amount of the commodity to a specific person on a specific date.

Over time, this type of contract tended to disappear at the large exchanges. It was replaced by a futures contract, which differs from a forward contract in that the commodity goes to a generic delivery point. Grain, pork, and cotton were the earliest commodities to have large numbers of futures contracts written. Other agricultural items were

added for futures trading, as benefits became apparent. As the United States became more industrialized, trading in natural resources such as oil, copper, and gold became important in the twentieth century. In the first decade of the twenty-first century, trading in energy commodities, such as oil, has grown appreciably. As with many financial areas, markets in the United States handle a larger percentage of commodity trades than any other country in the world.

During the late nineteenth and early twentieth centuries, certain exchanges came to dominate trade in specific commodities, so that smaller exchanges began to disappear. For example, the reliability of the Chicago Board of Trade for the purchase of high-quality grain allowed it to become the principal market for this commodity. By the end of the 1920's, three-fourths of all futures contracts were for grain. While the amount of grain traded on the exchanges has not decreased, the number of other futures contracts has increased to such an extent that the relative value of the grain contracts has decreased substantially. Estimates of the percentages for goods trading on global commodity exchanges in the twenty-first century (as measured in dollars) gives the breakdown as: energy, 75 percent; industrial metals, 7 percent; precious metals, 2 percent; agriculture, 13 percent; and livestock, 3 percent.

Various commodities were tried at some exchanges, but not always with success. Thus, the Chicago Mercantile Exchange, which was originally the Butter and Egg Exchange, added several other farm commodities. Some commodities experienced small demand, while others were in demand but primarily on other exchanges, and still others met stiff resistance. The latter category included onions, which were traded until onion producers forced the end to futures contracts on their crops. At one point after World War II, the Chicago Mercantile Exchange had shrunk so much it was principally an egg exchange, with dim prospects for the future. During the mid-1960's, new members sought out new trading opportunities, which allowed the exchange to survive.

COMMODITIES IN *TRADING PLACES*

The 1983 film *Trading Places* uses the trading of orange juice futures as the means of retribution by the protagonists. In the movie, the wealthy Duke brothers decide to make a rich man poor and a poor man rich to see how each will react. They bet each other a dollar over the outcome of the experiment. The bet is discovered by the two protagonists, the subjects of the bet, after the plan has been implemented. They also learn that the Duke brothers plan to profit illegally from advance knowledge of an orange crop report.

The two protagonists obtain the real report and give the Duke brothers a false report that indicates there will be a shortage of oranges. As the Duke brothers buy contracts for the delivery of orange juice at a moderately high price, the protagonists sell contracts to provide juice at that price. Because the protagonists sell so many contracts to supply juice, the price starts to fall. At the same time, other traders see the real report and learn that there will be a good supply of oranges. With the price down about $1 per pound, the protagonists begin to buy juice futures to cover the contracts to deliver juice they sold at the much higher price. The Duke brothers are stuck with expensive contracts that will deliver orange juice to them and must dispose of this juice by selling it at a greatly decreased price. This results in their bankruptcy, resolving the central plotline of the film.

TRADING FINANCIAL INSTRUMENTS

In 1972, a subdivision of the Chicago Mercantile Exchange offered futures trading on foreign exchange rates, ending the reliance on trades solely based on physical resources. The development of this type of futures contract spread quickly to other exchanges. Areas such as interest rates and mortgages were added during the upcoming decade. Many see the culmination of this move being the trading of stock futures that began in 1982. Early critics of this form of commodity charged that future trading on stocks increased the price swings for the underlying stocks. However, once established the trading of financial instruments, or derivatives, became a staple of most commodity exchanges. The importance of trading financial "commodities" has increased dramatically.

During most of history, items being bought and sold were present for the buyer to examine, to make certain they were of the type and quality that the seller claimed. Early commodity markets worked this way. With the development of futures contracts as the trade mechanism of choice, however, no items can be physically present to be examined, since they do not yet exist. What are bought and sold are electronic entries, formerly paper certificates, giving ownership of a preset amount of goods of a certain quality at a specific date in the future at a specific location.

Modern commodity markets work only because buyers have confidence that the exchanges (and government regulators) will enforce the contract in terms of the quality of the goods that will be delivered. Without this type of enforcement mechanism, modern commodity markets could not operate. At times in the past, the government attempted to limit participation in commodity trading to those who already had, or would have, goods to sell or those who could take delivery of the goods. However, from the 1960's on, this type of regulation of the commodity markets gradually decreased, so that anyone with adequate financial resources was able to trade on the markets.

Individuals, often called speculators, can buy or sell commodity contracts even if they do not have any of the commodity or have any use for it. As long as they do not have an open contract to ship a commodity they do not have, or conversely, receive the commodity on the delivery date, any amount of buying or selling futures contracts is legal. This means that only a small percentage of the contracts sold on commodity exchanges actually result in the delivery of the commodity. Most contracts are canceled out by individuals purchasing the opposite type of contract prior to the delivery date of the commodity.

REGULATION

Initially, commodity markets were regulated by the state in which they were located. Although the basic task of ensuring honest transactions was part of each state's laws, different rules applied for each market. During the 1920's, the federal government passed a law applying the same regulations to all agricultural markets. During the Great Depression, additional federal regulations were created. However, with the growing importance of natural resource markets and then the development of trading "commodities" based on financial instruments, such as currency exchange rates, the government realized that more regulation was needed.

In 1975, the Commodity Trading Futures Commission began operating to regulate all aspects of commodity exchanges. As with its predecessor, the CTFC is charged with making certain all exchanges operate so that the rules of the markets and all financial transactions are fair and honest. During the early twenty-first century, new "commodities" were being traded, such as financial instruments or the right to produce polluting emissions. The novelty of this type of market made regulating such trades difficult.

Donald A. Watt

FURTHER READING

Baer, Julius B. *Commodity Exchanges and Futures Trading: Principles and Operating Methods.* Seattle: Baer Press, 2007. This text covers the history of commodity exchanges, how they work and some societal effects.

Bouchentouf, Amine. *Commodities for Dummies.* Indianapolis: Wiley, 2007. One of the numerous Dummies books, this one focuses on how commodity markets work and how they should be approached.

Fontanills, George A. *Getting Started in Commodities.* Indianapolis: Wiley, 2007. Seeking to give advice to investors, Fontanills begins with an overview of what commodities are and how the markets work.

Geman, Helyette, ed. *Risk Management in Commodity*

Markets: From Shipping to Agriculturals and Energy.
Indianapolis: Wiley, 2009. Dealing with a variety
of commodity markets, this book examines the
factors that affect trades.

Kline, Donna. *Fundamentals of the Futures Market.*
New York: McGraw-Hill, 2001. Although written
to guide investors in the futures market, this text
also contains material on market history, defini-
tions of terms, and regulatory agencies.

SEE ALSO: Agribusiness; Agriculture; Agriculture,
U.S. Department of; Banking; Bond industry; Farm
subsidies; Mineral resources; Stock markets.

Computer industry

DEFINITION: The businesses involved in designing
and manufacturing computers and computer
networks, developing computer software, and
providing information technology services

SIGNIFICANCE: The computer industry is a major locus of innovation that has enabled all kinds of
American businesses to manage information
more efficiently.

The computer industry had its beginnings during
the 1880's, when the United States government
faced an insurmountable prob-
lem in counting its population.
By law, the government was required to perform a census every ten years to determine apportionment in the House of
Representatives. However, the
1880 census had taken nine
years to tabulate by hand, while
immigration and new births
were almost doubling the national population. It was recognized that tabulating the 1890
census rapidly enough to make
its data actually useful would require mechanical assistance.

THE FIRST COMPUTERS
Herman Hollerith, an engineer hired by the U.S. Bureau
of the Census to collect and analyze industrial statistics, de-

vised a machine that could input the necessary information in the form of punched cards and show
the resulting count on clocklike dials. After lengthy
negotiations, he installed a number of his machines
and kept them working throughout the tabulation
process. As a result of his diligent work, the 1890
census was tabulated in a year and a half.

Hollerith was soon receiving requests from other
countries for his machines to be used in their periodic censuses. In addition, the railroads and other
large companies were interested in such equipment
to streamline their accounting departments. As a result, Hollerith formed a business, the Tabulating
Machine Company, to build and market his machines. After a series of mergers, it would ultimately
form part of International Business Machines
(IBM), an early giant of the computer industry. The
best-known computing companies were known as
the Seven Dwarfs: Burroughs, Control Data Corporation (CDC), General Electric, Honeywell, National Cash Register (NCR), the Radio Corporation
of America (RCA), and Sperry Rand.

During the early decades of computing, each device was built specially for the agency or corporation
that would use it. These devices were in many ways as
experimental as those built by research institutions
to study computing. The lack of uniformity among
installations meant their production and operation

*The world's first computer, the Electronic Numerical Integrator and Calculator
(ENIAC) pictured here, was built in 1946.* (National Archives)

were more craft than an industry. Individual components might be mass-produced, but beyond that level, economies of scale could not be brought to bear.

In 1964, IBM introduced the System/360, the first mass-produced mainframe computer using a standardized architecture and instruction set. For the first time, it was possible for a business or government agency to order a computer and software from stock. The shift from computer as a custom-designed item to computer as a product was as critical to the creation of the modern computer industry as the technological progression from electromechanical relay to vacuum tube to transistor. However, mainframe computers and their smaller siblings, the minicomputers (machines about the size of an entire desk) were all sold on the same service-contract model as the original computers. The computer company did not sell its customers a device, but a long-term relationship of integrated software and support.

This concept is critical to understanding just how revolutionary the microcomputer was. Rather than being the end of a steady shrinking of the mainframe, the microcomputer had its roots in the youth culture of electronics enthusiasts in California's Silicon Valley. Like the radio enthusiasts of the 1920's, they were in love with the pioneering spirit of the new technology. With the development of the microprocessor, which put all the components of the traditional mainframe central processing unit onto a single piece of silicon, they could build up from this one chip to create a tiny computer.

MICROCOMPUTERS

Apple Computer (later simply Apple) had its beginnings when Steve Wozniak built the original Apple I to prove to his friends in the Home Brew Computer Club that he could build a better computer with fewer parts, but his friend Steve Jobs saw a potential market for a preassembled computer that could be used by anyone. That computer became the Apple II, and it took off in the market so rapidly that it soon made the founders of Apple wealthy. Their success was noted by other companies, and soon there were a large number of microcomputers on the market, all using incompatible formats and proprietary software.

Once IBM entered the microcomputer market in 1981 with the Personal Computer (PC), its reputation landed it a solid market among businesses who wanted to put small computers on the desks of their workers. Eager to cash in on this market, a number of other companies took advantage of certain loopholes in IBM's patent and licensing arrangements to build machines that would work the same way as an IBM PC. These low-cost IBM compatibles, often called "clones," secured a major portion of the market, to the point that competing approaches to the microcomputer were driven from the market, with one notable exception.

Jobs of Apple Computer refused to get on the bandwagon of IBM compatibility. In the Orwellian year of 1984, Apple showed a puzzling but prophetic advertisement in one of the coveted Superbowl advertising slots. Known as "Big Brother," the advertisement featured hordes of gray-clad drones listening to a corporate talking-head in a vast grimy theater, when they are interrupted by a muscular youth who flings a sledgehammer into the screen. A poke at the corporate domination of IBM, this advertisement introduced the Macintosh, a revolutionary new design in computing.

Jobs had become convinced that the microcomputer could succeed in the mass market only if it became an appliance. It must require no more understanding of its technology on the part of the user than a refrigerator or washing machine did. The Macintosh did away with the command line and its arcane commands, replacing them with an object-oriented graphical user interface built on a desktop metaphor. Anyone could sit down at a Mac and start doing useful work without needing to memorize commands.

However, the Mac's success in the marketplace was limited by its high cost. Unlike IBM, Apple jealously guarded its proprietary architecture. Although Apple did license the technology for connecting peripherals to a Macintosh, consumers could buy the computer itself only from Apple, on its terms. Even with deep educational discounts, the Mac remained beyond the reach of many cash-strapped students. Many people chose an IBM-compatible computer on the basis of price (and because of IBM's domination of the business market).

Apple did try some innovative marketing strategies to push the Macintosh in its early years. One of the most unusual was Test Drive a Mac, in which people could take a Mac for two days and try it out in the comfort of their home before deciding to buy it. The idea was that consumers would be so enchanted

VALUE OF SHIPMENTS OF ELECTRONIC COMPUTERS, 2000-2005, IN MILLIONS OF DOLLARS

Product	2000	2001	2002	2003	2004	2005
Host (multiuser) computer	22,877	16,469	13,053	12,237	10,993	11,759
Single-user computer	38,981	31,492	26,586	25,164	26,309	25,906
Other computers	999	582	809	870	593	721
Electronic computers (total)	64,857	48,543	40,448	38,271	37,895	38,386

Source: Data from U.S. Census Bureau, *Current Industrial Reports, Computers and Peripheral Equipment,* Series MA334R (Washington, D.C.: Author, 2006)

with the Mac experience that they could not bear to part with the Mac at the end of the trial period. However, Apple made one disastrous mistake: It rolled out the campaign during the 1985 Christmas season. Computer dealers already busy with the Christmas rush did not want the additional hassle of processing applications for loaner computers. As a result, the loaner program failed and was soon discontinued.

At the same time, users of the disk operating system (DOS) looking to simplify their experience were buying and installing shell software to interpret the command line for them. Most DOS shells offered a simplified set of menus, but Bill Gates's company, Microsoft, offered one that used the visual metaphor that had been so successful for Apple. The earliest versions of Windows were primitive, but by Windows 3.1, the interface was smooth enough that Apple sued Microsoft for copyright infringement on the basis of look and feel. In a ferocious court battle, Microsoft won on the basis that Apple had taken the Macintosh Finder largely from the experimental Alto interface developed by Xerox. After that legal battle secured its future, Windows became the dominant microcomputer operating system, capturing 85 percent of the market by 1995.

By the middle of the 1990's, Apple Computer seemed to have lost its way and was in danger of being put out of business altogether. Ironically, it was Microsoft's own success that saved Apple. Because of its dominant position in the microcomputer operating system market, Microsoft became the target of a U.S. Department of Justice antitrust suit alleging that it had used illegal monopolistic practices to secure its predominance. As a result, Gates became increasingly willing to work out a joint venture deal

with Jobs, who had returned to Apple as its new chief executive officer. The newly reinvigorated Apple simplified its line of products with the four-cell grid marketing scheme (personal vs. business, desktop vs. laptop) and secured its small but steady portion of the market share.

MAINFRAMES AND MORE

Although by 1990 the microcomputer in its various permutations had become people's primary image of a "computer," the mainframe had not vanished. In this market sector, IBM remained the dominant driving force. Critical as the IBM PC and its successors may have been in establishing microcomputer standards, mainframes remained IBM's bread and butter. The use of microprocessors and superscalar architecture permitted mainframes to shrink from the size of entire rooms to that of small cabinets, but they generally continued to be purchased on the full-service model. With the growth of the Internet and particularly the World Wide Web, mainframes grew popular once again for use as server farms by companies such as Yahoo!, eBay, and Google, running the infrastructure that served the information superhighway.

At the uppermost end of the mainframe market, a new subtype of computer had appeared—the supercomputer. These giant number crunchers were more the descendants of the university research computers such as ILLIAC than of the business mainframes, but with the rise of companies such as Cray, they became manufactured items that research universities could order from an established model line.

The beginning of the twenty-first century saw the convergence of several information technology industries. The bottom of the mainframe industry began to blur into the high end of the microcomputer workstation market, and some of the smallest laptop and notebook microcomputers began to share features with high-end scientific calculators, digital cellular telephones, and digital cameras. In addition, an increasing portion of the computer industry was devoted to the production and implementation of ubiquitous yet almost entirely invisible microcontrollers built into ordinary household appliances, automobiles, and other mechanical systems to make them run more efficiently and serve their users better. It was often cheaper for manufacturers to buy bulk lots of a standard microcontroller and hire a programmer to write a program to control the appliance's operations than to design and build a mechanical control system.

Leigh Husband Kimmel

FURTHER READING

Berlin, Leslie. *The Man Behind the Microchip: Robert Noyce and the Invention of Silicon Valley.* New York: Oxford University Pres, 2005. Argues that Noyce and Fairchild Semiconductor were primarily responsible for Santa Clara County, California, becoming a major center of the computer industry.

Chandler, Alfred D., Jr. *Inventing the Electronic Century: The Epic Story of the Consumer Electronics and Computer Industries.* New York: Free Press, 2001. Overview of the rise of the computer industry.

Cringely, Robert X. *Accidental Empires: How the Boys of Silicon Valley Make Their Millions, Battle Foreign Competition, and Still Can't Get a Date.* Reading, Mass.: Addison-Wesley, 1992. Focuses on the business culture of the computer industry.

Malone, Michael S. *Infinite Loop: How Apple, the World's Most Insanely Great Computer Company, Went Insane.* New York: Doubleday, 1999. Business history of Apple, the first company to make a microcomputer for consumers.

Pugh, Emerson W. *Building IBM: Shaping an Industry and Its Technology.* Cambridge, Mass.: MIT Press, 1995. Business history of IBM, the giant of computer companies.

Reid, T. R. *The Chip: How Two Americans Invented the Microchip and Launched a Revolution.* New York: Random House, 2001. A basic history of the development of the microchip, critical to the development of modern computers.

Wallace, James, and Jim Erickson. *Hard Drive: Bill Gates and the Making of the Microsoft Empire.* New York: Harper Business, 1993. Looks at Gates's role in dominating the microcomputer operating system market.

SEE ALSO: Apple; Automation in factories; Business crimes; Digital recording technology; eBay; E-mail; Fiber-optic industry; Gates, Bill; Google; International Business Machines; Internet; Online marketing.

Confederate currency

DEFINITION: Currency used by the Confederacy during the American Civil War

SIGNIFICANCE: Confederate currency—produced by the Confederate government and by individual states in the Confederacy—was critical to the South during the U.S. Civil War in its attempts to establish its own union. This currency was to be credited after the Confederacy's victory but became worthless after its defeat.

It later became a collector's item, fetching prices from a few dollars to tens of thousands of dollars for the rarest denominations.

The Confederate government began to issue currency in April of 1861, the month the Civil War began. The main printing press for central government-issued currency was in Richmond, Virginia, but currency was also printed by states, local municipalities, and merchants. Paper money was printed as well as coins, and both included symbolic representations of the Old South, including images of historical figures, military technology, and slavery.

Because it was philosophically opposed to federalism, the Confederate government was not able to tax its citizens sufficiently to prepare for the war effort. In addition, European markets were gaining access to alternative sources of cotton, such as India and Egypt. As a result, American cotton was selling for lower prices overseas, exacerbating the South's financial problems. Thus, Confederate currency was sure to experience high inflation should the South struggle in the war.

Counterfeiting of Confederate currency was common. Since Confederate currency was printed at a number of different venues and by different levels of government, Northern counterfeiters were easily able to buy Southern goods with replica money. The resulting increase in the amount of currency in circulation contributed to the high inflation that began to mount as the tide of the war turned in the North's favor.

Confederate money was relatively valuable when the Civil War began. The gold dollar was the standard of value at the time, and a Confederate dollar was worth as much as 95 cents against the gold dollar. Shortly after the Battle of Gettysburg (1863), as the likelihood of a Southern victory decreased, the value of a Confederate dollar dropped to roughly 33 cents against the gold dollar. Investors shied away from trading for currency that could become worthless if the South lost the war. Instead, they began to accumulate goods and services that would be redeemable regardless of the war's outcome. At the end of the war, the value of a Confederate dollar was about one penny against the gold dollar, and the currency ceased to be traded soon thereafter.

Brion Sever

FURTHER READING

Shull, Hugh. *Guide Book of Southern States Currency.* Florence, Ala.: Whitman, 2006.

Slabaugh, Arlie. *Confederate States Paper Money.* Lola, Wis.: Krause, 1998.

Tremmel, George. *Confederate Currency of the Confederate States of America.* Jefferson, N.C.: McFarland, 2003.

SEE ALSO: Civil War, U.S.; Currency; Inflation; Mint, U.S.

Confederation, Articles of. *See* Articles of Confederation

Congress, U.S.

IDENTIFICATION: Legislative branch of the federal government

DATE: First met in 1789

SIGNIFICANCE: As the lawmaking body of the U.S. national government, Congress is responsible for all legislation that affects American business. Its investigative powers and role in the appointment process also affect business.

Since the adoption of the U.S. Constitution in 1789, Congress has had a powerful impact on economic policy in the United States. That impact has generally increased, largely in response to economic problems such as depressions, business scandals, or the public's desire to improve the social welfare of the American people. Members of Congress have generally been quite supportive of business interests, although some business leaders have been critical of some efforts at regulation or taxation.

LAISSEZ-FAIRE AND SUPPORT FOR BUSINESS

For most of the nineteenth century, Congress rather than the president shaped economic policy. Congress's approach to American business during the nineteenth century was essentially laissez-faire—a hands-off, supportive attitude that did not interfere in business operations.

Congress's approach, however, was not entirely laissez-faire. To support nascent American industry during the early years of the republic, it adopted a policy of protective tariffs. Tariffs made foreign goods more expensive than American goods and thus protected American businesses from foreign competition. They also provided most of the income for the national government throughout the nineteenth century. This support for protective tariffs continued into the twentieth century, reaching a high point with the Smoot-Hawley Tariff Act of 1930. Protective tariffs may have been essential during the early years of the republic, but their continued imposition as American industries became more mature often led American business to neglect innovative practices and led some foreign countries to impose tariffs on American goods. The Smoot-Hawley Tariff Act led to a trade war with Europe, worsening the Great Depression.

In the years before the U.S. Civil War, Congress rarely acted to regulate the American business community, nor did it impose taxes that might have inhibited business profitability. Congress established the Second Bank of the United States in 1816 as a means of providing a national currency, but President Andrew Jackson allowed it to lapse. In the absence of a centralized approach to banking, Congress left banking regulation to state governments, often producing a chaotic approach to finance.

Congress began to change its approach during the Civil War, when the financial stress of the war prompted Congress in August, 1861, to create an income tax as a means of raising revenue to fight the war, although it was a tax on individuals not corporations. The tax was eliminated in 1872.

In 1862, Congress acted to support the settlement of the West with the Homestead Act that provided for free land for people who settled on it for a period of time. In 1864, Congress provided for subsidies for American railroads to encourage the construction of intercontinental rail lines. These subsidies were tinged at times with scandal as agents for various railroads succeeded in bribing members of Congress to gain increased benefits. Taken in combination, these two acts furthered the settlement of the West and provided impetus to the developing railroad industry.

Businesses, such as steamship companies or textile mills, were allowed to operate with no national governmental oversight, in spite of poor safety records or unsafe working conditions. Only when some aspect of the business world, such as railroads during the 1880's, became so abusive as to be harmful to other segments of the economy did Congress try to apply any sort of regulation. Congress passed the Interstate Commerce Act in 1887 to try to help consumers and farmers deal with discriminatory pricing by some railroads. Congress was trying to level the playing field between business, farmers, and consumers because railroads were viewed as possessing too much economic power when it came to setting their rate structure. However, in 1895, the Supreme Court weakened the operation of the Interstate Commerce Act as impermissible interference with the railroads' property rights.

Congress went further in 1890, passing the Sherman Antitrust Act with only a single dissenting vote, although both houses of Congress were controlled by probusiness Republicans. Although Congress was still probusiness during the 1890's, the various abuses by American railroads had led to such a clamor for reform that it could not be ignored. However, the Sherman Antitrust Act was largely unenforced for the rest of the decade.

THE GROWTH OF ACTIVISM

In the first decade of the twentieth century, Presidents Theodore Roosevelt and William Howard Taft used the Sherman Antitrust Act to break up various monopolies such as the Standard Oil Trust. As was often the case with much of the legislation affecting business, Congress legislated, but the execu-

tive branch was responsible for enforcement. The election of several progressives to Congress during the early twentieth century, coupled with the activism of Presidents Roosevelt and Taft, led to congressional action to protect American consumers from abusive practices by business and to enable the market to work more efficiently than was the case under the increasing power of monopoly capitalism. Although some business leaders such as the banker J. P. Morgan were critical of this government intervention, most Americans saw it as necessary to deal with an increasingly complex economy.

The legislation establishing the ineffective Interstate Commerce Commission had been one of Congress's first efforts at regulating an industry. The Pure Food and Drug Act of 1906 was another early twentieth century piece of legislation that took aim at health abuses that existed in the meatpacking and drug industries. Over the years, additional legislation has flowed from these beginnings that has been directed at protecting consumers' health and the environment, and maintaining competition. This legislation has arisen not from an antibusiness attitude in Congress but from a need to represent consumers, deal with environmental problems, and protect small businesses.

PRESIDENTIAL LEADERSHIP

During the twentieth century, it was often presidents who took the lead in establishing economic policy, as they sent legislative packages to Congress. Individual representatives and senators continued to be protective of business interests in their home states, but the balance of policy-making power was slipping into the hands of the presidents.

Spurred on by President Franklin D. Roosevelt, Congress took major action after 1933 in trying to find means to bring the United States out of the Great Depression. One example was the reestablishment of a national banking apparatus with the Federal Reserve System set up by the Glass-Steagall Act in 1933. New Deal legislation was directed at creating jobs, at times via public works projects such as the construction of the Hoover Dam that benefited corporations involved in the projects; reforming the banking system; and regulating the stock market to help ensure that a future crash would not occur.

In the years after World War II, Congress, often in response to presidential legislative initiatives, continued to be supportive of American business although it also displayed a concern for consumers and workers. For example, some business owners criticized congressional increases in the minimum wage, the imposition of health and safety standards in the workplace, or consumer product safety legislation, but the majority of Americans considered this sort of legislation necessary to even the balance among business and labor and consumers. Congress continued to be supportive of low corporate tax rates and still protected favored industries from foreign competition.

Late in the twentieth century, Congress began to produce environmental legislation such as the Clean Air Act of 1963 or the Resource Conservation and Recovery Act of 1976, which was designed to regulate industry conduct directly or to provide incentives for business to operate in a more environmentally friendly fashion. Some business leaders complained that such legislation interfered unjustly in their operations. Supporters of the legislation pointed out that much environmental legislation was designed to force businesses to pay for the costs of operation such as air or water pollution that they imposed on others (what economists call externalities). Debate also swirled around the 1994 North American Free Trade Agreement (NAFTA). Opponents such as the textile industry said that Congress was hurting their industry by allowing cheaper foreign goods to enter the U.S. marketplace. Businesses that profited from foreign trade were, however, supportive of NAFTA.

The operation of NAFTA helps illustrate the impact of Congress on American business. Legislation has, at times, benefited particular industries to the disadvantage of others. On occasion, Congress has granted special benefits to certain industries, often as a result of lobbying by these businesses. The American sugar industry, for example, has long benefited from protective tariffs that have kept the price of sugar artificially high. Lobbyists for the sugar industry have been quite effective at influencing enough members of Congress to maintain this situation.

American businesses have always been effective at presenting their case to Congress through lobbying, campaign contributions, advertising, and turning out the vote. Campaign reform legislation in the twentieth century has imposed some limits on the use of corporate power such as contribution limits,

but corporate American remains effective at often influencing the course of legislation. As the economy has become more complex, the business community is at times divided in its objectives as different businesses take opposing sides in trying to influence legislation before Congress. The rise of labor unions and consumer and environmental groups has provided some checks on business influence in Congress so that the legislative playing field became more equal by the late twentieth century than it had been before.

Congress during the early twenty-first century remained supportive of American business but also tried to maintain a broader view that takes into account the concerns of all Americans. Senators and Representatives were also responsive to nonbusiness interests among their constituents. Political scientists have long labeled this situation "interest group pluralism" to describe the various influences brought to bear on Congress. Even during the early years of the republic, business interests were often balanced by other interests, such as those of farmers. Some business leaders, aware of the benefits that may accrue to themselves from this balance, have been supportive of this balanced path followed by Congress.

John M. Theilmann

FURTHER READING

Arnold, R. Douglas. *The Logic of Congressional Action.* New Haven: Yale University Press, 1990. Develops a theory of congressional policy making with two chapters devoted to economic and tax policy.

Burda, Joan M. *An Overview of Federal Consumer Law.* Chicago: American Bar Association, 1998. Practical guide prepared by the American Bar Association. A useful overview of the types of laws passed by Congress that affect business.

Bureau of National Affairs. *U.S. Environmental Laws.* Washington, D.C.: Author, 1988. Compilation of laws passed by Congress that affect the environment.

Davidson, Roger H., Walter J. Oleszak, and Frances E. Lee. *Congress and Its Members.* 11th ed. Washington, D.C.: CQ Press, 2007. Standard institutional analysis of Congress and its lawmaking activities.

Gordon, John Steele. *An Empire of Wealth.* New York: Harper Collins, 2004. Comprehensive history of American economic development that often emphasizes the role of congressional action.

Quirk, Paul J., and Sarah A. Binder, eds. *The Legislative Branch.* New York: Oxford University Press, 2005. Part of a three-volume set dealing with three branches of government. Several useful chapters concerning the legislative role of Congress and its impact on economic policy.

Vogel, David. *Fluctuating Fortunes.* New York: Basic Books, 1989. Examination of the political power of American business.

SEE ALSO: Civil War, U.S.; Constitution, U.S.; Presidency, U.S.; Sherman Antitrust Act; Supreme Court and banking law; Supreme Court and commerce; Supreme Court and contract law; Supreme Court and labor law; Supreme Court and land law; Taxation.

Congress of Industrial Organizations. *See* AFL-CIO

Constitution, U.S.

IDENTIFICATION: Foundation document that established the structure and principles governing the national government of the United States
DATE: Ratified in 1789
SIGNIFICANCE: The U.S. Constitution provides a stable rule of law and an economic framework that makes American business and finance possible.

From the earliest recorded times, successful business activities have depended on the existence of peaceful and stable legal environments. When human societies moved beyond the hunter-gatherer stage to primitive agriculture, their members recognized that peace and security were extremely important to the growing and harvesting of crops. Without such security, farmers might expend their labor planting and weeding only to have neighbors steal their crops when they ripened. Within the United States, the federal Constitution has provided the basis for such an environment.

The Constitution was drafted during the summer of 1787, because the nation's previous foundation document, known as the Articles of Confederation, failed to provide a secure environment for living and for conducting business. Tariff barriers and trade wars among the states dampened economic development and threatened outright civil war. The lack of a national currency and the inability of the weak national government to protect contracts and private property made conducting business across state lines extremely difficult. Moreover, the absence of a national court system meant that disputes between citizens of different states could not be reliably resolved, as each state's courts tended to uphold the interests of its own citizens against those of other states. National economic activity was becoming stagnant.

The Framers of the U.S. Constitution addressed business and financial security in a number of specific ways. For example, Article I, section 9, prohibits taxes and duties on items exported from states. This clause promotes business by protecting the value of agricultural and manufacturing goods from being eroded by taxes. Article I, section 8, known as the commerce clause, gave the U.S. Congress authority to regulate commerce among the states, centralizing that critical power at the federal level. These two sections of the Constitution went a long way toward ending the dangerous trade wars among the original thirteen states and created one of the world's largest free trade areas.

THE CONSTITUTION AND CONTRACT LAW

Article I, section 10, of the Constitution prohibits states from passing any law impairing the obligation of contracts. This clause is vitally important for financial and business activity. Without enforceable contracts, almost any transaction beyond simple barter requires some way to allow transactions over time. Transactions often must take place over months or years, as is true, for example, in buying expensive properties, such as a home or an automobile.

Article III provides for a single Supreme Court and such other federal courts as Congress may decide to create, generating a national court system to resolve—among other things—disputes between citizens in different states. The Supreme Court also interprets the language in the Constitution and arbitrates disputes between the federal government and the various states. For example, early in U.S. history, the Supreme Court in *Fletcher v. Peck* (1810) voided a Georgia state law in which the Georgia legislature attempted to nullify a contract a previous legislature had made. Virtually every legislator in the previous legislature had taken a bribe to give away 35 million acres of state land for 1.5 cents per acre. No matter how corrupt the contract, however, the Court held that contracts were sacrosanct, thereby underscoring how important contracts are to the business life of a nation.

Protecting private property is a major concern of the Constitution that is exemplified by the Fourth Amendment, which prohibits, among other things, unreasonable searches and seizures. Private property is further protected by the Fifth Amendment's guarantee that it cannot be taken for a public purpose without just compensation. The Fifth Amendment also prohibits the federal government from taking property without due process of law.

About eighty years after the nation's founding, the Fourteenth Amendment was added to the Constitution, enacting two important provisions that have had a great impact on business and finance. This amendment guarantees that no state can deprive any "person[s]" of their property without due process of law. The Supreme Court held during the late nineteenth century that a corporation was a legal "person" entitled to Fourteenth Amendment protection, powerfully advancing the power of corporations in the United States. This decision meant that states were limited in the amounts and kinds of regulations they could impose on corporations, and it allowed for a dramatic increase in corporate power well into the twentieth century.

By the middle of the twentieth century, the Supreme Court decided that the Fourteenth Amendment's "equal protection" clause guaranteed individuals a number of important rights that have served to limit corporate power. This decision demonstrates that the U.S. Constitution can both

An 1867 print of the Constitution of the United States. (Library of Congress)

strengthen and weaken business interests. Despite these and other limits on business and finance, the basic rule of law provided by the Constitution remains the most important underpinning for the stable peaceful environment in which American business and finance operate.

Richard L. Wilson

FURTHER READING

Amar, Akhil Reed. *America's Constitution: A Biography.* New York: Random House, 2005. Provision-by-provision study of the Constitution that incorporates the events and issues that have helped shape each portion of the document.

Berkin, Carol. *A Brilliant Solution: Inventing the American Constitution.* New York: Harcourt, 2002. History of the Constitutional Convention of 1787, describing the conflicts and compromises among delegates, the disagreements between Federalists and anti-Federalists, and the development of the document itself. Contains one hundred pages of appendixes, including the full text of the Constitution and brief biographies of convention delegates.

Ely, James W., Jr. *The Guardian of Every Other Right: A Constitutional History of Property Rights.* 3d ed. New York: Oxford University Press, 2008. Scholarly history of property rights under the Constitution and its interpretation by the Supreme Court.

_____, ed. *Contract Clause in American History.* New York: Garland, 1997. Scholarly study of the impact of the Constitution's contract clause on American business history.

Farrand, Max. *The Records of the Federal Convention of 1787.* 4 vols. New Haven, Conn.: Yale University Press, 1966. The definitive set of primary source documents for the convention.

May, Christopher N., and Allan Ides. *Constitutional Law—National Power and Federalism: Examples and Explanations.* 3d ed. New York: Aspen, 2004. Examination of the U.S. federal system that analyzes the federal government's power to regulate interstate commerce.

Rakove, Jack N. *Original Meanings: Politics and Ideas in the Making of the Constitution.* New York: A. A. Knopf, 1996. Examines the concerns that shaped constitutional decision making during the late 1780's, exploring federalism, representation, executive power, civil rights and liberties, and other issues confronting delegates.

SEE ALSO: Annapolis Convention; Articles of Confederation; Congress, U.S.; Presidency, U.S.; Supreme Court and banking law; Supreme Court and commerce; Supreme Court and contract law; Supreme Court and labor law; Supreme Court and land law; Tariffs; Taxation.

Construction industry

DEFINITION: Enterprises that plan, finance, construct, repair, maintain, and demolish buildings and infrastructure

SIGNIFICANCE: All aspects of American business require locations at which businesspeople can work and the means to travel among these locations. The construction industry creates both these locations (buildings) and the roads and other infrastructure that make travel between them possible.

In the earliest days of European colonization, all building resembled that of Native Americans in that almost everyone carried out building by themselves using the simplest construction of materials readily at hand from nature. Although some Native Americans used animal hides as a part of their building construction, most of their early structures were of wood or stone depending on the availability of each substance. Colonists followed the same pattern. The early pioneer settlements on the great prairies were not infrequently made of sod. Only much later would clay products such as bricks and tiles be used in those areas where suitable clay was available. Two hundred and fifty years went by before steel was used as a critical structural material. Although such do-it-yourself building continues in the shadow of modern industrial construction, a specialization in the construction industry has emerged.

BUILDINGS AND INFRASTRUCTURE

In total number of units built, residential housing outstrips all other buildings in the modern world. The specialized character of home building means that such construction is financed and managed differently from the rest of the construction industry. In the twentieth century, government involvement in the nature and location of such building has increased substantially.

In addition to homes, people need a wide variety of shops and buildings, including offices, factories, warehouses, apartment buildings, and hotels. While some home building may still be done on a do-it-yourself basis, all large-scale construction has come to require diverse and sophisticated components assembled by specialized craftspeople. The financing of such large buildings is also necessarily far more complex, and these buildings are subject to government regulation as to both quality and location.

In addition to large commercial and governmental buildings, modern society also requires roads, airports, dams, canals, ports, locks, and irrigation systems. Although there is some private funding of these infrastructure projects, the great majority are built with public or government financing. As society has grown more complex, so have the demands on architects and civil engineers to produce this infrastructure.

As construction has moved from the simple to the complex, demand has increased for a far wider range of building materials. No longer does the building industry count on timber from naturally occurring forests; instead, vast tree farms have been created to supply society's demand for lumber. Mining and quarrying operations are more complex and involve clay, stones, gravel, and metallic ores. Glass, plastics, adhesives, metallic foils, and manufactured woods are all critical parts of sophisticated modern buildings and other construction projects.

COMPONENTS AND TRANSPORTATION

The modern construction industry uses a wide variety of components for plumbing, electricity, heating, air-conditioning, security, and telecommunications for private residences and for large commercial and public buildings. The manufacture of these components creates a multiplier effect that ripples throughout the economy. Each of the components that is manufactured for end-user buildings—whether public or private—must be built to suit the building that requires construction. Because natural materials such as wood and stone are increasingly replaced by glass, plastics, manufactured wood, and other artificial materials, the factories that manufacture these products must also be constructed, further amplifying a multiplier effect.

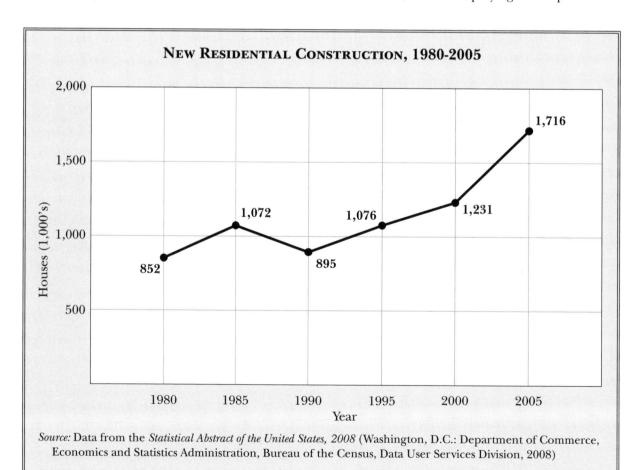

NEW RESIDENTIAL CONSTRUCTION, 1980-2005

Source: Data from the *Statistical Abstract of the United States, 2008* (Washington, D.C.: Department of Commerce, Economics and Statistics Administration, Bureau of the Census, Data User Services Division, 2008)

Modern building also requires a wide range of power tools, ranging from power screwdrivers used for the smallest projects to gigantic cranes used in the largest projects. Electrical, compressed air-, diesel-, and gasoline-powered equipment must be manufactured to support the wide variety of construction projects in the United States. The factories in which these products are manufactured also need to be constructed, so that construction has become a major part of the American economy.

Workers must transport all of the products, components, and equipment necessary for a project from the factories in which they are created to the warehouses in which they are stored to the work sites where they are used. Still other workers must move the raw materials to manufacture these products from the forests, quarries, and mines to the factories where the components and equipment are manufactured. The transportation industry in the United States is massive. Whenever possible, bulky goods are moved by rail, driving the expansion of railroads to accommodate such shipment. Still other goods are moved by long-distance commercial trucks, while delivery to the final destination is by short-distance trucking companies. Again, factories must be built to produce the equipment for railroads or trucking companies.

The complex, sophisticated building process leads to the construction of facilities for wholesale and retail merchants, further stimulating the construction industry. The wholesale and retail merchants themselves add significantly to the economic activity of the nation.

FINANCING AND REGULATION

Because construction, whether of a private home or a large commercial building, is a lengthy process and few projects can be paid for by the consumer in advance, financing is necessary. As the construction industry has evolved, home mortgage financing has generally been conducted in a significantly different fashion than financing of commercial and public projects. Banks, savings and loan associations, credit unions, and major investment firms all participate to a greater or lesser degree in the construction industry.

The increasing size and complexity of commercial and public buildings in particular has spawned a major industry of architects and civil engineers to design and plan construction projects. Educational institutions that train architects and civil engineers are another spinoff of the construction industry. Educational institutions for all of the other aspects of the construction industry are also a major part of the economic life of the nation.

The sophistication of modern construction means that consumers are increasingly unqualified to judge the quality of construction. The risk of buildings collapsing or otherwise exposing end users to great danger means that regulation of the building industry is increasingly important. Simple building codes have existed in cities for the last few hundred years, but even the smallest of contemporary buildings is subject to code requirements. The construction industry requires quality control personnel and building inspectors. Governmental entities at all levels provide many of these, but again educational institutions are required to train the necessary personnel.

The earliest buildings could be constructed wherever the owners of property wished them to be built, but as people began to live closer together and construction became more complex, such freedom was no longer possible. The zoning regulations were simple in the beginning but have become much more complicated over time. Population density and other factors have led to the establishment of sizable bureaucracies of the federal state and local levels. Although many chafe at government intrusion, nearly everyone recognizes that this is necessary. All of these public employees require specialized educational training, and educational facilities have expanded to meet these needs

At each step in the processes of construction, contractual relations are required and government bureaucracies are increased. These factors have a required a larger, more sophisticated legal profession, which is another economic activity that flows out of the construction industry. Educational institutions have expanded to apply the training for these additional legal personnel.

Richard L. Wilson

FURTHER READING

Bon, Ranko. *Building as an Economic Process.* 2d ed. Englewood Cliffs, N.J.: Prentice Hall, 2001. Process is the key variable examined in this study of building from an economic perspective.

Bon, Ranko, and David Crosthwaite. *The Future of International Construction.* London: Thomas Telford, 2000. This book examines American construction from an international perspective.

Dow, Louis A., and Fred Hendon. *Economics and Society.* Englewood Cliffs, N.J.: Prentice Hall, 1991. These coauthors, strongly influenced by the free-market economics of Adam Smith, examine economics in a societal context.

Hillebrandt, Patricia A. *Economic Theory and the Construction Industry.* 3d ed. London: Macmillan, 2000. This book takes a theoretical look at building from an economic perspective.

Ive, Graham, and Stephen Gruneberg. *The Economics of the Modern Construction Sector.* London: Macmillan, 2000. All aspects of construction are placed in a theoretical economic framework.

Willis, James. *Explorations in Microeconomics.* 5th ed. Redding, Calif.: North West, 2002. This mainstream text examines construction from a microeconomic perspective explaining the impact of construction on the individual firm.

SEE ALSO: Army Corps of Engineers, U.S.; Crédit Mobilier of America scandal; Government spending; Highways; Housing and Urban Development, U.S. Department of; Kaiser, Henry J.; Real estate industry, commercial; Real estate industry, residential; Woodworking industry.

Contract law

DEFINITION: Body of legislation and common law concerning agreements that create legal obligations of performance

SIGNIFICANCE: Contracts are vital to and at the heart of business and business dealings. Millions of contracts are made and executed daily to facilitate the completion of work and the distribution of goods and services. Without enforceable contracts, the American enterprise system could not operate. So important is the right to contract that the U.S. Constitution protects it. Article I, section 10, of that document states that freedom to contract may not be abridged.

Contract law is based on the principle that people should be secure in the knowledge that promises will be legally enforced when made between persons in order to provide each with some sort of benefit. Contract law has pervaded nearly all aspects of society, and as technology grows and society changes, the essential principles of contract law are necessarily modified or adapted to reach a fair and equitable result.

NATURE OF CONTRACTS

A contract is a promise or set of promises for the breach of which the law affords a remedy. That is, a contract is a promise or set of promises enforceable in a court of law. A contract should be distinguished from a moral obligation, which defines the code of conduct of an ethical person but falls short of constituting a binding promise. A handshake may constitute an agreement, but it does not rise to the level of a legally enforceable contract. Likewise, at common law, certain arrangements or understandings with regard to social obligations might be recognized as agreements but not contracts because the purpose of the understanding is of minor importance or constitutes undesirable social conduct. In contrast, a contract is normally made when two parties exchange binding promises in which each party declares that he or she will take or refrain from taking a specific action in the future. If the contractual promise is not performed, the contract has been breached, and money damages must be paid. The nonbreaching party is entitled to compensation. In situations in which money damages cannot make the victim of the breach "whole," a court of equity may order actual performance of the contract (specific performance).

NATURE AND CLASSIFICATION

Contracts can be classified in terms of validity and enforceability. A valid contract is a binding and enforceable agreement meeting all the necessary contractual requirements. A void contract is one from which a necessary contractual element is absent. In that case, the contract has no legal effect. A voidable contract is one that can be voided because of the manner in which the contract was made (fraud, duress, undue influence). Contracts made by those who are underage may also be voidable at the option of the party lacking legal capacity.

Bilateral contracts consist of mutual promises to perform some future act. A unilateral contract exists when one party makes a promise in exchange for the other performing an act or refraining from doing something. The intention of the parties is the primary factor involved in determining the nature of the contract. That is ascertained not only from the words used but also from the surrounding circumstances, including the acts and conduct of the parties. Invitations for social events, when accepted, do not, however, give rise to a binding contract because they lack contractual intention. A promise to make a gift does not normally create a contract. An exception exists, for example, in the case where a philanthropist promises to donate a large sum of money for a project and in reliance on that promise, funds are committed. If the entity has justifiably relied on the promise to its detriment, the promisor/philanthropist may be estopped from reneging on the promise to make a gift. This is the concept of promissory estoppel or detrimental reliance.

A written promise enforceable by law is called a formal contract. A familiar example of a formal contract is a contract under seal such as a check or a negotiable promissory note. Each has a required form and must contain certain elements. A type of formal contact called a "contract under seal" did not require the standard elements to prove its validity or enforceability. It was presumed that anyone (generally nobility) who pressed a signet ring into wax on a contractual document became bound to the obligation contained in the document. Merchants who wished to enter into contracts had to prove their intent to be bound in another manner, so the concept of "consideration" developed. An informal or simple contract, such as an employment contract, is not required to be in any particular form.

ANALYSIS

An offer is a proposal to make a contract. It is a promise conditional on a return promise, act, or forbearance (refraining from doing an act or giving up a right). It is important to distinguish between an offer and the solicitation of an offer. The willingness to make or receive an offer is not in itself an offer, but merely an invitation to negotiate. An offer can be made to one specific person or to the general public, as in an advertisement. Publication of an item for sale at a specific price, however, does not constitute an offer, but merely an invita-

tion to negotiate. Offers can be terminated by revocation, lapse of time, subsequent illegality, destruction of the subject matter, death or incapacity, rejection, or a counteroffer. In an option contract an offeror (person making the offer) agrees to hold the offer open for a specific time. The offer terminates on expiration of that time.

An acceptance is the agreement by the offeree (person to whom the offer is made) to be bound by the terms of the offer. Consent must be communicated to the offeror. Silence or inaction on the part of the offeree does not generally constitute acceptance. The offeror generally has the power to stipulate the means and methods of acceptance and the acceptance must conform to those stipulations. At early common law, an acceptance had to be a "mirror image" of the offer, any changes in terms of the offer acted as a counteroffer. Under the Uniform Commercial Code, however, new or different terms added to contacts involving the sale of goods are treated as proposals that must be accepted separately.

Every state has statutes called statutes of frauds

ELEMENTS OF AN ENFORCEABLE CONTRACT

For a contract to be enforceable under the law, certain elements must be present. These include the following:

- an agreement, or expression of the parties' willingness to be bound to the terms of the contract;
- an offer, in which one of the parties submits a proposal;
- an acceptance, in which the other party agrees to the terms of the offer;
- consideration, constituting the bargained-for element (generally money, a reciprocal promise, or an act)

The consideration cannot involve something that is prohibited by law (agreements to commit crimes, agreements to slander or defraud another, or agreements dealing with patent or trademark infringement are invalid).

In addition, contracts must also be executed by competent individuals. That is, the parties to the contract must have the capacity to bind themselves contractually, unimpeded by minority or mental disability. Genuine assent by the parties is presumed unless one of the parties is induced to agree because of misrepresentation, fraud, duress, undue influence, joke, or mistake.

requiring that certain contacts be in writing to be enforceable. These include an agreement by an executor or administrator to answer for the debt of a decedent; an agreement made in consideration of marriage; an agreement to answer for the debt of another; an agreement that cannot be performed in one year; an agreement for the sale of an interest in real property; and an agreement for the sale of goods above a certain dollar amount. Specific requirements vary by state.

If parties reduce their agreement to writing, they are presumed to have included their entire understanding. The writing is presumed to have integrated all prior agreements or terms. Under the parol (word-of-mouth) evidence rule, evidence of prior agreements or terms not contained in the writing is not admissible to prove anything within the contract.

Quasi-contract is a legal doctrine that allows courts to treat certain transactions as if a contract exists, even though one or more elements may be missing. Based on the equitable principle that one party should not be unjustly enriched at the expense of another or through violation of another's rights, the law requires restitution of the property. Unjust enrichment is the doctrine holding that one person should not profit inequitably at another's expense. If one party has received something of value at another's expense, or benefited unjustly, the nonenriched party may seek the remedy of restitution or reimbursement. To prevent unjust enrichment of one party at the other's expense, the party who provides services may recover in quantum meruit or the reasonable value of the services rendered if it can be shown that the services were rendered with the expectation of monetary reward. The proper measure of recovery in restitution cases is the amount by which the defendant was enriched, not the amount of the plaintiff's loss.

Uniform Commercial Code

Certain elements of contract law vary from state to state and according to the nature of the contract; that is, personal service agreements, contracts for securities, corporate financial transactions, and real estate dealings. Most contracts, however, involve the sale or purchase of goods (all movable personal property that consists of things other than money and securities). Those contracts are governed by the Uniform Commercial Code (UCC), a document dealing with the sale of goods, leases, banking, bills of lading, negotiable instruments, bulk transfers, warehousing, and mortgages, embodying the generally accepted statutes in all the states and adopted (at least in part) by all fifty states as part of their statutory law.

The UCC imposes an obligation of good faith in every contract arising under it. In most cases of breach, the injured party is awarded monetary damages. The UCC, however, provides special rules for breaches of contracts involving the sale of goods. If a seller breaches his or her contract to deliver goods, the buyer is entitled to rescission or cancellation of the contract, suit for damages, and restitution for any payments already made. If the goods are unique, such as rare artwork, or custom-made, a court may order specific performance to compel or coerce performance of the contract. If a buyer breaches a sales contract by not accepting delivery of goods, or wrongfully revokes a prior acceptance, the injured seller is entitled to cancel the contract, stop delivery of goods, and recover monetary damages from the buyer.

Under the UCC, contracts for the sale of goods often contain an implied promise that the goods are of a certain quality, called the implied warranty of merchantability and that they are suitable for the purpose for which they are bought, called the implied warranty of fitness for use. These implied warranties are not stated in the contract, but if applicable, a party may seek damages if the goods do not meet certain standards.

An unconscionable contract for the sale of goods under the UCC is a contract that courts may refuse to enforce or that courts may modify because one of the parties is in an unequal bargaining position or because the bargain is so one-sided in its benefit to one party as to shock the court's conscience. An example of this situation is the so-called adhesion contract in which the consumer has little if any bargaining power against big business. The once familiar and harsh concept of caveat emptor, or let the buyer beware, has been softened and continues to erode. That concept is being replaced by the concept of caveat venditor, or let the seller beware.

In addition to the UCC, other statutes that have as their purpose the protection of the consumer and therefore affect the conduct of business include the Consumer Product Safety Act of 1972 (which created the Consumer Product Safety Commission to review consumer products and their use) the Truth-in-Packaging Act of 1966 (to regulate and establish standards regarding contents of information shown on packages and encourage the development of standards for package sizes), the Federal Trade Commission Act of 1914 (creating the Federal Trade Commission to regulate deceptive trade practices), the Securities Act of 1933, and labor relations acts such as the National Labor Relations Act of 1935 (also called the Wagner Act) and the Taft-Hartley Act of 1947.

THIRD-PARTY CONTRACTS

Sometimes parties who enter into contracts transfer their rights or obligations under the contract. This is known as assignment. Because parties to a contract often prefer not to deal with assignees, it is not unusual for a contract to prohibit or restrict assignment. Sometimes a party to a contract transfers his or her obligations under a contract to another. This is known as delegation of duties. The law generally permits delegation except in cases in which the transfer of personal service contracts would change the basic agreement between the parties. For example, if a particular person such as an artist is hired to paint a portrait, the artist cannot delegate the obligation to another painter. Also, even if obligations or duties are delegated, the original party remains liable under the original contract unless specifically released from liability by the other party.

Marcia J. Weiss

FURTHER READING

Altschuler, Bruce E., and Celia A. Sgroi. *Understanding Law in a Changing Society.* 2d ed. Upper Saddle River, N.J.: Prentice Hall, 1996. Written for those who wish to gain basic knowledge of legal concepts, illustrated with case excerpts, and containing a chapter on contract law.

Carper, Donald L., Norbert J. Mietus, T. E. Shoemaker, and Bill W. West. *Understanding the Law.* 2d ed. St. Paul, Minn.: West, 1995. Contains basic legal principles and short illustrations from case law containing a chapter on contract law.

Hames, Joanne Banker, and Yvonne Ekern. *Introduction to Law.* Upper Saddle River, N.J.: Prentice Hall, 1998. Aimed at paralegals and containing legal principles, case excerpts, and a chapter on contract law.

Rohwer, Claude D., and Anthony M. Skrocki. *Contracts in a Nutshell.* 5th ed. St. Paul, Minn.: West Group, 2000. An excellent and succinct explanation of the law, written for those with some basic knowledge in the field.

Schubert, Frank A. *Introduction to Law and the Legal System.* 8th ed. Boston: Houghton Mifflin, 2003. An introductory text for the study of law with broad scope, good explanations, and case illustrations; contains a chapter on contract law.

SEE ALSO: Bankruptcy law; Commodity markets; Congress, U.S.; Constitution, U.S.; Derivatives and hedge fund industry; Indentured labor; Supreme Court and contract law.

Contract law, Supreme Court and. *See* Supreme Court and contract law

"Coolie" labor

DEFINITION: Derogatory term used to refer to Chinese immigrant laborers in the United States, especially during the second half of the nineteenth century

SIGNIFICANCE: During the second half of the nineteenth century, Chinese immigrants played a significant role in the economic growth and development of the western part of the country. However, their presence also led to an outpouring of racial prejudice and violence, and to the eventual passage of legislation at both the state and national levels to restrict Chinese immigration.

Chinese workers began immigrating to the United States in significant numbers in the years following the Opium Wars (1839-1842; 1856-1860) between China and Great Britain and the Taiping Rebellion (1851-1864). Although frequently referred to as "coolies"—a derogatory term used for enslaved Chinese and other Asians taken against their will to various parts of the world—these individuals came to the United States voluntarily because of the extreme poverty existing in their homeland and the economic opportunities offered by the new country.

The California gold rush during the late 1840's provided an initial incentive for some, but in the long run, it was employment as manual laborers that drew the majority of them. The vast majority were men, and those who were married generally left their wives and families in China, planning to remain in the new land only temporarily. By 1882, when the first federal law restricting Chinese immigration was passed, approximately 300,000 Chinese had come to the United States.

These Chinese immigrants provided an important labor source for a number of economic enterprises. Following the gold rush, large numbers were employed during the 1860's by the Central Pacific Railroad in the building of the western leg of the transcontinental railroad. During the 1870's, they provided an important source of labor for the construction of the levees of the Sacramento-San Joaquin River Delta, helping to create the fertile farmlands of that region. Many also turned to fishing, playing a key role in the development of the coastal fisheries. Others opened small businesses, such as restaurants or laundries, or found work as domestic servants.

Very soon after their initial arrival, Chinese immigrants began to experience racial and economic prejudice. In 1862, California passed the Anti-Coolie Act, which established a special tax for Chinese workers. In addition, Chinese were not allowed to own land in that state, and special regulations and taxes were imposed on Chinese fishermen. Violent attacks against Chinese immigrants also took place. Among the most notorious of these was a violent labor dispute in the mining town of Rock Springs, Wyoming, in September of 1885, which left twenty-eight Chinese miners dead and seventy-five homes of Chinese in the area destroyed. Reacting to these racial and economic tensions and to the lobbying ef-

Chinese mine workers travel on a railroad handcart. (Asian American Studies Library, University of California at Berkeley)

forts put forth by western states, Congress enacted the Chinese Exclusion Act in 1882, formally ending Chinese immigration to the United States. This remained in effect until its repeal by the Magnuson Act in 1943.

Scott Wright

FURTHER READING

Chang, Iris. *The Chinese in America: A Narrative History.* New York: Penguin Books, 2004.

Gyory, Andrew. *Closing the Gate: Race, Politics, and the Chinese Exclusion Act.* Chapel Hill: University of North Carolina Press, 1998.

Pfaelzer, Jean. *Driven Out: The Forgotten War Against Chinese Americans.* New York: Random House, 2007.

SEE ALSO: Asian trade with the United States; California gold rush; Chinese trade with the United States; Farm labor; Fishing industry; Immigration; Japanese trade with the United States; Labor history; Railroads; Transcontinental railroad.

Copyright law

DEFINITION: Body of statutes and common law that determines when creative works can be copyrighted and the enforceable rights of the copyright owner

SIGNIFICANCE: Copyright law, which promotes and protects creative expression by rewarding authors and artists for their efforts with exclusive legal rights to control the use of their work, has played an important role in the development of the media, publishing, and entertainment industries.

Copyright is a form of legal protection for authors and creators of original expressive works. Under law, the types of works protected by copyright are literary, musical, dramatic, artistic, choreographic, architectural, and audiovisual works, as well as sound recordings. In no case, however, does copyright protection extend to any idea, procedure, process, system, method of operation, concept, principle, or discovery, regardless of the form in which it is explained or illustrated. Rather, copyright protection applies only to an original expression of an idea or concept. For instance, the idea of two people falling in love cannot by copyrighted, but a particular expression of that idea in the form of an original short story, painting, or song can be copyrighted.

ORIGINS

The origin of American copyright law extends back to England. The history of copyright has been closely tied to the development of technology and business involving entertainment and information goods. When the printing press was invented and introduced in England in 1476, it became possible to reproduce works for mass circulation. Quite naturally, the interests of printers and authors in those works came to the forefront. More specifically, in 1556, the Stationers' Company was created by royal decree to control the printing industry. Printing of all published works became subject to the oversight of the Church of England and the government, and the stationers (printers and booksellers), rather than authors, had the sole right to print and publish the works in perpetuity. In 1710, however, Parliament enacted the Statute of Anne, which ended the stationers' monopoly and, for the first time, recognized the exclusive right of authors to control the printing of their works for a limited period of fourteen years, with the possibility of a fourteen-year renewal term.

English copyright law was later exported to the American colonies. After independence, all of the states except Delaware passed copyright laws modeled on the Statute of Anne. These laws were limited because they applied only within each state and authors had to register their works in each state and comply with a variety of state laws that often contained conflicting requirements. By the time that the drafters of the Constitution met, they recognized the importance of creating a uniform, national body of copyright law for the United States. Article I, Section 8, clause 8, of the U.S. Constitution empowers Congress to "promote the Progress of Science and useful Arts, by securing for limited Times to Authors . . . the exclusive Right to their respective Writings. . . ."

Based on this constitutional grant of power, the first Congress enacted the first federal copyright statute in 1790. This law granted copyright protection to the authors of maps, books, and charts for fourteen years. Authors were required to register the work with the government, publish notice of the registration, and deposit a copy of the work with the secretary of state within six months of publication. In addition, authors were also allowed to renew their copyright for another fourteen years.

As the American economy expanded throughout the nineteenth century, the scope of copyright protection was gradually broadened as well. In 1802, prints became protected by copyright, and in 1831, musical compositions were included. Dramatic compositions and the right publicly to perform them, were added in 1856. The extension of copyright protection also paralleled the invention of new technologies and media. For instance, Congress extended copyright to photographs in 1865. By 1870, paintings, drawings, sculptures, and models and designs in fine arts were protected. Other amendments during this period extended the initial copyright term to twenty-eight years, with a possible renewal for an additional fourteen years, and invested the Library of Congress with the administration of the copyright registration system and made it the repository of copyright deposits.

By 1909, Congress decided to pass a new and comprehensive copyright statute that incorporated all of its earlier amendments to the 1790 copyright statute and eliminate the inconsistencies in its provisions. The Copyright Act of 1909 made several important improvements to prior law. For example, under the new law, the term of copyright protection began with the publication of the work with a notice of copyright (such as © or "Copr."), rather than with registration of the work. Moreover, renewal of the copyright term was extended to twenty-eight years, thereby increasing the maximum duration of copyright protection to fifty-six years upon renewal.

Once again, technological developments and the growth of the U.S. economy in new directions during the twentieth century began to push the limits of copyright law. Inventions such as motion pictures, phonographs, radio, and television, along with the emergence of new media forms and the entertainment industry, made the 1909 statute increasingly obsolete. Almost immediately after its enactment, for instance, the 1909 statute was amended to include motion pictures. A later amendment extended copyright protection to sound recordings. Moreover, the advent of international markets for American authors and creators made it imperative that U.S. law conform to the standards set out in various international copyright treaties. In 1976, therefore, the Copyright Act of 1909 was repealed and replaced by the current statute.

THE STATUTE OF 1976

The Copyright Act of 1976 set forth two important requirements for copyright protection. First, the work must be fixed in a tangible medium of expression. This means that the author or artist must record the work in a material, physical form that is sufficiently stable and permanent to last more than a short time. Examples include a sculpture fixed in marble, a poem written on a sheet of paper, a song recorded on a compact disc, a videotape of dance choreography, or a computer program stored in a computer's hard drive. By contrast, a sculpture created in a medium such as ice or sand, or a picture created by skywriting is too transient and unstable to be considered fixed. Similarly, live performances that are purely impromptu or that are not recorded are not fixed.

The second principal requirement for copyright protection is that the work be original, meaning that it must have been independently and directly created by the author or artist. Moreover, the work must reveal some minimal level of creativity. The standard for originality is not particularly high, and it is not necessary that the work be novel, unique, or aesthetically pleasing. In fact, a work may be considered original even if it closely resembles another work or several different works. Instead, it must be apparent that the author or artist made some minimally creative choices in crafting or composing the work.

Under the Copyright Act of 1976, ownership of a copyright in a work vests initially in its actual creator, who owns all of the exclusive rights afforded by copyright protection. In some cases, a work is created by more than one author or artist. When a work is created by two or more authors who intend that their separate contributions be merged together into a single, complete work, the copyright is shared by the co-owners of the joint work. Each co-owner is entitled to exercise all of the exclusive rights, or to license other persons to exercise those rights.

Although the actual creator of the work is usually also the author or artist, there two situations when he or she is not the owner of the copyright in the work. If an employee (rather than an independent contractor) prepares a work that can be copyrighted within the scope of his or her employment, then the employer is the owner of the resulting copyright. Usually, an employee who creates a work as part of his or job, at the direction of the employer, for work-related purposes, has created the work within the scope of employment. A second type of work made for hire results when the work has been specially commissioned and the parties have agreed in writing and signed that the work is made for hire. Only certain types of works made for hire may be specially commissioned, including contributions to collections; parts of movies or audiovisual works; translations; supplementary works such as prefaces and illustrations; compilations; and instructional texts and tests.

Initially, the 1976 statute provided for a term of copyright protection consisting of the author's life plus 50 years beyond death, but the term was extended by 20 years as a result of an amendment in 1998. The term of copyright became the remainder of the author's life, plus 70 years after the date of death. This allows the author or artist's family to benefit from his or her creative efforts. In a work made for hire, the copyright lasts for a term of 95 years from the year of its first publication, or a term of 120 years from the year of its creation, whichever expires first.

COPYRIGHT HOLDER RIGHTS

Ownership of a valid copyright provides the copyright owner with five exclusive rights, which are set out in the Copyright Act. Those rights are known as the reproduction right, adaptation right, public distribution right, public performance right, and public display right. Accordingly, copyright owners have the exclusive right to reproduce their works by making copies or phonorecords of them. Copyright also affords the author or artist the exclusive right to make adaptations or derivatives of his or her preexisting work. A derivative work, therefore, is one that is based on or derived from another work due to reformatting, transforming, or revision of the earlier work. Examples of derivative works include a translation of a poem from one language to another, a rearrangement of a sonata, the production of a movie based on a novel, or a digitization of print photograph.

Copyright owners also have the exclusive right to distribute copies of their works to the public through sales, rentals, leases, or lending. The distribution right often goes hand in hand with the reproduction right, and in many cases, unauthorized reproductions only become known to the copyright owner once there are multiple copies that have been distributed publicly. In addition, the public

display and performance rights give copyright owners the exclusive right to show their work to members of the public. The Copyright Act defines "publicly" broadly to include places open to the public or where a large number of persons outside of the normal circle of a family and its social acquaintances are gathered. This would include film screenings in a theater, music performances at a concert hall, museum exhibitions, and public transmissions such as television broadcasting or video streaming over the Internet to a public location.

The Copyright Act of 1976 made a critical change as to when copyright protection begins. The 1909 statute had required publication of the work with a copyright notice affixed before copyright vested. Under the 1976 statute, copyright ownership vests as soon as an original work of authorship is fixed. The term of protection begins automatically and immediately upon creation of the work. Although registration of the work is not required to secure copyright ownership, it is nevertheless advisable. In addition, a registered copyright is required before a copyright owner may bring suit for infringement in federal court. Publication of the work is no longer required, nor is affixing a copyright notice to the work. Finally, the 1976 statute explicitly codified the fair use defense to infringement suits. One of the rights accorded to the owner of copyright is the right to reproduce or to authorize others to reproduce the work in copies or phonorecords. This right is subject to certain limitations, including that of "fair use." The Copyright Act contains a list of the various purposes for which the reproduction of a particular work may be considered "fair," such as criticism, comment, news reporting, teaching, scholarship, and research.

NEW TECHNOLOGIES

The new technologies and media forms that emerged during the late twentieth century have had an enormous effect on copyright law. The widespread adoption and use of personal computers and photocopiers were quickly followed by the proliferation of software tools, digital audiovisual recording media, satellite communications, and the Internet. Around each of these technologies have emerged new consumer markets and business models. At the same time, the limits of copyright law have been tested and Congress has responded by enacting numerous amendments to the Copyright Act. In 1980, for instance, the Copyright Act was extended to protect computer programs. In 1995, Congress added provisions governing the licensing of digital audio transmissions and, in 1998, prohibited circumvention of technological devices used to protect copyrighted digital works. In large part, such amendments reflect the growing influence and economic importance of information technology and the entertainment industries that have spurred these changes. Whether the 1976 statute will remain durable as the pace of technological development accelerates or will need to be replaced by a comprehensive new copyright law remains an open question at this time.

Kurt M. Saunders

FURTHER READING

Alpern, Andrew. *101 Questions About Copyright Law.* Mineola, N.Y.: Dover, 1999. A complete guide to copyright law written for nonlawyers using a question-and-answer format and containing practical advice about registering and protecting copyrights.

Leaffer, Marshall A. *Understanding Copyright Law.* 4th ed. Newark, N.J.: LexisNexis, 2005. This book contains a comprehensive summary and explanation of U.S. copyright law, written in concise, understandable language.

Nimmer, Melville B., and David Nimmer. *Nimmer on Copyright.* New York: Matthew Bender, 2003. A multivolume treatise on the law of copyrights, with detailed explanation of all aspects of copyright law and practice, including forms and text of relevant statutes.

Patry, William F. *Patry on Copyright.* St. Paul, Minn.: Thomson West, 2007. This treatise provided a thorough and understandable treatment of all aspects of copyright protection and enforcement.

Warda, Mark. *How to Register Your Own Copyright.* 3d ed. Naperville, Ill.: Sphinx, 2004. Written for nonlawyers, this book is a step-by-step guide to registering creative works with the U.S. Copyright Office, including sample forms and instructions.

SEE ALSO: American Society of Composers, Authors, and Publishers; Book publishing; Digital recording technology; Magazine industry; Music industry; Patent law.

Cotton gin

IDENTIFICATION: Machine designed to separate cotton seeds from cotton fibers

DATE: Patented on March 14, 1794

SIGNIFICANCE: By reducing the time required to process raw cotton into usable stock, the cotton gin revolutionized the economy of the antebellum South, quickly establishing cotton as the dominant American export. The corresponding enormous increase in the demand for cotton helped make the institution of slavery an entrenched part of the southern economy. In addition, the problems the gin's inventor faced exposed significant loopholes in newly enacted U.S. patent legislation.

After the American Revolution, southern planters faced an economic dilemma: The kind of cotton that could be grown abundantly in the vast inland farms of the Deep South, called short-staple, was prohibitive to grow, as an enormous investment of time was required to separate its sticky seedpods from its short, stubby fibers. Eli Whitney, a Massachusetts-born, Yale-educated aspiring lawyer, in 1793 had reluctantly accepted a tutoring post at a Georgia plantation. He was intrigued by the problem presented by short-staple cotton and, working with crude designs for hand-cranked machines that had already been tried, created a working model for a cotton "gin" (short for "engine"). Whitney's gin pulled the cotton through a series of screen meshes with holes too small for the seeds to pass through, while continuously rotating brushes pulled the fibers cleanly off. Whitney calculated that the hand-cranked machine could clean close to fifty pounds of cotton daily. Whitney applied for and received a government patent in 1794.

By mechanizing the laborious work of separating cotton seeds and fibers, the gin made an immense and immediate impact in the southern economy, which at the time depended largely on tobacco and rice. Recognizing the potential for major profits, Whitney and his partners attempted to establish throughout the Deep South a string of ginning depots, farming centers to which planters could bring their crops for processing. However, because Whitney charged a hefty fee (roughly two-fifths of the crop's profit), farmers quickly took advantage of loosely written patent laws to make minor alterations to the gin's design and then set up gins on their own property, asserting that their alterations protected them from claims of patent infringement.

Although Whitney saw little profit from his design, the gin revolutionized the South. In each decade leading up to the U.S. Civil War, raw cotton production doubled—an astounding growth record—and by 1860 America was producing three-quarters of the world's supply, helped by corollary developments in transportation, textile processing, and weaving. Bigger and more efficient gins were designed, powered by horses and then by water.

Because the gin so vastly increased the amount of cotton that could be processed, its adoption into the southern economy increased the need for slaves to work cotton plantations. Historians credit the boom in the cotton industry for expanding the number of slave states from six to fifteen. The gin also greatly increased the hardships under which slaves were compelled to live, as plantation owners sought huge profits from increasingly larger crops. The cash crop potential also retarded the South's urban growth, as farmland was too valuable to convert into cities. It also slowed the evolution of other industries in the region, making the South virtually dependent on the crop. This dependence led ultimately to the Civil War and the economic collapse of the South in the war's aftermath.

Joseph Dewey

This early drawing of a cotton gin shows African Americans working while two white businessmen examine the ginned cotton. (Library of Congress)

SEE ALSO: Agriculture; Civil War, U.S.; Cotton industry; Industrial Revolution, American; Inventions; Patent law; Plantation agriculture; Slave era; Slave trading.

Cotton industry

DEFINITION: Farmers and businesses responsible for growing, processing, and selling cotton

SIGNIFICANCE: The cotton industry, aided by the invention of the cotton gin, enriched the American South before the Civil War. Although it suffered setbacks during the war, the industry recovered to provide a significant source of American exports.

The early history of the cotton industry revolves around the introduction of African slaves to the American South in an effort to provide inexpensive labor for the cotton fields. Despite the use of the slaves, cotton farming was not highly noted or profitable before the late eighteenth century.

THE INVENTION

The cotton gin, widely believed to have been the invention of Eli Whitney alone, industrialized the harvesting of cotton. The invention was introduced in 1793, and a patent was filed in 1794. The patent

FURTHER READING

Green, Constance. *Eli Whitney and the Birth of American Technology.* London: Longman, 1997.

Howe, Daniel Walker. *What Hath God Wrought: The Transformation of America, 1815-1848.* Oxford, England: Oxford University Press, 2007.

Lakwete, Angela. *Inventing the Cotton Gin: Machine and Myth in Antebellum America.* Baltimore: Johns Hopkins University Press, 2005.

was finally upheld in 1802, but by that time, many other inventors had copied the idea and sold their machines to southern farmers. This was partially Whitney's fault, as he and a partner had set up ginning facilities across the South, charging farmers a fee for processing the cotton, rather than selling the machines directly to the growers. Although scholars continue to debate whether the cotton gin was Whitney's original design, whether it included parts copied from the machines of other inventors, or whether it was adapted from African and Asian contraptions, the cotton gin produced a revolution in the industry. The easier separation of the cotton fiber from the seeds increased the yield, thereby speeding up production. This allowed more cotton to be readied for sale, creating higher profits. The credit for the improvement in the South's economic status has popularly been given to Whitney and his invention.

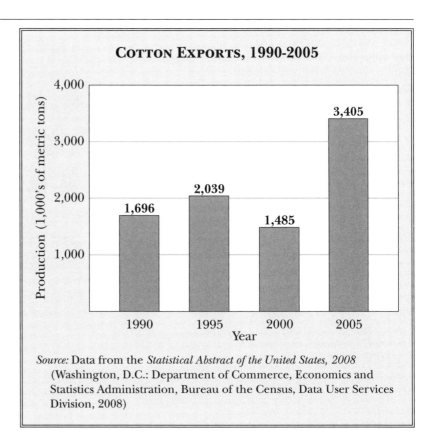

COTTON EXPORTS, 1990-2005

Source: Data from the *Statistical Abstract of the United States, 2008* (Washington, D.C.: Department of Commerce, Economics and Statistics Administration, Bureau of the Census, Data User Services Division, 2008)

By the middle of the nineteenth century, the cotton industry was one of the largest industries in the world, employing as many as twenty million workers. In the years just before the U.S. Civil War, the American South provided most of the cotton to textile mills both within the country, primarily in Massachusetts, and outside the country. The main export customers were Britain, France, Germany, and Russia. American cotton provided more than three-fourths of the necessary supply for textile mills in the countries that imported it.

The cotton industry's success has been blamed, in part, for the Civil War, as industries in the North were purportedly envious of the South's financial success. The onset of the Civil War caused a number of problems in the cotton industry. As the war progressed and the slaves became emancipated, the production of cotton in the South plummeted, dragging the economy with it. The loss of approximately four million unpaid laborers destroyed the plantations' ability to keep up with world demand. Production continued to be limited in the South as workers refused to labor in the cotton fields, even with pay. The drop in production resulted in international panic and unemployment. British and French textile workers rioted as the lack of cotton closed the doors of their mills. Because the countries that imported the cotton needed it to keep their mills running, they found other sources, and after the war, it took almost a decade for the cotton industry to recover. Fortunately for the United States economy, the cotton industry bounced back in the years after the Civil War with small farms, sharecroppers, and recovering plantations producing increasingly larger crops.

MODERN ISSUES

In the latter part of the twentieth century and the first part of the twenty-first century, the cotton industry has dealt with a number of issues. The World Trade Organization has repeatedly called for fewer government subsidies for American cotton growers. The organization claims that the U.S. government is illegally subsidizing American cotton farmers, which drives down cotton prices on the world market, creating poverty in other cotton-producing countries. The Food, Conservation, and Energy Act of 2008 (known as the 2008 Farm Bill), which was voted into law on May 22, 2008, attempted to make concessions to the World Trade Organization and to American growers, but a true compromise was not reached.

American cotton growers have been plagued by elevated energy costs for irrigation, higher fertilizer prices, and hikes in the minimum wage. Stagnant prices and increasingly pesticide-resistant weeds have also caused problems. Weather and reduced acreage (caused by increases in the acreage planted with corn) have also created trouble for American cotton growers. However, export demands have increased, with China continuing to be one of the country's biggest customers. In addition, although less acreage is being used for cotton crops, production has increased because of technological advances and newer farming methods that lower soil loss and water and pesticide usage.

Theresa L. Stowell

FURTHER READING

Broadus, Mitchell. *The Rise of Cotton Mills in the South.* Columbia: University of South Carolina Press, 2001. Looks at the history, the laborers, and the economic functions of cotton mills in America's southern states.

Jeremy, David J. *Technology and Power in the Early American Cotton Industry: James Montgomery, the Second Edition of His "Cotton Manufacture" (1840), and the Justitia Controversy About Relative Power Costs.* Philadelphia: American Philosophical Society, 1990. Provides historical information about eighteenth century writer James Montgomery and the conclusions he drew about American cotton manufacturing.

Lakwete, Angela. *Inventing the Cotton Gin: Machine and Myth in Antebellum America.* Baltimore: Johns Hopkins University Press, 2003. Argues that Eli Whitney's cotton gin was not the first model introduced to the South and, thus, not as responsible for Southern cotton production increases during the late 1700's as history books suggest.

Lichtenstein, Jack. *Field to Fabric: The Story of American Cotton Growers.* Lubbock: Texas Tech University Press, 1990. An account of the cotton industry, from the farmers to the finished product.

Yafa, Stephen. *Cotton: The Biography of a Revolutionary.* New York: Viking, 2005. Provides a general overview of the cotton industry in the United States from the seventeenth through the twenty-first centuries.

SEE ALSO: Agriculture; Civil War, U.S.; Commodity markets; Cotton gin; Panic of 1819; Panic of 1837; Plantation agriculture; Slave era; Tariff of Abominations; Tariffs.

Counterfeiting

DEFINITION: Illegal copying of currency or of brand-name or designer goods for the purpose of committing fraud or creating political and economic instability

SIGNIFICANCE: Counterfeiting of money weakens the foundation of a financial system by devaluing its currency. Counterfeiting products causes loss of profits, damage to a brand, and possible injury to unwitting consumers.

Counterfeiting of currency has very deep roots. Coinage was the only form of currency issued by governments for most of history. The early European Americans relied on coins rather than paper money, with Spanish, French, and British coins circulating widely until U.S. coinage became common. Coins could be reproduced with less valuable metals, but such forgery required some skill with metalworking and was apparently not common.

HISTORICAL BACKGROUND

Paper money is much easier to counterfeit, but it was not widely used in the United States until the end of the eighteenth century. By 1750, most of the North American colonies had experimented with forms of paper currency, but there was little in America that resembled the wide array of banknotes then available in Europe. Business in the colonies was conducted largely by credit in the forms of bills of exchange. Essentially, these were promissory notes in which one merchant pledged to pay another an agreed-upon sum on demand. Bills of exchange, easy to counterfeit, circulated much as paper money does. Despite harsh laws against counterfeiting, few counterfeiters were caught, because few government officials were looking for them. In

1775, the Continental Congress began issuing paper money, known as Continentals, but it did not take any procedures to protect the currency against counterfeiters. In 1792, the U.S. Congress passed the Mint Act, which established the coinage system and the dollar as the principal unit of currency. Without an agency dedicated to protecting the currency, counterfeiting remained a problem.

The federal government did not print paper money until 1861, despite a nationwide demand for such easy-to-transport currency. The government would occasionally issue Treasury notes during periods of financial stress, such as the War of 1812, the Mexican War, and the Panic of 1857. The federal government did not regulate the regional banks that did issue paper money in an effort to assist traders. This lack of federal interest in paper currency created a nation of counterfeiters, as it became next to impossible to distinguish legally produced paper money from illegally produced paper money.

Paper money is far more difficult to protect against forgers than is coinage. By the 1850's, more than ten thousand types of cheaply printed paper money were used legally in the United States. Unlike modern currency, this paper money was not printed on specially marked paper with specially designed inks and patterns. As a result, counterfeiters had a field day. The U.S. Treasury estimates that one-third of paper money in circulation in 1860 was counterfeit. This situation threatened to spark inflation by devaluing the currency. The chaos did not end until 1861, when Congress attempted to finance the U.S. Civil War by passing legislation permitting the Treasury to issue and circulate paper money.

From 1863 to 1929, the federal government again permitted thousands of banks to issue their own paper currency under the National Banks Acts. This money, known as national banknotes, was produced on paper authorized by the U.S. government and carried the same basic design, thus supposedly reducing the risk of counterfeiting. However, this

The huge variety of banknotes, such as these six, printed by the Confederacy during the Civil War made counterfeiting easy. (Library of Congress)

currency was counterfeited so widely that Congress established the U.S. Secret Service in 1865 to put a stop to the counterfeiting. The Secret Service largely succeeded, and counterfeiting dropped dramatically.

MODERN TECHNOLOGY

The emergence of high-quality laser printers and color photocopying during the late twentieth century aggravated the problem of counterfeit paper money, as it has become much easier to reproduce a bill with an altered denomination or to create an entirely counterfeit piece of currency in vast quantities. However, distinct differences usually remain. In genuine currency, the details of the designs are sharper with a clear background. Counterfeit currency often has blurred borders, shaded backgrounds, and fuzzy designs, as well as red and blue marks on the surface of the paper. Genuine currency has red and blue fiber as part of the paper itself. Most counterfeit coins in the modern era are produced to imitate rare objects and fool coin collectors. The most common changes in counterfeit coins are the removal, addition, or alteration of the coin's date or mint marks.

Counterfeit goods are more complicated to combat than is counterfeit currency, partly because of the worldwide scale of the problem. By the millennium, the counterfeiting of American goods had become a major concern of businesses ranging from clothing designers to film studios. Some of the "knockoffs" were sold so cheaply and under such circumstances that consumers could reasonably be expected to know that they were purchasing counterfeits. Other consumers, such as those purchasing pharmaceutical products on the Internet, were unaware. Counterfeit products have proven costly to manufacturers, who lose both profits and reputations for quality and, perhaps, exclusiveness.

Caryn E. Neumann

FURTHER READING

Bender, Klaus W. *Moneymakers: The Secret World of Banknote Printing.* New York: John Wiley & Sons, 2006. Revealing exploration of how currency notes—both American and foreign—are produced, with fascinating anecdotal material.

Mihm, Stephen. *A Nation of Counterfeiters: Capitalists, Con Men, and the Making of the United States.* Cambridge, Mass.: Harvard University Press, 2007. Excellent source providing a historical perspective, this volume presents true stories of counterfeiting during the early years of the independent United States and discusses the impact counterfeiting had on the economy and growth of the nation.

Scott, Kenneth, and David R. Johnson. *Counterfeiting in Colonial America.* Philadelphia: University of Pennsylvania Press, 2000. Lively study of counterfeiting in Britain's North American colonies.

Tremmel, George B. *Counterfeit Currency of the Confederate States of America.* Jefferson, N.C.: McFarland, 2003. Among the many financial problems that the Confederacy had during the Civil War was the rampant counterfeiting of its currency. This book examines how the Confederacy's treasury department tried to stop counterfeiting. Includes illustrations of the counterfeit currency and information on the methods used to produce it.

The Use and Counterfeiting of U.S. Currency Abroad. Washington, D.C.: U.S. Department of the Treasury, 2003. Federal government publication on the growing problem of foreign counterfeiting of U.S. currency.

Warner, Richard D., and Richard M. Adam. *Introduction to Security Printing.* New York: Graphic Arts Center, 2005. Study of the technical aspects of printing currency notes that are difficult to counterfeit.

Williams, Marcela M., and Richard G. Anderson. *Handicapping Currency Design: Counterfeit Deterrence and Visual Accessibility in the United States and Abroad.* St. Louis: Federal Reserve Bank of St. Louis, 2007. Discusses the various trade-offs that governments make when deciding how best to design currency and the necessity of periodic design changes to help protect currency against counterfeiting. Pays special attention to currency design in relation to the needs of persons who are visually impaired.

SEE ALSO: Banking; Civil War, U.S.; Confederate currency; Currency; Gold standard; Inflation; Mint, U.S.; Organized crime; Secret Service, U.S.; Treasury, U.S. Department of the.

Coxey's Army

THE EVENT: First mass protest march on Washington, D.C., in which unemployed people from across the United States converged on the Capitol to lobby for the creation of a federally supported public works program

DATE: March 26-May 1, 1894

PLACE: Washington, D.C.

SIGNIFICANCE: Coxey's Army advocated the then-radical notion that the federal government should take direct responsibility for aiding in economic recovery by creating programs for the unemployed. The demonstration was the first national protest by unemployed persons in response to what they perceived as employers' indifference to their welfare, and their use of the Capitol as a venue for protest foreshadowed later labor and civil rights protests of the twentieth century.

The protest march and demonstration that would become known as Coxey's Army was begun by three hundred unemployed men organized by Populist businessman Jacob Coxey and labor activist Carl Browne in Massillon, Ohio. Their ranks were augmented by similar groups inspired across the United States, chiefly the Western states, bringing the total number of participants to five hundred. The group publicized the plight of the unemployed and urged Congress (unsuccessfully) to create a federal program of public works, chiefly road building. The program, to be instituted by cities, towns, and county governments, would have been financed by non-interest-bearing bonds.

During the last three decades of the nineteenth century, the United States transitioned away from being a predominantly rural and agrarian society, as the nation's production and consumption both came to be centered increasingly in urban industrial areas. This transition created the economic conditions that Coxey's Army was organized to protest. In addition to public works programs, the group demanded the institution of a livable minimum wage. It was not unique in this regard, as many citizens struggled during the decade.

Federal positions regarding the proper response to economic crises at this time ranged from Republican preferences for levying additional taxes on imports to proposals to curb government spending when revenues fell. In general, unemployment was regarded as akin to a natural phenomenon whose causes were beyond humans' abilities to affect, and politicians were reluctant to intervene. Government intervention in labor problems in the past had often taken the form of instituting probusiness monetary policies and opposing strikes by the working class, sometimes with federal troops.

The disciplined behavior of the marchers in Coxey's Army gave the lie to the popular belief that being unemployed and poor was the result of individuals being lazy or weak, as many were professional men simply unable to find work of any kind above the menial level. Moreover, numerous incidents of seizure of property by Coxey's affiliates in the West (such as the commandeering of trains) forced the recognition that the frontier could no longer be relied on as an economic safety valve. Earlier, it had been believed that the endless frontier of the West could absorb all persons seeking a new life and unable to find it in the East. The manifest failure of the West to support all its residents rendered that belief a thing of the past.

Robert B. Ridinger

FURTHER READING

Barber, Lucy G. *Marching on Washington: The Forging of an American Political Tradition.* Berkeley: University of California Press, 2002.

Folsom, Franklin. *Impatient Armies of the Poor: The Story of Collective Action of the Unemployed, 1808-1942.* Niwot, Colo.: University Press of Colorado, 1991.

Schwantes, Carlos A. *Coxey's Army: An American Odyssey.* Lincoln: University of Nebraska Press, 1985.

SEE ALSO: Boycotts, consumer; Labor history; Labor strikes; New Deal programs; Poor People's Campaign of 1968.

Crash of 1929. *See* Stock market crash of 1929

Credit card buying

DEFINITION: Use of cards, attached to revolving charge accounts, to purchase goods and services for which payment is remitted to the card issuer at a later date, usually on a monthly basis

SIGNIFICANCE: General-purpose credit cards, unknown in the United States before 1958, have become an essential feature of commerce. Credit card purchases totaled more than $4 trillion in 2007, and total indebtedness on credit cards stood at $880 billion. Revenue from interest, cardholder fees, penalties, and merchant interchange fees made the institutions responsible for issuing credit cards among America's most profitable for investors. Credit cards stimulated personal consumption but also encouraged individuals to incur unprecedented levels of debt.

Credit card buying has contributed to one of the most profound social and cultural revolutions of post-World War II America. Credit and debt have been integral parts of the American economy since colonial times, but the general-purpose bank credit card, allowing individuals to obtain goods and services from multiple retailers on credit, dates from only 1958.

EARLY CREDIT PRACTICES

A Puritan bias toward thrift that stigmatized consumer debt characterized American attitudes in the nineteenth and early twentieth century. For the sake of convenience, merchants allowed regular customers to record purchases in an account book, paying at the end of the month. In 1926, Sears, Roebuck and Company went a step further, issuing an embossed metal charge card that could be used to make a purchase at any Sears store nationwide or from any Sears catalog. Other retail chains followed suit. Such store cards rarely charged interest or fees, counting on customer loyalty to offset costs. Stores also offered installment-sales con-

tracts for big-ticket items such as appliances. The premium a person paid for an installment-sales purchase was typically modest, in contrast to modern-day rent-to-own agreements, which can easily double the price of an item.

In 1950, an association of New York restaurants catering to business customers began issuing the Diners Club card, good at any participating establishment. This was a charge card rather than a credit card, requiring that balances be paid in full within thirty days. Over the years, Diners Club expanded to other aspects of travel and entertainment within the United States and abroad. Diners Club still operates as a subsidiary of MasterCard.

The first national general-purpose charge card was the American Express Green Card, issued by American Express in 1958. The idea of a general-purpose charge card arose naturally from the company's existing traveler's check and international money-transfer operations. Also in 1958, Bank of America in Fresno, California, began issuing BankAmericard, a credit card. In contrast to Diners Club and American Express, Bank of America targeted its BankAmericard toward middle-class consumers rather than business travelers.

In 1965, Bank of America expanded its opera-

Credit cards, such as these depicted outside a New York parking garage in 2006, are used by many consumers. (AP/Wide World Photos)

tions outside California. Banks in other states oper-ated Bank of America's card services as a franchise. In 1977, BankAmericard's licensees banded to-gether to form Visa. Meanwhile, in 1967, a group of rival California banks had begun offering MasterCard as both a charge and credit card. Sears, Roebuck launched the Discover card, chronologi-cally the last of the major bank credit cards, in 1985.

Credit card usage in the United States exploded around 1980, when companies started aggressively marketing cards outside the original middle-class base. In the twenty-first century, total purchases us-ing credit and debit cards amount to trillions of dol-lars annually. Aggregate credit card debt in the United States rose from $55 billion (15.8 percent of total consumer debt) in 1980 to $239 billion (30.2 percent) in 1990 and to $880 billion in 2007. Revenue generated by interchange fees (charged to service providers), interest, penalties, and arrange-ments with corporations providing consumer ser-vices make the parent companies of the major credit cards in the United States among the fastest-grow-ing and most profitable corporate entities in the world.

MARKETING STRATEGIES

Marketing credit is a huge business in its own right. Credit card companies direct-mailed 5.3 bil-lion credit card solicitations to Americans in 2007, roughly 20 per adult. Students, people who have re-cently filed for bankruptcy, retirees, and those whose credit reports show recent defaults receive a disproportionate share of solicitations, while low-income wage earners with indifferent credit ratings and convenience users with long histories of prompt repayment receive very few. Credit card so-licitations and billing statements constitute about 7 percent of the U.S. Postal Service's letter mail vol-ume. Card issuers also advertise heavily in the press and on television. They have found that unsolicited e-mail is ineffective and avoid it, but they have a high level of presence on the Internet as Web site spon-sors.

A typical solicitation touts personal convenience, associates modern technology with professional suc-cess, and encourages emotional spending. It may appeal to altruism, either by picturing the card-holder bringing joy to friends and family through spending, or by embedded giving, that is, contribut-ing some small fraction of total purchases to a wor-

thy cause. A very successful partnership between Discover and the Smithsonian Institution raised funds for the Smithsonian's one-hundredth anni-versary (in 1999) through a card ironically bearing the image of Benjamin Franklin, a great proponent of thrift.

Colleges and other nonprofits derive substantial income from credit card companies in return for ac-cess to clients, who are subjected to carefully tai-lored campaigns. Some colleges go so far as to com-bine a bank credit card with a student body card, allowing students to charge tuition and fees—and pay credit card interest rates on the balance. Cash-strapped nonprofit hospitals routinely include an application for a medical credit card with admis-sions paperwork. On discharge, the uninsured indi-vidual discovers that the medical bill is subject to the high interest rates and lack of flexibility characteris-tic of credit card debt.

Bank cards offer a bewildering array of incen-tives, including cashback offers, frequent flier miles, travel insurance policies, and discounts at certain re-tailers, as well as complicated rate structures giving some customers low interest rates. Despite provi-sions of the Truth in Lending Act in its various itera-tions, credit card solicitations continue to wave the rewards carrot in a customer's face while carefully hiding the penalties stick in a mass of contractual fine print. Most contracts offering low interest rates provide for reset on default to rates averaging 18 to 19 percent but potentially as high as 37 percent. For a number of years, many contracts also included a universal default clause, whereby failure to pay the minimum on one card triggered the higher rate on all cards, even those issued by different companies. Facing consumer outrage and a cry for federal regu-lation, the major credit card companies have since backed off on universal default clauses.

CREDIT CARDS AND CONSUMERS

Credit card buyers may be roughly grouped into two classes: convenience users, who usually pay their balances in full at the end of the month and pay very little in interest and fees, and revolvers, who use their cards to borrow money longer term and pay heavily for the privilege in high interest rates and penalties. Until the early 1980's, companies issued credit cards conservatively, and the majority of bor-rowers were convenience users. Later they discov-ered that revolvers generated more profit and be-

FAMILY USAGE OF GENERAL-PURPOSE CREDIT CARDS, 1995-2004

Age of Family Head	Percentage Having a Card	Median Charged in Previous Month ($)	Percentage Having an Unpaid Balance	Median Balance ($)	Percentage of Families Who . . .		
					Almost Always Pay Off the Balance	Sometimes Pay Off the Balance	Hardly Ever Pay Off the Balance
Less than 35	60.6	200	66.1	1,500	49.0	20.4	30.6
35-44	73.3	300	70.8	2,400	41.6	26.2	32.2
45-54	77.5	300	61.2	3,000	49.3	23.9	26.8
55-64	78.2	400	46.1	2,500	66.8	16.8	16.5
65-74	75.5	300	37.7	2,300	70.7	13.4	15.9
75 and older	65.4	200	32.2	1,100	77.5	12.9	9.7

Source: Data from the *Statistical Abstract of the United States, 2008* (Washington, D.C.: Department of Commerce, Economics and Statistics Administration, Bureau of the Census, Data User Services Division, 2008)

Note: Definition of family includes single-person families. General-purpose credit cards include MasterCard, Visa, Optima, and Discover cards; cards used only for business purposes are excluded. Dollars are given in constant 2004 dollars based on consumer price index data published by the U.S. Bureau of Labor Statistics.

gan aggressively marketing cards to low-income and less creditworthy individuals, such as students. Both credit card buying and credit card indebtedness rose steeply as a consequence. Despite this, nearly half of cardholders could be classified as convenience users in 2007, and although the average credit card debt per American household was $8,940 in 2004, the median was only $1,900, another indication that the system works favorably for large numbers of people.

Some economists see the subsidy of convenience users by revolvers as an important factor in the widening gap between the rich and poor in the United States, but this is only partly true. The ability to budget, matching expenditures to income, is only weakly correlated to absolute income. The critical factor in credit card debt is a cognitive disconnect between earnings and consumption. The people most vulnerable to the credit card's buy-now, pay-later pitch are those with fluctuating, unpredictable incomes, and young people just embarking on careers. Successive generations have shown themselves more ready to incur nonmortgage consumer debt, partly in response to changing attitudes about financial obligations and the morality of borrowing, and partly in response to the growing difficulty in making ends meet in an economy characterized by

stagnant entry-level salaries, poorer job security, sky-rocketing housing costs, and unstable families. Using a credit card to avoid facing the consequences of problems caused by any of these leaves a person drowning in debt.

Credit card debt is generally unsecured consumer debt and can be discharged in bankruptcy. In 2005, credit card companies, faced with growing levels of default involving tens of thousands of dollars worth of debt, lobbied for changes to bankruptcy laws intended to discourage people from filing.

Some of the impetus came from a weakening housing market. To minimize default on high-interest income-generating loans, credit card companies encouraged people to take out low-interest home equity loans to pay off their credit cards. When housing prices plateaued in 2006 and then began to decline, this source of credit dried up. An unsecured loan, which would have been discharged in bankruptcy, became a secured loan, contributing to home foreclosure. Some of the impetus behind aggressive marketing of credit cards to students lies in the assumption that the student (who has minimal current income and unknown job prospects) will spend extravagantly and then take out a low-interest, nondischargeable student loan to pay off the credit card.

One area in which credit cards have had a positive impact is small business. As of 2000, credit cards had supplanted direct bank loans as the top source of start-up capital for small entrepreneurial businesses. In contrast, loans from the United States Small Business Administration accounted for only 2 percent of total volume. Information technology companies, which are not highly capitalized, have been notable beneficiaries. Some of these have been highly successful. Some experts suspect that banks may have curtailed business loan availability to enable them to take advantage of more lucrative credit card contracts, especially when the business applying for a loan has some track record as a going concern.

In the twenty-first century, an increasing proportion of credit "card" purchases take place over the Internet. These transactions do not generate interchange fees and involve a higher proportion of debit card and convenience users than transactions at conventional stores. The convenience of these electronic transactions stimulates commerce generally but does not generate much revenue for the issuing financial institution.

Martha Sherwood

FURTHER READING

Bertolo, Giusseppe, Richard Disney, and Charles Grant, eds. *The Economics of Consumer Credit.* Cambridge, Mass.: MIT Press, 2006. A multiauthored work covering Italy and Great Britain as well as the United States.

Evans, David S., and Richard Schmalensee. *Paying with Plastic: The Digital Revolution in Buying and Borrowing.* Cambridge, Mass.: MIT Press, 2005. Includes a good history of the development of credit cards, with clear explanations of all levels of the process of using credit cards from the individual consumer to global investment markets.

Kamenetz, Anya. *Debt Generation: Why Now Is a Terrible Time to Be Young.* New York: Riverhead Books, 2006. A young journalist examines the impact of credit card and student loan debt on young people in an era of declining career opportunities.

Manning, Robert D. *Credit Card Nation: The Consequences of America's Addiction to Credit.* New York: Basic Books, 2000. Has a consumer bias; traces the history of credit cards and their impact on society.

Sullivan, Theresa, Elizabeth Warren, and Jay Westbrook. *As We Forgive Our Debtors: Bankruptcy and Consumer Credit in America.* Oxford, England: Oxford University Press, 1989. Based on a large study of consumer bankruptcies, this work focuses on economic trends and has a good treatment of women's issues.

_____. *The Fragile Middle Class: Americans in Debt.* New Haven, Conn.: Yale University Press, 2000. This volume by a consumer-oriented, socially conscious group of economists explores the impact of skyrocketing debt, including consumer debt, on American families.

SEE ALSO: Banking; Bankruptcy law; Catalog shopping; Diners Club; Drive-through businesses; Interest rates; Internet; Retail trade industry; Sears, Roebuck and Company; Small Business Administration; Truth-in-lending laws.

Crédit Mobilier of America scandal

THE EVENT: Revelation by the *New York Sun* that a construction company had bribed U.S. representatives with cheap stock to facilitate the company's illegal manipulation of railroad contracts

DATE: 1872

PLACE: Washington, D.C.

SIGNIFICANCE: The Crédit Mobilier of America scandal entered the annals of American business as an example of corruption typical in post-Civil War commerce, especially in railroad construction.

During the 1860's, westward expansion of the railroad system was of prime importance to the economy of the United States, and the government was prepared to provide substantial subsidies to ensure the project's completion. In 1862, George Francis Train, a vice president for publicity of Union Pacific Railroad, created two companies, Crédit Mobilier of America and Crédit Foncier, to oversee the railroad's western expansion. Both companies were modeled after French companies and introduced new concepts of corporate organization into the American system. Crédit Mobilier was one of the first companies to take advantage of limited liability in its financial structure. Stockholders were liable only for the amount of their investment in the company, rather than to the full extent of their personal assets.

Seeing an opportunity for enormous profit,

Thomas C. Durant, Union Pacific's major investor, quickly assumed control of Crédit Mobilier, the company involved with financing the railroad's construction. In 1864, he arranged for Herbert W. Hoxie to bid on construction of one hundred miles of rail from Omaha, Nebraska, west. There were no other bidders. Hoxie obtained a contract, which he signed over to Durant, who immediately transferred it to Crédit Mobilier as a subcontractor. Crédit Mobilier billed Union Pacific twice the normal fees for track work. The company also sold members of Congress shares of stock at extremely low cost in exchange for their advocacy of additional funding for the project.

When construction failed to proceed at a reasonable pace, President Abraham Lincoln asked U.S. representative Oakes Ames to remedy the situation. In 1867, Ames arranged for his brother Oliver Ames II, to become president of Union Pacific and he became president of Crédit Mobilier. Ames continued the practices of giving stock options to representatives and of overcharging for the construction.

In 1872, Ames got into a serious disagreement with one of his associates, Henry Simpson McComb, who gave information to the *New York Sun* newspaper. During the presidential campaign, the newspaper, which opposed the reelection of President Ulysses S. Grant, revealed that Crédit Mobilier had charged Union Pacific $72 million for $53 million worth of work, almost bankrupting the railroad company. It also exposed the fact that members of Congress had received large amounts of the resulting profit. The congressional investigation by chief counsel Aaron F. Perry resulted in accusations against thirteen representatives and a recommendation that Ames be expelled from Congress. Congress, however, decided merely to censure him.

Shawncey Webb

FURTHER READING

Crawford, Jay Boyd. *The Crédit Mobilier: Its Origin and History, Its Work of Constructing the Union Pacific Railroad, and the Relation of Members of Congress.* Providence, R.I.: AMS Press, 1980.

Martin, Edward Winslow. *Behind the Scenes in Washington: Being a Complete and Graphic Account of the Crédit Mobilier Investigation.* Whitefish, Mont.: Kessinger, 2007.

SEE ALSO: Business crimes; Congress, U.S.; Construction industry; Railroads; Stock markets.

Credit unions

DEFINITION: Cooperative financial establishments under the control of their membership

SIGNIFICANCE: Initially designed to provide credit to needy households, credit unions gradually became more like banks, representing a viable alternative to banks for consumers seeking a community-based financial establishment.

Credit unions were created as a means of dealing with the credit problems of low-income families, particularly industrial workers. Each institution formed around a cohesive social group, such as employees of the same businesses, members of churches, members of trade unions, or members of fraternal organizations. The cooperative principle emphasized that members were committing their savings to create a pool of loan funds for people whom they already knew. The implicit social pressure made borrowers more likely to repay. Putting money into the credit union involved acquiring shares, although they very much resembled deposits. For many years their chief business was extending personal loans to members. Group cohesiveness helped keep down credit risks and transactions costs. Credit unions were and remain not-for-profit organizations.

ORIGINS

Credit unions originated in Western Europe during the late nineteenth century. The idea spread to Canada and from there to New Hampshire, where the St. Mary's Bank Credit Union was formed in November, 1908. Massachusetts adopted enabling legislation in 1909. Edward Filene, a prominent retailer and philanthropist, was an influential promoter. He recognized that many low-income persons were victimized by loan sharks. State "usury" laws prohibiting high interest rates on loans caused banks and other reputable lenders to avoid the personal loan market, where credit risks were high and loans typically very small.

Initially, the credit union movement spread slowly—there were only 190 in 1921. Employers encouraged credit unions in the workplace, giving them office space and management advice. By 1931, there were 1,244 credit unions, but their total assets were only $34 million, so the average size was less than $30,000. However, the Great Depression of the 1930's brought many new members, fleeing the disastrous problems among banks and other deposit institutions. Congress adopted in 1934 the Federal Credit Union Act, which authorized federal charters for credit unions, giving some assurance of regulatory oversight (but not deposit insurance), and opening the entire country to credit union organization. Credit unions were exempt from the federal corporate income tax—a condition that has infuriated the banking industry. When tax rates went sky-high during the 1930's, tax exemption became attractive to many entrepreneurs who could achieve high salaries and favorable borrowing opportunities through organizing credit unions.

The number of credit unions grew rapidly from two thousand in 1934 to more than nine thousand by 1941. The numbers actually declined during World War II and passed ten thousand only in 1950, at which point they had about $1 billion of total assets— so average assets were still less than $100,000 per institution.

After 1950, market interest rates moved steadily higher, but regulations prevented banks and other deposit institutions from matching the increases. Credit unions were able to pay higher rates, and steadily increased market share. By 1970, there were nearly twenty-four thousand credit unions. Their assets had risen to about $16 billion. This was still only about 10 percent as large as the savings and loan industry. In 1970, Congress created the National Credit Union Administration (NCUA) to charter and regulate federal credit unions. A National Credit Union Share Insurance Fund was created to insure federal credit unions. The new insurance covered 22 million credit union members. Many state-chartered credit unions chose not to take federal insurance, and by 1981, sixteen states had created their own share-insurance programs.

GOVERNMENT DEREGULATION

Credit unions shared in the changes brought about by deregulation in and after 1980. In particular, they were able to offer the equivalent of interest-bearing checking accounts and to make mortgage loans. In 1982, the NCUA allowed individual credit unions to expand their membership to include multiple unrelated employer groups. A Supreme Court decision in 1998 invalidated this latitude, but Congress responded in the same year by passing the Credit Union Membership Access Act, which permitted broad membership.

Credit unions shared in the adverse developments affecting other deposit institutions after 1980. The state share-insurance programs were overwhelmed, and virtually all surviving credit unions migrated into the federal insurance program.

By the new millennium, credit unions had become much more like banks in terms of services provided, but served primarily households rather than business customers. In addition to the range of deposit and loan services, they were providing automatic teller machines (ATMs), credit cards, and online banking. Many had become big businesses— there were more than one hundred with more than $1 billion of assets apiece. Some large credit unions provided operational services to other credit unions. Some credit unions converted into commercial banks, a process criticized for giving windfall benefits to top management to the detriment of ordinary members. In 2004, there were about sixteen thousand

Customers and workers at a credit union in Greenhills, Ohio, in 1939. Credit unions enjoyed growth in the 1930's. (Library of Congress)

credit unions with about $655 billion of assets. Most tried to maintain a user-friendly style and to promote good financial management by their members.

Paul B. Trescott

FURTHER READING
Fountain, Wendell V. *The Credit Union World: Theory, Process, Practice—Cases and Applications.* Bloomington, Ind.: AuthorHouse, 2007. Examines all aspects of credit unions, from history to their future, covering topics such as governance and marketing.
Mishkin, Fredric S., and Stanley G. Eakins. *Financial Markets and Institutions.* 6th ed. Boston: Pearson Prentice Hall, 2009. Basic work on the financial world and its institutions, contains a chapter on savings and loan associations and credit unions.
Moody, J. Carroll, and Gilbert Fite. *The Credit Union Movement: Origins and Development, 1850-1970.* Lincoln: University of Nebraska Press, 1971. This scholarly study emphasizes the idealistic motivation of many credit union developers.
Pugh, Olin S., and F. Jerry Ingram. *Credit Unions: A Movement Becomes an Industry.* Reston, Va.: Reston, 1984. Rich in detail on the transition from philanthropy to business.
Wilcox, James. "Credit Union Conversions: Ripe for Abuse . . . and Reforms," *Credit Union Times*, July, 2006. This newsletter provides a good view of current credit union conditions. The article documents criticisms of conversions to banks.

SEE ALSO: Banking; Farm Credit Administration; Savings and loan associations.

"Cross of Gold" speech

THE EVENT: Speech delivered by William Jennings Bryan at the Democratic National Convention, advocating that the federal government adopt a free silver policy

DATE: July 9, 1896

PLACE: Chicago, Illinois

SIGNIFICANCE: Attacking the gold monetary standard in favor of bimetallism, Bryan defended Western farmers and the "common man" against banks and the wealth of the Eastern United States.

U.S. representative William Jennings Bryan of Nebraska spoke at the Democratic National Convention of 1896, contending that the gold standard should be abandoned in favor of free silver coinage. This change, he believed, would ease the burden of American farmers and debt-ridden laborers. In a carefully prepared speech incorporating balanced phrases and biblical allusions, Bryan appealed to logic, American history, patriotism, and populism. An accomplished orator, he invoked the names of Thomas Jefferson and Andrew Jackson, Democratic Party saints, in support of his "righteous cause."

Speaking directly to the romantic pastoral sentiments of his audience, Bryan praised the pioneers of the American West, who lived close to nature, unlike city dwellers and Eastern bankers. In monetary policy, he asserted that Americans should be leaders in bimetallism rather than abject followers of Great Britain and other nations. Bryan brought his address to a rousing conclusion, with a statement that would always thereafter be associated with him: "You shall not press down upon the brow of labor this crown of thorns, you shall not crucify mankind upon a cross of gold."

The speech catapulted Bryan, a thirty-six-year-old congressman, into national prominence. After hearing it, the party chose him as its presidential candidate in 1896. It thereby committed itself to incorporating bimetallism as a key plank in its platform, shaping the national debate on the gold standard.

Bryan would run for the presidency unsuccessfully three times and serve as Woodrow Wilson's first secretary of state. He remained a national figure until his death in 1925. His later defense of religious fundamentalism and his participation in the Scopes trial at the end of his life, when his powers were diminished, tarnished his reputation. However, with his resonant voice, impeccable diction, and ability to turn a memorable phrase, he is remembered as both "the American Cicero" and "the Great Commoner."

Allene Phy-Olsen

FURTHER READING
Kazin, Michael. *A Godly Hero: The Life of William Jennings Bryan.* New York: Knopf, 2006.
Leinward, Gerald. *William Jennings Bryan: An Uncertain Trumpet.* Lanham, Md.: Rowman and Littlefield, 2006.

Springen, Donald K. *William Jennings Bryan: Orator of Small-Town America.* New York: Greenwood Press, 1991.

SEE ALSO: American Bimetallic League national convention; *Coin's Financial School*; Currency; Gold standard; Klondike gold rush; Mint, U.S.; Monetary policy, federal.

Cumberland Road

THE EVENT: Building of a toll-free road, with federal funding and planning, to link the eastern seaboard with the western territories

DATE: 1811-1818

PLACE: From the Potomac River at Cumberland, Maryland, to the Ohio River at Wheeling, later in West Virginia

SIGNIFICANCE: One of the first toll-free highways in the United States, the Cumberland Road offered Americans overland passage and access to new markets. A stable road surface made the route attractive for entrepreneurs looking to transport people and goods to the expanding western frontier.

As early as 1802, the U.S. Congress discussed the need for a federally maintained road to connect the eastern seaboard with the expanding western territories. Existing overland routes were in need of repair and expansion, and they lacked connections to other turnpikes. The growth of population in the territories that became the states of Ohio (1803), Indiana (1816), and Illinois (1818) further spurred the need to connect the east with the west.

With President Thomas Jefferson's support, in 1806, Congress approved an act to construct a road from the Potomac River in Cumberland, Maryland, to the Ohio River in Wheeling, in what later became West Virginia. The act specified that the road would measure 4 rods (about 66 feet) in width, with a raised surface of stone, earth, gravel, or sand, and with drainage ditches on either side. Congress appropriated $30,000 for the cost of construction. Jefferson appointed three commissioners to direct the project. The commissioners assembled a surveying team to plot the route of the road, and in 1808, the six-member team completed its expedition.

Construction of the road began in 1811 near Cumberland. Two years later, the first 10-mile section opened to travelers. Road builders erected massive stone arches to traverse rivers, streams, and valleys. By 1818, the road, which stretched approximately 130 miles, reached the Ohio River in Wheeling.

The Cumberland Road provided an important overland link between the centers of commerce in the east and the expanding markets on the western frontier, long before the advent of railroads. Although the path was treacherous in places, it was not as unreliable as canal and riverboat routes, and attracted multitudes of settlers, business owners, and explorers to the western frontier.

Expansion and improvement of the Cumberland Road continued during the antebellum period. The

Part of the Cumberland Road, just east of Washington, Pennsylvania, in 1910. (Library of Congress)

path stretched east to Baltimore and west toward St. Louis, stopping in 1839 for lack of funds in Vandalia, Illinois. During the 1820's, road builders improved sections of the path using the macadam paving process. The route became known as the National Pike and later as the National Road. Much of the original path of the Cumberland Road is today part of U.S. Highway 40.

Aaron D. Purcell

FURTHER READING

Carvell, Clarence. *The National Road: A Photographic Journey.* Baltimore: Heritage Special Edition/ American Literary Press, 2007.

Day, Reed B. The Cumberland Road: A History of the National Road. Apollo, Pa.: Closson, 1996.

Raitz, Karl, ed. *A Guide to the National Road.* Baltimore: Johns Hopkins University Press, 1996.

SEE ALSO: Canals; Highways; Railroads; Transportation, U.S. Department of; Turnpikes; Wilderness Road.

Currency

DEFINITION: The paper money and coins that constitute a major part of a country's circulating money supply

SIGNIFICANCE: The money supply is an important determinant of aggregate demand and business conditions in general. Until 1935, a significant proportion of U.S. paper money was issued by commercial banks. The opportunity to issue banknotes was an important source of lending power for banks.

Before the United States gained its independence, paper money was issued by the various British colonial governments. Massachusetts made the first issue in 1690 to finance military expenditures: The bills could simply be paid out to soldiers and suppliers. Most colonies issued currency in the wartime period of 1713-1718, causing significant price inflation. Issuing paper money was a means of financing government deficits before the development of well-ordered interest-bearing government bonds. The notes were not formally convertible into gold and silver (specie) but could be used to pay taxes. Several colonial governments established loan of-

fices, mostly for mortgage loans secured by land. The borrowers received paper money. The new issues of paper were withdrawn as the loans were repaid. Some colonies managed their money creation with restraint, and the money supply grew enough to facilitate the spread of a market economy, specialization, and exchange. Real inflationary abuses occurred in Rhode Island, the Carolinas, and Massachusetts. The British government tried to stamp out the practice and issued a general prohibition in 1764. This enraged many colonists and was one of the many grievances precipitating the move for independence. During the 1770's, the total money supply was about $12 million, of which half was British and foreign coins and half was paper money.

REVOLUTIONARY WAR AND CONFEDERATION

During the Revolutionary War, both the Continental Congress and individual states issued paper money to pay troops and purchase supplies. About $11 million was issued in 1775 and $44 million in the next two years, about 70 percent of it by the national government. Congress persuaded northern states to halt their own issues in 1778-1779, but Congress poured out $60 million in 1778 and $140 million in 1779. Severe inflation resulted: By 1780, wholesale prices in Philadelphia were about one hundred times their level in 1776. Efforts to curb depreciation of paper issues involved making them legal tender and imposing price controls. However, many farmers and merchants simply refused to accept the government's paper.

In 1780, Congress shifted to borrowing by issuing interest-bearing securities and stopped issuing paper money. The last phase of the war was concentrated in the South, and Virginia issued more than $150 million of currency in 1780-1781. With the end of the war in 1781, most of the currency was withdrawn through taxation and through the issue of bonds. The Federal Funding Act of 1790 provided for acceptance of continental currency toward purchase of federal bonds, at a rate of one cent on the dollar.

Congress decreed that the dollar should be the national monetary unit. In 1780, it chartered the first modern commercial bank, the Bank of North America, in Philadelphia. Two more banks were created in 1784, one in Boston and one in New York. Each began issuing banknote currency, typically paying out the notes to borrowers. The notes were convertible on demand into specie. Coins issued in Great Britain, in Europe, and in Latin America circulated extensively.

A serious economic depression swept the country during the mid-1780's. Seven states resumed issuing paper money, partly to make loans to distressed citizens and partly to cover government deficits created when tax revenues declined. Nearly $3 million of government paper was issued in 1785-1786, creating alarm that the wartime financial disorder would be repeated. In response, the U.S. Constitution of 1787 gave Congress the power to coin money and regulate its value and forbade state governments from coining money, issuing bills of credit, or making anything except gold or silver legal tender.

THE NEW REPUBLIC

Alexander Hamilton, the first secretary of the Treasury, initiated major policies regarding currency. At his urging, in 1791, Congress chartered the First Bank of the United States, which opened offices in major port cities, where its banknotes became an important payment medium. Hamilton also shaped the Coinage Act of 1792, which created the United States Mint. The law provided for a variety of gold, silver, and copper coins. Private individuals could bring gold or silver to the mint and it would be coined for them. However, the government did not initiate the process. Coinage output was not large, and foreign coins continued to circulate extensively.

The number of banks and the volume of banknote currency grew steadily. By 1811, there were eighty-eight state-chartered banks. By then, circulating currency comprised about $15 million in gold and silver coins and $28 million in banknotes. The War of 1812 generated inflationary pressure from large federal military spending financed by borrowing heavily from the banks. More than one hundred new banks were created. In 1814, most of the banks ceased redeeming their notes in specie, which freed them to expand their loans and note issues still more.

To restore order to the monetary situation, Congress chartered the Second Bank of the United States in 1816 (the charter of the first had expired in 1811). The new bank was larger than its predecessor and had as many as twenty-five branches. Its banknote issues were redeemed in specie, and it pressured the other banks to do the same. However, the Second Bank of the United States contributed to a severe boom-and-bust cycle of credit expansion and contraction in 1817-1818. President Andrew Jackson strongly opposed the bank and prevented its recharter. It ceased operation in 1841.

The number of state-chartered or unchartered banks increased greatly during the 1830's, and the quality of banknote currency deteriorated. "Wildcat" banks were established in remote areas, making note redemption difficult. Many banks failed during a severe business contraction beginning in 1837. Bank expansion resumed during the 1840's, to be interrupted by another bank panic in 1857. By 1860, there were more than 1,500 banks, almost all issuing their own notes. Coinage legislation during the 1850's created the hierarchy of copper-nickel penny and silver dime, quarter, and half-dollar. (The nickel was added in 1866.) Circulation of foreign coins was prohibited in 1857.

CIVIL WAR DEVELOPMENTS

No formal government paper money was issued after 1787, although the Treasury notes issued during some business recessions temporarily performed that function. The outbreak of the Civil War in 1861 generated a huge increase in federal spending, and part of the resulting deficit was financed by issuing paper money. There were several different types, but the most nearly permanent were United States notes. In February, 1862, Congress authorized the issue of $150 million in legal-tender notes, soon named greenbacks for their distinctive design. More issues followed.

Monetary expansion generated inflation, and by 1864 consumer prices in the North were 75 percent higher than they had been in 1860. The Confederacy relied even more heavily on paper money issues, which totaled more than a billion dollars and generated far worse inflation—prices in early 1865 were nearly a hundred times those of 1861.

The war provided a basis for government efforts to reform banknote currency. In 1863, Congress authorized the creation of the National Banking system. A bank could obtain a federal charter that permitted it to issue national bank notes that were standardized in design (except for the name of the issuing bank) and secured by U.S. government bonds. In 1865, a punitive tax was imposed on note issues by nonnational banks, and notes from these banks soon disappeared. Between federal paper money and national banknotes, the nation's paper currency achieved very high quality—especially since the Secret Service effectively combated counterfeiting.

At the end of the war, neither greenbacks nor national banknotes were convertible into specie at par. Political pressure to restore par convertibility was strong, but even greater was the pressure to avoid a deflationary monetary contraction. Market forces gradually brought down the price of gold, and par convertibility was achieved in 1879. Congress authorized new forms of paper money: silver certificates (1878—redeemable in silver coin) and gold certificates (1863, but important only after 1882—redeemable in gold coin).

Women examining currency at the Bureau of Engraving and Printing in 1929. (Library of Congress)

The economy continued to experience strong business cycles and periodic depressions, and there was pressure for monetary expansion to relieve depressions. During the 1890's this pressure underlay the campaign for "free silver"—a proposal to allow unlimited coinage of silver into dollars at a ratio of sixteen to one with gold—a ratio that significantly overvalued silver and would have led to extensive coinage. The proposal was a major part of William Jennings Bryan's presidential campaign in 1896. Bryan's defeat and restoration of prosperity and rising prices put an end to the silver agitation. The Gold Standard Act of 1900 declared gold to be the country's monetary standard and ordered that all other forms of money be maintained at parity with gold.

THE FEDERAL RESERVE SYSTEM

The United States continued to be plagued by bank panics. The panic of 1907 led to renewed effort for currency and banking reform, culminating in the Federal Reserve Act of 1913. The act created a new type of paper money—Federal Reserve notes. These were supposed to be an "elastic" currency, capable of expansion during a panic when the banks were being pressed to redeem deposits in currency.

Banks that chose to become members of the Federal Reserve system would maintain reserve deposits with their regional Federal Reserve bank. They could always draw currency from their reserve deposits, borrowing from the Federal Reserve if they needed more.

The new system seemed to work well. When the economy entered a brief but severe depression in 1920 following the end of the inflationary pressures arising from World War I, there was no banking panic. By 1920, Federal Reserve notes constituted about three-fifths of outstanding coin and currency.

As the United States slid into depression in 1929, the most severe bank panic in American history occurred. Numerous bank failures had taken place during the 1920's but they were generally of small banks in rural areas. In 1930 failure struck numerous urban banks as well. The Federal Reserve was well designed to aid banks that were solvent but lacked cash. However, the bank failures that spread after 1930 generally involved insolvent banks—those whose assets were less than their liabilities, often because they had made speculative investments in stocks and real estate. Spreading bank failures led to massive withdrawals of currency from the banks, forcing them to sell investments and refuse to renew loans. Deflationary pressure was worsened by U.S.

adherence to the international gold standard. Britain's departure from the gold standard in 1931 set off a large effort to buy U.S. Treasury gold, a process that reduced bank reserves and the money supply. To protect the nation's gold reserve, the Federal Reserve imposed credit restraints that worsened the economic downswing and accelerated bank failures.

NEW DEAL AND AFTER

Franklin D. Roosevelt was inaugurated president in March, 1933, in the midst of the bank collapses. One of his first actions was to take the country off the gold standard. People were ordered to turn in their gold coins; contracts calling for payment in gold were declared invalid. Other forms of money were no longer convertible into gold. The official price of gold was raised from $20.67 an ounce, where it had stood since the 1830's, to $35 an ounce. American citizens could no longer buy Treasury gold, and even private gold transactions were severely regulated. Gold coins, gold certificates, and national banknotes were withdrawn from circulation.

After the Depression, U.S. currency became more routine and less interesting. The public can "buy" as much currency as it wants, supplied by the Federal Reserve through the banks. Links to precious metals were disconnected, except for gold and silver coins produced for collectors or investors and not intended to circulate as money. Beginning in 1965, silver was removed from U.S. coins, and silver certificates were discontinued. In 1971, the Treasury ceased to maintain a fixed price for gold or to sell it on demand to international buyers. After United States notes were discontinued in 1969, all paper currency consisted of Federal Reserve notes.

Paul B. Trescott

FURTHER READING

Friedman, Milton, and Anna J. Schwartz. *A Monetary History of the United States, 1867-1960.* Princeton, N.J.: Princeton University Press, 1963. The definitive monetary history, with lots of attention to the economic causes and effects of policy decisions.

Goodwin, Jason. *Greenback: The Almighty Dollar and the Invention of America.* New York: Henry Holt, 2003. Colorful, anecdotal history of American money; mostly pre-1900.

Hessler, Gene. *The Comprehensive Catalog of U.S. Paper Money.* 6th ed. Port Chester, Ohio: BNR Press, 1997. This catalog has many color illustrations of the various historical paper money issues.

Nussbaum, Arthur. *A History of the Dollar.* New York: Columbia University Press, 1957. A nice mix of scholarship and readability, this contains lots of detail on all the complexities of U.S. currency history.

Trescott, Paul B. *Money, Banking and Economic Welfare.* New York: McGraw-Hill, 1960. Chapters 14-17 of this college textbook put currency evolution in a full context of economic and political history.

SEE ALSO: Bank failures; Bank of the United States, First; Bank of the United States, Second; Confederate currency; Federal Reserve; Gold standard; Inflation; Mint, U.S.; Monetary policy, federal; Panic of 1907; Treasury, U.S. Department of the.

Cycles. *See* Business cycles

D

Dairy industry

DEFINITION: All industries that produce milk and cheese and other products made from animal milk

SIGNIFICANCE: Because of the importance of milk products in American diets, the dairy industry occupies a special place in the national economy. Since the mid-nineteenth century, the government has played a growing role in policing and supporting the industry, which has been largely removed from the dynamics of normal market forces. At the same time, government price supports of the industry have placed a growing burden on taxpayers that has become increasingly controversial.

Milk products have been important nutritional staples of human diets for thousands of years. As early as 9000 B.C.E., human societies domesticated cattle, which are one of the principal sources of milk products consumed by humans. Cattle were not bred in the Western Hemisphere until after Europeans began settling the Americas. The Italian explorer Christopher Columbus introduced cattle to the Caribbean islands during his second voyage to the Americas in 1493. In North America, cattle were brought over by British settlers at Jamestown in 1611 and at Plymouth colony in 1624.

The early years of European settlement in North America found most colonists living in small towns or on rural farms. Small dairy farms supplied the needs of towns, and many individual families owned their own dairy cows. After the colonies became independent to form the United States, urban centers grew in size, and the new nation needed more efficient methods to increase food supplies and improve distribution of agricultural and dairy products. The American Industrial Revolution of the nineteenth century changed the social and economic fabric of the country and advanced centralized and industrialized methods of food production. As new factories and mills were built, increasing numbers of people worked in large cities. By the mid-nineteenth century, large numbers of cattle were raised specifically for dairy production. As urban demand for milk and dairy products increased, small, family-owned dairy farms that had been the main sources of commercially supplied milk, were replaced by large dairy enterprises that functioned much like factories.

INDUSTRIALIZATION AND RESEARCH

Although American dairy farms were increasingly operated as large businesses, the dairy herds supplying milk were still based in rural areas that provided the space for cattle to be raised and fed. Many dairy herds were considerable distances from cities. Because milk and dairy products are highly perishable commodities, reliable methods to preserve and transport milk and dairy foods over long distances were needed.

Through the nineteenth century, as the dairy industry became more complex, new demands arose for standardizing milk and dairy foods and agricultural produce to make them safe for humans to consume. In response to these demands, the federal government created the U.S. Department of Agriculture (USDA) in 1862 to regulate farming methods and establish research centers. In 1895, the department added the Dairy Division and the Division of Agrostology, which studied grass feed and its effect on the flavor, odor, and quality of milk. Meanwhile, ongoing agricultural research, in the United States and elsewhere, led to improved breeding and feed methods that substantially increased the milk production of dairy cows. Tests developed by Nicklaus Gerber in Switzerland in 1888 and Stephen M. Babcock of the University of Wisconsin in 1890 established the fat percentages of milk and led to changes in price structures of milk products.

Cheeses have been made from cattle and goat milk products for millennia, but the first American cheese factory came into existence in the United States only in 1851, in Rome, New York, a small town northwest of Utica. Other advances in the manufacture of milk products soon followed. In 1856, for example, the first dried and condensed milks were developed and patented. In 1878, a process to separate cream from milk was developed. Milk bottles were invented in 1884, and tuberculin testing of all dairy cows, to prevent the spread of tuberculosis, began in 1890.

The Mehring milking machine, which was devel-

MILK PRODUCED, BY VOLUME AND VALUE, 1990-2005

Year	Volume (billion lbs)	Value ($ billions)
1990	148	20.4
1995	155	20.1
2000	167	20.8
2005	177	26.9

Source: Data from the *Statistical Abstract of the United States, 2008* (Washington, D.C.: Department of Commerce, Economics and Statistics Administration, Bureau of the Census, Data User Services Division, 2008)

Note: One gallon of milk is about 8 pounds of milk.

oped during the 1890's, made it possible to extract milk from cows more efficiently and to reduce milk contamination. Around this same time period, the French microbiologist Louis Pasteur discovered that microscopic germs were the causes of many diseases and invented the technique using heat to sterilize milk partially to kill possible disease germs and to make it easier to preserve the milk. That technique, which was soon adopted by virtually all industrialized dairy farms, came to be known as "pasteurization" after its discoverer. Indeed, in 1895 the pasteurization of milk became a public health mandate after commercial pasteurizing machines became available. The first pasteurization law in the United States was implemented in 1908 in Chicago.

Meanwhile, methods of transporting milk products to markets were advancing. In 1841, the first regular shipments of milk by railcar began. By the second decade of the twentieth century, refrigerated tanker trucks were being used to carry milk. At the same time, continued innovations in breeding methods substantially increased milk production. Packaging methods were also improving, using vacuum and ultra-high-temperature pasteurization techniques. Refrigerated transportation and automatic bottling machines permitted distribution of fresh milk and dairy products to all regions of the United States and to other countries.

By the mid-1920's, the United States had 21.5 million dairy cows that each produced an average of 4,218 pounds of milk per year. By 2007, the number of dairy cows had dropped to only 9.1 million, but their average milk production was more than 20,000 pounds of milk per year (a gallon of milk is about 8 pounds).

GOVERNMENT PRICE SUPPORTS

In 1922, passage of the federal Capper-Volstead Act allowed dairy farmers for the first time legally to combine small, family-owned dairy farms into cooperatives that marketed fluid milk and protected their pricing structure. However, the industry was soon set back by new challenges. The stock market crash of 1929 was followed by the Great Depression, which was aggravated by drought conditions in the Midwest. Market milk pricing fell so low that many dairy farmers were in danger of losing their farms. Federal intervention became necessary to sustain the dairy industry through these difficult times.

Originally designed as a temporary measure, the federal government's Agricultural Adjustment Act of 1933 provided economic relief to all U.S. farmers, including dairy farmers. Under the new law, the federal government set a uniform minimum milk price for raw milk. This price was paid to dairy farmers by dairy processors in ten U.S. regions, regardless of actual cost variations among the regions. In 1935, the federal government continued to support the dairy industry by purchasing milk and dairy products that were not sold on the open market. In later years, these surplus milk and dairy products would be used to feed financially needy Americans enrolled through the National School Lunch Program (1946), the Food Stamp Program (1961), and the School Breakfast Program (1966). Large amounts of the surplus products were also given to impoverished countries.

The Agricultural Act of 1949 mandated permanent federal support of dairy farms through uniform pricing programs for raw milk mainly to promote exports and improve environmental quality. These price supports have continued in the twenty-first century. The intent of federal price support programs was to support milk prices at levels that would maintain adequate supplies for American consumers while guaranteeing income levels to dairy farmers that would encourage them to continue production, so as to ensure future supplies. The federal law forbade independent dairies from supplying milk at lower prices than the government-set prices, and producers operating in lower-cost regions were not allowed to pass along price savings to higher-cost regions. The law also prohibited the importation of raw milk from other countries.

State milk price controls also began around the same time as the federal controls. These programs have operated essentially the same as the federal program. California is an example of a state that uses state milk price controls to establish raw milk prices. Federal and state agencies work together to establish the minimum prices paid to farmers for four tiers of raw Grade A milk based on weight and fat content. These tiers include the following:

- Class I (fluid milk)
- Class II (ice cream and soft products)
- Class III (cheeses)
- Class IV (butterfat and dairy powder)

Under the market order pricing system, dairy farmers are paid for raw milk in two parts—they are paid for the class value of the raw milk sold and given a price differential for the difference in value of the milk on the open market. A differential price adjustment is made for raw milk used in the other classes of raw milk use and a location differential is added to represent the manufacturing value of the milk in the state it is produced in. Dairy cooperatives are allowed to negotiate higher prices.

The 1980's brought the implementation of the federal government's Dairy Export Incentive Program (DEIP), which provided subsidies for dairy product exports. However, dairy price supports and import prohibitions distort market economics and insulate the dairy industry from market forces. As a result, American taxpayers are increasingly burdened and consumers pay much higher prices for milk and dairy products than they would if market forces alone prevailed.

Growing frustration with the dairy support programs led to the Federal Agriculture Improvement and Reform Act (FAIR Act), also called the Freedom-to-Farm Act, in 1996. The FAIR Act phased out dairy price supports, along with other commodity crops, gradually reducing payments until all federal pricing payments were intended to end in 1999. However, the dairy support program was extended as emergency assistance to the end of 2000, and then extended again until 2001 because of low market prices affecting dairy farmers. The Farm Security and Rural Investment (FSRI) Act of 2002 continued to extend dairy price supports through 2007, after which Congress continued to debate the continuation of federal subsidy programs.

TWENTY-FIRST CENTURY POLICY

In 2007, American dairy farms produced 186 billion pounds of raw milk. The continued Dairy Price Support Program (DPSP) and Milk Income Loss Contract (MILC) program continued to subsidize dairy farmers and maintain low raw milk prices on the open market. The federal government also continued to restrict foreign imports of milk, but the United States has remained among world leaders in its exports of dry milk to other countries. In 2007, Russia led the world in milk production, with about 22 percent of total world production, followed by the United States at 17.5 percent. Other major milk-producing nations include France, Germany, Poland, Great Britain, Italy, and Canada.

Controversy continues to surround the continued dairy farm economic supports. Research studies show that U.S. consumers pay more for their milk

Computerized milking allows two employees to milk about 160 cows per hour at this Cleveland, Minnesota, farm. (AP/Wide World Photos)

and dairy products than other countries with open market pricing. During the early twenty-first century, Americans have tended to buy less milk because of high retail prices and their increased use of milk substitutes, such as soy milk. At the same time, cheese consumption in the United States has continued to rise. However, cheese prices are affected by raw milk prices, so cheese consumption could yet decline.

Another twenty-first century change in the landscape of the dairy industry has been increased consumer demand for milk products free of pesticides and the hormones and drugs used to increase dairy production in cows. The production of organic milk and dairy products has also changed. Organic milk and dairy products are mainly produced by dairy cooperatives, but these small farms are struggling financially because of increased farming costs and raw milk price restrictions. Continued subsidization of dairy farms removes farmers from supply-and-demand market forces in the economy, ultimately creating a drain on taxpayers and a negative impact on the national economy and foreign exports.

Alice C. Richer

FURTHER READING

Apps, Jerry. *Cheese: The Making of a Wisconsin Tradition.* Amherst, Wis.: Amherst Press, 1998. Folksy history of the cheese industry in Wisconsin from the early 1940's through the end of the twentieth century, when Wisconsin was the leading producer of cheese among American states.

Bailey, Kenneth W. *Marketing and Pricing of Milk and Dairy Products in the United States.* Ames: Iowa State University Press, 1997. Useful survey of all aspects of marketing dairy products of all types, with attention to dairy cooperatives, federal milk marketing orders, price supports, and international trade.

Dupuis, E. Melanie. *Nature's Perfect Food: How Milk Became America's Drink.* New York: New York University Press, 2002. Lively and authoritative study that provides a balanced history of American milk production and consumption that considers changing public perceptions of the benefits of drinking milk.

Fuquay, John W., Patrick F. Fox, and Hubert Roginski, eds. *Encyclopedia of Dairy Sciences.* 4 vols. New York: Academic Press, 2002. Perhaps the single-most comprehensive reference source available on the dairy industry, this 2,500-page work addresses almost every imaginable topic in the field. Includes an article by Daniel A. Sumner and Joseph V. Balagtas titled "United States' Agricultural Systems: An Overview of U.S. Dairy Policy."

Schwarzweller, Harry K., and Andrew P. Davidson, eds. *Dairy Industry Restructuring.* New York: JAI Press, 2000. Collection of articles examining the special problems of the dairy industries of Western nations including the United States. Among the problems considered are changing technologies, withdrawals of government price supports, globalization of markets, and impact of food processing industries.

Turkey Hill Dairy. *Turkey Hill: A Family Vision.* Lincoln: Schiffer Publishing, 2006. Brief but entertaining and informative history of a small Pennsylvania dairy's growth from a family farm to a major manufacturer of ice cream and refrigerated teas. Includes many details on how dairies operate.

SEE ALSO: Agribusiness; Agriculture; Agriculture, U.S. Department of; Beef industry; Farm subsidies; Food and Drug Administration; Food-processing industries.

Dams and aqueducts

DEFINITION: Structures to control and guide the flow of water

SIGNIFICANCE: Pure water is essential for human health and the functioning of many businesses, and throughout American history aqueducts have been built to supply water to agricultural areas and to large urban areas, such as New York and Los Angeles. Many dams have been constructed to prevent floods, improve the navigability of rivers for commercial transportation of goods and people, and provide power for developing cities, businesses, and farms.

Dams are barriers, usually constructed of earth, rock, masonry, steel, concrete, or combinations of these materials, that are placed across watercourses to control their flow or create reservoirs. Aqueducts are systems of channels, ditches, tunnels, and pipes constructed to transport water by gravity and with pumps from a plentiful source to a population center. Because reliable sources of pure water are indispensable for many businesses, from agriculture to industries, ways of conveying water from these sources to places where it is needed have been important throughout American history. As the United States grew as a nation, its cities and industries required more and more water, so businesses and, more often, local and state governments constructed aqueducts to meet these needs.

EARLY PROJECTS

New York State, which constructed the Erie Canal between 1817 and 1825, required eighteen aqueducts to provide efficient transportation of goods from the East to the Midwest, thus facilitating the economic development of not only New York City but also Utica, Syracuse, Rochester, and Buffalo. New York City officials were behind the Croton Aqueduct, built from 1836 to 1843, to bring nearly a billion gallons of water every day from a reservoir created by a dam on the Croton River via a 40.5-mile aqueduct system through Westchester County to New York City. Though designed to satisfy the city's water needs for centuries, the Croton Aqueduct, within several decades, proved inadequate to meet the growing water demands of people and businesses in the New York City area, and a New Croton Aqueduct had to be built, three times the size of the original system and having the world's longest and largest tunnel. The much larger Catskill and Delaware aqueduct systems had to be built in the twentieth century because of the phenomenal growth in New York City businesses and population.

A similar pattern of population and business growth characterized the settling of the American West. One of the earliest aqueducts, a large wrought-iron pipe, supplied water to the mining town of Virginia City, Nevada, in 1873. Because of the arid conditions of the West, water was a scarce commodity that was fiercely fought over. Businessmen who speculated in land tried to discover when and where aqueducts would be built, because marginal lands would increase dramatically in value when water rights became available. A good example is the Los Angeles Aqueduct, completed in 1913, which brought water from the Owens Valley near the Sierra Nevada across two hundred miles of desert to southern California. Without this water, business and population growth in Los Angeles would not have been possible.

Los Angeles's experience mirrored that of New York City. Commercial development, which involved extensive amounts of water for the irrigation of massive agricultural areas and for urban industries, outstripped the water supplies much more quickly than was initially envisioned. As a result, the California Aqueduct, the largest in the world, was begun in 1957. These and other projects involved large dams that created reservoirs, huge pumping plants, concrete-lined open and covered channels, and subsidiary aqueducts that supplied water to such new cities as San Diego. During this time, environmentalists such as John Muir and others opposed the building of dams and aqueducts, the most famous example being the Hetch-Hetchy dam and aqueduct, designed to transport water from the Sierra Nevada to San Francisco. In this and other instances, commercial and political interests prevailed, and the dams and aqueducts were built.

Besides their connections to aqueduct systems, dams were specifically involved in various businesses. During the colonial period, dams provided power for various commercial enterprises. The earliest American dam was built in 1634 to power a sawmill in South Berwick, Maine, and during the early history of the United States, from its founding until well after the U.S. Civil War, ironworkers, sawyers, and mill operators relied on waterpower to drive bellows, saws, machine tools, and looms. A dam on the Blackstone River in Rhode Island provided the power that ran the textile machinery of Samuel Slater, which initiated the American Industrial Revolution. Much more extensive textile-manufacturing facilities were constructed and powered by the

---

A CLOSER LOOK AT THE FIRST LOS ANGELES AQUEDUCT

- Year completed: 1913
- Construction duration: 5 years
- Capacity: 485 cubic feet per second
- Construction cost: Less than $23 million
- Total length: 223 miles

Source: Los Angeles Department of Water and Power

water pressure created by dams throughout New England and the northeastern United States, most notably the Lowell Mills in Massachusetts.

During the late nineteenth and throughout the twentieth century, dam construction became an important part of the economic development of the American West. In 1888, John Wesley Powell, the renowned explorer of the Colorado River, who had authored a report on the arid regions of the West, convinced Congress to authorize a survey of Western rivers and potential reservoir sites, with a view toward developing irrigable lands for large farms. During the twentieth century many dams were built in the Western states by the federal government and private power companies to provide water for irrigation and electricity for new cities and industries. The most famous of these dams, built between 1931 and 1936 by the Bureau of Reclamation, was first known as Boulder Dam, and later as Hoover Dam. It was located on the Colorado River between Nevada and Arizona, and it increased water supplies and electricity for neighboring regions as well as for Southern California, especially Los Angeles.

GOVERNMENT INVOLVEMENT

Although entrepreneurs were responsible for the early construction of aqueducts and dams, during the twentieth century, the federal government undertook the largest projects. Private electric utilities increasingly came into conflict with social and environmental progressives who wanted the federal government to take over electric-power-generating projects. This trend is well exemplified by the Tennessee Valley Authority (TVA), commissioned by Congress in 1933. This grand endeavor was intended to control floods, create electric power, deepen rivers for shipping, and accelerate a multistate region's economic development. Because the TVA was a federal corporation, it represented a great change in government policy, provoking much controversy, especially from critics who believed that such undertakings were best left to private enterprise.

Even private enterprises could provoke controversy. When, in 1962, Consolidated Edison Company and Central Hudson Gas and Electric revealed plans to construct the world's largest hydroelectric plant near Storm King Mountain on the Hudson River to alleviate New York's chronic electricity shortages, several environmental groups banded together to stop the project, which, in a landmark class-action lawsuit, they succeeded in accomplishing. Those in favor of dams and aqueducts, especially business interests, emphasize their necessity in helping a region's economic progress, but those against these constructs, especially environmentalists, emphasize the damage that they do to scenic locations and wildlife. Most analysts now agree that dams and aqueducts have both costs and benefits for businesses, the environment, and people, and it will be a major task for future generations to balance these conflicting interests in ways that best serve the needs of all.

Robert J. Paradowski

FURTHER READING

Goldsmith, Edward, and Nicholas Hildyard. *The Social and Environmental Effects of Large Dams.* San Francisco, Calif.: Sierra Club Books, 1984. An analysis of the economic and social benefits of dams as well as their great environmental costs. Thirty-seven pages of notes, with many primary and secondary references, and an index.

Hundley, Norris. *The Great Thirst: Californians and Water—A History.* Rev. ed. Berkeley: University of California Press, 2001. Update of the story of how feuds over the control and use of water shaped the economic history of California. Notes, bibliography, and index.

Lowry, William R. *Dam Politics: Restoring America's Rivers.* Washington, D.C.: Georgetown University Press, 2003. This analysis of how water marketing and public policy have influenced decisions about dam building and dam removal reveals the significance of dams to America's urban and rural regions. Bibliography and index.

Reisner, Marc. *Cadillac Desert: The American West and Its Disappearing Water.* New York: Penguin Books, 1987. This book, honored as one of the most notable nonfiction works in the twentieth century, is a revisionist account of the settling of the West, as due not to rugged individualists but to the creation of an expensive and environmentally detrimental "hydraulic society." Index.

Schnitter, Nicholas J. *A History of Dams: The Useful Pyramids.* Rotterdam, The Netherlands: A. A. Balkema, 1994. The story of dams, their construction and uses, from antiquity to the present, with a focus on changing engineering practices. Illustrated with photos, graphs, and tables.

See also: Colorado River water; Construction industry; Erie Canal; Irrigated farming; Mississippi and Missouri Rivers; Public utilities; Tennessee Valley Authority; Water resources.

Daylight saving time

Definition: Practice of moving clocks ahead one hour during summer months

Significance: Daylight saving time was instituted in the United States as an energy-saving measure to allow people to take maximum advantage of available daylight. Although its effects in that regard remain questionable, the practice has been a boon for summertime retail business, increasing the length of the shopping day for consumers and thereby allowing stores to increase their sales volume.

Daylight saving time has often been traced to a proposal written by Benjamin Franklin in 1784. However, he was actually satirizing the Parisian lifestyle, urging the French to rise earlier in the morning. The first serious modern daylight saving proposal was put forth in 1907 by British house builder William Willett, who sought to encourage greater outdoor activity during the summer months. In spite of considerable lobbying, he was unable to convince the British government to adopt his plan.

Only the fuel shortages brought about by World War I convinced several of the belligerent nations to put daylight saving time into effect. However, it was so unpopular that all governments dropped it after the armistice. The United States reinstated mandatory daylight saving time as an energy-conservation measure during World War II, but after the war ended, the federal government left the decision to retain daylight saving time up to the individual states. In 1966, Congress passed the Uniform Time Act, which required all states observing daylight saving time to begin and end it on the same day each year. During the 1973 Arab oil embargo, the federal government temporarily mandated an early beginning to daylight saving time for 1974 and 1975.

Opponents have criticized daylight saving time as saving nothing, since it merely moves the observed hours forward rather than adding a real hour. In addition, there are serious questions about whether it realizes any energy savings in a society in which lighting is a relatively minor consumer of power compared with computers and other technology. By contrast, retail businesses tend to favor daylight saving, because it often results in consumers shopping later in the afternoon and evening, producing more revenue for stores.

Several U.S. states do not observe daylight saving time. For decades it was resisted by Indiana, which straddles the eastern and central time zones, but the state has adopted a unified time except for a few counties adjacent to Chicago or Louisville. In 2005, a law was passed by the Indiana General Assembly putting all of Indiana on daylight saving time beginning in 2006. Arizona also does not observe daylight saving time, except in several of the nominally sovereign Native American reservations.

The Energy Policy Act of 2005 lengthened the duration of daylight saving time in the United States beginning in 2007. From 1966 to 2006, daylight saving time began in the United States on the first Sunday in April and ended on the last Sunday in October. After 2006, it began on the second Sunday in March and ended on the first Sunday in November. The law, designed to increase energy savings, was motivated by concern over the nation's growing energy problems and the possibility of a looming crisis.

Leigh Husband Kimmel

Further Reading

Barnett, Jo Ellen. *Time's Pendulum: From Sundials to Atomic Clocks, the Fascinating History of Timekeeping and How Our Discoveries Changed the World.* San Diego, Calif.: Harcourt Brace, 1999.

Dolan, Graham. *The Greenwich Guide to Measuring Time.* Chicago: Heinemann Library, 2001.

See also: Arab oil embargo of 1973; Energy, U.S. Department of; Energy crisis of 1979; Franklin, Benjamin; Public utilities; Time zones.

DC-3 aircraft

DEFINITION: Twin-engine passenger plane that was the most successful aircraft in early American airline history

SIGNIFICANCE: The DC-3 provided the developing airline industry with a reliable and versatile craft. It was so popular with both customers and companies that it consolidated the industry's place in America's transportation network.

The DC-3 was the result of cooperation between a business, Douglas Aircraft Company, and a customer, American Airlines. American Airlines wanted to compete with TWA, which was flying the smaller DC-2, and United Airlines, which was flying the Boeing 247. American therefore approached Douglas with a proposal for a superior plane that would be roomy enough for sleeping berths and that could fly at least halfway across the country without stopping for gas. At the time, transcontinental flights normally made two or three stops along the way, allowing passengers to sleep overnight in hotels, so it typically took three or four days to make the trip.

With sales to American guaranteed in advance, Douglas engineers were able to commit the necessary time and costs to develop a remarkable new plane. The DC-3 made its maiden flight on December 17, 1935. It was big, fast, comfortable, and remarkably reliable. It could cruise at 230 miles per hour, fast enough to fly from Los Angeles to New York in only sixteen hours of flying time. It had variable-pitch propellers, allowing excellent control, and partially retractable landing gear. With a wing span of 64 feet 5 inches, it dwarfed the competition, and its large size allowed the airline to offer sleeping berths in some planes and hot meals prepared in an on-board kitchen.

The DC-3 was an instant success. Its efficiency and appeal meant that airlines could for the first time make money carrying passengers without a government mail subsidy. By the end of 1938, almost all airline traffic in America was on DC-3s. The plane's high safety margin meant that air travel was perceived to be as safe as train travel, and the pendulum began to swing away from the railroads to the airlines. More than eleven thousand DC-3s were eventually built.

After the start of World War II, most new aircraft construction was for military purposes. The Army version of the DC-3 was called the C-47, and it played an important part in the war effort. As a troop transport and freight plane, it was essential to the Allied efforts.

At the end of World War II, most C-47s were transformed into DC-3s and adopted for commercial transportation. The infusion of so many excellent airplanes jump-started the reemerging civilian airline industry. The DC-3 continued to play an important role in the air travel business for many years. Even into the early twenty-first century, seventy years after the plane's introduction, several hundred DC-3s remained in flying condition, though they were no longer used for commercial flights.

Paul W. Hodge

FURTHER READING

Gradidge, Jennifer M. *The Douglas DC-1/DC-2/DC-3: The First Seventy Years.* London: Air-Britain, 2006.

Holden, H. M. *The Legacy of the DC-3.* Brawley, Calif.: Wind Canyon Books, 1996.

A DC-3 in flight in 1959. (Library of Congress)

Pearcy, Arthur. *Douglas Propliners: DC-1 to DC-7.* Shrewsbury, Shropshire, England: Airlife, 1995.

SEE ALSO: Air transportation industry; Aircraft industry; Airships; Railroads; Supersonic jetliners; World War II.

DDT banning

THE EVENT: Federal revocation of the registration of the pesticide DDT, thereby prohibiting its use in the United States
DATE: June 14, 1972
PLACE: Washington, D.C.
SIGNIFICANCE: DDT's ban signaled a new political strength for the growing environmental movement.

Organic pesticides such as dichloro-diphenyl-trichloroethane (DDT) came into widespread use after World War II. DDT played a major role in the Allied war effort, helping the troops control malaria and other insect-borne diseases during the war. It became so popular among returning servicemen that it was thrown at weddings in place of rice. Federally subsidized aerial spraying programs to control gypsy moths, however, led to increasing conflicts between pest control programs and organic farmers, homeowners, and environmentalists.

After a series of lawsuits in New York state during the early 1960's failed to stop the spraying, activists focused on reforming the Federal Insecticide, Fungicide, and Rodenticide Act of 1947. They sought to add public and environmental health considerations to the statute's requirement that products be effective and safe for users. Rachel Carson's 1962 best seller, *Silent Spring,* argued that pesticides caused environmental damage, and Carson particularly targeted DDT. After a multiyear campaign marked by bitter division and months of Environmental Protection Agency (EPA) and congressional hearings, the Richard M. Nixon administration's EPA, led by William D. Ruckelshaus, canceled the pesticide's registration, effectively banning its use. Some antimalaria activists have challenged the ban, however, arguing that DDT is an essential element in the fight against malaria in developing countries. Use of the chemical is again increasing.

Andrew P. Morriss

FURTHER READING
Carson, Rachel. *Silent Spring.* 1962. Reprint. Boston: Mariner Books, 2002.
Dunlap, Thomas R. *DDT: Scientists, Citizens, and Public Policy.* Princeton, N.J.: Princeton University Press, 1981.
World Wildlife Fund. *Resolving the DDT Dilemma: Protecting Biodiversity and Human Health.* Washington, D.C.: Author, 1998.

SEE ALSO: Agribusiness; Agriculture; Chemical industries; Environmental movement; Environmental Protection Agency; World War II.

Debs, Eugene V.

IDENTIFICATION: Socialist labor leader
BORN: November 5, 1855; Terre Haute, Indiana
DIED: October 20, 1926; Elmhurst, Illinois
SIGNIFICANCE: Perhaps America's best-known socialist, Debs offered a strong critique of American capitalism during the late nineteenth and early twentieth centuries. His role as a strike leader—most notably during the Pullman Strike of 1894—and as a five-time candidate for president gained him both notoriety and a sizeable political following.

Although Eugene V. Debs was considered bright in school, his formal education ended in 1870, when, at the age of fourteen, he entered the employment of the Indianapolis Railway Company in Terre Haute, Indiana, first as a shop laborer and then as a locomotive fireman. This early experience fueled his interests in the rights of the working class and the embryonic labor movement. In 1875, Debs began serving as secretary of the local branch of the newly formed Brotherhood of Locomotive Firemen, and by 1880, he had become the secretary-treasurer of the national union as well as the editor of its publication, the *Locomotive Firemen's Magazine.*

As the 1880's progressed, labor strife throughout the country grew in response to the ruthless labor practices of the Gilded Age. In response, Debs became increasingly involved in the effort to bring about the federation of the major railroad unions. When this was finally accomplished in 1893 with the formation of the American Railway Union (ARU),

Eugene V. Debs. (Library of Congress)

Debs was chosen as the union's president. In April of 1894, under Debs's leadership, the ARU was successful in forcing James Jerome Hill and the Great Northern Railroad to submit to arbitration in a major labor dispute.

Mere months later, the union suffered a major defeat in the Pullman Strike of 1894, arguably the most significant effort of organized labor during the period. In the aftermath of this event, Debs was sentenced in Illinois to a six-month jail term for contempt. After supporting William Jennings Bryan in his unsuccessful bid for the presidency in 1896, Debs announced, on January 1, 1897, his conversion to socialism, seeing it as the best vehicle for achieving the types of economic reforms he felt the country required.

For the rest of his life, Debs fought for the socialist cause, becoming the country's best-known socialist leader. He ran five times for president as a socialist, in 1900, 1904, 1908, 1912, and 1920. Debs made his greatest impact in the 1912 presidential race, when he won 6 percent of the popular vote with a vote tally of 897,011. He was also one of the founders of the Industrial Workers of the World (IWW), a rad-

ical labor organization, in 1905, and he wrote extensively for the socialist publications *Appeal to Reason* and the *National Rip-Saw.*

Scott Wright

FURTHER READING

Chace, James. *1912—Wilson, Roosevelt, Taft, and Debs: The Election That Changed the Country.* New York: Simon & Schuster, 2004.

Papke, David Ray. *The Pullman Case: The Clash of Labor and Capital in Industrial America.* Lawrence: University Press of Kansas, 1999.

Salvatore, Nick. *Eugene V. Debs: Citizen and Socialist.* Urbana: University of Illinois Press, 1982.

SEE ALSO: AFL-CIO; Gilded Age; Gompers, Samuel; Industrial Workers of the World; Labor history; Labor strikes; Pullman Strike; Railroad strike of 1877; Railroads; Supreme Court and labor law.

Deming, W. Edwards

IDENTIFICATION: American statistician and business consultant

BORN: October 14, 1900; Sioux City, Iowa

DIED: December 20, 1993; Washington, D.C.

SIGNIFICANCE: Through his innovative ideas about quality control, Deming helped rebuild the Japanese economy after World War II, and decades later his ideas contributed to the transformation of American business as well.

After earning his undergraduate degree in electrical engineering from the University of Wyoming in 1921, W. Edwards Deming studied mathematical physics, receiving a master's degree from the University of Colorado in 1925 and a doctorate from Yale University in 1928. Influenced by Walter Shewhart's ideas about "statistical process control," Deming worked for the next decade for the U.S. Department of Agriculture and then, from 1939 to 1946, for the Census Bureau, where he helped develop its statistical sampling methodology. After the war, he began his half-century career as a consultant on statistics, and in 1950, Deming persuaded Japanese businessmen that their path to economic recovery lay in putting emphasis on quality control. Deming's methods seemed to enable Japanese firms to produce higher-quality products than had been feasible in the past, at lower cost. Within a year, Japan had established the Deming Prize in his honor.

Thirty years later, in June, 1980, as America began to wrestle with the challenge of superior Japanese industrial practices, a television documentary, *If Japan Can . . . Why Can't We?*, made Deming's ideas famous in his homeland. He enjoyed belated popular recognition in the United States and played a major role in the decade's "quality revolution," through extensive consulting and through his books, including *Out of the Crisis* (1982) and *The New Economics for Industry, Government, Education* (1993). Talk about Deming's "fourteen points for management" soon became commonplace. He remained an active proselytizer for his ideas about "continuous quality improvement" and systematic "profound knowledge" until his death in 1993. He received numerous awards for his theoretical and practical contributions to statistics and industry.

Although Deming is often credited with revolutionizing Japanese business practices after World War II, there has been some debate about the nature of Japan's economic turnaround and the extent of Deming's influence on it. A few critics have viewed the alleged superiority of Japanese quality-control processes, including those encouraged by Deming, as mythical, and "quality guru" Joseph M. Juran, who also served as a consultant in Japan during the early 1950's, in retrospect insisted:

> Japan created its own quality revolution. If Ed Deming and I hadn't gone there, they'd still be right where they are now, because the chief contributors to the revolution have been the Japanese managers. I learned a lot more from Japanese managers than they learned from us.

Perhaps the actual dynamic is suggested by a story told by Deming: He told a group of Japanese managers that, if they followed his suggestions, they could achieve their objectives in five years. In fact, they succeeded in four.

Edward Johnson

Further Reading

Dobyns, Lloyd, and Clare Crawford-Mason. *Thinking About Quality: Progress, Wisdom, and the Deming Philosophy.* New York: Times Books/Random House, 1994.

Eberts, Ray, and Cindelyn Eberts. *The Myths of Japanese Quality.* Upper Saddle River, N.J.: Prentice-Hall PTR, 1995.

Wood, John C., and Michael C. Wood, eds. *W. E. Deming: Critical Evaluations in Business and Management.* London: Routledge, 2004.

See also: Japanese trade with the United States; Management theory.

Depression. *See* Great Depression

Depression of 1784

The Event: Severe economic downturn resulting from low production, an insufficient hard money supply, and few opportunities to export goods
Date: 1784
Place: United States
Significance: The Depression of 1784 helped convince the nation that the central government created by the Articles of Confederation was too weak and that a new, stronger federal government with the power to issue currency, create tariffs, and regulate commerce was essential to national prosperity.

At the end of the Revolutionary War, the United States faced serious economic problems. Farmers had lost much of their livestock and had suffered destruction of their property as armies marched across the country. They lacked money to rebuild their farms. Manufacturers who had prospered during the conflict found that their war-related products were no longer needed. Once peace was made with Great Britain, the newly free colonists evinced a preference for British goods, which were cheaper and considered to be of better quality than those made in America.

Great Britain closed the markets of the West Indies and the North Atlantic fisheries to Americans and severely limited the importation of American goods into England. There was a shortage of hard currency, which had been used to pay for imports, and an overabundance of unregulated, worthless paper money, which creditors refused to accept. Merchandise remained on merchants' shelves, as

Americans became more impoverished. This set of economic problems combined to create the depression of 1784.

During the Revolutionary War, the government had used loan-office certificates and continental certificates to pay for supplies as well as to pay soldiers and officers. These non-interest-bearing notes quickly lost their value after the war. The holders of the certificates were for the most part farmers, small businessmen, and merchants who needed cash to operate their farms and businesses. Therefore, they had little recourse but to sell their certificates at rates of ten or twenty cents on the dollar. By the mid-1780's, the majority of these certificates were in the possession of a few wealthy speculators.

The federal government had not been able to either fund the war or pay the war debt under the Articles of Confederation. The states—which had borrowed money from individual creditors to fund the war—were by the mid-1780's heavily taxing landowners, farmers in particular, to pay their debts. They were demanding hard money, not paper. Impoverished farmers were unable to pay and feared loss of their land. This situation resulted in Shays's Rebellion in Massachusetts, which some historians view as a major impetus to the replacement of the Articles of Confederation by the Constitution. Once the Constitution was ratified, control of funding and repayment of the debt passed to the federal government.

Shawncey Webb

FURTHER READING

Brown, Richard D. *Major Problems in the Era of the American Revolution, 1760-1791: Documents and Essays.* 2d ed. New York: Houghton Mifflin, 1999.

Morris, Richard B. *The Forging of the Union, 1781-1789.* New York: Harper & Row, 1987.

Szatmary, David P. *Shay's Rebellion: The Making of an Agrarian Insurrection.* Amherst, Mass.: University of Massachusetts Press, 1984.

SEE ALSO: Annapolis Convention; Articles of Confederation; Constitution, U.S.; Depression of 1808-1809; Panic of 1819; Revolutionary War; Shays's Rebellion.

Depression of 1808-1809

THE EVENT: Economic downturn caused by the collapse of the United States' foreign trade
DATE: 1808-1809
PLACE: United States
SIGNIFICANCE: The depression of 1808-1809, brought on by an embargo that cut off international markets for U.S. business, led to the development of a number of domestic industries.

The 1780's were a period of great difficulty for the American colonies. Although they had secured a military victory, formally recognized in 1783 in the Treaty of Paris, the economy of the new republic remained in difficulty. The new country experienced high inflation because of multiple state currencies and the heavy debt carried by the states from funding the Revolutionary War.

By the early 1790's, things had changed. The ratification of the Constitution and the inauguration of George Washington as the first president in 1789 led directly to the adoption of Alexander Hamilton's financial reforms in 1790, consolidating debt and issuing a federal paper currency. Exports, which had fueled the colonial economy, revived and rapidly exceeded earlier levels, especially to the Caribbean.

From 1793 to 1807, Great Britain and France maintained a state of war with each other, except for a brief respite in 1803 and 1804. American ships profited enormously from the conflict. American exports (many of them re-exports) doubled between 1792 and 1795 and doubled again by 1801. By 1807, U.S. exports were five times what they had been in 1792. This burgeoning trade and the resulting prosperity was based largely on trade in finished commodities, although there was some export of raw materials to Europe as well.

The British Royal Navy, which dominated international waters, made life difficult for American ships. British naval vessels stopped American ships whenever they encountered them, removed some of their sailors, and forced them to serve on British vessels—a process known as impressment. Some vessels were taken over completely and forced to sail into British ports, where their cargoes were confiscated. The young American government protested these actions, but the protests proved largely futile. In late 1806, President Jefferson decided to em-

President Thomas Jefferson is depicted defending his embargo policy to a group of disgruntled men. (Library of Congress)

bargo all shipping from American to British and French ports.

America's overseas trade collapsed, causing the U.S. economy to fall into a deep depression by 1808. Foreign trade fell from $108 million in 1807 to $22 million in 1808. Some smuggling occurred, but it was not sufficient to replace the legitimate trade of the preceding years. Although the federal government tried to negotiate on behalf of neutral shipping, a category claimed for American ships, Britain and Napoleonic France were committed to mutual blockades, leading the United States eventually to declare war on Britain in 1812. It was not until after the end of that war, in 1815 and especially in 1816, that American international trade began to revive.

The depression of 1808-1809 had an unexpected consequence: With the American market closed to British manufactured goods, Americans began to make their own. The beginning of America's textile industry dates to this period. As a result, American prosperity no longer rested as heavily on international trade as it had before 1808.

Nancy M. Gordon

FURTHER READING

Hickey, Donald R. *The War of 1812: A Forgotten Conflict.* Urbana: University of Illinois Press, 1989.

Matson, Cathy. "The Revolution, the Constitution, and the New Nation." In *The Cambridge Economic History of the United States,* edited by Stanley Engerman and Robert E. Gallman. Vol. 1. New York: Cambridge University Press, 1996.

SEE ALSO: Depression of 1784; Embargo Acts; Great Depression; International economics and trade; Panic of 1819; War of 1812.

Deregulation of financial institutions

The Event: Federal government's removal or relaxation of many 1930's restrictions on banks' and savings and loans' ability to branch, lend, and make interest payments

Date: Began in 1980

Place: United States

Significance: Deregulation contributed to efficiency and innovation in the financial sector, but also to economic crises. Deposit institutions became less differentiated from one another, but each offered more diverse services to business and household customers.

During the Great Depression of the 1930's, the federal government imposed many restrictions on the conduct of banks and other deposit institutions. For banks, these fell chiefly into five categories. First, entry into banking was severely limited. Chartering authorities such as the U.S. Comptroller of the Currency (for national banks) and state banking departments made it difficult to start a new bank so that existing institutions were protected from competition. Second, types of assets were severely restricted. In general, banks were forbidden to invest in stocks or real estate directly, and loans on such collateral were also subject to stringent limitations. Commercial banks were barred from engaging in investment banking (marketing new securities issues), and from providing brokerage, insurance, or real estate services. Thrift institutions were largely restricted to home mortgages and bonds.

Third, federal law gave states authority to set rules for establishing bank branches. Some states prohibited branching altogether (Illinois). Even where regulations were liberal (California) branches were limited to one state. Fourth, ceilings were imposed on interest rates paid on deposits. No interest could be paid on demand deposits. Time deposit rates were set by the Federal Reserve under Regulation Q, and were generally held at low levels to safeguard bank profits. Finally, all deposits of Federal Reserve member banks were subject to reserve requirements set by the Federal Reserve, and required reserves were to be held on deposit with the Federal Reserve banks. Nonmember banks had much lower requirements set by state authorities.

After World War II

Interest rates were extremely low during the 1930's and 1940's, then they trended steadily upward. Reserve requirements were held at high levels during the inflationary conditions of 1942-1952. Requirements softened as the economy returned more nearly to normal. In 1959-1960, banks were allowed to count vault cash toward their required reserves. Banks experimented with holding companies as a way of participating in nonbank business activities and operating the equivalent of branches across state lines.

However, it was the severe inflation that erupted during the late 1960's that precipitated serious deregulation. Market interest rates rose to unprecedented high levels—far beyond the ceiling rates permitted on deposits. In 1966, Congress extended deposit-rate ceilings to thrift institutions to try to forestall a bidding war for deposits. The invention of money market mutual funds in 1971 provided savers with safe, liquid, high-interest assets, and deposit institutions found themselves losing time and savings deposits. Problems were especially severe for savings institutions, which held most of their funds in mortgages or long-term bonds. Deposit withdrawals pressured the institutions to try to sell off assets, but those asset prices were falling as interest rates rose.

The focus of deregulation was the Depository Institutions Deregulation and Monetary Control Act of 1980 (DIDMCA). The law and Federal Reserve actions pursuant to it brought these deregulations: All banks were brought under Federal Reserve rules for reserve requirements, but these were substantially reduced. Requirements on time and savings deposits were gradually eliminated by 1986. Checking deposits required a 10 percent reserve, but most corporate checking deposits escaped this by using sweep accounts. Ceiling interest rates under Regulation Q were phased out. Interest could now be paid on checking accounts of nonbusiness depositors. Savings institutions were now able to offer checking deposit services.

Though not an instance of deregulation, another provision of DIDMCA raised the coverage of deposit insurance of banks and thrift institutions to $100,000. This enabled deposit institutions to cash in on the two major deregulatory aspects of the law. They began issuing large, fully insured certificates of deposit (CDs), which they sold in the open market.

In 1982, the Garn-St. Germain Act greatly liberalized the range of permitted assets for thrift institutions (savings and loans, or S&Ls, and mutual savings banks). These were now permitted to have as much as 40 percent of their assets in commercial real estate loans, 30 percent in consumer loans, and 10 percent in commercial loans and leases. The 1982 law authorized banks and thrifts to offer money-market deposit accounts, designed to compete with money-market mutual funds.

The 1982 law was undertaken in an effort to rescue savings and loan associations from insolvency resulting when the market value of their mortgage loan portfolios declined. Perhaps half the S&Ls in the country were technically insolvent by 1982. The result was that many S&Ls undertook very risky lending and failed. In 1989, the Financial Institutions Reform, Recovery, and Enforcement Act undertook to clean up the mess, at a cost to the public of some $150 billion. Most of the 1982 liberalizations of the thrift industry were repealed.

In 1994, the Interstate Banking and Branching Efficiency Act removed the previous restrictions on interstate bank branching. In 1999, the 1933 prohibitions against banks engaging in nonbank financial business activities were largely eliminated.

As a result of all these laws, the financial system changed dramatically between 1975 and 2000. Legislated distinctions among different deposit institutions largely disappeared. A massive wave of bank consolidation reduced the number of institutions. In 1970, there were more than 13,000 commercial banks and more than 5,000 S&Ls. By 2006, there were about 7,400 commercial banks and 1,300 thrift institutions.

Deregulation gets very mixed reviews from financial experts. It opened the financial world to innovation and competition, paving the way for fuller participation in the global economy. However, it overwhelmed management and regulatory competence, as was evident in both the S&L crisis of the 1980's and the subprime mortgage crisis of 2007-2008.

Financial Crisis of 2008

Financial deregulation was heavily criticized as contributing to the financial crisis of 2008, which centered on subprime mortgage lending. In 2000, Congress passed a bill prohibiting federal and most state regulation of loan-guarantee contracts (credit default swaps) and similar derivatives. Such contracts were central to the crisis. Some potentially beneficial existing regulations were not effectively enforced, notably the requirements for minimum capital of financial firms. All regulation is subject to political pressure, and all the pressure was toward expanding credit for subprime borrowers. Some regulations were criticized as aggravating the crisis, notably the accounting regulation known as marking to market. This required that asset values be recalculated frequently based on estimates of their current market price. Valuations of assets with no real markets were arbitrary and may have contributed to the perception that firms were insolvent. New regulations are likely to emerge in response to the crisis.

Paul B. Trescott

Further Reading

Barth, James R., R. Dan Brumbaugh, Jr., and James A. Wilcox. "The Repeal of Glass-Steagall and the Advent of Broad Banking." *Journal of Economic Perspectives* 14, no. 2 (Spring, 2000): 191-204. Detailed examination of the 1999 legislation which removed barriers to the activities banks can engage in.

"Financial Market Deregulation." In *Economic Report of the President*. Washington, D.C.: Government Printing Office, 1984. A very readable and systematic overview, stressing links to monetary policy.

Litan, Robert E. "Financial Regulation." In *American Economic Policy in the 1980s*, edited by Martin Feldstein. Chicago: University of Chicago Press, 1994. Develops the interaction between deregulation and the thrift crisis; two commentators provide additional perspective.

Markham, Jerry W. *A Financial History of the United States*. Armonk, N.Y.: M. E. Sharpe, 2002. 3 vols. Largely chronological, this work is a gold mine of details, but not very analytical.

Mishkin, Frederic. *The Economics of Money, Banking, and Financial Markets*. 7th ed. New York: Pearson Addison Wesley, 2006. Chapter 10 of this college-level text places deregulation in the context of financial innovation, regulatory policy, and the S&L crisis.

See also: Bank failures; Banking; Federal Deposit Insurance Corporation; Financial crisis of 2008; Merger and corporate reorganization industry; Mortgage industry; New Deal programs; Savings and loan associations; Trickle-down theory.

Derivatives and hedge fund industry

DEFINITION: Enterprises dealing with financial instruments whose prices derive from the price of some other asset or measurable quantity (derivatives), and with private investment pools not subject to the full range of restrictions on investment activities and disclosure obligations imposed by the federal securities laws (hedge funds)

SIGNIFICANCE: Financial derivatives and hedge funds have played an increasingly important and often interrelated role in American business history. Hedge funds in particular have exploded in size, number, and relevance since the beginning of the twenty-first century. The funds have been leaders in financial innovation and have helped reduce overall risks in the economy.

Financial derivatives have enabled the growth of businesses by allowing companies to make specific investments that reduce the risks to which they are exposed and by making available more information about the value of assets to be transmitted throughout the economy. A common type of derivative is an employee stock option, which gives employees the right to purchase stock in their own company at a predetermined price. Another type of derivative is a futures contract, which obligates one party to deliver an asset to another on a specified date. Two other types of derivatives are swaps and forwards. Derivatives may be traded on an organized exchange or bilaterally negotiated over-the-counter (OTC) between purchasers and sellers.

RISK MANAGEMENT

Derivatives facilitate production and investment activities by allowing companies and investors to reduce and manage risk exposure. Derivatives trading also benefits the economy by revealing information about the value of derivatives contracts' underlying assets, thereby allowing market participants to make more informed decisions.

On March 13, 1851, the Chicago Board of Trade became the first American exchange on which a derivatives contract was traded. Until the 1970's, futures were based mostly on agricultural commodities and livestock. Since the 1970's, the derivatives markets have witnessed a rapid proliferation of new products, including derivatives of foreign currencies, common stocks, interest rates, and stock indices. The stock market crash of October 19, 1987, commonly called Black Monday, was widely blamed on derivatives serving as portfolio insurance.

By 1991, the notional amount of OTC derivatives became greater than exchange-traded derivatives. At the turn of the century, difficulties in valuing energy derivatives in part contributed to Enron becoming a symbol of deficiencies in American corporate governance. On March 16, 2008, the Federal Reserve arranged a fire sale of Bear Stearns, one of Wall Street's oldest and most prominent securities firms, to J. P. Morgan Chase in part because of Bear Stearns' involvement with a type of derivative known as a credit default swap.

HEDGE FUNDS

Hedge funds are active traders of derivatives. Hedge funds compensate management in part with annual performance fees and typically engage in the active trading of financial instruments. By law, they may accept capital only from wealthy individuals and institutions. Although Alfred Winslow Jones is widely regarded has having established the first hedge fund in 1951 by purchasing stocks he believed were undervalued and short-selling those he thought were overvalued, Jones was preceded by at least two decades when, on December 17, 1930, Karl Karsten established a private fund in Connecticut employing an early form of a trading strategy known as statistical arbitrage.

The hedge fund industry received notoriety in 1998, when the Federal Reserve of New York coordinated a $3.5 billion private bailout of the hedge fund Long-Term Capital Management. In part because hedge funds preserved their investors' wealth through the recession of 2000 to 2002, institutional investors increasingly sought them out as tools to preserve wealth in downmarkets, and they began to grow rapidly in size and number. Hedge funds approximately tripled in size from 2002 to 2007, when they managed an estimated $2 trillion in assets spread across about ten thousand funds. In September of 2006, the hedge fund Amaranth Advisors experienced $6.6 billion in losses stemming from its investments in natural gas derivatives, the largest losses ever for a U.S. hedge fund. Despite notable hedge fund losses, the hedge fund industry has primarily helped contribute to the stability and growth of the U.S. economy by ferreting out inefficiencies and taking risks other institutions are incapable of taking.

Houman B. Shadab

FURTHER READING

Hull, John C. *Options, Futures, and Other Derivatives.* 6th ed. Englewood Cliffs, N.J.: Prentice Hall, 2006.

Lhabitant, Francois-Serge. *Handbook of Hedge Funds.* Hoboken, N.J.: Wiley Finance, 2006.

SEE ALSO: Black Monday; Bond industry; Commodity markets; Enron bankruptcy; New York Stock Exchange; Securities and Exchange Commission; Stock markets.

DHS. *See* Homeland Security, U.S. Department of

Digital recording technology

DEFINITION: System for recording audio data in which the analog signal of sound is converted into binary numbers for storage or processing

SIGNIFICANCE: Digital recording has made possible much higher quality sound reproduction on much smaller and less expensive media but, at the same time, has made it easier for users to make high-quality copies of copyrighted materials, thereby cutting into sales of these materials.

Digital sound recording required several important developments seemingly unrelated to audio reproduction. The first foundational discovery was Claude Elwood Shannon's development of information theory, which provided the tools for translating the continuous variation of sound into discrete ones and zeros, a process known as digitizing. The second innovation was the development of small, lightweight computers that could be produced economically in large numbers, making them affordable to the average consumer. The third component was the development of cheap, reliable low-power lasers, creating a mechanism for reading recorded data without mechanical contact and its resultant wear.

LASER DISCS

The earliest laser discs were developed during the 1970's to hold analog television information. However, they failed as a consumer product because the laser playback mechanism was expensive and delicate, and therefore could not be brought down to a price that any but the wealthiest consumers could afford. Furthermore, a twelve-inch disc, the size of a long-playing phonograph record, could hold only twenty-five minutes of programming. A feature-length motion picture required five discs, resulting in constant interruptions, whereas videocassettes not only could hold an entire motion picture but also could be used to record television broadcasts.

However, executives at Phillips saw a potential for laser technology as a recording medium for the digital audio technology they were developing. In 1982, Phillips unveiled the first digital audio compact disc (CD). Smaller than a 45-revolutions-per-minute (rpm) single, it could hold as much music as an entire long-play (LP) record. Furthermore, the fidelity of sound reproduction was limited only by the quality of the amplifier and speakers. Because users could not record music on CDs, audio cassettes, which could be used to tape music, continued to sell briskly. Recording industry executives became increasingly concerned about loss of income due to piracy, and numerous congressional hearings about copyright protection for sound recordings were held during the late 1980's.

The real piracy problem came from advancements in personal computer technology. Computer companies quickly recognized the value of the CD to carry information other than music. Because CDs were write-protected by design, an unwitting user could not corrupt original disks. The 1990's saw increasing numbers of consumer computers equipped with CD-ROM (compact disc read-only memory) drives as standard equipment. The inability to write to a CD hit the computer industry even harder, resulting in the CD burner, which used a higher-power laser to record data onto special blank discs. As a result, people with the right software could copy digital music files from a commercial audio CD and burn it onto their own CD.

IPOD NATION

The marriage of computers and sound recording was completed by Apple Computer in 2001. Only weeks after the September 11 terrorist attack, Apple's chief executive officer Steve Jobs announced the iPod, a music player that would allow people to upload music directly from their computers and carry a thousand or more songs in their pockets with no discs to switch. Along with this remarkable device, he introduced the iTunes Music Store, at which people could buy individual songs as well as albums, all as digital files that could be downloaded onto their computers without the need for manufacturing or transporting a physical disc.

The iPod was a tiny computer with a limited operating system, which stored music files on a miniature hard drive and allowed users to control how they were played back. Sleek and beautiful, it quickly made Apple Computer a leader in the consumer electronics industry, to the point where the company dropped "Computer" from its name. Throughout the first decade of the twenty-first cen-

tury, Apple improved the iPod. As flash memory became cheaper, hard-drive-based iPods gave way to solid-state ones. As market research discovered that many iPod users rarely used the playlist function, instead preferring the shuffle feature, the smallest iPods were made with a simplified interface that allowed only shuffle play. At the same time, high-end iPods such as the iPod Touch, introduced in 2008, became more similar to the iPhone, a high-end smartphone that combined digital telephony and handheld computer functions.

Digital recording also made it easier for small players to enter the recording business. Although professional-grade analog audio recordings required an entire system of expensive equipment, a professional-grade digital recording could easily be recorded and mixed on a consumer-grade computer with software such as Apple's Garage Band, then burned to a CD to send to a recording company. The only special investment a band would need was the high-quality microphones to accurately capture the sound of their voices and nonelectronic instruments for digitization, since most electric guitars and synthesizers generally could be jacked directly into the digital mixer board. Whereas aspiring bands in the analog era generally had to rent a professional recording studio to produce suitable demo tapes, the rise of digital recording technology meant that bands could produce a demonstration CD using the equipment and skills of a computer-adept friend.

Leigh Husband Kimmel

Apple CEO Steve Jobs holds a new iPod with video capabilities during an address in 2005. (Hulton Archive/Getty Images)

FURTHER READING

Day, Timothy. *A Century of Recorded Music: Listening to Musical History.* New Haven, Conn.: Yale University Press, 2000. Sets digital recording in the larger context of sound recording.

Espejo, Roman, ed. *What Is the Future of the Music Industry?* Detroit, Mich.: Greenhaven, 2008. This collection of articles discusses the music industry's future. Covers illegal file sharing, CDs, and digital rights.

Levy, Steven. *The Perfect Thing: How the iPod Shuffles Commerce, Culture, and Coolness.* New York: Simon & Schuster, 2006. A study of Apple's iPod and its role in making MP3s popular.

Morton, David L., Jr. *Sound Recording: The Life Story of a Technology.* Westport, Conn.: Greenwood Press, 2004. Although this work contains substantial material on the predigital era, it also looks at the development of digital recording.

Pohlmann, Ken C. *The Compact Disc Handbook*. Madison, Wis.: A-R Editions, 1992. A specific study of the compact disc.

SEE ALSO: Apple; Computer industry; Copyright law; Electronics industry; Google; International Business Machines; Music industry; Photographic equipment industry; Radio broadcasting industry; Video rental industry.

Diners Club

IDENTIFICATION: First multiple-business charge card

DATE: Founded in 1950

SIGNIFICANCE: As the first multiple-business charge card, Diners Club revolutionized the American economy and consumer culture by creating a means of effecting cash-free transactions and permitting consumers ready access to credit.

The use of charge cards began during the 1920's, when department stores and gasoline retailers began issuing cards to their customers. By the 1930's, some companies had begun accepting cards from other businesses on a limited basis. Until the establishment of Diners Club in 1950, however, no system existed by which a single charge card could be used at multiple businesses.

The event that led to the founding of Diners Club reportedly occurred in 1949, when Frank X. McNamara was unable to pay for his dinner at a New York restaurant because he had forgotten his wallet. He subsequently resolved to devise a system by which consumers could pay for goods and services without cash by presenting a charge card that would allow member merchants to secure reimbursement from a central source. By 1950, McNamara and his partner, Ralph Schneider, had established Diners Club, enrolling the restaurant at which McNamara conceived the idea as one of its first member merchants and adding over twenty thousand cardholders to its rolls in its first year of operation.

By the mid-1950's, Diners Club had enrolled thousands of member merchants and issued over 200,000 cards worldwide. The cards were promoted to salespeople and other frequent business travelers as a means of paying for and keeping track of expenses. After the Internal Revenue Service issued regulations requiring detailed accounting of business expenses in 1958, the number of Diners Club accounts being opened per year increased drastically. The card became a fixture of American culture, gaining prominence as a status symbol and as a representation of a modern consumer society characterized by mobility, affluence, and convenience.

Diners Club and early competitors such as American Express, which issued the first general-purpose charge card, required users to pay their outstanding balances in full within thirty to sixty days, and they were known among industry insiders as "travel and entertainment cards." They were charge cards used primarily by business travelers and wealthy consumers as a convenient substitute for cash. In 1958, Bank of America issued the BankAmericard, a true credit card, which allowed customers to carry balances over time in exchange for interest charged to the balances. Credit cards linked to revolving-charge accounts became the industry standard during the late twentieth century. As credit cards became more widely available to consumers, nonrevolving charge cards such as Diners Club gained an increasing reputation for exclusivity while losing market share to an increasing number of revolving-charge credit cards.

During the early 1960's, Diners Club became the first credit card company to sell franchise rights to its brand name, increasing its presence in international markets. By the early 1970's, credit card companies such as BankAmericard (later Visa), MasterCharge (later MasterCard), and American Express had surpassed Diners Club in popularity. In 1981, Citigroup purchased the rights to the Diners Club name, and in 2008, Discover purchased the Diners Club network from Citigroup. Diners Club cards remained in limited use, primarily outside the United States.

Michael H. Burchett

FURTHER READING

Evans, David S., and Richard Schmalensee. *Paying with Plastic: The Digital Revolution in Buying and Borrowing*. 2d ed. Cambridge, Mass.: MIT Press, 2005.

Mandell, Lewis. *Credit Card Industry: A History*. New York: Macmillan, 1990.

SEE ALSO: Banking; Catalog shopping; Credit card buying; Restaurant industry; Retail trade industry; Truth-in-lending laws.

Disney, Walt

IDENTIFICATION: Entertainment industry entrepreneur
BORN: December 5, 1901; Chicago, Illinois
DIED: December 15, 1966; Burbank, California
SIGNIFICANCE: A commercial artist and cartoonist, Disney founded the Walt Disney Company, which would become one of the most influential media and entertainment corporations in the world.

Walt Disney was an influential force in the entertainment industry in the twentieth century. At the beginning of his entrepreneurial days, during the early 1920's, Disney collaborated with another talented artist, Ub Iwerk, in creating a small cartoon-production company. Although their first business ventures failed, the two artists acquired enough knowledge and expertise in the industry to convince Disney that success was possible. He moved to Hollywood, California, and recruited his brother Roy O. Disney to assist him. Together, Walt and Roy founded the Disney Brothers Studio. This company survived, creating such cartoon series as *Alice in Cartoonland* and *Oswald the Rabbit*. Disney's first major success, in 1928, was the cartoon character Mickey Mouse.

By this point in his career, with a staff of animators in place, Disney was no longer sketching his characters himself. Instead, he devoted his attentions to finding innovative ways to enhance his productions. In his third Mickey Mouse production, *Steamboat Willie* (1928), Disney used music and his own voice to create the first sound cartoon. Over the next few years, Disney's cast of characters expanded to include Minnie Mouse, Donald Duck, Goofy, and Pluto. His keen imagination, groundbreaking use of color and other technologies, creation of full-length animated films, and production of live-action films made him a leader in the industry. He also exploited merchandising opportunities, marketing toys and souvenirs based on his characters.

Business was not always rosy: During the 1940's, Disney created several works, including *Fantasia* (1940), that were fiscal failures in their initial re-

leases. During this difficult period, Disney stayed in production by creating training and educational films for the federal government, including the armed forces. Business improved during the 1950's, and Disney branched out into other forms of entertainment, including television. Television shows such as *The Mickey Mouse Club* and *Disneyland* (later known as *The Wonderful World of Disney*) became popular, particularly the episodes of the latter show featuring Fess Parker as Davy Crockett.

For his next venture, Disney planned a theme park that would outshine all other existing amusement parks. This park would capitalize on his other financial interests, using Disney themes and characters already familiar to the public and placing them in a clean and magical land for family entertainment. Disneyland opened in 1955.

Disney's empire was particularly influential in that it integrated various media, using the same core characters as a bridge. Disney produced films, television programs, books, comic books, theme parks, and merchandise. Each success also served to promote the success of related ventures, and each fail-

Walt Disney. (Library of Congress)

ure was mitigated by diversification. As a result, Walt Disney was a twentieth century pioneer in the entertainment industry, demonstrating the power of integration and the ability of a strong brand, character, or icon to drive entertainment revenues.

Cynthia J. W. Svoboda

FURTHER READING

Barrier, Michael. *The Animated Man: A Life of Walt Disney.* Berkeley: University of California Press, 2007.

Gabler, Neal. *Walt Disney: The Triumph of the American Imagination.* New York: Alfred A. Knopf, 2007.

Peri, Don. *Working with Walt: Interviews with Disney Artists.* Jackson: University Press of Mississippi, 2008.

SEE ALSO: Disneyland; Motion-picture industry; Television broadcasting industry; Tourism industry.

Disneyland

IDENTIFICATION: Amusement park in Anaheim, California

DATE: Opened to the public on July 18, 1955

SIGNIFICANCE: Disneyland set a new standard for theme parks, combining rides and other attractions with famous Disney characters and themes to create a magical, otherworldly setting for family entertainment. The park became a tourist destination, bringing visitors to Southern California, and it helped perpetuate Disney's brand, demonstrating that the brand could be successful in a variety of arenas.

Walt Disney first conceived the idea of a new amusement park during the 1930's. Disillusioned with the unkempt entertainment facilities of the day, Disney envisioned a clean, well-lit place that would cater to the needs of its customers. In December, 1952, Disney created WED Enterprises to oversee the design and development of such a theme park. Disney anticipated erecting the park in the vicinity of Burbank, California, but hired the Stanford Research Institute to recommend the most suitable location and to estimate start-up expenses.

Anticipating the need for extra revenue to fund his venture, Disney made an agreement with the American Broadcasting Company (ABC) to pro-duce the weekly *Disneyland* television show. This show would help market the park and provide Disney with additional start-up revenue. After securing financial support from his brother Roy O. Disney and other funding sources, Disney eagerly began transforming 160 acres of orange groves in Anaheim, California, into his fantasy land. Construction began on July 21, 1954, with a scheduled opening date planned for just under a year later.

Creating a massive theme park with five distinct areas was no easy feat. The design plan had visitors entering the park at Main Street, U.S.A., a seeming replica of a turn-of-the-twentieth-century Midwestern town. From there, guests could choose to explore Frontierland, an Old West pioneer town; Adventureland, which offered a tropical cruise with lifelike mechanical animals; Tomorrowland, which featured a visit to Mars; or Fantasyland, which contained Sleeping Beauty's castle and amusement rides based on Disney stories and characters. Another popular attraction was the Disneyland railroad that encircled the park.

On Sunday, July 17, 1955, Disneyland celebrated its opening day with a special event for the press and invited guests, and ABC premiered the first episode of *Disneyland.* Well-known news anchors were on hand to endorse and promote the glamorous new park, but all was not well. Many people showed up with counterfeit tickets, leading to the event becoming overcrowded. Water problems, lengthy lines, food shortages, a gas leak, a plumber's strike, and problems associated with hot, uncured asphalt plagued the park. The day was a near fiasco, and media coverage was not flattering.

Despite this initial setback, Disneyland's popularity mounted, and by the second year it was realizing a profit. Fun family entertainment, a strong business commitment to quality control, a well-trained courteous staff, and well-orchestrated marketing transformed a former orange grove into one of the most visited attractions in America. Disneyland spawned other Disney resorts in Florida, Tokyo, Hong Kong, and Paris. Disney Parks became a multimillion-dollar operation and a part of American culture.

Cynthia J. W. Svoboda

FURTHER READING

Bryman, Alan. *Disney and His Worlds.* New York: Routledge, 1995.

_____. *The Disneyization of Society.* Thousand Oaks, Calif.: Sage, 2004.

Gabler, Neal. *Walt Disney: The Triumph of the American Imagination.* New York: Alfred A. Knopf, 2007.

SEE ALSO: Disney, Walt; Motion-picture industry; Television broadcasting industry; Tourism industry.

Distiller's Securities Corporation. *See* Whiskey Trust

DJIA. *See* Dow Jones Industrial Average

DOE. *See* Energy, U.S. Department of

Dot-com bubble

THE EVENT: Rapid rise and sudden fall in the price of Internet sector stocks resulting from overvaluation and the indiscriminate distribution of venture capital

DATE: 1995-2001

PLACE: United States

SIGNIFICANCE: During the 1990's, Internet-related businesses were viewed as a way for investors to make quick profits, and millions of dollars were pumped into nascent businesses. After the bubble burst and many of these businesses failed, dotcoms were regarded as bad investments. Ultimately, as the markets settled, it became clear that Internet stocks offered both good and bad investment opportunities.

The period from 1995 to 2001 saw a stock market bubble develop in the Internet sector. A temporary overvaluation of stocks in a particular industry is called a bubble because it acts like a bubble, which grows and then bursts. During much of the 1990's, however, the growth in the value of Internet stocks was not seen as a bubble but simply as the energetic growth of a promising new industry.

Investors had become enamored with the industry. Following the rise of Netscape and its massive initial public offering (IPO), they were more than willing to invest venture capital in companies that had never made a profit. Some economists said that America was entering the era of a "new economy" in which the old rules of investing no longer applied. The fervor was also fueled by low interest rates and by day traders who bought stocks with borrowed money. Many companies that were formed at the time operated at a net loss to build their market share. In such a business model, one company would have to monopolize a niche to make a profit. The new companies spent their venture capital and then made their IPOs as quickly as possible to raise more cash. The public eagerly bought these new stocks. In 1999 alone, of the 457 IPOs made, 117 doubled in value on the first day of trading. The result was that these stocks became grossly overvalued.

The Pets.com sock puppet, shown in 2000, was a familiar figure during the dot-com boom. The puppet spokesperson, like many in his industry, soon found himself out of work. (AP/Wide World Photos)

The index tracking the value of stocks on the NASDAQ stock exchange, which includes many technology stocks, reached its all-time high, 5048.62, on March 10, 2000. The index had stood at less than half that value just a year earlier. However, online retailers reported poor results from the previous Christmas season, and some of the bellwether technology stocks processed massive sell orders for billions of dollars. March 13 saw the NASDAQ decline in value by four percentage points, triggering a long slide in the Internet sector.

Some companies were found to have used accounting tricks to overstate their profits. The public quickly lost its faith in technology, and by October, 2002, the NASDAQ had lost 78 percent of its peak value to close at a low of 1114.11. The Federal Reserve cut interest rates to stop the decline, and the economy entered a recession. Ultimately, the bubble wiped out $5 trillion in market value. Very few Internet companies survived the dot-com bubble, with some of the notable exceptions being Amazon.com and eBay. Although the losses in market value and jobs were tremendous, many analysts view the dot-com bubble as a necessary part of learning about the new technology of the Internet and its effect on the economy. As many Internet-only companies disappeared in the wake of the bubble, many brick-and-mortar retailers developed major Internet presences, using their established brands and resources to succeed where firms relying solely on venture capital had failed.

James J. Heiney

FURTHER READING

Cassidy, John. *Dot.Con: The Greatest Story Ever Sold.* New York: HarperCollins, 2002.

Kuo, J. David. *Dot.Bomb: My Days and Nights at an Internet Goliath.* Boston: Little, Brown, 2001.

Munroe, Tapan. *Dot-Com to Dot-Bomb: Understanding the Dot-Com Boom, Bust, and Resurgence.* Moraga, Calif: Moraga Press, 2004.

SEE ALSO: Catalog shopping; Computer industry; Fiber-optic industry; Google; Internet; Online marketing; Telecommunications industry.

Dow Jones Industrial Average

IDENTIFICATION: Index that measures the performances of thirty representative American stocks

DATE: Introduced on May 26, 1896

SIGNIFICANCE: The Dow Jones Industrial Average tracks stock market trends and, by extension, economic trends in American business, thereby providing an overall indication of the status and health of the stock market and of the U.S. economy.

The Dow Jones Industrial Average (DJIA), devised by financial analyst Charles Henry Dow, first appeared in Dow's *Customers' Afternoon Letter* on May 26, 1896. Variously referred to as the Dow, the Dow Jones, or the Dow 30, the Dow Jones Industrial Average originally consisted of twelve representative stocks, only one of which, General Electric, remains in the index as of 2008. The word "industrial" is perhaps misleading because the stocks in the index are not necessarily involved in heavy industry but include holdings in such diverse areas as pharmaceuticals, energy, health care, mining, minerals, technology, and finance.

In its earliest days, the DJIA was determined by adding the prices of each of the dozen stocks in the index and dividing by twelve. On the day the index was first published, the index closed at 40.94. By 1914, the DJIA stood at 71.42, but just before World War I broke out in Europe, on July 30, 1914, the stock market closed and remained closed until December 12, 1914, when the DJIA stood at 74.56.

THE TWENTIETH CENTURY

To more accurately reflect the state of business in the United States, the DJIA was reformulated in 1916 to include twenty representative stocks and in 1928 to include thirty stocks. Although the original means of measuring stock market activity was simple and straightforward, it soon had to be altered because, as stocks in the index split or issued stock dividends, the simple process of dividing the total value of one share of each of the stocks in the index by the number of stocks in it became misleading and inaccurate. When a stock split takes place, if the split is two-for-one, stockholders receive two shares for every share they hold. There are also occasional reverse splits in which stockholders end up with fewer shares than they originally held. In such situations, the overall value of stockholders' positions in a stock remains unchanged, but unless provision is made for the index to reflect these splits, the index can be misleading.

The DJIA grew at a compounded annual rate of 5.3 percent during the twentieth century, reflecting the nation's industrial growth. When the number of investment grade stocks—usually referred to as blue chips—in the DJIA was raised to thirty, a more sophisticated means of gauging their performance, called a flexible divisor, was put into use. It provides for splits and other actions that might affect the overall representativeness of the DJIA.

In the latter part of the century, huge stores of information about the stock market began to be available nearly instantaneously through the Internet. The major index averages are entered and updated every few seconds on the Internet. Stock traders who follow these indexes can buy and sell nearly immediately by communicating with their brokers through their personal computers. They can transact business from anywhere in the world as long as they have their computers up and running.

THE EARLY TWENTY-FIRST CENTURY

The thirty companies represented on the Dow Jones Industrial Average during the early twenty-first century are drawn from a variety of fields. Computer technology is represented by such stocks as Microsoft, Intel, United Technologies, and International Business Machines (IBM). Retail sales are reflected by holdings like Home Depot, Procter and Gamble, and Wal-Mart. Pharmaceuticals are represented by Johnson and Johnson, Merck, and Pfizer. Among the energy stocks on the index are Chevron and Exxon Mobile. Entertainment and leisure are reflected in the Dow's holding Walt Disney and McDonald's. Communication is represented by American Telephone and Telegraph (AT&T) and Verizon Communications.

Among the financial stocks in the DJIA are Amer-

DOW JONES INDUSTRIAL AVERAGE HISTORIC CLOSINGS

Benchmark Closing	First Day Exceeded	Actual Average at Closing
100	January 12, 1906	100.25
500	March 12, 1956	500.24
1,000	November 14, 1972	1,003.16
2,000	January 8, 1987	2,002.25
3,000	April 17, 1991	3,004.46
5,000	November 21, 1995	5,023.55
8,000	July 16, 1997	8,038.88
10,000	March 29, 1999	10,006.78
11,000	May 3, 1999	11,014.69
12,000	October 19, 2006	12,011.73
13,000	April 25, 2007	13,089.89
14,000	July 19, 2007	14,000.41

Source: Data from the New York Stock Exchange

ican Express, American International Group, Bank of America, Citigroup, and General Electric. There is some overlapping of categories, as for example with General Electric, which is both a manufacturing corporation and a major financial organization that is also involved in entertainment. Heavy industry is represented by Boeing and Caterpillar. As the status of industries changes, some stocks are dropped from the index and others are added so that the DJIA will be reflective of American business.

R. Baird Shuman

FURTHER READING

Hamilton, William Peter. "Charles Dow." In *Eyewitness to Wall Street: Four Hundred Years of Dreamers, Schemers, Busts, and Booms,* by David Colbert. New York: Broadway Books, 2001. In this brief but useful essay, Hamilton outlines Dow's approach to scoping the stock market and comments on his creating the Dow Jones Industrial and Transportation Indexes.

Kindleberger, Charles Poor. *Manias, Panics, and Crashes: A History of Financial Crises.* New York: John Wiley & Sons, 2000. Kindleberger analyzes market trends as they are reflected by various stock market indexes.

Shiller, Robert J. *Irrational Exuberance.* 2d ed. Princeton, N.J.: Princeton University Press, 2005. Of particular interest is Chapter 3, "Precipitating Factors: The Capitalist Explosion, the Internet, and Other Events." Well written, clear, thorough.

Soros, George. *The Crisis of Global Capitalism: Open Society Endangered*. New York: PublicAffairs, 1998. Provides information about the role of indexes in plotting market performance.

Stevens, Leigh. *Essential Technical Analysis: Tools and Techniques to Spot Market Trends*. New York: John Wiley, 2002. See especially Chapter 3, "Charles Dow and the Underlying Principles of Market Behavior," in which Dow's method of analyzing stock market trends is discussed.

Weiss, Martin D. *Crash Profits: Make Money When Stocks Sink and Soar*. Hoboken, N.J.: John Wiley & Sons, 2003. Weiss emphasizes the cyclical nature of stock markets and shows how the indexes that reflect them can guide investors during turbulent times.

SEE ALSO: CNBC; New York Stock Exchange; Securities and Exchange Commission; Standard & Poor's; Stock markets; *The Wall Street Journal*.

Drive-through businesses

DEFINITION: Commercial establishments at which customers may complete transactions while remaining in their automobiles

SIGNIFICANCE: With the rise of American automobile culture and consumers' increasing need for convenient and speedy services during the twentieth century, drive-through businesses proliferated and revolutionized major industries. Drive-through establishments became a profitable part of the American landscape and economy, from fast-food dining to banking and more.

In 1923, J. G. Kirby and Dr. Reuben Wright Jackson opened the first drive-in eatery, the Pig Stand, in Dallas, Texas. A&W opened a drive-in diner in 1923, and Maid-Rite had a drive-through window when it opened in 1926. In 1951, Jack in the Box introduced the drive-through system of ordering at a two-way intercom in the parking lot and then driving to a service window to pay for and pick up an order. Sonic opened its first drive-in diner, complete with carhops, in 1952.

FOOD AND GAS

By 2008, most of the major American fast-food chains offered drive-through service at some or all of their outlets. *QSR Magazine* (whose name stands for quick-service restaurant) published a statistical analysis of speed, accuracy, and customer service that listed the ten "speediest drive-thru chains" in the year 2007. They were Wendy's, Checkers, Taco Bell, McDonald's, Long John Silver, Burger King, Arby's, Bojangles', Taco John's, and Chick-Fil-A.

Another early major drive-through industry was gasoline retailing. In 1905 in St. Louis, Missouri, Clem Laessig and Harry Grenner opened the first gas station. By the late 1920's, there were twenty-four-hour gas stations. In 1947, Frank Ulrich founded the first modern self-serve gas station. However, there were fewer than 3,000 self-serve stations in operation during the early 1970's. Some 226,000 traditional full-service stations were in operation in the United States in 1973, but more than half of these businesses disappeared between 1970 and 1990. Their decline was caused partly by the rise of another drive-through phenomenon, the convenience store.

In 1927, the first modern convenience store was founded when Southland Ice Company dock manager Jefferson Green began selling "convenience" products such as milk, eggs, and bread on evenings and Sundays, when local grocery stores were closed. His chain of stores was open from 7:00 A.M. to 11:00 P.M., which led to the chain's officially adopting the name 7-Eleven in 1946. After World War II, convenience stores grew rapidly. In 1961, the first twenty-four-hour convenience store opened. During the 1970's, increasing numbers of convenience stores began to sell gasoline. By 2002, 80 percent of stores were using the pay-at-the-pump credit/debit card reader system, enabling speedier customer transactions. According to 2008 industry reports, motor fuel sales at convenience stores reached $405.8 billion in 2006, and convenience stores sold more than 80 percent of all gasoline purchased in the United States.

OTHER BUSINESSES

Founded in 1901, Walgreen's introduced the concept of freestanding stores with drive-through pharmacy service in 1992. This was a significant development that made it more convenient for customers to drop off and pick up prescriptions. After 1994, most new Walgreen's stores included this service. In 2008, Walgreen's was the nation's largest retail pharmacy chain, and 80 percent of its stores offered drive-through service. This innovation became an industry standard. In 2001, CVS offered drive-through service in twelve hundred of its forty-two hundred U.S. stores. In 2006, drugstore chain Rite Aid offered the service in 43 percent of its stores.

The Donut Hole, pictured in 1970, was a popular coffee and donut drive-through shop in Los Angeles. (AP/Wide World Photos)

The drive-through concept revolutionized American banking. The first drive-through bank, the Exchange National Bank of Chicago, opened on November 12, 1946. Customers could deposit or withdraw money at drive-through teller windows.

Richard Hollingshead opened the first drive-in movie theater on June 6, 1933, in Camden, New Jersey. After World War II, drive-ins, which provided a leisure activity the whole family could enjoy, reached their peak in popularity, with more than four thousand such theaters in the United States in 1958. With the invention of videocassette recorders in 1971, drive-in theaters started to fade in popularity.

By the twenty-first century, the drive-through concept permeated the American economy, in mom-and-pop operations as well as in national chains. Drive-through businesses included dry cleaners, car washes, liquor stores, coffee shops, casinos, and even a wedding chapel: In 1991, Charolette Richards created a drive-up window at her Little White Wedding Chapel in Las Vegas, Nevada, to accommodate handicapped patrons. The novelty soon became popular, especially among film stars and celebrities.

Alice Myers

FURTHER READING

Bacon, John. *America's Corner Store: Walgreen's Prescription for Success.* Hoboken, N.J.: Wiley, 2004. History of Walgreen's, which pioneered the concept of the drive-through pharmacy. Bibliography, appendix, notes, and index.

Hinckley, Jim, and Jon Robinson. *The Big Book of Car Culture: The Armchair Guide to Automotive Americana.* St. Paul, Minn.: Motorbooks, 2005. This entertaining compendium includes chapters on service stations, dinner in the car, drive-through windows, and other aspects of road culture. Illustrated with over one hundred photos. Index.

Jakle, John A., and Keith A. Sculle. *Fast Food: Roadside Restaurants in the Automobile Age.* Baltimore: Johns Hopkins University Press, 1999. Written by a geographer and a historian, this is a well-researched study of the culture of the automobile and quick-service restaurants. Illustrated, with over 100 photos. Bibliography.

_____. *The Gas Station in America.* Baltimore: Johns Hopkins University Press, 1994. Comprehensive history, with over 150 illustrations, including vintage ads and postcards of gas stations. Notes, bibliography, and index.

Russell, Tim. *Fill 'er Up: The Great American Gas Station.* St. Paul, Minn.: Voyageur Press, 2007. Written by an eminent petroliana historian and collector, this entertaining chronicle covers the early decades of the twentieth century through the beginning of the twenty-first century. Includes vintage photography and advertisements. Illustrated. Index.

Segrave, Kerry. *Drive-In Theaters: A History from Their Inception in 1933*. Jefferson, N.C.: McFarland, 1992. Covering the history of drive-in theaters through the 1980's, this study includes copies of the original theater patents. Illustrated. Appendixes, notes, and extensive bibliography.

Witzel, Michael, and Tim Steil. *Classic Roadside Americana: Car Hops, Fast Food, Drive-in Restaurants, Road Trips, Route 66*. St. Paul, Minn.: Crestline, 2006. Pictorial history, including descriptions of businesses, architecture, and automobile travel. Illustrated, mostly in color. Index.

See also: Automotive industry; Banking; Fast-food restaurants; Motion-picture industry; Petroleum industry; Retail trade industry.

Drug trafficking

Definition: Criminal trade in controlled and illegal substances

Significance: The illegal production and distribution of drugs has become a multibillion-dollar industry that has allowed criminal organizations to generate exorbitant profits while evading payment of taxes, thereby placing additional tax burdens on American citizens and legitimate business enterprises. Further, the illegal drug trade has taxed the resources of law-enforcement organizations at the local, state, and national levels and has forced many American businesses to spend considerable sums to combat the effects of drugs in the workplace.

Drug trafficking is not a new phenomenon in the United States. In the eighteenth and nineteenth centuries, narcotics such as opium and morphine were often-prescribed medications, and both legal and illegal networks were established to import these drugs from the Middle East and Asia. At that time, most Americans were unaware of the long-term ill effects of addiction and turned a blind eye to the establishment of opium dens and the widespread availability of morphine and other narcotics. By the early twentieth century, however, the public became alarmed at the dangers of addiction, and the U.S. government began taking serious steps to curb the importation and sale of narcotics.

Congress passed the Harrison Act of 1914 and the Narcotic Drugs Import and Export Act of 1922 to regulate production and distribution of certain narcotic substances. In 1930, the Federal Bureau of Narcotics (FBN) was established to enforce laws regarding drug sales and use. Trafficking persisted, however, largely because enormous profits were available to those willing to risk penalties and jail time to supply a population addicted to substances such as opium, heroin, and morphine.

Organized Trafficking Operations

Although early traffickers were often loosely organized to facilitate the importation, distribution, and sales of illegal drugs, over time groups engaged in illegal trafficking developed more sophisticated models for managing the drug trade. Surprisingly, despite their involvement in protection rackets, prostitution, illegal gambling, and loan sharking, until the 1940's most Italian Mafia leaders insisted that their outfits avoid dealing drugs. A few, notably Charlie "Lucky" Luciano of New York, defied this prohibition and used their organizations to oust other gangs from the drug trade and develop sophisticated networks for importing and selling drugs in the United States. As a consequence, in some cities, drugs were readily available to ordinary working men and women whose habits had an impact on their effectiveness in the workplace.

During the early decades of the twentieth century, most businesses did not take steps to help rehabilitate drug users, preferring simply to assist law enforcement in dealing with users as criminals. During the 1930's, some forward-looking companies such as Eastman Kodak and E. I. DuPont established employee-assistance programs designed to aid workers whose performance was being affected by drugs and alcohol. There was not widespread recognition, however, of the deleterious effect that an easily accessible supply of drugs was having on the workforce.

During World War II, drugs became less readily available in the United States, as traffickers found it exceedingly difficult to import drugs from overseas areas where conflict was raging. Almost immediately after the war ended, however, trafficking picked up again. At this time, the Mafia became the principal supplier of illegal drugs. Its extensive network, organized in a fashion similar to an American corporation, provided a means for smuggling drugs into the country through ports (and later air terminals), where it controlled many of the operations. The Mafia also developed an efficient system for distributing drugs to users and an effective, sometimes ruthless, method for collecting payments. Frequently, traffickers used legitimate businesses such as pizza parlors as "fronts" for the sale of their products. By 1970, the Mafia controlled 80 percent of the market.

The availability of illegal drugs made possible one of the most important revolutions in American lifestyle during the 1960's, the creation of the "drug culture" associated with Vietnam War protests and with a general rebellion among young people against established social norms. In addition to illegal narcotics, users began experimenting with mind- and mood-altering substances such as amphetamines, barbiturates, and the hallucinogen lysergic acid diethylamide (LSD). The presence of more than a half-million Americans in Vietnam facilitated the establishment of a strong network between American traffickers and suppliers in the Golden Triangle—Thailand, Burma (later Myanmar), and Laos. At the same time, a movement to deal with drug users by employing a social-services model of treatment and rehabilitation began to gain favor across the country. The public began to recognize that the real criminals were traffickers, who were profiteering on the illicit sales of addictive substances.

THE WAR ON DRUGS

In 1971, President Richard M. Nixon declared a War on Drugs, and in 1973, the Drug Enforcement

DRUG ENFORCEMENT ADMINISTRATION DRUG SEIZURES, 1986-2007

Year	Cocaine (kilograms)	Heroin (kilograms)	Marijuana (kilograms)	Methamphetamine (kilograms)	Hallucinogens (dosage units)
1986	29,389	421	491,831	235	4,146,329
1987	49,666	512	629,839	198	6,556,891
1988	60,951	728	347,306	694	16,706,442
1989	73,587	758	286,371	896	13,125,010
1990	57,031	535	127,792	272	2,826,966
1991	67,016	1,174	98,592	289	1,297,394
1992	69,324	722	201,483	352	1,305,177
1993	55,529	616	143,055	560	2,710,063
1994	75,051	491	157,181	768	1,366,817
1995	45,326	876	219,830	876	2,768,165
1996	44,735	320	192,059	751	1,719,209
1997	28,670	399	215,348	1,147	1,100,912
1998	34,447	370	262,180	1,203	1,075,457
1999	36,165	351	338,247	1,489	1,736,077
2000	58,674	546	331,964	1,771	29,307,427
2001	59,430	753	271,849	1,634	13,755,390
2002	63,640	710	238,024	1,353	11,661,157
2003	73,725	795	254,196	1,678	2,878,594
2004	117,854	672	265,813	1,659	2,261,706
2005	118,311	640	283,344	2,161	8,881,321
2006	69,826	805	322,438	1,711	4,606,277
2007	96,713	625	356,472	1,086	5,636,305

Source: Data from the Drug Enforcement Administration

Administration (DEA) was created by combining a number of federal agencies that had been involved in combating the sale and use of illicit substances, including the Federal Bureau of Narcotics. The need for interdiction was apparent: A 1977 study of drugs in the workplace revealed that substance abuse was responsible for lost productivity, increased medical and accident insurance expenses, and an increase in property crimes—both by employees who pilfered from their employers and by others who stole to generate money to support their habits. Neighborhoods known for heavy drug trafficking and use were seen as unsafe for many business operations. Under President Ronald Reagan, efforts to eradicate drug trafficking increased during the 1980's, and the federal government began what became a multibillion-dollar investment in enforcement and education to deal with the problem. Both the DEA and the U.S. military began active operations in foreign countries to destroy crops from which illegal drugs could be manufactured.

During the 1970's and 1980's, as the federal government began a campaign to eliminate Mafia influence in the United States, new groups—mainly African American, Asian, and Latino gangs—took over the drug trade. Many of these groups received their drugs from Latin American countries via Mexico, although sources in Asia and the Middle East continued to supply American markets. As the Mafia had done in America decades earlier, supplier organizations in Latin America and Asia developed complex, hierarchical business structures that permitted those at the top to accumulate significant wealth, much of which was reinvested in legitimate businesses or used to buy protection from complicit government officials. In some developing nations, drug production was a means of generating income for much of the population, so participation in drug trafficking was often ignored or even quietly abetted by the government.

Between 1980 and 2000, a steady influx of drugs into the United States caused the price for many substances to fall. It thus became easier for users to support their habits, and the number of drug users increased, exacerbating the problem for law enforcement and, by extension, for American businesses. Although it is difficult to obtain precise figures, one 2000 estimate placed the value of worldwide drug trafficking at $400 billion. DEA estimates for 2005 suggested the value of illegal drugs sold in the United States was $64 billion.

While law-enforcement officials stepped up their attempts to curb trafficking, businesses became more aggressive in establishing programs to assist users. Pre-employment screening and random testing were introduced into the workplace at a number of companies. By 2000, nearly 90 percent of America's larger firms were conducting some form of screening or testing. Substance-abuse treatment and counseling programs proliferated nationwide in response to the perceived epidemic of drug use, creating jobs for thousands in the social work field and generating millions of dollars in expenditures on cures and rehabilitation. Concurrently, during the last decades of the twentieth century, an increasing number of habitual users and traffickers—mostly low-level street dealers—were imprisoned, creating an additional drain on tax dollars but creating jobs as well in both state-run and privately managed prisons. Indeed, private prisons constituted a new industry that sprang up to deal with the country's growing prison population, a population in which many inmates were guilty of drug-related offences.

Laurence W. Mazzeno

FURTHER READING

Battacharya, Gargi. *Traffick: The Illicit Movement of People and Things*. London: Pluto Press, 2005. Explains the relationship of drug trafficking in America to the worldwide network involved in promoting the growth, distribution, and sales of illegal substances.

Bauder, Julia, ed. *Drug Trafficking*. New York: Greenhaven Press, 2008. Collection of essays examining the nature and ramifications of drug trafficking in the United States and other countries. Examines the economic impact of the drug trade and its relationship to international terrorism.

Booth, Martin. *Opium: A History*. New York: Simon & Schuster, 1996. Includes a chapter on America's century-long struggle to control drugs, as well as one on the business aspects of drug trafficking.

Clutterbuck, Richard. *Drugs, Crime, and Corruption: Thinking the Unthinkable*. New York: New York University Press, 1995. Traces the history of drug trafficking worldwide. Examines the economic impact of that trade and efforts by the United States and other countries to thwart those engaged in it.

Kopp, Pierre. *Political Economy of Illegal Drugs*. New York: Routledge, 2004. Concentrates on the economic impact of drug trafficking and consumption worldwide. Analyzes problems posed by this enterprise in the United States. Includes a bibliography of additional source materials.

Lyman, Michael D., and Garry W. Potter. *Organized Crime*. Upper Saddle River, N.J.: Prentice-Hall, 1997. Includes a chapter on the involvement of organized crime in the sale of illicit drugs in the United States. Describes methods of importation, manufacture, and distribution and provides a history of the growth of illegal drug sales in America.

Reppetto, Thomas A. *Bringing Down the Mob: The War Against the American Mafia*. New York: Henry Holt, 2006. Describes the Mafia's involvement in the sale of illegal drugs. Explains how the drug trade exploded during the 1970's and 1980's and how the Mafia was displaced in drug trafficking activities by other crime groups.

SEE ALSO: Food and Drug Administration; Justice, U.S. Department of; Organized crime; Pharmaceutical industry; Prohibition; Racketeer Influenced and Corrupt Organizations Act.

DST. *See* Daylight saving time

Dust Bowl

THE EVENT: Drought in the American South and Midwest that caused the regions to encounter recurring and sometimes devastating dust storms, destroying many farms and exacerbating the effects of the Great Depression

DATE: 1931-1938

PLACE: Midwestern and southern plains of the United States

SIGNIFICANCE: The Dust Bowl caused hundreds of thousands of Americans to become homeless and resulted in millions of inhabitants leaving the Great Plains in search of better living conditions elsewhere. It also led to a greater awareness of the negative impact that industry can have on the environment.

Although the precise date of origin of the Dust Bowl is a matter of controversy, the phenomenon began during the early 1930's, at the height of the Great Depression. The states that were hardest hit were Texas, Oklahoma, Nebraska, Kansas, New Mexico, and Colorado, although the impact of the Dust Bowl could be felt throughout the northern plains.

Drought began damaging crops in the South and Midwest in 1931, causing some farmers to revert to producing dairy and other products that did not directly rely on soil conditions. The combination of the drought and poorly strategized plowing of fields led to a situation that was ripe for natural disaster. Winds began creating powerful dust storms, the strongest of which occurred between 1933 and 1936. The impact of a few of these storms was actually felt as far northeast as New York City. During this period, the area also saw an increase in other natural phenomena, including tornado activity.

The dust storms destroyed crops and caused farms to fail throughout the affected region. Some 2.5 million Americans became economic refugees in their own country, as they packed their few possessions and traveled to other parts of the country in search of a way to support themselves and their families. These refugees became known in the communities to which they moved by the pejorative term "Okies," referring to the origin of some of them in Oklahoma.

In 1937, President Franklin D. Roosevelt introduced a tree-planting campaign in the area to minimize soil erosion caused by the winds. The program had some success, but the end of the drought was probably the most important factor in ending the Dust Bowl by 1938. World War II then helped solidify America's resurgent economy and officially ended the Great Depression.

The Dust Bowl was in part a result of new technology that allowed farmers to plow a greater portion of the land than they had in the past. The technologies resulted in greater loss of soil, because farmers did not take adequate steps to minimize such loss. The destruction of the Dust Bowl resulted in new techniques being developed to decrease soil loss through recycling. These new proce-

A collage of 1930's headlines about the Dust Bowl. (Library of Congress)

dures, combined with the inhabitation of the area, decreased the likelihood of similar disasters in the future.

Brion Sever

FURTHER READING

Egan, Timothy. *The Worst Hard Time: The Untold Story of Those Who Survived the Great American Dust Bowl.* Boston: Mariner Books, 2006.

Levey, Richard, and Daniel Franck. *Dust Bowl! The 1930's Black Blizzards.* New York: Bearport, 2005.

Worster, Donald. *Dust Bowl: The Southern Plains in the 1930's.* Oxford, England: Oxford University Press, 2004.

SEE ALSO: Agriculture; Dairy industry; Farm labor; Farm protests; Great Depression; Internal migration; Literary works with business themes.

E

eBay

IDENTIFICATION: Online auction site that uses the World Wide Web to bring individual sellers and buyers together

DATE: Launched on September 3, 1995

SIGNIFICANCE: During the mid-1990's as more and more people gained access to the Internet, online retailers began to proliferate. On September 3, 1995, computer programmer Pierre Omidyar and businessman Jeffrey Skoll launched AuctionWeb, later known as eBay, and the largest online auction house was born.

In concept, eBay is very similar to traditional auction houses, except that its bidding process is handled by online software and the bidders and sellers can be located anywhere in the world. eBay earns its profits from insertion and final value fees on items listed by the sellers.

This eBay teddy bear celebrates the company's ten-year anniversary in 2005. (AP/Wide World Photos)

The eBay auction site started with 41,000 registered users in 1996 and a merchandise volume of $7.2 million. Meg Whitman joined eBay in 1998 as president and chief executive officer (CEO), and in September, 1998, eBay had its initial public stock offering. In April, 1999, the company bought the auction house of Butterfield and Butterfield for $260 million to help extend its auctions on a global scale. eBay Motors was launched, and by 2006, 2 million vehicles had been sold. In 2002, eBay purchased Paypal, an electronic payment service, for $1.5 billion. Since then, Paypal has become one of the preferred methods of payment for online purchases and is an example of how eBay influences other online retailers. In 2007, Paypal continued to expand by handling almost $50 billion in payments, an increase of more than 30 percent from the prior year, indicating the growing popularity of electronic payment services among consumers and retailers. In June, 2007, eBay, in partnership with GE Money, the financial services unit of General Electric, launched an eBay MasterCard rewards credit card.

As of 2006, eBay had a gross merchandise volume of $52.5 billion, with 222 million registered eBay users and 13,200 employees. It has spawned much competition, and as eBay's fees continue to rise, several smaller online auction houses are seeing an increase in business. Paypal processed $6.1 billion in payments during the fourth quarter of 2007 for World Wide Web retailers, such as Dell, Blue Nile, and Yahoo!'s shopping sites. Changes in 2008 to eBay's fee structure and feedback system have resulted in notable dissatisfaction, negative press, and boycotts. In March, 2008, CEO Whitman resigned, although she remained on the board, and was replaced by John Donahue. In October, the company announced employee layoffs of 10 percent of its global workforce and acquisitions of an online payment company and online classified businesses. eBay's third-quarter revenues were on the low end of projections, partly because of the loss of consumer confidence caused by the financial crisis and also because of competitors.

Linda M. Kelley

FURTHER READING

Griffith, Jim. *The Official eBay Bible: The Newly Revised and Updated Version of the Most Comprehensive eBay*

How-to Manual for Everyone from First-Time Users to eBay Experts. 3d ed. New York: Gotham, 2007.

Hillis, Ken, Michael Petit, and Nathan Scott Epley, eds. *Everyday eBay: Culture, Collecting, and Desire.* New York: Routledge, 2006.

Russell, Cheryl L. *eBay Income: How Anyone of Any Age, Location, and/or Background Can Build a Highly Profitable Online Business with eBay.* Ocala, Fla.: Atlantic, 2006.

SEE ALSO: Computer industry; Dot-com bubble; E-mail; Gates, Bill; Google; Home Shopping Network; Internet; Jewelry industry; Online marketing; Thrift stores.

Economic Growth and Tax Relief Reconciliation Act of 2001. *See* Bush tax cuts of 2001

The Economist

IDENTIFICATION: London-based weekly financial newsmagazine

DATE: Launched in September, 1843

SIGNIFICANCE: With more than half of its 1.3 million subscribers in the United States, *The Economist* represents and influences the economic and sociopolitical views and interests of American corporations and executives as part of an Anglo-American, free-market business tradition. The neoliberal perspective it espouses has come to penetrate the greater part of globalized commercial operations and thinking.

Since its nineteenth century inception, *The Economist* has been located in London. Over the course of the twentieth century, however, as New York City replaced London as the world financial center, the publication has become representative of Anglo-American business perspectives, issues, and interests. Throughout its existence, it has been a leading advocate of free trade, supporting market factors and private enterprise as the axis of economic activity.

Founded in 1843 by the Scottish free-trade advocate James Wilson, it initially appeared as *The Economist: A Political, Commercial, Agricultural, and Free-Trade Journal.* In 1861, famed economist and constitutional scholar James Bagehot became editor. At its founding, the magazine had a circulation of approximately two thousand. It reached the one million mark in 2005. The newsmagazine has become part of a larger media conglomerate known as the Economist Group (half owned by the *Financial Times*), which publishes periodicals such as *Intelligent Life* and *Roll Call* and includes the business research agency, the Economist Intelligence Unit.

The magazine's focus has primarily been business, finance, and politics, but its subject matter has grown to include science, technology, and the arts. Printed each week on Thursdays, it appears simultaneously around the world in numerous regional editions and is available online. News items incorporate robust editorial viewpoints. Articles usually appear without a byline and bear a uniform writing style known for its taut economy and ironic wit. These qualities contribute to the stylish, cosmopolitan appeal *The Economist* holds for its globalized executive readership.

Edward A. Riedinger

SEE ALSO: Bloomberg's Business News Services; *Coin's Financial School*; *Forbes*; *Fortune*; Newspaper industry; *Reader's Digest*; *USA Today*; *The Wall Street Journal.*

Edison, Thomas Alva

IDENTIFICATION: American inventor and innovator

BORN: February 11, 1847; Milan, Ohio

DIED: October 18, 1931; West Orange, New Jersey

SIGNIFICANCE: Using his entrepreneurial skills to implement business diversification and divisional structure in the format of mass production, Edison dramatically influenced modern society by developing, manufacturing, and marketing practical products, particularly electric lightbulbs, electric generating systems, phonographs, and motion-picture projectors.

Selling newspapers, candy, and vegetables on the Grand Trunk Railway and later working as a telegraph operator for the same company helped young Thomas Alva Edison recognize his skills as a businessman and motivated him to develop an intense work ethic, resourcefulness, and creativity. In his spare time, he concentrated on reading and experimenting with printing presses, electrical systems, and mechanical apparatuses.

Through his invention and sale of improved telegraphic devices, Edison earned the money necessary to establish an industrial research lab in Menlo Park, New Jersey, in 1876 with the goal of inventing, manufacturing, and marketing useful products. He did not want to be an inventor who just turned ideas into patents; rather, he wanted to reap the financial benefits that would result from also producing and selling practical inventions. After initially manufacturing incandescent lightbulbs in Menlo Park, Edison set up a large factory in Harrison, New Jersey, to pursue that task. He learned that the cost of manufacturing a product could be significantly lowered by implementing mass production technology. Attracting several financial backers, Edison established the Edison Electric Light Company in New York City in 1878. The company was incorporated as the Edison Electric Illuminating Company in 1880.

In 1887, Edison moved his industrial laboratory to West Orange, New Jersey, where he concentrated on making useful small products, such as his electric fan and phonograph, that had a high profit potential and low capital requirement. Edison was one of a very few American businessmen during the 1890's who were willing to gamble on new ideas and new markets for consumer goods in rapidly growing American cities. By 1906, Edison had manufactured more than one million phonographs.

Another important product produced at the West Orange laboratory was Edison's motion-picture camera. After he experienced financial disasters in the electrical industry and the ore-milling business, motion pictures reestablished Edison's fame and fortune as an inventor and a businessman. By 1910, Edison had expanded and diversified his business into a stream of assembly-line products, including film projectors, motion pictures, phonographs, electric fans, storage batteries, and Portland cement. He quickly established new companies and built factories for each new product, and in 1911 he formed Thomas A. Edison, Inc., as the umbrella organization to consolidate his many business ventures. Although Edison failed to keep up with changing consumer expectations during the 1920's,

Thomas Alva Edison. (Library of Congress)

he was responsible for pioneering the model for the successful development and management of industrial research. His diversified, divisional business structure became the standard of business organization in the twentieth century.

Alvin K. Benson

FURTHER READING
Alvarado, Rudolph. *The Life and Work of Thomas Edison.* Indianapolis, Ind.: Alpha, 2002.

Millard, Andre. *Edison and the Business of Innovation.* Baltimore: Johns Hopkins University Press, 1993.

Pretzer, J. William S. *Working at Inventing: Thomas A. Edison and the Menlo Park Experience.* Baltimore: Johns Hopkins University Press, 2002.

SEE ALSO: Bell, Alexander Graham; General Electric; Industrial research; Industrial Revolution, American; Inventions; Motion-picture industry; Music industry; Public utilities.

Education

SIGNIFICANCE: Education has played a central role in shaping the abilities and attitudes of owners, managers, workers, and consumers. It also has become a major business, encompassing private schools at all levels, technical and trade institutes, and producers of educational supplies and books.

Education is a search for ways in which society can both benefit from as well as limit the variety of individual experience. Accordingly, American attitudes toward education have always been ambivalent. In *America as a Civilization* (1957), cultural historian Max Lerner made the following comment:

> While most Americans value education as the road to "know-how" and business advance, they suspect it when carried into political action or expressed in social attitudes.

The early impetus to education in the United States derived from the practical needs of what was still a predominantly rural, agricultural society. The need for applied knowledge in areas such as agriculture was a central motivation in the establishment of land-grant institutions of higher learning in the nineteenth century, despite the earlier view that education ruined people for agricultural work. However, education was perceived as essential in producing the informed and intelligent voters democracy requires, the key to promoting social mobility, and a way for the country to assert its status among other nations.

Spiritual needs also encouraged educational development. Founded by immigrants who espoused a variety of religious viewpoints, the United States established a long tradition of valuing religious freedom. Many educational institutions in the United States began with religious missions, and religious values (such as family, patriotism, and professional ethics) for a long time provided a counterweight to strictly economic considerations. The proper relationship between private, especially religious, education and public education has been the subject of continuing debate. During the course of the twentieth century, the United States completed its transformation from a rural to an urban, and from an explicitly religious to a nominally secular society.

AFTER WORLD WAR II

The history of American education since World War II has been one of ever-greater federal concern over and involvement in local educational practice. The war brought home the importance of science and technology in national defense and made the ongoing development of expertise in those areas a national priority. In addition, the postwar G.I. Bill encouraged veterans to go back to school, building up the middle class and transforming American higher education in the process. A massive infusion of federal dollars into education during the 1940's effectively created the research university. As corporate-sponsored work came in later years to supplement or supplant government-funded research, universities gradually learned to recoup some of the profits of their breakthroughs by technology-transfer partnerships and other forms of participation in commercialization.

During the 1950's, educational policy became entangled with the debate about racial discrimination, as the U.S. Supreme Court in *Brown v. Board of Education* (1954) forsook its longtime contentment with the separate-but-equal provisions of *Plessy v. Ferguson* (1896). The slow implementation of the new requirements resulted in controversies over busing and, in some parts of the country, white students enrolling in private rather than public schools. Residentially based mechanisms for educational support, such as property tax, were partially reformed, but real educational equality remained elusive. Debates about the merits of affirmative action programs proliferated, as immigration shifts and demographic patterns ensured that increased diversity would be sought in the worlds of both business and education. A controversial emphasis on multiculturalism drew on both concern about racial (and other) diversity and commitment to religious freedom.

At the same time, the emergence of the space race, subsequent to the launch of the Soviet satellite *Sputnik* in 1957, resulted in a frantic effort to beef up American education, especially in science and math. However, in the ensuing decade, increased governmental support of education was colored by student activism growing out of the Civil Rights movement and the anti-Vietnam War movement, new demands for educational relevance, and a series of student rebellions on college campuses during the late 1960's. The end of the Vietnam War and the subsequent abolition of the military draft

SCHOOL SPENDING, 1980-2005, IN MILLIONS OF DOLLARS

Year	Elementary and Secondary Schools	Colleges and Universities
1980	254,727	140,531
1985	270,772	163,028
1990	348,993	203,287
1995	385,403	233,190
2000	467,123	268,115
2005	536,900	341,400

Source: Data from the Statistical Abstract of the United States, 2008 (Washington, D.C.: Department of Commerce, Economics and Statistics Administration, Bureau of the Census, Data User Services Division, 2008)
Note: Dollars are constant 2004-2005 dollars.

seemed largely to quell middle-class student protest. The later 1970's and the 1980's saw the transformation of radical yippies (members of the Youth International Party) into ambitious yuppies (conservative young urban professionals), as social discontent came to be viewed by advertisers as merely another market segment (exemplified by Nike's controversial use in 1987 of the Beatles' song "Revolution" as a jingle in a commercial for athletic shoes).

In 1983, the U.S. Department of Education's report A Nation at Risk renewed the critique of American educational practices and called for a return to fundamentals. Conservative pundits were soon arguing that the 1960's radicals had taken over the educational establishment, substituting social engineering and political correctness for teaching the skills required in the modern workplace. In 1992, the U.S. Department of Labor produced the Secretary's Commission on Achieving Necessary Skills (SCANS) report, which sought to promote workforce development by aligning American secondary education with anticipated business needs for the coming century. In 2001, the No Child Left Behind Act gave schools across the country the mandate to develop and meet specific measures of educational outcomes. Whether these initiatives helped or hindered educational progress has not been definitively determined.

During the 1990's and after, the effects of computerization came to be felt in both business and education. Computers began to be used by both school administrators and students. Computers could be used to write papers, perform complex statistical and mathematical functions, and to do research. Computer and technology savvy students and college administrators communicated through e-mail and cell phones. In addition, efficient communications, effective process control at a distance, and cheap transportation combined to free both business and educational activities from their traditional limitation to particular localities. This led to distance learning, from online courses at colleges and universities to online learning at the elementary level.

EDUCATION AS A BUSINESS

The twentieth century saw much criticism of the influence of businessmen and corporations on schools, colleges, and universities. The increasing emphasis on business models and methods in education after 1900 has been associated with the declining influence of classical (Greek and Roman) content, as well as with the increasing emergence of practical or technical courses of instruction. William H. Maxwell, superintendent of the New York City schools, complained in 1913 that manufacturers were no longer using the apprenticeship method of training workers and were finding it difficult to find skilled workers. Instead, he said, manufacturers were asking the public school system to assume the task of training workers.

Under the pressure of business and political concerns, educators have often learned to see their own activities in managerial terms. They were, some suggest, thereby capitulating to the sway of money. However, as people have come to view education as primarily about increasing their earning power rather than enhancing personal discovery, social engagement, or civic responsibility, it is no surprise that business models of efficiency and effectiveness play an increasing role in education. Proponents view this change in education, like the similar transformation in medicine, as welcome and long overdue. To its supporters, the business model in education has not only been the harbinger of greater economic efficiency but also has led the way to greater concern with the actual needs of students, who, perhaps increasingly, do not fit traditional models and are instead working students, first-generation college students, and students from underrepresented populations. Critics charge that any such benefits come at a high cost, as the business model imposes its standards on what ought to be understood in terms of other, noneconomic values.

Some enthusiasts for the business model, however, believe that it alone can save educators from themselves by imposing discipline and returning power to the consumer. This is often associated with an argument that anything run by the government must go awry. Critics may concede this, while still insisting that private enterprise is also subject to distorting factors. Because this is one of the fundamental debates about the role of business in American society—and people often change their view depending on whether the latest scandal involves bureaucratic inefficiency or contractor fraud—the question of education's role in a business society that is also a democracy will not be settled soon.

Edward Johnson

FURTHER READING

Berg, Gary A. *Lessons from the Edge: For-Profit and Nontraditional Higher Education in America*. Westport, Conn.: Praeger, 2005. Sympathetic account of the rapid development of the for-profit university at the end of the twentieth century.

Bok, Derek. *Universities in the Marketplace: The Commercialization of Higher Education*. Princeton, N.J.: Princeton University Press, 2003. The former president of Harvard University argues that at the beginning of the twenty-first century, American universities showed signs of excessive commercialization.

Bowie, Norman E. *University-Business Partnerships: An Assessment*. Lanham, Md.: Rowman & Littlefield, 1994. Measured assessment of the advantages and dangers of academic-industrial joint undertakings such as technology transfer.

Callahan, Raymond E. *Education and the Cult of Efficiency: A Study of the Social Forces That Have Shaped the Administration of the Public Schools*. Chicago: University of Chicago Press, 1962. Classic analysis of the shift to business values and methods in education at the beginning of the twentieth century, including the establishment of a managerial self-image within the newly emerging discipline of educational administration.

Coulson, Andrew J. *Market Education: The Unknown History*. New Brunswick, N.J.: Social Philosophy and Policy Center/Transaction Publishers, 1999. Detailed history of the free-market approach to schooling, which argues that "government involvement in education tends to interfere with the very principles it is meant to advance" (391).

Veblen, Thorstein. *The Higher Learning in America: A Memorandum on the Conduct of Universities by Business Men*. 1918. Reprint. New York: Cosimo, 2007. Critique of the influence of business on higher education, by one of the twentieth century's most famous radical social critics.

Whittle, Chris. *Crash Course: Imagining a Better Future for Public Education*. New York: Riverhead Books/Penguin, 2005. Enthusiastic defense of a market-based approach to school problems by the founder of Edison schools, an innovator in private, for-profit secondary education.

SEE ALSO: Affirmative action programs; Business schools; Child labor; Education, U.S. Department of; G.I. Bill; Industrial research; Junior Achievement; National Science Foundation; Space race.

Education, U.S. Department of

IDENTIFICATION: Cabinet-level department of the U.S. government charged with creating and monitoring federal financial aid programs for education, collecting data on schools, and ensuring equal access to education

DATE: Established in 1867; became a cabinet-level department in 1979

SIGNIFICANCE: Because it is the responsibility of the Department of Education (ED) to establish and disseminate educational policy and to inaugurate and oversee federal funding designated for educational assistance, this department has direct responsibility both for identifying the needs of personnel to join the American workforce and developing means to train people to fill these needs.

Although public education in the United States has always been the responsibility of the individual states, the federal government first became officially involved in overseeing it, however minimally, on March 2, 1867. On that day, President Andrew Johnson signed into law a bill that established the Department of Education, a government agency without cabinet status headed by a commissioner of education, the first of whom was Henry Barnard. He served from 1867 until 1870 with a staff of three and an initial budget of $15,000.

The establishment of this department was controversial. Many people did not want their communities to lose control of their schools. Congress was not impressed by the new department and changed its name to the Office of Education in 1868, reduced its budget, and attached it to the Department of the Interior. In 1870, Congress again reduced its budget, this time to $5,000 a year. During the last quarter of the nineteenth century, however, the Office of Education regained some respect from Congress during the sixteen-year tenure of a politically savvy commissioner, John Eaton. Many school districts had already ceded a modicum of local control to state control as some states established centralized departments to oversee education within their boundaries.

Gaining Cabinet Status

Although the Office of Education served significant educational functions for more than a century, it did not have cabinet status, being rather an adjunct of the Department of Health, Education, and Welfare. During World War II, this agency gained prestige by becoming directly involved in developing programs to train people needed to staff vital wartime occupations. At war's end, however, its staff of 500 was slashed to 286.

With increasing governmental involvement in enforcing civil rights laws and ensuring all people equal access to educational facilities, the Office of Education won back some of the luster it had achieved during the war years. Support built for a cabinet-level agency that would oversee education on a national level but would leave crucial educational decisions in the hands of state and local agencies.

On October 17, 1979, President Jimmy Carter, who led the initiative to support a cabinet-level department for education, signed a bill, the Department of Education Organization Act, passed earlier by Congress, that called for the creation of a cabinet-level Department of Education. On December 6, 1979, Carter appointed Shirley Hufstedler secretary of education. She was instrumental in the official creation of the Department of Education that opened on May 7, 1980.

Headquartered in Washington, the department has ten regional offices. Its early budget of $29 billion had reached $56 billion by 2007. In that year, the department had a workforce of approximately five thousand and administered more than two hundred programs dealing with the nation's educational needs.

A major thrust of the department is to ensure that the United States has a well-trained workforce to meet the country's industrial, commercial, and financial needs. Although local control of the nation's schools presumably is preserved, the Department of Education has become increasingly involved in establishing minimal educational standards and in the competency testing that was part of the No Child Left Behind initiative of the George W. Bush administration.

The government has taken an active role in promoting education. This 1930's Work Projects Administration poster promotes adult education classes. (Library of Congress)

Friends and Foes

Early impetus for a cabinet-level department to deal with education came from President Lyndon B. Johnson's emphasis on building a great society that ensured all Americans equality of opportunity. The civil rights legislation that grew out of the Johnson administration mandated such equality. A strong central agency was needed to accomplish this ideal.

The advances the department made during Carter's administration were threatened upon Ronald Reagan's election to the presidency in 1981. Reagan advocated reducing the size of the federal government and attempted to dismantle the department but could not win congressional approval to do so. He managed instead to get the Education Consolidation and Improvement Act of 1981 through Congress as a compromise measure. This act increased the ability of state and local agencies to determine how they would use federal funds for education and diminished the power of the Department of Education.

Under the administrations of George H. W. Bush and Bill Clinton, education regained the important national position it had held when Carter was president. The Department of Education remains a viable department that operates major units dealing with such matters as bilingual education, civil rights as they are affected by educational institutions, special education, education of the handicapped, vocational and adult education (including the reeducation of those whose skills are no longer in demand), and educational research and its dissemination.

R. Baird Shuman

Further Reading

Bell, Terrel. *The Thirteenth Man: A Reagan Cabinet Memoir.* New York: Free Press, 1988. Memoir of Bell's service as secretary of education from 1981 to 1984. Useful insights.

Bennett, William J. *Our Children and Our Country: Improving America's Schools and Affirming the Common Culture.* New York: Simon & Schuster, 1988. Conservative view by a former secretary of education (1985-1988) of what American education should seek to achieve.

Boyer, Ernest L. *College: The Undergraduate Experience in America.* New York: Harper & Row, 1987. Plan by a former U.S. commissioner of education (1977-1978) for overhauling higher education in the United States.

No Child Left Behind: A Desktop Reference. Washington, D.C.: U.S. Dept. of Education, Office of the Under Secretary, Office of Elementary and Secondary Education, 2002. A program-by-program look at the reforms created by the legislation.

Riley, Richard W. *Design for Learning: Building Schools for the Twenty-First Century.* Washington, D.C.: Department of Education, 1998. Blueprint for educational change by a former secretary of education (1993-2001).

Sniegoski, Stephen J. *The Department of Education.* New York: Chelsea House, 1988. Although directed toward young-adult readers, this overview is thorough and readable.

See also: Affirmative action programs; Business schools; Civil Rights movement; Education; G.I. Bill.

EEOC. *See* Equal Employment Opportunity Commission

Electrical power industry. *See* Nuclear power industry; public utilities

Electronics industry

Definition: The companies that make and sell products that contain circuits or systems using electron devices, including magnetic amplifiers and transistors

Significance: The electronics industry, from its start in telephones, to the development of the transistor, the microchip, and the microcontrollers embedded in automobiles, appliances, and power tools, has had a profound influence on telecommunications, entertainment, and the products people use everyday.

Modern electronics began with Alexander Graham Bell's telephone, which could transmit the human voice across wires. The telegraph required mastery of an arcane code, but anyone who could speak could use the telephone, creating an enormous market. For a person to make a telephone call, a circuit had to be created to the recipient's telephone. At first, circuits were created by hand, but as telephone networks grew, the Bell System developed direct-dialing systems.

The second great driver of electronics development was radio. When Guglielmo Marconi first demonstrated that radio waves could carry a meaningful signal, he was thinking in terms of a wireless telegraph. Reginald Aubrey Fessenden imagined creating a carrier wave and modulating it to bear a complex audio signal. To accomplish that end, he designed an alternator that would produce high-frequency radio waves onto which information could be imposed.

Decoding the signal used two types of devices: the crystal detector, a primitive semiconductor that was often used by hobbyists, and the vacuum tube, a modified lightbulb originally developed by Thomas Alva Edison in 1882. In 1912 Lee De Forest added a third element, the grid, between the cathode and the plate of the vacuum tube, and demonstrated its ability to amplify a faint signal.

During World War I, the United States government seized all the American Marconi Company's radio patents and stations, on the grounds of national security. After the war ended, several leading industries formed a new company to control that vital patent pool. The Radio Corporation of America (RCA), with its visionary general manager David Sarnoff, became the driving force of the electronics industry throughout the 1920's. Sarnoff realized the potential of radio as entertainment, like a phonograph with an infinite number of records.

Even as radio was taking American society by storm, Sarnoff was looking toward the possibility of transmitting images by radio waves. By 1928, primitive mechanical television systems had been demonstrated in the United States and abroad. Sarnoff knew such systems were a technological dead end and backed the all-electronic system of fellow Russian immigrant Vladimir Zworykin. At the same time, Mormon schoolboy Philo T. Farnsworth independently conceived the idea of electronic television while working the fields. When Farnsworth refused to sell out to RCA. Sarnoff brought all the corporation's legal leverage to bear against this maverick, delaying television's commercial emergence until after World War II.

DREAMING IN DIGITAL

Although De Forest had thought of his triode primarily as an amplifier, it was also a fast-acting electronic switch, capable of turning a current on and off hundreds of times a second. Properly wired together, vacuum tubes could perform calculations far more rapidly than any electromechanical system. However, vacuum tubes were fragile, and in computer operations, their usefulness was limited by their demand for power.

That solution was the transistor, invented in 1947 by John Bardeen, William Shockley, and Walter H. Brattain at Bell Laboratories, the research arm of American Telephone and Telegraph (AT&T). However, this discovery introduced its own problem, the tyranny of numbers: Thousands of tiny transistors had to be assembled into each circuit. Two men working independently, Robert Norton Noyce of Fairchild Semiconductor and Jack St. Clair Kilby of Texas Instruments, realized that the solution lay in manufacturing all the components of a circuit on a single piece of silicon. The integrated circuit, or microchip, made possible a range of consumer products, from digital watches to pocket calculators.

MICROPROCESSORS

When Marcian Edward "Ted" Hoff, Jr., of Intel put all the circuits of a computer's central processing unit on a single chip and created the microprocessor, he opened the door to the microcomputer industry. The first company to recognize the enormous consumer market for microcomputers was Apple Computer, but once Steve Jobs proved that a computer could be an appliance, microcomputers for consumer and business use became a large portion of the electronics industry. At the same time, old standbys such as radio and television benefited from the microchip revolution, becoming smaller and more reliable. Vacuum tubes vanished from everything but a few specialized applications such as the magnetron of a microwave oven. By the twenty-first century, even the cathode ray tubes of televisions and computer monitors gave way to flat-panel liquid crystal displays (LCDs) and plasma displays.

The microprocessor also made possible the embedded runtime controller, a small, cheap computer that could automate various aspects of the operation of ordinary devices such as automobile

U.S. CONSUMER ELECTRONICS SALES BY PRODUCT, 2003-2006, IN MILLIONS OF DOLLARS

Product Category	2003	2004	2005	2006
In-home technologies (total)	58,806	64,022	67,135	73,297
TV sets and displays [a]	14,528	16,783	19,022	25,085
Video components [b]	4,862	4,668	4,491	4,498
Home information technologies and security [c]	33,428	36,315	38,187	38,947
Audio separates/systems	3,000	3,390	2,862	2,634
Communications [d]	2,988	2,866	2,573	2,133
In-vehicle technologies (total)	6,388	7,062	7,860	8,809
Entertainment devices [e]	5,842	6,426	7,140	7,556
Information and security systems [f]	546	636	720	1,253
Other technologies (total)	29,600	32,037	39,026	47,899
Digital imaging [g]	5,923	6,390	7,315	9,492
Portable entertainment [h]	1,779	2,281	5,003	6,105
Electronic gaming	10,253	10,512	11,070	13,022
Portable communication [i]	11,645	12,854	15,638	19,280
Consumer electronic enhancements [j]	11,524	13,911	14,874	15,740
Total	106,318	117,033	128,895	145,744

Source: Data from Consumer Electronic Association, *U.S. Consumer Electronic Sales and Forecasts, 2002-2007* (Washington, D.C.: Author, 2008)
Note: Numbers may not add up due to rounding.
[a] Includes digital and analog TV sets and displays.
[b] Includes DVD players/recorders and set-top boxes.
[c] Includes personal computers, computer monitors and printers, moderm, computer peripherals and software, and home security systems.
[d] Includes telephone answering devices and fax machines.
[e] Includes aftermarket and factory-installed auto sound systems.
[f] Includes portable and transportable navigation.
[g] Includes digital cameras and camcorders.
[h] Includes MP3 players.
[i] Includes wireless telephones.
[j] Includes accessories and blank computer and flash media.

engines and home appliances. A microcontroller could adjust the operation of an engine or transmission far more rapidly and precisely than the gears and cams of older automobiles. On such devices as washing machines, it was often cheaper for the designers to buy bulk lots of a standard microcontroller and hire a programmer than to design an electromechanical control.

By the end of the twentieth century, the center of gravity of the electronics industry had shifted heavily toward the West Coast, particularly to the area south of San Francisco commonly known as Silicon Valley. Vast fortunes were made in the electronics industry, although it was hit hard by the burst of the dot-com bubble at the end of 2001.

Leigh Husband Kimmel

FURTHER READING

Chandler, Alfred D., Jr. *Inventing the Electronic Century: The Epic Story of the Consumer Electronics and Computer Industries.* New York: Free Press, 2001. A general history of electronics and its impact on consumer products.

Corbin, Alfred. *The Third Element: A Brief History of*

Electronics. Bloomington, Ind.: AuthorHouse, 2006. Covers the industry from its beginnings in radio through the computer age. Looks at applications in music, timekeeping, medicine, and navigation.

De Forest, Lee. *Father of Radio: The Autobiography of Lee De Forest.* Chicago: Wilcox and Follett, 1950. Primary source of the early days of radio.

Riordan, Michael, and Lillian Hoddeson. *Crystal Fire: The Birth of the Information Age.* New York: W. W. Norton, 1997. Looks specifically at the use of the transistor and computer technology in various applications.

Seitz, Frederick, and Norman G. Einspruch. *Electronic Genie: The Tangled History of Silicon.* Urbana: University of Illinois Press, 1998. Focuses on semiconductor electronics, although it contains some discussion of the vacuum tube age that preceded it.

See also: Apple; Bell, Alexander Graham; Bell Labs; Computer industry; Digital recording technology; Edison, Thomas Alva; E-mail; International Business Machines; NASDAQ.

E-mail

Definition: Electronic messages sent or received over a computer network and stored on the network until read

Significance: E-mail has replaced voice and physical mail as the primary means of communication in many businesses. It has spawned support industries that earn billions of dollars per year.

E-mail started in 1965 as a way for users who were time-sharing a single mainframe computer to communicate with one another. The ability to communicate with others who were on different time schedules was of immense value, and the technology was soon expanded to allow users to pass messages between different servers. Although initially e-mail was used in government and research institutions, businesses soon adopted it when the benefits became evident.

Much of the business world relies on communication between parties in separate physical locations. E-mail provides a fast and efficient method of information exchange at little cost per message.

It also eliminates the need for communicating parties to interface with one another at the same time, as is required in telephone calls or teleconferences.

The technology's savings in time alone was enough to motivate most businesses to adopt e-mail as their standard medium of communication. As the medium developed, the ability to store and quickly access e-mail messages as well as attached documents, files, and other information created more cost savings for companies. E-mail quickly became such a vital resource that many business professionals are estimated to spend up to 50 percent of their working time using e-mail. Internet-based businesses estimate that tens of thousands of dollars can be lost per hour if there is an outage of their e-mail servers. The drop in communications can also reduce the ability of workers to complete their tasks, resulting in a loss of person-hours and damaging customer relations.

Businesses have also capitalized on the ability to mass market to consumers via e-mail. More customers can be reached at little or no cost by e-mail than by previous methods such as telephone calls and traditional media advertising. The business of selling lists of e-mail addresses has become a staple of the mass-mailing industry and makes millions of dollars yearly.

Abuse of mass e-mailing has created problems as well as business opportunities. Unsolicited commercial e-mail, commonly called "spam," comes from a business or individual misusing the system. Spam has the potential to clog users' e-mail inboxes, wasting valuable work hours that must be spent separating important messages from unwanted advertisements. The ability to attach files to e-mail messages has also led to the propagation of computer viruses, another potential danger to businesses that rely on computers. The need to guard against these problems, however, has itself spawned an industry that makes billions of dollars per year. The servers and software that support e-mail are equally profitable.

James J. Heiney

Further Reading

Cortada, James W. *The Digital Hand: How Computers Changed the Work of American Manufacturing, Transportation, and Retail Industries.* Oxford, England: Oxford University Press, 2004.

Nussey, Bill. *The Quiet Revolution in E-Mail Marketing.* New York: IUniverse, 2004.

Okin, J. R. *The Internet Revolution: The Not-for-Dummies Guide to the History, Technology, and Use of the Internet.* Winter Harbor, Maine: Ironbound Press, 2005.

SEE ALSO: Advertising industry; Catalog shopping; Computer industry; Online marketing; Pony Express; Postal Service, U.S.; Telecommunications industry.

Embargo Acts

THE LAWS: Federal legislation banning American ships from trading with Great Britain, largely to protest British attempts to dominate international waters

DATE: 1806-1813

SIGNIFICANCE: The embargoes created an economic recession, but ultimately American industry became more reliant on the domestic market and less dependent on foreign trade.

When the nineteenth century began, Britain had mobilized to stop Napoleonic France's increasing control of continental Europe and sought to stop trade with France. British warships overpowered ships of other countries, demanded their surrender, boarded them, seized control, and forced sailors of various nationalities to work against their will until they were released in home ports, penniless.

The United States was at peace with Britain but often accepted British deserters as crew members, and the British sought to recapture these men. In response to high-handed British behavior in international waters to conscript Americans to serve on British ships, Congress in 1806 authorized a limited embargo of British imports.

In 1807, after Britain's Privy Council demanded an embargo of French ports by all countries, Congress passed an Embargo Act to disallow American ships from trading abroad by requiring that a bond be posted for each ship's value, subject to forfeit by ships violating the ban. In early 1808, the law was amended to double the value of the bond and to ban trade with Canada. However, shippers refused to comply, so Congress passed a third Embargo Act,

increasing penalties and empowering federal port authorities to seize cargos without a warrant, pending a trial of merchants and shipowners on suspicion of contemplating an embargo violation.

The embargo was still flouted, so Congress relented by authorizing President Thomas Jefferson to call off the embargo if conditions improved. He did so in 1809 just before leaving office. Congress then passed the Nonintercourse Act, officially lifting the embargo from all countries but Britain and France. Congress ended the still unpopular embargoes on both countries in 1810, while authorizing the president to reinstitute an embargo if either country reimposed restrictions.

Meanwhile, from 1807 to 1812, Britain seized 389 more American trading ships, and 775 additional sailors were forced into British service. Consequently, Congress supported President James Madison's request for war with Britain, unaware that London had already rescinded orders to conscript foreign sailors.

After the war declaration, British ships attacked American ports during the War of 1812, prompting a full-scale American embargo of Britain in 1813. The final embargo act was repealed in April, 1814, and an Anglo-American peace treaty was signed at the end of that year, though word reached North American after the Battle of New Orleans in early 1815. Meanwhile, Britain had subdued Napoleonic France by April, 1814, and no longer sought extreme measures in international waters.

Michael Haas

FURTHER READING

Craughwell, Thomas J., with M. William Phelps. *Failures of the Presidents: From the Whisky Rebellion to the War of 1812 to the Bay of Pigs to the Iran-Contra Affair.* Beverly, Mass.: Fair Winds Press, 2008.

Sears, L. M. *Jefferson and the Embargo.* Reprint. New York: Octagon Books, 1966.

Spivak, Burton. *Jefferson's English Crisis: Commerce, Embargo, and the Republican Revolution.* Charlottesville: University Press of Virginia, 1979.

SEE ALSO: Boston Tea Party; Depression of 1808-1809; European trade with the United States; International economics and trade; Navigation Acts; Shipping industry; War of 1812.

Energy, U.S. Department of

IDENTIFICATION: Federal cabinet department that deals with all aspects of energy policy in the United States

DATE: Established in 1977

SIGNIFICANCE: The Department of Energy is charged with developing the overall energy policy for the United States. Much of its attention is directed toward coal, nuclear energy, and oil policy, although it also concerns itself with alternative sources of energy. It is also in charge of administering the repositories for nuclear waste and the operational aspects of nuclear weapons development.

The Department of Energy (DOE) is a relatively new federal department with roots that go back to the Atomic Energy Commission (AEC), which was founded in 1946 to provide for civilian control of nuclear energy. From the founding of the AEC onward, the United States has pursued an approach to energy policy in which industry often shapes energy policy as much as does any government agency. The energy crisis of the mid-1970's led to calls for a unified energy policy for the United States. At President Jimmy Carter's urging, Congress combined several energy-related agencies into an umbrella cabinet department in 1977. Although the DOE was charged with overall oversight for energy policy, much of its attention has been devoted to nuclear energy, reflecting the continuing impact of the AEC's legacy.

After a strong start during the Carter administration with James Schlesinger as secretary of energy, the DOE developed a checkered character. The department was, in many ways, under siege during the Ronald Reagan administration, as several members of the administration, including the president, wished to abolish the DOE, or at least privatize energy policy as much as possible. The DOE's reputation regained some luster during the George H. W. Bush and Bill Clinton years, but it had to devote a good deal of attention to issues stemming from the dismantling of the nation's nuclear weapons complex as the Cold War wound down. During the administration of George W. Bush, the DOE often came under fire for its policies regarding coal mining and global warming.

EARLY YEARS

Partially in response to energy shortages during the mid-1970's, the Carter administration presented a legislative package to Congress that included creating a cabinet-level department to be responsible for energy policy and research. The DOE incorporated the old AEC and thus had oversight responsibility for the nuclear power industry and aspects of the nuclear weapons complex, such as weapons production. The new department also included the Federal Energy Regulatory Commission, which dealt with the licensing of hydroelectric power projects and natural gas transmission. The Economic Energy Regulatory Commission dealt with oil pricing and importation, and the Energy Information Administration centralized federal data-gathering concerning energy. The DOE faced the continuing challenge of energy shortages, at times with efforts at mandated energy allocations, throughout the 1970's, although these efforts were beginning to abate by 1979. The department also dealt with the 1979 accident at the Three Mile Island nuclear power plant that effectively ended the already-declining demand for nuclear power plants.

During the 1980 presidential campaign, Reagan attacked many of Carter's energy policies, such as price and allocation controls on gasoline, and even advocated the abolition of the DOE. James Edwards, Reagan's energy secretary in 1981-1982, worked to return much of American energy policy to the private sector by weakening the department's oversight of the energy industry. The Reagan administration also emphasized the use of coal and nuclear power as means of generating energy self-sufficiency. The administration supported efforts to use coal by supporting research directed at curbing pollution generated by its burning. Its advocacy of nuclear power led to the passage of the Nuclear Waste Act of 1982, which offered a long-term solution to the management of high-level nuclear waste. Three possible repository sites were selected in 1986. The DOE also began considering how to dispose of low- and medium-level nuclear waste.

When it took over the AEC's mandate, the DOE had also assumed responsibility for oversight of the nuclear weapons industry. Nuclear weapons production had been handled by private firms as government contractors since the end of World

War II, but they often operated with little oversight from the AEC. A report commissioned by the DOE in 1987 criticized the safety standards for several weapons-production facilities and conceded that weapons-production reactors were not always in compliance with federal safety standards for reactor operation. Standards for the disposal of nuclear waste at these sites were generally poorly enforced. In 1988, some weapons facilities had to be shut down because of radiation leaks and other safety concerns. These safety issues became intertwined with Reagan's efforts to restart nuclear weapons production.

POST-COLD WAR ISSUES AND GLOBAL WARMING

With the election of George H. W. Bush in 1988, the DOE adopted a policy of cleaning up the contaminated weapons complex. It also moved to further research in nuclear power and to implement a high-level nuclear waste site at Yucca Mountain, Nevada. The DOE's broader energy strategy was caught up in the oil shortage produced by the Gulf War in 1991. Nonetheless, the Energy Policy Act of 1992 enunciated a broad-based energy policy that advocated developing multiple sources of energy, as well as pursuing energy conservation, as means of ensuring American energy self-sufficiency. President Bush proclaimed that the Cold War was over, but cleaning up the remnants of several decades of nuclear weapons production remained a major challenge for the DOE, and it was forced to change weapons-facility contractors in some cases to find companies more amenable to a concern for safety.

Beginning in 1993, President Clinton's secretary of energy, Hazel O'Leary, engaged in a reorganization of the department that helped revitalize the DOE's central role in energy policy. The Clinton DOE emphasized use of natural gas, development of alternative energy sources, and energy conservation as means for ensuring energy self-sufficiency and decreasing environmental degradation. Concern for this latter issue was a new departure for the DOE, which had generally not considered environmental issues in its policies in the past.

Agencies within the DOE that dealt with the nuclear weapons complex still accounted for a large share of the department's budget, as much remained to be done to deal with lingering problems of nuclear weapons production. The DOE also

Global warming is one problem the Department of Energy must face. The village of Shaktoolik, Alaska, shown in 2006, is facing the same erosion problem due to climate change that forced it to relocate in the 1960's. (AP/Wide World Photos)

turned its attention to global warming caused by burning hydrocarbons such as coal and oil. Its emphasis was on achieving more efficient energy generation as well as decreasing pollution. Part of this attention was devoted to helping industries compete effectively in the global marketplace through efficient energy use. The department also provided increased funding for basic research for alternative energy sources in areas such as solar and wind power. Because of the stagnant demand for nuclear power, the DOE decreased research dollars for programs such as the development of a gas-cooled reactor. The new strategic plan for the DOE integrated four areas that had not been well-coordinated in the past: science and technology, energy resources, defense programs, and environmental restoration. The plan placed science and technology at the core but emphasized the interrelated nature of the four areas, as well as adding an emphasis on maintaining industrial competitiveness.

INTO THE TWENTY-FIRST CENTURY

The election of George W. Bush in 2000 brought yet another shift in energy policy and the focus of the DOE. Aside from some changes dealing with renewable energy sources and the environmental problems arising from some energy sources such as coal, American energy policy had not changed for some time. It was apparent, however, that the United States needed a coherent, broad-based energy policy that went beyond the plans of the Clinton years in dealing with issues of both energy self-sufficiency and environmental protection. Several Bush DOE and Environmental Protection Agency (EPA) appointees came from the energy industry, as did Vice President Dick Cheney, who often consulted representatives from U.S. energy companies in making policy. They quickly moved to redirect energy policy once again.

The DOE shifted its approach to energy development to one concentrating on opening Western federal lands to energy development, massive extraction of coal, and drilling for oil and gas wherever possible—including the Arctic National Wildlife Refuge—often ignoring any resulting environmental problems. Other forms of energy received short shrift at the hands of the Bush DOE. For example, when $135,000 was needed to print copies of the 2001 energy plan, the funds were taken from the DOE's solar and renewable energy conservation funds.

The energy plans of the Bush DOE had the merit of constituting a coherent approach to energy development. The plans tended to neglect renewable energy in favor of coal, oil, and natural gas, and they were usually prepared with scant concern for environmental consequences or long-term economic costs. The DOE worked with the EPA to relax environmental regulations so as to make it easier to extract coal, oil, or natural gas. For example, regulations were relaxed to make it easier for coal companies to engage in the coal mining approach known as mountaintop removal, in which mountaintops are literally blown into nearby valleys to more readily reach subsurface coal deposits. DOE spokespeople, in addition to those from other agencies in the Bush administration, denied the impact of global warming, which is caused in large part by burning oil and coal, despite the opinions of the scientific community.

The Department of Energy has been plagued by continually shifting policies, making it difficult to construct a long-term approach that would provide for reliable sources of energy at a reasonable cost. In addition to numerous policy swings, the DOE's leadership has often been short-lived. Most secretaries have served no more than two years before moving on to other positions, further complicating issues of policy continuity. Started in an era of perceived energy scarcity, the DOE rarely addressed the question of U.S. energy needs in a broad-based way that included conservation.

During the late 1970's and during the 1980's, the DOE was forced to devote a good deal of money and attention to cleaning up problems within the nuclear arms complex, some of which had existed since World War II, further diluting its efforts. At times, DOE policies have clearly favored the energy industry. At other times, efforts were made to rein in industry and to protect consumer interests or deal with environmental issues. Energy consumers were often ignored after Carter left office.

The Energy Information Agency provides a good deal of reliable information concerning energy consumption and supply of use to a variety of businesses. In addition, the DOE summer fellowship program for undergraduate and graduate students in the sciences and mathematics encourages able students to pursue study and careers in energy-related fields.

John M. Theilmann

FURTHER READING

Fehner, Terrence R., and Jack M. Hall. *Department of Energy, 1977-1994: A Summary History.* Oak Ridge, Tenn.: Department of Energy, 1994. Detailed coverage of the DOE from its inception to 1994, albeit with little analysis.

Kraft, Michael E., and Sheldon Kamieniecki, eds. *Business and Environmental Policy.* Cambridge, Mass.: MIT Press, 2007. Collection of essays, several of which emphasize that business often has had a large impact on energy policy.

Macfarlane, Allison M., and Rodney C. Ewing, eds. *Uncertainty Underground.* Cambridge, Mass.: MIT Press, 2006. Essays from several different perspectives concerning the development of the high-level nuclear waste facility at Yucca Mountain.

Morgenstern, Richard D., and Paul R. Portney, eds. *New Approaches on Energy and the Environment.*

Washington, D.C.: Resources for the Future, 2004. Good analysis of several potential futures for energy policy and the role of the DOE in developing policy.

Rosenbaum, Walter A. *Environmental Politics and Policy.* 7th ed. Washington, D.C.: Congressional Quarterly, 2008. Puts energy policy and the Department of Energy in the larger context of U.S. environmental policy.

SEE ALSO: Coal industry; Energy crisis of 1979; Environmental Protection Agency; Interior, U.S. Department of the; Nuclear power industry; Petroleum industry; Presidency, U.S.

Energy crisis of 1979

THE EVENT: Oil shortage during which prices soared, the government imposed price controls, and U.S. economic growth stagnated

DATE: December, 1977-January, 1981

PLACE: United States

SIGNIFICANCE: The sharp rise in prices after the Iranian Revolution, combined with the Iran-Iraq War and U.S. government actions that exacerbated the problem, produced gas lines, shortages, and dramatically higher energy prices for U.S. businesses and consumers.

World crude oil prices rose sharply after the Arab oil embargo of 1973 and continued a steady climb through the mid-1970's, spurring government intervention in the form of price, allocation, and import controls. President Jimmy Carter attempted to increase U.S. crude production by scaling back the complex system of government regulation of the oil industry to allow domestic crude prices to rise.

President Carter's efforts at reform were stalled by a series of events in the Middle East: In December, 1977, riots broke out in Iran; they were followed by the Iranian Revolution and the overthrow of the shah in January, 1978. In September, 1980, Iran was invaded by Iraq. Together, these events disrupted the world's crude oil supply. Iran had provided approximately 15 percent of internationally traded crude oil and 9 percent of U.S. crude imports before the revolution. The loss of Iranian crude oil—which were particularly "light" (low in wax content)

and "sweet" (low in sulfur content) and thus inexpensive to refine into gasoline—shifted the market toward heavier, more sour crude oils that were more expensive to refine. U.S. refineries were able to produce less gasoline per day from these crude oils, so the decrease in supply of gas was greater than the decrease in supply of crude oil.

The result of these events was soaring crude oil, gasoline, diesel, and home heating oil prices that led to a general economic decline in the United States. Inflation rose to a rate of more than 13 percent, and the U.S. unemployment rate reached 6.1 percent in 1979. As a result of the oil shortages, consumers were forced to wait in long lines to buy gasoline, and in some regions of the country, restrictions were placed on industrial energy use.

Iranian and Iraqi oil production gradually recovered and partly eased the world crude shortage. However, most economists date the end of the energy crisis to President Ronald Reagan's issuance of Executive Order 12287 on January 28, 1981, terminating federal price and allocation controls and leading to a lengthy decline in real crude prices as domestic crude production increased. Declining energy prices helped spur the economic recovery of the early 1980's. Although Reagan is given credit for this deregulation, the outgoing Carter administration had already begun the process, and the crisis would have probably abated regardless of which candidate won the 1980 election.

Andrew P. Morriss

FURTHER READING

Bradley, Robert L. *Oil, Gas, and Government: The U.S. Experience.* 2 vols. Washington, D.C.: Cato Institute, 1995.

Katz, James Everett. *Congress and National Energy Policy.* Piscataway, N.J.: Transaction, 1983

Morriss, Andrew P., and Nathaniel Stewart. "Market Fragmenting Regulation: Why Gasoline Costs So Much (and Why It Is Going to Cost More)." *Brooklyn Law Review* 72, no. 3 (2007): 939-1060.

Yergin, Daniel. *The Prize: The Epic Quest for Oil, Money, and Power.* New York: Free Press, 1993.

SEE ALSO: Arab oil embargo of 1973; Organization of Petroleum Exporting Countries; Petroleum industry.

Enron bankruptcy

THE EVENT: Financial failure of Enron, one of the world's largest energy distributors, as a result of fraud perpetrated by its managers
DATE: Filed for bankruptcy on December 2, 2001
PLACE: New York City
SIGNIFICANCE: The collapse of Enron, an energy conglomerate with reported revenues of $100 billion, is one of the largest bankruptcy and accounting fraud cases in U.S. history.

Enron Corporation began as a traditional natural gas supplier in 1985 in Houston, Texas. In less than two decades, it evolved into the seventh largest of the *Fortune* 500 companies in the United States. What had started as a simple natural gas operation grew into a e-commerce superpower, which traded in energy commodities (such as wind, water, and electricity) and eventually in Internet bandwidth for communication purposes

Between 1998 and 2000, the stock price of Enron experienced unprecedented increases, making it one of the most profitable corporations on Wall Street. However, many of the deals Enron made were based solely on unrealistic projections regarding future supply and demand. By the beginning of 2001, the federal government began to become suspicious of Enron's accounting practices, in large part because of a whistle-blower inside the company, who uncovered suspicious accounting practices.

Enron's accounting practices were rife with fraud and misrepresentation. Many investigators have referred to Enron as a massive pump-and-dump scheme: Company officials used various misleading accounting practices to drive up (pump) stock prices, then insiders would quickly sell (dump) their own stocks at the top of the market, leaving many misinformed investors to suffer huge losses when the stock prices began to drop. Equally culpable was the prestigious accounting firm of Arthur Andersen, which was responsible for assisting Enron officials with the accounting scheme that netted extensive financial gains for certain company officials

An employee carries a box from Enron's headquarters in Houston in November, 2001. (AP/Wide World Photos)

and their high-ranking government friends. In the end, millions of American investors, including long-time loyal Enron employees, lost billions in savings, investments, and retirement plans.

Enron filed Chapter 11 bankruptcy on December 2, 2001, with $6.8 billion in assets, making it the largest bankruptcy in U.S. history (this record would later be broken by WorldCom in 2002 and Lehman Brothers in 2008). The stock had fallen from almost $140 a share to pennies on the dollar. The crimes carried out by top Enron executives have been prosecuted in both criminal and civil courts.

Paul M. Klenowski

FURTHER READING

Fox, Loren. *Enron: The Rise and Fall.* Hoboken, N.J.: Wiley, 2003.

Fusaro, Peter C., and Ross M. Miller. *What Went Wrong at Enron: Everyone's Guide to the Largest Bankruptcy in U.S. History.* Hoboken, N.J.: J. Wiley, 2002.

Swartz, Mimi, and Sherron Watkins. *Power Failure: The Inside Story of the Collapse of Enron.* New York: Doubleday, 2003.

SEE ALSO: Accounting industry; Bankruptcy law; Business crimes; Chrysler bailout of 1979; Derivatives and hedge fund industry; Incorporation laws; Justice, U.S. Department of; WorldCom bankruptcy.

Environmental movement

DEFINITION: Grassroots, organized attempts to protect the natural world from damage by humans

SIGNIFICANCE: The environmental movement has often been criticized by business interests for hampering the growth of American business. Environmentalists, by contrast, argue that the movement has helped point out the true costs of economic development and in doing so has helped make some industries more efficient.

The environmental movement in the United States dates from the early twentieth century formation of conservationist organizations such as the Sierra Club. Environmentalism gained force during the 1960's and 1970's and helped achieve the passage of

legislation that halted or reduced pollution. Environmental groups' goals vary widely, from land preservation, to halting various forms of pollution, to full-scale attacks on industry. Some business leaders have gone so far as to label environmental groups a danger to the American economy because of their advocacy of regulating industrial pollution. Other business leaders have tried to work with environmental leaders in areas of common interest and go so far as to acknowledge that some regulations have caused industry to become more efficient (for example, by using less of some materials), as well as benefiting society as a whole.

AN ENVIRONMENTAL CONSCIOUSNESS

Most early environmental groups were concerned with the preservation of natural habitats and in a few cases with local pollution issues. Coming out of the social activism of the 1960's, existing environmental groups often adopted new issues, and new groups arose. Many of these groups were concerned with the impact that industry had on the environment. They cited numerous cases of industries polluting streams with hazardous materials such as heavy metals or petroleum compounds, or of air pollution generated by burning coal or oil. Environmental groups indicated that the pollution generated by an industry (which economists label "externalities") should be taken into account as an internal factor when the cost of a power plant or factory was computed. Most business spokespersons argued against taking externalities into account and indicated that efforts to do so through governmental regulation introduced unfair costs.

During the 1970's, several environmental groups engaged in lobbying, lawsuits, public-relations efforts, and demonstrations to pressure government to adopt environmental regulations. Some of their actions led to the adoption of legislation such as the Clean Air Act of 1970, water-quality legislation, and efforts designed to clean up pollution such as the Resource Conservation and Recovery Act of 1976. These tactics proved to be more effective than some of the direct-action tactics of 1970's activists, such as a person known as "the Fox" who blocked pipes that were emitting toxic material into streams. The legislative approach was often coupled to efforts to increase public awareness of environmental concerns.

During the 1980's, the business community struck back, aided by the receptive presidential administration of Ronald Reagan. Business leaders argued that environmental regulations should be weakened because they harmed productivity and made the United States less competitive. Their approach was directed toward lobbying government and changing the public's perception of environmental issues.

Even though the environmental movement made some gains in combating problems such as the depletion of the ozone layer during the Bill Clinton administration, it was not as strong as it once had been. In some cases, the memberships of individual organizations had declined from their late-1970's levels. Business leaders had become more adept at combating the message of environmentalists, as they emphasized that environmental regulation led to job loss.

Although environmental groups had found a ready audience in the Clinton administration, the administration of George W. Bush often took positions that environmental groups regarded as harmful. Efforts to lobby agencies in the Bush years were usually fruitless, as federal officials emphasized economic development even when it led to environmental harm. Some environmental leaders turned again to trying to raise public consciousness of environmental issues, most notably of global warming. In some cases, these efforts paid off, and membership in environmental groups began to increase once again.

PRESERVING THE ENVIRONMENT

Although some environmental groups have advocated sharply curtailing economic growth because of potential harm to the environment, most have taken a more nuanced stand. In some cases, environmentalists have overstated risks from industries such as the nuclear power industry. For the most part, environmentalists have been critical of industries that pollute the environment or use large amounts of natural resources. They do not urge the abolition of these industries but instead advocate

A number of corporations and businesses are "going green" by adopting business practices favorable to the environment or producing environmentally aware products. Earthdoggy.com, an online pet store, offers this eco-friendly dog bed in 2008. (AP/Wide World Photos)

that means be found to decrease pollution or use fewer resources. In the short run, these changes often have meant additional costs for business. In the long run, changes such as using less of a natural resource such as copper have often meant cost savings for a business. Because air or water pollution often harm areas at some distance from the polluter, gaining business acceptance of pollution regulation has been difficult at times. Nonetheless, some businesses have emphasized that they are part of a larger whole and have a duty to be environmentally responsible in their operations.

American business and environmental groups will continue to be at odds regarding some business practices. There are also some common areas for agreement. Some oil companies now emphasize a need to conserve oil and seek out other energy sources, because of the threat of global warming. In sum, the environmental movement has often provided a needed check on the power of business in dealing with environmental issues.

John M. Theilmann

FURTHER READING

Dowie, Mark. *Losing Ground.* Cambridge, Mass.: MIT Press, 1996. Good analysis of the reverses that the environmental movement suffered during the 1980's and some prescriptions for change.

Gottlieb, Robert. *Environmentalism Unbound*. Cambridge, Mass.: MIT Press, 2001. Advocates a new approach to forming business and environmental group partnerships in dealing with environmental problems.

_____. *Forcing the Spring*. Rev. ed. Washington, D.C.: Island Press, 2005. Examines the changes that have taken place in the environmental movement over time.

Rosenbaum, Walter A. *Environmental Politics and Policy*. 7th ed. Washington, D.C.: CQ Press, 2008. Broad-based approach to environmental politics that incorporates the perspectives of industry and the environmental movement.

Speth, James Gustave. *Red Sky at Morning*. New Haven: Yale University Press, 2004. Written by a former environmental activist and governmental leader, this book details an agenda for environmental groups and government in dealing with the global environment.

SEE ALSO: Alaska Pipeline; Coal industry; DDT banning; Energy, U.S. Department of; Environmental Protection Agency; Nuclear power industry; Water resources.

Environmental Protection Agency

IDENTIFICATION: Independent agency of the U.S. government founded to safeguard the nation's environment from pollution

DATE: Established in 1970

SIGNIFICANCE: The Environmental Protection Agency regulates and punishes companies whose practices damage the environment, while it encourages businesses to research and develop environmentally friendly technologies and products. Its oversight has forced many companies to change the way they do business, costing individual firms money but saving the nation billions of dollars in environmental damage control.

The U.S. Environmental Protection Agency (EPA) grew out of the environmental movement of the 1960's. Books such as Rachel Carson's *Silent Spring* (1962) had alerted the public to the environmental

dangers of certain pesticides produced by American chemical companies. By 1970, the U.S. Congress had passed laws designed to protect humans and their environment from chemical pollutants, but these laws had been administered piecemeal through a variety of federal programs. In 1970, President Richard M. Nixon issued Executive Order 11548 and Reorganization Plan No. 3, which unified these programs under the aegis of the Environmental Protection Agency. After this reorganizational plan met with congressional approval, the EPA began operations on December 2, 1970.

MISSION OF THE AGENCY

The EPA's purpose was to conserve pristine air, water, and land where they existed and to return polluted air, water, and land to a healthy state, while educating the public about the risks of environmental degradation and how these risks could be minimized and managed. William D. Ruckelshaus, the EPA's first administrator, viewed his primary duty as protecting the environment, not as promoting American business interests, and during the EPA's early years a contentious state existed between the agency and many of the businesses that were sometimes adversely affected by the agency's regulations. American businesses and the public had for some time been grappling with frequently contradictory aspirations for a clean environment and a prosperous economy.

Even before the EPA began functioning, the Clean Air Act of 1970 had been signed into law, giving the new organization formidable power to create and implement national air-quality standards. These standards had a direct effect on those "smokestack industries" that polluted the air. The Clean Water Act of 1972 had an effect on those industries that traditionally dumped their wastes into rivers. When the EPA banned the insecticide dichloro-diphenyl-trichloroethane (DDT) in 1972, chemical companies were forced to develop alternatives. Officials in some American businesses objected to the costs of developing environmentally friendly (or "green") products, and they asserted that some banned substances were irreplaceable.

Some American industries responded to EPA regulations by forming organizations, such as the American Industrial Health Council, to challenge the regulations they found particularly burdensome. The Chemical Industry Institute of Toxicology was founded to support scientific research to generate data that would counter what businesses viewed as an exaggeratedly negative estimation of many of their successful chemical products. Even coin laundry centers, restaurants, gas stations, and other small businesses that generated pollutants experienced the restrictive regulations of the EPA.

Despite objections from the business community, the EPA's regulatory powers continued to increase during the 1970's. For example, in 1976, Congress passed the Resource, Conservation, and Recovery Act (RCRA), which empowered the EPA to oversee the production, transportation, storage, and disposal of hazardous wastes. Congress also passed the Toxic Substances Control Act (TSCA) of 1976, which gave the EPA regulatory power over the production and use of toxic substances.

During the late 1970's, hazardous wastes that had been buried by Hooker Chemical Corporation at Love Canal in Niagara Falls, New York, were discovered to pose a health threat to many local families, who were relocated at great government expense. The Love Canal incident provoked a controversy that eventually led Congress to enact the Comprehensive Environmental Response, Compensation, and Liability Act (CERCLA) of 1980. Commonly known as the Superfund, the act provided financing for hazardous waste cleanups, and it authorized the EPA to find toxic-waste sites and prosecute companies responsible for the contamination.

CONTROVERSIES AND POLITICIZATION

After Ronald Reagan became president in 1980, he sought to reduce government bureaucracies and minimize their interference in American business. He appointed Anne Burford to head the EPA and put his policies into effect there. Burford's policies, especially her handling of the Superfund program, were heavily criticized by public interest groups, leading to a congressional investigation that uncovered illegal collusion between EPA officials and polluting companies. Burford was forced to resign in 1983. Ruckelshaus returned as the EPA's administrator, and he oversaw the Superfund Amendments and Reauthorization Act (SARA) of 1986, which increased cleanup funding, as well as providing the agency with greater legal authority to prosecute polluting companies.

During the 1980's, the EPA increased its cooperation with the states, businesses, and international organizations to better achieve its mission. Environmental issues were the subjects of nearly one-third of all federal legislative mandates affecting the states. EPA officials also reduced their reliance on inflexible "command and control" regulations and shifted to market-based methods of enhancing environmental quality, such as tradable permit systems, which were used in programs designed to phase out asbestos and chlorofluorocarbons (CFCs).

For smokestack industries, the EPA permitted emissions banking, in which businesses earned credits for keeping their pollutants below a certain level. Incentives were also offered to companies to create green technologies. In 1992, the EPA and various businesses helped introduce the Energy Star program to aid consumers in identifying energy-efficient appliances and products. Through such cooperative measures as the Design for Environmental Progress and the Green Chemistry Program, the EPA sought to stimulate the

EPA coordinator Robert Wise points at a creek bed at the Greka Oil and Gas site in Santa Maria, California, that was contaminated with hazardous waste. The EPA engaged in a two-month cleanup in 2008. (AP/Wide World Photos)

creation and dissemination of green technologies and chemicals.

Perhaps the most serious environmental problem confronting American businesses and the EPA is global warming. Most scientists agree that economies deeply dependent on fossil fuels have been increasing the carbon dioxide content of Earth's atmosphere, resulting in a rise in the average global temperature with possible dire consequences for coastal cities, agriculture, and the survival of many wildlife species. During the late twentieth and early twenty-first century, EPA officials, politicians, businesspeople, and the public were becoming sensitive to the need for everyone to cooperate so that these environmental problems could be solved. A sign of such collaboration was Partners for the Environment, a collection of national and regional projects promoted by the EPA and involving more than eleven thousand organizations.

The EPA began as a large organization, with about fifty-seven hundred employees and a $4.2 billion budget. By the early twenty-first century, it employed more than eighteen thousand people and had an annual budget in excess of $7 billion. During its relatively brief existence, the EPA has achieved notable success, bringing Americans cleaner urban air, more swimmable lakes and fishable rivers, and a reduction in the illegal dumping of hazardous wastes. American businesses have begun to participate—some reluctantly, others with enthusiasm—in the EPA's efforts to improve the environment. However, no single policy, market-based or conventional, is appropriate for all environmental problems. Because no federal or commercial panaceas exist, the EPA must continue to analyze each environmental problem and determine the best way to solve it.

Robert J. Paradowski

FURTHER READING

Anderson, Terry L., and Donald L. Leal. *Free Market Environmentalism*. 1991. Rev. ed. New York: Palgrave Macmillan, 2001. Explains how markets can be used to improve environmental quality.

Cohen, Steven. *Understanding Environmental Policy*. New York: Columbia University Press, 2006. Uses case studies, such as "Why Companies Let Valuable Gasoline Leak Out of Underground Tanks," to explore the relationship between businesses and regulatory agencies such as the EPA. References and index.

Eisner, Marc Allen. *Governing the Environment: The Transformation of Environmental Regulation*. Boulder, Colo.: Lynne Rienner, 2007. Argues that future improvements in environmental quality will require "the integration of public regulation and private sector initiatives." Bibliography and index.

Morgenstern, Richard D., ed. *Economic Analyses at EPA: Assessing Regulatory Impact*. Washington, D.C.: Resources for the Future, 1997. Experts assess the role that cost-benefit analyses have played in the EPA's decision-making in such controversial areas as regulating lead in gasoline and water, asbestos, and stratospheric ozone depletion. No index.

Sussman, Glenn, Byron W. Daynes, and Jonathan P. West. *American Politics and the Environment*. New York: Longman, 2002. Explores how political decisions affecting the environment are made within political institutions, such as the EPA. Bibliographic references and index.

SEE ALSO: DDT banning; Energy, U.S. Department of; Interior, U.S. Department of the; Occupational Safety and Health Act; Tobacco industry; Water resources.

EPA. *See* Environmental Protection Agency

Equal Employment Opportunity Commission

DATE: Established in 1964

IDENTIFICATION: Federal agency given the task of enforcing laws that prohibit businesses from discriminating on the basis of race, gender, ethnicity, age, or disability

SIGNIFICANCE: The EEOC is responsible for many late twentieth century changes in the hiring, promotion, and dismissal procedures of American businesses. By enforcing antidiscrimination laws, the agency has forced businesses to diversify their workforces and to follow regulations that allow the government to intervene into some of the most basic business decisions.

The Civil Rights Act of 1964 placed employment discrimination at the forefront of the legal system. The act forbade discrimination in hiring, promotion, or dismissal on the basis of race, gender, ethnicity, national origin, or religion. Suddenly, business practices once deemed lawful became grounds for a federal lawsuit. To aid in the enforcement of this law, Congress created the U.S. Equal Employment Opportunity Commission (EEOC) and granted it the authority to define the different elements of employment discrimination, establish the procedures for investigating claims of discrimination, and collect evidence of illegal acts.

COMMISSION FUNCTIONS

The EEOC changed the relationship between employer and employee, creating and enforcing rules affecting some of the basic policies used by business. Prior to passage of the 1964 Civil Rights Act and the formation of the EEOC, employers could hire, fire, promote, or demote employees for a variety of reasons or for no reason at all. Employers could dismiss employees based on their religious beliefs, gender, race, or ethnicity. Many corporations limited job opportunities and promotions for women, placing them in clerical jobs and preventing them from overseeing male employees. Racial and ethnic minorities also had their employment opportunities limited to low-paying, low-skill jobs that reduced their chances for promotion. Such policies were considered part of business, the right of employers to choose their employees without government interference.

The EEOC changed that philosophy, enforcing federal laws that limited the rights of business and created a right to a job free from discrimination. Suddenly, business decisions once considered part of the private domain became public record. Complying with government regulations and satisfying government record-keeping requirements placed severe limitations on the justifications businesses could use for choosing new employees. Personnel departments became integral and growing parts of businesses, as hiring became a formal process. The involvement of the EEOC in hiring decisions made hiring employees more tedious and time-consuming for any business.

ENFORCEMENT

As the commission became more powerful, it regulated the most minute parts of the interviewing and hiring process, creating guidelines for the wording of advertisements for job openings and rules governing where and for how long ads were to be placed. Companies were required to maintain records for all applicants, including information on their gender and race, as proof that they were following EEOC rules. The choosing and interviewing of applicants raised even more issues for businesses, as the EEOC forbade interviewers from asking questions pertaining to age, marital status, previous employment, and a host of other topics previously used to gauge the employability of an applicant.

Failure to abide by these regulations would result in federal lawsuits being filed, charging a company with discrimination. The EEOC forced many corporations to pay fines and large settlements to applicants who were not hired. They then had to restructure their hiring processes to prevent the continued appearance of discrimination.

The threat of legal action also affected how and when employees were dismissed from their positions. Because dismissed employees could sue, claiming discrimination in their removal from their job, many employers were forced to document closely the work habits of employees, collecting information that might be used to support the decision to fire them. Such a long process harmed businesses by increasing the time and costs associated with firing employees while forcing them to keep workers deemed incompetent or inefficient simply out of fear that a dismissal might provoke a lawsuit.

Promotion policies were also affected. Women and racial or ethnic minorities rarely rose through the corporate ranks prior to enactment of the 1964 law, as the "glass ceiling" kept these groups in a subordinate position. With discrimination in promotion forbidden after 1964, businesses began to adopt deliberate policies of dividing promotions according to gender and racial factors, publicizing the number of nonwhite and women employees who held high-level corporate jobs as proof of nondiscrimination. Promotion policies changed more slowly than did hiring, as rising through the corporate system required years of seniority and achievement.

During the 1970's, the relationship between the EEOC and business turned more negative, as the agency was granted the authority to sue private businesses when employees claimed discrimination in hiring, firing, or promotion decisions. The 1972

Equal Opportunity Act granted that authority, then expanded the scope of antidiscrimination law to include state and local governments and public educational institutions. The agency aided those claiming discrimination, enforcing their civil rights and no longer requiring employees to engage in expensive court litigation to enforce their bias claims. The EEOC could also appeal unfavorable rulings from trial courts, having the resources to carry those appeals through the process, an opportunity few private litigants enjoyed. The threat of a lawsuit would also pit businesses against the unlimited funds of the government, usually forcing a business to settle out of court and agree to further government regulation of its practices.

Business faced a change in discrimination law in 1971. A Supreme Court decision involving the Duke Power Company changed the standard of proof in discrimination cases. Under the decision, a business was considered guilty of employment discrimination if it was statistically shown that its employment policies led to a smaller percentage of minority-group members being employed by the company than lived in the area. The disparity between the racial, gender, or ethnic makeup of a company's workforce and that of the local population constituted evidence of discrimination. This ruling made it easier for the EEOC to win lawsuits against employers.

CHANGING EEOC

The EEOC was also responsible for promoting affirmative action programs, either on a voluntary basis or as part of a legal settlement. These programs emphasized race and gender in hiring, promotion, and dismissal, favoring women and racial minorities over men and nonminority workers. Businesses found it easier to institute affirmative action policies, as they would protect the businesses from EEOC lawsuits. The change from a Democratic to a Republican administration in Washington, D.C., during the 1980's saw the EEOC switch its enforcement to a new form of discrimination.

The Ronald Reagan administration changed the agency's focus on discrimination against minorities to a focus on the consequences of antidiscrimination policies. Affirmative action, once seen as a solution to past discrimination, became a target of the EEOC. Another change came as the commission focused on individual claims rather than group asser-

tions of discrimination, clearing a backlog of cases while no longer emphasizing group rights. Suddenly, business found itself caught between a government that saw affirmative action as a form of racial discrimination and private individuals who threatened lawsuits if affirmative action policies were not carried out.

By the 1990's, business had adapted to the demands of the EEOC, even as the agency had acquired additional duties. The passage of the 1990 Americans with Disabilities Act (ADA) created an entirely new class of employment discrimination, as businesses were required to make reasonable accommodations to allow disabled persons to work. A whole range of accommodations were mandated to allow the blind, the deaf, and those in wheelchairs to use the workplace. Disabilities became another topic that could not be discussed in job interviews. By the beginning of the twenty-first century, the EEOC had become an established federal agency, having dramatically changed the methods used by businesses in hiring, firing, and promotions, while changing the face of the workforce through enforcement of antidiscrimination principles.

Douglas Clouatre

FURTHER READING

Burstein, Paul. *Discrimination, Jobs, and Politics.* Chicago: University of Chicago Press, 1998. Describes the political aspects of job discrimination lawsuits and how enforcement of these laws against business has affected the economic climate.

Busse, Richard. *Employees' Rights.* Napierville, Ill.: Sourcebooks, 2004. General guide to the antidiscrimination laws that apply to employees and how those laws are used to defend employees' rights if discrimination occurs.

Cavanagh, Matt. *Against Equality of Opportunity.* New York: Oxford University Press, 2002. Challenging the view that equality is a positive force in society, Cavanagh criticizes government's attempts to force equal outcomes through legislation.

Guerin, Lisa, and Amy Delpo. *Essential Guide to Federal Employment Law.* Berkeley, Calif.: NOLO, 2006. Broad-based examination of race, gender, age, and disability laws as applied to employment and business.

Segrave, Kerry. *Age Discrimination by Employers.* Jefferson, N.C.: McFarland, 2001. One of the duties of the EEOC is investigating age discrimination in the workplace, and this book defines age discrimination and discusses how the government has sought to ban it.

SEE ALSO: Affirmative action programs; Civil Rights Act of 1964; Civil Rights movement; Supreme Court and labor law; Women in business.

Erie Canal

IDENTIFICATION: A system of artificial waterways from Buffalo on Lake Erie to Albany on the Hudson River providing transportation between the less-developed interior of New York and the eastern seaboard

DATE: Completed in 1825

SIGNIFICANCE: The Erie Canal allowed goods to be shipped between the Great Lakes and the Atlantic Ocean faster and cheaper than by mule-drawn carts. It resulted in the settling of western New York and helped establish New York City as the main port on the East Coast.

Until the construction of the Erie Canal, travel westward for both people and goods was by stagecoach or cart and was slow and expensive. General Philip Schuyler's Western Inland Lock Navigation Company became the first to seek easier, smoother, and cheaper travel by waterway when it started improving some of the natural waterways in upstate New York. Although the company's improvements by no means constituted a statewide waterway, they encouraged merchant Jesse Hawley in 1807 to publish a series of essays envisioning how a waterway connecting Lake Erie with the Hudson River would yield tremendous economic growth for the nation.

"FIFTEEN YEARS ON THE ERIE CANAL"

The construction of the Erie Canal caught the popular imagination, as it symbolized both American ingenuity and the labor necessary to put that ingenuity into action. Such labor is emphasized in the 1905 folk song "Low Bridge, Everybody Down: Or, Fifteen Years on the Erie Canal," by Thomas S. Allen, excerpted below.

I've got an old mule and her name is Sal,
Fifteen years on the Erie Canal,
She's a good old worker and a good old pal,
Fifteen years on the Erie Canal.
We've hauled some barges in our day,
Filled with lumber, coal and hay—
And every inch of the way I know
From Albany to Buffalo.

Low bridge, everybody down,
Low bridge! We're coming to a town!
You can always tell your neighbor, you can always tell your pal
If you've ever navigated on the Erie Canal.

We'd better look around for a job, Old Gal,
Fifteen years on the Erie Canal.
You bet your life I wouldn't part with Sal,
Fifteen years on the Erie Canal.
Giddap there, Gal, we've passed that lock,
We'll make Rome 'fore six o'clock—
So one more trip and then we'll go
Right straight back to Buffalo.

Low bridge, everybody down;
Low bridge, I've got the finest mule in town.
Once a man named Mike McGintey tried to put over Sal,
Now he's way down at the bottom of the Erie Canal.

Oh! where would I be if I lost my pal?
Fifteen years on the Erie Canal,
Oh, I'd like to see a mule as good as Sal,
Fifteen years on the Erie Canal.
A friend of mine once got her sore,
Now he's got a broken jaw,
'Cause she let fly with her iron toe
And knocked him in to Buffalo.

Low bridge, everybody down;
Low bridge, I've got the finest mule in town.
If you're looking for trouble, better stay away,
She's the only fighting donkey on the Erie Canal.

Source: Poets' Corner.

A year later, New York assemblyman Joshua Forman successfully proposed an expenditure of $600 for a survey of possible canal routes across the state. This was followed in 1810 by an act appointing commissioners to study the possibility of limited inland waterway improvements, and in 1811, the commissioners were given a mandate to study a waterway from the Hudson River to Lake Erie. As a result of their work and the vision of Governor DeWitt Clinton, the legislature authorized construction of the Erie and Champlain Canals in 1817. The first 94 miles from Utica to Salina opened in 1820, and local business owners experienced an immediate and substantial reduction in shipping costs. In 1823, a 250-mile section from Brockport to Albany was opened, and the Champlain Canal, from Lake Champlain to the Hudson, also opened. The remaining sections of the Erie Canal were completed in October, 1825.

THE ORIGINAL CANAL

The Erie Canal was 363 miles long, 4 feet deep, and 40 feet wide, and built at a cost of $7.1 million. It had 83 locks, 17 toll booths, 18 aqueducts to carry the canal over ravines and rivers, a rise of 568 feet from Hudson River to Lake Erie, and a 10-foot-wide towpath for horses, mules, and oxen. In October, 1825, Governor Clinton, who had suffered ridicule for what was termed "Clinton's Big Ditch," rode the packet boat *Seneca Chief* on the eight-day trip from Buffalo to New York City and emptied two casks of Lake Erie water into the Atlantic Ocean, celebrating the ceremonial "marriage of the waters" from west to east.

The governor was immediately vindicated by an explosion of trade. Freight rates from Buffalo to New York were $10 per ton, compared with $100 per ton by road, and time was cut from twenty to ten days. In 1829, a total of 3,640 bushels of wheat were

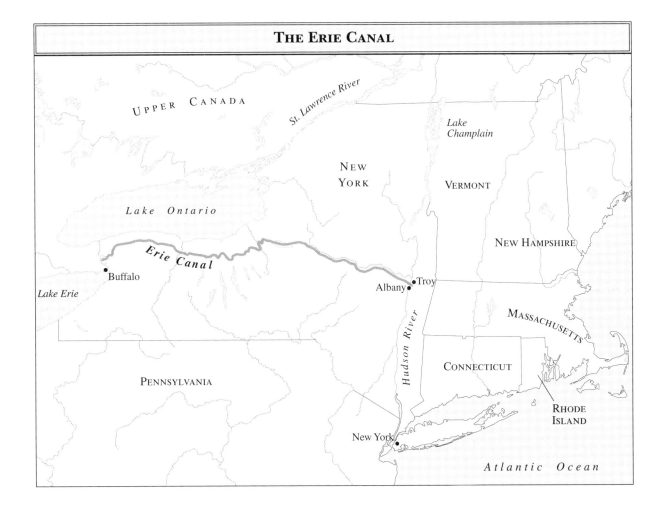

THE ERIE CANAL

transported; by 1837, the volume of wheat had increased to 500,000 bushels and by 1841 to one million bushels. In nine years the canal tolls more than recouped the entire cost of construction. Within fifteen years of the opening of the Erie Canal, New York City had become the busiest port in the United States, moving more tons of freight than Boston, Baltimore, and New Orleans combined. In addition, the New York towns of Albany, Schenectady, Utica, Syracuse, Rochester, and Buffalo morphed from small outposts to major industrial cities.

LATER VERSIONS

The canal's success spawned the construction of a number of feeder canals during the 1830's, creating a system of canals. However, it soon became clear that the Erie Canal was too small, and so in 1835, major enlargement was authorized. When the enlargement was finished in 1862, the canal was 70 feet wide and 7 feet deep and could handle 240-freight-ton boats. However, the new transcontinental railroad system provided a faster alternative for shipment of goods westward, and canal use never reached its new capacity. The canal was used primarily by those who sought lower rates and were not as concerned about the speed of delivery. By the time sharply higher railroad freight rates caused shippers to regain interest in the canal, large sections had fallen into disrepair, and it was being used only for local trade.

However, the state of New York, far from abandoning the canal system, decided to restructure it in 1903. For the next fifteen years and at a cost of $101 million, much of the old Erie Canal route was redirected and engineered to include not only the original Champlain Canal, but also the state's Oswego, Cayuga, and Seneca canals. The restructuring also "canalized" sections of the Mohawk, Oswego, Seneca, Genesee, Clyde, and other rivers that had been avoided by the original canal, dredging a uniform channel, 12 to 14 feet deep and 120 to 200 feet wide, adding dams with new locks of from 6 to 40 feet. The completed project was renamed the New York State Barge Canal. In the process, the canal bypassed the centers of the major cities through which it had once passed.

The canal can accommodate barges carrying up to 3,000 tons of cargo, but commercial traffic on the canal declined dramatically after the completion of the New York State Thruway in 1956 and the opening of the St. Lawrence Seaway in 1959. By the end of the first decade of the twenty-first century, the canal was used primarily by recreational boats, and the state had begun developing parks around the canals to create a major recreational area and tourist attraction. The majority of the canal system, known as the New York State Canal System, became part of the Erie Canalway National Heritage Corridor in 2000.

Erika E. Pilver

FURTHER READING

Bernstein, Peter L. *Wedding of the Waters: The Erie Canal and the Making of a Great Nation.* New York: W. W. Norton, 2005. Examines the social ramifications, political squabbles, and economic risks and returns of the canal.

Bourne, Russell. *Floating West: The Erie and Other American Canals.* New York: W. W. Norton, 1992. This series of histories of canals covers the Erie.

Hecht, Roger W., ed. *The Erie Canal Reader, 1790-1950.* Syracuse, N.Y.: Syracuse University Press, 2003. Essays, travelogues, poems, and fiction by major American and British writers; part celebration of the men and women who worked the canal and part social observation.

Shaw, Ronald E. *Erie Water West: A History of the Erie Canal, 1792-1854.* Lexington: University Press of Kentucky, 1990. Examines the canal from its development to its use during the mid-nineteenth century.

Sheriff, Carol. *The Artificial River: The Erie Canal and the Paradox of Progress, 1817-1862.* New York: Hill & Wang, 1996. Innovative use of archival research to document the varied responses of ordinary people who lived along the waterway.

SEE ALSO: Canals; Dams and aqueducts; Highways; Mississippi and Missouri Rivers; Panama Canal; Railroads; Shipping industry; Stagecoach line, first; Transcontinental railroad; Water resources.

European Recovery Program. *See* Marshall Plan

European trade with the United States

SIGNIFICANCE: Europe has always been an important trading partner of the United States, consistently providing a major import-export market. As the United States and Europe have increased investment in each other's domestic economy through corporate globalization, their trading relationship has become more open and free of barriers, resulting in economic growth for both.

The United States' primary import-export market has been Canada and the European nations, especially Great Britain. After World War II, the United States began to trade with more countries, including those in Latin and South America, Asia, Australia, and Africa; however, until that time, foreign trade was generally understood to mean trading with Canada and Europe.

HISTORICAL BACKGROUND

The United States followed a policy of protectionism until the 1940's. Tariffs and import-export policy were considered domestic issues until the 1920's, and the government's chief objective was to protect farmers and manufacturers from foreign competition. The Constitution prohibited duties on exports but not tariffs on imports. In 1789, the United States Congress passed its first Tariff Act. The tariff, set relatively low at 5 percent, was a means of collecting revenue for the nation.

During the War of 1812, American manufacturers operated without any competition from British manufacturers. In 1816, after the war concluded, tariffs were raised to protect American manufacturers by keeping imports from Britain low. The increased tariff was also seen as a means for paying the war debt. However, British goods appeared in American markets in spite of the tariffs. Not all members of Congress were in favor of high tariffs. A battle over tariffs ensued in 1828; those opposed to tariffs encouraged the protectionist members of Congress, who were preparing a new tariff bill, to place in the language of the bill excessively high tariffs on every possible commodity. They believed that the bill would defeat itself. They were wrong, and a bill known as the Tariff of Abominations passed. In 1833, Congress reduced these tariffs. By 1861, higher tariffs were once again being authorized.

The high tariffs caused both domestic and international problems for the United States. Europe was a major market for the cotton and tobacco grown on the plantations in the southern states. The high tariffs angered the European markets and made export sales difficult as retaliatory tariffs and duties were implemented. Domestically, the southern farmers viewed the tariffs as an attack on their economic and cultural base. This widened the chasm between North and South in the United States.

PROTECTIONISM AND NEW POLICIES

From 1870 through the 1920's, the U.S. stance on tariffs depended on which political party had control of Congress. A pattern of lower tariffs under Democratic Party control and higher tariffs under Republican Party control developed. However, the United States became more and more isolationist, and tariffs began to decline less during periods when the Democrats were in control. In 1930, the Smoot-Hawley Tariff Act raised tariff duty to 53 percent of the value of the import. European countries retaliated by raising their tariffs and adding quotas. By 1933, because of its unwillingness to import goods, the United States saw its export trade decline significantly.

In 1934, the United States changed its policy on trading. European countries were not willing to trade with the United States as long as such high tariffs were in force. Cordell Hull, secretary of state under President Franklin D. Roosevelt, obtained an amendment to the Smoot-Hawley Tariff Act that would cut tariffs equally with trading partners. This became the Reciprocal Trade Agreements Act, which, for the first time, gave the president the power to reduce tariffs. By the early 1940's, the United States had entered into bilateral trading agreements with approximately twenty-five countries, primarily European.

During World War II, trade was seriously interrupted. After the war, the role of the United States in international affairs and trading changed dramatically. The war-torn countries of Europe were trying to rebuild their economies and their countries. Cooperation became the action plan between European countries and the United States. The United States looked on Europe as its ally, from both a defense and an economic standpoint. The United States modified its trading policy and encouraged imports. By 1948, the General Agreement on Tariffs and Trade (GATT) was in place, with twenty-three countries, seven of which were European, signing it. The treaty reduced tariffs, quantitative restrictions, and subsidies, and has been repeatedly modified. On January 1, 1995, the members of GATT, in association with the European Community (EC) countries, formed the World Trade Organization (WTO), which replaced the GATT. The WTO is headquartered in Switzerland and oversees the implementation of treaties and adherence to trade agreements.

Until 1958, the United States had entered into trading agreements primarily with individual European countries. However with the signing of the Treaty of Rome, the situation changed. France, West Germany, Italy, Belgium, Luxembourg, and the Netherlands formed the European Economic Community (EEC). The EEC set a policy of no tariffs between member countries, common external tariffs, and shared policies in regard to agriculture, transport, and trade. In 1962, in the Dillon Round of the GATT negotiations, the EEC negotiated as a representative for all its member nations. In 1973, the United Kingdom, Ireland, and Denmark joined the EEC, and during the 1980's, Greece, Spain, and Portugal became members. The economic influence of the European countries increased steadily. The United States, from the end of World War II, supported the concept of a European union because it had come to realize that international cooperation, not isolationism, was the best policy for defense, modernization, and prosperity.

Although the United States favored a united Europe and was willing to make many concessions, including tariff reductions as described in the Trade Expansion Act of 1962, problems continued to arise in trade relations. During the 1980's, disputes arose, particularly in regard to agricultural products. The EEC, from its creation in 1962, protected European farmers from foreign competition. The Common Agricultural Policy (CAP) ensured the free movement of agricultural products within the European community, gave member-country products priority over imports, and imposed market restrictions on foreign products. These policies resulted in a decline in U.S. agricultural exports to Europe. Disputes about trade in canned fruit, wine, wheat flour, pasta, and other products were brought to the attention of the GATT but not easily solved.

THE EUROPEAN UNION

On February 7, 1992, with the signing of the Treaty of Maastricht, the European Union (EU) was formed. Its membership included new members as well as the EEC countries, eventually bringing the membership to twenty-seven. The European Union and the United States represent the largest interdependent trade and investment relationship in the world. The increase in investment in the United States by European companies and by American companies in European countries has done much to stimulate trade between the United States and the European Union. A good portion of the trade between the United States and the European Union stems from imports and exports between parent companies and their affiliates in the other country.

The two trading units, which are basically on the same socioeconomic level, engage in a considerable amount of intraindustry trade. Many similar products are both imported and exported by the two trading partners. The European Union is the United States' second-largest trading partner in merchandise and goods and its largest trading partner in services. Although since 1993, the United States has imported more goods than it has ex-

---

UNITED STATES TRADE WITH THE EUROPEAN UNION, 1997-2007, IN MILLIONS OF DOLLARS

Year	Exports	Imports	Balance
1997	143,931	160,896	−16,965
1998	151,967	180,549	−28,582
1999	154,824	200,052	−45,228
2000	168,181	226,900	−58,719
2001	161,931	226,568	−64,637
2002	146,621	232,313	−85,692
2003	155,170	253,042	−97,872
2004	172,622	281,959	−109,337
2005	186,437	308,776	−122,339
2006	213,996	330,482	−116,486
2007	247,242	354,409	−107,167

Source: Data from U.S. Census Bureau, Foreign Trade Division, Data Dissemination Branch, Washington, D.C.
Note: Trade figures are from the U.S. perspective.

ported to the European Union, it also has exported more services than it has imported from the European Union.

Although the United States and the European Union enjoy a cooperative trade relationship, disputes continue to arise between the trading partners. Many of these result from regulations and policies adopted to protect various segments of the members' domestic economies. Agriculture-related problems remain the biggest area of discord, particularly because of the subsidies granted to farmers or agricultural producers of specific products. The 1994 Uruguay Round of trade talks solved part of the problems created by subsidies. However, export subsidies and market-access quotas remain issues. Other problems that came into prominence after the Uruguay Round include hormone-treated beef and bioengineered foods.

Areospace is another trade area in which the United States and the European Union have argued over subsidies. This dispute has centered on subsidies provided by the United States to Boeing Aircraft and by various European Union nations (France, Spain, the United Kingdom, and Germany) to Airbus Industrie. Each trading partner maintains that the subsidies are necessary for the aircraft manufacturers to remain competitive

Differing attitudes toward social and environmental protection have also caused trading problems between the United States and the European Union. Domestic health and safety standards often vary widely between the trading partners. The United States tends to apply fewer regulations than does the European Union. In an attempt to be a homogenous single market, the European Union prefers to set standards and legal guidelines to be followed by its members in all areas, but the United States intervenes in production only when health concerns or other problems become apparent. One example of this difference is found in the issue of hormone-treated beef. Although this type of beef is considered safe for human consumption in the United States, it is not welcomed in European Union countries. Bioengineered food crops have also been an issue. The European Union is opposed to importing them because of the lack of proof regarding their long-range safety. However, the United States argues that bioengineering of food products has become a necessity for its farmers to be able to grow crops profitably.

The interdependency of the United States and the European Union has significantly affected the trade relationship between the two political entities, and this relationship is highly influential in the global economy.

Shawncey Webb

FURTHER READING

Baldwin, Robert E., Carl B. Hamilton, and Andre Sapir, eds. *Issues in U.S.-EC Trade Relations.* Chicago: University of Chicago Press, 1988. Discusses the European Community (European Union's predecessor) and its relation with the United States. Essays with commentaries giving both U.S. and EC opinions on issues. Author and subject indexes.

Cohen, Stephen D., et al., eds. *Fundamentals of U.S. Foreign Trade Policy.* Boulder, Colo.: Westview Press, 2002. Chapters on U.S.-EU relations, U.S. legislation regulating imports and exports, and who does what in U.S. trade policy. Index. Appendix of Web sites on international trade.

Featherstone, Kevin, and Roy H. Ginsberg. *The United States and the European Union in the 1990's.* New York: St. Martin's, 1996. Discusses economic interdependence of the United States and the European Union. Tables, appendixes.

Hamilton, Daniel S., and Joseph P. Quinlan. *Partners in Prosperity: The Changing Geography of the Transatlantic Economy.* Baltimore: Johns Hopkins University Press, 2004. Looks at the ever-increasing dependency and interconnectedness of the United States and Europe. Discusses investment, trade, and employment links.

Petermann, Ernst-Ulrich, and Mark Pollack, eds. *Transatlantic Economic Disputes: The EU, the U.S., and the WTO.* New York: Oxford University Press, 2004. Examines disputes such as the beef-hormone case, how the WTO functions, sources of dispute, and possible future remedies.

SEE ALSO: Asian trade with the United States; Canadian trade with the United States; Chinese trade with the United States; Colonial economic systems; General Agreement on Tariffs and Trade; International economics and trade; Japanese trade with the United States; Latin American trade with the United States; Marshall Plan; Mexican trade with the United States; Tariffs; World Trade Organization.

Exploration

SIGNIFICANCE: Before 1492, the Americas were a largely unexploited region, full of resources that promised opportunity and prosperity. Early European explorers were often motivated by curiosity about unknown and undiscovered lands, but most great exploration ventures were essentially business trips, in which the search for new resources, new trade routes, and new trading partners were the paramount goals. Even modern exploration of the land and sea benefits business in many ways. As new techniques for exploration are developed, new biological and mineral resources are being found beneath the ground and beneath the coastal waters.

More than thirteen millennia ago, a land bridge connected North America and Asia across what later became the Bering Strait, and the first immigrants into the Western Hemisphere crossed from Siberia. The first explorers of North America, these people were primarily hunters who followed the moving herds of big game. Over the ensuring millennia, they spread into South America, becoming isolated tribes with individual customs and languages. Though often separated by large distances, many of these societies communicated with one another through trade; they had common currencies and special trade languages.

The first European exploration of the Americas was accomplished by the Vikings, who reached the northeast shores of Canada around the year 1000. The Vikings may also have explored inland as far as the Great Lakes, though the evidence is considered tentative. They are thought to have made their explorations more for the sake of finding new lands to settle than for trade. However, their explorations had no lasting impact on North America, which would remain outside world trade routes until the sixteenth century.

The voyages of the Italian navigator Christopher Columbus finally opened the Western Hemisphere to the rest of the world during the 1490's. Columbus, like many of the explorers who came later, was motivated primarily by a desire to find a shorter route to East Asia's spice markets. Following his discoveries, many expeditions were sent to the new lands, both in pursuit of trade with the presumed Asian spice merchants and later for the purpose of taking gold and other valuables, including territory, from the native residents.

The Englishman Henry Hudson was a remarkably competent and adventurous early seventeenth century explorer whose voyages were primarily business-oriented. His two most famous voyages, the 1609 exploration of the Atlantic coast and the Hudson River and his 1610 voyage to northern Canada and Hudson's Bay, were searches for a trade route to the Far East. Hudson's 1609 voyage was sponsored by the Dutch East India Company because Hudson could not find an English company to back him. Afterward, he was put under house arrest in England for working for the Dutch company. His 1610 exploration was sponsored by the English East India Company, which arranged for his release so that he could find a new route to East Asia. Neither of Hudson's voyages found the elusive Northwest Passage, but they opened up some of the best fur-trading regions of the New World. Some historians believe that Hudson's trip to Hudson's Bay was possibly less aimed at the discovery of a Northwest Passage and more oriented toward exploration of mineral resources in the Canadian north. Hudson's own views on that question are unknown; he died after the crew of his ship mutinied and set him, his son, and some loyal crew members adrift on a small boat on the huge Canadian bay that now bears his name.

COLONIAL EXPLORATION AND WESTWARD EXPANSION

The settlers of Britain's North American colonies were primarily confined to the Atlantic coast and did not penetrate deeply into their colonies' hinterlands. Deeper exploration of the interior regions was accomplished mostly by French traders and missionaries from the north and from the Mississippi River Valley, Spanish conquerors and seekers of gold in the Southwest and the Pacific coast, British seagoing explorers on the northwest coast, and Russians in Alaska. Their activities sowed the seeds of continental business and trade, which at first was centered on extracting new resources in the vast and thinly populated mid-continent and the West.

After President Thomas Jefferson purchased the vast Louisiana Territory from France for the United States in 1803, he realized the importance of exploring it to learn about its characteristics and its resources. He appointed his secretary, Meriwether

Lewis, and wilderness-savvy William Clark to lead an exploratory expedition through the Louisiana Territory and thence on to the Pacific Ocean. The success of their journey is well known. Lewis and Clark explored and mapped an immense territory, enabling the young United States to lay claim to all the land between the Mississippi and Columbia Rivers, thereby ensuring American access to the wealth of much of the continent.

With the return of Lewis and Clark and the publication of their journals, other frontiersmen followed, exploring the many large areas not covered by Lewis and Clark's route. A colorful example of the overland explorers was the famous outdoorsman Jim Bridger, who ranged widely over the American West, establishing several routes through the Rockies and the Sierras that are still in use, such as that followed by Interstate Highway 80. He also explored the remarkable area that became Yellowstone National Park. Bridger's various routes across

Jim Bridger was an explorer and scout. (Courtesy, Denver Public Library)

the plains and mountains were important keys to the development of trade, especially the fur trade and the establishment of mining activities throughout the West.

MINERAL EXPLORATION

From the business point of view, an important kind of exploration is the discovery and recovery of natural mineral resources. This work depends heavily on the techniques used in geological research. Whether the materials sought are hard-rock minerals, such as gold, silver, and iron; liquids, such as petroleum and water; or gases, such as natural gas and helium, the locations of these resources are found by hard-rock geology, as in prospecting, or by the study of geological maps or the results of remote sensing.

Much modern mineral exploration takes advantage of geophysical and geochemical techniques. Geophysical exploration allows the geologist to explore the properties of subsurface materials. Instruments can measure the magnetic properties of the rocks, their density, conductivity, and resistivity, revealing clues about the location and nature of possible veins or layers of desirable materials. For uranium and other radioactive minerals, Geiger counters and related instruments are used. Frequently the geophysical exploration for minerals is carried out from low-flying aircraft, which allow large areas to be surveyed quickly.

Satellite-borne instruments are powerful tools for mineral exploration, especially when infrared spectroscopy provides information of the mineral composition of land masses. This method can be used to search for key spectroscopic signals anywhere on the earth where surface materials are sufficiently free of vegetative cover.

Geochemical techniques are also important in the discovery of mineral deposits that are contained in ground-level samples. Traditionally, the geochemist analyzes a sample of surface material to search for either traces of the mineral being sought or for tracers (called pathfinder elements), which are often associated with the mineral. A very old example of the geochemical technique is to search for microscopic particles of gold in streambeds that indicate the presence of gold-bearing veins higher up. Also a person can test a sample for the presence of arsenic, which is a pathfinder for gold, as they are often found together. Using geochemical tools requires that the geologist have access to the rocks or to soil that has been formed by erosion from the rocks.

The final act in mineral exploration is often drilling, in some cases to bring up rock cores that can be analyzed in the laboratory, or in the case of oil or water, to determine the depth and volume of the resources. When deposits are evaluated and found to be both economically and physically feasible to be extracted and to pass various environmental tests, the owners can proceed with extraction.

Paul W. Hodge

FURTHER READING

Dennen, W. H. *Mineral Resources: Geology, Exploration and Development.* London: Taylor and Francis, 1989. Overview of mineral exploration that gives useful information with an emphasis on the economic aspects of the field and discusses the modern ways of ensuring financial success.

Hayes, Derek. *America Discovered: A Historical Atlas of Exploration.* Vancouver, B.C.: Douglas & McIntyre, 2004. Through a collection of historical and contemporary maps, this book presents a history of the discovery and exploration of America. It includes sections of diaries and narratives that illuminate the maps and reveal how the exploration of the coasts, the rivers, the mountains, and the resources brought about the development of the continent.

Isserman, Maurice, and John S. Bowman, eds. *Across America: The Lewis and Clark Expedition.* New York: Facts On File, 2004. Comprehensive reference work on the Lewis and Clark expedition.

Lewis, Meriwether, and William Clark. *The Journals of Lewis and Clark.* Edited by Bernard DeVoto. Boston: Mariner Books, 1997. The 1804-1806 expedition of Lewis and Clark was one of the world's great explorations, and the journals kept by the two explorers make fascinating reading. Their journey into the little-known lands of the Louisiana Territory and the unknown lands of the Far West paved the way for American claims to the vast lands of present-day Oregon, Washington, and Idaho.

Moon, Charles J., Michael K. G. Whateley, and Anthony M. Evans, eds. *Introduction to Mineral Exploration.* 2d ed. Oxford: Blackwell, 2006. This basic book covers all aspects of exploration for mineral resources, from coal to diamonds. It gives details

of procedures for initial selection of areas to explore and for methods of exploration, including direct sampling as well as remote sensing. Several case studies are included.

SEE ALSO: Black Hills gold rush; California gold rush; Coal industry; Fur trapping and trading; Jewelry industry; Lewis and Clark expedition; Mineral resources; Pike's western explorations; Space race.

Export-Import Bank of the United States

IDENTIFICATION: Federal agency charged with financing and insuring foreign purchases of American commodities

DATE: Established in 1934

SIGNIFICANCE: The Export-Import Bank of the United States helps encourage and maintain trade between the United States and other nations by reducing the risks associated with that trade. The bank guarantees transactions that are too risky for commercial banks but that still have a reasonable assurance of repayment, thereby helping maintain employment in the U.S. manufacturing and agricultural sectors.

Since its inception, the Export-Import Bank of the United States (Ex-Im Bank) has struggled to strike a balance between its financial responsibilities and its foreign policy responsibilities. Various presidential administrations have used the bank's credit facilities to increase American power and influence abroad. The bank was originally chartered to facilitate trade between the United States and the newly recognized Soviet Union, as well as between the United States and Cuba. These attempts at fostering international trade and diplomacy were not successful, so the trading focus of the bank quickly became more global. Prior to the beginning of the Marshall Plan, President Harry S. Truman used the bank to supply capital to rebuild Western Europe after World War II. President Lyndon B. Johnson used the bank to finance development projects in Latin America as a way to counteract Soviet influence in the region during the 1960's.

Until the 1970's, the bank relied on U.S. Treasury funds to finance its credit activities. Since then, the bank has shifted its focus to work with commercial banks both in the United States and abroad to share risk and ensure repayment.

During the 1990's, the bank provided development funds to start private companies in the recently collapsed Soviet Union, when commercial lenders refused to lend without a certainty of repayment. When Asian economies declined during the late 1990's, the bank provided substantial short-term credit for customers to continue to purchase U.S. goods.

The Export-Import Bank, while undeniably helping foster international trade and American influence abroad, is not without its critics. Many of the U.S. exporters it has helped are giant, profitable defense contractors such as Boeing, Lockheed, and General Electric, whose foreign sales were essentially subsidized by U.S. taxpayers through the bank. In the past, the bank has also helped guarantee financing for gigantic development projects without due regard to the environmental impact of those projects. In response to criticism, the bank has come to emphasize U.S. export transactions that more directly benefit smaller U.S businesses.

Victoria Erhart

FURTHER READING

Baker, James C. *Financing International Trade.* Westport, Conn.: Praeger, 2003.

Becker, William H., and William M. McClenahan, Jr. *The Market, the State, and the Export-Import Bank of the United States, 1934-2000.* New York: Cambridge University Press, 2003.

Hufbauer, Gary Clyde, and Rita Rodriguez, eds. *The Ex-Im Bank in the Twenty-First Century: A New Approach?* Washington, D.C.: Institute for International Economics, 2001.

SEE ALSO: Agency for International Development, U.S.; Arms industry; Asian financial crisis of 1997; Asian trade with the United States; Bank of the United States, First; Bank of the United States, Second; Banking; Insurance industry; Military-industrial complex.

F

Factories. *See* Automation in factories; Industrial Revolution, American

Farm Credit Administration

IDENTIFICATION: Federal government agency responsible for regulatory oversight of all financial institutions that provide credit facilities to farmers, farming co-ops, rural landholders, and rural utilities

DATE: Established in 1933

SIGNIFICANCE: The Farm Credit Administration is the federal agency that regulates all other government entities providing credit facilities for farmers, other rural landholders, and rural-based businesses.

After the end of the U.S. Civil War in 1865 and the opening of the West for settlement, homesteaders needed access to long-term credit to purchase farmland. They also needed shorter-term credit to purchase equipment, livestock, and seed, as well as to make necessary improvements on the land. Credit facilities were available for businesses but not for agricultural enterprises. Although the federal government knew farming was part of a healthy and balanced national economy, the government did very little to help rural landholders until President Woodrow Wilson signed the Federal Farm Loan Act of 1916 into law.

FEDERAL FARM LOAN ACT OF 1916

The Federal Farm Loan Act authorized the creation of twelve federal land banks spread throughout the country. The act also created hundreds of national farm loan associations, which acted as retail agents to loan money to individual farmers and to supply long-term credit for land purchases. Although helpful over the long term, the act offered no short-term loans to purchase livestock or seed. Nor did it provide loans for tractors as farming in the United States became mechanized after World War I. This deficiency was not rectified by the Agricultural Credits Act of 1923, which made money available to federal intermediate credit banks, as these institutions did not lend to individual farmers.

When the Great Depression hit America during the 1930's, it hit rural America particularly hard. Few institutions offered agricultural loans, and farmers owed more than their depreciating land was worth. Many simply walked away from their farms. Banks, already crippled by losses due to defaults on business loans, were forced to carry foreclosed farms on their balance sheets. This drove many smaller rural banks into insolvency and eventual failure.

President Franklin D. Roosevelt signed the Emergency Farm Mortgage Act and the Farm Credit Act into law in 1933 as part of his New Deal plan to resurrect the moribund U.S. economy. The two acts made the federal government a guarantor of last resort for institutions providing agricultural credit facilities. Few lending institutions were enthusiastic about such a program. The Farm Credit Act established the Farm Credit System, through which federal money, via local agricultural lending boards, would be loaned to individual farmers and other rural landholders for short-, intermediate-, and long-term needs.

The Farm Credit Administration (FCA), created by executive order, was originally created as an independent federal agency and made responsible for all existing agricultural credit organizations. From 1939 until 1953, the FCA was part of the Department of Agriculture, but it later reverted to being an independent agency. The Farm Credit System served as the regulator of all later federal credit unions, until this function was given to the Federal Deposit Insurance Corporation (FDIC) in 1942. The Farm Credit System was the vehicle through which federal money would reach qualifying individual farmers. The Farm Credit Act of 1933 was updated and extended to include fishers and other types of rural landholders by the Farm Credit Act of 1971. This 1971 act, as amended, also provided the authority for the Farm Credit Administration.

The 1970's were a boom time for American farmers. Grain harvests in the Soviet Union failed repeatedly, and worldwide demand for U.S. agricultural exports reached record levels. Farmers received record prices for their products. Many farmers borrowed heavily to expand operations, thinking that the boom would be of indefinite duration.

CHANGING CREDIT AVAILABILITY

Beginning in 1979, the Federal Reserve tightened the availability of credit in U.S. markets to control domestic inflation. Tightened credit drove up prices for agricultural goods both in the United States and abroad. As a result, developing countries that had previously purchased U.S. agricultural goods cut back on their purchases. These countries improved their own national agricultural productivity to become food exporters themselves. As labor costs in developing countries are a fraction of labor costs in the United States, agricultural products from developing countries were much cheaper to purchase, further reducing international demand for U.S. agricultural exports. Faced with rising costs, declining demand, and tightened availability of credit, U.S. farmers were in grave financial trouble by the mid-1980's. Some 300,000 American farmers were billions of dollars in debt and facing foreclosure.

The Farm Credit Amendments Act of 1985 and the Agricultural Credit Act of 1987 provided $4 billion in federal money to agricultural lending agencies and streamlined the Farm Credit System that had been in place since 1933. It also created the Federal Agricultural Mortgage Corporation (Farmer Mac) to provide a secondary financial market for the securitization and purchase of farm and rural home mortgages. The sales of these mortgage-backed securities provided liquidity in order for Farmer Mac to continue to make new agricultural loans for mortgages and rural land improvements.

The Farm Credit System is solvent and receives no federal government appropriations. The Farm Credit System does not take deposits. Through regional farm credit banks, the Farm Credit System raises money for new agricultural loans for issuing bonds and notes in U.S. capital markets. These bonds are backed by the federal government but are different from U.S. Treasury bonds and notes. The various lending institutions within the Farm Credit System are allowed to pool their funds in order to share risk and more easily absorb losses. The Farm Credit System, of which Farmer Mac is a part, has grown to carry more than $135 billion in loans to over 500,000 rural borrowers.

Victoria Erhart

FURTHER READING

Bishoff, Jonathan M., ed. *Agricultural Finance and Credit.* New York: Nova Science Publishers, 2008. Discusses the importance of credit in capital-intensive farming.

Farm Credit Administration. *The Director's Role: Farm Credit System Institutions.* McLean, Va.: Author, 2006. Looks at the governmental institutions designed to help farmers and examines their effects.

Gardner, Bruce L. *American Agriculture in the Twentieth Century: How It Flourished and What It Cost.* Cambridge, Mass.: Harvard University Press, 2002. Takes a long look at agriculture and discusses agricultural credit and other economic issues.

Hurt, R. Douglas. *Problems of Plenty: The American Farmer in the Twentieth Century.* Chicago: Ivan R. Dee, 2002. Discusses the economics and social aspects of farming during the twentieth century, including the loan process.

Sunbury, Ben. *The Fall of the Farm Credit Empire.* Ames: Iowa State University Press, 1990. Looks at the effects of the Agricultural Credit Act of 1987 on credit and farmers.

SEE ALSO: Agriculture; Agriculture, U.S. Department of; Farm labor; Farm protests; Farm subsidies; Great Depression; New Deal programs.

Farm labor

DEFINITION: Body of agricultural workers, including self-employed farmers and their families, regular and migratory wage earners, indentured servants, and slaves

SIGNIFICANCE: The United States is one of the most productive agricultural nations in the world, and its ability to produce food and other cash crops has been a direct function of the labor available and its relationship to the means of production. The southern states in particular have found themselves at various points dependent on slavery and other forms of labor to continue the agricultural productivity underlying their traditional way of life.

The use of some kind of farm labor other than farm owners themselves to help plant and harvest crops has been a part of the agricultural history of the United States from colonial times. Various sources provided that help, which can be divided into at least six categories: indentured servants, both black and white; African slave labor; sharecroppers; immigrant Asian laborers; braceros; and undocumented immigrants.

INDENTURED SERVANTS

Indentured servitude was a reality in America from early in the country's colonial era. White laborers—British, Irish, Scottish, and German—emigrated to America, having been guaranteed passage into colonies in exchange for years of hard labor, usually in the fields. In fact, up to 75 percent of the populations of some colonies were made up of indentured servants. Used principally in the Middle Colonies and the tobacco-growing colonies, these "bound" laborers, or indentured servants, were either voluntary or involuntary laborers. Voluntary laborers (redemptioners or "free willers"), bound themselves for terms varying from two to seven years or more in return for passage to America. It has been estimated that from 60 to 75 percent of the total immigrant population until 1776 were of this group. In addition, apprentices—minors who were given training in exchange for services—were considered voluntary laborers.

The involuntary laborers generally fell into one of four groups. Some British convicts were allowed transportation to the colonies to avoid a death penalty. Between 1655 and 1699, forty-five hundred such servants entered the colonies, and between 1700 and 1750, around ten thousand came to Maryland alone, with many others going to Virginia or the West Indies. Convicted criminals, especially those charged with larceny or debt, and victims of kidnapping by overzealous recruiters also became involuntary indentured servants.

Throughout the first half of the seventeenth century, these white indentured servants performed most of the arduous labor of clearing the land and cultivating tobacco crops in Virginia in particular. Thanks to this cheap labor, tobacco quickly became a cash crop, with over 500,000 pounds being exported by 1627. Indeed, it was said that indentured servants' contributions in the raising of tobacco saved the Virginia colony. The golden age for the indentured servant ended during the mid-seventeenth century, however.

In South Carolina, the decline was due largely to the nature of the work involved in rice production.

Rice cultivation is well suited to gang labor, and the hard work in the hot summers in the colonies may have been an important deterrent to those considering migration to South Carolina. The Restoration of King Charles II and the subsequent passage of the Navigations Acts deprived Virginia and Maryland of the free world market they had enjoyed for tobacco, and this, along with other conditions, led to an irreversible decline in the number of indentured laborers.

A new wave of indentured migrants began to arrive in the United States around the 1830's. These were largely Asian, and, unlike the earlier European laborers, the nineteenth century arrivals received wages, housing, medical care, and clothing. Although these new indentured laborers resembled members of the earlier European labor trade in some ways, there was no historical connection; instead, they replaced African slavery. By the 1850's, however, holding laborers in indentured servitude came to be perceived as equivalent to slavery, and the Anti-Peonage Act of 1867 prohibited both voluntary and involuntary servitude in all states and territories of the United States. Indentured servitude, however, played a significant role both in making the United States successful economically and in populating it.

SLAVE LABOR

Slavery in the British colonies began on August 20, 1619, when about twenty Africans were delivered by a Dutch ship to the Jamestown, Virginia, settlement and sold as indentured servants. Although these people did not become slaves immediately, they were the first permanent involuntary African immigrants in what would become the United States. Over the course of the next 150 years or more, however, slave labor came to be the answer to the need for cheap agricultural labor, especially in the South. With the emergence of cotton, first as a small specialized crop in the Sea Islands of South Carolina and Georgia and then as the "king" of cash crops, slavery became ever-more important to the southern economy.

Few would have dared to believe that all sectors of the national economy would be transformed by cotton during the early years of the nineteenth century. It quickly became clear that large numbers of slave laborers would be needed to clear the land and plant cotton on new acreage being acquired. Because the Founding Fathers had written into the Constitution

MEDIAN HOURLY WAGES FOR AGRICULTURAL WORKERS AS OF MAY, 2006, IN DOLLARS

Job Title	Median Hourly Wage
Agricultural inspectors	18.32
Animal breeders	13.02
Agricultural equipment operators	9.72
Farmworkers, farm and ranch animals	9.17
Graders and sorters, agricultural products	8.27
Farmworkers and laborers, crop, nursery, and greenhouse	7.95

Source: Data from U.S. Bureau of Labor Statistics, Office of Occupational Statistics and Employment Projections

a twenty-year moratorium on even considering an end to the transatlantic slave trade, importation continued unchecked into the early nineteenth century. Initiatives by the United States government to acquire additional land, including the Louisiana Purchase, the annexation of West Florida, the purchase of East Florida, and the annexation of Texas, permitted the expansion of both cotton cultivation and slavery. The cultivation of cotton in the United States had a powerful impact on both the domestic economy and international trade as well.

Although cotton was the dominant cash crop under cultivation by slave labor, the slaves raised other profitable crops: sugarcane in southeastern Louisiana; tobacco in Virginia, North Carolina, Tennessee, and Kentucky; rice in South Carolina and Georgia; and corn and wheat in the Shenandoah Valley, the "breadbasket" of the Confederacy during the U.S. Civil War. All contributed to the nation's economic viability and prosperity. However, Reconstruction laws, specifically the Thirteenth, Fourteenth, and Fifteenth Amendments to the Constitution, would bring slave labor to an end, as the rights of citizenship and the vote were enacted for all natural-born Americans.

SHARECROPPING AND DEBT PEONAGE

After slavery fell into disrepute, free-labor plantations came into use. In the aftermath of the Civil War, planters often had to borrow money at high interest rates to produce crops. One way to be able to work all of the land was to establish a system of agricultural labor whereby a landlord provided a plot of land to a poor agricultural worker or farmer to work

in exchange for the sharecropper's paying the landowner a certain percentage, usually from one-third to one-half, of each crop. Historically, the tenants were both white and black. At one point during the early twentieth century, there were more than 5 million such white laborers and about 3 million black sharecroppers.

During the Dust Bowl era of the 1930's, the number of white tenant farmers and sharecroppers increased, because so many sold their own farms and began migrating to harvest crops on other farmers' farms. The system had benefits and costs for both the landlords and the tenants. It assured that the tenant would remain on the land throughout the harvest season, but because the tenant paid in shares of the harvest, the owner was not immune from the effects of a bad harvest. Because sharecroppers benefited from large harvests, they had more incentive to work hard and use better farming methods than did plantation slaves. Debt peonage resulted when a sharecropper's share was insufficient to repay the landlord for seed and supplies. Sharecropping laws required indebted croppers to remain on the land until their debt was retired. Although there was often a perception that sharecropping was exploitative, the system could be mutually beneficial.

LARGE-SCALE FARMING IN THE WEST

Between the 1860's and the 1920's, farming, especially in California, developed into a large-scale industry that resulted in a series of importations of Asian labor. The first wave of imported workers were Asian Indians, followed by Chinese. By 1876, seven out of eight farmworkers in California were Chinese. Between the 1890's and 1903, Japanese workers joined the labor force, followed during the 1920's by Filipino and a few Mexican workers. Thus, Asian Pacific American history is inextricably interwoven with American labor history. These workers planted some of the first crops in California's San Joaquin Valley, and although they toiled for generations helping build the country, the U.S. labor movement historically opposed including Asian American workers in unions.

The Chinese Exclusion Act of 1882, supported by labor unions, was the first immigration law in U.S. history to explicitly forbid an entire group based on nationality. In 1903, Japanese American farmworkers in Oxnard, California, along with some Mexicans, tried to form a multiracial union, but when they applied for a charter, they were rejected because of the Japanese American members. In 1934, Chinese and Japanese American workers participated in a strike. During this same period, Filipino workers established the Filipino Labor Union and

A Mexican farmworker holding carrots in Edinburg, Texas, in 1939. (Library of Congress)

played a key role in organizing agricultural workers throughout the Central Valley and the number of Mexican workers saw a huge increase. In 1924, the U.S. Border Patrol was created, an act that would have an important effect on their lives and give rise to the term "illegal alien."

Between 1942 and 1964, because of labor shortages arising from World War II, the bracero program was established. Under this program, temporary laborers from Mexico were brought in to harvest crops; more than 4 million Mexican farmworkers left their own lands and families to chase the dream of a better life in the United States. Their arrival altered the social and economic environment of a number of border towns. Because the contracts were written in English, many workers signed papers without understanding the terms of employment and the rights they were forfeiting. Eventually, the program ended because of gross humanitarian violations by bracero employers. The end of the bracero program was followed by the formation of the United Farm Workers union, and subsequent changes of the American migrant labor system were made under the leadership of César Chávez, a bracero program critic.

Between the 1970's and 1990's, many African American workers moved into other industries, and Latin American immigrants became the primary source of labor in agriculture. In 1994, the North American Free Trade Agreement (NAFTA) was implemented, eliminating nontariff barriers to agricultural trade between the United States and Mexico; the final provisions of the agreement were fully implemented on January 1, 2008. Proponents hail NAFTA as one of the most successful trade agreements in history, citing large increases in agricultural trade and investment between the United States, Canada, and Mexico. Detractors observe that 2 million Mexican farmers and farm laborers lost their livelihood and were forced off the land by heavily subsidized U.S. farm products being imported to Mexico. Although agricultural workers in the United States have been a disenfranchised group by any measure, the Mexican hand helped the United States become the most lush agricultural center in the world.

Victoria Price

FURTHER READING

Buss, Fran Leeper, ed. *Forged Under the Sun/Forjada Bajo el Sol: The Life of Maria Elena Lucas.* Ann Arbor: University of Michigan Press, 1993. The autobiography of a migrant farmworker who endured the struggles and the injustices of such a life, and who grew up to become a champion for farmworkers through organized labor groups. Also a writer, she incorporates some of her poems and a play into the text. Photographs.

Eaton, Clement. *A History of the Old South: The Emergence of a Reluctant Nation.* 3d ed. Prospect Heights, Ill.: Waveland Press, 1987. Traces the colonial origins of southerners, the evolution of the plantation, the rise of a native aristocracy, and the southern Federalists. Discusses slave labor and later changing attitudes toward slavery. Bibliography and index.

Kiser, George C., and Martha Woody Kiser, eds. *Mexican Workers in the United States.* Albuquerque: University of New Mexico Press, 1979. A collection of essays and brief commentary, organized chronologically, traces the use of Mexican labor from the World War I era through the bracero era of 1942 to 1964. Addresses the illegal Mexican worker and the Mexican commuter situations. Reports on the Mexican Border Industry Program enacted by the United States government.

Lewis, Sasha G. *Slave Trade Today: American Exploitation of Illegal Aliens.* Boston: Beacon Press, 1979. Analyses the reality of slave trade in contemporary times in the United States, pointing out that it is international in scope. Discusses the problems inherent in the undocumented alien labor situation, with employers wanting to reap the financial benefits of hiring illegal aliens, leaving the law-enforcement sector feeling helpless. Suggests ways to addresses the broken system. Extensive list of sources and resources.

Northrup, David. *Indentured Labor in the Age of Imperialism, 1834-1922.* New York: Cambridge University Press, 1995. Compares the different indentured migrations of the nineteenth century and relates their experiences to those of more contemporary migrant groups. Presents indentured labor as a distinct historical phenomenon, not as a continuation of slavery.

SEE ALSO: Agribusiness; Agriculture; Bracero program; Dust Bowl; Farm protests; Farm subsidies; Indentured labor; Plantation agriculture; Sharecropping; Slave era; United Farm Workers of America.

Farm protests

THE EVENT: Demonstrations by farmers throughout America against falling prices, the rise of indebtedness, and general business trends they believed to be detrimental to their economic opportunities

DATE: Culminating during the 1880's and early 1890's

PLACE: U.S. agrarian states, especially in the Midwest, the western plains, and the South

SIGNIFICANCE: Although the population of the United States grew dramatically during the late nineteenth century, the vast expansion of land being farmed and the beginnings of mechanized agriculture soon led to overproduction and falling prices. Farmers protested these developments, blaming government policies, the railroads, and the processors of agricultural products.

During the 1870's and 1880's, a series of bad weather cycles plagued American farmers. Compounding these cycles was the general downward trend of prices from the end of the U.S. Civil War to the early 1890's. The amount of land being farmed in the United States more than doubled as the Great Plains were settled and brought into production. Prices for many farm commodities fell by 50 percent over a thirty-year period, before reaching some stability during the mid-1890's. Many farmers became involved in the crop lien system, and farm indebtedness rose dramatically.

In the West, farming and cattle ranching would have hardly been possible without railroad connections to the markets of the East, yet producers felt at the mercy of the railroads, the grain elevator operations, and the millers, meatpackers, and other agricultural processors. Farm organizations that had begun as social and educational ventures, such as the National Grange of the Patrons of Husbandry and the various farmers' alliances, became politically active during the late 1870's and into the 1880's.

These alliances organized protests and other political activities designed to make their voices heard. They backed the political candidates of both the Republican and the Democratic Parties who promised to represent their interests. The major farmers' alliances were the Northern Farmers' Alliance, with about two million members; the Southern Farmers'

Alliance, with about two million white members; and a separate Colored Farmers' National Alliance that represented about one million southern black farmers. These organizations had some success in electing state and local legislators and governors and in passing state laws regulating railroads and grain elevator operations.

During the early 1890's, representatives from several of these farm organizations helped form the People's Party, also known as the Populist Party. The Populists never achieved much of their agrarian reform agenda, although some of their proposals were later adopted in the Progressive and New Deal eras. During the mid-1890's, agricultural production began to level off and commodity prices rose, ending much of the discontent that had fueled the earlier protests.

Mark S. Joy

FURTHER READING

Argersinger, Peter H. *The Limits of Agrarian Radicalism: Western Populism and American Politics.* Lawrence: University Press of Kansas, 1995.

Kazin, Michael. *The Populist Persuasion: An American History.* Rev. ed. Ithaca, N.Y.: Cornell University Press, 1998.

Schwartz, Michael. *Radical Protest and Social Structure: The Southern Farmers' Alliance and Cotton Tenancy, 1880-1890.* Chicago: University of Chicago Press, 1988.

SEE ALSO: Agriculture; Farm labor; Food-processing industries; Granger movement; Railroads.

Farm subsidies

DEFINITION: Supplemental income paid to American farmers by the U.S. Department of Agriculture for commodities such as wheat, corn, soybeans, cotton, and rice in an effort to manage supply and control prices

SIGNIFICANCE: Farm subsidies help control the price of crops, ensure farmers of a consistent income, and keep the United States free from dependence on foreign countries for its food supply.

During the 1930's, the United States had 6 million farms on which one-quarter of the population lived. However, by the end of the twentieth century, only 2 percent of the population resided on the nation's 157,000 farms. Various United States farm bills, dating back to the Agricultural Adjustment Act of 1933, supplement the income of growers and producers of more than twenty commodities, including sugar, wheat, rice, peanuts, soybeans, dairy products, tobacco, wool, honey, and vegetable oils. These agricultural subsidy programs, which amount to more than $25 billion annually, ensure that farmers receive a base minimum price, called a price floor, for their crops, as well as a financial supplement that is funded by tax revenues. For instance, if farmers receive $3.50 for a bushel of wheat on the market, the government might pay them an extra 50 cents per bushel to ensure a certain level of payment. These programs, created by farm bills, are the subject of great controversy.

THE PROS AND CONS

Those who favor farm subsidies believe that farmers could not compete with low-priced foreign imports unless they received subsidies. They would be bankrupted and lose their farms, and American agriculture would all but disappear. Consequently, the United States would become dependent on other countries for its food supply, and this would severely upset the nation's balance of trade. Some argue that farm subsidies are vital because although farmers have a large capital investment and therefore high fixed costs of production, weather can produce severe fluctuations in crop yield. When weather reduces production levels, the market price goes up, but farmers have less to sell, and their income would drop if not for subsidies. When weather boosts production, the market price falls, and farmers would make less if not for subsidies. Farm subsidies mean that food and animal producers pay less for crops (as the government makes up the difference), ensuring that lower-income people, who spend a higher percentage of their income than do wealthier people on food, are able to afford to purchase groceries. Farm subsidies, partly by encouraging overproduction, also allow U.S. agricultural products to be competitive exports.

Some Americans insist that subsidies are simply against the principles of free trade and are angry that their tax dollars are spent on farm subsidies. They believe that farmers should not rely on government financial support and look on farm subsidies

GOVERNMENT SPENDING ON FARM INCOME STABILIZATION, 1990-2006, IN BILLIONS OF DOLLARS

Year	Spending
1990	9.7
1995	7.0
2000	33.4
2003	18.3
2004	11.2
2005	22.0
2006	21.4

Source: Data from the *Statistical Abstract of the United States, 2008* (Washington, D.C.: Department of Commerce, Economics and Statistics Administration, Bureau of the Census, Data User Services Division, 2008)

as a costly form of welfare. Consistent income for farmers, they insist, should be maintained through insurance programs and the futures market. Besides, the argument continues, the image of the poor single-family farm is out of date. These critics argue that, in the twenty-first century, much farming is done by agribusinesses or large farming operations. Subsidies, critics insist, go mostly to the biggest, most productive farms, which simply do not need them. Farmers, they insist, will grow anything, even if it is not demanded by the public, just to get the subsidies.

Critics also assert that providing farmers with subsidies causes problems in the proper allocation of resources. For instance, instead of using land as pastures for cattle, farmers grow corn to use as livestock feed. Also, subsidies encourage farmers to grow corn for conversion to ethanol, which is used as automotive fuel, instead of for food.

Beyond the question of whether crops should be subsidized, a serious question remains as to which crops should be subsidized. Because 90 percent of subsidy money goes to corn, wheat, soybeans, and rice, those are the cheapest and most abundant crops produced. These crops are often used as feed for cows, pigs, and chickens, thus supporting the dairy and meat industries. Fresh vegetables and fruit, by contrast, are not significantly subsidized.

Thus, many less nutritious foods are lower priced in American supermarkets and fast-food restaurants, whereas fresh, nutritious food is more difficult to afford. Were subsidy money to be reallocated, this situation could be reversed.

WORLD MARKETS

The World Trade Organization has determined that keeping the price of food low through the use of export farm subsidies can help American farmers while providing low-priced food for people in developing countries. However, these same export subsidies also encourage these poorer countries to remain dependent on food from wealthier countries. They can in fact ruin poorer farmers and force them off their land, thus contributing to an increase in poverty. For example, it is estimated that 2 million Mexican agricultural laborers have been forced off their land by the combination of American corn subsidies and the North American Free Trade Agreement (NAFTA).

In 2008, however, the problem was not excess supply of grains and oilseeds (including soybeans) and low prices but rather high prices and increasing demand. Low agricultural productivity in the poorest countries, higher cost of agricultural production (higher fuel costs), diversion of corn and other grains to make biofuels, droughts in Australia and Europe, and rising populations and incomes have caused commodity prices to rise and created worldwide food shortages. These shortages were felt most in the poorest countries, which could no longer afford to import food, but were also evident in the prices Americans paid for food. The food consumer price index, created by the U.S. Department of Labor, rose at a seasonally adjusted annual rate of 7.5 percent for the first eight months of 2008, compared with 4.9 percent in 2007.

M. Casey Diana

FURTHER READING

Ikerd, John E. *Crisis and Opportunity: Sustainability in American Agriculture.* Winnipeg, Alta.: Bison Books, 2008. Collection of essays dealing with the sustainability of food and farming systems. Penetrating discussions of the results of farm subsidies.

Pawlick, Thomas F. *The End of Food: How the Food Industry Is Destroying Our Food Supply—And What We Can Do About It.* Fort Lee, N.J.: Barricade Books,

2006. Written by an investigative science journalist and professor of journalism; uses scientific research that demonstrates the negative effects subsidized crops can have on the food supply of the United States.

Pollan, Michael. "The Way We Live Now: You Are What You Grow." *The New York Times*, April 22, 2007. Pollan blames the rising rate of American obesity on the overabundance of junk food brought about by the wrong kind of farm subsidies.

Pyle, George B. *Raising Less Corn, More Hell: Why Our Economy, Ecology, and Security Demand the Preservation of the Independent Farm.* New York: Public Affairs Press, 2005. Veteran journalist Pyle argues that American farmers can feed the world by growing fewer crops and that growing too much food contributes to world hunger, because farmers in developing countries cannot compete against subsidized American food.

Roberts, Paul. *The End of Food.* Boston: Houghton Mifflin, 2008. Roberts, author of *The End of Oil*, makes a plea for rethinking food systems by analyzing the global food economy and the effect of farm subsidies worldwide, especially on the poor.

SEE ALSO: Agribusiness; Agriculture; Agriculture, U.S. Department of; Cereal crops; Cotton industry; Dairy industry; Farm Credit Administration; Farm labor; Farm protests; Government spending; Rice industry.

Farming. *See* Agriculture

Fast-food restaurants

DEFINITION: Restaurants that offer convenience and speed in serving food, usually including hamburgers, pizza, fried chicken, or submarine sandwiches

SIGNIFICANCE: During the twentieth century, fast-food restaurants, or quick service restaurants (QSR), became one of the fastest-growing American industries. The major chains and franchises purchased prime real estate, thus transforming the American landscape. Along with the rise of automobiles, QSRs changed consumer behavior and spending. Major QSRs invested billions of advertising dollars to create brand-name recognition, shaping popular culture as well.

America's first major fast-food chain was the Horn & Hardart Automat, which opened in 1902 in Philadelphia. These waiterless restaurants in Art Deco style had coin-operated glass-and-chrome vending machines offering freshly made food.

During the 1920's, the American lifestyle began to change, as automobiles became affordable and the federal government funded new highway systems. A new, mobile society that valued convenience and speed needed quick meals. In 1921 in Dallas, Texas, the first drive-in restaurant chain, the Pig Stand, opened, with carhops taking customers' orders. Their first drive-through window appeared in 1931.

In 1921, White Castle, the first fast-food hamburger chain, opened in Wichita, Kansas. In 1932, it introduced fast-food coupon advertising. The chain was the first to sell one billion hamburgers, and it comprised 380 restaurants in 2007. Celebrated in art and film, the iconic Automat—another waiterless coin-operated restaurant—was popular during the Great Depression but could not compete with the modern fast-food franchises that began proliferating during the 1950's. The last Automat would close in 1991.

MODERN HAMBURGER CHAINS

Two hamburger restaurants inaugurated the modern fast-food industry. In 1948, brothers Maurice and Richard McDonald opened their McDonald's hamburger stand in San Bernardino, California. They used a self-service, assembly line system called the "Speedee Service System," which established the basic format of the modern fast-food restaurant. In 1954, Ray Kroc, distributor of the Multimixer milkshake mixer, observed how quickly McDonald's produced inexpensive meals for a constant stream of customers. On April 15, 1955, Kroc opened the first franchised McDonald's restaurant in Des Plaines, Illinois. In 1961, he purchased the McDonald brothers' equity in the business. Many McDonald's products became known worldwide, including the Big Mac sandwich (launched in 1968), the Egg McMuffin (1973), and Happy Meals for children (1979). When Kroc died in 1984, there were more than seventy-five hundred McDonald's restaurants globally. By 2008, McDonald's was the leading QSR, with thirty thousand restaurants in more than one hundred countries and serving more than 54 million customers daily.

Like Ray Kroc, James McLamore and David Edgerton had admired the first McDonald's hamburger stand. They subsequently founded the Burger King (BK) Corporation in Miami, Florida, in 1954. However, the unique BK hamburger was "flame-broiled" rather than fried, and BK served onion rings. In 1957, Burger King introduced its signature product, the Whopper, and franchising began in 1959. When Pillsbury bought BK in 1967, it was the third-largest fast-food chain in the United States. In 1974, BK launched its successful Have It Your Way marketing campaign, promoting its customized offerings. In 2007, Burger King's revenues were $2.234 billion, and it served more than 11 million customers per day. By 2008, BK had become the second-largest hamburger chain, with more than 11,200 restaurants throughout the United States and in sixty-nine countries.

Founder Dave Thomas opened the first Wendy's in November, 1969, in Columbus, Ohio, and sold the first franchise in 1972. Wendy's offered old-fashioned, square hamburgers, and its Big Classic rivaled Burger King's Whopper. The famous tagline Where's the Beef? became part of American pop culture. In 2006, Wendy's had revenues of $2.45 billion, and it was the third-largest burger chain, with sixty-seven hundred locations. In April, 2008, Tirarc Companies, owner of Arby's, announced it had purchased Wendy's for $2.34 billion. Founded in 1964, Arby's was famous for its roast beef sandwiches.

In 1956, Carl N. Karcher opened the first Carl's Jr. charbroiled burger restaurants in Anaheim and Brea, California. Carl's Jr. created the Six Dollar burger, the first sit-down-restaurant-style burger at a QSR. In 1997, parent company Carl Karcher Enterprises acquired Hardee's, a hamburger chain with twenty-five hundred locations. Carl Karcher Enterprises made $1.52 billion in sales in 2006. Other burger QSRs have flourished, including Sonic Drive-In, founded in 1953 and known for its carhops and Toaster sandwiches. Jack in the Box, founded in 1951, was the first QSR to introduce a breakfast sandwich and a portable salad.

OTHER MAJOR BRANDS

Dairy Queen featured soft ice cream when it opened in 1940 in Joliet, Illinois. Other dairy-based

In the 1970's, many Jack in the Box fast food restaurants, like this one in Los Angeles, featured eye-catching signs. (AP/Wide World Photos)

dessert items were added over time, and the menu eventually expanded to include hamburgers and other cooked foods. One of the first chains to use the franchise model, Dairy Queen had twenty-six hundred stores by 1955 and over fifty-nine hundred internationally by 2007. Berkshire Hathaway purchased Dairy Queen in 1998.

Founded by Fred DeLuca and Peter Buck, Pete's Super Submarines opened in Bridgeport, Connecticut, in 1965. In 1968, the name was changed to SUBWAY. Large sandwiches on long rolls were popularly known as "submarines" because of their shape. SUBWAY introduced sandwiches that were customized for each customer, who could select from ingredients on display. SUBWAY competed against other QSRs by emphasizing the health benefits of its ingredients, including fresh vegetables. By 2008, the company had more than twenty-nine thousand restaurants in eighty-six different countries, and it was the second-largest fast-food chain and the largest sandwich chain in the world. Quiznos Sub, founded in 1981, was the second-largest sandwich chain, and in third place was Blimpie, founded in 1964.

In 1997, PepsiCo's fast-food giants KFC, Taco Bell, and Pizza Hut were made subsidiaries of Tricon Global Restaurants, which became Yum! Brands in 2002. By 2008, Yum! Brands had become the world's largest restaurant company, with over thirty-five thousand restaurants in over 110 countries.

The KFC brand was originally the Kentucky Fried Chicken fast-food franchise founded by Colonel Harland Sanders in 1930. In 1940, he developed a secret recipe of eleven herbs and spices for his "finger lickin' good" chicken, fried in a pressure cooker. The famous buckets appeared in 1957. By 1979, there were six thousand Kentucky Fried Chicken restaurants worldwide with sales of over $2 billion annually. By 2006, over one billion KFC chicken dinners were served annually in over eighty countries. Other chicken-based chains followed: Chick-Fil-A opened in 1967, Popeye's Chicken and Biscuits started in 1972, and Bojangle's opened in 1977.

In 1962, Glen Bell opened the first Taco Bell in Downey, California. This QSR offered alternative menu items such as tacos, burritos, and other Mexican dishes. The first franchise was sold in 1964, and the famous Taco Bell tagline was Think Outside the Bun. By 2008, Taco Bell was the leading Mexican-style QSR chain, with more than fifty-eight hundred restaurants in the United States, serving more than 2 billion consumers annually.

Pizza Hut was America's first national pizza chain. Brothers Dan and Frank Carney opened the first Pizza Hut in 1958 in Wichita, Kansas. In 2007, Pizza Hut was the world's leading pizza restaurant company, with more than sixty-five hundred restaurants in the United States and more than four thousand in one hundred other countries. Domino's Pizza, founded by James Monaghan in 1961, became the world leader in pizza delivery and the second-largest chain. In 1985, John Schnatter created Papa John's Pizza to offer a superior traditional pizza; it became the third-largest chain. Founded by Mike and Marian Ilitch in 1959, Little Caesars became the fastest-growing chain in 2007.

Other specialty chains developed, including Starbucks, the world's largest coffee retailer, and Dunkin' Donuts, serving coffee, breakfast foods, and smoothies. Founded in 1983, Panda Express became the first national Chinese QSR chain, with over eight hundred locations in 2008. By the early twenty-first century, the industry included approximately 200,000 restaurants with a combined annual revenue of about $120 billion.

Alice Myers

FURTHER READING

Darden, Bob. *Secret Recipe: Why KFC Is Still Cookin' After Fifty Years.* Irving, Tex.: Tapestry Press, 2002. Complete history of KFC, including business secrets and narratives about founder Colonel Harlan Sanders. Illustrated. Index.

Jakle, John A., and Keith A. Sculle. *Fast Food: Roadside Restaurants in the Automobile Age.* Baltimore: Johns Hopkins University Press, 1999. With over one hundred photos, this is a well-researched study of the culture of roadside eateries, fast-food chains, and the automobile. Bibliography.

Love, John F. *McDonald's: Behind the Arches.* Rev. ed. New York: Bantam Books, 1995. Comprehensive chronicle of the rise of McDonald's, including behind-the-scenes stories. Illustrated. Index.

McLamore, James. *The Burger King: Jim McLamore and the Building of an Empire.* New York: McGraw-Hill, 1997. Detailed autobiography of a cofounder of Burger King and detailed history of the company from its beginning in 1954. Illustrated. Index.

Schlosser, Eric. *Fast Food Nation: The Dark Side of the All-American Meal.* Boston: Houghton Mifflin, 2001. Well-researched *New York Times* bestseller that reveals the cultural, social, economic, and health consequences of the fast-food trend. Notes and index.

Spurlock, Morgan. *Don't Eat This Book: Fast Food and the Supersizing of America.* New York: G. P. Putnam's Sons, 2005. Humorous account of how the author lived on fast food alone for thirty days and the effect on his health. The subsequent documentary film broke box-office records. Appendixes and notes.

Tennyson, Jeffrey. *Hamburger Heaven: The Illustrated History of the Hamburger.* New York: Hyperion, 1993. Includes the history of hamburger fast-food chains such as Burger King, McDonald's, and Wendy's. Beautifully illustrated.

SEE ALSO: Drive-through businesses; Food-processing industries; McDonald's restaurants; Restaurant industry.

FCA. *See* Farm Credit Administration

FDA. *See* Food and Drug Administration

FDIC. *See* Federal Deposit Insurance Corporation

Federal Communications Commission

IDENTIFICATION: Independent federal agency charged with regulating interstate and international communications that use radio, television, wire, satellite, or cable
DATE: Established in 1934
SIGNIFICANCE: Because the Federal Communications Commission has the power to allocate frequency bands and to grant (or deny) licenses to radio and television stations, it has had a profound effect on these and other communications businesses, which commission officials are legally required to monitor so that they serve the public interest.

Before the formation of the Federal Communications Commission (FCC), American communications businesses evolved mainly through private enterprise, with minimal government regulation. The proliferation of radio stations with increasingly powerful transmitters, however, caused interference from overlapping transmissions and led Congress to pass the Radio Act of 1927, which gave a federal commission power to license stations, assign operating frequencies, and, through a 1928 amendment, establish both high-powered interstate stations and low-powered local stations. Because laws governing radio, telegraph, and telephone communications were inconsistent and out of date, the Congress, at the request of President Franklin D. Roosevelt, passed the Communications Act of 1934, which put all electronic communications businesses under the purview of a single agency, the Federal Communica-

tions Commission. The commission, through its power to grant or terminate licenses, had the responsibility of ensuring that communications businesses served the public good.

FCC OBJECTIVES

FCC officials were charged with allocating frequency bands for radio stations, approving (or disapproving) rate increases for interstate telephone communications, and monitoring radio broadcasts for unlicensed operations and corrupting content. The Communications Act of 1934 also had a direct effect on businesses through its mandate to preserve healthy competition by facilitating the multiplication of stations throughout the United States, not just in cities, and by encouraging quality and diversity in programming. During the early history of the FCC, and indeed throughout its entire existence, these multifarious objectives have often proved incompatible, and FCC officials often encountered difficulties in implementing them.

Among the FCC's earliest missions was the improvement of programming. Though forbidden by law from censoring broadcasts, FCC officials could alert stations when their programs and policies harmed the commonweal. For example, in 1935 the FCC criticized an astrology program on a Missouri station, and in 1937, in a highly publicized case, it expressed its displeasure over Mae West's racy remarks on *The Edgar Bergen and Charlie McCarthy Show,* which had offended many listeners, but it took no punitive action. Indeed, cases in which stations lost licenses were rare, though the FCC did issue warning lists of practices, such as the use of racially or religiously derogatory language, that could lead to license revocation.

During the late 1930's and into the 1940's, the FCC became involved in a number of important issues, from investigations of monopolies in communications businesses to the regulation of new technologies, such as television and frequency-modulated (FM) radio. Its investigation into "chain broadcasting," which was begun in 1938 and resulted in regulations that were upheld by the Supreme Court in 1943, led to rules designed to combat abuses, such as a network's control over its affiliates. The FCC also forced the National Broadcasting Company (NBC) to sell its Blue Network, which became the American Broadcasting Company (ABC).

FM transmission, which Edwin Armstrong had invented in 1933, provided high-fidelity sound, and in 1939, the FCC studied the problem of allocating parts of the very high frequency (VHF) spectrum for FM broadcasts. By 1941, a small number of FM stations were in operation, but, with the American entry into World War II, the FCC stopped authorizing any new FM stations. Television presented more difficult problems than FM, since several companies had developed incompatible systems for transmitting and receiving television signals. In 1940, the FCC began a study of these systems, and its National Television Standards Committee (NTSC) devised a plan for television broadcasting, but commercial television's development was also halted by World War II.

Businesses that owed their start to FCC regulations or whose progress had been hampered by monopolistic networks tended to approve FCC actions, whereas other businesses, whose operations were hampered by these regulations, tended to disapprove. For example, when the FCC restricted radio stations from owning newspapers in the same market, some radio stations and newspapers objected, while their competitors applauded the decision. Some members of Congress also felt that the FCC

had exceeded its prerogatives, and they began investigations into allegations that FCC officials had assisted friends in obtaining station licenses. The hearings resulted in some changes to the FCC, but they also made the agency overly cautious in regulating businesses.

During World War II, the FCC attacked so-called "black" stations (those that were covertly pro-Nazi). The commission also pressured broadcasters to insert patriotic announcements into popular network programs, insisting that such propaganda was crucial to the war effort. Scholars have questioned the effectiveness of such FCC-stimulated actions, but they did help the networks remain commercially successful during wartime.

CHANGES AND CONTROVERSIES

After World War II, the same pent-up consumer demand that led to the rapid growth of American steel and automobile businesses also fueled the communications industries, especially the new fields of FM radio and television. In 1945, the FCC allocated new channels to FM stations, which used them so effectively that, by 1948, about a thousand stations were in operation. The FCC also allocated thirteen VHF channels to commercial television stations, and by 1948, twenty such stations were on the air, with many more applications pending.

Because of the unexpectedly high demand for licenses and because the FCC needed a just and technically efficient way of allocating channels, a freeze on the licensing of new television stations began on September 20, 1948. The freeze lasted from 1948 to 1952, during which time FCC technicians developed scientific standards to assign urban channels so that stations would not interfere with each other. Experts from the FCC and affected companies also studied competing formats for color television, and, after some missteps, the FCC adopted a new NTSC color standard in 1953 that met with wide approval.

The FCC was created to deal with the development of radio. This 1945 photograph shows a broadcast in progress at an NBC studio in New York. (Library of Congress)

Other FCC actions did not generate such approval. For example, in allocating channels, the FCC—strictly interpreting a law that had regulated radio—used a system of priorities that ignored population density and relied on balanced geographical apportionment. In an attempt to foster competition among ultra high frequency (UHF) stations, the FCC actually contributed to conditions that led to three-quarters of them losing money. Although it issued reports highly critical of television networks, the FCC itself was attacked for collusion with the businesses it was supposed to monitor. For instance, in 1958 the FCC commissioner had to resign after it became known that he had accepted a bribe from an applicant for a television-station license. On the other hand, a success resulted when, in 1959, the FCC held hearings on the quiz show scandals, revealing how producers had rigged the results of some shows. These hearings led to regulations that prevented a recurrence of the scandals.

Mismanagement of the enforcement of regulations and conflict-of-interest scandals had tarnished the FCC's reputation when John F. Kennedy assumed the presidency during the early 1960's. He appointed Newton Minow, an idealistic young lawyer, as FCC chairman. Minow bravely attempted to transform television programming from the "vast wasteland" it had become, but, frustrated by FCC bureaucrats and business opponents, he returned to private life in 1963.

LATE TWENTIETH CENTURY CHALLENGES

Similar problems confronted other FCC commissioners during the rest of the 1960's and into the 1970's, and they also encountered several new issues, such as the poor representation of minorities both on television programs and in the management positions of communications firms. These problems emerged alongside the development of new technologies, and FCC officials had to decide on ways to regulate communications satellites and cable television. New FCC regulations restricting alcohol and cigarette advertising on television had a direct effect on the producers and resellers of those products, and the implementation of the "fairness doctrine" caused controversy over such issues as equal time for candidates from various political parties. Groups such as Action for Children's Television (ACT) alerted the public to the potential dangers of allowing children to watch violence on television, leading to regulations limiting the hours during which certain kinds of adult programming could be aired.

During the 1980's and 1990's, the FCC had a profound influence on American communications businesses, largely through their regulation of new technologies. For example, even though American Telephone and Telegraph (AT&T) had introduced the first mobile phone system in 1946, cellular telephone systems did not become commercially viable until 1983, and by 1996 these systems, regulated by the FCC, were serving over 100 million mobile phone customers. During the 1980's, the Ronald Reagan administration facilitated a shift at the FCC toward more business-friendly practices than in the past. Some of these changes, such as the removal of the fairness doctrine, were controversial.

After the forced breakup of AT&T in an antitrust suit, members of Congress became concerned that the Communications Act of 1934 had become outdated in an era of new technologies and increased national and global competition in communications businesses. Some critics even argued for abolishing the FCC and returning to totally free markets. The Telecommunications Act of 1996 aimed to replace laws that were seen as antibusiness and anticonsumer with laws designed to invigorate market competition, but the new laws and policies met with little success and much criticism. Some analysts diagnosed the dilemma as being due to the FCC's formidable task of balancing its responsibilities toward the business community, the public, and many governmental agencies.

Throughout its history the FCC has been accused of capitulating to improper influence from Congress, businesses, and public-interest groups, and an ideal balance among regulations, regulators, and the regulated has never been achieved. In the twenty-first century, the multiplication of new communications technologies shows no sign of abating, making the FCC's task of creating a progressive and just environment for mass communications even more challenging.

Robert J. Paradowski

FURTHER READING

Barnouw, Erik. *The Golden Web: A History of Broadcasting in the United States, 1933-1953.* New York: Oxford University Press, 1968. This second volume of the author's social and business history of American broadcasting focuses on radio, and the FCC's sometimes controversial relationship with communications businesses is very much a part of the story he tells. Chronology, list of FCC laws, bibliography, and index.

_____. *The Image Empire: A History of Broadcasting in the United States from 1953.* New York: Oxford University Press, 1970. This third volume of the author's series emphasizes television and traces the uneasy relationship of the FCC to politicians, businesspersons, and the public during the tumultuous 1960's. Chronology, list of laws, bibliography, and index.

Furchtgott-Roth, Harold W. *A Tough Act to Follow? The Telecommunications Act of 1996 and the Separation of Powers.* Washington, D.C.: American Enterprise Institute Press, 2006. The author evaluates the FCC's successes and failures in deregulating the telecommunications industry, revealing how difficult it is to make regulated businesses responsive to consumer interests. Extensive endnotes and index.

Inglis, Andrew F. *Behind the Tube: A History of Broadcasting Technology and Business.* Boston: Focal Press, 1990. This book is organized according to different communications technologies, and the author makes excellent use of his experience in various communications businesses. Glossary, bibliography, and index.

Noll, Roger C., Merton J. Peck, and John J. McGowan. *Economic Aspects of Television Regulation.* Washington, D.C.: Brookings Institution, 1973. According to its authors, this book presents "the first comprehensive economic analysis of the television broadcast industry, its interaction with the Federal Communications Commission, and the prospects for change." Extensive footnotes and tables, with three appendixes and an index.

Sterling, Christopher, and John M. Kittross. *Stay Tuned: A Concise History of American Broadcasting.* 3d ed. Mahwah, N.J.: Lawrence Erlbaum Associates, 2002. This narrative history surveys the chief events and themes in the evolution of the American broadcasting industry, including the role of regulation played by the FCC. The third edition contains new material from the 1980's and 1990's. Chronology, glossary, broadcasting statistics, selected bibliography, and index.

SEE ALSO: Congress, U.S.; Federal Trade Commission; National Broadcasting Company; New Deal programs; Radio broadcasting industry; Securities and Exchange Commission; Television broadcasting industry; Tobacco industry.

Federal Deposit Insurance Corporation

IDENTIFICATION: Federal agency that increases public confidence in the financial system by insuring deposits in banks and savings and loans up to a specified dollar amount per depositor

DATE: Established in 1933

SIGNIFICANCE: Establishment of the Federal Deposit Insurance Corporation helped eliminate bank panics, which had been a major contributor to business depressions. There has been no repetition of the deluge of bank failures that occurred in 1929-1933.

Although federal deposit insurance did not formally begin until 1933, there had been numerous earlier attempts to achieve the same results. Since early in the nineteenth century, banknotes and bank deposits were an important part of the nation's supply of money. These bank liabilities cost very little to create and could be used to acquire valuable assets, so there was a chronic tendency for banks to create more notes and deposits than they could redeem in cash.

HISTORICAL BACKGROUND

Periodic bank panics became a characteristic of the nineteenth century economy. Consequently, state governments experimented with the equivalent of deposit insurance. A notable example was the Safety Fund system established by New York State in 1827. This provided insurance for banknotes and bank deposits, financed by an assessment on bank capital and supported by bank examination to monitor the quality of bank loans. However, a wave of bank failures broke the system in 1842. Other states protected depositors by imposing the requirement that banks keep cash reserves equal to a percentage of their deposit liabilities.

Federal government protection for holders of banknotes was established by U.S. Civil War legislation. The National Banking Acts of 1863 and 1864 created a system of national banks whose banknote issues were protected by the deposit of government securities. A tax on nonnational banknotes in 1865 drove those out of existence. National banks were also subject to substantial required cash reserves. However, bank panics persisted. During panics in 1873, 1893, and 1907, many banks resorted to "suspension of specie payments"—that is, they temporarily refused to pay out cash to depositors, while continuing the rest of their normal banking operations.

These suspensions focused attention on the "inelasticity" of currency supply—there was no way to increase the amount of currency in times when depositors wanted more cash. The desire to create an "elastic currency" was embodied in the Federal Reserve Act of 1913. Proposals for federal insurance of bank deposits were advanced as early as 1886, and federal insurance was advocated by William Jennings Bryan in his unsuccessful presidential campaign in 1908. Creation of the Federal Reserve system improved depositor protection by strengthening reserve requirements and bank examination, and by permitting the Federal Reserve to lend to banks and create additional currency in a crisis.

Individual states started experimenting with deposit insurance, beginning with Oklahoma in 1907. By 1918, eight states had such programs. An important motive was to preserve the large number of small unit banks by maintaining restrictions on branch banking. Extending branch banking was frequently proposed as a way to reduce bank risks and failures. The farm depression of the 1920's led to a large increase in the number of bank failures, and the state deposit-protection programs were unable to handle the claims against them. So all had shut down by 1929. However, most of the bank failures of the 1920's involved small banks in small towns. In most of the country, bank deposits became more widely used. The number of checking accounts increased from 11 million in 1909 to more than 23 million in 1920.

As the economy slid into the Great Depression after 1929, an avalanche of bank failures occurred. Large-bank failures in 1930 involved banks that had taken unduly risky positions speculating in stocks or real estate. As bank failures escalated, depositors withdrew cash, putting pressure on the banks to contract their loans and to hold larger cash reserves.

These tendencies, along with actual losses of deposit funds, worsened the economic downswing.

NEW DEAL ACTIONS

In the final months of 1932, a number of states imposed "bank holidays," suspending cash payout in an effort to protect banks from the heavy currency withdrawal. On his inauguration in March, 1933, President Franklin D. Roosevelt extended the bank holiday to the entire country. Every bank was required to undergo examination of its assets and would be allowed to reopen only when found to be solvent. In 1933, 4,000 banks closed permanently, involving $3.6 billion of deposits and inflicting a half-billion of losses on depositors. Most banks were reopened within a few days. The shock therapy was effective. Panic ended, and currency flowed back into the banks. However, the banking system had experienced a severe shakeout. From a high of around 30,000 in 1920, the number of banks had declined to half that number.

Congress quickly moved to try to reform the structure of the banking system. The Banking Act of 1933 created the Federal Deposit Insurance Corporation (FDIC), with capital provided by the Treasury, the Federal Reserve, and the banks. All member banks of the Federal Reserve system were required to have their deposits insured, and other banks could join the system if approved (and most of them did). Coverage began January 1, 1934. Initially, coverage was limited to $2,500 for each depositor; it was increased to $5,000 in mid-1934 and to $10,000 in 1950. Each bank was required to pay a premium based on deposits. The initial level of 0.5 percent of deposits proved far higher than necessary. From 1934 the premium was 0.085 percent. After 1950 premiums became flexible based on experience.

Within the first year, 1934, insurance covered 97 percent of commercial-bank deposits, and the proportion moved still higher. The FDIC was authorized (in cooperation with other banking agencies) to examine insured banks, and this power helped sustain bank solvency. The agency soon developed two ways of dealing with failing banks. One was simply to pay off covered deposits without delay and try to cash in the bank's assets. Deposits exceeding the coverage limit might suffer some loss. The second approach was to merge the failing bank into another solvent institution. The latter arrangement would protect all depositors from loss.

The FDIC began operation under favorable conditions. Bad banks had been purged from the system, and surviving bankers were strongly risk averse. In the first decade of FDIC operation, an average of forty-nine banks failed each year. Between 1944 and 1960, there were fewer than ten failures each year, with negligible depositor losses. Never again would the financial system experience the kind of deflationary tidal wave experienced in 1929-1933.

In 1980, deposit insurance coverage was extended to $100,000 in the Depository Institutions Deregulation and Monetary Control Act. Deregulation permitted banks to take greater risks in the hope of higher profits. As a result, the number of bank failures increased sharply during the 1980's. In 1984, Continental Illinois, one of the nation's ten largest banks, became insolvent. The FDIC was able to arrange a merger on terms that averted depositor loss. This kind of bailout of large depositors came under criticism as weakening their motivation to monitor the banks' risky activities. Banks' experience had parallels with the savings and loan crisis. The number of failures confronting the FDIC exceeded two hundred a year in 1987-1989, then dropped rapidly. In 1991, Congress adopted the Federal Deposit Insurance Corporation Improvement Act. This increased insurance premiums and restricted the FDIC's latitude in large-bank settlements. The FDIC was given more restrictive guidelines for monitoring bank capital. As a result, bank failures after 1995 returned to negligible levels, ranging from two to twelve per year from 2000-2007.

FINANCIAL CRISIS OF 2008

The financial crisis of 2007-2008 raised bank failures to the highest level since 1994. The failures generally stemmed from bank involvement in subprime mortgage lending. The FDIC was involved in each case, trying to arrange mergers that would protect all depositors. They were able to do this for Wachovia, which was absorbed by Wells Fargo in October, 2008. However, IndyMac, which failed in July, 2008, had roughly $1 billion in uninsured deposits held by 10,000 depositors. Washington Mutual ("WaMu") failed in late September, 2008. With more than $300 billion of reported assets, it was the largest bank failure in U.S. history. WaMu was merged into JPMorgan Chase on terms that wiped out WaMu stockholders and some of their nondeposit creditors.

The FDIC protected the deposits of customers at Washington Mutual, which failed in October, 2008. (AP/Wide World Photos)

The financial rescue package adopted by Congress on October 3, 2008, the Emergency Economic Stabilization Act, increased federal deposit insurance coverage from $100,000 to $250,000. A few days earlier the government had created temporary insurance for existing accounts with money-market mutual funds, but this was not put under FDIC.

Paul B. Trescott

FURTHER READING

Friedman, Milton, and Anna J. Schwartz. *A Monetary History of the United States, 1867-1960.* Princeton, N.J.: Princeton University Press, 1963. Pays extensive attention to banking evolution and particularly the developments of the 1920's and 1930's.

Golembe, Carter. "The Deposit Insurance Legislation of 1933: An Examination of Its Antecedents and Purposes." *Political Science Quarterly* 75, no. 2 (1960): 181-200. Good detail on pre-1933 developments; stresses that deposit insurance was long seen as a way of preserving the country's system of small, independent banks.

Mishkin, Frederic S. *The Economics of Money, Banking, and Financial Markets.* 7th ed. New York: Pearson/ Addison Wesley, 2004. This college textbook thoroughly covers recent developments in bank supervision and deposit insurance.

Redburn, F. Stevens. "Never Lost a Penny: An Assessment of Federal Deposit Insurance." *Journal of Policy Analysis and Management* 7, no. 4 (1988): 687-702. Very critical of the existing deposit insurance arrangements, which the author claims "threaten to destabilize the U.S. banking system."

Seidman, L. William. *Full Faith and Credit.* New York: Random House, 1993. Seidman served as FDIC chair from 1985 to 1991. This is a colorful and entertaining memoir of a turbulent period.

Sprague, Irvine H. *Bailout: An Insider's Account of Bank Failures and Rescues.* Washington, D.C.: Beard Books, 2000. A former chair and director of the FDIC (1972-1985) describes a number of bank bailouts and failures, beginning with Commonwealth in 1972.

Trescott, Paul B. *Financing American Enterprise: The Story of Commercial Banking.* New York: Harper & Row, 1963. A nontechnical narrative that identifies the major steps in depositor protection from the 1820's.

SEE ALSO: Bank failures; Banking; Currency; Deregulation of financial institutions; Farm Credit Administration; Financial crisis of 2008; New Deal programs; Panic of 1907; Savings and loan associations.

Federal Emergency Management Agency

IDENTIFICATION: Federal government agency in charge of providing humanitarian aid to disaster victims

DATE: Established in 1979

SIGNIFICANCE: Through mismanagement, waste, cronyism, budget slashing, and fraud, the Federal Emergency Management Agency has been largely ineffectual, causing businesses as well as individuals to suffer needlessly in the wake of disasters.

Created on April 1, 1979, by President Jimmy Carter, the Federal Emergency Management Agency (FEMA) was a federal government response to the need for a centralized emergency management system. Formed from a combination of a number of relief agencies that had previously been ineffective in natural disasters, FEMA was named the nation's primary disaster-response agency, charged with providing relief from hurricanes, floods, tornadoes, and earthquakes, and aid for civil defense. To begin the process, the afflicted state's governor must declare a state of emergency and ask the government for assistance, which comes in the form of emergency services for the disaster area and later with financial help for recovery.

CRITICISMS OF FEMA

Criticisms of ineffectiveness began to dog FEMA. The slowness of FEMA's response to the devastation of South Carolina by Hurricane Hugo in 1989 brought angry assertions of ineptitude. Category 5 Hurricane Andrew's swath across South Florida in 1992 left thousands stranded without food or water. Confused and unprepared, FEMA officials designated duties to special subgroups but did not establish a presence at the disaster site. Federal assistance finally arrived five days after the catastrophe.

As a result of its disappointing performance, FEMA was restructured by President Bill Clinton in 1993 to include twenty-two federal agencies. Clinton nominated James Lee Witt, a former emergency management director from Arkansas, as its director. Witt's success at reducing bureaucracy and emphasizing community preparedness led to FEMA's advancement to the rank of cabinet-level department in 1996. With a budget of $4 billion, FEMA was an independent agency whose responsibilities expanded continuously.

Witt left his position when President George W. Bush took office and was replaced by Joe Allbaugh, Bush's former campaign director, who, at Bush's direction, cut FEMA's budget for 2001 to $2.1 billion. Allbaugh considered the three most likely disaster areas would center around a hurricane in New Orleans, an earthquake in California, or a terrorist attack in New York, and planned a practice exercise for FEMA. In May, 2001, FEMA's duties were expanded to include a response to terrorism.

Consequently, FEMA was one of the first responders to the terrorist attacks on the World Trade

Center on September 11, 2001, but relinquished command of the recovery to the New York City Office of Emergency Management. FEMA later approved the distribution of $5.5 billion to local and state governments to help with the costs of recovery.

REORGANIZATION

Following the terrorist attacks, President Bush created the Department of Homeland Security (DHS), and FEMA was downgraded to a subdepartment within DHS. Allbaugh resigned, and his friend Michael Brown assumed the directorship of FEMA. Downsizing of FEMA continued, as well as the shifting of money from it to other agencies. A planned disaster exercise for "Hurricane Pam," a catastrophic hurricane in New Orleans that would leave 100,000 people stranded in the city, was scratched because Bush had cut the funding. Emphasis in FEMA had shifted to terrorism, rather than natural disasters, and Brown saw FEMA as an impending failure.

FEMA came under fire again in 2004, following a succession of hurricanes that swept Florida in a period of six weeks. The disbursement of recovery funds was later found to have been indiscriminately made, sending $31 million to residents who were largely unaffected by Hurricane Frances, including millions for residents whose homes were undamaged. When Hurricane Katrina ravaged the Gulf Coast on August 29, 2005, FEMA earned the ire of Americans for its slow response and, later, for its mismanagement and waste.

Shortly after Hurricane Katrina's landfall, Congress sanctioned $62.3 billion in disaster relief for FEMA, whose allocations were $23 billion for temporary housing and household costs; $8 billion for rescue, roads, and bridges; $3 billion for evacuation; $5 billion for urban recovery; and $15 million for Homeland Security's monitoring of spending. Aware of its discouraging track record, FEMA dispatched thirty auditors to the Gulf Coast to keep

A FEMA inspector stands in the rubble of a San Leon, Texas, home destroyed by Hurricane Ike in September, 2008. (FEMA/ Greg Henshall)

track of the money. In an effort to minimize abuse, the DHS was required to report weekly to Congress on spending.

Although Brown was blamed for most of the disastrous results of FEMA's mismanagement of the Hurricane Katrina operation and was removed from his responsibilities by Homeland Security Secretary Michael Chertoff, the problem proved to be larger than Brown. Money was free-flowing. One estimate determined that the government handed out about $800 million a day for everything deemed a necessity.

FEMA issued more than ten thousand charge cards worth more than $20 million to evacuees, later increasing the spending amount on each card from $15,000 to $250,000. FEMA chose to engage three ships from Carnival Cruise Lines for $220 million to accommodate seven thousand relief workers, despite the fact that the government of Greece had offered the use of two ships for free. Also, a sharp controversy arose between FEMA and Kathleen Blanco, the governor of Louisiana, concerning sluggish removal of dead bodies. The controversy resulted in the loss of some FEMA contracts.

Critics of FEMA attacked its outsourcing of recovery, handled largely through no-bid contracts to companies with strong ties to the Bush administration. This outsourcing in effect prevented local residents whose employers had been shut down by the disaster from gaining employment helping their city. It also stymied efforts to monitor spending. Moreover, FEMA critics maintained that generous contracts to rebuild encouraged the rebuilding of homes in disaster-prone areas whose owners would then refuse to buy natural disaster insurance, expecting the government to come to their aid. FEMA was loudly condemned when, with generous allocations from Congress, it purchased for storm victims almost 300,000 trailers—a demand that outstripped the builders' abilities to supply them. When they arrived, residents were sickened by chemical residues in the trailers. Investigations revealed the trailers were products of shoddy construction using inferior materials.

Mary Hurd

FURTHER READING

Burns, Linda A., ed. *FEMA: An Agency in the Crosshairs.* New York: Novinka, 2007. A collection of essays examining the agency's history and its programs.

Craig, Steven J. *Chronicles of Katrina: Lessons Learned from the Hurricane Katrina Disaster for Your Home Preparedness.* Denver, Colo.: Outskirts Press, 2007. Detailed instructions and tips for home preparedness.

Marzilli, Alan. *Disaster Relief.* New York: Chelsea House, 2007. A point-counterpoint discussion of the role of federal and state governments, the adequacy of financial aid, and the role of flood insurance.

Redmond, Robert. *The Katrina Puzzle: America's Disgrace.* Denver, Colo.: Outskirts Press, 2007. Criticizes the lack of response by FEMA to the area of devastation and the attempts at recovery.

White, Jonathan R. *Terrorism and Homeland Security: An Introduction.* 6th ed. Boston: Wadsworth, 2008. Discusses the backgrounds of modern terrorism and contemporary conflicts and provides detailed information on the organization of the Department of Homeland Security.

SEE ALSO: Great Depression; Homeland Security, U.S. Department of; New Deal programs; September 11 terrorist attacks.

Federal Reserve

IDENTIFICATION: U.S. central bank
DATE: Founded on December 23, 1913
SIGNIFICANCE: As the central bank of the United States, the Federal Reserve is the institution in which the federal government and private banks do their banking. Central banks are responsible for monitoring banks and ensuring they remain solvent. They also control interest rates and thus borrowing costs for consumers and business firms. This, in turn, affects unemployment and inflation, giving the Federal Reserve substantial control over the U.S. economy.

The First Bank of the United States was established by Congress in 1791 through the efforts of Secretary of the Treasury Alexander Hamilton. A bill to renew the bank's charter was defeated by one vote in 1811. The Second Bank of the United States was authorized by Congress and opened in 1816. However, it was opposed by President Andrew Jackson, and it ceased operation in 1841. These national banks were privately owned and mainly served as the bank for the federal government. Because they competed with other banks and could regulate the amount of currency in the country, private banks opposed the two national banks, which is why their charters did not get renewed.

Lacking a national bank, the United States was ravaged by a series of financial panics during the late nineteenth and early twentieth centuries. People ran to their banks to withdraw their money, but because banks had lent the money out, they could not pay their depositors. This led to more bank runs and many bankruptcies. After the severe 1907-1908 panic, Congress created a commission to study how future panics might be prevented. When the Democrats swept to power in the 1912 election, they pushed for one key recommendation from the commission—the creation of a central bank. Passage of the Federal Reserve Act in 1913 (mainly along party lines, with Democrats supporting the legislation and Republicans opposing it) created the Federal Reserve, or "the Fed" for short.

STRUCTURE

At the bottom of the Federal Reserve System are all the banks and financial institutions in the United States that are subject to regulation and control by the Federal Reserve. Twelve regional Federal Reserve Banks have been established throughout the country to monitor individual banks. These banks are actually owned by the area banks but are not controlled by them. Regional Federal Reserve Banks serve as banks for private banks, doing for them what banks do for people and businesses. Banks deposit their money into regional Federal Reserve Banks, just as people deposit their money into banks. Regional Federal Reserve Banks lend money to banks, just as banks lend to the public; and they cash checks for banks (which is easy as they have all the money), just as each person's bank cashes that individual's checks.

Overseeing the entire Federal Reserve System are seven directors or governors. Governors are nominated by the U.S. president and approved by the Senate. They serve fourteen-year terms that are staggered so that one term ends every other year. Lengthy terms mean that governors are not subject to political pressure and do not have to seek reappointment (or reelection) on a regular basis. Staggered terms ensure that people with a good deal of experience will always be on the board of governors.

Governors may serve only one full term, but any governor appointed to complete an unexpired term can be reappointed to a full term.

The Federal Reserve governors set U.S. monetary policy by using several tools to control bank lending and interest rates. The chair is the chief executive officer of the board of governors and chief spokesperson for monetary policy. The Federal Reserve chair is regarded as the second most powerful individual in the United States, after the president.

Another important group is the open market committee, which determines the interest rate on overnight loans among banks, or the federal funds rate. This committee consists of the seven governors plus five regional Federal Reserve Bank presidents. The president of the New York Federal Reserve always sits on the open committee, since the hard work of controlling the federal funds rate is done by the New York Federal Reserve Bank in lower Manhattan; four other regional Federal Reserve Bank presidents serve on a rotating basis.

FEDERAL RESERVE POWERS

The Federal Reserve has both monetary and supervisory powers. In addition, as with the original national banks, the U.S. government uses the Federal Reserve to make deposits and write checks. The Federal Reserve has three main tools to control bank lending and interest rates.

The first tool is through setting the reserve ratio (within some limits set by Congress). Banks typically want to lend out as much of their deposits as possible, because that is how they earn money. However, banks with too little cash are subject to bank runs and panics. The reserve ratio was meant to solve this problem. It requires banks to hold a fraction of their deposits rather than lending them all out. Controlling this ratio lets the central bank control bank lending. At the end of 2007, the reserve ratio was 0 percent on the first $9.3 million of deposits in the bank, 3 percent on total deposits between $9.3 million and $43.9 million, and 10 percent on deposits in excess of $43.9 million. This system of multiple ratios was one of the political compromises made when creating the Federal Reserve. Small banks wanted no restrictions on their lending; larger banks wanted their wealthy depositors to be confident that money would be there for them. Each side got some of what it wanted.

The second is through lending money to private

banks at the discount rate, an interest rate set by the board of governors. This lending by the regional Federal Reserve Banks serves two purposes: It helps stem bank runs and panics because it provides money to banks, and discount rate changes allow the Federal Reserve to control bank lending and the interest rates charged by private banks. When the Federal Reserve lowers the discount rate, banks are encouraged to borrow money. With more money to lend out, and with a cheaper source of funds, private banks will lend at lower interest rates. However, with a higher discount rate, banks are less likely to borrow from the central bank and tend to repay any money they borrowed from the Federal Reserve. This means that banks have less money to lend out and therefore will give loans to the highest bidders, which are borrowers willing to pay higher interest rates.

The third method of control is open market operations, which are controlled by the open market committee. These involve the Federal Reserve's buying and selling government securities or bonds. These are printed up and then sold whenever the government runs a budget deficit and needs to borrow money. Banks own many government securities, which they see as highly liquid (they can be easily sold) and as providing a safe return (the federal government is not likely to go bankrupt). When the Federal Reserve buys securities, it offers higher and higher prices until some bank sells its securities for cash. When the Federal Reserve sells securities, it lowers the price of the securities it owns until it finds a buyer.

These actions enable the Federal Reserve to control the federal funds rate. Overnight loans between banks occur because some banks invariably fail to meet their reserve requirements, and others have extra or excess reserves at the end of the banking day. Overnight lending enables banks to meet their requirements while allowing banks with extra reserves to earn some interest. When the Federal Reserve sells government securities, banks pay for them with cash and therefore have fewer excess reserves to lend out. As a result, the federal funds rate will rise. However, when the Federal Reserve buys securities, it gives cash to banks, which then have more reserves to lend out. With a greater supply of excess reserves, the cost to banks of obtaining funds to meet their reserve requirements will fall.

The Federal Reserve also has many supervisory powers. It sets margin requirements, which limit the use of borrowing to purchase corporate stocks and bonds. It examines the books of private banks to make sure that they are safe and sound, thus protecting depositors. This involves checking to see whether the banks have adequate capital and performing assets (that is, loans that are getting repaid), and have not made risky loans. The Federal Reserve also makes sure that banks do not discriminate in lending or give false or misleading information to borrowers.

A final responsibility of the Federal Reserve is to ensure that the check-clearing system in the United States functions effectively. Because the Federal Reserve holds most bank deposits, it is relatively easy for it to cash checks—basically, it moves money from the pile it is holding for one bank to the pile of another bank.

The most important actions of the Federal Reserve involve lowering the discount rate and the federal funds rate to deal with unemployment problems or financial crises, and raising them when the economy experiences inflationary problems. Lowering these rates make it cheaper for banks to obtain

---

CONSUMER DEBT, 1945-2007, SEASONALLY ADJUSTED, IN MILLIONS OF DOLLARS

Date	Outstanding Credit
December, 1945	6,567
December, 1950	23,229
December, 1955	41,869
December, 1960	60,025
December, 1965	95,955
December, 1970	131,552
December, 1975	204,002
December, 1980	351,920
December, 1985	599,711
December, 1990	808,231
December, 1995	1,140,744
December, 2000	1,717,483
December, 2005	2,284,876
December, 2007	2,523,632

Source: Data from "G.19: Consumer Credit," Federal Reserve Statistical Release, 2008

money to lend out. Banks can then lend money at lower interest rates, which encourages borrowing and spending by individuals and business firms. This generates more production, profits, employment, and economic growth. In contrast, higher rates make it more expensive for banks to obtain money, and this means that they will raise interest rates on consumer and business loans. This curtails borrowing and spending in the economy, slows down economic growth, and puts a damper on inflation. The power of the Federal Reserve to control interest rates gives it tremendous control over the performance of the U.S. economy.

CRITICISMS

Over the years, the Federal Reserve has been criticized by both the left and the right. Free-market economists argue that the market can monitor and control banks better than central bankers can. Milton Friedman criticized the Federal Reserve for supporting a massive stock market bubble during the 1920's. Then, when the bubble burst, the Federal Reserve did not provide the cash that banks needed after the stock market crashed, leading to the Great Depression.

From the left, the main criticism of the Federal Reserve has been that it protects banks and the U.S. financial system but not average citizens. The Federal Reserve tends to worry more about inflation (which hurts banks, whose loans get repaid in dollars that are worth less) than about unemployment (which hurts the average citizen through job loss and stagnating wages). It also protects financial institutions (for example, bailing out Bear Stearns when it was near default from making bad mortgages) but does little to help individuals unable to make mortgage payments.

Steven Pressman

FURTHER READING

Eccles, Marriner. *Beckoning Frontiers.* New York: Alfred Knopf, 1966. This autobiography by the seventh Federal Reserve chair tells of acrimonious political battles with the Department of the Treasury over monetary policy, and how Eccles was essentially forced to resign from his position.

Friedman, Milton, and Anna Schwartz. *A Monetary History of the United States, 1867-1960.* Princeton, N.J.: Princeton University Press, 1963. In this historical account of the creation of the Federal Reserve, Friedman holds the institution responsible for causing the Great Depression and then prolonging it.

Galbraith, John Kenneth. *Money.* Boston: Houghton Mifflin, 1975. A history of money and its regulation in the United States. Galbraith focuses on the politics leading to the creation of the Federal Reserve and its political role.

Greenspan, Alan. *The Age of Turbulence.* New York: Penguin Press, 2007. Autobiography of the thirteenth Federal Reserve chair and an insider's account of the institution from 1987 to 2002, as it struggled with the Asian financial crisis, stock market booms and busts, and the impact of 9/11.

Greider, William. *Secrets of the Temple.* New York: Simon & Schuster, 1987. A description of the functions and history of the Federal Reserve, focusing on Paul Volcker's term as chair. Sharply critical of the institution's secrecy and how it favors Wall Street.

Moore, Carl. *The Federal Reserve System: A History of the First Seventy-five Years.* London: McFarland, 1990. A history of events leading up to the creation of the Federal Reserve, a discussion of the politics involved in passing the Federal Reserve Act, and an account of the changing role of the Federal Reserve in controlling banks and the economy.

Wells, Donald. *The Federal Reserve System: A History.* London: McFarland, 2004. A comprehensive history of the Federal Reserve that emphasizes how it has evolved to become a valued and powerful institution and how it gained independence from political pressures over time.

SEE ALSO: Bank failures; Bank of the United States, First; Bank of the United States, Second; Banking; Bond industry; Federal Deposit Insurance Corporation; Greenspan, Alan; Inflation; Interest rates; Monetary policy, federal; Panic of 1907; Securities and Exchange Commission.

Federal Trade Commission

IDENTIFICATION: Federal agency created to protect consumers from unfair commercial practices

DATE: Established on September 26, 1914

SIGNIFICANCE: The Federal Trade Commission is charged with protecting consumers from unfair competition and unfair or deceptive acts in commerce. It promotes free and fair competition through the prevention of price-fixing agreements, combinations in restraint of trade, interlocking directorates, unfair acts of competition, false advertising, and other deceptive business practices.

The passage of the Federal Trade Commission Act was the result of a program by President Woodrow Wilson to curtail the growth of business trusts and monopolistic businesses, and to preserve competition as an effective regulator of business. The underlying philosophy of the act was that markets should be left to competitive market forces and that anticompetitive market structures should be prevented. The intent was to prevent unfair practices rather than punish perpetrators. The Federal Trade Commission (FTC), created by the act, took over some of the work being performed by the Bureau of Corporations in the Department of Commerce. Joseph Davies was the initial FTC chair. The FTC began operating on March 16, 1915.

FTC OBJECTIVES

The fundamental objectives of the FTC are to initiate antitrust actions and to protect the consumer public. In 1938, the Wheeler-Lea Act amended the act by prohibiting a variety of deceptive practices in commerce. The law does not require an actual deception; a company may be held liable for unfair and deceptive acts when there is a possible likelihood that a consumer might be deceived. The FTC can hold a company liable for the unfair and deceptive acts of its employees, agents, or other representatives. The act applies to interstate and foreign commerce but does not apply to banking institutions, savings and loan associations, federal credit unions, or common carriers—all of which are regulated by other federal agencies.

The FTC consists of five commissioners who are appointed by the president with the advice and consent of the Senate. Not more than three of the commissioners can be from the same political party. Commissioners serve seven-year terms. Among the FTC's activities are the enforcement of the provisions of the Sherman Antitrust Act of 1890, the Clayton Antitrust Act of 1914, and amendments to these acts. The FTC also enforces the Truth-in-Lending Act of 1968 and some aspects of the Foreign Corrupt Practices Act of 1977. The FTC has

also enforced other laws at times over the years, including the Trading With the Enemy Act during World War I and the 1918 Webb-Pomerene Act, which created antitrust exemptions for export trade associations.

To enforce legislation, the FTC can investigate corporate conduct, hold hearings, and issue cease-and-desist orders. If a person or company fails to comply with the cease-and-desist order, the FTC turns to the Federal Circuit Court of Appeals for enforcement. The first major initiative of the FTC was at the behest of an association of advertising agencies, which urged the new agency to challenge misrepresentations in advertisements. A February 19, 1918, sweep alleged deception and commercial bribery in thirty-nine complaints. The 1920's were a contentious time at the FTC. Part of the problem was political; there was a Democratic majority during the early part of the decade despite the fact that there were Republican presidents.

There were also some judicial setbacks during the 1920's, including the Supreme Court's decision in *Federal Trade Commission v. Eastman Kodak Co.* (1927). The Court eliminated the commission's ability to challenge mergers effectively by ruling that the agency could not issue divestiture orders. During the 1930's, there was further turmoil because of President Franklin D. Roosevelt's New Deal and the subsequent passage of the Securities Act of 1933. Initially, the FTC enforced the Securities Act, but in 1934, the Securities and Exchange Commission took over that job. Prior to the Securities Act of 1933, the FTC had been active in enforcing "blue sky" cases and was thus the originator of federal securities regulation.

The 1936 Robinson-Patman Anti-Price Discrimination Act provided more work for the FTC, as did the 1939 Wool Products Labeling Act. Still, it was the 1938 Wheeler-Lea Act that was the most important in granting additional power to the agency. The 1938 act provided greater civil penalties to be assessed by the FTC and stipulated that deception need not be harmful to competitors to be unlawful. Also, precomplaint injunctions could be filed for the first time. Despite its accomplishments, the FTC was often criticized for not accomplishing enough. The decade of the 1940's closed with the agency being publicly criticized by the Hoover Commission, which studied all federal executive department agencies.

THE 1950'S AND LATER

In 1950, based partly on the Hoover Commission recommendations, there was a change in the administration of the FTC. Formerly, the chair of the commission had been elected by the other commissioners, and the role was essentially rotated among all the members. President Harry S. Truman changed that methodology by appointing a chair. Additional laws designed for FTC enforcement were passed in 1951 (the Fur Products Labeling Act) and 1958 (the Textile Fiber Products Identification Act). The enforcement of these labeling laws led to criticism that the agency was overly enthusiastic in enforcing the laws. In 1969, the American Bar Association report condemned the FTC's enforcement of textile and fur labels as being a "glaring example of misallocation of resources and misguided enforcement policy."

The FTC has been quite active in developing and enforcing consumer protection laws through litigation and other actions. Studies of antibiotics pricing during the 1950's led to self-regulation within the pharmaceutical industry. The agency suffered additional criticism in late 1960, when President-elect John F. Kennedy asked a former commissioner, James Landis (who had served briefly in 1933-1934 and worked primarily on securities regulation), to evaluate the organization's performance. While working for President Kennedy, Landis developed a number of agency reorganization plans, one of which provided new authority for the FTC to delegate functions to its staff. At about the same time, the agency came under attack from the forces of Ralph Nader, who argued that there was inadequate regulation over product quality, particularly in automobiles.

The FTC was led by seven different chairs during the 1970's, but it accomplished much, and most of what it accomplished was controversial. The result was a tidal wave of restrictive legislation in 1980. There was also important legislation during the 1970's, including a 1973 law to broaden FTC authority to obtain preliminary injunctions. The 1975 FTC Improvement Act prescribed a variety of new remedies, including civil penalties for violations of trade regulations. The 1976 Hart-Scott-Rodino Act required that the FTC be notified in advance of mergers and prescribed a waiting period before mergers could be consummated. This latter act greatly expanded the FTC's ability to maintain competition when a merger occurred.

Later laws have further expanded the FTC's realm of responsibility. These acts have included the Fair Credit Reporting Act of 1970 and the Fair Debt Collection Practices Act. The 1994 Telemarketing and Consumer Fraud and Abuse Prevention Act became the basis for what is known as the National Do Not Call Registry. In the eyes of the general public, it is this registry for which the FTC became best known. The agency has also taken the lead on new issues such as Internet fraud.

Over its history, the FTC has found its work frustrated by several Supreme Court decisions, but the commission has done much to rid the economy of anticompetitive business practices. The agency has been an aggressive advocate of competition and consumer protection, but it has constantly been criticized for not doing enough. Such criticism has led to more laws to strengthen the agency. Therefore, the FTC is much stronger than it was at its founding, and covers a greater variety of issues, but the overall role is still consumer protection and the advocacy of fair competition.

Dale L. Flesher

FURTHER READING

Clarkson, Kenneth W., and Timothy J. Muris. *The Federal Trade Commission Since 1970: Economic Regulation and Bureaucratic Behavior.* New York: Cambridge University Press, 2008. Calling the pre-1970 FTC dormant and ineffective, this volume is a comprehensive analysis of the revitalized agency.

Henderson, Gerard Carl. *The Federal Trade Commission: A Study in Administrative Law and Procedure.* New Haven, Conn.: Yale University Press, 1924. This 382-page volume is old, but is still used in law schools to teach issues arising from the FTC's mandates to enforce certain laws.

Holt, William Stull. *The Federal Trade Commission: Its History, Activities, and Organization.* New York: D. Appleton and Company, 1922. This is a good early history of the FTC's founding and is widely available, but it covers only the first seven years.

Jones, Mary Gardiner. *Tearing Down Walls: A Woman's Triumph.* Lanham, Md.: Hamilton Books, 2008. This autobiography provides an insider's view of the FTC through the eyes of its first female commissioner.

Kanwit, Stephanie W. *Federal Trade Commission.* 2 vols. St. Paul: Thomson West, 2008. Practice manual for those who are worried about being in violation of FTC requirements; probably only available in large business or law libraries.

Katzmann, Robert A. *Regulatory Bureaucracy: The Federal Trade Commission and Antitrust Policy.* Cambridge, Mass.: MIT Press, 1981. This volume deals with the competitiveness issues of mergers and antitrust violations.

SEE ALSO: Antitrust legislation; Business crimes; Child product safety laws; Commerce, U.S. Department of; Congress, U.S.; Funeral industry; Identity theft; Supreme Court and commerce.

FedEx

IDENTIFICATION: Private package-delivery and logistics service

DATE: Founded in 1971

SIGNIFICANCE: FedEx was the first company to integrate air and ground transportation to enable overnight, door-to-door delivery of time-sensitive parcels.

Until the 1960's, the transportation of freight by commercial airliners was an adjunct to the transportation of passengers. Because accommodating freight was a lower priority than was accommodating passengers' luggage, deliveries could easily be delayed. Thus, there was no practical advantage to sending a parcel by plane rather than by train or truck, since it might take just as long either way.

While still a student at Yale during the 1960's, Frederick W. Smith began arguing that this arrangement could not persist indefinitely and that there was a vast potential market for specialized airfreight services. When he graduated, he set out to provide such services, and in 1971, he founded Federal Express (better known as FedEx), choosing the name in the hope of winning contracts from the Federal Reserve system, which shipped large numbers of checks throughout the country. To avoid difficulties with the Civil Aviation Board, the regulatory agency that controlled airlines at the time, he specifically chose business jets just small enough to escape regulation.

FedEx sorted packages using nonunion workers to keep costs low, and the company's planes flew at night. After some initial rough spots, including an incident in which Smith gambled in Las Vegas and wired his winnings back to Memphis to support the company, FedEx began to show a profit by 1976. President Jimmy Carter's airline deregulation permitted FedEx to grow beyond the artificial limits imposed by earlier regulations.

In 1984, FedEx introduced Zapmail, a facsimile service that allowed companies to transmit copies of documents electronically. However, changes in telephone regulations soon made it possible for companies to install their own fax machines on regular phone lines. The market for Zapmail quickly eroded, and in 1986, FedEx wrote off a $320 million loss.

The emergence of e-mail cut into the U.S. Postal Service's revenues, but FedEx found the Internet a boon as the result of online shopping. For instance, it partnered with Amazon.com to provide expedited delivery of books and other merchandise. When each of the last four Harry Potter books was released, Amazon.com received hundreds of thousands of preorders for the books. Each order had to be fulfilled on—but not before—the book's official release date.

FedEx has expanded beyond package delivery. In 2004, FedEx purchased Kinko's, a chain of copy shops frequently found on college campuses. As a result, FedEx had an immediately visible market presence for individual customers as well as businesses. A person who came into a FedEx Kinko's to make copies was that much more likely to choose FedEx rather than its competitors, such as UPS (United Parcel Service) and DHL, when it came time to ship a package.

Leigh Husband Kimmel

FURTHER READING
Birla, Madan. *FedEx Delivers: How the World's Leading Shipping Company Keeps Innovating and Outperforming the Competition.* New York: John Wiley & Sons, 2005.

Carrison, Dan. *Deadline! How Premier Organizations Win the Race Against Time.* New York: AMACOM, 2003.

Heppenheimer, T. A. *Turbulent Skies: The History of Commercial Aviation.* New York: John Wiley, 1995.

SEE ALSO: Air transportation industry; Catalog shopping; Postal Service, U.S.; Shipping industry.

FEMA. *See* Federal Emergency Management Agency

Fiber-optic industry

DEFINITION: Industry built on a method of communication that transmits data using light through optical fibers

SIGNIFICANCE: The fiber-optic industry transformed communication and data transmission, allowing more data to be sent using a greater bandwidth for longer distances with lower interference and attenuation. This increased the efficiency of business communications and allowed the formation of businesses that used this technology to provide services or products.

The fiber-optic industry developed during the 1970's as a result of a number of significant scientific and technological breakthroughs during the 1960's. Scientists first demonstrated that data could be sent through glass if a proper light source could be invented. Then, in 1966, other scientists developed the laser to provide that light source. The Corning Glass Corporation developed a glass fiber with a low enough attenuation to be used to send data in 1970. In 1977, the first live telephone communication through a fiber-optic cable occurred in Long Beach, California. The successful use of lasers as a light source was achieved in 1980.

During the 1980's, fiber-optic cable was laid in low-density areas because it was difficult to lay in densely populated areas where the copper wire infrastructure was extensive. This was also cost-effective because fiber-optic cable had a comparative advantage over long distances. The first transatlantic fiber-optic cable was laid and became operational in 1988. From that point on, fiber-optic cables were laid across the globe even though the capital costs were high.

Between 1990 and 2000, researchers and industry promoters predicted increased demand for greater bandwidth because of the use of the Internet and the commercial possibilities for consumer services, such as video on demand. They predicted that data traffic would increase exponentially, promising enormous profits to those who made the extremely expensive investment. These promises lead to a large infusion of venture capital, which was

Corning's Donald Keck was the first scientist at his company to discover a glass formulation pure enough for fiber optical communication. (AP/Wide World Photos)

lost when the commercial possibilities were not realized. The fiber-optic industry suffered in what became known as the dot-com bubble by the end of the decade.

Although the initial investors lost a great deal of money when the bubble burst, other investors who bought up the cable infrastructure at discount rates were able to make reasonable profits while offering the services of the fiber-optic infrastructure to customers in underdeveloped countries that could not have afforded them previously. With development of new computer platforms that interconnected easily, those with suitable training and access to computers were able to sell their services in the developed world in a way that they previously could not. New communication industries grew up around the globe. This dramatically increased the globalization of skilled labor throughout the developing world.

Richard L. Wilson

FURTHER READING

Agrawal, Govind P. *Fiber-Optic Communication Systems.* New York: John Wiley & Sons, 2002.

Baiman, Ron, Heather Boushey, and Dawn Saunders. *Political Economy and Contemporary Capitalism.* Armonk, N.Y.: M. E. Sharpe, 2000.

Friedman, Thomas L. *The World Is Flat: A Brief History of the Twenty-First Century.* New York: Farrar, Straus and Giroux, 2006.

SEE ALSO: Computer industry; eBay; E-mail; Internet; Outsourcing, overseas; Telecommunications industry.

Film industry. *See* Motion-picture industry

Films with business themes

SIGNIFICANCE: Films treating economic subjects tend to reflect popular American attitudes toward business during the periods in which they are made. For example, during eras of social and economic unrest, cautionary tales are popular. Rags-to-riches narratives have always been popular but are especially so during hard economic times, such as the Great Depression.

In a scholarly essay published in 2000, Mary Pileggi, Maria Grabe, Lisa Holderman, and Michelle de Montigny argued that all American business films can be traced back to the myth of the American Dream—the notion that with hard work and determination, every American has an equal chance to obtain prosperity. Pileggi and her coauthors went on to argue that the narrative of every business-themed film fits at least one of these four categories:
- rags to riches
- power and wealth corrupts
- money can't buy happiness
- poor little rich boy (or girl)

Rags-to-riches narratives began proliferating during the late nineteenth century, thanks to the popularity of the juvenile literary works of Horatio Alger. One of the great promoters of the American Dream, Alger wrote more than one hundred books for young people with such suggestive titles as *Ragged Dick: Or, Street Life in New York with the Bootblacks* (1868), *Risen from the Ranks: Or, Harry Walton's Success* (1874), and *The Errand Boy: Or, How Phil Brent Won Success* (1888). Rags-to-riches themes remained popular in both literature and film during the twentieth century. Film versions of these stories generally depict characters succeeding through hard work, ambition, and sacrifice. They have been especially popular during eras of comparative prosperity and stability, such as the 1950's and early 1990's. They were also popular during the Great Depression of the 1930's, when many Americans sought escapism. Notable examples of late twentieth century rags-to-riches films include *How to Succeed in Business Without Really Trying* (1967), *Trading Places* (1983), *Secret of My Success* (1987), and *Working Girl* (1988).

MONEY CAN'T BUY HAPPINESS

Money-can't-buy-happiness films typically depict successful people who discover that even great wealth does not always bring them the friendships and love that they crave. Films with this theme are often closely related to films with power-corrupts narratives. In the latter, characters who strive for financial power at all costs become evil, unhappy, and unsympathetic. Such films tend to gain in popularity during eras beset with social or political problems, such as World War I, when the emphasis was on the collective, not the individual; the years immediately following World War II; the Cold War era; and the Vietnam War years. Such films were also popular during the Ronald Reagan era of the 1980's, when Americans were reacting to unemployment and Reagan's new policies. Among notable films with the money-can't-buy-happiness narratives are *The Man in the Gray Flannel Suit* (1956), *Baby Boom* (1987), and *In Good Company* (2003). Notable power-corrupts films include *Executive Suite* (1954) and *The Apartment* (1960).

In addition to the four narrative types previously described, two other popular types of business films are whistle-blower and labor-strife stories. It might be argued that these are merely variations of the rags-to-riches theme in that they usually depict characters with almost nothing who speak out against corporate corruption or unfair labor practices, but for every *Erin Brockovich* (2000) that ends happily, there are several films with unhappy endings, such as *Matewan* (1987) and *Silkwood* (1983). Additional examples of this genre are *On the Waterfront* (1954), *The Insider* (2000), and *The China Syndrome* (1979).

FROM SILENT FILMS TO THE DEPRESSION ERA

Early silent films often looked at labor issues, with titles such as *Capital Versus Labor* (1910) and *The Girl Strike Leader* (1910). Because of the loss of many silent films, it is difficult to determine with which side many of these films tended to sympathize. However, films reflecting both points of view still survive. Especially popular with members of the working class were the films of Charles Chaplin, many of whose early films centered around work—or the lack thereof. In shorts such as *Making a Living* (1914), *The Tramp* (1915), and *The Pawnshop* (1916), Chaplin portrayed workers who tried to get by doing as little as possible. In *Work* (1915), he played a man who had to do most of his employer's work while his boss did nearly nothing. Every time Chaplin's character slapped his boss in the face with his paintbrush in that film, he expressed the anger of many workers. Chaplin's 1936 feature film *Modern Times*, which is essentially a silent film, although it has a sound track, is one of the classic films of the Depression era. In this film, Chaplin's tramp character begins literally as a cog in the dehumanizing machinery of the modern industrial age.

Charles Chaplin starred in several films with business themes. (Library of Congress)

Rags-to-riches tales were particularly popular during the Depression. One variation on this theme occurred in musicals, such as *Forty-Second Street* (1933), in which a plucky chorus girl becomes the star of a Broadway show, thanks to a lucky break. Popular rags-to-riches comedies of the era include Frank Capra's *Mr. Deeds Goes to Town* (1936), in which Gary Cooper plays a small-town man who inherits a fortune. Another classic of the era is Capra's *It Happened One Night* (1934), a money-can't-buy-happiness story in which Claudette Colbert plays the spoiled heir to a fortune.

WORLD WAR II AND AFTERWARD

During World War II and shortly thereafter, a large part of the films with business themes had money-can't-buy-happiness stories that promoted the notion that the common good was more important than individual success. One of the best-known examples of this theme is Capra's *It's a Wonderful Life* (1946). In this film, James Stewart plays the manager of a small-town savings and loan institution who considers himself a failure until an angel helps him realize how much good he has done for his community—in contrast to the town's wealthy and unloved villain.

The roles of women in business films have often differed from those of men. A survey of 120 business films made between 1927 and 1995 found that businesspeople rarely broke the law, betrayed others, lied, or used sex to get ahead, unless they were women. A blatant early example of this is in *Baby Face* (1933), wherein the main character, played by Barbara Stanwyck, uses sex to rise from her job in the filing room of a bank to become secretary to the bank's chief officer. Nearly fifty years later, the female protagonists of *Nine to Five* (1980) succeed by kidnapping their male boss.

During the postwar era, films questioning the roles of women in the workplace, such as Ann Sothern's character in *A Letter to Three Wives* (1949), served as reminders for wives to concentrate on being homemakers, while allowing their husbands—then returning from the war—to take back their rightful places in the workforce. Director William Wyler's *The Best Years of Our Lives*, which won the Academy Award for best picture for 1946, also addresses this theme. In it, returning war hero Fred (played by Dana Andrews) has difficulty finding a job, while his wife, Marie (played by Virginia Mayo), who had gotten a job while he was away, is portrayed as selfish and angry. It is not surprising that after their marriage falls apart, Fred takes up with a more complacent, younger woman (played by Teresa Wright).

Not all films of the postwar era portrayed women in business in a negative light. For example, *The Solid Gold Cadillac* (1956) depicts a corporate shareholder played by Judy Holliday as a smart employee, who is given a figurehead position in the company in the hope that she will go away, but instead uncovers corruption within the corporation. Although *Nine to Five* portrays its female protagonists as lawbreakers, it also depicts them as supremely competent in business, despite their unorthodox methods.

The Reagan Era

With many factories closing or being taken over by foreign companies during the 1980's, films focusing on the plight of exploited factory workers, such as *Take This Job and Shove It* (1981) and *Gung Ho* (1986), were popular. At the same time, the era of young urban professionals, or "yuppies," was taking hold, and films about them were made. Examples include *Bright Lights, Big City* (1988) and *Wall Street* (1987). Despite the clear power-corrupts narrative of *Wall Street*, the "Greed Is Good" speech by Gordon Gecko (played by Michael Douglas) in the film was received as a rallying cry by many yuppies of the period, and Douglas won an Oscar for his performance as a corrupt corporate raider. As the 1980's stretched into the 1990's, both rags-to-riches tales, such as *Secret of My Success* (1987), and money-can't-buy-happiness and power-corrupts narratives, such as *Nothing in Common* (1986), *Baby Boom* (1987), and *Head Office* (1985), all featured yuppies as characters.

Toward the end of the 1990's, a new genre of business film began to emerge that featured temporary workers and cubicle employees. *Clockwatchers* (1998), for example, is a story told from the point of view of temps working in a large firm. A quirky film with elements of the rags-to-riches narrative (the main characters eventually find their way out of temporary employment), *Clockwatchers* reflected an employment reality that was becoming increasingly common throughout the United States, as the temp-placement industry, led by companies such as Kelly and Manpower, continued to grow. *Office Space* (1999) revolves around a group of cubicle workers at a firm in Texas who are being evaluated by an efficiency expert firm and their subsequent decision to embezzle from the company. The central character decides that he no longer wants to go to work. However, instead of getting fired for not being productive, he is seen as a maverick with potential for management. This spoof of corporate cubicle culture evolved into a cult classic, with major companies such as Dell and International Business Machines (IBM) holding *Office Space* showings and theme parties for their employees. Like the early Chaplin films about characters who did not want to work that had delighted members of the working class during the early twentieth century, *Office Space* entertained early twenty-first century audiences with its depiction of office workers who do not want to fill out routine reports.

Julie Elliott

Further Reading

Bergman, Andrew. *We're in the Money: Depression America and Its Films.* New York: Harper, 1971. Study of the film industry and the American films made during the Great Depression.

Casper, Drew. *Postwar Hollywood, 1946-1962.* Malden, Mass.: Blackwell, 2007. Exploration of the American film industry through the optimistic era following World War II.

Mintz, Steven, and Randy Roberts. *Hollywood's America: United States History Through Its Films.* St. James, N.Y.: Brandywine Press, 1999. Illuminating study of the complex interplay of history and film in twentieth century America.

Pileggi, Mary S., Maria Grabe, Lisa Holderman, and Michelle de Montigny. "Business as Usual: The American Dream in Hollywood Business Films." *Mass Communication and Society* 3, no. 2/3 (2000): 207-228. Overview of business films made between 1927 and 1995. The essay does not discuss specific films but instead examines the predominant themes of the films made during each decade.

Welch, Sara J. "The Ultimate Four Letter Word." *Successful Meetings* 55, no. 2 (February, 2006): 14. Article describes the *Office Space* party phenomenon.

See also: Great Depression; Literary works with business themes; Motion-picture industry; Radio broadcasting industry; Television broadcasting industry; Television programming with business themes; Video rental industry.

Financial crisis of 2008

THE EVENT: Throughout 2008, declining prices for houses and increasing defaults on home-mortgage loans led to a wave of failures involving banks and other mortgage-market participants. The crisis phase crested in mid-October after the U.S. Congress authorized the Treasury Department to use up to $700 billion to buy troubled assets or inject capital into banks.

DATE: September-October, 2008

PLACE: United States, also Europe and Asia

SIGNIFICANCE: The crisis disrupted housing markets, mortgage markets, and finance and credit markets generally. These developments reduced aggregate demand and brought on an economic recession that adversely affected most businesses and shook public confidence in financial institutions and government.

Beginning during the summer of 2007, worsening conditions in the United States housing and home-finance sectors led to an escalation of financial distress. Average house prices had doubled between 1997 and 2005, and many people expected the increases to continue. Then the market for houses turned around, and house prices declined by 18 percent from mid-2006 to mid-2008. An increasing number of borrowers could not meet their mortgage payments—or chose not to. Major financial institutions with hundreds of billions of assets and liabilities became insolvent, unable to pay their debts. Federal government agencies, notably the Federal Reserve and the Treasury, intervened at many points to try to prevent matters from getting worse. At the same time, stock prices were falling rapidly. By then the panic had spread to Europe.

Government intervention was not primarily motivated by concern for the failing institutions. Rather, it was undertaken in an effort to prevent a decrease in aggregate demand (as measured by gross domestic product—GDP) that would cause a decrease in production and employment. There was fear that loans would not be available for business spending for new capital equipment. More specifically, government interventions sought to prevent a serious decrease in the construction and sale of new homes—an important component of GDP. Surprisingly, even by mid-2008, GDP was still increasing. Another objective was to prevent foreign investors from selling off their holdings of American securities, which would increase interest rates in the U.S. and drive down the international value of the dollar. This objective was achieved.

FANNIE AND FREDDIE

At the center of financial turmoil were two giant financial firms. The Federal National Mortgage Association ("Fannie Mae") had been created in 1938 as a government enterprise. It was privatized in 1968, meaning it had private stockholders and very highly paid executives. To create competition, the federal government established the Federal National Mortgage Corporation ("Freddie Mac") in 1970. Both institutions operated by borrowing money and using it to buy home mortgages from the grassroots lenders. Although technically private, they were able to borrow on favorable terms because investors believed their debts were guaranteed by the federal government. From 1970, they increasingly raised money by issuing mortgage-backed bonds.

In 1977, Congress passed the Community Reinvestment Act, which put pressure on banks and other lenders to expand loans to racial minorities and low-income borrowers. In 1995 the Department of Housing and Urban Development (HUD), required banks to meet numerical quotas in lending and provide evidence of the diversity of their borrowers. By 2005, HUD required that 22 percent of all mortgages bought by Fannie and Freddie represent borrowers with incomes below those of 60 percent of their area's median income.

Traditionally, mortgage lenders wanted to be sure the loans that they made would be repaid and evaluated loan applicants on the basis of their incomes, wealth, and credit experience. Now those standards were increasingly set aside, particularly in view of the rapid increase in house prices that was raising the market value of borrowers' collateral. In 2007, 45 percent of first-time home buyers made no down payments; they were thus borrowing the entire prices of their houses. The rapid rise in house prices generated demand for houses by speculators who expected to be able to resell the houses at still higher prices.

COLLATERALIZED DEBT OBLIGATIONS

The expansion of subprime lending was financed in large degree by the creation of collateralized debt obligations (CDOs). Invented in 1987, mortgage-backed CDOs were issued by Fannie,

Freddie, and a number of private investment firms. A pool of mortgages worth $10 million could be the basis for issuing a stratified mix of securities with different levels of priority. The issuer might create $8 million of bonds with top priority claims for principal and interest. Credit risk for these bonds would be much lower than the average for the entire mortgage pool. Consequently, they could carry a very high rating and be purchased by conservative investors such as insurance companies, foreign governments and central banks, who would be willing to buy them at relatively low interest rates. Perhaps $1 million of additional bonds ("mezzanine tranche") would be sold with second priority. Investors in this bond would receive payment only after the first bonds were paid in full. The risk would be substantial and thus a higher interest rate would need to be paid. The securities in the third layer ("equity tranche") would receive payment only after both the others were paid in full. The equity level appealed to hedge funds and other investors who sought high returns from high risk.

The opportunity to issue low-interest CDOs to finance high-interest mortgages created large profit opportunities, and private firms flocked to the field in the new millennium. Whereas in 2003, Fannie and Freddie accounted for three fourths of CDO issues, by mid-2006 their share had fallen to 43 percent. In 2003, prime (top-grade) mortgages were half the basis for CDOs, but by 2006, they were down to one fourth.

CDO PROBLEMS

In retrospect, many problems can be identified in CDO issues. Often the issuers offered guarantees to persons buying their bonds. Such loan guarantees became a big business in themselves, in the form of "credit-default swaps." Fannie and Freddie guaranteed many privately issued CDOs. Both issuers and bond buyers lacked adequate information about the risk characteristics of the various CDO issues. Not only did the mortgage pools contain debts of persons of diverse credit standing, but the mortgages themselves were often loaded with complex provisions such as adjustable interest rates or interest-only payment schedules.

The national securities rating agencies, such as Moody's or Standard and Poor's, usually gave the high-priority bonds top investment grades—again without adequate information. The opportunity to

purchase "insurance" against loan defaults, often at low cost, enabled many investors to ignore considerations of credit risk. The nominal value of credit-default swaps reached $62 trillion by the end of 2007. Many of these were simple financial speculations, for the volume of corporate debt was only about $6 trillion. Some of these speculations were unbelievably profitable: According to *Fortune* magazine, "Hedge fund star John Paulson . . . made $15 billion in 2007, largely by using [credit-default swaps] to bet that other investors' subprime mortgage bonds would default."

The security issues arising from CDOs were subject to surveillance by the Securities and Exchange Commission. However, this only involved confirming that issuers accurately described the new securities, not trying to assess their riskiness. In contrast, credit-default swaps had been explicitly exempted from government regulation by federal legislation in 2000.

INSTITUTIONAL FAILURES

In March, 2008, Bear Stearns, a prominent investment banking firm, was rescued from imminent failure by being merged into JPMorgan Chase, a merger assisted by the Federal Reserve. In July, 2008, Countrywide, a major mortgage-lending bank, was taken over on the brink of collapse by Bank of America. The settlement was noteworthy for the fact that Bank of America agreed to offer many Countrywide borrowers improved terms on their loans. That same month the Federal Deposit Insurance Corporation (FDIC) supervised the closing of IndyMac, a large West Coast bank with heavy mortgage involvement.

On September 7, 2008, the federal government (through Treasury Secretary Henry Paulson) took control of Fannie and Freddie. The Treasury provided each with a $100 billion line of credit in exchange for an ownership share. Existing stockholders lost most of their investment. The two firms had liabilities exceeding $5 trillion and were providing as much as 80 percent of new mortgage financing. They continued operating under supervision from the Federal Housing Finance Agency. A week later, Lehman Brothers, a noted investment banking firm, filed for bankruptcy after efforts to arrange a rescue merger fell through. With total assets of $630 million, Lehman was the largest bankruptcy in U.S. history. Lehman had borrowed heavily by issuing short-term commercial paper. When these debts went into default, their market value fell by 80 percent. This spread crisis to money-market mutual funds (MMMFs) that held large amounts of commercial paper. When Reserve Primary Fund, a money-market mutual fund, found their net asset value per share falling below a dollar, most of their account holders demanded payment, and Reserve was unable to pay them. Federal authorities responded by extending deposit-insurance coverage to existing money-market mutual fund accounts, estimated at $3.4 trillion.

The Lehman failure led to an avalanche of security sales by financial firms desperate to raise cash, driving down stock prices and bond prices. Firms that had provided loan guarantees were under pressure to make good. One such troubled firm was AIG (American International Group), a large insurance company. On September 16, the Treasury agreed to lend AIG $85 billion, taking an 80 percent ownership interest in return. AIG's stock had fallen from $37 to $3 a share in four months. Simultaneously, Merrill Lynch, an old and respected brokerage and investment-banking firm, was absorbed by Bank of America.

On September 25, 2008, the FDIC presided over the forced merging of Washington Mutual (WaMu), into JPMorgan Chase. With $300 billion in assets, WaMu represented the largest bank failure to date. Experts predicted its stockholders and some of its creditors would lose their investments.

The spectacle of financial institutions trying to sell assets and driving markets down finally provoked major federal intervention. On October 3, Congress approved a Treasury plan to use as much as $700 billion to buy distressed financial assets and to inject capital into banks. Included in the Emergency Economic Stabilization Act was an increase in the coverage of federal insurance of bank deposits from $100,000 to $250,000. For the week following, stock prices experienced one of their most severe declines, prompting the Federal Reserve to lower its already-low target interest rate. Another large troubled bank, Wachovia, was absorbed by Wells Fargo.

On November 25, an additional initiative was undertaken, chiefly involving a commitment by the Federal Reserve to buy up to $600 billion in debts issued by or backed by Fannie, Freddie, and other housing lenders. It committed an additional $200 billion to enable investors to carry securities backed by student loans, automobile loans, credit card debt and small-business loans.

Almost simultaneously, a major rescue effort was directed toward banking conglomerate Citigroup, with the government providing $20 billion in capital and a guarantee covering about $250 billion in real estate loans and securities held by Citi.

On February 17, 2009, President Barack Obama signed into law the American Recovery and Reinvestment Act, a $787 billion recovery package that included funds for renewable energy, infrastructure, education, and health care, as well as about $282 billion in tax relief for individuals and businesses. The next day, Obama announced a $275 billion housing relief plan designed to help people refinance their mortgages and stay in their homes.

WHY THE COLLAPSE WAS SO SEVERE

One of the primary questions that this crisis raised is how a relatively minor increase in mortgage defaults—as measured by dollar magnitude—developed into a worldwide financial meltdown. One contributing factor was the layering of debts through several stages of finan-

A Dow Jones news ticker in New York's Times Square displayed news about AIG and Lehman Brothers on September 16, 2008. (AP/Wide World Photos)

cial intermediation. Grassroots lenders initiated mortgages, some of which they held pending resale, borrowing 80 to 90 percent of the value of their holdings. Fannie and Freddie bought mortgages using mostly borrowed money. They and other firms pooled some mortgages into CDOs, some of which they held pending resale, financed by borrowing. Hedge funds bought the high-risk equity tranches of CDOs, financed by borrowing. For every $100 of underlying mortgage debt, there could easily be $500 or more of interlocking institutional debts. Interwoven with these were the debts implicit in the purchase and sale of credit-default swaps.

Firms that were deeply involved in CDOs were most likely to experience a crisis. Relatively small increases in mortgage defaults became magnified for several reasons:

- Firms that made major investments in CDOs or in mortgages were heavily dependent on short-term loans that needed to be rolled over continuously. Inability to renew loans precipitated most of the firm closures.
- The firms did not have capital accounts sufficient to their risk exposure. The capital account shows the amount by which the value of assets exceeds the value of liabilities. Fannie and Freddie had capital accounts less than 2 percent of their assets. A decline of 2 percent in the value of their assets would make them technically insolvent. Government regulations establish minimum capital requirements, but in many cases these were not large enough. A major reason was that many firms had extensive "off-balance-sheet" liabilities, such as loan guarantees. Firms like AIG had more liabilities than they acknowledged, and the rules for minimum capital failed to adjust for these invisible liabilities.
- Firms that sold large amounts of credit-default swaps, such as Fannie, Freddie, and AIG, believed they were providing "insurance." They had elaborate computer algorithms to calculate probabilities of loss. The calculations were simply wrong, and the sellers did not have enough solid assets to cover their bad bets.

When financial markets are smoothly functioning, many transactions and relationships substitute trust in place of information. Few Americans, after all, carefully scrutinize the asset portfolios of their automobile insurance providers. The crisis of 2007-2008 broke down trust in many relationships. In particular, potential suppliers of short-term loan funds lost trust in the potential borrowers, particularly after the Lehman collapse.

The crisis occurred in a context that included the extremely low saving rate in the United States and the large flow of international capital into the U.S. CDOs and credit-default swaps experienced explosive growth in part because they facilitated marketing American CDOs to foreign investors. In 2007, the financial services industry received 40 percent of all U.S. corporate profits. It seems unlikely the sector contributed to American economic welfare in such a proportion.

Critics blamed the crisis in part on the federal government policy of trying to expand home ownership. Many people may prefer or are better off living in rental housing because they move frequently, lack financial decision-making skills, have better use for their capital than a house, or do not want to spend time maintaining the property. The government's programs increased spending for housing and increased home prices—so first-time home buyers had to pay more and did not really gain from the underlying policies. Capital that flowed into overpriced and underfunded homes could have gone into productive capital assets, buildings, and machines to raise labor productivity and real wages. A substantial share of the losses from asset defaults were experienced by foreign investors.

Paul B. Trescott

FURTHER READING

Bandler, James. "Hank's Last Stand." *Fortune* 158, no. 7 (October 13, 2008): 112-131. A play-by-play look at the collapse of AIG from the perspective of its longtime head, Maurice "Hank" Greenberg.

"Briefing: A Short History of Modern Finance." *The Economist*, October 18, 2008, 79-81. Excellent overview, stressing long-term and international aspects.

Dodd, Randall. "Subprime: Tentacles of a Crisis." *Finance and Development* (December, 2007): 15-19. Clear and detailed explanation of the emergence and role of collateralized debt obligations.

Mizen, Paul. "The Credit Crunch of 2007-2008: A Discussion of the Background, Market Reactions, and Policy Responses." *Review* (Federal Reserve Bank of St. Louis, September/October, 2008): 531. Detailed scholarly examination of long- and short-term aspects, with attention to the international dimension.

Varchaver, Nicholas, and Katie Benner. "The $55 Trillion Question." *Fortune* 158, no. 7 (October 13, 2008): 135-140. Explains everything about credit-default swaps except why they are called "swaps."

SEE ALSO: Asian financial crisis of 1997; Bank failures; Banking; Congress, U.S.; Deregulation of financial institutions; Federal Deposit Insurance Corporation; Federal Reserve; Monetary policy, federal; Mortgage industry.

First Bank of the United States. *See* Bank of the United States, First

Fishing industry

DEFINITION: Enterprises engaged in the harvesting, processing, and distribution of seafood

SIGNIFICANCE: The American fishing industry expanded in response to the growing popularity of seafood, but many of the areas rich in seafood have become overfished. As fisheries decline, the world fish supply will decrease, driving up prices and rendering a significant, nutritious part of the human diet inaccessible to many people.

In 2008, the American fishing industry comprised twenty-five thousand commercial fishing vessels, seven hundred fish processors, twenty-eight thousand distributors, and seventy-three thousand employees, and it generated annual revenue of $14 billion. On average, Americans ate about twelve pounds of seafood annually. Despite these impressive numbers, the commercial fishing industry in the United States is in decline. As America's population increases, there is a greater demand for both fresh and frozen fish, as well as fishmeal products. Large investments in fishing fleets during the 1970's and 1980's, speculators demanding record annual harvests, and government subsides helped increase marine harvests for many years, but in many fishing regions, harvests quickly began to exceed estimated sustainable yields. The end result of this process was

that for too many years too many fishing fleets were chasing too few fish, until stocks collapsed and fishing businesses began to go bankrupt.

Many fisheries traditionally harvested by American fishing fleets have been decimated, including haddock, capelin, Atlantic cod, Atlantic herring, Pacific perch, rockfish, red snapper, California sardines, Atlantic salmon, and Pacific salmon. Industrialized fishing has literally destroyed some of the most productive fisheries in the world. To compensate for declines in traditional fisheries, harvesting of other species has increased, often at nonsustainable rates. The United States has begun actively restricting commercial fishing, thereby eliminating thousands of jobs.

The collapse of fisheries along North American coasts is not entirely the fault of U.S. fishing fleets. For many years, foreign fishing fleets have also overfished U.S. waters. In 1976, the U.S. government enacted the Magnuson Fishery Conservation and Management Act, and in 1983, it established the U.S. Exclusive Economic Zone, all but ending exploitation of U.S. waters by foreign vessels. However, the result of removing foreign fishing boats from U.S. waters was a 40 percent increase in domestic commercial fishing boats and a 60 percent increase in employment rates in the U.S. commercial fishing industry. Essentially, foreign overfishing was replaced by domestic overfishing. By 1998, the U.S. government reported that for three hundred species of fish for which it had data, one hundred were being fished beyond sustainable yields. As fuel costs continue to escalate, many smaller fishing businesses will be forced out of existence.

The Georges Bank, off the coast of New England, was once one of the world's most productive fisheries. Stocks of flounder, haddock, and cod there fell so low in 1992 that their harvest was banned. Rockfish have become so endangered that the United States enacted an emergency ban on bottom fishing in 2003. Pacific salmon stocks have become so low that a ban on their commercial harvest was established in 2008. The Magnuson-Stevens Fishery Conservation and Management Reauthorization Act of 2006 required overfishing to be eliminated by 2011 for all domestic fisheries.

Overfishing is not the only threat to U.S. and world fisheries. Environmental pressures, pollution, and destruction of near-shore nursery grounds affect North American fishery productivity and thus the livelihood of fishermen. Additionally, climate change seriously affects commercial fishing, as warming surface waters alter currents and shift plankton populations. The use of artificial industrial fertilizers in U.S. agriculture also contributes to the problem, because the chemicals that make up these fertilizers eventually wash out to sea, nourishing algae and creating blooms that rob the water of oxygen. As a result, vast "dead zones" in which fish cannot survive have been created in the Gulf of Mexico and elsewhere.

Randall L. Milstein

FURTHER READING

Blum, M. C., and E. L. Bodi. *The Northwest Salmon Crisis: A Documentary History.* Corvallis: Oregon State University Press, 1996.

Gimbel, K. *Limiting Access to Marine Fisheries: Keeping the Focus on Conservation.* Washington, D.C.: Center for Marine Conservation, 1994.

Rogers, R. *The Oceans Are Emptying: Fish Wars and Sustainability.* Montreal: Black Rose Books, 1995.

SEE ALSO: Agribusiness; Agriculture; Alaska purchase; Beef industry; Canadian trade with the United States; Fur trapping and trading; Hurricane Katrina; Interior, U.S. Department of the; Pork industry; Poultry industry.

Food and Drug Administration

IDENTIFICATION: Agency of the federal government attached to the Department of Health and Human Services and responsible for protecting the public from dangerous, unsanitary, and mislabeled drugs, cosmetics, and mechanical products such as pacemakers

DATE: Established in 1906

SIGNIFICANCE: The oversight provided by the Food and Drug Administration affects directly such businesses as agriculture, tobacco, meat processing and packing, pharmaceuticals, the cosmetics industry, and the makers of much of the biomedical hardware commonly found in modern medical facilities.

The creation of a federal agency to oversee the food and drug industries is largely a product of the twentieth century. As early as the Vaccine Act of 1813, which was short-lived, the federal government had some interest in controlling activities related to the health of Americans, but the question of states' rights always loomed, as citizens shied away from a federal government that might become too large and powerful.

Nevertheless, in the last quarter of the nineteenth century, one influential scientist, Harvey Wiley, attached to the United States Department of Agriculture as its chief chemist, was vitally concerned with the safety of the nation's food supply. During his term in office, which ran from 1883 to 1912, Wiley created "poison squads" to test foods that were suspected of causing illnesses.

Wiley's efforts were bolstered substantially in 1906 with the publication of Upton Sinclair's muckraking novel, *The Jungle*, an exposé of the meatpacking industry in Chicago. Pointing out the unsanitary and inhumane conditions that prevailed in slaughterhouses and meatpacking facilities at that time, Sinclair's novel horrified people who read it and had previously paid little attention to the conditions under which their food was produced. Sinclair quipped that he wrote a novel that he hoped would touch the hearts of his readers, but instead it touched their stomachs.

Among the most influential readers of *The Jungle* was President Theodore Roosevelt, whose reaction was immediate. He goaded Congress, many of whose members read Sinclair's novel, into passing the Pure Food and Drug Act of 1906 months after the novel first appeared. This act, which applied only to the interstate sale of contaminated foods and drugs, made a wary public more conscious of the health dangers that some food products and drugs posed.

This act also demanded that food and drugs be labeled accurately and honestly, which was a blow to many charlatans who had been selling magical cures—things like snake oil—to an unsuspecting public. Between 1906 and 1927, the enforcement of the Pure Food and Drug Act fell to the Bureau of Chemistry, an agency within the United States Department of Agriculture. In 1927, the Bureau of Chemistry was renamed the Food, Drug, and Insecticide Administration, and in 1930, the name was shortened to the Food and Drug Administration.

The Food, Drug, and Insecticide Administration

In 1928, Congress, through the passage of the Food, Drug, and Insecticide Act, authorized the federal government to establish a separate agency to carry out research relevant to the Pure Food and Drug Act. This agency was concerned not only with food and drugs but also with biomedical devices used in the treatment of various conditions.

In 1931, during Herbert Hoover's presidency, Congress passed the Agricultural Appropriation Act, which changed the agency's name to the Food and Drug Administration (FDA). During the presidency of Franklin D. Roosevelt, Congress passed the Food, Drug, and Cosmetics Act of 1938, which increased the types and number of commodities that fell under the jurisdiction of the federal government. This act increased the penalties that could be exacted against those who violated its provisions.

Special interest groups attempted to apply pressure to the agency and to encourage it to overlook some of their infractions of clear-cut rules, the enforcement of which would cost them dearly. In 1940, to circumvent such pressure, the agency became a part of the Federal Security Agency, where it remained until 1953, when it became officially attached to the Department of Health, Education, and Welfare. It remained attached to this cabinet-level department until 1980, when it became an adjunct of the Department of Health and Human Services, also a cabinet-level department, to which it remains attached.

Criticisms

Through the years, the federal Food and Drug Administration has undergone a great deal of public scrutiny and criticism. Because its findings affect the lives and welfare of millions of people, the public demands high standards of this agency. Sometimes, to maintain such standards, the FDA is forced to take actions that cost various affected industries millions of dollars.

In the first half of 2008, for example, two major criticisms were leveled against the FDA. In the first instance, an epidemic of human salmonella poisoning afflicted 1,294 people in forty-three states as well as in Canada and the District of Columbia. The FDA undertook an immediate investigation and initially proclaimed that tainted tomatoes might be the source of this epidemic.

Only two years earlier, the agency had cast a similar suspicion on the $180-million-a-year spinach crop from California's Salinas Valley, resulting in an embargo that led to the bankruptcy of many of those involved in the production and distribution of spinach. The outbreak of illness caused by e-coli was traced to spinach from California's Salinas Valley and destroyed the businesses of many farmers dependent on the spinach crop for their economic survival. Their losses were estimated by some to exceed $1 million for each day the embargo was in effect.

In 2008, as a result of the suspicion cast on tomatoes, several varieties of tomatoes were withdrawn from markets and restaurants in many areas. The tomato industry lost millions of dollars because of these recalls. After several weeks, it was determined that tomatoes were probably not the cause of the epidemic and suspicion then fell on two other possible sources, jalapeño peppers and cilantro, both ingredients in the salsa that is a frequent accompaniment of Mexican food.

Finally the FDA pinpointed jalapeño peppers and cilantro imported from Mexico, to which contaminated irrigation water was traced, as the probable culprits, but there was no conclusive evidence that such was the case. The FDA declined to exclude tomatoes categorically from its list of suspects. Importers and those involved in Mexican agriculture took an enormous financial hit because of the FDA's investigation. Meanwhile, the FDA declared that jalapeños and cilantro grown in the United States were safe to eat.

By this time, however, the damage had been done, and the financial losses to farmers were substantial. Given the ambiguity of the FDA's investigation, many people avoided altogether the vegetables that had been mentioned as possible sources of the epidemic. Rather then trying to check the origins of vegetables on the list of suspects, many shoppers played it safe by not buying any of the suspected vegetables.

Conflicts of Interest

Critics have pointed out that many illnesses and even deaths occur every year when drugs are prescribed by physicians to treat conditions for which the prescribed drugs were not intended and for which they have not been field tested. This is a grave problem with extremely dangerous consequences

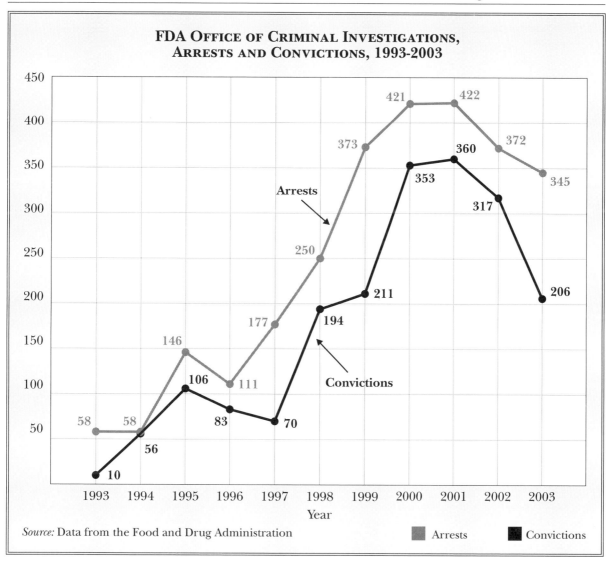

FDA OFFICE OF CRIMINAL INVESTIGATIONS, ARRESTS AND CONVICTIONS, 1993-2003

Arrests

Convictions

Year

Source: Data from the Food and Drug Administration   Arrests   Convictions

for many people who receive these off-label drugs. Despite the dangers involved, the FDA has been powerless to take action against physicians who prescribe drugs for unintended uses because the agency is not legally authorized to question the authority of physicians in prescribing legal medications. Also, with the growth of the pharmaceutical industry, the agency has been severely understaffed, so it has had to cut back on many of its investigative efforts.

Field testing is a long and, at times, unwieldy process. Although some side effects are apparent almost immediately when a person has taken a drug, in many cases it takes months or even years for side effects to occur. In matters of health, the public often expects immediate results, but the FDA should not hasten field testing to produce such results nor should it be pressured into doing so.

Of additional concern to the FDA has been a suspected correlation between the regular use of cell phones and brain cancer. Millions of people use cell phones and the cell phone industry generates many hundreds of million dollars in profits for both the manufacturers and service providers of cell phones and cell phone service. The public has become dependent on cell phones for much of its communication. In this matter, the FDA has the responsibility of trying to assess the hazards that cell phones might pose, but such an assessment would involve broad longitudinal studies tracing the health records of cell phone users over periods of time that might extend to decades. Meanwhile, the FDA cannot ban cell phones even though it cannot give its categorical approval to their use.

One must remember that the links between the use of tobacco products and certain types of cancer took decades to be established. As a result, many Americans found fault with the FDA for not acting more aggressively to discourage the use of tobacco products, but a thriving tobacco industry lobbied strenuously to thwart the kind of ban that some people thought was necessary. Lawsuits relating to the use of tobacco and cancer often involved histories of tobacco use that went back forty or fifty years. In cases of this sort, it is difficult to isolate a single cause of an illness that occurs in one's later life.

PROBLEMS IN KEEPING CURRENT

With dramatic increases in research, the FDA frequently has had to reverse some of its earlier advisories. For many years, it recommended that women have diets high in calcium and that they take calcium supplements to strengthen their bones and to forestall such conditions as osteoporosis. It was assumed that men could also benefit from such a recommendation.

After several years, however, a link was discovered between high calcium intake among men and the incidence of prostate cancer. Presumably, high calcium intake in men can result in inhibiting their absorption of vitamin D. Reductions in the absorption of this vitamin are thought to increase the occurrence of prostate cancer in men. The FDA, therefore, cautions all men nineteen or older to control their intake of foods high in calcium—mostly dairy products—and not to take calcium supplements. Such reversals raise serious public concerns, but they are quite understandable in the light of continuing research.

Although the FDA's reversals of some of its long-standing edicts shake public confidence in the agency, there is no justification for suppressing recent research findings merely to save face. If the agency is to function effectively and is to have the full confidence of the public it serves, it must admit previous errors that have sometimes resulted in its need to countermand some of its earlier recommendations and edicts.

R. Baird Shuman

FURTHER READING

Johnson, Cathy Marie. *The Dynamics of Conflict Between Bureaucrats and Legislators.* Armonk, N.Y.: M. E. Sharpe, 1996. Chapter 4 focuses on the Food and Drug Administration. It is interesting to compare Johnson's account with the later account of Richard Rettig noted below.

King, Paul H., and Richard Fries. *Design of Biomedical Devices and Systems.* New York: Marcel Dekker, 2003. Chapter 14 is devoted to the role of the FDA in its oversight of biomedical devices.

Rettig, Richard A. *The Food and Drug Administration Confronts Homeland and National Security.* Santa Monica, Calif.: RAND, 2003. A spirited discussion of how the FDA sometimes is thought to intrude on the responsibilities of other governmental agencies.

Wannisky, Kathleen E. *Department of Health and Human Services, Food and Drug Administration, Bar Code Label Requirement for Human Drug Products, and Biological Products.* Washington, D.C.: U.S. General Accounting Office, 2004. A forthright presentation of how bar code labeling of drugs reduces the danger that prescriptions will be filled inaccurately, resulting in the wrong drugs being administered to patients.

Warner, John W., and Beverly Sweatman. *Federal Jobs in Law Enforcement.* 2d ed. Lawrenceville, N.J.: Arco/Thomson Learning, 2002. A comprehensive listing of government jobs in law enforcement with a full listing of such jobs available in the Food and Drug Administration

SEE ALSO: Food-processing industries; Genentech; Health care industry; Pharmaceutical industry.

Food for Peace

IDENTIFICATION: Federal program designed to help American farmers sell surplus food

DATE: Signed into law on July 10, 1954

SIGNIFICANCE: Food for Peace succeeded in facilitating the sale of increasingly large American agricultural surpluses to foreign buyers. It also established the principle that promoting American business abroad was linked to U.S. national security goals and demonstrated the political clout of U.S. agricultural producers.

The Agricultural Trade Development and Assistance Act (Public Law 480, 83rd Congress) was signed into law by President Dwight D. Eisenhower on July 10, 1954, establishing a program to help farmers sell surplus food abroad. When President John F. Kennedy expanded the program in 1961, he renamed it Food for Peace.

The Food for Peace program grew out of the Marshall Plan, which included exporting large amounts of American wheat to European countries recovering from World War II. The main purpose of Food for Peace was initially to address the problem of substantial agricultural surpluses in the United States. At the time of its adoption, alleviating world hunger was only a secondary goal of the legislation. It appeared to have immediate success, as U.S. agricultural exports grew from $449 million in 1952 to $1.9 billion in 1957. In addition to farmers, the program benefited such other professions as truckers and operators of barges and grain elevators.

Eisenhower was mostly concerned with helping American farmers sell their surpluses when he signed the law. As the number of Americans living in rural areas began to decline, their voting power diminished as well. However, other objectives besides helping rural Americans arose to ensure the continued importance of the program. Though assisting American farmers was still important to him, President Kennedy wanted to use the Food for Peace program as a tool to achieve U.S. foreign policy goals and to reduce global hunger.

The merits of Food for Peace have been hotly debated. Its supporters argue that it has provided food assistance to 3.4 billion people suffering from malnutrition. They also state that it has helped open foreign markets for American farmers while simultaneously obtaining allies needed for U.S. national security interests. Critics contend, however, that most of the program's funds go to the sale of food to wealthier markets instead of feeding malnourished people. Furthermore, they argue that only a small minority of American farmers actually receive money from the program, and approximately 67 percent of the funds are distributed to the wealthiest 10 percent of American agricultural producers.

Regardless of this debate, Food for Peace has had an impact domestically and internationally. Since its beginning, it has been responsible for exporting more than 106 million metric tons of U.S.-produced food to more than 150 countries. The total cost of the program has been approximately $33 billion.

Kevin L. Brennan

FURTHER READING
Picard, Louis A., et al., eds. *Foreign Aid and Foreign Policy: Lessons for the Next Half-Century.* Armonk, N.Y.: M. E. Sharpe, 2008.
Stanford, Claire, ed. *World Hunger.* Washington, D.C.: H. W. Wilson Company, 2007.
Wallerstein, Mitchel B. *Food for War—Food for Peace: United States Food Aid in a Global Context.* Cambridge, Mass.: The MIT Press, 1980.

SEE ALSO: Agribusiness; Agriculture; Agriculture, U.S. Department of; Export-Import Bank of the United States; International economics and trade; Marshall Plan; World War II.

Food-processing industries

DEFINITION: Enterprises that transform raw plant and animal products into marketable forms suitable for direct human consumption or for use as ingredients

SIGNIFICANCE: From its modest beginnings during the American Industrial Revolution, the food-processing industry in the United States evolved into a trillion-dollar enterprise exercising enormous economic, political, social, and cultural influence over people's eating habits as well as their health.

Throughout the early history of the American colonies and the United States, food production and processing were largely in the hands of individuals on small farms. Over time, farmers increasingly made use of mills to grind their wheat into flour, and as urban areas grew in population, many families could no longer produce all the food they needed. Various industries stepped in to meet this demand. Some scholars also single out the military needs of large armies and navies as another impetus for the growth of mass-market food processing.

EARLY TECHNOLOGY

An early example of the development of modern food-processing technology was the inventor Oliver Evans's automated flour mill outside Philadelphia.

Patented during the late eighteenth century, this factory, consisting of an ingenious system of integrated conveyors, elevators, and scales, was not just the first fully automated food-processing system but the first process of any kind to be automated. Evans's widely infringed system spread throughout the young country, and Buffalo and Rochester, New York, became national flour-milling centers. With the growth of these and other cities, consumers welcomed nationally distributed, inexpensive foodstuffs, even though small, local processors often suffered.

Because many foods deteriorated during storage and transport, ways of preserving them after processing became essential. Developed in Europe, hermetic canning of food was brought to the United States in 1817 by William Underwood, and in 1825, Thomas Kensett received the first American canning patent. He used cylindrical tin cans to hold various foods, which were heated before the cans were sealed. Initially, such canned foods as lobster were affordable only to the wealthy, but during the 1840's and 1850's, canned fruits, vegetables, and fish were marketed to travelers, especially those crossing the continent to California in search of gold.

Early in the nineteenth century, the processing of meat took place mostly in local slaughterhouses that provided their customers with not only fresh meat but also such processed meats as smoked, pickled, and salted beef, pork, and mutton. However, by mid-century, the processing of meats had become the domain of large enterprises in Cincinnati, Chicago, and St. Louis. In these and other cities the processing of meats had become automated, and a national system was established to distribute the products. Particularly significant was the way in which pork was processed. Workers hung gutted pigs from hooks attached to an overhead moving device that brought the carcasses to one butcher after another, who removed various body parts (this disassembly line would later influence Henry Ford's assembly line for automobiles).

Because food was a necessity for soldiers and civilians of the North and South during the U.S. Civil War, heightened wartime demands stimulated the food-processing industry. Although fresh foods continued to be consumed, shortages occurred because so many men left farms to fight. The food industry expanded to mitigate the crisis, and midwestern mechanized agricultural production and canneries proved to be very important to the ultimate Northern victory. The Underwood Company produced deviled ham, the Borden Company made condensed milk, and the Van Camp Company produced pork and beans. Other companies created sauces that rendered the dried and salted meats palatable, such as Len and Perrins's Worcestershire Sauce and the McIlhanny Company's Tabasco Sauce. Despite these efforts, many soldiers and civilians suffered from malnutrition during the war, especially in the Confederate states.

THE SECOND PHASE

From the Civil War to World War I, a period that some scholars have called the second phase of the American Industrial Revolution, food processing became more scientific and systematic. Alongside large California farms and ranches, food-processing facilities proliferated, canning such items as tomatoes and olives. Firms created and marketed synthetic foods, touting their superiority to natural products. For example, Procter and Gamble's Crisco vegetable shortening did not become rancid as butter and lard did. Henry John Heinz founded a company that produced such popular processed foods as ketchup, sauerkraut, and pickles, and the company began using its famous "57 varieties" slogan in 1896. Alphonse Biardot, a French chef who came to America in 1887, founded the Franco-American Company, which had initial success in marketing oxtail and green-turtle soups to gourmets. During the late nineteenth and early twentieth centuries, other food-processing companies had success with such cereal products as Quaker Oats, Grape-Nuts, Shredded Wheat, and Corn Flakes. The Campbell company's condensed soups became so popular that the firm was able to absorb the Franco-American Company as its subsidiary.

The rapid growth of the food industry was due to scientific and technological research that provided the means for making more kinds of convenience foods. Increasingly food processing moved from the home to large factories. For example, more commercial than homemade baked products were made during this time. Aunt Jemima pancake mix was very popular, as well as the gelatin dessert Jell-O and such canned meats as corned beef. The phenomenal growth of the food-processing industry did not come without problems. Foods contaminated with infectious agents for botulism and typhoid fever sometimes caused serious illnesses and even deaths, as did certain food additives. In his 1906 novel, *The Jungle*, Upton Sinclair attacked the unsanitary conditions of Chicago's meatpacking industry, but his criticisms helped to give the entire food industry a tainted reputation. As a consequence of these and other revelations, legislators passed the Pure Food and Drug Act of 1906, which created the Food and Drug Administration (FDA), one of whose purposes was to ensure the purity and safety of American foods.

The involvement of the federal government in the food-processing industry increased during World War I through such agencies as the Food Administration, headed by Herbert Hoover. He tried to increase the quantity and quality of food by encouraging companies and citizens to increase production and minimize waste. His agency also regulated the wheat-processing industry, for example, by limiting the amount of grain going into the production of alcoholic beverages.

WORLD WAR I THROUGH WORLD WAR II

The 1920's constituted a time of rapid technological innovation in food-processing businesses. For example, rendering, the process by which waste animal products are transformed into marketable materials, increased profits, and dry rendering, in which raw foods are cooked in steam-jacketed cylinders, gave high protein yields, thus increasing nutritional content. Improved canning techniques, especially short, rapid heating, preserved the fresh flavor of foods. Through his 168 patents, Clarence Birdseye perfected a process for freezing foods, which ultimately became the property of General Foods. As the food-processing businesses improved their mass-production methods, more and more families came to depend on their products. The food business grew in variety and complexity, as processors handled, transformed, and distributed gigantic amounts of the nation's food. The Great Depression adversely affected raw foods more than processed ones, and by 1940, more than two-thirds of all American food passed through some processing.

During World War II, the federal government converted many American industries, including food-processing companies, to a war status, so that people supporting and fighting the war would be well fed. The need for safe, transportable, easy-to-prepare rations for soldiers forced the industry to develop new techniques for manufacturing, preserving, and packaging various foodstuffs. Scientists had discovered the importance of balanced diets and vitamins, and the Food Administration used this information to pressure companies into formulating nutritious foods. Civilian shortages of meat, sugar, and canned goods characterized wartime, though such companies as Wrigley's and Coca-Cola managed to circumvent restrictions on sugar by convincing regulators that soldiers and sailors needed chewing gum and soda. The frozen-food industries also prospered because metal shortages led to limitations on the sales of canned goods. In general, the war was beneficial to the food-processing industry because the industry was able to develop many new products and improve its mass-production and distribution techniques.

Canning peas at a factory in Sun Prairie, Wisconsin, in 1937. (Library of Congress)

AFTER WORLD WAR II

The growth of the food-processing industry in the decades after World War II was part of what some scholars have called the "Consumer Revolution," in which food, like so much else in modern American life, was reengineered to maximize choice, speed, and convenience. The trend to transfer food production, processing, and preparation from the home to the factory intensified, so that, within the home, meals increasingly consisted of canned, instant, pre-cooked, ready-mixed foods, and outside the home, Americans flocked to such fast-food restaurant chains as McDonald's and Kentucky Fried Chicken (later KFC), in which foods such as hamburgers, French fries, and fried chicken were served, often with high-sugar sodas made by Coca-Cola and Pepsi. Some feared that the phenomenal growth of the fast-food business would lead to the decline of small ethnic restaurants, further "homogenizing" American life. Evidence certainly exists that the huge purchasing power of fast-food chains transformed how cattle are born, raised, fed, slaughtered, and processed.

During this time, many food manufacturers used increasingly sophisticated chemicals in their processing: emulsifiers gave foods a consistent texture, artificial flavors enhanced taste, retardants prolonged storage times, and vitamins raised nutritional value. Advertisers helped create the desire for new processed foods such as Minute Rice and Cool Whip, which was neither whipped nor cream but a nondairy synthetic. Supporters of the food industry insisted that because of these scientifically produced foods, Americans were "the best-fed people on Earth."

During the 1960's and succeeding decades, various activists, often associated with the environmental movement, raised serious questions about the healthfulness of an American diet increasingly dominated by processed foods. In 1970, Jim Turner, an advocate in Ralph Nader's group of lawyers, published *The Chemical Feast: Ralph Nader's Study Group Report on the Food and Drug Administration*, which was extremely critical of the American food industry and the FDA that was supposed to monitor it for the benefit of the public. The American food industry was also facing intense competition from such countries as China, Brazil, and Argentina. Nutritionists accused the food-processing industry of helping to create the "fattest nation on Earth," in which 60 percent of American adults were overweight and 30

percent were obese. These nutritionists encouraged consumers to eat natural foods and to avoid processed foods. To a certain extent, businesses responded by reformulating some of their products as reduced-fat, cholesterol-free, and sugarless.

At the start of the twenty-first century, the American food industry was one of the largest in the world, employing several million workers. This industry had grown and prospered because it provided consumers with the new and convenient foods they desired, even creating "fun foods" for young children. These companies had become masters of a supply network that stretched from large farms throughout the world via many food-processing factories to the American consumer. Ironically, the growing criticism of processed foods did not result in substantial increases in the use of fresh foods but to an increase in the variety of take-home foods, some of them labeled "organic" or "healthy." Whether health concerns can become an effective force in transforming the food industry remains to be seen. Market pressures will, as they have always done, play a pivotal role, but individual consumers often create these market forces, and an educated public can make food decisions that have the potential to create a healthier world.

Robert J. Paradowski

FURTHER READING

Connor, John, and William A. Schiek. *Food Processing: An Industrial Powerhouse in Transition*. 2d ed. New York: Wiley-Interscience, 1997. Better as a source of statistical information about the food-processing industry than a narrative treatment, this book centers on the research, development, and management of an often-overlooked American business. The many footnotes serve as a guide to much fascinating industrial data.

Levenstein, Harvey A. *Paradox of Plenty: A Social History of Eating in Modern America*. Rev. ed. Berkeley: University of California Press, 2003. This new edition of a work originally published by Oxford University Press in 1993 focuses on the interactions between American consumers and the businesses that supplied them with processed foods in the period from 1930 to the early twenty-first century. Illustrated, with notes and an index.

Nestle, Marion. *Food Politics: How the Food Industry Influences Nutrition and Health*. Rev. ed. Berkeley: University of California Press, 2007. This book has been called a major contribution to the understanding of the relationship between science and politics in an industry that is vital to all Americans. An appendix on "Issues in Nutrition and Nutrition Research," notes, and an index.

Roberts, Paul. *The End of Food.* Boston: Houghton Mifflin, 2008. Though his focus is on the global food economy, the author analyzes how the American food industry is part of a system of making, marketing, and moving what people eat, and this system is increasingly incompatible with the health of consumers. Notes, bibliography, and index.

Schlosser, Eric. *Fast Food Nation: The Dark Side of the All-American Meal.* Boston: Houghton Mifflin Company, 2001. The author argues that the fast-food industry has brought about the "homogenization" of American society and played an important role in "American cultural imperialism" around the world. Fifty-five pages of notes, bibliography, and index.

Turner, James S. *The Chemical Feast: Ralph Nader's Study Group Report on the Food and Drug Administration.* New York: Viking Press, 1970. Criticizes the FDA for sponsoring industrial food-processing and marketing practices that have harmed consumers. Notes and index.

SEE ALSO: Agribusiness; Agriculture, U.S. Department of; Beef industry; Cereal crops; Dairy industry; Food and Drug Administration; Meatpacking industry; Pork industry; Poultry industry; Sugar industry; United Food and Commercial Workers.

Food Stamp Plan

THE LAW: Legislation creating a federal government program designed to solve two economic problems by providing food for needy families and creating a market for surplus agricultural products during the Great Depression

DATE: 1939

SIGNIFICANCE: Because of widespread unemployment during the Great Depression, many families in the United States were unable to buy enough food. The Food Stamp Plan increased the purchasing power of these families and reduced the agricultural surplus, thereby stimulating the economy.

The Food Stamp Plan of 1939 began during the Great Depression under the administration of President Franklin D. Roosevelt. It was part of the New Deal program called the Federal Surplus Commodities Corporation and its first administrator was Milo Perkins. The federally funded program was operated by each state through the United States Department of Agriculture (USDA). The program issued orange and blue stamps that people could purchase. For each dollar of orange stamps purchased, a person would receive 50 cents worth of blue stamps. People could buy any type of food with the orange stamps but only food that the USDA deemed surplus with the blue stamps.

The Food Stamp Plan was meant both to ease hunger and to provide a market for surplus farm products. The plan was in operation for four years and helped millions of people at its peak. Because of other New Deal programs, which provided jobs for many Americans, and the United States' entrance into World War II, the Food Stamp Plan ended in the spring of 1943. However, the 1939 plan became the foundation for the later Food Stamp Program. Studies, reports, and proposed legislation for a new program followed the plan's end in 1943. A pilot program was initiated in 1961, under the administration of President John F. Kennedy. In this pilot program, food stamps were still purchased; however, surplus foods were no longer part of the program.

Melinda Swafford

FURTHER READING

DeLorme, Charles D., Jr., David R. Kamerschen, and David C. Redman. "The First U.S. Food Stamp Program: An Example of Rent Seeking and Avoiding." *American Journal of Economics and Sociology* 51, no. 4 (October, 1992): 421-433.

Landers, Patti S. "The Food Stamp Program: History, Education, and Impact." *Journal of the American Dietetic Association* 107, no. 11 (November, 2007): 1945-1952.

Poppendieck, Janet. *Breadlines Knee Deep in Wheat: Food Assistance in the Great Depression.* New Brunswick, N.J.: Rutgers University Press, 1986.

SEE ALSO: Agriculture; Agriculture, U.S. Department of; Farm subsidies; Government spending; Great Depression; New Deal programs.

Forbes

IDENTIFICATION: Business and financial magazine
DATE: Founded in September, 1917
SIGNIFICANCE: *Forbes* is one of the most influential business and financial magazines in the United States, known for its many lists, including its list of the world's richest people.

In large measure, the history of *Forbes* is the history of the magazine's founder, B. C. Forbes, and his famous family. A Scottish immigrant and prodigious business writer, Forbes attracted the attention of publishing giant William Randolph Hearst. Hearst thought that the very popular columnist would boost his newspaper sales, so he syndicated the writer's column in 1911 and paid Forbes a premium salary, equivalent to $185,000 in 1990 dollars.

In 1917, using his salary as a stake, Forbes started *Forbes*, a magazine designed to profile the "doers and doings" of American capitalism, giving prominent business leaders a human face. From its start, *Forbes* was a stalwart champion of capitalism. The magazine had virtually no rivals until the late 1920's, when *BusinessWeek* entered the scene. *BusinessWeek*, however, had a starkly different orientation from that of *Forbes*, which generally portrayed businessmen as heroes. Forbes thought it necessary to expand, and the magazine shifted from investment to industry stories.

After World War II, Forbes's eldest son, Malcolm S. Forbes, figured prominently in the management of the company. The younger Forbes was an innovator, and the company diversified. He began the *Forbes* Investor Advisory Institute, which was quite profitable. The magazine's circulation grew steadily, reaching 265,000 by 1957, with about $1 million in advertising. In 1964, the younger Forbes took the reins of the company after convincing family members to sell him their stakes in the company. He immediately began an aggressive advertisement campaign, promoting the magazine as "*Forbes*: Capitalist Tool." Circulation skyrocketed to 500,000 by the magazine's fiftieth anniversary in 1967. By 1976, the magazine could claim close to $20 million in advertising-generated revenues alone.

During the late 1970's, business publishing expanded, and *Forbes*'s competition grew fiercer. In 1979, *Inc.* magazine, targeted toward small-business owners, reached the stands. In 1978, *Forbes*'s great rival, *Fortune* magazine, known for its *Fortune* 500 list of America's biggest corporations, went from a monthly to a bimonthly. The *Fortune* 500 list was the center of industry speculation and gossip; Forbes envied the list's popularity. In 1982, he countered (despite numerous threats of lawsuits) with a compilation of the richest Americans, the *Forbes* 400. The "rich list" was enormously successful, although, critics claimed, of doubtful accuracy.

With the death of Malcolm S. Forbes in 1990, his son Steve Forbes (Malcolm Stevenson Forbes, Jr.) became editor-in-chief and created international editions of the magazine to keep abreast of the rapidly globalized marketplace. A Web site begun in 1996 bloomed into several other profitable Internet ventures thanks to Forbes's ever-novel marketing schemes. In 2006, the Forbes family sold a 40 percent stake in the company to Elevation Partners, which is believed to have paid between $250 million and $300 million. An Elevation manager is alleged to have quipped that his company was buying into a Web site with a magazine attached. *Forbes* magazine reached 900,000 subscribers in North America with an average age of forty-three and an average annual income of more than $88,000.

Edward W. Maine

FURTHER READING
Jones, Arthur, and Malcolm Forbes. *Peripatetic Millionaire*. New York: Harper & Row, 1977.
Winans, Christopher. *Malcolm Forbes: The Man Who Had Everything*. London: Peter Owen, 1991.

SEE ALSO: *Barron's*; Buffett, Warren; *The Economist*; *Fortune*; Internet; Magazine industry; Muckraking journalism; *Reader's Digest*; *The Wall Street Journal*.

Ford, Henry

IDENTIFICATION: First U.S. businessman to mass-produce and market automobiles
BORN: July 30, 1863; Springwells Township, Michigan
DIED: April 7, 1947; Dearborn, Michigan
SIGNIFICANCE: The methods Ford used to make and sell cars revolutionized American manufacturing and marketing. Consumer mobility provided by his cars and the increase of leisure time provided by his farm machinery helped create

suburban sprawl and spawned roadside eateries, motels, and other consumer-oriented enterprises.

Henry Ford's early life was spent on the family farm in Dearborn, Michigan. Ford became obsessed with machinery and ways to use it to improve people's lives. At the age of twenty-four, he married Clara Bryant, who became a major force in his business successes by acting as a sounding board and consultant, and the couple moved to Detroit to pursue his goals.

The bicycle had become extremely popular during the late nineteenth century. Ford was disappointed that his motorized bicycle was not the first and became determined to make the fastest and most streamlined gasoline-powered version. Ford's quadricycle, his first "automobile," hit the Detroit streets in 1896. Soon after, and with substantial backing, Ford started a car company that produced a domestic road model in 1903, and the successful Ford Motor Company was born. The Ford Model T, the most successful car in automotive history, was introduced to an enthralled public in 1908.

Henry Ford. (Library of Congress)

Intended to appeal to the masses rather than the wealthy, most Ford automobiles were sturdy, affordable, and of simple design. Ford created and produced cars for average people and provided the first nationally known installment payment plan to make cars even more affordable, while increasing his company's sales and name recognition.

Ford cars were soon in huge demand, which could be satisfied only by mass production and speedy delivery to dealers. To ensure that his company always had parts in stock, Ford bought raw materials, such as iron ore, copper, and sand (used to make glass for car windows), and made parts for assembling cars on-site. This practice obviated dependence on suppliers and made Ford Motor Company largely self-sufficient. Ford revolutionized industrial standards by perfecting integrated assembly-line production. Previously, a product was stationary while the factory worker moved around it attaching parts; in Ford's factories, the product moved along a line of workers who remained stationary. When the tedium of this practice caused a large workforce turnover, Ford raised worker income to a minimum of five dollars a day and lessened work hours from nine to eight—at the time, these were shockingly good wages and hours in American industry. As a result, the cost of living for all Detroit citizens increased dramatically; Ford assisted his employees by providing company stores stocked with excellent quality goods and foods at prices well below those of public stores. He also assisted his employees in acquiring good housing near his factories, facilitating the rise of Detroit suburbs.

In addition to cars, Ford also designed and built farm machinery and airplanes that were widely used by both private and military operations. Ford's personal and business style affected American business in the realms of workforce and labor policies and had a far-reaching impact on governmental regulation of industry.

Twyla R. Wells

FURTHER READING

Brinkley, Douglas. *Wheels for the World: Henry Ford, His Company, and a Century of Progress, 1903-2003.* New York: Penguin Books, 2004.

Ford, Henry. *My Life and Work.* 1922. Reprint. New York: Arno Press, 1973.

Marquis, Samuel S. *Henry Ford: An Interpretation.* Detroit, Mich.: Wayne State University Press, 2007.

SEE ALSO: Automation in factories; Automotive industry; Chrysler bailout of 1979; Ford Model T; Ford Motor Company; General Motors; Iacocca, Lee; Industrial Revolution, American.

Ford Model T

IDENTIFICATION: First automobile produced by the Ford Motor Company
DATE: Produced 1908-1927
SIGNIFICANCE: The Ford Model T was the first automobile to be manufactured on an assembly line. This innovation not only made it the most affordably priced automobile on the market at the time but also made it possible for more of the members of the middle class to purchase automobiles.

The Ford Motor Company unveiled the Ford Model T on October 1, 1908, at the Piquette Plant in Detroit, Michigan. The vehicle, also known as the Tin Lizzie or the Flivver, was designed by Henry Ford, Childe Harold Wills, Joseph A. Galamb, and Eugene Farkas. The assembly of the Model T during its first years of production was slow and costly, because like all other automobiles at the time, it was built by hand. Ford ingeniously applied the assembly-line technique to the building of the Model T, and by 1913, the company could build a Model T in one hour and thirty-three minutes. By 1927, the company could produce a completed car every twenty-four seconds.

Ford's use of mass production and of interchangeable automobile parts lowered the manufacturing costs of building a car and reduced the price at which a car could be sold. In 1908, the Model T sold for $850, but by the 1920's, the car was sold for less than $300. The Model T became the most popular vehicle of its time and was produced until May 26, 1927. The engine continued to be manufactured until August 4, 1941. Ford's use of the assembly line in the production of the Model T—often called the "universal car"—not only revolutionized the manufacturing industry but also transformed the economic and social framework of the American middle class by allowing more Americans to own a car.

Bernadette Zbicki Heiney

FURTHER READING
Brinkley, Douglas G. *Wheels for the World: Henry Ford, His Company, and a Century of Progress.* New York: Penguin Books, 2004.
Hooker, Clarence. *Life in the Shadows of the Crystal Palace, 1910-1927: Ford Workers in the Model T Era.* Bowling Green, Ohio: Bowling Green University Popular Press, 1997.
Lacey, Robert. *Ford: The Men and the Machines.* Boston: Little, Brown, 1986.

SEE ALSO: Automation in factories; Automotive industry; Ford, Henry; Ford Motor Company.

Ford Motor Company

IDENTIFICATION: Major U.S. automobile manufacturer
DATE: Founded on June 17, 1903
SIGNIFICANCE: The first successful mass-production automaker, Ford Motor Company introduced a number of manufacturing and sales techniques that revolutionized production and sales of automobiles worldwide.

When Henry Ford and a group of investors incorporated the Ford Motor Company in 1903, they began a transportation revolution. An automobile enthusiast who began building prototypes in 1896, Ford had grandiose plans for the company. His vision was to build cars that would be inexpensive but reliable and easy to maintain, allowing him to build a large and loyal customer base. To promote sales, Ford created a system for franchising dealerships. The introduction of the inexpensive Model T in 1908 launched Ford into the top position among car manufacturers, a ranking it held for more than two decades. By the time production of the Model T ended in 1927, Ford had sold 15 million of the cars. Ford began producing trucks in 1908 and quickly became a national leader in that market as well. In 1919, Ford bought out the other investors, making the company a truly family-owned business.

Perhaps Ford's most important innovation was the establishment of the moving assembly line in 1913, improving efficiency and increasing worker productivity. Ford was also the first international automobile company, establishing a plant in Canada in 1904 and in various European cities within a decade. The company revolutionized labor practices by increasing wages, introducing the eight-hour workday and five-day workweek. During the Great Depression, however, Ford instituted harsh business practices, and the company resisted unionization of its workforce until 1941. During World War II, the company transferred much of its production capacity to manufacturing Jeeps and aircraft, but after hostilities ceased, it returned to full-scale automaking.

In the three decades following the war, Ford was comfortably situated among America's Big Three automakers, ranking second to General Motors and ahead of Chrysler. Over the years, Ford diversified its offerings by creating the Mercury line of mid-priced vehicles and purchasing or gaining controlling interest in other companies, including Lincoln, Opel, Mazda, Volvo, Land Rover, and Jaguar. Over the last quarter of the twentieth century, however, Ford has had mixed success in attracting buyers to new brands, scoring a hit with its Thunderbird in 1954 and Mustang in 1964 but failing with the Edsel in 1958. As the price of gasoline began to rise steadily during the 1970's and more Americans began purchasing Japanese and European cars, largely because they obtained better gas mileage, Ford began to lose market share. Ford introduced the very popular Taurus in 1985, but during the 1990's, it decided to capitalize on popularity of sport utility vehicles (SUVs) among American consumers. This, however, led to financial difficulties when customers began turning away from these vehicles after 2001. Consequently, Ford was forced to undergo a radical restructuring that included sell-offs of some brands and drastic reductions in the workforce. Although Ford joined Chrysler and General Motors in appealing to the federal government for financial help in October, 2008, its efforts at restructuring meant that it was in better financial shape than the other two automakers and was not expected to use any of the $17.4 billion in emergency loans that President George W. Bush made

A woman boards a Ford sedan in about 1923. (Library of Congress)

available to the Big Three in return for major concessions on December 19.

Laurence W. Mazzeno

FURTHER READING

Brinkley, Douglas. *Wheels for the World: Henry Ford, His Company, and a Century of Progress, 1903-2003.* New York: Viking, 2003.

Magee, David. *Ford Tough: Bill Ford and the Battle to Rebuild America's Automaker.* Hoboken, N.J.: John Wiley & Sons, 2005.

Marquis, Samuel S. *Henry Ford: An Interpretation.* Detroit, Mich.: Wayne State University Press, 2007.

SEE ALSO: Automotive industry; Chrysler bailout of 1979; Ford, Henry; Ford Model T; General Motors; Labor history.

Forestry industry

DEFINITION: Companies involved in timber production, forestry economics and marketing, firefighting, and pest control; companies that operate timber tracts or tree farms; forest nurseries; and companies that gather forest products such as gums, barks, seeds, mushrooms, and plants

SIGNIFICANCE: The forestry industry in the United States dates back to the colonial era and remains integral to the economy. An abundance of wood aided in the rapid expansion of the United States. Wood was used to build everything from homes and factories to ships and wagons, and it also supplied chemicals such as tannin, potash, and lye for use in industry. In the twenty-first century, forest products are used primarily in the production of lumber, paper, and many plastics and chemicals.

The first forest products that American colonists shipped to Europe were masts for ships cut from New England pines and potash manufactured by burning hardwoods in the coastal mid-Atlantic region. From its earliest days, the American forestry industry has included more than simply wood for building. For example, tanneries used hemlock bark for processing leather, and wood ashes were leached to produce lye, a chemical necessary for making soap and for other industrial applications.

HISTORICAL BACKGROUND

During the seventeenth and eighteenth centuries, foresters marked trees in North American forests to show that they were reserved for use by the British crown, although colonists often ignored the marks as settlements grew and land was cleared for farming. The timber resources of the North American continent appeared so vast that colonial governors quickly abandoned efforts to impose timber-cutting laws in the colonies similar to the regulations enforced in Europe. The early forestry industry was fragmented, with wood harvesting done on a small scale. Settlers clearing land for farming would sell timber to local sawmills or to wood yards, where people could purchase fuel for fireplaces. Potash was produced on individual farms, and brokers would travel the countryside collecting it. As the country grew, however, the forest product industries increased in size and emerged as distinct full-time business enterprises rather than one of many part-time activities undertaken on farms and plantations.

Even as lumbering operations grew in size, however, until the mid-nineteenth century the forestry industry functioned as it had for millennia: Trees were felled by axmen or sawyers and the timber was moved by brute force. Railroad ties, for example, were squared by tie hackers using adzes to cut each tie to length and shape before the ties left the woods for market. The ties were then hand loaded onto

sledges or wagons for transport. Although subtle differences in logging practices existed from region to region, sometimes dictated by the local topography or species of timber being harvested and sometimes by personal preference, generally forestry workers could travel from Maine to Louisiana, from the Carolinas to the Pacific Northwest, and not be surprised by the equipment being used. No matter where the logger was employed, in-woods equipment used for felling consisted of axes, crosscut saws, and bucksaws, and the work was organized similarly regardless of whether the timber being felled was located in Pennsylvania or California.

In the heyday of white pine logging in Michigan, for example, the operations involved in cutting and moving one log might involve a dozen different men. A two-man crosscut saw team felled the tree, then it was limbed and cut to saw-log lengths by the bucking crew. Other men using logging tongs or a two-man come-along would move it to a point where a chain could be attached, then a teamster with a horse would skid the log to a temporary landing in the woods. From that landing, logs would be hauled out to a larger landing to await final transport to the mill. A small two- to four-man crew piled the logs at the landing. This crew consisted of two men who attached and detached the cabling or chains to the logs and directed the guide cables, and the operator who controlled the winch. The winch was variously powered by horses, steam engines (donkey engines), or gasoline engines, depending on the time period and the resources of the company doing the logging. The larger firms, such as Diamond Match Company or Weyerhauser, were more likely to invest in power equipment than the small, independent contractors. If the winch was horse-powered, the crew also included a teamster.

In any region of the country, topography and the type of timber harvested could affect the size of the logging crew involved in harvesting each stem. In the smaller timber of the South and the pulpwood forests of Canada, instead of a two-man crosscut saw team, individual sawyers armed with bow saws felled trees, while the large timber of the Pacific Northwest required additional workers who would prepare the path where the tree would fall. High-lead and skyline cable logging systems and logging that use river drives called for workers with additional and different skills. Not every logger wanted to—or could be—a drover. Before the development of railroad logging, in northern climates much of the lumbering took place during the winter months, when snow and ice made it easier to drag logs out of the woods to a landing on a riverbank. When the snow melted, the logs would be floated downstream to the mills.

Nineteenth Century Innovations

Following the U.S. Civil War, several innovations emerged that, when combined, sped up the pace of production and encouraged the emergence of large forest product companies, many of which survive into the twenty-first century, such as Weyerhauser. Raker teeth on crosscut saws, big wheels, steam-powered donkey engines, railroad logging, and cable yarding systems were all developed during the 1870's. All five innovations corresponded with the boom years of the lumber industry. The big wheel and high-lead cable skidding were both based on the desire to make logs easier to move by lifting the leading ends off the ground and eliminating the need to wait to log in the winter, when snow and ice could be used for skidways. High-lead cable systems made logging possible on the rugged mountain slopes of the Pacific Northwest. The raker tooth cleared sawdust from the cut and dramatically reduced sawing time per tree, and donkey engines replaced horses and oxen to provide skidding and loading power that never became fatigued. The first recorded use of a donkey engine occurred when John Dolbeer of the Dolbeer and Carson Lumber Company of Eureka, California, began snaking logs out of the redwoods along Salmon Creek in August, 1881.

The Lake George and Muskegon River Railroad established in October, 1876, was the first successful logging railroad in the United States. Railroad logging freed the forestry industry from the geographical limitations of river drives, although loggers could be quite ingenious in using extremely small streams of water to transport timber during the spring run-off in areas where no railroads yet existed. Indeed, the forestry industry succeeded in cutting vast reaches of Maine, Pennsylvania, Michigan, Wisconsin, Minnesota, and other states before any rails were ever laid in those regions. Where no natural bodies of water existed, loggers would construct flumes and canals, and when water was particularly scarce, as in the mountains of Wyoming and Montana, or the wood unsuitable for floating (for example, the redwoods of California), greased skidways.

More significant than removing seasonal restrictions, railroads removed species limitations in the lake states and elsewhere. Many varieties of wood were not sufficiently buoyant to be transported by river drives. Before railroad logging, these trees were viewed as unusable by lumbermen. Almost all green wood will not float, and even when dry, many hardwoods are too dense for water transport. Therefore, in many frontier areas, mixed stands of hardwoods had been considered commercially useless.

The growth of large lumber companies operating multiple camps and employing hundreds of men paralleled the growth of railroad logging. Equipment developed for use with railroad logging, such as the Barnhart and McGiffert loaders, was large, steam powered, and capital-intensive. Large volumes of wood had to harvested and processed to make railroad logging operations profitable. Lumbermen who were able to continually expand their business and take advantage of the economies of scale that railroad logging represented, including Frederick Weyerhauser, thrived during the late nineteenth century. From primitive temporary clusters of shacks in the woods, Weyerhauser logging camps evolved into stable company towns, such as Shelton, Washington, set up to efficiently process, from the stump right through the mill, large amounts of timber.

Weyerhauser was also one of the first in the forestry industry to recognize the need to practice sustainable forestry. Rather than doing what had been common practice—harvesting large tracts of land and then moving on—Weyerhauser pioneered tree farming. As the supplies of old-growth, untouched forest dwindled, other companies followed Weyerhauser's lead. By the mid-twentieth century it was common practice for the major forest product companies, such as Georgia-Pacific, Union Camp, Mead, and others, to manage plantation forests covering many thousands of acres. As mature trees are harvested, young trees are planted to replace them.

An Industry in Transition

The era of railroad logging was short-lived. Highly capital intense, railroad logging needed large harvests to be profitable, and by the 1930's those large harvests were gone. Except for the Pacific Northwest region, the thick stands of old-growth timber no longer existed. Also, along with the disappearance of the unlimited supply of timber, the demand for wood had changed. Other

A CLOSER LOOK AT TIMBER-BASED MANUFACTURING IN THE UNITED STATES

Type of Manufacturer	Number of Establishments	Value of Shipments ($ billions)
Millwork maker	4,725	22.6
Paper bag or coated and treated paper maker	929	18.2
Paper mill	327	45.2
Paperboard container maker	2,669	43.5
Paperboard mill	203	21.2
Pulp mill	31	3.7
Sawmill	3,805	21.4
Stationery product maker	636	8.0
Veneer, plywood, or engineered wood product maker	1,925	20.2
Wood container or pallet maker	2,948	5.1

Source: Data from U.S. Census Bureau, 2002 Economic Census, *Manufacturing, General Summary* (Washington, D.C.: Author, 2005)

building materials, such as brick and concrete, had supplanted pine and spruce in new construction. In urban areas, the wooden buildings of the nineteenth century were replaced by the brownstones and skyscrapers of the twentieth century. The demand for lumber peaked in 1910 and steadily declined for the next forty years.

The decline in the demand for saw timber was counterbalanced by a steadily increasing demand for pulpwood and chemical wood, but the species utilized for pulpwood as well as the size of the trees harvested often differed from those used for saw timber. Processes for manufacturing paper from wood pulp came into wide use during the late nineteenth century, and the papermaking industry grew rapidly. Trees too small to be cut for lumber could be used for making paper or for chemical wood for the growing plastics industry, which in turn meant harvesting previously cut-over regions could be profitable. However, while railroad logging to clear-cut thousands of acres of virgin white pine for lumber made economic sense, railroad logging to harvest much smaller stands of second-growth forest did not.

At the same time, improvements in the internal combustion engine brought trucks and tractors to the woods. By the 1930's power chain saws were being introduced. The forestry industry became increasingly mechanized as hydraulic loaders, skidders, and other equipment eliminated the need for hand labor. The process was gradual, but by the end of the twentieth century much of the work that one hundred years earlier was done by workers on the ground, from felling trees to loading them for transport to a mill, was now accomplished by a machine with an operator sitting safely in a climate-controlled cab.

As the forestry industry entered the twenty-first century, it remained an integral part of the U.S. economy. The demand for wood products, both in their most natural forms and for use in producing paper and synthetic materials like rayon, continued to grow. Sustainable forestry practices will ensure the industry continues to meet consumer needs well into the future.

Nancy Farm Mannikko

FURTHER READING

Brown, Nelson Courtland. *Forest Products: The Harvesting, Processing, and Marketing of Materials Other than Lumber.* New York: John Wiley & Sons, 1950. A good discussion of the various uses for wood in plastics, paper, and other applications.

Clary, David. *Timber and the Forest Service.* Lawrence: University of Kansas Press, 1986. An engaging, highly readable history of the U.S. Forest Service that includes an explanation of why it sometimes seems to pursuing conflicting goals.

Connor, Mary Roddis. *A Century with Connor Lumber:*

Connor Forest Industries, 1872-1972. Stevens Point, Wis.: Worzalla, 1972. An interesting account of one particular lumber company with a long history in the upper Midwest.

Hickman, Nollie W. *Mississippi Harvest.* Montgomery, Ala.: Paragon Press, 1962. A fascinating look at the forestry industry in an often overlooked region of the country, the southern pine forest.

McEvoy, Thomas J., and James Jeffords. *A Sustainable Approach to Managing Woodlands.* Washington, D.C.: Island Press, 2004. A contemporary discussion of sustainable forestry.

Williams, Michael. *Americans and Their Forests: A Historical Geography.* New York: Cambridge University Press, 1992. An excellent overview of the United States and forests that while remarkably thorough is nonetheless accessible to the general reader.

SEE ALSO: Agribusiness; Agriculture; Colonial economic systems; Construction industry; Papermaking industry; Woodworking industry.

Forgery. *See* Identity theft

Fort Knox

IDENTIFICATION: Federal gold bullion depository

DATE: Founded in December, 1936

SIGNIFICANCE: Although four other sites also store the nation's gold bullion holdings, the federal depository at Fort Knox, Kentucky, has served as the primary U.S. gold safeguarding facility since the first years of the New Deal, with assets during the early twenty-first century estimated at 147.3 million ounces of gold valued at more than $123 billion.

In 1933, the new administration of President Franklin D. Roosevelt, along with the Democratic Congress, acted to stabilize a national economy reeling from the Wall Street collapse four years earlier. The president and legislature reoriented the United States' monetary policy, abolishing the gold standard. Although gold had been freely circulated in the American economic system since the nation's beginnings, since 1900 it had been established as the nation's standard unit of currency. In a series of controversial congressional acts that culminated in January, 1934, the federal government embargoed gold shipments coming into the United States, recalled all circulating gold in the country, and then removed gold coinage as the standard currency for covering federal debts. Further, the government instructed banks to turn in their gold holdings and ultimately made it a federal offense for private citizens, except jewelers and metal merchants, to own or hold gold.

Despite conservative outcry against these actions, the federal government had by the mid-1930's accumulated a considerable hoard of gold bullion and coin. In 1936, the Treasury Department authorized construction of a massive, two-story underground vault near Fort Knox, in north central Kentucky, which had been an U.S. Army post since the American Civil War. The facility, which cost a Depression-era federal government the equivalent of $7 million, incorporated unprecedented security

A view of Fort Knox from outside its gated entrance in 1939. (Library of Congress)

measures, including more than sixteen thousand cubic feet of granite, four thousand cubic yards of concrete, and fourteen hundred tons of reinforced steel (the blast-proof vault door alone weighed more than twenty tons). The main vault itself was 105 feet by 121 feet, with a 42-foot ceiling—the gold bars inside were to be arranged unwrapped on pallets. The facility opened with little fanfare in December, 1936, and transportation of the nation's gold holdings to the vault was completed by rail within a year.

Fort Knox, rumored to hold more than five thousand tons of gold (only the Federal Reserve in Manhattan holds more), is not open to the public. It is considered the most secure facility within the federal government. In addition to being located on a federal Army post and permanently guarded by a carefully screened detachment of the United States Mint police, the facility is ringed by numerous security fences and monitored by video. The vault is accessible only through a series of secured doors, and the combinations to the principal vault require a number of depository staff members to key. The technology protecting the holdings is updated annually. Fort Knox is a hallmark for fortification and as such has been the subject of numerous fictional and cinematic theft attempts. Despite persistent rumors that the government long ago moved the gold holdings to less well-known facilities overseas, the Fort Knox reserve continues to serve as the principal reservoir of the nation's gold holdings.

Joseph Dewey

FURTHER READING

Bayoumi, Tamim, et al. *Modern Perspectives on the Gold Standard.* New York: Cambridge University Press, 2008.

Eichengreen, Barry. *Golden Fetters: The United States and the Great Depression.* Oxford, England: Oxford University Press, 1996.

Hamby, Alonzo. *For the Survival of Democracy: Franklin Roosevelt and the World Crisis of the 1930's.* New York: Free Press, 2004.

SEE ALSO: *Coin's Financial School;* "Cross of Gold" speech; Currency; Gold standard; Great Depression; Mint, U.S.; Treasury, U.S. Department of the.

Fortune

IDENTIFICATION: Financial newsmagazine
DATE: Launched in February, 1930
SIGNIFICANCE: *Fortune* was the first true American financial magazine. Although the existing trade periodicals of the 1930's were black-and-white compilations of statistics and facts, *Fortune* offered artistic covers, beautiful photographs, compelling advertisements, and literary articles with economic, political, and social analyses. *Fortune* became a global business brand, with significant franchises, worldwide readership in the millions, and an online presence.

In February, 1930, only four months after the stock market crash of October, 1929, America's first real business magazine appeared. *Fortune*'s founder was the legendary publisher Henry Luce, who had founded *Time* magazine in 1923 and would introduce *Life* magazine in 1936.

Fortune embodied Luce's bold new idea of business journalism. This stylish, upscale magazine was eleven inches by fourteen inches in size and featured art, culture, and literature, along with financial and economic news. Instead of hiring economists, Luce recruited talented writers such as John Kenneth Galbraith, Archibald MacLeish, Alfred Kazin, and James Agee. As a result, articles were often provocative and critical. Topics included munitions factories, the U.S.S.R, Herbert Hoover, farm life, and social issues.

Another innovation was the use of photography to document industrialization and business. *Fortune*'s first photographer was Margaret Bourke-White, a pioneer photojournalist who became famous for her poignant photos of the Great Depression. Renowned photographer Walker Evans, known for his images of the poor and everyday life, was an editor from 1945 until 1965.

A fervent believer in the potential of industrial design for the manufacturing industry, Luce conceived of covers with beautiful, original designs, unrelated to the contents inside. Cover artists included Herbert Bayer, Lester Beal, Fernand Leger, Diego Rivera, Ben Shahn, Charles Sheeler, and Gyorgy Kepes. However, in 1950, Luce redefined *Fortune* as a professional magazine with the mission of helping develop American business, and the art covers were discontinued.

Fortune developed into one of most influential business magazines. The first issue had 30,000 subscribers. By the mid-1930's, with more than 450,000 subscribers, *Fortune* was making a profit of about $500,000. *Fortune* also developed significant business lists. First published in 1955, the *Fortune* 500 is an annual comprehensive list of the five hundred largest U.S. corporations, ranked by revenues, profits, assets, stockholders' equity, market value, profits as a percentage of revenues, earnings per share, and total return to investors. Global 500 ranks the world's largest companies. The magazine's other lists include One Hundred Best Companies to Work For, One Hundred Fastest-Growing Companies, and the Fifty Most Powerful Women in Business.

By the early twenty-first century, *Fortune* had a readership of almost 5 million, with editions in Asia and Europe. It had also established online leadership as part of CNN.Money.com.

Alice Myers

FURTHER READING

Augspurger, Michael. *An Economy of Abundant Beauty: "Fortune" Magazine and Depression America.* New York: Cornell University Press, 2004.

Okrent, Daniel. *"Fortune": The Art of Covering Business.* Salt Lake City, Utah: Gibbs Smith, 1999.

Swanberg, W. A. *Luce and His Empire.* New York: Scribner, 1972.

SEE ALSO: *Barron's*; Bloomberg's Business News Services; *The Economist*; *Forbes*; Magazine industry; Muckraking journalism; *Reader's Digest*; Stock market crash of 1929.

401(k) retirement plans

DEFINITION: Accounts that take advantage of a provision of the U.S. tax code that allows private-sector employees to make pretax contributions to employer-sponsored retirement plans

SIGNIFICANCE: Most businesses with pension plans have replaced traditional defined-benefit plans with 401(k) retirement plans, or what are classified as defined-contribution pension plans. They have thus become the primary method whereby private-sector employees save for retirement.

Section 401(k) of the U.S. Internal Revenue Code was created by the Revenue Act of 1978. The law went into effect on January 1, 1980, and after the Internal Revenue Service (IRS) issued formal rules regarding 401(k) retirement plans in November, 1981, these plans quickly became the fastest growing type of employer-sponsored retirement plans. By the year 2000, more than 50 percent of private-sector employees with employer-sponsored retirement plans had 401(k) plans.

Section 401(k) of the tax code outlines a method for private-sector employees to save for retirement. It allows for employees to contribute a portion of their income into investment options available from an employer-sponsored plan. In addition to the employee's contribution, many employers also make contributions of cash or company stock. As long as the employee remains in the plan, these contributions, and the subsequent investment gains, are not subject to income tax. Taxes are paid when the funds are withdrawn during retirement years. To discourage the withdrawal of funds before retirement, amounts withdrawn before the employee reaches the age of $59\frac{1}{2}$ are subject to a 10 percent penalty in addition to the payment of income tax. There are, however, provisions that allow individuals to borrow money from their plans before retirement or to withdraw specific amounts to pay for the purchase of a first home.

The rapid growth of 401(k) plans is attributable to features of the plans that appeal to both employees and employers. Not only do contributions to these plans reduce taxes during working years, but 401(k) plans also are portable, which means that employees can roll the money into another employer's 401(k) plan or an individual retirement account (IRA) if they move from one job to another before retirement. A benefit to employers is the ability to offer employees a retirement plan that avoids the risks employers face with a traditional pension plan. The risks associated with investment losses are borne by employees under 401(k) plans.

Unlike traditional pension plans, which provide a fixed income to retired employees, 401(k) plans offer no guarantee regarding the amount of retirement income, which may fluctuate along with financial markets. Thus, although these plans offer a means to retain retirement savings for job changers, they can make retirement planning more challenging for employees. The attraction for employers in shifting the risks associated with traditional retirement plans to employees and the appeal of portability for employees have caused 401(k) retirement plans to supplant traditional retirement plans for a majority of private-sector employers.

Randall Hannum

FURTHER READING

Munnell, Alica H., and Annika Sundén. *Coming Up Short: The Challenge of 401(k) Plans.* Washington, D.C.: Brookings Institution Press, 2004.

Wise, David A., ed. *Perspectives on the Economics of Aging.* Chicago: University of Chicago Press, 2004.

Wolman, William, and Anne Colamosca. *The Great 401(k) Hoax.* Cambridge, Mass.: Perseus Books, 2002.

SEE ALSO: Bond industry; Funeral industry; Mutual fund industry; Pension and retirement plans; Social Security system; Stock markets; Taxation.

Benjamin Franklin. (Library of Congress)

Franchising. *See* Retail trade industry

Franklin, Benjamin

IDENTIFICATION: Printer, statesman, scientist, and entrepreneur
BORN: January 17, 1706; Boston, Massachusetts
DIED: April 17, 1790; Philadelphia, Pennsylvania
SIGNIFICANCE: Before becoming one of America's Founders, a scientist, and a statesman, Franklin was one of America's first entrepreneurs. Business practices he developed have continued to be successful tools almost three hundred years later.

Benjamin Franklin was a self-educated, self-made man. As a young boy, he worked as an apprentice in his brother's printing shop in Boston. It was during these early years that he developed one of his most important, yet simplest, principles: The path to wealth is through hard work and frugal living. After a falling-out with his brother, Franklin ran away to Philadelphia, where he was hired in another print shop. He continued to work hard and live simply, eventually opening his own store in 1729.

Always interested in improving himself and helping others, Franklin organized a club of young tradesmen like himself. Known as the Junto, members met to discuss current events and share business ideas and opportunities. The Junto provided mutual self-improvement and is considered to be the first example of networking.

During his years in business, Franklin developed many successful strategies involving values such as integrity, honesty, and a having good reputation. He demonstrated these values in his everyday actions, often working late into the night when necessary to make sure that orders were filled on time. One important strategy was the concept of using rewards to motivate an employee's performance. He showed in his own rise to success that hard work was rewarded with wealth.

Franklin understood that being a good business manager meant being able to manage himself first. "The Art of Virtue" was a list he created, consisting of thirteen personal traits he felt he needed to work on to make him a better person. He shared this list with his friends, and it became one of his most popular publications. It is often considered the first self-improvement program. Although he never quite achieved perfection in all of the traits he sought to improve, Franklin found that the effort of trying greatly enhanced his life.

As his business grew, Franklin recognized that to continue to be successful, he needed to diversify. He created his own media empire by purchasing a newspaper and a stationer's shop and publishing *Poor Richard's Almanck* (1732-1758). He also drafted a profit-sharing contract in which he furnished start-up funds for his employees to open their own businesses. In return he received a percentage of the profits, thereby creating the franchising concept.

Franklin believed it was the duty of any successful businessman to give back to the community. After retiring at the age of forty-two, he used his talents and connections to help build the first American hospital, establish the University of Pennsylvania, and help young entrepreneurs start their own businesses. Franklin's business practices were so sound and valuable that they have been adopted by such notable figures as Henry Ford, Andrew Carnegie, and Thomas Mellon.

Maryanne Barsotti

FURTHER READING

Issacson, Walter. *Benjamin Franklin: An American Life.* New York: Simon & Schuster, 2003.

McCormick, Blaine. *Ben Franklin: America's Original Entrepreneur—Franklin's Autobiography Adapted for Modern Business.* Irvine, Calif.: Entrepreneur Press, 2005.

_____. *Ben Franklin's Twelve Rules of Management.* Irvine, Calif.: Entrepreneur Press, 2000.

SEE ALSO: Catalog shopping; Daylight saving time; How-to-succeed books; Literary works with business themes; Management theory; Newspaper industry; Postal Service, U.S.; Printing industry; Revolutionary War.

French and Indian War

THE EVENT: Conflict between Great Britain and France over colonial control of much of North America

DATE: 1754-1763

PLACE: Northeastern North America (now in the United States and Quebec)

SIGNIFICANCE: The British victory in the French and Indian War led to greater economic opportunities for Great Britain's North American colonies, but it ironically also helped the nation's thirteen American colonies eventually to become independent. It also facilitated the ability of the American colonists to trade.

The French and Indian War was the North American portion of a larger war between Great Britain and France. The larger war, known as the Seven Years' War, was fought in Europe as well as North America. Britain's North American forces were supported by troops from the thirteen colonies and Nova Scotia, while the French were aided by troops from New France, which included Quebec, Louisiana, the Ohio River Valley, and some Atlantic islands. Various Native American tribes also participated in the fighting, with some supporting the British and others aiding the French.

The French and Indian War broke out over a long-standing dispute concerning territory west of the Appalachian Mountains. As the thirteen British colonies increased in population, they started to expand into the Appalachian region in a search for more land and trade, particularly in the Ohio River Valley. The colonists had the support of the British government, which argued that this uncharted territory should be open to them as well as to the French. By the mid-1750's, however, France stationed soldiers in the area.

The fighting began in 1754, when George Washington attacked French forces at Fort Duquesne, which had previously belonged to Great Britain. Neither side issued a formal declaration of war, however, until 1756. France had the advantage for the first half of the war. The momentum in the war shifted toward Great Britain in 1758. The most important battle of the war occurred in September, 1959, when British forces won on the Plains of Abraham in what became modern-day Quebec City. On February 10, 1763, France and Great Britain, among other belligerents, signed the Treaty of Paris. As a result, Great Britain acquired Quebec, Cape Breton, and all other French territory east of the Mississippi River, thus making the British the only European power on the Atlantic coast of North America.

Ironically, the relationship between the thirteen colonies and Great Britain began to deteriorate soon after the war. The colonists did not want to bear any of the financial burden for the war or for maintaining a British troop presence, especially when they believed these soldiers were preventing them from moving west. These issues contributed to the eventual decision of the colonies to seek independence and the creation of the United States.

Kevin L. Brennan

FURTHER READING

Dale, Ronald J. *The Fall of New France: How the French Lost a North American Empire, 1754-1763*. Halifax, N.S.: James Lorimer, 2004.

Marston, Daniel. *The French-Indian War, 1754-1760*. Oxford, England: Osprey, 2002.

Schwartz, Seymour I. *The French and Indian War, 1754-1763: The Imperial Struggle for North America*. Edison, N.J.: Book Sales, 1999.

SEE ALSO: Boston Tea Party; Canadian trade with the United States; Fur trapping and trading; Parliamentary Charter of 1763; Revolutionary War; Wars.

FTC. *See* Federal Trade Commission

Fuller Brush Company

IDENTIFICATION: Home products manufacturer and distributor

DATE: Founded on January 1, 1906

SIGNIFICANCE: The Fuller Brush Company produced its own high-quality goods for sale, based on what the users needed, raising the level of door-to-door sales of household, cleaning, and personal products.

Like many revolutionary movements in American entrepreneurial history, the Fuller Brush Company began with a remarkably simple premise: Design a quality product that will last. In 1903, twenty-one-year-old Alfred C. Fuller left the fruit farms of Welsford, Nova Scotia, where he had grown up, to try his hand at sales in the lucrative markets of the Boston area. Fuller began by selling cleaning brushes door-to-door at a time when such a sales technique lacked industry respect. He soon conceived of a radical new approach: To improve the quality of the brushes by designing them to accommodate the specific needs of their users, based on anecdotal data gathered from the housewives along his routes.

When his employer saw little promise in such an endeavor, Fuller struck out on his own. He took orders by day and by night, in his sister's basement, actually made the high-quality brushes (including new designs for spittoon cleaners, baby brushes, and long-handled dusters for furniture and fixtures). Response was immediate. Within three years, Fuller had expanded his operation to nearly three hundred sales representatives nationwide. To meet orders, he opened a major manufacturing plant in East Hartford, Connecticut, and within a decade, the Fuller Brush Company was a national enterprise. By 1923, it was a $15 million business.

The Fuller Brush man, a trusted and personable representative toting a suitcase stocked with samples of quality home care products, became an icon of American business. During the heyday of the Fuller Brush Company from 1930 to 1950, its sales representatives were regularly featured in cartoons, comic strips, films, and eventually television. During the Great Depression, when jobs were scarce, many people saw selling with the Fuller Brush Company as a way to succeed. The company, even as it continually expanded its line of products, pioneered innovative door-to-door sales techniques. Because Fuller's sales force did not draw a salary but rather were paid by commission, they were encouraged to develop a strong work ethic and effective sales pitch.

In 1973, the year Fuller died, the company moved its production operations from Connecticut to a twelve-acre facility in Barton County, Kansas. The Fuller Brush Company still uses direct sales through its distributors, but has added catalog and Internet sales. More than a century after its modest start, the company maintains its commitment to developing a wide variety of durable domestic products and catering directly to consumers.

Joseph Dewey

FURTHER READING

Boyer, Kenneth Karel, Markham T. Frolich, and G. Thomas M. Aukt. *Extending the Supply Chain: How Cutting-Edge Companies Bridge the Critical Last Mile into Customer's Homes.* New York: AMACOM, 2004.

Friedman, Walter A. *Birth of a Salesman: The Transformation of Selling in America.* Cambridge, Mass.: Harvard University Press, 2005.

Spence, Hartzell, with Alfred Fuller. *A Foot in the Door: A Life Appraisal of the Original Fuller Brush Man.* New York: McGraw, 1960.

SEE ALSO: Catalog shopping; Great Depression; Home Shopping Network; Retail trade industry; Tupperware.

Funeral industry

DEFINITION: Enterprises that prepare bodies for burial or cremation and that provide ceremonial and related services to plan and facilitate memorial rituals

SIGNIFICANCE: Death is, in the aggregate, predictable and universal—not disposed to revolutionary trends and practices. However, the funeral industry in the United States experienced significant changes during the U.S. Civil War and during the 1960's after an exposé on the industry was published. Changing attitudes toward funerals may produce changes as the baby boomers face death.

Christian rites and European customs prevailed in nineteenth century Canada and the United States. Death rites were observed lovingly in the home, and the body was consigned to a local cemetery. However, the U.S. Civil War produced alarming numbers of corpses, many of which could not be identified, and many soldiers died far from their hometowns and families. Embalming techniques were available but uncommon, and carpenters could not produce enough coffins after battles. The ideal of a "good death" was threatened.

AN INDUSTRY BEGINS

Thomas Holmes, a former New York coroner's assistant, recognized the increased demand for corpses to be preserved and shipped long distances so that they could receive a "decent burial" at home. (The railroads were reluctant to ship coffins holding unpreserved corpses because of the resultant odors and leaking fluids.) Recognizing the commercial potential of embalming, Holmes developed a better chemical embalmer, resigned his Army commission, and offered his services to the bereaved for $100.

Embalming fell into relative disuse after the Civil War because of its unfamiliarity and expense. It was especially rare in the American South and rural areas. However, the bundling or "undertaking" of funeral services—laying out, transportation, grave-digging, and coordinating rites—by commercial businesses became more common.

Undertaking developed into family businesses that thrived on genteel yet increasingly profit-oriented arrangements. The funeral director would guide grieving families in purchasing embalming (to disinfect, preserve, and restore the body for a "lifelike" appearance), cosmetics, caskets, vaults, transportation, and other products and services. These professional arrangements were largely unexamined and unregulated, until Jessica Mitford was persuaded to inquire into the funeral industry during the late 1950's.

Seldom has a writer been better matched to a topic or produced more explosive results. Mitford interviewed funeral home directors, read their professional publications, sampled their products ("Fit-a-Fut" oxfords), and produced a witty, scathing exposé, *The American Way of Death* (1963). It became a surprise best seller that put the industry on its guard, despite her insistence that the book reflected insiders' own points of view. Mitford showed how funeral directors were motivated to guide consumers to the maximum number of services and the more expensive models of caskets and other products. Because the bereaved had a pressing need for the products and services, they were in no position to comparison shop, reflect on their choices, or object to unsatisfactory performances.

There was immediate public demand for federal regulation of the funeral industry; such was the industry's opposition, however, that not until 1975 did the Federal Trade Commission (FTC) even propose rules of fair practice. Even this might not have happened without Ralph Nader's 1970 critique of the FTC for failing in its mission to protect consumers. Only in 1984 did the FTC finally rule that funeral directors could not lie to prospective clients and that services must be itemized so consumers could select or decline each option. Further federal legislation in 1994 forbade funeral homes from refusing to handle caskets purchased elsewhere.

Mitford's *The American Way of Death Revisited* was published posthumously in 1998. It considered the industry's changes ("not many . . . for the better"), such as the trend toward international funeral conglomerates and the failures of the FTC to enforce new legislation passed largely in reaction to the original book.

THE MAKEUP OF THE INDUSTRY

The funeral industry is dominated by two or three international corporations, representing about 10 percent of all funeral homes but more than 20 percent of all funerals. Funeral homes owned by the conglomerates tend to be more rigid about their rules and have a reputation for stonewalling questions or requests that may lessen their profit on a funeral package. Because individual funeral homes retain their family or local titles after corporate acquisition, it may be difficult for consumers to identify or avoid these corporate services. The average cost of a funeral as of 2007 was $6,195, including embalming, transportation, a casket, and use of the funeral home facilities, but without cemetery costs.

Many people are prearranging and paying for their own funerals. Doing so locks in cost and may shelter assets from probate delays or Medicaid eligibility. Contract provisions can oblige survivors to pay any difference between the agreed-upon fee and actual costs.

Some baby boomers have nontraditional attitudes toward death and funerals, and they have introduced changes into the traditional funeral. Modern funerals tend to be less formal and more personalized. Visitation, or wakes, often feature the deceased's prized possessions, hobbies, or accomplishments, and pictures and portraits may be preserved on a "celebration of life" digital versatile disc (DVD). The viewing is increasingly likely to be at a home or a church, as in earlier times, and there may be Internet visitation. Nearly one-third of Americans choose cremation (which is increasing in cost). Finally, more people seek natural, biodegradable burial in conservation cemeteries and nature preserves, or similar options such as burial at sea or interment of ashes in "reef balls."

The National Burial Company USA's Web site guides consumers to "green" cemeteries in each state. The Funeral Consumers Alliance, founded to promote nonprofit burial services, publishes a newsletter, advises and advocates for consumers, monitors trends, and exposes abuses in the funeral industry.

Jan Hall

FURTHER READING

Faust, Drew Gilpin. *This Republic of Suffering: Death and the American Civil War.* New York: Alfred A. Knopf, 2008. Examines how the "harvest of death" affected Americans' views on death and ritual.

Harris, Mark. *Grave Matters: A Journey Through the Modern Funeral Industry to a Natural Way of Burial.* New York: Scribner, 2007. Analyzes the aftermath of embalming from an ecological viewpoint and accompanies mourners as they consign their loved ones to cremation, burial at sea, memorial reefs, or natural cemeteries using simple, biodegradable materials.

Laderman, Gary. *Rest in Peace: A Cultural History of Death and the Funeral Home in Twentieth-Century America.* New York: Oxford University Press, 2003. Traces the evolution from home funerals to funeral homes, and, counter to Mitford's view, asserts that funeral homes largely give people what they want.

Mitford, Jessica. *The American Way of Death Revisited.* New York: Vintage, 1998. Update of the hilarious 1963 original laments that not much has changed, and not for the better. New chapters discuss the prepaid funeral trend and federal regulation, and provide the basis for the funeral reform movement.

Roach, Mary. *Stiff: The Curious Lives of Human Cadavers.* New York: W. W. Norton, 2003. Witty but respectful account of all the useful things bodies have done after their owners were done with them.

SEE ALSO: Civil War, U.S.; 401(k) retirement plans; Health care industry; Wars.

Fur trapping and trading

DEFINITION: The capturing and slaying of animals for their coats and the selling of these pelts

SIGNIFICANCE: Beginning with the French who settled along the St. Lawrence River during the early seventeenth century and continuing with the British in the second half of the same century, the fur trade constituted a major force underlying the European exploration, settlement, and economic development of the North America continent. The involvement of the United States in this trade, which began during the late eighteenth century and extended to the mid-nineteenth century, coincided with the last stage of this vast commercial enterprise.

Trading for furs with the peoples of the New World began during the earliest period of French contact in the sixteenth century. As the French led by Samuel de Champlain began to establish permanent settlements along the St. Lawrence River during the early years of the seventeenth century, this trade took on a special significance. Europe at this time was developing an insatiable desire for furs as its own population of fur-bearing animals was being depleted. As French explorers penetrated the Canadian wilderness and knowledge of the upper St. Lawrence and the Great Lakes region expanded, the possibilities of conducting a more organized system of trade developed. By the 1630's and 1640's, regular shipments of furs were leaving from the French embarkation points of Montreal and Quebec for Europe, and ever-broadening patterns of trade with the indigenous peoples of the interior were taking shape.

BRITISH TRADERS

British competition with the French in the conduct of the fur trade began in the second half of the seventeenth century. During the late 1650's, two French traders—Pierre Esprit Radisson and Médard Chouart des Groseilliers—embarked on an unauthorized journey to the area south of Hudson Bay in an attempt to open up new areas to the fur trade. When they returned to Montreal, heavily laden with furs and with a plan for extending the trade into the new region, the French authorities rejected their scheme and confiscated their furs. Angered and disappointed, the two then took their plan to the British, who already possessed claims to the Hudson Bay region as a result of the explorations of Henry Hudson earlier in the century. The British quickly took steps to exploit this new dimension of the trade, and they soon emerged as major competitors to the French. Although the French method of conducting trade involved the use of the St. Lawrence-Great Lakes water system as a means of penetrating the interior and trading with the Native Americans, the British sailed their ships into Hudson Bay and encouraged the natives to bring their furs to them at trading posts such as York Factory (established during the 1680's) to be loaded directly onto their ships. The Hudson's Bay Company, formed in 1670, was given a monopoly over this British trade.

The French and the British thus competed in the fur trade in Canada until the British took control of the entire area at the conclusion of the French and Indian War in 1763. Other early players in the trade included the Dutch, who conducted it using the Hudson River in New York during the middle years of the seventeenth century, and the Russians, who played a key role in developing it in the western part of the continent, principally in Alaska, beginning in the second half of the eighteenth century.

BRITISH EXPANSION AND CONTROL

Following its conquest of French Canada in 1763, Great Britain took over the vast St. Lawrence-Great Lakes fur trading system formerly controlled by the French. The British made various attempts over the course of the twenty years that followed to develop an effective means of control over this system, but it was not until the formation of the North West Company during the 1780's that any degree of real order was established. From that point, the North West Company and the Hudson's Bay Company competed in much the same manner as the French and the British had earlier.

Using Grand Portage on the Pigeon River near the western end of Lake Superior as their rendezvous point, the North West Company for the next twenty years carried on the vast seasonal trade that began each spring when the large lake canoes, filled with trade goods, set out from Montreal for the west. When they arrived in midsummer at Grand Portage, the voyagers who piloted the canoes met the traders from the interior who had spent the winter months trading with the Native Americans. The trade goods were exchanged for furs, and then the long journey of the canoes back to Montreal began, the trip coming to an end as autumn set in. During this period, individuals working for the North West Company pushed ever farther into the Canadian northwest, setting the stage for the eventual expansion of the trade westward to the Pacific. The most famous of these eighteenth century explorers, Alexander Mackenzie, completed the first overland journey across the northern portion of the continent, reaching the Pacific Ocean in the summer of 1793.

During these years the American Revolution also took place, and in the years following that event, the fur trade quickly came to play an important role in the new country's growth and development.

EARLY AMERICAN DEVELOPMENT

The Treaty of Paris (1783) that concluded the War for Independence brought the United States a vast amount of western territory—west to the Mississippi River and north to the region of the Great Lakes. As a result, the new country and Great Britain bumped into each other in an area, then known as the Old Northwest, where the fur trade was still being conducted. This collision reflected the very different outlooks of the two nations regarding the importance of this region. While the British, interested primarily in the fur trade, had built forts throughout

the area to protect their conduct of the trade, the new country was poised to embark on a process of western expansion and settlement that threatened to bring that trade to an end. Thus, one of the major problems facing the United States government during its early years was the continued British occupation, despite the terms of the peace treaty, of their forts in the region. Although this matter was not fully resolved until the conclusion of the War of 1812 several decades later, some temporary reduction in tensions occurred with the signing of Jay's Treaty in 1794, which, among other things, allowed the fur traders of both countries to pursue the trade without concern for each other's borders.

Although the continued pursuit of the fur trade east of the Mississippi conflicted with the long-term direction of American development in that region, the new country was at the same time eager to become a major player in the trade farther west. With the Louisiana Purchase in 1803, the United States gained another enormous tract of new land, extending westward from the Mississippi River to the Rocky Mountains. American exploration of the new territory—and the area beyond—quickly began. The Lewis and Clark expedition of 1804 to 1806 was the most famous of these explorations, but many others also took place with the expansion of the fur trade frequently providing a driving force behind them.

The explorations of Jedediah Smith during the mid-1820's offer a good example of this. Sponsored by American fur trader William Ashley, Smith's journeys led eventually to the creation of a fur-trading network in the Rocky Mountain area similar in many ways to that conducted earlier by the North West Company in the Great Lakes region. With either Green River or Jackson Hole, in what would later become the state of Wyoming, serving as rendezvous points, trappers and traders came from points as far distant as Santa Fe to the south and Canada to the north to carry on this trade. During these years, a number of overland trade routes developed to

This illustration from an eighteenth century atlas of North America shows Englishmen trading for furs with a member of a local tribe. (Library of Congress)

carry on the trade between specific locales. Two examples were the Santa Fe Trail running from Santa Fe to St. Louis and the Red River oxcart trail extending from Fort Garry (located near the modern day Winnipeg) to St. Paul.

ASTOR AND THE AMERICAN FUR COMPANY

American business acumen and entrepreneurial skill found an early focus in the fur trade. Without question the most successful American fur trade entrepreneur of the period was John Jacob Astor. Arriving in New York City in 1783 as an impoverished twenty-year-old German immigrant, Astor entered the fur business at the bottom rung of the ladder. Within a remarkably short period of time, he rose to become a dominant figure in the trade. From the normal export of furs to Europe, he also connected into the growing China trade of the period and greatly expanded fur markets. In 1808, while still in his mid-forties, he formed the American Fur Company, which would eventually become one of the largest American companies of its time. Two years later, in 1810, he founded the Pacific Fur Company in an attempt to expand the trade by sea into the Pacific Northwest.

As a part of this latter plan, he built Astoria, a fur post at the mouth of the Columbia River, the following year. Although the post never achieved the success that Astor had intended and was eventually sold to the North West Company in 1813, it later became famous as a result of American author Washington Irving's popular history entitled *Astoria*, published in 1836. The explorations Astor sponsored in the area led to the discovery of the famous South Pass by which vast numbers of settlers would later cross through the Rocky Mountains on their way to California, Oregon, and Utah.

After abandoning Astoria, Astor refocused his energies on the interior fur trade, gaining control over the last stages of the Great Lakes trade and eventually building a fur trading empire that extended to the Missouri River, the Rocky Mountains, and beyond. The merger of the North West Company and the Hudson's Bay Company in 1821 was at least in part a response to the American Fur Company's presence in the trade. In 1834, Astor relinquished his control of the company and used his fortune to speculate in New York City real estate. At the time of his death in 1848, he was considered to be the wealthiest person in the country, with a net worth of more than $20 million (about $115 billion in modern dollars).

DECLINE OF THE TRADE

The fur trade fell off steadily during the 1830's and 1840's as the numbers of fur-bearing animals declined and settlement moved steadily westward. Although it continued in isolated areas and especially in Canada into fairly modern times, its long run as a major economic force had come to an end. Beginning during the 1860's, fur farming replaced trapping as a major source of furs. In the twenty-first century, mink, fox, and chinchilla were still being raised commercially in the United States. Since the 1980's and 1990's, however, the raising of animals for this purpose has come under increasing attack by animal rights groups, and the demand for furs has fallen off significantly.

Although the fur trade has diminished in importance, its historical effects were enormous. It stimulated exploration of the continent, provided an economic base for early settlement, and made tremendous fortunes for those who organized and controlled it. At the same time, it also contributed significantly to the decline of Native American cultures, as large numbers of native peoples gave up their traditional lifestyle in the pursuit of furs, becoming increasingly dependent on whites and ultimately losing their lands as the trade gave way to permanent settlement. Perhaps no other economic enterprise had a larger impact on the early history of the continent.

Scott Wright

FURTHER READING

Chittenden, Hiram Martin. *The American Fur Trade of the Far West.* 2 vols. 1902. Reprint. Whitefish, Mont.: Kessinger, 2006. A classic treatment of the American fur trade in the area west of the Mississippi.

Huck, Barbara. *Fur Trade Routes of North America.* Winnipeg, Ont.: Heartland Publications, 2000. A beautifully illustrated volume that is much more than simply an interesting travel book. Its coverage of sites associated with the North American fur trade is very complete. The accompanying historical summaries are accurate and well written, and the inclusion of numerous maps is extremely useful.

Madsen, Axel. *John Jacob Astor: America's First Multi-*

millionaire. New York: John Wiley & Sons, 2001. A solid and well-researched biography of an important figure in the American dimensions of the trade.

Phillips, Paul C., and J. W. Smurr. *The Fur Trade.* 2 vols. Norman: University of Oklahoma Press, 1967. An exhaustive treatment of all aspects of the fur trade in North America.

Robertson, R. G. *Competitive Struggle: America's Western Fur Trading Posts, 1764-1865.* Boise, Idaho: Tamarack Books, 1999. Covers much of the same ground as Huck's book but in greater detail and depth. Particularly strong in providing information on the major companies involved in the trade. Also contains excellent and very detailed maps.

Van Kirk, Sylvia. *Many Tender Ties: Women in Fur Trade Society, 1670-1870.* Winnipeg, Man.: Watson and Dwyer, 1980. Offers an interesting perspective on the role of women—both European and Native American—in the trade.

Wishart, David J. *The Fur Trade of the American West, 1807-1840: A Geographical Synthesis.* Lincoln: University of Nebraska Press, 1979. This work focuses on what the author refers to as the two main fur "production systems" of the Trans-Missouri West—the beaver trapping and transport system of the Rocky Mountain region and the trade in bison skin robes that occurred in the upper Missouri River basin.

SEE ALSO: Alaska purchase; Astor, John Jacob; Canadian trade with the United States; Colonial economic systems; Fishing industry; French and Indian War; Lewis and Clark expedition; Louisiana Purchase; Native American trade; Parliamentary Charter of 1763; Pike's western explorations.

G

Gadsden Purchase

IDENTIFICATION: Treaty between the United States and Mexico giving the United States 29,640 square miles that later became part of Arizona and New Mexico

DATE: Treaty signed on December 31, 1853, ratified on June 29, 1854

SIGNIFICANCE: The acquisition of this territory was essential for the construction of a southern transcontinental railroad, eventually built by the Southern Pacific during the early 1880's. It is also a land rich in copper and valuable for agriculture and grazing.

The United States emerged from the Mexican War (1846-1848) with an additional one-half million square miles of territory containing excellent ports on the Pacific Ocean and tremendous mineral resources. Entrepreneurs in all sections of the nation saw the promise and viability of transcontinental railroads. It was also in the national interest to tie together the vast regions of the country. Proponents of these railroads competed to establish the eastern terminus at Chicago, St. Louis, or New Orleans.

Advocates of the southern route had an advantage during the early 1850's in that most of the route lay in organized territories and states. It also avoided extremely rugged mountain ranges and brutal winter weather. When the surveyors mapped out the best route, however, a substantial stretch lay south of the New Mexico Territory.

In May, 1853, James Gadsden, a former railroad executive from South Carolina, was appointed minister to Mexico by President Franklin Pierce. Secretary of War Jefferson Davis particularly encouraged Gadsden to negotiate the purchase of a substantial amount of land between Texas and the Pacific. Gadsden found President Antonio López de Santa Anna of Mexico in need of funds to prop up his regime. The initial agreement in December, 1853, would have cost $15 million, but the U.S. Senate reduced the amount of land and price to $10 million.

Sectionalism during the late 1850's prevented the construction of the southern route. The honor of the first transcontinental railroad went to the Union Pacific and Central Pacific in 1869. The advantages of a southerly route remained strong. Beginning at Los Angeles, the Southern Pacific reached the Arizona Territory in 1877. Despite political problems and occasional lack of steel rails, the Southern Pacific pursued a path through the Gadsden Purchase. It linked with the Atchison, Topeka, and Santa Fe Railroad at Deming, New Mexico Territory, on March 8, 1881, to become the second transcontinental route. The last 219 miles had been completed in less than nine months, which testifies to the geographical advantage of the Gadsden Purchase territory. Overall, railroad construction through that territory probably cost one-fifth that of the first transcontinental route. Remarkably, it was accomplished without federal land grants. El Paso was reached on May 19, 1881. The Southern Pacific pushed across Texas to connect with New Orleans on January 12, 1883, finally fulfilling the dreams of southern entrepreneurs before the American Civil War and justifying the wisdom of the Gadsden Purchase.

M. Philip Lucas

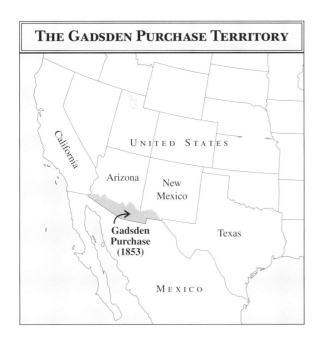

THE GADSDEN PURCHASE TERRITORY

California
UNITED STATES
Arizona
New Mexico
Gadsden Purchase (1853)
Texas
MEXICO

FURTHER READING

Devine, David. *Slavery, Scandal, and Steel Rails.* New York: iUniverse, 2004.

Garber, Paul N. *The Gadsden Treaty*. Reprint. Gloucester, Mass.: Peter Smith, 1959.

Schmidt, Louis B. "Manifest Opportunity and the Gadsden Purchase." *Arizona and the West* 3, Autumn (1961): 245-264.

SEE ALSO: Mexican trade with the United States; Mexican War; Railroads; Texas annexation; Transcontinental railroad.

Gambling industry

DEFINITION: Companies that provide legal gaming activities and associated facilities

SIGNIFICANCE: Gambling has become one of the most profitable American enterprises. For a time, it was legal only in the state of Nevada, but gambling has become legal in forty-eight states (although not Hawaii and Utah). Shares in some gambling corporations are traded on the New York Stock Exchange.

In the United States, Nevada became the first state to permit gambling in 1931. In large measure, the move was made to create revenue for a jurisdiction faced with the prospect of being unable to support itself. After gambling became legal, organized crime syndicates came into Nevada and took control of the gambling industry, using the experience they had gained by running illegal gambling operations elsewhere. Vast sums of money were regularly skimmed from casinos in Las Vegas and Reno and hidden from tax authorities. However, in time, it became obvious that casinos could be run profitably and legitimately, merely by predetermining the odds on any game and making certain that the house reaped the desired profit. By the twenty-first century, most of the gambling casinos in Nevada were owned by giant public corporations.

In 1978, Atlantic City, New Jersey, joined Las Vegas as a major site for casinos, and since then, many states have licensed various forms of gambling. The casinos draw people with slot machines and games such as baccarat, craps, keno, roulette, and blackjack. They also make use of clever tactics to enhance sales. For example, casinos do not have clocks on the wall that might remind gamblers how long they have been gambling. They sometimes provide free alcoholic beverages, served by attractive young women. The casinos also attempt to soften any moral concerns by saying that their patrons are engaged in "gaming" rather than "gambling."

Two firms—Harrah's Entertainment and MGM Mirage—dominate the gambling business, both in Nevada and in the rest of the United States. In 2007, Harrah's Entertainment, the largest gambling company in the world, had an estimated annual income of almost $9 billion; it employed 95,000 people and owned fifty-four casinos across the United States. It controlled more than half of the hotel rooms on the Las Vegas Strip. The transformation of the gambling industry from a shady business to a modern, corporate endeavor is demonstrated by the leadership (as of 2008) of Harrah's Entertainment and MGM Mi-

This sign welcomes visitors to Las Vegas, a major center of gambling in the United States. (© Davinci/Dreamstime.com)

rage. Gary Loveman, the chief executive officer of Harrah's Entertainment, was formerly a professor at the Harvard Business School, and J. Terrence Lanni, chief executive officer of MGM Mirage, holds a master's degree in business from the University of Southern California. Also, MGM Mirage describes itself on its Web site as a "respected hotel and gaming company," thereby distancing itself from the image of a gambling casino run by gangsters.

Las Vegas has also successfully marketed itself as something more than just a gambling mecca—as a fun family destination and a great place to hold conventions. The city has highlighted the celebrity performances, shops and restaurants, swimming pools, and family amenities (such as playgrounds for children) featured at its many casinos as well as the relatively low prices of its hotel rooms. Each day, Las Vegas's population of 793,000 is increased by 250,000 visitors.

SLOT MACHINES

About 70 percent of gambling casino income is derived from slot machines. The customer, who on average makes six plays a minute, presses a button that results in a winning or losing display. Slot machines have distinct advantages for the businesses that use them: They can generate revenue any time that the business is open, and they do not require the hiring of an employee (such as a dealer) to interact with the customers.

Manufacturing of slot machines largely is the province of International Game Technology, a Reno-based business. One of its best sellers is The Price Is Right, a slot machine designed to dispense a large number of small payouts to provide a great deal of positive reinforcement while nibbling away at the bettor's money. On the average, slots pay back about 90 percent of what is bet.

Slots are designed to appeal primarily to women over the age of fifty-five, who are believed to have considerable leisure time and disposable income. In cities such as San Diego and Phoenix, some casinos operate a fleet of vehicles that shuttle people between the casinos and retirement communities. For older people, casinos provide a safe environment, with numerous security guards and attractive shops and restaurants.

RIVERBOAT GAMBLING

The popularity of riverboat gambling in the United States can be traced in part to nostalgia for earlier times when boats traversed the major inner waterways. One gambling riverboat on Lake Charles in Louisiana has been designed to look as if it was created in the Victorian era. It features a huge paddle wheel, as required by state law, even though it is propelled by diesel engines and underwater propellers.

Most riverboat gambling came into being through voter referendums. For example, in 1962, 62 percent of the voters in Missouri endorsed a referendum favoring dockside and excursion gambling within the state on boats on the Mississippi and Missouri Rivers. At first, there were limited boarding times and a $500 ceiling on the amount of money any one person could lose, but the time restrictions were later abandoned. Only games of pure chance are permitted. The courts have upheld a ban against any games in which a player's expected return is increased by reasoning, foresight, dexterity, or any strategy.

OFF-TRACK BETTING

Although bets were allowed to be made at racetracks, bets on the same horse races were forbidden if placed elsewhere. This discrepancy seemed odd to many people. In 1971, legal off-track betting made its debut in New York. The state-operated Off-Track Betting Corporation (OTB) sought to popularize its business with catchy slogans. One OTB advertisement proclaimed, "Start a new morning routine—coffee and doughnuts and the daily double." Another advertisement read, "If you're in the stock market, you might find this a better bet."

The effects of legalized off-track betting are difficult to determine. However, organized crime's strength in the realm of illegal bookmaking has been greatly reduced. The impact on racetracks is harder to determine; however, tracks are experiencing lower attendance figures, an increase in the age of clientele, and a decrease in the number of foals registered each year. The drop in revenue at racetracks in Bangor, Maine, and in Pennsylvania has been offset somewhat by the installation of slot machines at the tracks.

NATIVE AMERICAN CASINOS

Casinos run by Native Americans on tribal land first appeared after Congress enacted the Indian Gaming Regulatory Act of 1981, which legalized gambling on Native American reservations. The

GAMBLING REVENUE, 1995-2006, IN BILLIONS OF DOLLARS

Year	Casinos	Gaming Total
1995	16.0	45.1
1996	17.1	47.9
1997	18.2	50.9
1998	19.7	54.9
1999	22.2	58.2
2000	24.3	61.4
2001	25.7	63.3
2002	26.5	68.6
2003	27.02	72.9
2004	28.93	78.8
2005	30.29	84.4
2006	32.42	90.9

Source: Data from American Gaming Association
Note: Revenue is gross revenue, the amount wagered minus the winnings returned to players. Gaming includes pari-mutuel wagering, lotteries, casinos, legal bookmaking, charitable gaming and bingo, and Native American reservations and card rooms.

law sought to promote tribal economic development, self-sufficiency, and strong tribal government. By 2008, there were 310 such casinos, run by 200 of the nation's 556 federally recognized tribes. States cannot tax Native American reservations, but many arrange to share in the revenue from these operations. During the early twenty-first century, some states were receiving more than $800 million a year from Native American gambling operations.

The most lucrative of the Native American gambling operations is Foxwoods Resort Casino, located in Ledyard, Connecticut, 110 miles south of Boston and 130 miles north of New York. Foxwoods is operated by the Mashantucket Pequot tribe. It hosts about 40,000 persons daily and has 6,000 slot machines as well as 350 table games located throughout its nineteen-story casino. From the profits, each of the three hundred members of the tribe receives at least $50,000 a year and some receive free homes, education subsidies, medical care, and retirement benefits.

One study found that, on average, in the first four years after a Native American casino was opened, employment in the county where the reservation was located grew by 24 percent, the population increased by 12 percent, and the mortality rate dropped by 2 percent. On the downside, bankruptcies, automobile theft, violent crime, and larceny increased 10 percent in the same time period.

INTERNET GAMBLING

The most controversial form of gambling in the twenty-first century is Internet gambling. Most Internet gambling takes the form of electronically placing wagers on sporting events or playing games of chance on personal computers. Fifty-four countries allow Internet gambling, but in the United States, federal and state laws forbid such activities. Some argue that these laws are constitutionally suspect as they violate the First Amendment guarantee of freedom of speech. Law-enforcement agencies object to Internet gambling because it is too accessible to minors. Although some legislators have proposed bills that would legalize and monitor online gambling, as of 2008, none had become law.

Despite the legal questions, Americans are believed to be some of the best customers of overseas Internet gambling operations. The small island of Antigua and Barbuda in the Caribbean has asked the World Trade Organization to issue a ruling that the American ban on Internet gambling is an unfair trade practice and contrary to the agreement by the United States to adhere to regulations that allow traffic in most goods between signatory countries. Although the World Trade Organization ruled in favor of Antigua and Barbuda's claim, it has no real power to enforce its decision.

It is estimated that illegal sports betting by Americans in the twenty-first century ranges somewhere between $80 billion and $300 billion annually. Some experts argue that if Internet gambling were permitted in the United States, many of those bets would be placed with Nevada casinos because of their name recognition, and the U.S. government would gain considerable revenue from the business.

Gilbert Geis

FURTHER READING

Adler, Peter J. *Gambling, Freedom and Democracy.* New York: Routledge, 2008. Adler argues that governments have a duty to protect their residents from the subtle degradation of legal gambling and advocates international conventions to monitor gambling activities.

Chafetz, Henry. *A History of Gambling in the United States from 1492 to 1955*. New York: Clarkson N. Potter, 1960. Chafetz offers anecdotes that bear on the historical development of gambling, noting Thomas Jefferson's backgammon losses while he was writing the Declaration of Independence and the start of the infamous Chicago fire, when a companion of Mrs. O'Leary's son (and not her cow) knocked over a lantern while rolling dice in the barn.

Darian-Smith, Eve. *New Capitalists: Law, Politics, and Identity Surrounding Casino Gambling on Native-American Land*. Belmont, Calif.: Wadsworth, 2004. An anthropologist looks at the implications for tribal life of casinos on Native American reservations, stressing the dramatic changes that have been introduced into a historically marginalized culture.

Grinols, Earl L. *Gambling in America: Costs and Benefits*. New York: Cambridge University Press, 2004. Grinols argues that others have used conceptually flawed concepts to measure the impact of gambling and that his approach indicates that its social harms outweigh its benefits.

McGowan, Richard A. *The Gambling Debate*. Westport, Conn.: Greenwood Press, 2008. Focuses on the ethical and rhetorical elements in debates regarding gambling and offers case studies from Missouri, Massachusetts, and Macao.

Morse, Edward A., and Ernest P. Goss. *Governing Fortune: Casino Gambling in America*. Ann Arbor: University of Michigan Press, 2007. A comprehensive examination of all facets of gambling practices, including practices in Nevada, other states, and on tribal lands, with emphasis on the role of casinos in economic development.

Walker, Douglas M. *The Economics of Casino Gambling*. New York: Springer, 2007. Argues that legal gambling "cannibalizes" other industries and therefore makes no net economic addition to economic well-being. Includes a comprehensive review of the costs and benefits of gambling.

SEE ALSO: Indian removal; Lotteries, state-run; Organized crime; Taxation; Tourism industry; Vending machines.

Garner, John Nance

IDENTIFICATION: U.S. representative, 1903-1933, Speaker of the House of Representatives, 1931-1933, and vice president of the United States, 1933-1941

BORN: November 22, 1868; Red River County, Texas

DIED: November 7, 1967; Uvalde, Texas

SIGNIFICANCE: More than any other single individual, Garner was responsible for the passage of the Glass-Steagall Act of 1933, which created the Federal Deposit Insurance Corporation, putting an end to widespread runs on banks in the United States.

The son of a former Confederate soldier and of a banker's daughter, John Nance Garner grew up in a family prosperous enough to send him to college at Vanderbilt University in Nashville, Tennessee. A respiratory ailment forced him to leave the damp Tennessee climate after a few months and to return to Texas, where he "read in the law"—that is, he studied on his own in a Clarksville, Texas, law office. At twenty years of age, he passed the bar, and a year later he ran unsuccessfully for city attorney. For health reasons, he moved to the drier Uvalde area, where he practiced law, bought a newspaper, and built a political base.

Employing his shrewd entrepreneurial skills, Garner bought thousands of acres of land, three banks, and several other businesses, becoming a very wealthy young man. After serving briefly as a judge, he was elected in 1898 to the state legislature, where he served until he became a member of the U.S. House of Representatives in 1903. He was re-elected fourteen times, including in 1932, when he was simultaneously elected vice president of the United States having run successfully with presidential candidate Franklin D. Roosevelt (1933-1945).

In 1928, Garner was elected House minority leader. In the year following the 1930 congressional elections, fourteen representatives died, and the Democrats won the subsequent special elections. As a result, Garner became Speaker of the House in 1931. In 1932, he was the southern states candidate for U.S. president, opposing Roosevelt in the primary elections. The Democratic National Convention that year deadlocked, with no candidate able to gain the necessary two-thirds vote to became the party's presidential nominee. Garner withdrew his name, and Roosevelt was nominated. Although both Roosevelt and Garner denied that any deal had been made between them, it seems probable that Garner threw his support to Roosevelt in return for the vice presidency.

Garner worked hard for the election of the Roosevelt-Garner ticket, convincing southerners to vote for a northern liberal New York governor, and Roosevelt relied on Garner's sage advice during the campaign and into his first term. As a former Speaker of the House with as many as twenty old friends in the Senate, Garner successfully guided Roosevelt's New Deal legislative package through the Congress during the administration's first Hundred Days.

Garner argued to Roosevelt's northern liberal advisers that the best way to avoid future runs on banks would be an insurance system. He knew that banks made money by paying their depositors a lower rate of interest on their deposits than the banks charged in interest to their borrowers. Banks naturally wanted to maximize their profits by loaning as much of their depositors' money as possible. If they loaned too much, however, they would be unable to pay the money back on demand. Conservative bankers always maintained a reasonable reserve, but even the most conservative banker could not maintain a reserve large enough to meet all depositors' demands simultaneously in the event that the depositors lost confidence in the bank. If most of the nation's depositors lost confidence in the entire banking system, the system itself would fail. This had happened every few decades since the nation was founded, including in 1933, during the Great Depression.

Garner favored a system in which all participating banks paid a premium to the Federal Deposit Insurance Corporation, which would then guarantee all deposits up to $100,000 per individual depositor. To protect the government from unwise bankers, banks were required to maintain a minimum reserve and to be audited to eliminate overly risky loans. Depositors would no longer need to worry that their money could disappear, so the motive for runs on banks was eliminated. Since the adoption of this system, there has been no general run on U.S. banks.

Roosevelt's more liberal advisers had favored more extreme measures, nationalizing the U.S.

banking system, and Roosevelt himself wavered until he discovered how popular Garner's solution was. Garner offered Roosevelt other significant economic advice during his tenure as vice president. Roosevelt ignored much of this advice, possibly lengthening the depression and contributing to the recession of 1937-1938.

Garner lost Roosevelt's confidence and retired to his home in Texas, where he lived longer than any other president or vice president, dying just fifteen days shy of his ninety-ninth birthday.

Richard L. Wilson

FURTHER READING

Champagne, Anthony. "John Nance Garner." In *Masters of the House: Congressional Leadership Over Two Centuries*, edited by Roger H. Davidson, Susan Webb Hammond, and Raymond W. Smock. Boulder, Colo.: Westview Press, 1998.
Timmons, Bascom N. *Garner of Texas: A Personal History*. New York: Harper, 1948.
Wilson, Richard L. "Garner, John Nance." In *American Political Leaders*. New York: Facts On File, 2002.

SEE ALSO: Federal Deposit Insurance Corporation; Great Depression; New Deal programs; Presidency, U.S.; Recession of 1937-1938.

Garvey, Marcus

IDENTIFICATION: Founder of a mass movement that advocated African American economic self-sufficiency
BORN: August 17, 1887; Saint Ann's Bay, Jamaica
DIED: June 10, 1940; London, United Kingdom
SIGNIFICANCE: Garvey built the world's largest activist organization for people of African descent, the Universal Negro Improvement Association, and promoted various business ventures. His economic ideas were largely dismissed by many subsequent black political leaders in favor of modified socialist theories.

The youngest child of a successful Jamaican mason, Marcus Garvey grew up watching his father's modest wealth being gradually consumed through a series of disastrous legal cases. This decline led Garvey to take work as a printing apprentice in Kingston, where he quickly rose to the rank of foreman. In 1908, he helped lead an unsuccessful strike by the local printers' union and was subsequently black-listed as a result. The episode left him doubtful about the power of labor unions. After a period of restlessness that saw him travel throughout the Caribbean, Latin America, and England, Garvey returned to Jamaica, where he founded the pan-Africanist Universal Negro Improvement Association (UNIA) in 1914.

The UNIA claimed to have had over four million members at one point, although actual membership has been estimated at about sixteen thousand. The group advocated black unity and economic self-dependency and promoted a number of economic ventures, including publications, stores, and even a shipping line. Most of these enterprises were failures, which led to criminal charges that sullied Garvey's reputation and weakened his movement. Two years after starting the UNIA, Garvey traveled to the homeland of one of his heroes, Booker T. Washington, in the hope of recruiting African Americans.

The movement rapidly grew as millions of African Americans became attracted to Garvey's ideas of racial, political, and economic independence. He believed one of the key causes of African American subjugation was their fiscal dependence on whites and believed it was impossible to ease social inequalities until the financial power of African Americans began to grow. Toward this end, in 1919, UNIA published newspapers and founded the publically traded Negro Factories Corporation, which owned a chain of grocery stores and various other small businesses. That same year a more ambitious plan was embarked on to create the Black Star Line, a shipping firm designed to promote trade among black people in the United States, the Caribbean, and Africa, and to assist African American emigration to Africa, with the independent West African nation of Liberia as the primary destination.

The U.S. government found these ideas threatening and investigated Garvey while it simultaneously pressured the Liberian government not to work with the UNIA. The Black Star Line had purchased old ships, and several subsequently proved to be unseaworthy. American authorities alleged that Garvey knew this while still promoting the sale of company shares. Garvey was eventually convicted

Marcus Garvey. (Library of Congress)

of mail fraud for selling stock in a ship the line did not own in 1923 and sentenced to five years in prison. The scandal took the wind out of UNIA's sails, and Garvey never managed to regain a high level of influence. Perhaps as a partial result, theories of economic independence in a strictly free-market context took a backseat to more socialist-oriented ideas in the subsequent civil rights and black independence movements of the twentieth century.

Roger Pauly

FURTHER READING

Grant, Collin. *Negro with a Hat: The Rise and Fall of Marcus Garvey.* New York: Oxford University Press, 2008.

Hill, Robert A., ed. *The Marcus Garvey and Universal Negro Improvement Association Papers.* 7 vols. Berkeley: University of California Press, 1983-1991.

Lewis, Rupert. *Marcus Garvey: Anti-Colonial Champion.* Trenton, N.J.: Africa World Press, 1988.

SEE ALSO: Carver, George Washington; Walker, Madam C. J.; Washington, Booker T.

"Gas wars"

DEFINITION: Price-cutting competitions that develop among gas stations, typically when global oil prices are high, as stations try to attract customers

SIGNIFICANCE: "Gas wars" have occurred many times throughout American history; one of the most memorable such times was during the 1970's, when oil prices began to rise as a result of economic and political strife. That gas war eventually ended with oil prices stabilizing, but gas wars continued to be a part of American life throughout the 1980's and reappeared during the early years of the twenty-first century.

Since the invention of the automobile, the United States has become increasingly dependent on oil for fuel. When the United States began searching for oil resources outside its own borders, American consumers were forced to adhere to global oil pricing that was out of their control. At times, when global prices are too high, America's fuel stations start "gas wars" to lower prices for consumers and draw business away from their competitors.

One of the largest American gas wars began during the economic recession of the 1970's, when the Organization of Petroleum Exporting Countries (OPEC) lessened oil production to raise prices in response to poor relations in the Middle East and with the United States. The higher oil prices led to oil shortages in the United States, and a gas war began as a method of bringing more customers to the gas pumps. The "war" escalated as gas stations continued to lower their prices until they could set them no lower without causing the station owners to lose money. In the end, the owners were forced to raise their prices, and consumers were forced to pay nearly the same or more than they had before the gas war.

The end of the gas war during the 1970's did not signal the end of gas wars altogether. Throughout the 1980's, small-scale price competitions occurred between gas stations in different regions of the United States, but a gas war as large as during the 1970's did not occur again until the early twenty-first century. The war in Iraq, natural disasters such as Hurricane Katrina, and a declining economy all contributed to the return of the gas wars in the United States. Once again, Americans were struggling to gain access to affordable fuel, and gas stations began to compete for customers. However, as was true during the 1970's, the gas wars did not offer a great deal of relief to consumers, and gas stations were ultimately forced to raise their prices again.

Jennifer L. Titanski

FURTHER READING

Castanias, Rick, and Herb Johnson. "Gas Wars: Retail Gasoline Price Fluctuations." *The Review of Economics and Statistics* 75, no. 1 (1993): 171-174.

Fleming, Harold M. *Gasoline Prices and Competition.* New York: Appleton-Century-Crofts, 1966.

Savoye, Craig. "Gas Wars: Mini-marts Fend Off Wal-Mart." *Christian Science Monitor* 93, no. 141 (2001): 1.

SEE ALSO: Arab oil embargo of 1973; Automotive industry; Drive-through businesses; Energy crisis of 1979; Organization of Petroleum Exporting Countries; Petroleum industry; Trucking industry.

Gates, Bill

IDENTIFICATION: Cofounder and chief executive officer of Microsoft

BORN: October 28, 1955; Seattle, Washington

SIGNIFICANCE: The software and the software company that Gates created dominated the market, partly because he realized the marketing potential for his own and other software.

Bill Gates was born into a family of modest but comfortable wealth and developed a fascination with electronics from an early age. In high school, he met Paul Allen and formed a partnership that would result in the founding of Microsoft. At that time, the only consumer microcomputer was the Altair, a toy that was operated by flipping switches on its front panel. Gates figured out how to run a BASIC compiler on the Altair, despite its extremely limited memory; this accomplishment became the foundation of his fortune.

From the beginning, Gates recognized that a piece of software did not have to be perfect to find a market. Equally, a software company did not have to develop all of its software in-house. In fact, it was often preferable to license merely adequate third-party software and sell one's products when the market was hot, rather than spend the time to develop superior, proprietary software but miss the market's peak of interest. The Microsoft Disk Operating System (MS-DOS) was a perfect example of that principle in practice. Microsoft obtained it from another company in order to have it ready in time for the release of the International Business Machines Personal Computer (IBM PC). As a result, MS-DOS dominated the market for IBM-compatible operating systems throughout the 1980's.

Apple's successful graphical user interface (GUI), the Macintosh Finder, presented an alternative to MS-DOS that was limited only by its higher price. As a result, Microsoft set to work developing its own GUI, Windows. The earliest versions were simple shell programs, and even the 1990 operating system Windows 3.1 was mocked by Mac users. Windows 95, however, proved to have such a smooth interface that Apple sued Microsoft for copyright infringement. A judge decided in Microsoft's favor, on the grounds that Apple had licensed core aspects of its GUI to Microsoft during the mid-1980's for use in Windows 1.0. However, the Federal Trade Commission began investigating allegations of monopolistic practices in Microsoft's software bundles.

In 1997, Gates worked out a joint venture agreement with Steve Jobs that saved Apple Computer and gained Microsoft some protection against antitrust suits. He began a program of charitable giving in an effort to improve public opinion of him and his company. In addition, he began to rethink his role in Microsoft, moving away from routine administrative work and concentrating on keeping his company innovative. He wrote *The Road Ahead* (1994) and *Business @ the Speed of Light* (1999), books in which he discussed the future of business and information technology and how businesses had to actively embrace information technology to survive and succeed in the digital age.

Leigh Husband Kimmel

FURTHER READING

Liebovich, Mark. *The New Imperialists: How Five Restless Kids Grew Up to Virtually Rule Your World.* Paramus, N.J.: Prentice-Hall, 2002.

Slater, Robert. *Microsoft Rebooted: How Bill Gates and Steve Ballmer Reinvented Their Company.* New York: Portfolio, 2004.

Wallace, James, and Jim Erickson. *Hard Drive: Bill Gates and the Making of the Microsoft Empire.* New York: Harper Business, 1993.

SEE ALSO: Apple; Buffett, Warren; Computer industry.

GATT. *See* General Agreement on Tariffs and Trade

Genentech

IDENTIFICATION: American biotechnology corporation

DATE: Founded on April 7, 1976

SIGNIFICANCE: The advent of recombinant deoxyribonucleic acid (DNA) technology created unprecedented opportunities to develop and market a new type of medicine. Genentech was the first company to take this promising but untried technology into the business world and thus started the multibillion-dollar biotechnology industry.

Bill Gates. (AP/Wide World Photos)

In 1973, Herbert Boyer and Stanley Cohen pioneered recombinant DNA technology when they spliced frog genes into a bacterium. In 1976, venture capitalist Robert A. Swanson met with Boyer for a ten-minute meeting that stretched into three hours. Swanson's infectious enthusiasm for recombinant DNA technology captivated Boyer, who left academia to cofound Genentech with Swanson.

Genentech used genetically engineered microorganisms to synthesize a new category of drugs. Its scientists succeeded in producing somatostatin, a human protein, in a microorganism in 1977 and in cloning human insulin and human growth hormone in 1978 and 1979, respectively. Genentech went public in 1980, and its stock rocketed from $35 to $88 a share in less than an hour, which constitutes one of the largest stock run-ups ever.

In 1982, Genentech licensed the right to market human insulin, the first drug made by recombinant DNA technology, to Eli Lilly, and in 1985, Genentech received Food and Drug Administration (FDA) approval to market its first product, Protropin (somatrem, a polypeptide hormone), for children with growth hormone deficiency. In the following years, it has created other products using DNA recombinant technology to treat diseases and conditions, including cancer, rheumatoid arthritis, stroke, heart attack, cystic fibrosis, allergic asthma, plaque psoriasis, and macular degeneration.

In 2007, Genentech's net income was $2.8 billion, a 31 percent increase from the previous year, and its total operating revenue was $11.7 billion, a 26 percent increase from the previous year. Its diluted earnings per share were $2.79, a 31 percent increase from 2006.

Michael A. Buratovich

See also: Food and Drug Administration; Genetic engineering; Health care industry; Industrial research; Patent law; Pharmaceutical industry.

General Agreement on Tariffs and Trade

Identification: Accord among several capitalist countries reached soon after World War II that established some goals for the exchange of goods and services across international borders

Date: Signed on January 1, 1948

Significance: The GATT helped reopen and maintain access to foreign markets and products following more than a decade of a global depression and an accompanying decrease in exports. The new guidelines for trade contributed to a period of strong performance by American businesses and the U.S. economy in general.

The General Agreement on Tariffs and Trade (GATT) was created in 1947 by twenty-three countries to facilitate the exchange of goods and services between countries. It attempted to create a free trade system. It primarily tried to achieve this broad goal by reducing tariffs, or taxes on imports, as these taxes were the main obstacles to trade at the time.

The GATT was based on three broad principles: expanding trade by reducing tariffs, granting most-favored-nation status to all members, and unconditional reciprocity. Thus, signatories to the agreement pledged to reduce taxes on imports while giving the same treatment to all other members as they provided to their best trading partner. To adhere to these principles, signatories to the GATT would hold periodic sets of multilateral talks. The participants would reach a series of agreements at the end of each set of negotiations to make progress toward a free trade system.

The early sets of talks made significant progress in cutting tariffs on trade in industrial goods between the United States and Western Europe. The Uruguay Round (1986-1993) was the last set of GATT negotiations. By this time, new trade issues had emerged. Agriculture, services such as banking, and the protection of copyrights and patents became points of contention among GATT signatories. The Uruguay Round ended with agreements to reduce trade barriers in all of these areas. Most important, however, it established in 1995 the successor to the GATT—the World Trade Organization.

Kevin L. Brennan

Further Reading

Bhagwati, Jagdish. *The World Trading System at Risk.* Princeton, N.J.: Princeton University Press, 1991.

Mavroidis, Peter C. *The General Agreement on Tariffs and Trade: A Commentary.* New York: Oxford University Press, 2005.

Schott, Jeffrey J., ed. *Free Trade Agreements: U.S. Strategies and Priorities.* Washington, D.C.: Institute for International Economics, 2004.

SEE ALSO: Asian trade with the United States; Canadian trade with the United States; European trade with the United States; International economics and trade; Japanese trade with the United States; Marshall Plan; Organization of Petroleum Exporting Countries; Tariffs; World Trade Organization.

General Electric

IDENTIFICATION: Diversified multinational American conglomerate that produces—among other things—electricity, consumer appliances, transportation technologies, and television and motion picture entertainment

DATE: Founded in 1892

SIGNIFICANCE: The first conglomerate in history, the General Electric Company has led the way in the development of breakthrough technologies and services that have had an impact on nearly every facet of contemporary life

In 1876, inventor Thomas Alva Edison opened his laboratory in Menlo Park, New Jersey, where he invented the incandescent electric lamp. The most influential invention of the time, it became the basis for his electrical business. He was also involved in various other enterprises, including transportation, industrial products, power transmission, and medical equipment. In 1890, Edison combined all his businesses and formed the Edison General Electric Company.

In 1879, Edwin J. Huston and Elihu Thomson formed the Thomson-Huston Electric Company, which became Edison's major competitor. In 1892, Edison General Electric and Thomson-Huston merged to become the General Electric Company (GE) with headquarters in Schenectady, New York. The rapid growth of General Electric earned it a place as one of the twelve original organizations listed on the Dow Jones Industrial Average when the index was first formed in 1896. General Electric expanded through mergers, acquisitions, and reorganizations. In 1911, General Electric acquired the National Electric Lamp Association (NELA) in Cleveland, Ohio. The business was located in Nela Park, which became the first industrial park in the United States. In 1919, General Electric and American Telegraph and Telephone Company (AT&T) partnered to launch the Radio Corporation of America (RCA). In 1930, General Electric formed its plastics department, and in 1932, the company introduced the first garbage disposal. General Electric transformed the aviation business with the development of the first American jet engine in 1942.

One of the leaders in cutting-edge technology, General Electric was numbered among the major computer companies during the 1960's. In 1986, General Electric reacquired RCA in order to obtain the National Broadcasting Company (NBC) television network. The acquisition was a precursor to the 2004 purchase of Vivendi Universal Entertainment's television and film divisions. The newly formed corporation became NBC Universal, the third-largest media company in the world.

General Electric has been led by many notable chief executive officers, but the most influential was Jack Welch, who was the chief executive officer from 1981 until his retirement in 2001. Welch systematically cut waste, shut down nonperforming units,

This GE photograph from around 1908 shows two women using the company's toaster, coffee pot, and egg poacher. (Library of Congress)

and transformed General Electric's corporate culture. He was criticized for what some perceived to be harsh methods. His innovative strategies, however, were later adopted by other corporate leaders as they sought to streamline their own operations to cut costs and increase profits.

General Electric is one of the best-known brands in the world, with many top-performing divisions, including GE Capital, GE Technology Infrastructure, GE Infrastructure, and NBC Universal. ITT, Westinghouse, Tyco, and other well-known conglomerates have tried to imitate General Electric's business model, but have not been as successful.

Pegge Bochynski

FURTHER READING

Gorowitz, Bernard. *The General Electric Story: A Heritage of Innovation, 1876-1999*. Schenectady, N.Y.: Schenectady Museum, 1999.

O'Boyle, Thomas F. *At Any Cost: Jack Welch, General Electric, and the Pursuit of Profit*. New York: Vintage Books, 1999.

Rothschild, William E. *The Secret to GE's Success: A Former Insider Reveals the Leadership Lessons of the World's Most Competitive Company*. New York: McGraw Hill, 2007.

SEE ALSO: Aircraft industry; Automotive industry; Dow Jones Industrial Average; Edison, Thomas Alva; Electronics industry; Multinational corporations; National Broadcasting Company; Public utilities.

General Motors

IDENTIFICATION: Dominant American manufacturer of automobiles and trucks and a pioneer in many aspects of business techniques

DATE: Founded on September 16, 1908

SIGNIFICANCE: Throughout the twentieth century, General Motors was the epitome of American big business. As the world's largest automobile manufacturer, General Motors was looked to as a gauge of the health of both the American economy and the automotive industry in general. The company's leaders were viewed as spokespeople for that industry as a whole.

General Motors (GM) was established by William Crapo Durant in 1908 to manufacture Buick auto-

mobiles. During its first year in operation, the company sold over twenty-five thousand vehicles. In 1910, Durant merged several other companies into GM, including Oldsmobile, Pontiac, Cadillac, and AC Spark Plugs. Sales increased by 60 percent in 1910, but Durant was ousted by bankers because of the company's heavy debt load. The company was incorporated as General Motors Corporation in 1916 when it merged with Chevrolet—a company that Durant had founded after his earlier ouster. Durant regained control.

Fisher Body was acquired in 1919, the same year that General Motors Acceptance Corporation (GMAC) was established to finance sales of cars. By 1921, GM accounted for 12 percent of the U.S. automotive market, thanks in part to a product scheme that aimed five main car lines at five different groups of buyers. In 1925, the company went international with its acquisition of Vauxhall Motors of Great Britain. Another international acquisition came in 1929, when Germany's Adam Opel was acquired. Plants were opened in China and India before 1930. In 1914, the DuPont company began purchasing GM shares, because the company's management saw a market for DuPont's products. By 1920, Dupont owned one-third of GM's stock. Eventually, the relationship attracted the attention of the Federal Trade Commission, which in 1949 sued DuPont and forced an end to the affiliation.

THE SLOAN YEARS

In 1923, Alfred P. Sloan became GM's president and chief executive officer—a position he was to hold until 1956. Much of the company's growth occurred during the Sloan era. Sloan, however, did not act alone; credit can also be accorded to the company's chief financial officer during this period, Donaldson Brown, who developed and applied his return-on-investment formula to every department within GM. A knowledge of the rate of return on investment was particularly important at GM, because the company was among the first to use discounted-cash-flow analysis to evaluate investment alternatives. Brown's return-on-investment reporting compared all of GM's operations with alternative capital investments. The result was a system that significantly decreased the cost of managing complex firms.

Brown also developed the concept of flexible budgeting, which in addition to being a financial tool was a way of communicating top management's expectations. The entire concept of business budgeting was unknown before the 1920's. Brown introduced a budgeting system at GM shortly after his move from DuPont in 1921. Year in and year out, despite radical fluctuations in the demand for automobiles, GM recorded a positive return on investment. During the Great Depression of the 1930's, GM was one of the few corporations not to register a loss.

One cause of GM's success in dealing with the problem of fluctuating demand was its accounting system. Before 1921, inventories had gotten out of control at many divisions—the result being heavy borrowing to finance unneeded inventories. Brown's 1924 requirement that dealers report inventories every ten days was a step toward eliminating inaccurate forecasts of future sales. That policy was a lasting one, eventually adopted by all automobile manufacturers. Using these periodic reports (initially from twenty thousand dealers), management was able to base production schedules and material commitments on the trend of retail sales. The result was that GM was able to use a centralized budgeting system to control decentralized operations. Every division made its own production decisions, but the budget and accounting system were policy tools that guaranteed goal congruence throughout the decentralized structure.

A violent strike at the Flint, Michigan, plant in 1937 led to GM workers gaining collective bargaining representation by the United Auto Workers union. By the start of World War II, GM had 41 percent of the U.S. automotive market, but civilian auto production dropped to zero in 1942, when factories turned their efforts to the war. Following the war, GM's market quickly grew; the newly designed cars of the late 1940's and early 1950's led the company to a 54 percent market share in 1954.

THE POST-SLOAN ERA

In 1960, GM introduced its first small car—the Chevrolet Corvair—in response to similar offerings from European manufacturers. The Corvair was later criticized by Ralph Nader in his book *Unsafe at Any Speed: The Designed-In Dangers of the American Au-*

U.S. MARKET SHARE OF TOP SEVEN AUTOMAKERS (%)		
Maker	*May, 2007*	*May, 2008*
General Motors	23.8	19.3
Toyota	17.2	18.4
Ford	16.5	15.4
Chrysler	12.8	10.7
Honda	9.3	12.0
Nissan	6.0	7.2
Hyundai	4.6	5.6

Source: Data from Rick Newman, "How Toyota Could Become the U.S. Sales Champ," *U.S. News & World Report,* June 9, 2008

tomobile, which led to a congressional investigation of automobile safety.

During the 1970's, GM was the largest private employer in the country, but sales declined during the decade because of a recession, an Arab oil embargo that led to higher gas prices, and competitive gains by Japanese automakers. During the 1980's, GM overhauled its North American operations, acquired Electronic Data Systems Corporation (EDS) from H. Ross Perot, formed a subsidiary company called Saturn, and bought Hughes Aircraft. EDS was subsequently spun off as a separate company in 1996, as was Delphi Automotive Systems, a parts-manufacturing subsidiary, in 1999. In 1997, Hughes Electronics was sold.

In 2002, GM acquired a controlling interest in South Korea's bankrupt Daewoo Motors. The GM product line was reduced in 2004, when the last Oldsmobile came off the line. The company suffered a loss of $38.7 billion in 2007, and sales declined even more in 2008. In October, 2008, General Motors joined Chrysler and Ford in appealing to the federal government for financial aid, as it and Chrysler faced possible bankruptcies. On December 19, President George W. Bush announced that $13.4 billion in emergency loans would be made available to keep the automakers afloat. However, the automakers were given the loans on condition that they make major concessions and organizational changes by March 31, 2009, to demonstrate that they could return to profitability. On February 18, 2009, General Motors and Chrysler asked for an additional $14 billion in aid.

Dale L. Flesher

FURTHER READING

Chandler, Alfred D. *Strategy and Structure: Chapters in the History of the Industrial Enterprise.* Cambridge, Mass.: Harvard University Press, 1962. Excellent history of business, with much discussion of the importance of GM.

General Motors, The First Seventy-Five Years of Transportation Products. Princeton, N.J.: Automobile Quarterly, 1983. Analysis of GM's transportation products, prepared by the Princeton Institute for Historic Research with the assistance of GM.

Gustin, Lawrence R. *Billy Durant: Creator of General Motors.* Rev. ed. Ann Arbor: University of Michigan Press, 2008. Biography of the man who created the General Motors Corporation.

Johnson, H. Thomas, ed. *System and Profits: Early Management Accounting at DuPont and General Motors.* New York: Arno Press, 1980. Excellent analysis of the internal business operations of GM.

Sloan, Alfred P. *My Years with General Motors.* Garden City, N.Y.: Doubleday, 1964. Autobiography of the man who led GM for a third of a century. This volume covers much of the company history during its growth years.

Wright, J. Patrick. *On a Clear Day You Can See General Motors: John Z. De Lorean's Look Inside the Automotive Giant.* Grosse Pointe, Mich.: Wright Enterprises, 1979. A view of GM during the 1970's.

SEE ALSO: AFL-CIO; Automotive industry; Chrysler bailout of 1979; Ford, Henry; Ford Motor Company; Multinational corporations; Petroleum industry; Sit-down strike of 1936-1937.

Genetic engineering

DEFINITION: Scientific and technological control of reproductive processes at the level of genes, allowing genetic modification of organisms for the introduction or exclusion of desired traits

SIGNIFICANCE: The techniques of genetic engineering are at the heart of biotechnology. Despite some controversy, genetic engineering has found many industrial applications in agriculture, medicine, and other biology-based businesses.

In 1953, English scientist Francis Crick and the American biologist James D. Watson discovered the structure of deoxyribonucleic acid (DNA), unlocking the secrets of the genetic mechanisms of reproduction. Within a few decades, the techniques of genetic engineering had increased scientists' understanding of biological processes and allowed for alterations to living creatures, thereby creating new products, services, and industries.

In *Diamond v. Chakrabarty* (1980), the United States Supreme Court upheld the right of companies to patent life-forms created or significantly modified through human invention. The result was a flood of genetically modified organisms (GMO), which altered the landscape of a number of business areas, including agriculture (where there was a good deal of opposition) and medicine (where there was less conflict). Research into the genetic manipulation of animals and plants proceeded vigorously and helped encourage partnerships between research universities and commercial developers. Early milestones included the production of synthetic human insulin in 1980, Harvard's development of the oncomouse (a mouse for cancer research) in 1984, and the commercial availability of the Flavr Savr tomato in 1994. In 1996, genetically engineered crops were grown on 3.8 million acres of American cropland, but by 1999, that number had reached 70.9 million acres. By the end of the twentieth century, genetically engineered soybeans and cotton made up more than half of the total crop, and 28 percent of corn was also grown from genetically engineered varieties.

Advances in bioscience often initially are criticized as meddling with nature. In the United States, genetic engineering became stigmatized because of an association with cloning (in which a genetically identical plant or animal is created), especially of human beings. Another related issue was the use in research of embryonic stem cells, which are favored for their ability to differentiate into other cell types. In 2001, President George W. Bush limited further research to sixty already existing embryonic stem-cell lines. Critics complained that such restrictions delay development of genetically based applications to treat illnesses or result primarily in shifting the locus of scientific work to nations without such restrictions.

Supporters of research in transgenic technology claim that critics succeed only in keeping from the world's disadvantaged from benefiting from the science they need to stave off poverty and famine. Some scientists believe that underdeveloped parts of the world may offer the greatest potential for discovering genetic treasures that can enrich humanity's medical resources while sustaining local economic development. Some critics argue that such technological fixes are ultimately counterproductive as they draw excessively on natural resources and run the risk of diminishing the gene pool, with the potential for catastrophic results.

However, many scientists think that genetic engineering is ultimately beneficial to agriculture, as it can help produce plants that are resistant to disease and insect infestation.

Edward Johnson

Oregon State University professor Steve Strauss is among scientists working on genetically engineered poplar trees that resist pollution and grow faster. (AP/Wide World Photos)

FURTHER READING

Paarlberg, Robert. *Starved for Science: How Biotechnology Is Being Kept Out of Africa.* Cambridge, Mass.: Harvard University Press, 2008.

Roberts, Paul. *The End of Food.* Boston, Mass.: Houghton Mifflin, 2008.

Wilson, Edward O. *The Future of Life.* New York: Alfred A. Knopf, 2002.

SEE ALSO: Agriculture; Cereal crops; Food and Drug Administration; Genentech; Health care industry; Rice industry.

Getty, J. Paul

IDENTIFICATION: American oil tycoon and billionaire

BORN: December 12, 1892; Minneapolis, Minnesota

DIED: June 6, 1976; Sutton Place, Surrey, England

SIGNIFICANCE: Getty amassed a personal fortune exceeding $3 billion, making him one of the first billionaires in the United States and one of the richest men in the United States from the 1950's to his death. He also played a role in deepening the link between American oil companies and Saudi Arabia.

J. Paul Getty graduated from Oxford University in 1914, majoring in economics and political science. He returned from England, and working independently of his father, president of Minnehoma Oil, he excelled at trading Oklahoma oil leases and by 1916 had earned his first million.

Getty quit the business and moved to Los Angeles to be a playboy. This period began a lifetime of failed romantic relationships, with five marriages ending in divorce. These failures always bothered Getty, who never had a bad word to say about his former wives, blaming only his own nature. In 1919, Getty grew tired of Los Angeles, moved back to Oklahoma, resumed his oil career, and devoted himself to his father's business, George F. Getty Oil. George F. Getty never forgave his son for wasting those years or for his divorces, and thought he would ruin the family business. Therefore, on his death in 1930, he left his son only $500,000 and a one-third share in the company.

Through the 1920's, J. Paul Getty increased his fortune by about $3 million. During the Great Depression, he continued to accumulate wealth by purchasing undervalued stock, focusing his attentions on acquiring Pacific Oil Corporation. This allowed to Getty to emerge from the Depression more powerful and richer than before. He continued to buy up oil leases and negotiated with his mother for control of her two-thirds of George F. Getty Oil, which he finally received in 1953.

Getty's most important deal was a 1949 rental agreement made privately with Saudi Arabia's Ibn Saʿūd. Getty paid $9.5 million for a sixty-year lease of apparently barren Saudi land near Kuwait, invested $30 million to develop the site, and discovered an untapped oil reserve, which proceeded to produce more than 16 million barrels a year for in excess of thirty years.

In 1953, Getty obtained Mission Oil and in 1967 combined it and Tide Water Oil, Skelly Oil, and his father's company, creating the Getty Oil Corporation, which remained independent from the major oil corporations.

Although one of the world's richest men, Getty had a reputation for tightfistedness, having a pay phone installed in his home for guests' use. In 1973 he refused to pay ransom for his kidnapped grandson, John Paul Getty III, until after an ear was sent as proof of the kidnappers' resolve. Getty claimed that

his initial refusal was not due to cheapness but to discourage copycat criminals and protect his fourteen other grandchildren.

Getty died in 1976, at his England estate, Sutton Place; he is buried in Malibu, California.

Leslie Neilan

FURTHER READING

De Chair, Somerset Struben. *Getty on Getty: A Man in a Billion.* New York: Sterling, 1989.

Getty, J. Paul. *As I See It: The Autobiography of J. Paul Getty.* Rev. ed. Los Angeles: J. Paul Getty Museum, 2003.

_____. *How to Be Rich.* 1966. Reprint. New York: Jove Books, 1986.

SEE ALSO: Energy, U.S. Department of; International economics and trade; Petroleum industry; Rockefeller, John D.; Standard Oil Company.

G.I. Bill

THE LAW: Federal legislation designed to provide benefits to veterans of the armed forces; also known as the Servicemen's Readjustment Act

DATE: Signed into law on June 24, 1944

SIGNIFICANCE: Besides providing economic relief and financial benefits to returning veterans, the G.I. Bill strongly stimulated the post-World War II economy as veterans spent their government benefits on education opportunities and private housing. As an ongoing program, the G.I. Bill continues to provide economic opportunities to former members of the armed forces.

The U.S. government has a long history of rewarding veterans of its wars. Veterans of the Revolutionary War and early nineteenth century wars received land bounties as compensation for their services, and the government promised veterans of World War I (1917-1818) a cash bonus that veterans would collect in 1945. The onset of the Great Depression caused many veterans to demand their money early, and the 1932 clash between protesting veterans demanding their bonuses (the Bonus Army) and the army caused great embarrassment for the government and the U.S. Army. To prevent a reoccurrence of the Bonus Army, the government decided to im-

J. Paul Getty. (AP/Wide World Photos)

plement a system of compensation to World War II veterans known as the G.I. Bill ("G.I." was a World War II slang term for a common soldier), that provided assistance immediately, instead of years later like the World War I bonus.

Although Franklin D. Roosevelt often receives the credit for the G.I. Bill as part of his New Deal programs, the G.I. Bill (officially the Servicemen's Readjustment Act, also known as the G.I. Bill of Rights) was the result of proposals by Henry W. Colmery, a World War I veteran and national commander of the American Legion, a veterans' advocacy group. Colmery formed a series of proposals during the legion's 1943 National Convention and presented them to President Roosevelt. Roosevelt convinced Congress to enact Colmery's proposals (both houses of Congress passed the legislation by unanimous vote), and Roosevelt signed the act into law on June 22, 1944. The first G.I. Bill included three main benefits for veterans. First, the government offered to subsidize education or career training for returning veterans. Second, the government offered guaranteed home, business, or agricultural loans at low interest rates. Third, if veterans could not find employment, the government offered one year of unemployment compensation, often known as "52-20" because veterans could receive $20 per week for up to fifty-two weeks while they searched for work. To qualify for benefits, a veteran had to have served for at least ninety days in the military and have received an honorable discharge.

IMPACT OF THE BILL

The G.I. Bill was a significant reason that American society and the economy changed so rapidly after World War II. Thanks to subsidized education, 7.8 million veterans received a college education they might otherwise not have received. Before the G.I. Bill, relatively few Americans went to col-

---

ROOSEVELT'S VIEW OF THE G.I. BILL

On signing the G.I. Bill on June 22, 1944, President Franklin D. Roosevelt described its benefits, one by one, then made the following comments on the government's general responsibility to the men and women who served in the military.

With the signing of this bill a well-rounded program of special veterans' benefits is nearly completed. It gives emphatic notice to the men and women in our armed forces that the American people do not intend to let them down.

By prior legislation, the Federal Government has already provided for the armed forces of this war: adequate dependency allowances; mustering-out pay; generous hospitalization, medical care, and vocational rehabilitation and training; liberal pensions in case of death or disability in military service; substantial war risk life insurance, and guaranty of premiums on commercial policies during service; protection of civil rights and suspension of enforcement of certain civil liabilities during service; emergency maternal care for wives of enlisted men; and reemployment rights for returning veterans.

This bill therefore and the former legislation provide the special benefits which are due to the members of our armed forces — for they "have been compelled to make greater economic sacrifice and every other kind of sacrifice than the rest of us, and are entitled to definite action to help take care of their special problems." While further study and experience may suggest some changes and improvements, the Congress is to be congratulated on the prompt action it has taken.

Source: U.S. Department of Veteran Affairs

---

lege, but the G.I. Bill started the process of expanding the system (and business) of higher education, making a college degree a middle-class expectation. University enrollments boomed as older veterans joined younger college students on campus. By 1948, the enrollment of Syracuse University had tripled, and veterans made up more than 60 percent of the students at the University of Iowa. Colleges had to expand their facilities to accommodate the new students. Government subsidization of education for veterans continued into the twenty-first century.

The availability of easy home loans also significantly changed the American economy and landscape, as 5.9 million veterans applied for housing loans. The shortage of existing homes meant that veterans used their G.I. Bill benefits to construct new homes, and the postwar housing boom fueled the economic surge of the 1950's and 1960's. The construction of new housing invigorated many associated industries. The construction of a home required the services of many different business entities, including construction firms, carpenters, electricians, landscapers, home furnishers, and the automobile industry. Relatively few single-family homes were available in American cities, so veterans used their loans to build new homes outside the city limits, starting the population shift out of American cities and into newly formed suburbs. The acquisition of new homes in the suburbs promoted larger families, and the G.I. Bill was, to a certain extent, responsible for the post-World War II baby boom.

CONTINUATION OF THE BILL

The original G.I. Bill of 1944 expired in 1956, but the concept of veteran compensation continued, with all subsequent legislation still referred to as G.I. bills. In 1952 Congress passed the Veterans' Adjustment Act to compensate veterans of the Korean War (1950-1953). There were some minor differences between the World War II and Korean G.I. Bills, but the outcome was broadly similar. More than two million Korean War veterans used the G.I. Bill to go to college, and 1.5 million financed new homes. The G.I. Bill underwent a significant change in 1966, when Congress passed the Veterans Readjustment Benefits Act (VRBA) as part of President Lyndon B. Johnson's Great Society slate of social programs. The VRBA removed the requirement of serving in combat to receive government benefits, and instead made G.I. Bill benefits available to anyone who served in the military, whether in wartime or peacetime. Since 1966 the G.I. Bill has undergone a series of modifications and adjustments, but the fundamental benefits subsidizing education and home ownership remain the same. The Montgomery G.I. Bill (MGIB), enacted by Congress in 1985, provides educational stipends to former members of the military who contribute a small portion of their pay during their time in the service. The Post 9/11 Veterans Assistance Act of 2008 (effective date August, 2009) substantially increased the amount of tuition and housing assistance, allows veterans to transfer benefits to their spouses and children, and provides tuition benefits for National Guard and Reserve members.

Steven J. Ramold

FURTHER READING

Humes, Edward. *Over Here: How the G.I. Bill Transformed the American Dream.* New York: Harcourt, 2006. Excellent study of the G.I. Bill that offers a full description of the political struggle to create the bill and a discussion of how the law changed America's definition of middle-class status.

Mettler, Suzanne. *Soldiers to Citizens: The G.I. Bill and the Making of the Greatest Generation.* New York: Oxford, 2005. An examination of the G.I. Bill from an economic standpoint, this book looks at how the G.I. Bill created a concept of civil virtue out of a successful government program.

Michel, Christopher. *The Military Advantage: A Comprehensive Guide to Your Military and Veterans Benefits.* New York: Simon & Schuster, 2006. An insider's look at the G.I. Bill, this book contains a good history of the G.I. Bill and a clear explanation of benefits offered to American military personnel.

Simon, Richard. "Bush Signs Emergency War Funding Measure: It Also Expands Veterans Benefits Under the G.I. Bill and Extends Unemployment Aid." *Los Angeles Times,* July 1, 2008, p. A5.

SEE ALSO: Automotive industry; Construction industry; Education; Government spending; Wars; World War I; World War II.

Gilded Age

THE ERA: Period of rapid economic growth in the United States that began in 1877 and began to give way to the Progressive Era in 1900

DATE: 1877-1900

PLACE: United States

SIGNIFICANCE: Taking its name from an 1874 novel by Mark Twain and Charles Dudley Warner, the Gilded Age was a period of rapid economic growth accompanied by a host of serious social problems and chronic economic dislocation. It gave way to the Progressive Era, a period in which selective federal regulation of American business became widespread.

The most spectacular growth in the United States during the Gilded Age occurred in heavy industry, transportation, and banking. Steel led the way, as new technology made steelmaking more economical than before. The major innovator was the United States Steel Corporation, led by the dynamic Andrew Carnegie, whose rags to riches story captivated the nation. Cornelius Vanderbilt was his counterpart in railroads and shipping, and J. P. Morgan reorganized American banking and finance on a massive scale.

American railroads grew at a dizzying pace during the Gilded Age. The major transcontinental lines received the most attention, but smaller railroads brought coal, iron, and food to factories and cities across the country. Many farmers decried the predatory freight prices but ultimately benefited from a national market for their products.

Labor unions never matched the pace of development of their management counterparts. The Knights of Labor grew rapidly at first but declined after the strike of 1877 failed. Samuel Gompers was a dynamic organizer of the American Federation of Labor during the 1880's, but he focused his efforts on skilled labor. Eugene V. Debs brought a militant approach to union organizing during the 1890's but found his efforts stymied by federal antistrike laws.

The Gilded Age is a generally neglected topic, and most studies of the era emphasize the aspects of capitalism gone wild and the resulting human cost. An objective view of the Gilded Age rests on the conclusion that rapid economic growth inevitably is accompanied by widespread human suffering.

Michael Polley

FURTHER READING

French, Bryant Morey. *Mark Twain and "The Gilded Age": The Book That Named an Era.* Dallas: Southern Methodist University Press, 1965.

Summers, Mark Wahlgren. *The Gilded Age: Or, The Hazard of New Functions.* Upper Saddle River, N.J.: Prentice Hall, 1997.

Wicker, Elmus. *Banking Panics of the Gilded Age,* New York: Cambridge University Press, 2000.

SEE ALSO: AFL-CIO; Carnegie, Andrew; Debs, Eugene V.; Gompers, Samuel; Gould, Jay; Knights of Labor; Labor history; Literary works with business themes; Morgan, J. P.; Railroads; United States Steel Corporation; Vanderbilt, Cornelius.

Gold rush. *See* Black Hills gold rush; California gold rush; Klondike gold rush

Gold standard

DEFINITION: Valuation of national currency by equating a specific monetary unit with a specific amount of gold

SIGNIFICANCE: Adoption of the gold standard stabilized international currency exchange rates and enabled free trade, thereby aiding the growth of American business during the late nineteenth and early twentieth centuries. However, as individual nations assumed greater control over monetary policy, the standard gradually fell into disuse and was discontinued.

The gold standard was both a means of regulating the currency value within an individual nation and a means of regulating international currency exchange rates. Historically, gold has been considered a reliable metal for use as currency because its supply has remained relatively stable over time. The gold standard came into international use during the late nineteenth century as the growth of nations and advances in transportation and communications rendered trade increasingly global in nature.

In the nineteenth century, the United States employed a bimetallic currency system based on gold and silver. American industry, aided by stable gold-based international exchange rates that made free trade between nations possible, prospered during the latter half of the century. However, as European nations turned away from silver and new discoveries of the metal in the United States created an oversupply, farmers and small-business interests suffered from deflation. Farmers and Populists who favored the increased coinage of silver to reverse deflation clashed with supporters of a pure gold standard. The supporters of a gold standard prevailed at the turn of the century, with the passage of the Gold Standard Act of 1900, which officially established gold as the only precious metal for which paper money could be redeemed in the United States.

World War I and its aftermath led to currency inflation in Europe, as nations struggled to finance their war efforts and to pay debts and reparations, leading to widespread suspension of the gold standard. When European nations returned to the gold standard during the 1920's, severe deflation resulted, contributing to the economic collapse that led to the Great Depression of the 1930's. Europe abandoned the gold standard during the early 1930's, and in 1933, president Franklin D. Roosevelt followed suit by effectively suspending the gold standard in the United States.

The gold standard remained in effect in modified form after World War II with the 1946 adoption of the Bretton Woods Agreement, under which the U.S. dollar became the preferred means of settling international debts, and the U.S. government promised to redeem dollars at a fixed rate of $35 per ounce. Inflation produced by the economic boom of the 1950's and 1960's combined with decreased national gold reserves and debts incurred as a result of the Vietnam War prompted the United States to abandon the gold standard in 1971. By then, most nations had moved to a fiat standard (not backed by any physical asset) of currency, in which the value of money was established strictly by government policy and global market forces.

Michael H. Burchett

FURTHER READING

Bayoumi, Tamim, et al. *Modern Perspectives on the Gold Standard.* New York: Cambridge University Press, 2008.

Bordo, Michael D., ed. *Money, History, and International Finance.* Chicago: University of Chicago Press, 1989.

Lewis, Nathan. *Gold: The Once and Future Money.* New York: John Wiley & Sons, 2007.

SEE ALSO: American Bimetallic League national convention; Black Friday; Black Hills gold rush; Bretton Woods Agreement; California gold rush; *Coin's Financial School;* "Cross of Gold" speech; Currency; Fort Knox; Klondike gold rush; Monetary policy, federal.

Gompers, Samuel

IDENTIFICATION: Labor leader and founder of the American Federation of Labor
BORN: January 27, 1850; London, England
DIED: December 13, 1924; San Antonio, Texas

SIGNIFICANCE: Gompers emphasized organizing skilled workers in craft or trade unions and advocated for practical benefits for workers, rather than embracing the radical activism of European labor movements.

Samuel Gompers was born in London to a Dutch Jewish family that had recently immigrated from Amsterdam. As a young man, he learned his father's trade of cigar making. The family emigrated to New York City in 1863, where Gompers continued working in the cigar trade and eventually became an official in the Cigar Makers International Union.

During the 1870's, cigar makers were threatened by technological advances that greatly simplified production. In 1871, Gompers was involved in a failed strike against the introduction of this automation. He also joined demonstrations for an eight-hour workday in September, 1871. In 1881, Gompers helped create the Federation of Organized Trades and Labor Unions of the United States and Canada. This organization sought to bring together many different unions, but it never flourished.

During the late 1880's, controversy with the Knights of Labor opened the way for the creation of the American Federation of Labor (AFL). The Knights of Labor sought to organize all workers, and it included some middle-class workers. Gompers believed the labor movement should concentrate on organizing the working class and focus primarily on skilled workers. Labor leaders meeting in December, 1886, disbanded the Federation of Organized Trade and Labor Unions and created the new American Federation of Labor. Gompers would be the president of the AFL from its beginning until his death, except during one year, 1895.

Gompers rejected the socialist agenda of many early labor activists. He believed labor's goals should be practical and attainable benefits for workers—higher wages, shorter hours, and better working conditions—an approach called "bread and butter unionism." Gompers also advocated craft or trade unionism—organizing skilled workers according to their craft or specialization. Skilled craftsmen could not be replaced by business owners as easily as unskilled craftsmen, and the emphasis on a separate union for each craft built solidarity among the workers. The AFL provided leadership and coordinated the activities of the various craft and trade unions that made up the organization.

Samuel Gompers. (Library of Congress)

Initially, Gompers put little emphasis on political activity, and he tried to keep the AFL politically neutral until 1908. That year, the AFL supported Democratic presidential candidate William Jennings Bryan, because his platform called for an end to judicial injunctions against union activism. Under the leadership of Gompers, the AFL quickly became the major labor organization in the United States, with more than 24 million members by the time of his death.

During World War I, Gompers initially called for the United States to remain neutral, but when the country entered the war, he worked to prevent strikes that would disrupt war production. After the war, he participated in the peace talks at Versailles, France.

Mark S. Joy

FURTHER READING

Gompers, Samuel. *The Samuel Gompers Papers.* 9 vols. to date. Urbana: University of Illinois Press, 1986-2003.

Greene, Julie. *Pure and Simple Politics: The American Federation of Labor and Political Activism, 1881-*

1917. New York: Cambridge University Press, 1998.

Livesay, Harold. *Samuel Gompers and Organized Labor in America.* Boston: Little, Brown, 1978.

SEE ALSO: AFL-CIO; Gilded Age; Hoffa, Jimmy; International Brotherhood of Teamsters; Labor history; Labor strikes; World War I.

Google

IDENTIFICATION: Private corporation specializing in information organization and search on the Internet

DATE: Founded in September, 1998

SIGNIFICANCE: Google, the leading Internet information organization and search company in the world, is one of the fastest growing companies in the world. It daily provides services to corporations, government agencies, nonprofit organizations, and individuals in a platform-independent manner.

Google emerged from pioneering work on an Internet search engine known as BackRub that was created in January of 1996 by Larry Page and Sergey Brin, two graduate students at Stanford University. They first sought to license their search technology to another company, but when that failed, they decided to form their own company. They received $100,000 in financing from Andy Bechtolsheim, one of the founders of Sun Microsystems. Because the check was made out to "Google, Inc.," which did not yet exist as a corporation, Page and Brin had to incorporate to cash it. They convinced family, friends, and others to invest, collecting a total of $1 million.

The company launched in rented garage space in Menlo Park, California, in September of 1998, starting with just 10,000 search queries a day and three employees. In June of 1999, when the company had eight employees and more than 500,000 Internet queries per day, it obtained an infusion of $25 million in venture capital from Sequoia and Kleiner Perkins. By 2000, when Google introduced a one-billion-page index to the World Wide Web and had more than 100 million search queries a day, it had come to control the world's largest search engine. On April 19, 2004, it became a publicly traded

The founders of Google, Sergey Brin (above) and Larry Page at the company's headquarters in Mountain View, California, in early 2004. (AP/Wide World Photos)

company on NASDAQ. In October, Google announced its first quarterly results as a public company, with revenues of nearly $806 million. By 2008, the company had grown to encompass more than seventeen thousand employees in twenty nations offering search services via 160 local country domains on the Internet and in more than 117 distinct languages from its Googleplex headquarters in Mountain View, California, and locations worldwide. Google reported revenues of $5.2 billion for the first quarter of 2008 (ending March 31, 2008), up 42 percent from the first quarter of 2007 and up 7 percent from the fourth quarter of 2007. Net income for the same period was $1.31 billion as compared with $1.21 billion in the fourth quarter of 2007.

Over the course of its evolution, Google has acquired more than fifty companies and annually spends about a third of its revenues on search technologies, a third on advertising technologies, and a fifth on businesses related to its interests in organizing the world's information. Major acquisitions in 2006 and 2007 included YouTube, a consumer media company; Postini, a communication security and compliance company; and DoubleClick, an Internet advertising service provider. Through its many products and services, Google provides search technologies for print, visual, and audio media. It has entered into a growing partnership with major libraries to make available fully searchable digital forms of the world's literature. The company has also launched into wireless technologies and created Google.org as a philanthropic arm of the corporation.

Dennis W. Cheek

SEE ALSO: Apple; Catalog shopping; Computer industry; Dot-com bubble; eBay; E-mail; Internet; NASDAQ.